D0152334

THE PAPERS OF

THOMAS JEFFERSON

RETIREMENT SERIES

THE PAPERS OF

Thomas Jefferson

RETIREMENT SERIES

Volume 4

18 June 1811 to 30 April 1812

J. JEFFERSON LOONEY, EDITOR

ROBERT F. HAGGARD AND SUSAN HOLBROOK PERDUE,
ASSOCIATE EDITORS

JULIE L. LAUTENSCHLAGER, ASSISTANT EDITOR

LISA A. FRANCAVILLA, MANAGING EDITOR

ELLEN C. HICKMAN AND DEBORAH BECKEL,
EDITORIAL ASSISTANTS

CATHERINE COINER CRITTENDEN, SENIOR DIGITAL TECHNICIAN

SUSAN SPENGLER, DIGITAL TECHNICIAN

PRINCETON AND OXFORD

PRINCETON UNIVERSITY PRESS

2007

Published by Princeton University Press, 41 William Street,
Princeton, New Jersey 08540
In the United Kingdom:
Princeton University Press, 3 Market Place,
Woodstock, Oxfordshire OX20 1SY

Library of Congress Cataloging-in-Publication Data

Jefferson, Thomas, 1743–1826
The papers of Thomas Jefferson. Retirement series / J. Jefferson Looney, editor . . .
[et al.] p. cm.
Includes bibliographical references and index.
Contents: v. 1. 4 March to 15 November 1809.
v. 2. 16 November 1809 to 11 August 1810.
v. 3. 12 August 1810 to 17 June 1811
v. 4. 18 June 1811 to 30 April 1812
ISBN 978-0-691-13565-6 (cloth: v. 4: alk. paper)
1. Jefferson, Thomas, 1743–1826—Archives. 2. Jefferson, Thomas, 1743–1826—Correspondence. 3. Presidents—United States—Archives. 4. Presidents—United States—Correspondence. 5. United States—Politics and government—1809–1817—Sources. 6. United States—Politics and government—1817–1825—Sources. I. Looney J. Jefferson. II. Title. III. Title: Retirement series.
E302.J442 2004b
973.4'6'092—dc22 2004048327

This book has been composed in Monticello

Princeton University Press books are printed on acid-free paper and meet the guidelines for permanence and durability of the Committee on Production Guidelines for Book Longevity of the Council on Library Resources

Printed in the United States of America

DEDICATED TO THE MEMORY OF

ADOLPH S. OCHS

PUBLISHER OF THE NEW YORK TIMES

1896–1935

WHO BY THE EXAMPLE OF A RESPONSIBLE

PRESS ENLARGED AND FORTIFIED

THE JEFFERSONIAN CONCEPT

OF A FREE PRESS

ADVISORY COMMITTEE

THIS EDITION was made possible by a founding grant from The New York Times Company to Princeton University.

The Retirement Series is sponsored by the Thomas Jefferson Foundation, Inc., of Charlottesville, Virginia. It was created with a six-year founding grant from The Pew Charitable Trusts to the Foundation and to Princeton University, enabling the former to take over responsibility for the volumes associated with this period. Leading gifts from Richard Gilder, Mrs. Martin S. Davis, and Thomas A. Saunders III have assured the continuation of the Retirement Series. For these essential donations, and for other indispensable aid generously given by librarians, archivists, scholars, and collectors of manuscripts, the Editors record their sincere gratitude.

FOREWORD

THE 580 DOCUMENTS printed in this volume cover the period from 18 June 1811 through 30 April 1812. Between these two dates, Thomas Jefferson found himself as busy as ever. Although he had to fight off several bouts of rheumatism and had difficulty walking long distances, he continued to be in relatively good health and to enjoy his life at Monticello and Poplar Forest. As Jefferson wrote to Charles Willson Peale on 20 August, "no occupation is so delightful as the culture of the earth, & no culture comparable to that of the garden." In the same letter he remarked that although he was "an old man, I am but a young gardener." In a letter to Peter Minor, Jefferson expressed eternal "hostility to dogs" and a willingness to "join in any plan for exterminating the whole race," and shortly thereafter he joined a group of Albemarle County residents who petitioned the Virginia legislature to put a tax on dogs in order to reduce their numbers and, thereby, protect sheep and improve domestic manufactures. Jefferson also calculated lines for a horizontal sundial for Poplar Forest; surveyed his Bear Creek lands in Bedford County; and drew up detailed slave lists, a catalogue of his landed possessions, and a schedule of the work he wanted done at Poplar Forest in 1812.

The arts and sciences continued to attract Jefferson. During this period he was reelected president of the American Philosophical Society and chosen president of the Philadelphia-based Society of Artists of the United States. Jefferson took readings of a solar eclipse in September 1811; attempted to determine Monticello's longitude with the assistance of William Lambert and Bishop James Madison; ordered an astronomical case clock from Philadelphia; and measured Willis Mountain with his grandson, Thomas Jefferson Randolph. On 10 November he wrote an impassioned letter to Robert Patterson concerning the need for a fixed international standard for measures, weights, and coins. Foreign correspondents such as Madame de Tessé, Valentín de Foronda, Pierre Samuel Du Pont de Nemours, and Antoine Louis Claude Destutt de Tracy continued their long-distance discussions with Jefferson about everything from chestnuts and the Spanish constitution to taxation and political economy.

Legal issues also took up a great deal of Jefferson's time. A developing controversy with Samuel Scott over the ownership of a piece of land in Campbell County threatened to disrupt Jefferson's plan to sell this tract. Of even greater significance, the litigation that grew out of Jefferson's eviction of Edward Livingston from the New Orleans batture in 1807 finally came to a head early in December 1811. United

States circuit court judges John Marshall and John Tyler, sitting in Richmond, dismissed Livingston's suit on jurisdictional grounds. Because the dispute had not been decided on its merits, Jefferson moved immediately to lay his case before the American people. He accordingly engaged a New York publisher, Ezra Sargeant, to print 250 copies of the lengthy statement he had prepared for his legal counsel. Jefferson arranged to have a copy given to each member of Congress, and he began distributing the remainder to various friends and acquaintances during the spring of 1812.

Nor was this the full extent of Jefferson's involvement in the publication of his own work and that of others. With his permission, Joseph Milligan published a revised second edition of Jefferson's *Manual of Parliamentary Practice* in March 1812. Jefferson received a second manuscript volume from Destutt de Tracy in February 1812 and began the laborious process of seeing it into print. In a belated response to William Wirt's request for information to assist him in writing a biography of Patrick Henry, Jefferson forwarded a lengthy, colorful, and largely negative portrait of his former colleague. James S. Gaines sent Jefferson a detailed plan for a revised constitution and legal code for the state of Virginia, and Jefferson and Virginia governor James Barbour had an important exchange on the proper limits of executive power.

Perhaps the most important development for posterity documented in this volume is the resumption of correspondence in January 1812 between Jefferson and his former rival for the presidency, John Adams. Although the two men had had little contact since Jefferson's inauguration in March 1801, their mutual friend Benjamin Rush's persistent efforts to heal the rift finally succeeded. Aided by reports that Jefferson's neighbors John and Edward Coles had found Adams open to reconciliation during a visit to Quincy, Rush urged Jefferson and Adams to "Bury in silence all the causes of your separation. Recollect that explanations may be proper between lovers but are never so between divided friends." Adams and Jefferson each came to relish the renewed opportunity to engage with a fellow founder whose mind was as wide-ranging, imaginative, and thought-provoking as his own. These first tentative letters initiated a body of correspondence that not only enriches the papers of Adams and Jefferson, but also provides a useful lesson to their political successors, that ideological differences can be overcome through a mixture of compassion, understanding, and patriotism.

ACKNOWLEDGMENTS

MANY INDIVIDUALS and institutions provided aid and encouragement during the preparation of this volume. Those who helped us to locate and acquire primary and secondary sources and answered our research questions include our colleagues at the Thomas Jefferson Foundation, especially Anna Berkes, Eric D. M. Johnson, Jack Robertson, Leah Stearns, and Endrina Tay of the Jefferson Library, Director of Gardens and Grounds Peter Hatch and Shannon Senior Research Historian Lucia C. Stanton; Marie Lamoureux at the American Antiquarian Society; Clare Sheridan at the American Textile History Museum in Lowell, Massachusetts; Mary Warnement at the Boston Athenaeum; Henry Scannell at the Boston Public Library; the Richardson-Sloane Special Collections Center at the Davenport (Iowa) Public Library; Wanda S. Gunning of Princeton, New Jersey; Olga Tsapina at the Huntington Library; Thomas E. Buckley, SJ, of the Jesuit School of Theology at Berkeley, California; John Buchtel, curator of rare books at Johns Hopkins University; Kevin B. Jones; Lewis Hobgood Averett at the Jones Memorial Library in Lynchburg; Jeff Flannery and his coworkers at the Library of Congress's Manuscripts Division; Virginia Dunn, William Luebke, Craig Moore, and Brent Tarter at the Library of Virginia; Christopher Kintzel and Robert Schoeberlein at the Maryland State Archives; Carrie Supple at the Massachusetts Historical Society; Janet Bloom at the Clements Library, University of Michigan; Nila Crouch, deputy clerk, Montgomery County, Kentucky; Zara Phillips and Martha Rowe of the Museum of Early Southern Decorative Arts in Winston-Salem, North Carolina; Eric Chamberlain and Ernie Price at the Natchez Trace Parkway in Tupelo, Mississippi; Wayne DeCesar, J. Dane Hartgrove, Jessica Kratz, Sally Kuisel, Fred Romanski, and Rodney Ross at the National Archives; David Dearborn at the New England Historic Genealogical Society; Irene Wainwright at the New Orleans Public Library; William Stingone at the New York Public Library's Manuscripts and Archives Division; Nancy Horan at the New York State Library; Robert Hitchings at the Norfolk Public Library; Jack Gumbrecht and Leslie Hunt at the Historical Society of Pennsylvania; Marcia Grodsky of the University of Pittsburgh's Darlington Library; Travis McDonald and Gail Pond at the Corporation for Jefferson's Poplar Forest; Father R. Christopher Heying, Saint Stephen's Episcopal Church, Forest, Virginia; Robin Copp at the South Caroliniana Library, University of South Carolina; Stephen G. Hague, director of Stenton,

George Logan's home in Philadelphia; Maria Paula Diogo of the Universidade Nova de Lisboa, Portugal; William Britten at the Special Collections Department of the University of Tennessee, Knoxville; David Turk of the United States Marshals Service; Bradley J. Daigle and Barbie Selby at the University of Virginia Library and their colleagues in the Special Collections Department, Christian Dupont, Edward Gaynor, Margaret Hrabe, Michael Plunkett, and Regina Rush; John M. Jackson and Bruce J. Turner at Virginia Polytechnic Institute and State University; and Susan Riggs at the Special Collections Department of the College of William and Mary. As always, we received advice, assistance, and encouragement from a large number of our fellow documentary editors, including Margaret Hogan from the Adams Papers; Ellen R. Cohn, Karen Duval, and Philipp Ziesche from the Papers of Benjamin Franklin; Martha J. King, James P. McClure, Linda Monaco, Barbara B. Oberg, and Elaine Weber Pascu from the Papers of Thomas Jefferson at Princeton University; Mary A. Hackett, Angela Kreider, David B. Mattern, and John C. A. Stagg from the Papers of James Madison; Charles F. Hobson from the Papers of John Marshall; Marlena C. DeLong from the Papers of James Monroe; and Philander D. Chase, Theodore J. Crackel, David R. Hoth, and Christine S. Patrick from the Papers of George Washington. Genevieve Moene and Roland H. Simon transcribed and translated the French letters included in this volume; David T. Gies, Jennifer McCune, and Pedro Alvarez de Miranda performed a similar service for those in the Spanish language; and John F. Miller assisted us with Latin quotations. The maps of Jefferson's Virginia and Albemarle County were created by Rick Britton. The other illustrations that appear in this volume were assembled with the assistance of Valerie-Anne Lutz at the American Philosophical Society; John Hutter of Hopewell, New Jersey; Peter Drummey and Kim Nusco at the Massachusetts Historical Society; the National Gallery of Art; Meredith Topper and Keri Butler at the Art Commission of the City of New York; and Wayne Mogielnicki and Carrie Taylor at the Thomas Jefferson Foundation. Stephen Perkins of Dataformat.com continued to assist in all things digital. Our departing and arriving colleagues at the Retirement Series, Kristofer M. Ray, Leigh Sellers, and Paula Viterbo, contributed to this volume in various ways. Finally, we would like to acknowledge the efforts both routine and extraordinary made by the able staff at Princeton University Press, including Sam Elworthy, Alison Kalett, Dimitri Karetnikov, Jan Lilly, Neil Litt, Elizabeth Litz, Brigitta van Rheinberg, and our production editor and special friend, Linny Schenck.

EDITORIAL METHOD AND APPARATUS

1. RENDERING THE TEXT

From its inception *The Papers of Thomas Jefferson* has insisted on high standards of accuracy in rendering text, but modifications in textual policy and editorial apparatus have been implemented as different approaches have become accepted in the field or as a more faithful rendering has become technically feasible. Prior discussions of textual policy appeared in Vols. 1:xxix–xxxiv, 22:vii–xi, 24:vii–viii, and 30:xiii–xiv of the First Series.

The textual method of the Retirement Series will adhere to the more literal approach adopted in Volume 30 of the parent edition. Original spelling, capitalization, and punctuation is retained as written. Such idiosyncrasies as Jefferson's failure to capitalize the beginnings of most of his sentences and abbreviations like "mr" are preserved, as are his preference for "it's" to "its" and his characteristic spellings of "knolege," "paiment," and "recieve." Modern usage is adopted in cases where intent is impossible to determine, an issue that arises most often in the context of capitalization. Some so-called slips of the pen are corrected, but in such cases the original reading is recorded in a subjoined textual note. Jefferson and others sometimes signaled a change in thought within a paragraph with extra horizontal space, and this is rendered by a three-em space. Blanks left for words and not subsequently filled by the authors are represented by a space approximating the length of the blank. Gaps, doubtful readings of illegible or damaged text, and wording supplied from other versions or by editorial conjecture are explained in the source note or in numbered textual notes. Foreign-language documents, the vast majority of which are in French during the retirement period, are transcribed in full as faithfully as possible, and followed by a complete modern translation.

Two modifications from past practice bring this series still closer to the original manuscripts. Underscored text is presented as such rather than being converted to italics. Superscripts are also preserved rather than being lowered to the baseline. In most cases of superscripting, the punctuation that is below or next to the superscripted letters is dropped, since it is virtually impossible to determine what is a period or dash as opposed to a flourish under, over, or adjacent to superscripted letters.

Limits to the more literal method are still recognized, however, and readability and consistency with past volumes are prime considerations. In keeping with the basic design implemented in the first volume of the *Papers*, salutations and signatures continue to display in large and small capitals rather than upper- and lowercase letters. Expansion marks over abbreviations are silently omitted. With very rare exceptions, deleted text and information on which words were added during the process of composition is not displayed within the document transcription. Based on the Editors' judgment of their significance, such emendations are either described in numbered textual notes or ignored. Datelines for letters are consistently printed at the head of the text, with a comment in the descriptive note when they have been moved. Address information, endorsements, and dockets are quoted or described in the source note rather than reproduced in the document proper.

2. *TEXTUAL DEVICES*

The following devices are employed throughout the work to clarify the presentation of the text.

[. . .]	Text missing and not conjecturable. The size of gaps longer than a word or two is estimated in annotation.
[ ]	Number or part of number missing or illegible.
[roman]	Conjectural reading for missing or illegible matter. A question mark follows when the reading is doubtful.
[*italic*]	Editorial comment inserted in the text.
<*italic*>	Matter deleted in the manuscript but restored in our text.

3. *DESCRIPTIVE SYMBOLS*

The following symbols are employed throughout the work to describe the various kinds of manuscript originals. When a series of versions is included, the first to be recorded is the version used for the printed text.

Dft	draft (usually a composition or rough draft; multiple drafts, when identifiable as such, are designated "2d Dft," etc.)
Dupl	duplicate
MS	manuscript (applied to most documents other than letters)

PoC	polygraph copy
PrC	press copy
RC	recipient's copy
SC	stylograph copy

All manuscripts of the above types are assumed to be in the hand of the author of the document to which the descriptive symbol pertains. If not, that fact is stated. On the other hand, the following types of manuscripts are assumed *not* to be in the hand of the author, and exceptions will be noted:

FC file copy (applied to all contemporary copies retained by the author or his agents)

Tr transcript (applied to all contemporary and later copies except file copies; period of transcription, unless clear by implication, will be given when known)

4. LOCATION SYMBOLS

The locations of documents printed in this edition from originals in private hands and from printed sources are recorded in self-explanatory form in the descriptive note following each document. The locations of documents printed from originals held by public and private institutions in the United States are recorded by means of the symbols used in the *MARC Code List for Organizations* (2000) maintained by the Library of Congress. The symbols DLC and MHi by themselves stand for the collections of Jefferson Papers proper in these repositories. When texts are drawn from other collections held by these two institutions, the names of those collections are added. Location symbols for documents held by institutions outside the United States are given in a subjoined list. The lists of symbols are limited to the institutions represented by documents printed or referred to in this volume.

CLU-C William Andrew Clark Library, University of California, Los Angeles

CSmH Huntington Library, San Marino, California
- JF Jefferson File
- JF-BA Jefferson File, Bixby Acquisition

CtY Yale University, New Haven, Connecticut

DeGH Hagley Museum and Library, Greenville, Delaware

DLC Library of Congress, Washington, D.C.
- TJ Papers Thomas Jefferson Papers (this is assumed if not stated, but also given as indicated

to furnish the precise location of an undated, misdated, or otherwise problematic document, thus "DLC: TJ Papers, 213:38071–2" represents volume 213, folios 38071 and 38072 as the collection was arranged at the time the first microfilm edition was made in 1944–45. Access to the microfilm edition of the collection as it was rearranged under the Library's Presidential Papers Program is provided by the *Index to the Thomas Jefferson Papers* [1976]), and this collection can also be viewed online at the Library's American Memory website

DNA — National Archives, Washington, D.C., with identifications of series (preceded by record group number) as follows:

CD	Consular Dispatches
CS	Census Schedules
DI	Diplomatic Instructions
DL	Domestic Letters
LAR	Letters of Application and Recommendation
MLR	Miscellaneous Letters Received
MLRSN	Miscellaneous Letters Received by the Secretary of the Navy
RWP	Revolutionary War Pension and Bounty-Land Warrant Application Files
SB	Surety Bonds

MdHi — Maryland Historical Society, Baltimore

MeHi — Maine Historical Society, Portland

MHi — Massachusetts Historical Society, Boston

MiD-B — Burton Historical Collection, Detroit Public Library, Michigan

MiU-C — Clements Library, University of Michigan, Ann Arbor

MoSHi — Missouri Historical Society, Saint Louis

TJC	Thomas Jefferson Collection
TJC-BC	Thomas Jefferson Collection, text formerly in Bixby Collection

MWA — American Antiquarian Society, Worcester, Massachusetts

NcU — University of North Carolina, Chapel Hill

NhD	Dartmouth College, Hanover, New Hampshire
NHi	New-York Historical Society, New York City
NjMoHP	Morristown National Historical Park, New Jersey
NjP	Princeton University, Princeton, New Jersey
NjVHi	Vineland Historical and Antiquarian Society, Vineland, New Jersey
NN	New York Public Library, New York City
NNGL	Gilder Lehrman Collection, New York City
NNPM	Pierpont Morgan Library, New York City
PHi	Historical Society of Pennsylvania, Philadelphia
PPAFA	Pennsylvania Academy of the Fine Arts, Philadelphia
PPAmP	American Philosophical Society, Philadelphia
PPiU	University of Pittsburgh, Pittsburgh, Pennsylvania
PPL	Library Company of Philadelphia
PPRF	Rosenbach Foundation, Philadelphia
PWacD	David Library of the American Revolution, Washington Crossing, Pennsylvania
RPB	Brown University, Providence, Rhode Island
ScU	University of South Carolina, Columbia
TU	University of Tennessee, Knoxville
Vi	Library of Virginia, Richmond
	USCC-OB — United States Circuit Court, Virginia District, Order Book
	USCC-RB — United States Circuit Court, Virginia District, Record Book
ViBlbV	Virginia Polytechnic and State University, Blacksburg
ViCMRL	Thomas Jefferson Library, Thomas Jefferson Foundation, Inc., Charlottesville, Virginia
ViFreJM	James Monroe Memorial Foundation, Fredericksburg
ViHi	Virginia Historical Society, Richmond
ViLJML	Jones Memorial Library, Lynchburg, Virginia
ViN	Norfolk Public Library, Norfolk, Virginia
ViU	University of Virginia, Charlottesville
	TJP — Thomas Jefferson Papers
	TJP-CC — Thomas Jefferson Papers, text formerly in Carr-Cary Papers
	TJP-ER — Thomas Jefferson Papers, text formerly in Edgehill-Randolph Papers

TJP-LBJM Thomas Jefferson Papers, Thomas Jefferson's Legal Brief in *Jefferson v. Michie*, 1804–13, deposited by Mrs. Augustina David Carr Mills

ViW College of William and Mary, Williamsburg, Virginia

TC-JP Jefferson Papers, Tucker-Coleman Collection

TJP Thomas Jefferson Papers

The following symbol represents a repository located outside of the United States:

PlKMN Muzeum Narodowe w Krakowie, Poland

5. *OTHER ABBREVIATIONS AND SYMBOLS*

The following abbreviations and symbols are commonly employed in the annotation throughout the work.

Lb Letterbook (used to indicate texts copied into bound volumes)

RG Record Group (used in designating the location of documents in the Library of Virginia and the National Archives)

SJL Jefferson's "Summary Journal of Letters" written and received for the period 11 Nov. 1783 to 25 June 1826 (in DLC: TJ Papers). This epistolary record, kept in Jefferson's hand, has been checked against the TJ Editorial Files. It is to be assumed that all outgoing letters are recorded in SJL unless there is a note to the contrary. When the date of receipt of an incoming letter is recorded in SJL, it is incorporated in the notes. Information and discrepancies revealed in SJL but not found in the letter itself are also noted. Missing letters recorded in SJL are accounted for in the notes to documents mentioning them, in related documents, or in an appendix

TJ Thomas Jefferson

TJ Editorial Files Photoduplicates and other editorial materials in the office of the Papers of Thomas Jefferson: Retirement Series, Jefferson Library, Thomas Jefferson Foundation, Charlottesville

d Penny or denier

f Florin

£ Pound sterling or livre, depending upon context (in doubtful cases, a clarifying note will be given)

s Shilling or sou (also expressed as /)
ʈ Livre Tournois
₱ Per (occasionally used for pro, pre)

6. SHORT TITLES

The following list includes short titles of works cited frequently in this edition. Since it is impossible to anticipate all the works to be cited in abbreviated form, the list is revised from volume to volume.

Acts of Assembly *Acts of the General Assembly of Virginia* (cited by session; title varies over time)

Albemarle County Cemeteries Fay Early and Constance Harris, *Record of Cemeteries in Albemarle County, Virginia, including Charlottesville*, 1968–ca. 1982, 14 vols. in 20

ANB John A. Garraty and Mark C. Carnes, eds., *American National Biography*, 1999, 24 vols.

Annals *Annals of the Congress of the United States: The Debates and Proceedings in the Congress of the United States . . . Compiled from Authentic Materials*, Washington, D.C., Gales & Seaton, 1834–56, 42 vols. (all editions are undependable and pagination varies from one printing to another. Citations given below are to the edition mounted on the American Memory website of the Library of Congress and give the date of the debate as well as page numbers)

APS American Philosophical Society

ASP *American State Papers: Documents, Legislative and Executive, of the Congress of the United States*, 1832–61, 38 vols.

Bashkina, *United States and Russia* Nina N. Bashkina and others, eds., *The United States and Russia: The Beginning of Relations, 1765–1815*, 1980

BDML Edward C. Papenfuse and others, eds., *A Biographical Dictionary of the Maryland Legislature, 1635–1789*, 1979–85, 2 vols.

BDSCHR Walter B. Edgar and others, eds., *Biographical Directory of the South Carolina House of Representatives*, 1974– , 5 vols.

Betts, *Farm Book* Edwin M. Betts, ed., *Thomas Jefferson's Farm Book*, 1953 (in two separately paginated sections; unless otherwise specified, references are to the second section)

Betts, *Garden Book* Edwin M. Betts, ed., *Thomas Jefferson's Garden Book, 1766–1824*, 1944

Biog. Dir. Cong. *Biographical Directory of the United States Congress, 1774–1989*, 1989

Black's Law Dictionary Bryan A. Garner and others, eds., *Black's Law Dictionary*, 7th ed., 1999

Brigham, *American Newspapers* Clarence S. Brigham, *History and Bibliography of American Newspapers, 1690–1820*, 1947, 2 vols.

Bruce, *University* Philip Alexander Bruce, *History of the University of Virginia 1819–1919: The Lengthened Shadow of One Man*, 1920–22, 5 vols.

Bush, *Life Portraits* Alfred L. Bush, *The Life Portraits of Thomas Jefferson*, rev. ed., 1987

Chambers, *Poplar Forest* S. Allen Chambers, *Poplar Forest & Thomas Jefferson*, 1993

Claiborne, *Letter Books* Dunbar Rowland, ed., *Official Letter Books of W. C. C. Claiborne, 1801–1816*, 1917, repr. 1972, 6 vols.

Clay, *Papers* James F. Hopkins and others, eds., *The Papers of Henry Clay*, 1959–1992, 11 vols.

Connelly, *Napoleonic France* Owen Connelly and others, eds., *Historical Dictionary of Napoleonic France*, 1985

CVSP William P. Palmer and others, eds., *Calendar of Virginia State Papers . . . Preserved in the Capitol at Richmond*, 1875–93, 11 vols.

DAB Allen Johnson and Dumas Malone, eds., *Dictionary of American Biography*, 1928–36, 20 vols.

Destutt de Tracy, *Commentary and Review of Montesquieu's Spirit of Laws* Antoine Louis Claude Destutt de Tracy, *A Commentary and Review of Montesquieu's Spirit of Laws. prepared for press from the Original Manuscript, in the hands of the Publisher. To which are annexed, Observations on the Thirty-First Book, by the late M. Condorcet; and Two Letters of Helvetius, on the merits of the same work*, Philadelphia, 1811; Sowerby, no. 2327; Poor, *Jefferson's Library*, 10 (no. 623)

DBF *Dictionnaire de biographie française*, 1933– , 19 vols.

Dexter, *Yale Biographies* Francis Bowditch Dexter, *Biographical Sketches of the Graduates of Yale College*, 1885–1912, 6 vols.

DNB Leslie Stephen and Sidney Lee, eds., *Dictionary of National Biography*, 1885–1901, 22 vols.

Dolley Madison, *Selected Letters* David B. Mattern and Holly C. Shulman, eds., *The Selected Letters of Dolley Payne Madison*, 2003

DSB Charles C. Gillispie, ed., *Dictionary of Scientific Biography*, 1970–80, 16 vols.

DVB John T. Kneebone and others, eds., *Dictionary of Virginia Biography*, 1998– , 3 vols.

EG Dickinson W. Adams and Ruth W. Lester, eds., *Jefferson's Extracts from the Gospels*, 1983, *The Papers of Thomas Jefferson*, Second Series

Ford Paul Leicester Ford, ed., *The Writings of Thomas Jefferson*, Letterpress Edition, 1892–99, 10 vols.

Hatch, *Fruit Trees* Peter Hatch, *The Fruits and Fruit Trees of Monticello*, 1998

HAW Henry A. Washington, ed., *The Writings of Thomas Jefferson*, 1853–54, 9 vols.

Heitman, *Continental Army* Francis B. Heitman, comp., *Historical Register of Officers of the Continental Army during the War of the Revolution, April, 1775, to December, 1783*, rev. ed., 1914

Heitman, *U.S. Army* Francis B. Heitman, comp., *Historical Register and Dictionary of the United States Army*, 1903, 2 vols.

Hening William Waller Hening, ed., *The Statutes at Large; being a Collection of all the Laws of Virginia*, Richmond, 1809–23, 13 vols.

Hortus Third Liberty Hyde Bailey, Ethel Zoe Bailey, and the staff of the Liberty Hyde Bailey Hortorium, Cornell University, *Hortus Third: A Concise Dictionary of Plants Cultivated in the United States and Canada*, 1976

Jackson, *Papers* Sam B. Smith, Harold D. Moser, and others, eds., *The Papers of Andrew Jackson*, 1980– , 6 vols.

Jefferson, *Proceedings* Thomas Jefferson, *The Proceedings of the Government of the United States, in maintaining the Public Right to the Beach of the Missisipi, Adjacent to New-Orleans, against the Intrusion of Edward Livingston. prepared for the use of counsel, by Thomas Jefferson*, New York, 1812; Sowerby, nos. 3501, 3508; Poor, *Jefferson's Library*, 10 (no. 604)

Jefferson Correspondence, Bixby Worthington C. Ford, ed., *Thomas Jefferson Correspondence Printed from the Originals in the Collections of William K. Bixby*, 1916

JEP *Journal of the Executive Proceedings of the Senate of the United States*

JHD *Journal of the House of Delegates of the Commonwealth of Virginia*

JHR *Journal of the House of Representatives of the United States*

JS *Journal of the Senate of the United States*

JSV *Journal of the Senate of Virginia*

L & B Andrew A. Lipscomb and Albert E. Bergh, eds., *The Writings of Thomas Jefferson*, Library Edition, 1903–04, 20 vols.

Latrobe, *Papers* John C. Van Horne and others, eds., *The Correspondence and Miscellaneous Papers of Benjamin Henry Latrobe*, 1984–88, 3 vols.

Lay, *Architecture* K. Edward Lay, *The Architecture of Jefferson Country: Charlottesville and Albemarle County, Virginia*, 2000

LCB Douglas L. Wilson, ed., *Jefferson's Literary Commonplace Book*, 1989, *The Papers of Thomas Jefferson*, Second Series

Leavitt, *Poplar Forest* Messrs. Leavitt, *Catalogue of a Private Library . . . Also, The Remaining Portion of the Library of the Late Thomas Jefferson . . . offered by his grandson, Francis Eppes, of Poplar Forest, Va.* [1873]

Leonard, *General Assembly* Cynthia Miller Leonard, comp., *The General Assembly of Virginia, July 30, 1619–January 11, 1978: A Bicentennial Register of Members*, 1978

List of Patents *A List of Patents granted by the United States from April 10, 1790, to December 31, 1836*, 1872

Longworth's New York Directory *Longworth's American Almanac, New-York Register, and City Directory.* New York, 1796–1842 (title varies; cited by year of publication)

MACH *Magazine of Albemarle County History*, 1940– (title varies; issued until 1951 as *Papers of the Albemarle County Historical Society*)

Madison, *Papers* William T. Hutchinson, Robert A. Rutland, John C. A. Stagg, and others, eds., *The Papers of James Madison*, 1962– , 29 vols.

Congress. Ser., 17 vols.
Pres. Ser., 5 vols.
Sec. of State Ser., 7 vols.

Malone, *Jefferson* Dumas Malone, *Jefferson and his Time*, 1948–81, 6 vols.

Marshall, *Papers* Herbert A. Johnson, Charles T. Cullen, Charles F. Hobson, and others, eds., *The Papers of John Marshall*, 1974–2006, 12 vols.

MB James A. Bear Jr., and Lucia C. Stanton, eds., *Jefferson's Memorandum Books: Accounts, with Legal Records and Miscellany, 1767–1826*, 1997, *The Papers of Thomas Jefferson*, Second Series

McGehee and Trout, *Jefferson's River* Minnie Lee McGehee and William E. Trout III, *Mr. Jefferson's River: The Rivanna*, 2001

McMahon, *Gardener's Calendar* Bernard McMahon, *The American Gardener's Calendar; adapted to the Climates and Seasons of the United States*, Philadelphia, 1806; repr. 1997; Sowerby, no. 810; Poor, *Jefferson's Library*, 6 (no. 273)

Notes, ed. Peden Thomas Jefferson, *Notes on the State of Virginia*, ed. William Peden, 1955

ODNB H. C. G. Matthew and Brian Harrison, eds., *Oxford Dictionary of National Biography*, 2004, 60 vols.

OED James A. H. Murray, J. A. Simpson, E. S. C. Weiner, and others, eds., *The Oxford English Dictionary*, 2d ed., 1989, 20 vols.

Papenfuse, *Maryland Public Officials* Edward C. Papenfuse and others, eds., *An Historical List of Public Officials of Maryland*, 1990– , 1 vol.

Peale, *Papers* Lillian B. Miller and others, eds., *The Selected Papers of Charles Willson Peale and His Family*, 1983– , 5 vols. in 6

Pierson, *Jefferson at Monticello* Hamilton W. Pierson, *Jefferson at Monticello: The Private Life of Thomas Jefferson, From Entirely New Materials*, 1862

PMHB *Pennsylvania Magazine of History and Biography*, 1877–

Poor, *Jefferson's Library* Nathaniel P. Poor, *Catalogue. President Jefferson's Library* [1829]

Princetonians James McLachlan and others, eds., *Princetonians: A Biographical Dictionary*, 1976–90, 5 vols.

PTJ Julian P. Boyd, Charles T. Cullen, John Catanzariti, Barbara B. Oberg, and others, eds., *The Papers of Thomas Jefferson*, 1950– , 31 vols.

PW Wilbur S. Howell, ed., *Jefferson's Parliamentary Writings*, 1988, *The Papers of Thomas Jefferson*, Second Series

Randall, *Life* Henry S. Randall, *The Life of Thomas Jefferson*, 1858, 3 vols.

Randolph, *Domestic Life* Sarah N. Randolph, *The Domestic Life of Thomas Jefferson, Compiled from Family Letters and Reminiscences by His Great-Granddaughter*, 1871

Rush, *Letters* Lyman H. Butterfield, ed., *Letters of Benjamin Rush*, 1951, 2 vols.

Shackelford, *Descendants* George Green Shackelford, ed., *Collected Papers to Commemorate Fifty Years of the Monticello Association of the Descendants of Thomas Jefferson*, 1965

Sibley's Harvard Graduates John L. Sibley and others, eds., *Sibley's Harvard Graduates*, 1873– , 18 vols.

Sowerby E. Millicent Sowerby, comp., *Catalogue of the Library of Thomas Jefferson*, 1952–59, 5 vols.

Stanton, *Free Some Day* Lucia Stanton, *Free Some Day: The African-American Families of Monticello*, 2000

Stein, *Worlds* Susan R. Stein, *The Worlds of Thomas Jefferson at Monticello*, 1993

Terr. Papers Clarence E. Carter and John Porter Bloom, eds., *The Territorial Papers of the United States*, 1934–75, 28 vols.

TJR Thomas Jefferson Randolph, ed., *Memoir, Correspondence, and Miscellanies, from the Papers of Thomas Jefferson*, 1829, 4 vols.

U.S. Reports *Cases Argued and Decided in the Supreme Court of the United States*, 1790– (title varies; originally issued in distinct editions of separately numbered volumes with *U.S. Reports* volume numbers retroactively assigned; original volume numbers here given parenthetically)

U.S. Statutes at Large Richard Peters, ed., *The Public Statutes at Large of the United States . . . 1789 to March 3, 1845*, 1855–56, 8 vols.

VMHB *Virginia Magazine of History and Biography*, 1893–

Washington, *Papers* W. W. Abbot, Dorothy Twohig, Philander D. Chase, Theodore J. Crackel, and others, eds., *The Papers of George Washington*, 1983– , 48 vols.

Colonial Ser., 10 vols.
Confederation Ser., 6 vols.
Pres. Ser., 12 vols.
Retirement Ser., 4 vols.
Rev. War Ser., 16 vols.

William and Mary Provisional List *A Provisional List of Alumni, Grammar School Students, Members of the Faculty, and Members of the Board of Visitors of the College of William and Mary in Virginia. From 1693 to 1888* [1941]

WMQ *William and Mary Quarterly*, 1892–

Woods, *Albemarle* Edgar Woods, *Albemarle County in Virginia*, 1901

CONTENTS

CONTENTS

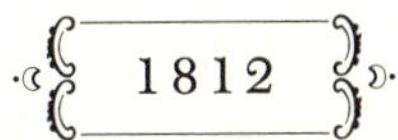

MAPS

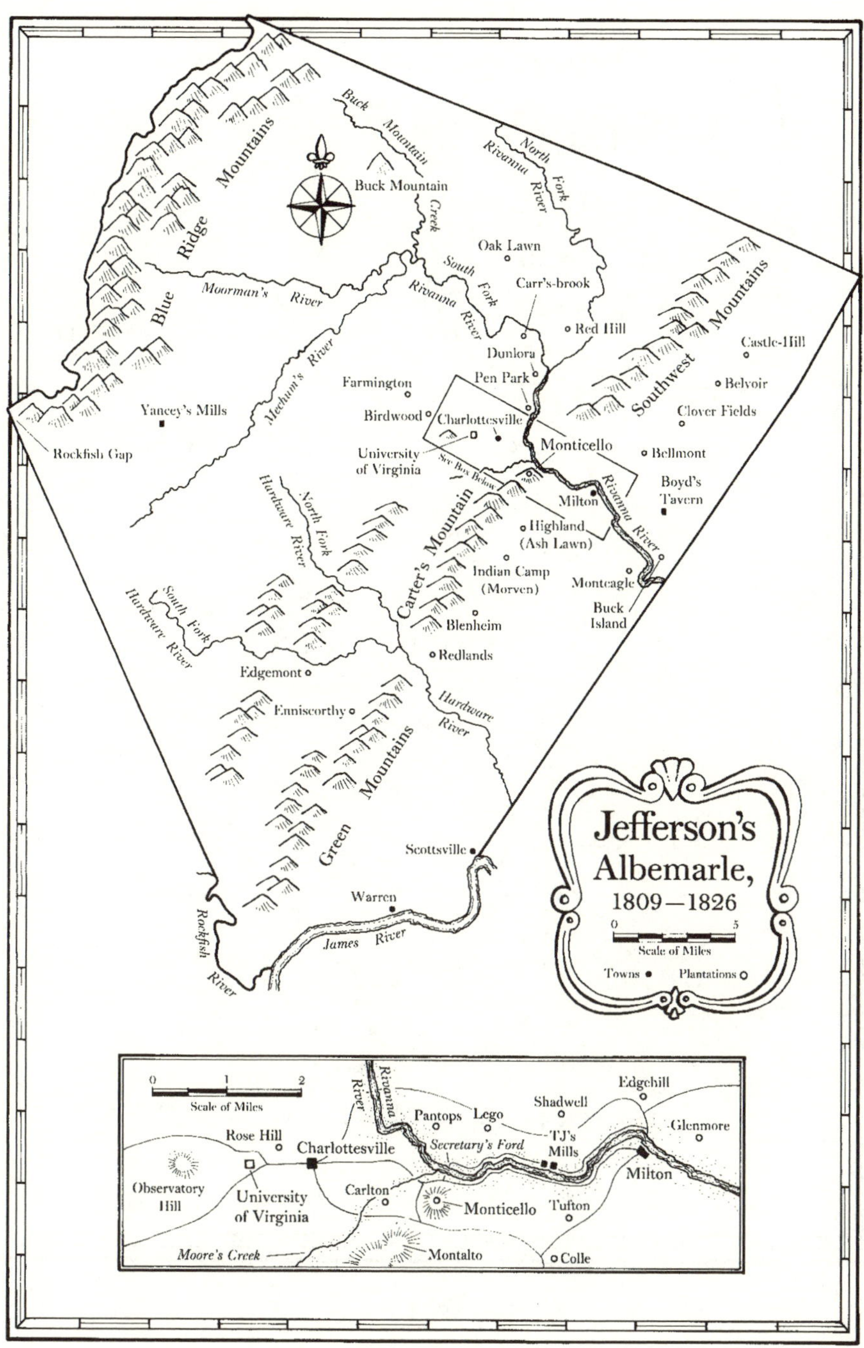

Jefferson's Albemarle, 1809–1826
0
5
Scale of Miles
Towns
Plantations
Blue Ridge Mountains
Buck Mountain Creek
Buck Mountain
North Fork Rivanna River
Oak Lawn
South Fork Rivanna River
Carr's-brook
Moorman's River
Red Hill
Southwest Mountains
Castle-Hill
Dunlora
Mechum's River
Farmington
Pen Park
Belvoir
Birdwood
Charlottesville
Clover Fields
Yancey's Mills
Monticello
Bellmont
Rockfish Gap
University of Virginia
See Box Below
Milton
Boyd's Tavern
Hardware River
North Fork
Carter's Mountain
Rivanna River
Highland (Ash Lawn)
Indian Camp (Morven)
Montcagle
Buck Island
South Fork Hardware River
Blenheim
Redlands
Edgemont
Enniscorthy
Hardware River
Green Mountains
Scottsville
Warren
James River
Rockfish River
0
1
2
Scale of Miles
River
Rivanna
Edgehill
Shadwell
Pantops
Lego
Glenmore
Rose Hill
Charlottesville
Secretary's Ford
TJ's Mills
Milton
Observatory Hill
University of Virginia
Carlton
Monticello
Tufton
Moore's Creek
Montalto
Colle

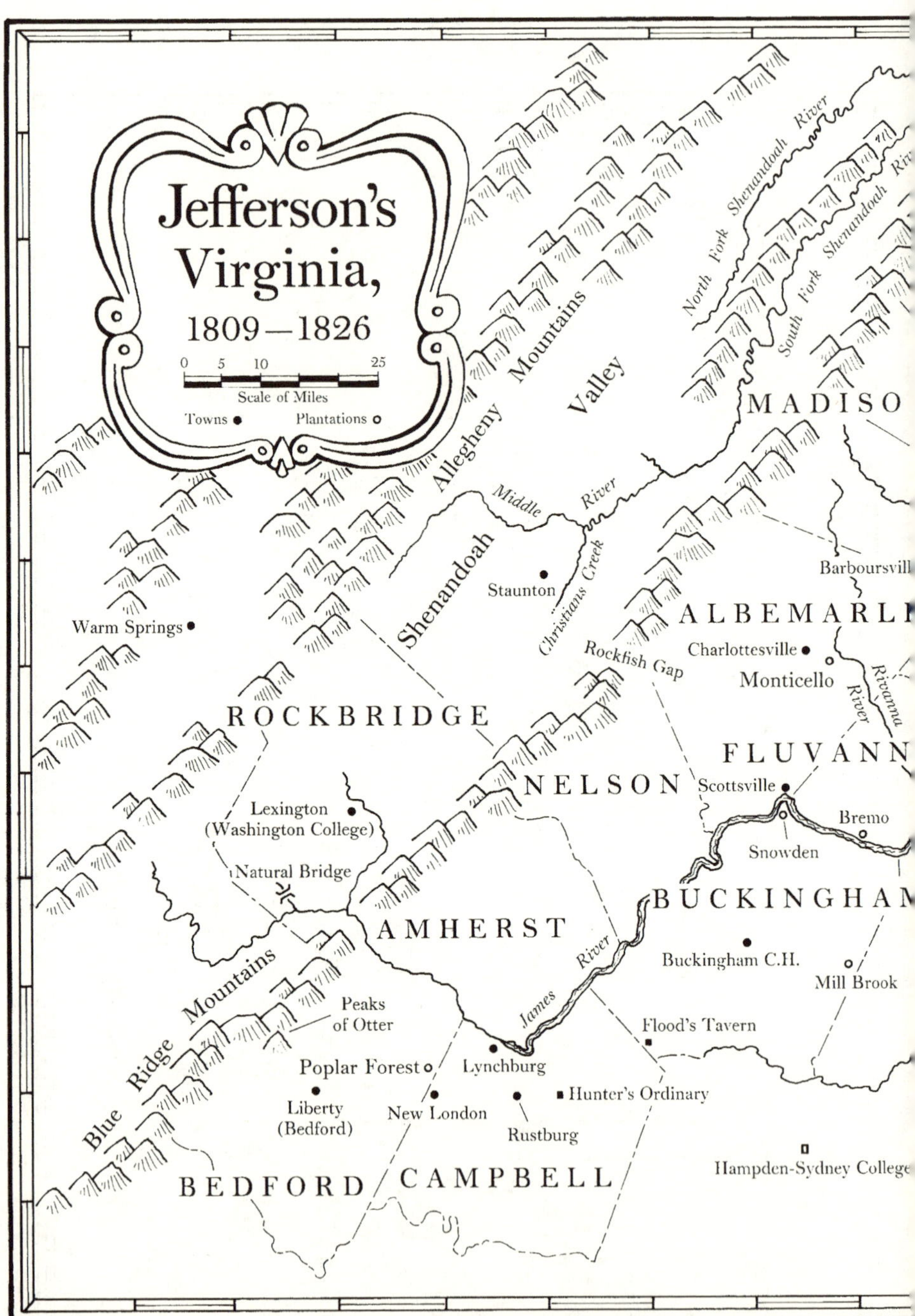
Jefferson's Virginia, 1809–1826
0 5 10 25
Scale of Miles
Towns
Plantations
Allegheny Mountains
Valley
North Fork Shenandoah River
South Fork Shenandoah River
MADISO
Middle River
Shenandoah
Staunton
Christians Creek
Barboursvill
Warm Springs
ALBEMARL
Rockfish Gap
Charlottesville
Monticello
Rivanna River
ROCKBRIDGE
FLUVANN
NELSON
Scottsville
Bremo
Lexington
(Washington College)
Snowden
Natural Bridge
BUCKINGHAM
AMHERST
James River
Buckingham C.H.
Mill Brook
Blue Ridge Mountains
Peaks of Otter
Flood's Tavern
Poplar Forest
Lynchburg
Liberty
(Bedford)
New London
Hunter's Ordinary
Rustburg
Hampden-Sydney College
BEDFORD
CAMPBELL

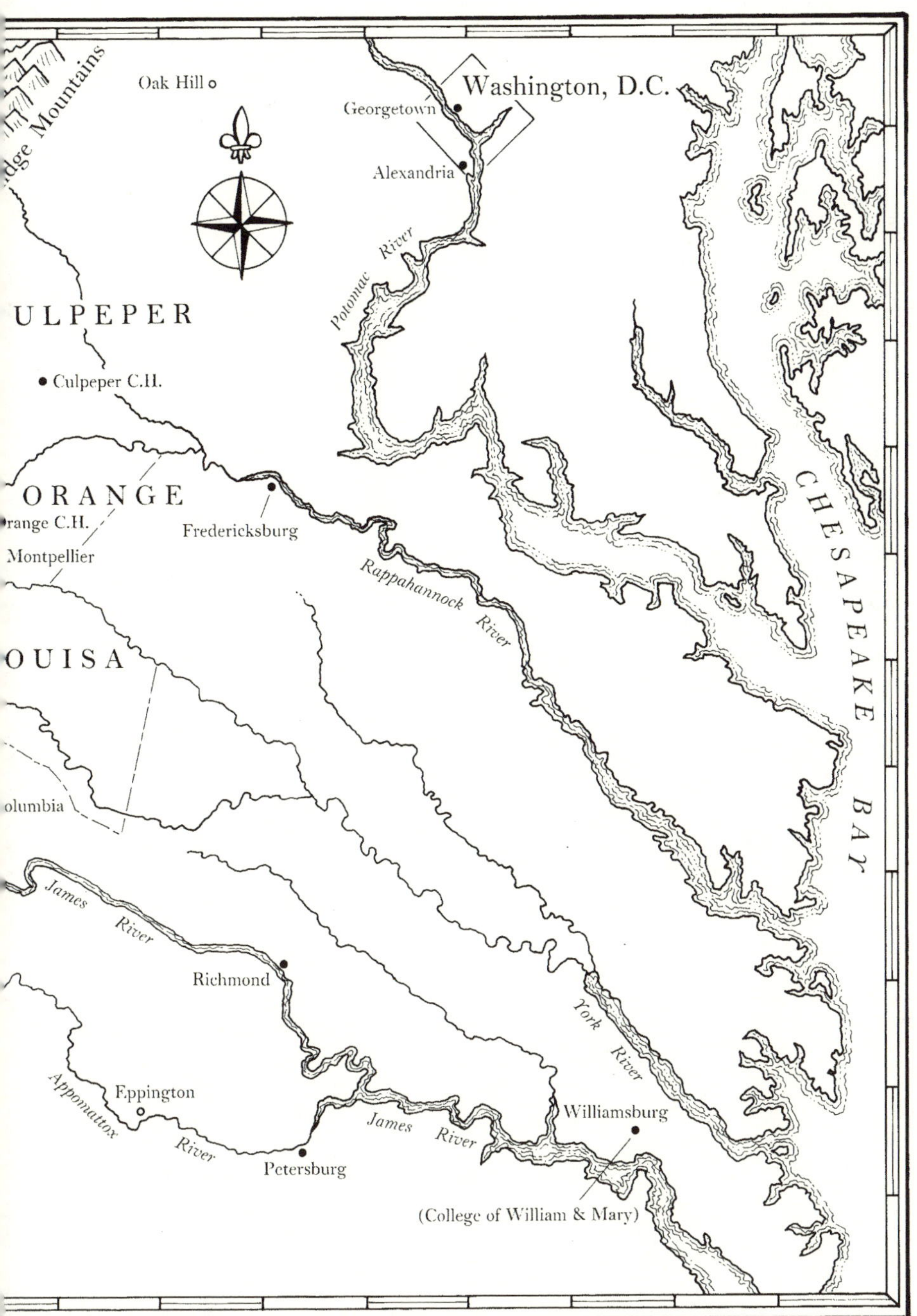

dge Mountains
Oak Hill
Washington, D.C.
Georgetown
Alexandria
Potomac River
ULPEPER
Culpeper C.H.
ORANGE
range C.H.
Montpellier
Fredericksburg
Rappahannock River
CHESAPEAKE BAY
OUISA
olumbia
James River
Richmond
York River
Eppington
Appomattox River
Petersburg
James River
Williamsburg
(College of William & Mary)

ILLUSTRATIONS

Following page 370

TITLE PAGE OF JEFFERSON'S MANUAL OF PARLIAMENTARY PRACTICE

In the winter of 1811–12 Jefferson received requests from two publishers, Mathew Carey, of Philadelphia, and Joseph Milligan, of Georgetown, for permission to print a second edition of his 1801 work, *A Manual of Parliamentary Practice. for the Use of the Senate of the United States.* Jefferson approved the requests and sent both men revisions amounting to approximately three additional pages of text. Carey decided to step aside after learning that Milligan had asked first and planned to proceed with the project. Milligan's revised edition appeared on 24 Mar. 1812. Although Jefferson's *Manual* has been republished often since 1812, all subsequent editions until 1988 seem to have been based on the 1801 edition. Milligan's text, however, contains Jefferson's last thoughts on a subject that was highly interesting to him and in which he made lasting contributions to American congressional procedure (*PW*, 32–5, 348–9; Carey to TJ, 21 Jan., 14 Feb. 1812; TJ to Carey, 27 Jan. 1812; Milligan to TJ, 2 Dec. 1811; TJ to Milligan, 7 Jan. 1812; Washington *National Intelligencer*, 24 Mar. 1812).

Courtesy of the University of Virginia.

TITLE PAGE OF JEFFERSON'S PAMPHLET ON THE BATTURE CASE

Jefferson's lengthy "Statement of the Usurpation of Edward Livingston on the Batture, or public Beach at New Orleans, and of the laws requiring his removal by the late Executive of the United States," which he had completed on 31 July 1810 and circulated to his legal counselors and others thereafter, provided the basis for his 1812 pamphlet on the controversy. Within three months of the dismissal of this case early in December 1811, Jefferson had composed a preface and arranged to have the pamphlet printed at his own expense by Ezra Sargeant, a publisher in New York. As requested by Jefferson, Sargeant sent the clerks of the United States House of Representatives and Senate copies of the finished work for distribution to every member of Congress. On 21 Mar. 1812 Sargeant sent additional copies to Jefferson, who began distributing them a month later to friends, politicians, and legal authorities.

Courtesy of the University of Virginia.

JEFFERSON'S MAP OF THE BATTURE

Jefferson made this and another copy of Charles V. Mansuy Pelletier's map of the Batture Sainte Marie in New Orleans (DLC: TJ Papers, 195:34665, 34659). Both of Jefferson's drawings are dated 15 Oct. 1808 and filed at the end of 1807 in his papers at the Library of Congress under the heading Batture Case, Reference Documents with Responses, 1807–13. This grouping of documents includes newspaper clippings, Jefferson's notes detailing various elements of the case, lists of legal precedents and exhibits, legal advice, and drafts of what would become Jefferson's pamphlet on the controversy. He believed that Pelletier's map documented massive, rapid, and dangerous changes in the channel of the Mississippi River resulting from Edward Livingston's construction projects on the batture. Jefferson therefore added the map to his Statement on the Batture Case, 31 July 1810, which he circulated to his legal counsel and to various political associates for their comments (Albert Gallatin's Notes on Thomas Jefferson's Statement on the Batture Case, [ca. 10 Sept. 1810]; TJ to Gallatin, 27 Sept. 1810).

Courtesy of the Library of Congress.

EDWARD LIVINGSTON BY JOHN TRUMBULL

Edward Livingston was a former political ally of Jefferson who labored under an enormous debt to the federal government after a clerk for whom he was responsible while serving as district attorney for New York absconded with public funds. Livingston moved to New Orleans to rebuild his fortunes and sued Jefferson for damages three years after the president ordered him removed from the batture in 1807. Livingston lost his suit against Jefferson but ultimately won a share of the land in question, paid his debts, reconciled with Jefferson, and attained the offices of United States secretary of state and minister plenipotentiary to France (*ANB*; *DAB*; Livingston's Bill of Complaint against Thomas Jefferson, enclosed in George Hay to TJ, 20 July 1810). John Trumbull created several likenesses of Jefferson when he visited him in Paris in 1786. He later painted four enormous historical paintings—including *The Declaration of Independence*—that were installed in the United States Capitol in 1826 (*ANB*; *DAB*; *PTJ*, 10:xxix–xxx, 466).

Collection of the City of New York. Courtesy of the Art Commission of the City of New York.

JEFFERSON'S FARM BOOK

Jefferson kept a record of his multitudinous agricultural activities in his farm book, a bound volume containing 178 pages of manuscript text (22 pages of which he left blank) followed by 202 additional blank pages, each measuring approximately 8 by 6.3 inches. The pages are not numbered after page 147. Jefferson made his first entry in 1774 and continued to add lists of slaves and landholdings, records of bread, beds, and blankets distributed, planting schedules, and notes on crops, animals, farm implements, and buildings until May 1826, just over a month before his death. In *Thomas Jefferson's Farm Book* (1953; repr. 1999), Edwin M. Betts provided a facsimile edition of the manuscript at the Massachusetts Historical Society, incorporated ten additional pages that had become separated from the bound work, and added full and partial transcriptions of many related documents. The page shown here contains Jefferson's Land Roll for 1810. He later struck through the last entry to indicate that he no longer owned the lot in Richmond that he sold to David Higginbotham in November 1811.

Courtesy of the Massachusetts Historical Society.

ILLUSTRATIONS

JEFFERSON'S MAP OF TOMAHAWK PLANTATION

This undated plat in Jefferson's hand bears an 1809 watermark and depicts the fields under cultivation at Tomahawk plantation, which was itself a part of his Poplar Forest estate in Bedford County. Jefferson drew most of the map with a pen and then used a pencil to assign the crops to be grown in the plantation's various fields, perhaps so that he could easily mark changes from year to year.

Courtesy of Mrs. Edwin C. Hutter.

TABLE WITH A REVOLVING TOP

Manufactured at the Monticello joinery by John Hemmings out of cherry, walnut, and southern pine, this table boasts tapered legs and a segmented decorative top. It was intended for use at Poplar Forest and is probably the "round table" referred to by Jefferson in his 5 Dec. 1811 letter from that place to Edmund Bacon. Jefferson's granddaughter Cornelia Randolph later sketched the table during one of her visits to his Bedford County retreat (Stein, *Worlds*, 262, 286–7).

Courtesy of the Thomas Jefferson Foundation.

ASTRONOMICAL CASE CLOCK

In a letter he wrote to his friend Robert Patterson on 11 Sept. 1811, Jefferson expressed his desire for a clock that kept perfect time and lacked "a striking apparatus, as it would be wanted for astronomical purposes only." Patterson's response recommended a fellow Philadelphian, Thomas Voigt, the son of a prominent clockmaker and coiner Jefferson had known during the 1790s. The completed eight-day clock, which Voigt made especially for Jefferson out of walnut with a mahogany veneer, was twice as expensive and much fancier than Jefferson had anticipated. Furthermore, the difficulty of shipping such a large object during the War of 1812 delayed its arrival at Monticello until December 1815. Jefferson placed the timepiece in his private suite of rooms and wrote the days of the week inside the clock so that its descending weight would mark the passage of the days (Stein, *Worlds*, 378–80).

Courtesy of the Thomas Jefferson Foundation.

BENJAMIN RUSH BY THOMAS SULLY

Benjamin Rush was a prominent physician in Philadelphia who promoted a wide range of reforms, including temperance, humane treatment of mental illness, the abolition of slavery, and the education of women. He had made periodic efforts to restore friendship between Jefferson and John Adams, his fellow signers of the Declaration of Independence. They both credited him as the prime mover in their reconciliation in 1812, which Rush regarded as one of the crowning achievements of his old age. Thomas Sully's portrait of Rush at his reading desk is listed twice in the artist's register of his works. He took Rush's likeness from life between 7 May and 20 July 1812. Two years after the doctor's death in 1813, Sully executed a replica of his earlier three-quarter length study. The painting depicted here was found in 1899 folded "amongst old papers &c. in the Library" of the American Philosophical Society. This unfinished portrait may be the original study made by Sully from life for use in later portraits and engravings (Rush to TJ, 3 May 1809; *A Catalogue of Portraits and other works of art in the possession of the American Philosophical Society* [1961], 86–7, 124).

Courtesy of the American Philosophical Society.

JOHN ADAMS BY GILBERT STUART

Jefferson's defeat of John Adams in the bitterly contested presidential election of 1800 led to a lengthy estrangement between the two men. Jefferson's attempt to effect a reconciliation in 1804 after Abigail Adams sent condolences on the death of his daughter Maria was eventually rebuffed. However, on 1 Jan. 1812 John Adams rewarded repeated entreaties by Benjamin Rush and wrote Jefferson a letter to which his erstwhile Revolutionary, congressional, and diplomatic colleague eagerly responded. The rich and extensive correspondence that resulted endured until their last days and is regarded as one of the pinnacles of their respective literary legacies. Gilbert Stuart was one of America's preeminent portraitists in the early decades of the new republic. He depicted Jefferson, the Washingtons, the Madisons, John Jay, Albert Gallatin, and many others during his long career. Stuart began an oil portrait of John Adams in 1798. Seventeen years elapsed and Stuart completed another likeness of Adams before he finished the portrait reproduced here. One authority suggests that the resulting painting "is a compromise between the Adams of 1798 and the Adams of 1815" (*ANB*; *DAB*; Andrew Oliver, *Portraits of John and Abigail Adams* [1967], 136, 140–1, 251).

Courtesy of the National Gallery of Art.

Volume 4

18 June 1811 to 30 April 1812

JEFFERSON CHRONOLOGY

1743 • 1826

1743	Born at Shadwell, 13 April (New Style).
1760–1762	Studies at the College of William and Mary.
1762–1767	Self-education and preparation for law.
1769–1774	Albemarle delegate to House of Burgesses.
1772	Marries Martha Wayles Skelton, 1 January.
1775–1776	In Continental Congress.
1776	Drafts Declaration of Independence.
1776–1779	In Virginia House of Delegates.
1779	Submits Bill for Establishing Religious Freedom.
1779–1781	Governor of Virginia.
1782	Martha Wayles Skelton Jefferson dies, 6 September.
1783–1784	In Continental Congress.
1784–1789	In France on commission to negotiate commercial treaties and then as minister plenipotentiary at Versailles.
1790–1793	Secretary of State of the United States.
1797–1801	Vice President of the United States.
1801–1809	President of the United States.

RETIREMENT

1809	Attends James Madison's inauguration, 4 March.
	Arrives at Monticello, 15 March.
1810	Completes legal brief on New Orleans batture case, 31 July.
1811	Batture case dismissed, 5 December.
1812	Correspondence with John Adams resumed, 1 January.
	Batture pamphlet preface completed, 25 February; printed by 21 March.
1814	Named a trustee of Albemarle Academy, 25 March.
	Resigns presidency of American Philosophical Society, 23 November.
1815	Sells personal library to Congress, 29 April.
1816	Writes introduction and revises translation of Destutt de Tracy, *A Treatise on Political Economy* [1818].
	Named a visitor of Central College, 18 October.
1818	Attends Rockfish Gap conference to choose location of proposed University of Virginia, 1–4 August.
	Visits Warm Springs, 7–27 August.
1819	University of Virginia chartered, 25 January; named to Board of Visitors, 13 February; elected rector, 29 March.
	Debts greatly increased by bankruptcy of Wilson Cary Nicholas.
1820	Likens debate over slavery and Missouri statehood to "a fire bell in the night," 22 April.
1821	Writes memoirs, 6 January–29 July.
1823	Visits Poplar Forest for last time, 16–25 May.
1824	Lafayette visits Monticello, 4–15 November.
1825	University of Virginia opens, 7 March.
1826	Writes will, 16–17 March.
	Last recorded letter, 25 June.
	Dies at Monticello, 4 July.

THE PAPERS OF
THOMAS JEFFERSON

From John Barnes

DEAR SIR— George Town 18th June 1811—

I am without any of your favors since that of the 4th April—Answered the 15th—on the 25th I had the Honor of inclosing to you Mrs Beckleys letter to me, respecting her Brothers unfortunate situation, since when nothing has transpired on that Acco^{t}—

Mr Barry called on me 21st Ult^{o} (since Married) when I paid him the $100– Messrs G & J. remitted me, Over and above, your $360. Int on Genl K. a/c

I have some thoughts of making a short Tour the insuing M^{o} to Philad^{a} (health permitting[1]) which of late I have not—as heretofore injoyed.—no Unusual[2] complaint (save weakness—&^{c}—the Natural affect, of advancd Age.)[3]—

as I expect to be—in Philad^{a} Middle July should you have any particular Commands—I should with pleasure Attend to them,—as well, whilst there—receive—via your Order—the good Gen^{l}s 6 M^{o}s dividend due 1st July—

I am Anxiously expecting to hear of your last years remittance to him—being safe in his Brokers hands—as well the present years—now—on its passage—

with great Respect, I am, Dear Sir, your most Obed^{t} servant

JOHN BARNES.

RC (ViU: TJP-ER); at foot of text: "Th: Jefferson Esqr Monticello Virg^{a}"; endorsed by TJ as received 27 June 1811 and so recorded in SJL.

Maria Prince Beckley's UNFORTUNATE brothers included Isaac Prince (Beckley to Barnes, 21 Apr. 1811, enclosed in Barnes to TJ, 25 Apr. 1811). G & J.: Gibson & Jefferson. K. A/C: Tadeusz Kosciuszko's account current.

[1] Manuscript: "permiitting."

[2] Manuscript: "Unsual."

[3] Omitted closing parenthesis editorially supplied.

To Hugh Chisholm

SIR Monticello. Tuesday June 18. 11.

We yesterday got up the wooden frame of our Pier-head compleat, and this morning mr Salmonds begins the stone-work. he will get to the spring of the arch this evening, or tomorrow morning before you can reach this from mr Madison's. I must pray you therefore to be with us tomorrow forenoon, the earlier the better. on arriving at the Pier head you will find your attendants on the spot, the same who attend Salmonds, as he must stop his work till you have turned the arch for him to proceed on. the mortar is there, ready made, the bricks & sand on the spot, and I shall probably be there myself. I must beseech you therefore not to fail us an hour, as besides Salmonds' work being stopped, I wait only for this job to be done to set out for Bedford, from whence I must be back to the beginning of our harvest. Accept my best wishes. TH: JEFFERSON

PoC (ViU: TJP); at foot of text: "M[r] Hugh Chisolm"; endorsed by TJ.

TJ kept a brief memorandum indicating that Chisholm "began to work with his negro boy 1811. May 7. or 8. plaistering the cisterns," that he finished 24 May, and that from "June 19. to 23." he "worked on the pier head" (MS in MHi, entirely in TJ's hand; on a small scrap; undated). In his Farm Book TJ noted completion of his mill's new pierhead this month, and that "it's floor is 9 f below the spring of the brick arch, and 10 f 2 I. below the crown of the arch" (Betts, *Farm Book*, pt. 1, 106). At this time Chisholm was also helping to renovate James Madison's Montpellier (Madison, *Papers, Pres. Ser.*, 3:318–9).

From John Martin Baker

SIR, Palma. Island of Majorca June 19th 1811—

I have the Honor to Enclose herewith a packet delivered to me at Cagliary by the professor Director General of His Sardinian Majesty's Cabinet of Natural History, at Said place, which accompanies a Box Containing Natural Petre productions of the mentioned Island—which will be forwarded to you sir, by William R Lee Esq[e] Collector at Salem—who will at the same time Send on One quarter Cask Albaflor Wine—One Bag Soft shell almonds 76.lb majorca weight, and One Box Olives: all which I hope may come Safe to hand, and I shall be particularly gratified that you approve of them—this opportunity Sir, is the very first, and the only direct one, from this Island to the United States, since my last return to my Station from America—per the first next that may offer I will not fail to remit

you the remainder of the Articles, I had the Honor to be Commissioned to send You. Times are very dull here, particularly in my Consular Station owing to the very few or no Arrivals of Vessels bearing our flag.—In the event of any Affrican, or European Commercial Seaport–Consular Vacancy, I pray You Sir, to hold me in view, and intercede in my behalf with His Excellency The President—
M[rs] Baker desires me sir, to present you her most Respectful Compliments—and I have the Honor to be, with the Highest Respect & Gratitude

Sir Your most obedient humble servant

John Martin Baker.

sir,
I am just informed, that the Consular office of Tripoly is vacant. If it be a truth, I pray you sir, to intercede for me for the appointment: & I beg leave to add, that I am conversant with the lengua-franca—now commonly used in Affrica, by the Cheifs &[c]—

RC (MHi); at foot of text: "To The Most Honorable Thomas Jefferson &[c] &[c] &[c] Monticello Virginia"; endorsed by TJ as received 15 Sept. 1811 and so recorded in SJL. Enclosure: Leonardo de Prunner to TJ, 15 Mar. 1810.

natural petre productions: in this context, mineral specimens. TJ commissioned Baker to send him goods from Majorca on 25 July 1809. George Davis had recently resigned his consular office at Tripoli for health reasons (Madison, *Papers, Pres. Ser.*, 4:54–5n).

From Charles L. Bankhead

Dear sir — Port Royal June 20th–11

I have recieved yours of the 10 June for which both my father and myself render you our gratefull acknowledgements. he thanks you sincerely for the information you have given him of Mr: Shorts intention to sell his land & to be remember,d by you will ever impose a debt of gratitude upon me, a debt which my heart most liberally repays. I should have answe[rd] you before this, but for the expectation of saying to you in person, what I now do by letter. M[r]: Radford of Lynchburgh[1] has lately written me on the subject of our land in Bedford, and express,d a strong desire to become a purchaser; supposing him acquainted with the price, Mr: Clay having promised to make that known, I had determined to set out immediately for Lynchburgh. As you are lately from the forest I should be obliged to you for any information you may have collected, as to the chances of finding a purchasor. M[r]: Radford requests me to fix a price. I must solicit your advice as to that also, as my answer will be determined by it. My father declines the purchase of Mr: Shorts land, both my mother and himself fearing at this time of their lives, to encounter the laborious & troublesome details of moveing, building, improveing &c. I wish indeed that there was a house on the place with some little improvements about it, for those are circumstances which I believe would make highlanders of us all. I am happy to hear Colo. Randolph is likely to succeed with the mill. I always thought from the adjacency of his farm, that the advantages resulting from the lease would be greater [to][2] him tha[n] to any other tenant. My warmest regards to Mr: & Mrs Randolp[h] and believe me my dear sir to be yours very affectionately CHAS: L BANKHEAD

RC (Robert Hill Kean, on deposit ViU: TJP); edge trimmed; at foot of text: "Mr: Jefferson"; endorsed by TJ as received 7 July 1811 and so recorded in SJL.

TJ was last at Poplar FOREST between 30 Jan. and 28 Feb. 1811 (*MB*, 2:1263).

Thomas Mann Randolph's Edgehill FARM was located close to TJ's Shadwell Mill.

[1] Manuscript: "Lyncburgh."
[2] Omitted word editorially supplied.

From George Jefferson

DEAR SIR Richmond 20th June 1811

I inclose an acct of the sales of 547 bbls of your flour, together with your acct current to this day, the last shewing a balance against you of \$:2671.$\frac{40}{100}$.—Deducting this sum from the 5800\$ obtained from the bank, (which is partly to be paid off with Harrisons dft, and the balance to be continued) leaves \$:3128.$\frac{60}{100}$ for which you are to draw.—You can likewise if you think proper draw for the probable amount of 54 barrels of flour received within these few days from Lynchburg; which I have not been able to sell, although very anxious to do so, both from a wish to close the sales of the whole together, and from a fear of holding it at this advanced season of the year, lest it should spoil. I suppose however that it has been but lately manufactured, and will therefore be safe for a short time at any rate. At present there is no demand whatever: no one will purchase except at a price greatly under the value—sales of small parcels having been made as low as \$:8.$\frac{1}{4}$.

I inclose a note for your signature, for renewal in the bank.—I have filled it up with 3000\$ as being a round sum.—if you prefer any other, you will of course make the necessary alteration. you will see from the date, when it will be wanted.

I am Dear Sir Your very humble servt GEO. JEFFERSON

I have bought the blankets, but at the very high price of 15/ each: this was not in consequence of an advance in the price, but of their great size, & very superior quality.—there are no common ones to be had.

G.J.

RC (MHi); between signature and postscript: "Thomas Jefferson esq^r"; endorsed by TJ as received 23 June 1811 and so recorded in SJL. Enclosures not found.

SJL records a missing letter of 17 June 1811 from TJ to Jefferson.

To Peter Minor

June. 20. 11.

Th: Jefferson presents his compliments to mr Peter Minor and sends him a bottle of oil of the last expression, in the wooden press placed under the beam of the cyder press. it's colour shews it preferable to the Iron press; and the ease with which this press is made is a further encoragement to the culture of the Benni. Th:J. will not make seed this year, owing to his having sowed it with a drill which covered it too deep.

RC (ViU: TJP); dateline at foot of text; addressed: "Mr Peter Minor Ridgeway." Not recorded in SJL.

From Robert Wash

D^R SIR St Louis June 20th 1811—

Your letter of the 11th may reached me by the last mail: from which I learn with considerable regret, that Mr Crafts changed the resolution he had formed, of passing by Monticello on his return to New york. That Gentleman's politeness & intelligence would have been an excuse for the haste & apparent negligence with which I had ventured to address you. From your letter, I am led further to conclude, that the N^os of the Louisiana Gazette containing a sketch of this country have never reached you. The News Papers containing those numbers could not be conveniently enclosed, and were therfore, entrusted to M^r C,— who promised to deliver them in person. It was that you might read Mr Breckenridge's remarks with more satisfaction, that induced me to submit to your inspection such an appology for a map.

I herewith enclose you seven N^os & will forward the rest in the course of a week or two. The Author I fear, has been rather too desirous of obtaining a reputation for writing truths with facility: But of his merit in this respect you are the better Judge. One thing tho' is most certain,—we need not blush at the coulour of his praise.—

We are so remote from the busy scenes of the world, & the mail establishments in this country So very defective, that we seldom get any thing like News. All is old before it reaches us.—The report of an engagement off the Capes of Virginia (which reached us by last nights Mail) has excited a lively interest in every class of people. The only wish expressed is, that it may be true.—

There are between 3 & 4 hundred men engaged in hunting on the head waters of the Missouri & Columbia, who meet with little or no opposition from the Indians.—A letter from Mr Bradburry received a few days since, informs us that he was within two or three days Journey of the Mandan Villages. He has sent down a number of valuable minerals & Indian curiosities, with a view to have them forwarded to his friends in Europe. I am truly sorry, that the scientifical labours of such a man as Mr Bradberry should depend upon Europe for their Just reward.—

Col. John Smith & F Morehead, Gentlemen of capital & great enterprise, left this place about ten days since, with 97 men to form an establishment at the lead mines on the Mississipi, about 40 miles this side of Prairie de Chien. It is expected that by the next winter, there will [be][1] 8 hundred or a thousand men engaged in raising mineral.—

we have had almost incessant rains for the last three months. Since the 1st of Freb^ry^ thirty five & a $\frac{1}{4}$ inches of water have fallen.—

with the most sincere respect & esteem y^rs^ &C R: Wash

P.S. The Potash, made in the manufactories which have been lately established at the U.S.'s Saline & other salt furnaces in this country, has been found to be so strongly impregnated with Marine acid as entirely to destroy it's utility. If a method could be suggested by which the M.A. might be seperated in the process, or its effects nutralized the labour of industrious w^d^ be richly reward & the public greatly benifits R: Wash

RC (DLC); addressed: "Thomas Jefferson Monticello Virginia"; endorsed by TJ as received 21 July 1811 and so recorded in SJL.

Henry Marie Brackenridge's REMARKS appeared in the 31 Jan., 7–28 Feb., 7–21 Mar., 4–25 Apr., and 20–27 June 1811 issues of the weekly Saint Louis *Louisiana Gazette*. He revised and republished them in his *Views of Louisiana; together with a journal of a voyage up the Missouri River, in 1811* (Pittsburgh, 1814; Sowerby, no. 4162).

MARINE ACID: muriatic, or hydrochloric, acid (*OED*).

[1] Omitted word editorially supplied.

To William Chamberlayne

SIR Monticello June 24. 11.

I have been longer than I had hoped in getting my produce to market & sold. it now enables me to inclose you a draught on Mess[rs] Gibson & Jefferson of Richmond for fifty nine dollars 74. Cents, the balance due according to the statement in my letter of Apr. 4. & your answer. I inclose you D[r] Everett's account for his attendance on the negro man, and Lewis's account for board & nursing with the award of the arbitrators to whom it was submitted by consent, and the receipt for the money. Accept the assurances of my great esteem & respect TH: JEFFERSON

PoC (MHi); at foot of text: "Gen[l] W[m] Chamberlayne"; endorsed by TJ. Enclosure: TJ's Account with Charles Everette, [ca. 23 Feb. 1810], enclosed in Everette to TJ, 1 Nov. 1810. Other enclosures not found.

Chamberlayne's missing ANSWER to TJ's letter of 4 Apr. 1811 is not recorded in SJL. The NEGRO MAN was Tom Buck, a slave TJ had rented from an estate managed by Chamberlayne and who had suffered a severe case of frostbite (TJ to Chamberlayne, 17 Aug. 1810).

To Charles Everette

DEAR DOCTOR Monticello June 24. 11.

My funds lying all in Richmond, I inclose you an order on Mess[rs] Gibson & Jefferson of that place for 42. D 20 c the balance of your account. but should it not be convenient to you to recieve the money in Richmond, I will on your intimation call for it by the first post. will you be so good as to sign the inclosed paper & return it to me by the bearer to be transmitted to Gen[l] Chamberlayne who, acting as executor for the estate of which the negro man was a part, informs me he must produce vouchers for the passing of his accounts. I hope you are recovering fast from the consequences of your fall. our good cherries are all gone, or we should have repeated the sending them. none remain but a few Morellas, too sour to be eaten. but if they would be acceptable they are at your service. Accept the assurances of my great esteem & respect TH: JEFFERSON

PoC (MHi); at foot of text: "D[r] Everett"; endorsed by TJ. Enclosures not found, but see Everette to TJ, 1 Nov. 1810, and enclosure.

William Chamberlayne was the EXECUTOR of Lyne Shackelford's estate. The NEGRO MAN was Tom Buck. TJ had cultivated morello cherries (MORELLAS) at Monticello since 1778. These late-season sour cherries were commonly used for pies, preserves, or brandy (Hatch, *Fruit Trees*, 95, 97–8; Betts, *Garden Book*, 75, 82n).

From Gideon Granger

Dear Sir General Post office June 24th. 1811

A few days past I rec'd your note acknowledgeing the receipt of my late list of Post offices, which was transmitted without my knowledge and in consequence of my suggesting a determination to furnish you, as I now do, by the volume herewith transmitted, a complete view of the present state of this Department.

Ever your friend G Granger

RC (DLC); in a clerk's hand, signed by Granger; at foot of text: "Thomas Jefferson Esqr late President of the United States"; endorsed by TJ as received 30 June 1811 and so recorded in SJL. Enclosure: *Table of Post Offices in the United States, with their distances from Washington City, and the names of the post-masters* (Washington, 1811).

TJ's brief note from Monticello, 7 June 1811, thanked Granger for "his new pamphlet of the Post offices" and described it as "a most valuable Manual" (PoC at DLC; endorsed by TJ).

To George Jefferson

Dear Sir: Monticello June 24. 11

Yours[1] of the 20th was recieved yesterday inclosing my account balance[2] 3128.60[3] and the estimated amount of 54. Barrels flour unsold, to be drawn for—there should be still[4] near 50. Barrels more to be recieved from Bedford. In consequence of your permission I am drawing on you as follows:

Dr. Everett of[5] Charlottesville	42.20
Gen.l Wm. Chamberlayne of N. Kent	59.74[6]
Jones & Howell Phila.	500.[7]
James Lyle	1000.
D. Higginbotham	1500.
	3101.94[8]

all those will present draughts, except Jones & Howell whom I inform by letter that you will[9] be so good as to remit them 500 Dol. immediately, which I must pray you to do. besides the order to D. Higginbotham, I give him one on you for the proceeds of the 7 hhds tob. sent from this place whenever you shall have sold it. they are supposed[10] to yield something upwards of 12,000 weight. if it is not too troublsome,[11] I will ask to know what has been the fate of the single hhd of tobo sent last, the overseer who made it, solliciting me to[12] enquire, as he supposes it much superior to that which went from another plantation. in addition to the above draughts I will pray you to forward me by post 150. Dollars. some symptoms of indisposition & the heat of the weather have induced me to defer my journey to Poplar Forest yours with combined[13] affection. TH. JEFFERSON

P.S. I returned the note for the bank signed at 3000D.

Tr (TJ Editorial Files); typescript by Isaac Mendoza Book Co., New York, 1941; between signature and postscript: "Mr. Jefferson."

SJL records letters of 24 June 1811 from TJ to JONES & HOWELL and to David HIGGINBOTHAM, not found, as well as Higginbotham's missing reply to TJ of 25 June 1811, received from Milton the same day.

[1] Typescript: "Upirs."
[2] Typescript: "balanxe."
[3] Typescript: "3124.60." Correct figure supplied from Jefferson to TJ, 20 June 1811.
[4] Typescript: "atill."
[5] Typescript: "pf."
[6] Typescript: "59.70." Correct figure supplied from *MB*, 2:1266, and TJ to Chamberlayne, 24 June 1811.
[7] Typescript: "200." Correct figure supplied from *MB*, 2:1266.
[8] Typescript: "3101.90."
[9] Typescript: "wull."
[10] Typescript: "suppose."
[11] Punctuation corrected from period by Editors.
[12] Typescript: "ti."
[13] Thus in typescript.

To James Lyle

DEAR SIR Monticello June 24. 11.

The process of getting my flour to market from Bedford and this place, and of getting it sold, has been slower than I had hoped. it is now so far effected as to enable me to inclose you an order on Gibson & Jefferson for one thousand Dollars. I shall not fail to make as great an exertion from my future crops as they will enable me to do for the completion of the paiment of my debt to you. 3000.D. still unpaid in the bank will cramp me the ensuing spring, but that once discharged, I shall be able to make a close of this long indulged debt. I remark what you say of Edward Bolling's debt to me, assigned to you, & that you have to sue him for his father's debt. I beseech you to add mine to his debt to you so that it may be comprehended in the recovery, or I shall lose it. this letter shall secure you against being accountable to me for it, unless you recover it from him. wishing you a continuance of life and health, I add the assurance of my continued affection & respect TH: JEFFERSON

PoC (MHi); at foot of text: "James Lyle esq."; endorsed by TJ. Enclosure not found.

From William McGehee

SIR June 24th 11

your boy came down today while I was in the woods geting timber for the Sithes with a line concening Bens absence from the Conmll[1] my family informed me that he wanted an answer which I now prseed to give I stoped Ben for the purpose of assisting about planting the Tobacco tryd to find Fill also but could not this was done in conciquence of finding that the seasson would be gone before I could get done unless I raised all the hands I could & then to hurrey them another reason why I did so is notwithstanding I am doing your bisness for a certain sum feel it much more my intrest to make you a good crop than a sorry one & that I feel a greater regard for my Character than I do for only this one years wages & I hope it will be no offence if I further observe that if you cant see it I plainly can that the way your matters are at present planed you are to loose wheet considerably after you have read this I am perfectly willing that you Should do as you see cause I can but do as well as I can

am Sir Sincerely your well wisher WM MCGEHEE

RC (MHi); dateline at foot of text; addressed: "Conl Jefferson"; endorsed by TJ as an undated letter received 24 June 1811; with notes by TJ on verso:

"wages for 1811	£65–0–0
12. geese, 2. turkies	2–2–0
3½ doz. eggs	1–9
	67–3–9
By 70.℔ beef	1–0–5
	66–3–4"

and his calculations of the dollar equivalent of this sum. On 6 Apr. 1812 TJ settled his account with McGehee by giving him an order on Gibson & Jefferson for $220.56, the dollar equivalent of £66.3.4 (*MB*, 2:1275).

McGehee was gathering wood to construct cradle scythes (SITHES), a tool larger than the common scythe that was used to harvest heavier crops such as wheat and barley. TJ's LINE to McGehee is not recorded in SJL and has not been found. FILL: Phill Hubbard.

A missing letter from McGehee to TJ of 13 Mar. 1812 is recorded in SJL as received from Columbia on 19 Mar. 1812.

[1] Abbreviation for "Corn mill."

From George Jefferson

DEAR SIR Richmond 27th June 1811

I have sold your last 54 barrels of flour to Wm McKenzie at 8.½ & 9$. (5 barrels being fine only)[1] on a credit of 60 days, his note to be endorsed by Jno Lesslie.—For the reasons before assigned you will be pleased to consider this likewise as a Cash sale.

I am Dear Sir Your Very humble servt GEO. JEFFERSON

RC (MHi); at foot of text: "Thomas Jefferson esq^{r}"; endorsed by TJ as received 10 July 1811 and so recorded in SJL. Dupl (MHi); entirely in James Ligon's hand; on verso of RC of Jefferson to TJ, 4 July 1811, and received by TJ with that letter on 7 July 1811.

[1] Parenthetical phrase omitted in Dupl.

From Edmund M. Blunt

SIR, New-York, June 28, 1811

Permit me to enclose for inspection a copy of the Nautical Almanac for 1812—I confess myself governed principally by interest, in soliciting your opinion of a work which, if incorrect, is not only useless, but extremely dangerous. I was this day informed at the Navy Office the Officers were furnished by government, and they used that published by Mr John Garnett—His Almanac for 1811 contains Nine, and for 1812, Thirteen Errors, one of which is an error of 90°—Should you consider my work entitled to the patronage of the country your approbation will sanction its sale; if, like the one to which I refer, you should discover the least deviation from what it should be, I will consign the whole edition to the flames, where every work should be that misleads the Mariner on the pathless ocean.

Respectfully your obt sert EDM. M. BLUNT

P.S. A reply will confer an honor on one who has ever appreciated your talents

RC (DLC); between dateline and salutation: "Thomas Jefferson, Esq"; endorsed by TJ as received 2 July 1811 and so recorded in SJL. Enclosure: Blunt, *The Nautical Almanac and Astronomical Ephemeris for the year 1812* (New York, 1811; Sowerby, no. 3810).

Edmund March Blunt (1770–1862), a native of Portsmouth, New Hampshire, published the *Impartial Herald* in Newburyport, Massachusetts, 1793–96. He also operated a bookstore and a circulating library there. In 1796 Blunt published the *American Coast Pilot*, a source that gave nautical directions for the most important harbors, capes, and headlands of North America and portions of South America. The work was translated into many languages and went through numerous editions during his lifetime. Blunt also printed other nautical works and an 1817 guide to New York City, to which he moved about 1810 (*DAB*; Brigham, *American Newspapers*, 1:379; *Longworth's New York Directory* [1810], 111; *New-York Times*, 6 Jan. 1862).

Blunt wrote a similar letter to President James Madison on the same day (Madison, *Papers, Pres. Ser.*, 3:361; see also same, 4:343).

From James Chamberlain

Mississippi Territory, Jefferson county 18 miles from Natchez & 7 miles from Greenville; the county town, [received 28 June 1811]

Worthy Sir—

This strange application will, I have no doubt, surprise you, but dire necessity compels me to it—being well acquainted with your benificence, makes me thus bold to apply to you to save me from ruin,—to detail the cause or causes of my present embarrasment perhaps wou,d be useless, inasmuch as you can not in the least be acquainted with the facts—but suffice it to say, that at the commencement of the Embargo system, tho, I much approved of it, and still shou,d, had it been persevered in, because I think it wou,d have had, completely, the effect contemplated by it.—I was at that time in debt for the purchase of property which was to be paid out of my crop of cotton then growing which woud have been sufficient if the then price had continued,

But behold the price of cotton in an instant reduced nearly two thirds from the price it was when those Debts were contracted. Add to this the loss of two valuable negroes, apart of the purchase; and unfortunately for me from that description of men that opposed the System and now sport with my embarrasments and laugh at my admiration of the measure, consequently will not give me further indulgence. I have used every proper exertion that lay within my reach to discharge my debts, and have annually paid all that I made, among my creditors. but last year an uncommon drought occured my fields yeilded in consequence an half crop of cotton & but one third of corn,—And then to crown the climactur—I sold my cotton on a credit in order to get a higher price, the firm shortly after failed, tho tis said they will be able to pay all, yet it will be several years before they can effect it; tis generally said[1] that they are honest, the best thing, or name they can possess.

there are two executions VS, me, the delay of payment is spun out to the last moment, on the third monday in July the money ought to be paid but by an indulgence of the Sheriff, he takes upon himself the responsibility of delaying it about two months longer;

If I am not releived by that time all my personal[2] property will be sacrafised, no property of any kind will at this time bring half its value; And then—Oh horrible—a prison more horrible than all. save me my great & good Chief and three little boys (my children) from such a dreadful catastrophe—by the aid of one thousand Dollars. I can save all of my Property and rise again sufficiently to educate my poor little boys by the time that their age may require it;—I can & will return it to you in one & two years, tho, if you will extend the payment of[3] it all, to two years, I will come in person and do myself the honor and exquisite pleasure[4] of laying it at the feet of my Chief and benefactor.—I am well aware that it woud be by the covetous, and iron hearted part of mankind, thot, madness to trust a man utterly unknown to them, but were I known to your honor, (excuse me) you wou,d not hesitate a moment in relieving me, Your Excellency are I presume directly, or indirectly acquainted with some of the most conspicuous characters of this Territory, to whom you can if you please entrust the transaction of this business[5] by forwarding the sum to them directing them if you chuse and they think proper, to take sufficient Security which I can easily give.—Allow me for that purpose to name to you Gen[l] Ferdinand Lee Claiborne, a Gentleman of the first[6] respectability and fortune—hasten my dear and renowned Chief and save me.

I will further state what are my Present circumstances Vzt, five negroes slaves (I,ll be[7] particular)—

Guy	35 years of age	all of them[8] are valuable Some horses horned cattle hogs, &[a]
Sam[l]	17 D[o]	
Peter	15 D[o]	
Philis & Liza—18 and 16 years of age		

I have two tracts of uncultivated land in West florida of 640 acres each[9] said to be good but can not convert them into cash at present; and one of five hundred in this Territory confirmed by the board of Commissioners, it is also in a state of nature.

I have no one to look to for assistance my father was ruined in the revolution by the British under the infamous Arnold, at the time of his incursion into Virginia, every thing that he had, (which was considerable)[10] a small plantation excepted, was either destroyed or taken off—while he was in arms against the foes of mankind, he never recovered his circumstances tho, he was assisted by the immortal Washington. he is now living in Kentucky, about 70 years of age—in low circumstances.

I emigrated to this country in the year 1800—with nothing but myself, and have made what I have before stated by my exertions—I know not what to say—but will add that I am a native of Loudoun County Virginia born near Leesburg 9th August 1778—my three children—are Louis—Ferdinand[11] and Jefferson, of the ages of 8—6—& 4 whether you relieve me or not, (of which I have great hopes.) may the Deity Smile on you in the climes of bliss & give you that seat among Angels which you so[12] justly merited among men is the sincere wish of JAMES CHAMBERLAIN

That the foregoing is a true and just statement of my embarrasments, that they [were] occassioned not by any improper conduct of mine, I do declare Solemnly before the great Deity of the Heavens

My Great & honorable Chief, let me add that one of the principle inducements to apply to you was—your declining a third Presidency, an allurement, exclusive of the honor that but few cou,d withstand your wealth is great—your Goodness greater—and a thousand Dollars for the space of two years is scarsely worth your recolecting—and still it will save me from ruin, I have 50. acres in cotton which will yield me about as many thousand wt. if I can keep my negroes & horses from being sold.—hasten great friend of the human race & relieve me, take nothing amiss in my uncouth stile, I sincerely beg of you, they are the pure Sentiments of my Heart, God bless you

JAMES CHAMBERLAIN

RC (MHi); mutilated at crease; adjacent to dateline: "The Honorable Citizen Thomas Jefferson Esqr"; undated; endorsed by TJ as received 28 June 1811 and so recorded in SJL.

James Chamberlain (b. 1778) was an overseer at Mount Locust in Jefferson County, Mississippi, when in about 1806 he married Paulina Ferguson, the widow of the previous owner and the mother of seven. The Chamberlains had three children of their own. According to family tradition, Chamberlain deserted his family in 1812. Paulina Ferguson was listed as head of household at Mount Locust in the 1820 census, when a James Chamberlain with a wife and daughter was living in Pike County, Mississippi (Marius M. Carriere Jr., "Mount Locust Plantation: The Development of Southwest Mississippi during the Frontier Period, 1810–1830," *Journal of Mississippi History* 48 [1986]: 187, 188n; Kelly Obernuefemann and Lynnell Thomas, *Travel, Trade, and Travail: Slavery on the Old Natchez Trace* [2001], 7, 11, 12n, 61; DNA: RG 29, CS, 1820).

On 4 July 1811 Chamberlain sent a similar letter from Mount Locust to James Madison. In that letter he requested $600 and gave the names of his sons as Ferdinand Lee, Louis Washington, and Jefferson Madison Chamberlain (Madison, *Papers, Pres. Ser.*, 3:369). Other records cited above give the latter two names as Louis Bonaparte and Thomas Jefferson Chamberlain.

CLIMACTUR: "climacteric."

[1] Manuscript: "said said."
[2] Manuscript: "peronal."
[3] Preceding three words interlined.
[4] Manuscript: "plasure."
[5] Manuscript: "busibess."
[6] Word interlined.
[7] Manuscript: "(be."
[8] Manuscript: "then."
[9] Preceding four words interlined.
[10] Omitted closing parenthesis editorially supplied.
[11] Manuscript: "Ferdinadand."
[12] Word interlined.

From Benjamin Rush

Dear Sir, Philadelphia June 28th 1811

I enclose you another Attempt to combat a greater enemy to the prosperity and liberties of the United states, than the fleets of Britain and the Armies of Bonaparte. It is intended to catch the eye of the Common people—upon the doors of School houses, Court houses and Churches. For this purpose suppose it were republished in your state. Bishop Madison would I have no doubt concur in it, for I know him to think humanely and piously upon this Subject.

Health and friendship! from Dear Sir Yours truly

RC (MHi); addressed (torn): "Thomas Jefferson Mo[nticello]"; postmarked Philadelphia, 28 June; endorsed by TJ as a letter from Rush received 2 July 1811 and so recorded in SJL. Enclosure: Rush, *A view of the physical, moral, and immoral effects of certain liquors upon the body and mind of man, and upon his condition in society* (Philadelphia, 1808), or an otherwise unknown later edition.

On this day Rush also sent a copy of his temperance broadside to John Adams, asking that he "Send it to the parson of your parish" or "any other person that you think will republish it and cause copies of it to be pasted upon the doors of your school and court and meeting houses in different parts of the state" (Rush, *Letters*, 2:1086).

To John Barnes

Dear Sir Monticello June. 29. 11.

Your favor of June 18th is recieved as had been in due time that of Apr. 25. I now inclose you the order on the bank of Pensva for Genl Kosciuzko's July dividend. I inclosed to him one copy of the bill of exchange you sent me by mr Barlow, & a 2d by mr Warden, both then expected to sail shortly & in different vessels. I have not however as yet heard of the actual sailing of either. the newspapers say they are detained till the arrival of the Essex hourly expected. still I think it would be better if you, in your visit to Philadelphia, could find some eligible conveyance for the 3d of Exchange, which with that view I now return to you. I recieved mrs Beckley's letter in yours. presuming her unable to pay what is due to me, I mean not to have it mentioned to her again. it's reciept would always have been & still would be a sensible convenience to me, as small sums give me difficulty while I am devoting every thing to my Washington debt, in order to get out of the bank: but impossible things must be thought no more of. you did right in paying Barry the hundred Dollars. I wonder mr Jefferson did not mention they were for him, as I had done in my order. I thank you for your kind offer of service in Philada, but at present have nothing particular for that place. expecting that the harvest we are now reaping will clear me of the bank, I am looking forward to the time, not distant I hope, when I may send to Philadelphia for every thing I use in my family. I pay 167 D. here for what costs 100.D. there. freight & charges add only 20. p[r] c[t]. if you could recommend any merchant there who would purchase for me on Commission as faithfully and kindly as you used to do, it would be a valuable service to me, as soon as I am in a state to avail myself of it. I learn with concern the increase of feebleness of which you complain. I may sympathize in it the more feelingly inasmuch as I am very sensible of it in myself. I have long lost the power of walking any distance, and feel that I do not ride now with as little fatigue as I used to do. providence is kindly withdrawing by degrees the enjoiments of life that we may leave it without reluctance. I wish you had thought a visit to Monticello as friendly to your views of health[1] as Philadelphia. I am persuaded it would have been as much so, and been recieved with more welcome in our tranquil situation, than the bustle & distraction of a great town will admit. try it the next experiment you make with the same view, and follow afterwards the course which shall have proved itself most favorable, and accept in the mean time my prayers for a longer continuance of the blessings of strength, health & happiness. TH: JEFFERSON

PoC (DLC); at foot of first page: "M[r] Barnes"; endorsed by TJ. Enclosure: TJ to Jonathan Smith, Monticello, 29 June 1811: "Be pleased to have paiment made to John Barnes or order of all dividends which shall become due on the 1st day of July ensuing for the shares of stock held by Gen[l] Thaddeus Kosciuzko in the bank of Pensylvania, for which this shall be your sufficient voucher" (RC at Christie, Manson and Woods International, Inc., New York, 1993; in TJ's hand and signed by him as "Atty for Gen[l] Thad. Kosciuzko"; below signature: "The Cashier of the Bank of Pensylvania"; with subjoined notation by Smith: "Pay $400 & Charge Tho: Jefferson").

On 15 Apr. 1811 Barnes sent TJ three sets of a bill OF EXCHANGE drawn by Bowie & Kurtz on William Murdock, of London, not found.

This month the physician Clark Sanford completed and at some point sent TJ an essay on Peruvian bark (*cinchona*), describing at length its various forms, methods of preparation, proper dosages, and use in treating intermittent fevers and other maladies common among the aged (printed circular letter dated Greenwich, Conn., June 1811, in DLC: Rare Book and Special Collections; with handwritten address: "Thomas Jefferson Esqr. Monticello"; endorsed by TJ: "Bark Peruvian").

[1] Manuscript: "heath."

From David Bailie Warden

SIR, Washington, 1 July, 1811—

I beg leave to inform you, that the Essex is arrived, and that we expect to sail in the course of eight, or ten days. I received, from Mr. Graham, the note which you were pleased to write, with the inclosed letter for Paris—Since that time, I took the liberty of sending you a copy of my translation of Gregoires' work on Blacks, in which he examines your opinions concerning their capacity for improvement. He proposes to write a Biographical-Dictionary of all Individuals who have distinguished themselves in the cause of freedom, of which he is still an enthusiast. He is obliged to keep this project a secret at Paris.

I have great hopes of being able to carry with me a copy of the commentary on[1] Montesquieus' spirit of laws, which you were pleased to mention to me—Mr. Duane recommended it to me in the highest terms—

I have amused myself lately in examining the productions and improvements of this district, and have some idea of writing a kind of Itinerarie, which may be useful to strangers who visit, or who propose to inhabit Washington. I do not find that there exists here any register of the temperature of the atmosphere, predominant winds & &—, and having been informed, that you paid great attention to this subject, you will oblige me much, if convenient, to furnish me a brief abstract of your observations on this subject—

I have lately seen chicoreé, Chicorium Intubus—in a luxuriant state, in a dry soil, at Masons' island—I suspect that it might be cultivated, in this district, with great advantage, as food for cattle—

It is well ascertained that the Captain of the Melampus declared to that of the Tamahamak, which he carried to Halifax, that he had received positive orders to capture all american vessels bound to France—

Mr. Pinkney is arrived in this City. He proposes to bring his family here on a visit. Mr. Foster has taken lodgings at Crawfords' Georgetown

I am, Sir, with respects to Mr & Mrs Randolph and family,—and with sincere thanks for the interest you have taken in my welfare

Your ever obliged & devoted Sevt D B: WARDEN

RC (DLC); at foot of text: "Thomas Jefferson Esquire"; endorsed by TJ as received 7 July 1811 and so recorded in SJL.

Both TJ's NOTE to Warden and the letter to Tadeusz Kosciuszko it covered are dated 12 May 1811. SJL records no covering letter from Warden SENDING TJ his translation of Henri Grégoire, *An Enquiry concerning the Intellectual and Moral Faculties, and Literature of Negroes* (Brooklyn, 1810; Sowerby, no. 1399), and none has been found. Warden eventually published his ITINERARIE as *A Chorographical and Statistical Description of the District of Columbia* (Paris, 1816; Poor, *Jefferson's Library*, 7 [no. 362]). On 21 June 1811 the British frigate *Melampus* captured the *Tamaahmaah* (TAMAHAMAK) off Sandy Hook, New Jersey. The British commander, Edward Hawker, reportedly stated that "his orders oblige him to send in all vessels bound to France" (New York *Public Advertiser*, 25 June 1811).

[1] Reworked from "of."

From Horatio Turpin

DEAR SIR Palmyra 2 July 1811.

This will be handed you by Mr Wm Harris the Grandson of your Old Acquaintance Col^o^ John Harris of the Mankin town who wishes to go on board of the Navy and if you could by a letter to the President be instrumental in Obtaining a birth for him he would be thankful to you to do so, he is a young Gentleman of good morals addicted to none of the prevalent vices & I think I can with Safety pledge myself for his intrepidity bravery and that he will never disgrace the American flag by Striking to inferior force whenever it may be his lot to have the command of a vessel

As Our present prospects with the belligerent powers will Justify an expectation of a Rupture young Men of his Undaunted courage will probably be Acceptable to his Country

As Offices to which danger is attach'd perhaps are not so frequently apply,d for, the difficulty of obtaining a Suitable birth would not be So great as those where more ease and safety and better pay are expected, Should you think this recommendation would Justify you for an Application in his favour you would confer an Obligation on me

Mrs Turpin Join me in presenting our best wishes to yourself, and also Mrs Randolph and family who we expect are with you and am respectfully thy friend HORATIO TURPIN.

PS. W^ms^ Father Jordan Harris and his Brother John Harris were both Revolutionary officers in Our last war HT—

RC (MHi); dateline above postscript; addressed: "Mr Thomas Jefferson Monticello Mr Harris"; with unrelated calculation by TJ on address cover; endorsed by TJ as received 5 July 1811 from "Palmyra. Powhatan" and so recorded in SJL.

MANKIN TOWN: Manakin Town, in Cumberland County (*MB*, 1:298n).

To James Madison

Dear Sir Monticello July 3. 11.

I have seen with very great concern the late Address of mr Smith to the public. he has been very ill advised both personally and publicly. as far as I can judge from what I hear, the impression made is entirely unfavorable to him. every man's own understanding readily answers all the facts and insinuations, one only excepted, and for that they look for explanations without any doubt that they will be satisfactory. that is Erving's case. I have answered the enquiries of several on this head, telling them at the same time, what was really the[1] truth, that the failure of my memory enabled me to give them rather conjectures than recollections. for in truth I have but indistinct recollections of the case. I know that what was done was on a joint consultation between us, and I have no fear that what we did will not have been correct & cautious. what I retain of the case, on being reminded of some particulars, will re-instate the whole firmly in my remembrance, and enable me to state them to enquirers with correctness, which is the more important from the part I bore in them. I must therefore ask the favor of you to give me a short outline of the facts which may correct as well as supply my own recollections. but who is to give an explanation to the public? not yourself certainly. the chief magistrate cannot enter the Arena of the newspapers. at least the occasion should be of a much higher order. I imagine there is some pen at Washington competent to it. perhaps the best form would be that of some one personating the friend of Erving, some one apparently from the North. nothing laboured is requisite. a short & simple statement of the case, will, I am sure, satisfy the public.—we are in the midst of a so so harvest; probably one third short of the last. we had a very fine rain on Saturday last. ever affectionately Yours Th: Jefferson

RC (DLC: Madison Papers); at foot of text: "The President of the US." PoC (DLC).

Among the facts and insinuations in his *Address to the People of the United States* (Baltimore, 1811), Robert Smith charged that, as secretary of state, Madison had improperly allowed the American claims agent in London, George W. Erving, to retain $2\frac{1}{2}$ percent of the sums paid by the British government between 1801 and 1805 to settle American claims, a commission totaling $22,392.67. Although Smith found no letters on this subject in the State Department files, in 1810 Erving sent him Madison's private letter of 3 Nov. 1804 authorizing the transaction (Smith, *Address*, 30–6; Madison, *Papers, Pres. Ser.*, 3:158–9, 255–65). Building on a 2 July editorial condemnation of Smith, Joel Barlow's anonymous explanation vindicated Madison. It appeared in the Washington *National Intelligencer*, 4–11 July 1811, and was reprinted as *A Review of Robert Smith's Address to the People of the United States* (Philadelphia, 1811).

[1] Manuscript: "the the."

From Robert Rives

Sir Oak Ridge July 3rd 1811

Under cover you have Invoice of Books which my Son inform'd me you wishd me to order for you from London—I am inform'd they are $\frac{1}{4}$tos instead of Octavo's as order'd—and should they not please on that account it will be not the least inconvenience to me to keep them myself

I am very respectfully Your mt obdt Ro Rives

RC (MHi); endorsed by TJ as received 20 July 1811.

Robert Rives (1764–1845), merchant and planter, was a native of Sussex County and the father of William Cabell Rives. He served in the Yorktown campaign during the Revolutionary War and later joined the Agricultural Society of Albemarle. By the 1790s his firm of Robert Rives & Company kept a store at Milton, and he was a longtime partner in the Richmond commission house of Brown, Rives & Company. TJ first did business with him in 1795, and he visited his large Nelson County estate, Oak Ridge, in the spring of 1817. At his death Rives owned land in Albemarle, Buckingham, Campbell, and Nelson counties and a personal estate valued at just over $100,000 (Alexander Brown, *The Cabells and their Kin*, 2d ed., rev. [1939, repr. 1994], 235–46; *MB*, 2:929, 1332; *PTJ*, 28:365–6, 30:27, 29n; *Richmond Enquirer*, 14 Mar. 1845; Nelson Co. Will Book, G:103–7, 123–9).

The enclosed invoice, not found, probably billed TJ for William Mitford, *The History of Greece*, 4 vols. (London, 1808; Sowerby, no. 23), and Catharine Macaulay, *The History of England from the Accession of James I. to that of the Brunswick Line*, 8 vols. (London, 1763–83; Sowerby, no. 386), both of which TJ acquired in quarto editions about this time (William C. Rives to TJ, 4 June 1811).

From Pierre Samuel Du Pont de Nemours

Mon respectable Ami, Paris 4 juillet 1811.

voici le dernier Volume des Œuvres de Mr Turgot. vous y verrez parce quil écrivait au docteur Price et au Sage Franklin combien il aimait votre Patrie.

Je fais passer à Monsieur le Président une copie corrigée de mon Mémoire sur les Finances des Etats-unis dont je vous ai envoyé la minute l'année derniere.

Et aussi une copie corrigée de l'ouvrage que vous m'aviez demandé sur l'éducation nationale.

On m'a dit que Mr Barlow avait traité le même Sujet. Je serais bien curieux de savoir en quoi nous nous raprochons et en quoi nous differons; et d'avoir votre jugement sur les deux ouvrages.

J'ai encore à donner pour completter l'edition actuelle[1] de Mr Turgot une seconde Edition très augmentée des Mémoires sur Sa vie, son Administration, et Ses Ouvrages. Et en retravaillant ces Mémoires j'ai pleuré comme la premiere fois.

La cessation du Ministere de ce Grand Homme et sa mort, ont été des malheurs bien graves pour le Genre humain.

quand vous recevrez le volume qui en contiendra les dernieres preuves, je serai vraisemblablement bien près de partir pour Monticello: car je veux être enterré en terre Sainte, c'est-à-dire en terre libre. Il me semble que j'y serai plus tranquille, et que mes os y porteront quelque bonheur.

agrez mon inviolable, et tendre, et bien respectueux attachement.

DuPont (de nemours)

EDITORS' TRANSLATION

My respectable Friend, Paris 4 July 1811.

Here is the final volume of Mr. Turgot's works. You will see by what he wrote to Doctor Price and the wise Franklin how much he loved your country.

I am forwarding to the President a corrected copy of my memoir on the finances of the United States, the draft of which I sent to you last year.

And also a corrected copy of the work you had requested of me on national education.

I was told that Mr. Barlow had treated the same subject. I would be very curious to know how we are similar and how we differ, and to have your judgment on these two works.

To complete the current edition of Turgot's writings, I have still to produce a second, much enlarged edition of his Memoirs on his Life, Administration, and Works. And upon returning once again to these memoirs, I cried like I had the first time I saw them.

The cessation of this great man's ministry and his death have been very serious misfortunes for mankind.

When you receive the volume that contains the final proof of this, I will probably be about to leave for Monticello: because I want to be buried in holy ground, that is to say in a free land. It seems to me that I will be more tranquil and that my bones will bring some happiness there.

Please accept my inviolable, tender, and very respectful attachment.

DuPont (de nemours)

RC (DLC); dateline at foot of text; at head of text: "a Son Excellence Thomas Jefferson ancien Président des Etats-Unis"; endorsed by TJ as received 9 Sept. 1811 and so recorded in SJL. Tr (DeGH: H. A. Du Pont Papers, Winterthur Manuscripts; posthumous copy). Translation by Dr. Genevieve Moene.

Enclosure: Du Pont, ed., *Oeuvres de Mr Turgot, ministre d'état, précédées et accompagnées de mémoires et de notes sur sa vie, son administration et ses ouvrages* (Paris, 1808–11; Sowerby, no. 2436; Poor, *Jefferson's Library*, 11 [no. 702]), vol. 9. Possibly enclosed in James Madison to TJ, 7 Sept. 1811, not found, which is recorded in SJL as received from Montpellier the following day.

On this day Du Pont sent Madison manuscript copies of his works on American finance and education, as well as four printed copies of the last volume of Turgot's *Oeuvres* for Madison, Du Pont's children, the APS, and TJ (Madison, *Papers, Pres. Ser.*, 3:369–70).

Turgot's letters to Richard PRICE and Benjamin FRANKLIN are in Du Pont, ed., *Oeuvres de Mr Turgot*, 9:376–404. Du Pont's MÉMOIRE SUR LES FINANCES DES ETATS-UNIS is printed above at 28 July 1810. Joel BARLOW advocated placing a university in the nation's capital in his *Prospectus of a National Institution, to be established in the United States* (Washington, 1806).

[1] Word added in left margin.

From George Jefferson

DEAR SIR Richmond 4th July 1811

I only yesterday received your favor of the 24th ultimo.—the note however was in time, but had one hour only to spare.—I suppose that your letters must have been too late for the mail, for the dft to Mr Lyle has not yet appeared.—the one to Mr Higginbotham did, in due time. I will tomorrow forward the 500.$ to Jones & Howell.—to day the bank does no business. I wrote you a few lines by last mail to Poplar Forest, a copy of which I subjoin.

The last Hhd of Tobacco is greatly superior in quality to the average of the other six, being indeed a very good one.—There was one of the others however as good as this.

Tobacco of an inferior quality is if possible becoming more & more unsaleable.—I really should not be at all surprised at its selling shortly at 2$.

If Mr Higginbotham will take yours, I think you had better let him have it almost at any price.

I would not willingly sell it if you would give me the whole proceeds.—I inclose you 150$ & am

Dear Sir Your Very humble servt GEO. JEFFERSON

RC (MHi); at foot of text: "Thomas Jefferson esqr"; with Dupl of Jefferson to TJ, 27 June 1811, on verso; endorsed by TJ as received 7 July 1811 and so recorded in SJL.

A missing letter of 6 July 1811 to TJ from Benjamin Jones of the firm of JONES & HOWELL is recorded in SJL as received from Philadelphia on 17 July 1811. SJL also records a letter from TJ to David HIGGINBOTHAM of 9 July 1811, not found, in which TJ forwarded "an order on Gibson & Jefferson for 124.29 of which 96.29 are on the order of Wm. Johnson for flour & tobo. carried to Richmond and 28.D. for Dabney Minor" (*MB*, 2:1267).

From William Duane

Sir, Phil[a] July 5, 1811

By the Mail of this day, I forward you a single copy of the Review of Montesquieu, I hope you will find it executed in a style of neatness not discreditable to the work nor to the American press. By printing it on a larger type and a smaller page, it might have been made a large volume, but I believe it will be considered as preferable in its present form by those who prefer a book for its contents rather than by weight or measure.

I have ventured to place two short paragraphs from Hobbes & Beccaria, as mottoes to the title page—containing applicable truths, and at least not inconsistent with its spirit; it was done merely to comply with a fashion, rather than any other motive.

The price which I have put it for sale at, is governed by two considerations, the expence incurred, and the expence to be incurred in circulating it; I have printed 750 copies, & must pay 25 per cent out of the price only for circulating it, that being the Sum agreed upon with the man I employ to obtain Subscribers and deliver works; should this edition sell sufficiently soon, it will determine whether or not it would be adviseable to print another edition at a lower price, and that will be known by the demand and the impression which the work makes; it is too soon to form any judgment here, as my political sins of several years prevents the light of my door from being ever darkened by federal shadows.

I trust you will excuse my not having written in answer to your two letters of 28 March and May 1. they excited in my breast very painful feelings, and as I could not touch the Subjects to which they related without expressing my sentiments[1] explicitly and fairly, I judged it preferable to be silent, perfectly satisfied with my own integrity and indifferent to the frowns or favors of mankind thus fortified.

If the book is in the form which you suggested as adapted for sending abroad, I shall send you the ten copies which you were pleased to order; or if there should be any other form of binding or putting together, with thinner covers in the manner of French works, I shall have them executed to your wish, having bookbinders in my own house. I am, Sir, with great respect

Your obed[t] Ser[t] W[m] Duane

RC (DLC); at head of text: "Thomas Jefferson Monticello"; endorsed by TJ as received 10 July 1811 and so recorded in SJL. Enclosure: Destutt de Tracy, *Commentary and Review of Montesquieu's Spirit of Laws.*

Duane added TWO SHORT PARAGRAPHS to the title page of Destutt de Tracy's commentary. The quotations were by Thomas HOBBES: "Ignorance of the signification of words, which is want of understanding, disposeth men to take on trust, not only the truth they know not, but also the errors, and which is more, the nonsense of them they trust: for neither error nor sense can, without a perfect understanding of words, be detected" (taken with slight variations from *Leviathan* [London, 1651], ch. 11, p. 50) and Cesare Bonesana, marchese di BECCARIA: "The most certain means of rendering a people free and happy, is to establish a perfect method of education" (adapted from *Dei delitti e delle pene* [Monaco, 1764]; English trans. as *An Essay on Crimes & Punishments* [New York, 1809]; Sowerby, no. 2349; Poor, *Jefferson's Library*, 11 [nos. 629–30], which maintained that "the most certain method of preventing crimes is, to perfect the system of education" [ch. 45, p. 133]). By MAY 1. Duane evidently meant TJ's letter to him of 30 Apr. 1811.

[1] Manuscript: "sentimemts."

From John Barnes

DEAR SIR George Town Colum[a]—6th July, 1811

Your esteemed fav[r] 29th Ult[o] inclosed Order on Bank of Pensyl[a]—as well 3[d] Bill of Ex—on Acco[t] of Gen[l] Kosciusko—respecting the latter—on paying my respects on the Memorable 4th Ins[t] to the good Presid[t] and conversing with M[r] Monroe—whose presense gave universal satisfaction—I took Occasion to mention the delay of Mess[s] Barlow and Warden—by whose conveyance the 1st & 2[d] setts were deposited—would not be protracted, but for a short time—under these circumstances, forwarding this 3[d] sett by a 3[d] conveyance, might possibly be attended with risque—by the possibility of its being presented, for Acceptance, by some unknown hand, prior to the receipt of either the 1st or 2[d] sett, by Mess[s] B & W—this 3[d] sett is therefore Retained—

The extreme heat of the Weather deterrs me for the present proceeding to Philadelphia—The disadvantages you labour Under Respecting your family supplies—I am fully persuaded may be considerably Reduced—by bei[g] procured here, you would scarsely Credit, the very extra increase of importations of every Article of family consumption to this place Coastwise from Boston New York Philad[a] Baltimore Charleston &c[a] &c[a] Owing to the Many Capital New buildings—Wholesale Stores, along the Wharfs above and below the ferry, since you left Washington, several of which contain Merchandize to the Amo[t] of 80, a 90,000 Dolls each—for my part I am at a loss to conceive, how the importers can dispose, of them: but so it is—the Back planters & farmers need not, nor in general do not, Now as heretofore resort, to Baltimore—or Alexandria—Moreover—the return flour Boats, take back vast quantities of Merchandize to Cumberland—on their Way to Kentucky &[a] &[a]—a source of great Commercial intercourse solely Appertaining to this place.—

The increasing population—and extra improvem[ts] in George Town and Washington—is in a great Measure Owing to these adventurous speculators Coastwise And were it not for the fatal—and I fear increasing Obstructions—to our foreign Navigation I mean—Obstructions in the Channel of our River—being such, as to compell our shipping Merchants (under, very great disadvantages—extra expences &c[a])—to Enter &, Reenter to load, & unload their Vessels—belonging to this port, bound to, & from a foreign port—to transact their business at the port of Alexand[a]—instead of George Town solely on Acco[t] of the Obstruct[n] in the Channel—Caused in part, by the New Bridge C[o]—could these difficulties but be removed—this Port and Town would most Assuredly Rival—if not out strip—the Invious pride of Alexandria—The Citizens of Washington, not less Invious—and unfriendly—are equally Jealous of this Town's superior situation—Unhappy, selfish—Views totally erronious—they ought most certainly to be one & the same—as in a Co-partnership—the One proportionably benefited by the improvements and prosperity of the other—the other <u>relative</u>—and envious Neighbour, instead of aiding our Mutual Comforts—do but laugh, at our folly and Madness—

If you want an early fall or immediate supply—do but give a little time to look about me—I will engage to put them up—as Usual good, and Reasonable—at least reduce your $167- to 147—The Stores on the Wharfs are Chiefly for the Storage of Flour Corn Salt Sugar & Molasses and Groceries—generally of all Kinds—here are also not less than 12 New Brick buildings on both sides Bridge Street Elegantly fitted up, and stored abundently—with every Article you can possibly stand in Need of,[1] <u>Wholesale and retail</u>—as Rivals, their prices & terms, are very Moderate, nearly if not equaly so, to the great Citys, if purchased by those Accustomed to purchase by the piece or package &c[a]—and altho some particular Articles must be paid for in Cash—the far greater part, w[d] be a 60 and others a 90 days Credit on Note—
upon the whole, I may safely Venture to say—that with M[rs] Ratcliffs Assistance—You could be furnish[d] with almost every family Article—<u>Wet</u> or <u>dry</u>—fine or Coarse—Linins—Muslins, Cottons, & Woolens, East, and West India produce & Manufacture—&[a] &c[a]—[2] The freight from hence to Richmond—as the Vessels Usually go in Ballast, would be very Moderate—and fixed here on the Spot—not as Customary—from New York or Philad[a]

In, The[3] fall every Needfull Article for the Blacks are in great abundance—

If then, from these several combined circumstances you should judge favorably of them—And Accept[4] my Offer—you may depend upon my best exertions for your Interest & satisfication, and while shipping your family supplies—The others at same time might in part be furnished Also—such as Ticklenbergs &[a] &[a]—always in Store—

Accept my Dear Sir my most gratefull thanks for your kind invitation Necessity not choice, alone, induced me to propose that of Philad[a] on Acco[t] of my unfortunate Tob[o] purchase By my latest advices, ℘ last Even[gs] post[5] I find no possible sale can be made—nor even a Barter one effected. of course I shall defer the Attempt—and[6] Anxiously wait the issue of events more favorable to my purpose,—

most Respectfully—and most sincerely—Be Assured I am Dear Sir—Your Obed[t] servant, JOHN BARNES.

RC (ViU: TJP-ER); at foot of text: "Th. Jefferson Esquire Monticello—Virginia"; endorsed by TJ as received 10 July 1811 and so recorded in SJL.

The FERRY crossed the Potomac River to Mason's (now Theodore Roosevelt) Island (Christian Hines, *Early Recollections of Washington City* [1866; repr. 1981], 4). The NEW BRIDGE company was most likely the Georgetown Potomac Bridge Company active at this time (Washington *National Intelligencer*, 9 May 1811). TICKLENBERGS (Ticklenburgs) are coarse linen fabrics named for their German town of origin (*OED*).

[1] Manuscript: "off."

[2] At foot of first sheet Barnes here noted: "Continued—2[d] Sheet," and he headed the second sheet "Continuation—6th July 1811."

[3] Thus in manuscript.

[4] Manuscript: "Acceept."

[5] Preceding four words interlined.

[6] Barnes here canceled "quietly &."

To Tadeusz Kosciuszko

MY DEAR GENERAL AND FRIEND Monticello July 8. 11.

I recieved your letter of Mar. 1. by our yesterday's post and by it's return of to-day I hasten a word of answer in the hope it may reach mr Barlow & mr Warden before they actually sail, which they are to do in the course of the week. it is principally to answer on a single point. you have thought my letters, while in office, rare, short & dry. they certainly were so. but it was purely from the fear that my correspondence might bring on you the suspicions or censure of the government under which you were living. it would have delighted me to have detailed to you from time to time, our measures and our views; because I knew that no one felt a livelier interest in our welfare: but I knew that my letters might fall into the hands of the English & be published, or into those of the French government who might make you responsible for what I wrote. I reserved therefore a free communication until I should be a mere private citizen, and made it fully in my letter of Feb. 26. of the last year, which I am rejoiced to hear you have recieved. from a fear that you had not, I inclosed a duplicate of it in mine of Apr. 16. of the present year, which has been ever since that date in the hands of mr Barlow & mr Warden, & I suppose will get to your hands at the same time with this.

I will write to mr Barnes to attend specially hereafter to your wish of recieving your remittances otherwise than thro' London. I am sorry that of the present year had been previously invested in a London bill & inclosed to you. I have recommended specially to mr Barlow to consider whether an exchange of funds here & there, might not be an accomodation to him as well as you.

I thank you most particularly for the last paragraph of your letter. it has relieved me from a load of uneasiness which rested on my mind till I could recieve your approbation of what I had done. nothing shall be so sacred to me as a regular paiment of the interest; and should your situation require at any time an anticipation of it, and the means occur of turning a draught on me to account, it shall always be punctually honored. accept the assurances of my unchanged affections & respect

Th: Jefferson

RC (PlKMN); at foot of first page: "Gen[l] Kosciuszko." PoC (MHi); endorsed by TJ. Enclosed in TJ to David Bailie Warden, 8 July 1811.

To Lafayette

My dear friend — Monticello July 8. 11.

I have just recieved your letter of Mar. 12. and learning by our yesterday's post that mr Barlow & mr Warden will sail in the course of the week, I endeavor by this day's return of the mail to get an answer into their hands before their departure. I feel very sensibly the reproaches of silence pressed in your letter. a few days before my departure from Washington (in Feb. 1809) I wrote you on the subject of your interests, in the moment of turning them over to my successor. I had never ceased to press on the proper agents the location, the survey, & the returns of your lands, in order to sign the grants before I quitted office. but they had not yet come on for signature. and as I had chiefly taken the business on myself, because I knew my station would give more effect to my urgencies, so I knew it to be for your interest to commit[1] the business then completely into the hands of mr Madison, who succeeding to the same station, would employ as much zeal in promoting your interests. whenever therefore I recieved a letter from you on the subject, instead of answering you, I wrote to him, & found him always on the alert & doing whatever circumstances rendered practicable. indeed I could not answer you, because the non-intercourse then existing, admitted no conveyance by private vessels, and if ever a public vessel went, it was from N. York 500. miles from Monticello, & my first information would be from the newspapers, that on such a day, <u>sailed</u> such a vessel E^t^c. as soon as the President's proclamation permitted a revival of intercourse, I began my letter of Jan. 20. but kept it open, till I learned the appointments of mr Barlow & mr Warden to France, and concluding it the 27th of Mar. forwarded it to them in expectation they were to sail immediately. I at the same time wrote to Made de Tesse, & others of my friends with you. I had written to mr Tracy Jan. 26. that letter, which like the rest, is only now on it's departure, tho' delivered from my hands so long ago, will prove to M. Tracy how little disposed I was to delay the publication of his work, the extraordinary value I placed on it, & my anxiety that he should extend his commentaries thro' the whole of Montesquieu's work. such were the real causes of the intermission of my letters, which render unnecessary the addition of any other. yet there exists another cause and a growing one for a remission at least in my correspondencies. I know that after long absence, we are apt to consider our friends as still being what they were when we saw them last, with undiminished vigour of body & mind. but 22. years have made a great alteration in me, my friend, much greater than with you I hope. one birth-day more commits me to my 70th year. I have enjoyed good health; but I am greatly enfeebled. I can barely walk out into my garden and grounds appurtenant to the house. retaining the power of riding on horseback, I have passed from breakfast to dinner chiefly in that way, and when within doors, I read much more willingly than I write. I am therefore grown remiss in my correspondencies, and disposed to indulge a debility which is gaining on me. I hope therefore you will impute the silence complained of to it's true causes, and by no means to any relaxation in my friendship to you, or in my zeal for your interests and happiness. I rejoice that you have obtained so good a price as is mentioned in your letter, for the portion of your lands at Point Coupée disposed of to mr Baring. it justifies my recommendation of all the delay in selling which your situation would admit. you have got at least six times as much as you could have sold for in the first instant, & therefore may well have afforded to pay common interest for the delay. having attained this height, their further advance will be more slow, because more nearly on a level with prices in our older possessions, and if you could free yourself entirely by a further sale on as good terms, it could not but be a great relief to your mind. their value will still rise faster than common interest, but whether that may requite the uneasiness of your present situation, you are best judge. at least mr Madison's judgment on that point will deserve far more weight than mine from the superior state of his information. referring to my former letter which has been so long delayed, and will go at length[2] with this I shall only repeat the assurances of my constant & affectionate friendship and respect. TH: JEFFERSON

RC (CLU-C); addressed: "M. de la Fayette." PoC (DLC); endorsed by TJ. Enclosed in TJ to David Bailie Warden, 8 July 1811.

The letter TJ wrote Lafayette just before his DEPARTURE FROM WASHINGTON is dated 24 Feb. 1809 (DLC). James Madison's proclamation of 2 Nov. 1810 authorized a REVIVAL OF INTERCOURSE with France (Madison, *Papers, Pres. Ser.*, 2:612–3).

[1] Word interlined in place of "turn."
[2] Preceding two words interlined.

From James Madison

DEAR SIR Washington July 8. 1811

Your favor of the 3[d] came duly to hand. You will have noticed in the Nat: Intelligencer that the wicked publication[1] of M[r] Smith is not to escape with impunity. It is impossible however that the whole turpitude of his conduct can be understood without disclosures to be made by myself alone, and of course, as he knows, not to be made at all. Without these his infamy is daily fastening itself upon him; leaving no other consolation than the malignant hope of revenging his own ingratitude and guilt on others. The case of Erving, will probably be better explained in the Newspaper, than I can here do it. The general facts of it I believe are, that the three offices at London were centered in him, with one of the salaries only; it being understood at the time that he would be made Assessor to the Board under Jay's Treaty, in which case he would be well recompenced. The Board declined to appoint him, giving preference to Cabot. Still however a certain portion of business passed thro' his hands. On this he charged, the usual commission of $2\frac{1}{2}$ per C[t] accruing from the individuals, and not from a public fund.[2] Having paid over the whole of the money of individuals in his hands, to the public, instead of retaining his Commission, a resort to Cong[s] became necessary. Whilst the subject was before them, doubts were excited as to the merits of the case, and a call made on M[r] Gallatin for information. His report put an end to the difficulty. the appropriation was immediately made, and but for the perverted view of the matter now before the public, would never more been thought of. The Treasury officers, tho' politically adverse to M[r] E. do him much justice on the occasion, declaring that his official transactions throughout[3] as presented in his acc[ts] are models of clearness and exactness, that he appears to have saved or gained to the public by his vigilance & assiduity[4] 60. or 70,000 dol[rs] that there remains a surplus of unclaimed monies, to a considerable amount, the greater part of which will probably never be claimed, & finally that the only error committed by M[r] E. was his not avoiding the necessity of asking Cong[s] to give back the amount[5] of his Commission, by deducting it himself from the sums paid into the public Coffers.

It has been thought best, whilst M[r] Monroe is in communications with the B. & F. Ministers here, to be silent on the subject. As the latest information from Russel, is prior to the arrival of the non-importation Act, the state of our affairs at Paris[6] may be conjectured. Pinkney brings, of course, nothing; Foster being the channel of English news. I do not know that he has yet opened himself compleatly[7] to M[r] Monroe; but from the conciliatory disposition of the Prince Regent, and the contrary one of his Cabinet, still deriving an ascendency from the convalescence[8] of the King, you will be very able to dive into the character of the mission. You will perceive[9] in the printed paper enclosed, a step by the British Minister, which, very unseasonably it would seem, denotes an increasing rigor towards this Country. According to a preceding interposition with the Court of Admiralty, cases under the orders in Council, had been suspended

I had promised myself a release from this position immediately after the 4th July. It will be some days yet before I shall be able to set out. Considering the excessive heat for some days past, no time has yet been lost. The weather has been as dry as hot. In general the drought has been so severe as to ruin almost the oats & flax. The crop of wheat, tho' shortened, will be tolerable, in tolerable land, where the Hessians have not committed their ravages. Be assured of my most affectionate esteem.

JAMES MADISON

RC (DLC: Madison Papers); endorsed by TJ as received 10 July 1811 and so recorded in SJL. Enclosure not found.

On 7 Feb. 1811 the United States Senate asked Madison to provide information on George W. Erving's accounts as American claims agent in London. Secretary of the Treasury Albert Gallatin delivered his REPORT to the president the following day, and on 11 Feb. 1811 Madison forwarded it to the Senate along with supporting documents. The packet included Robert Smith's endorsement of the account as secretary of state on 1 Dec. 1810, with Smith's opinion at that time that $22,392.67 should "be admitted to Mr. Ervings credit" (Madison, *Papers, Pres. Ser.*, 3:158–9; *JS*, 4:565, 569).

HESSIANS: Hessian fly (*Mayetiola destructor*).

[1] Word interlined in place of illegible word.

[2] Madison here canceled "In stating his account however."

[3] Manuscript: "througout."

[4] Preceding five words interlined.

[5] Preceding two words interlined in place of "what they had improperly [re?]."

[6] Preceding two words interlined.

[7] Word interlined.

[8] Manuscript: "conalescence."

[9] Manuscript: "perceiv."

To David Bailie Warden

DEAR SIR Monticello July 8. 11.

I recieved your favor of the 1st by our yesterday's post and have hastily written the two inclosed letters to Messrs La Fayette & Kosciuszko, in the hope that the return of the post may still find you at Washington.

I kept, during the last half dozen years of my residence at Washington a diary of the weather. I cannot in the instant make any thing of it which could be useful to you, but, with the first leisure, will furnish you with such general results from it as may answer your views.

Arthur Young carried the Sichorium Intubus from France to England, & sent some seed to Genl Washington who gave me a part. it has been growing here in abundance & perfection now 20. years without any cultivation after the first transplanting. I know no plant so valuable for green feeding, and mr Strickland told me they cut up the dry plant in England, & fed their horses with it. to get my letter to the office before the departure of the mail I must here conclude with my wishes for a happy passage, & an assurance of my great respect & esteem. TH: JEFFERSON

RC (MdHi: Warden Papers); at foot of text: "Mr Warden"; endorsed by Warden. PoC (DLC); endorsed by TJ. Enclosures: (1) TJ to Tadeusz Kosciuszko, 8 July 1811. (2) TJ to Lafayette, 8 July 1811.

A DIARY OF THE WEATHER that TJ kept from 1 Nov. 1802 to 31 Dec. 1816 is at MHi. SICHORIUM INTUBUS: *Cichorium intybus*, commonly known as chicory or succory (*Hortus Third*, 262). On 28 Apr. 1794 TJ sowed chicory seed he had received from George WASHINGTON. It remained a staple fodder crop at Monticello well into his retirement (*PTJ*, 28:68–9, 232–3, 464; Betts, *Garden Book*, esp. 211; TJ to Henry E. Watkins, 27 Nov. 1818).

To Philip Mazzei

Monticello July 9. 11.

I recieved, my dear friend, the day before yesterday, your favor of Feb. 15. it is the only one I have recieved from you since that of Oct. 28. 1808. so long a silence had excited apprehensions which this letter removes. I shall take the best measures I can for the sale of your house & lot in Richmond. it is in a part of the town where property sells low. for it is a curious fact, that Richmond instead of extending itself downwards towards the lower navigation has built to meet the upper navigation. the body of the town is now on Shockoe hill. I will immediately write to mr Bracken on the subject of Bellini's effects; but the result cannot go with this letter, because a frigate sailing this week with mr Barlow appointed minister & mr Warden Consul to Paris, allows me but the single post of tomorrow to get this letter into their hands. it is the more unfortunate as the few opportunities which occur are rarely known to me but by the newspapers announcing their departure. your friend Woollaston arrived safely in this country, and sent me the wines you were so kind as to commit to his care. they were delicious, such bottles as preserved their quality, and served to excite the regret you have often heard me express, that the monopoly of our commerce by a single nation, should exclude us from the good things of all others. mr Woolaston called on me afterwards at Washington, but making no stay there, gave me no other opportunity, than at a single dinner, of becoming acquainted with him. the Monthly strawbery seed you sent me in a phial, I determined to keep unopened till I should come home myself to take care of them, because I found it impossible from repeated trials, to have such things attended to in my absence. I sowed the seeds in an earthen box, and one single one only germinated, from which I have now two beds, and loaded at this time with fruit. I shall be enabled, the ensuing season, to stock the neighborhood. all the other articles you were so kind as to send me, being of necessity confided to servants here, have left me with a few vines only, and about half a dozen peach trees, which not having yet borne fruit, are as yet unknown as to their qualities. I learn with great pleasure that you have such a source of happiness in your daughter. her age, her education, her prospects & her love, must be so many interesting links binding you to life. altho' I doubt whether a person brought up in European society & habits can themselves be as happy here as there, yet I have no doubt of the blessings they prepare for their posterity by transplanting them hither. but my visions of going to bring you all here are dissipated by the hand of time. one birthday more places me in my 70th year, and tho' I have constantly enjoyed good health, I am much enfeebled. I am little able to walk about. most of my exercise is on horseback, and the powers of life very sensibly decayed. rest and tranquility now constitute the summum bonum for me, and my only wish a quiet[1] descent to that asylum which has recieved some more of your acquaintances since my last. mr John Walker and his wife left us the last year, within a few days of each other. I am not certain whether the deaths of John Page & mr Wythe have been made known to you. Daniel Hylton is also gone, and my affectionate connections, mr & mrs Eppes, and indeed I recollect none of your intimate acquaintance now living but T. Lomax & myself. make me known favorably to your daughter if you please, to whom the affectionate dispositions of an old man can do no harm, and accept my sincere prayers for the continuance of your life & health as long as yourself shall wish. TH: JEFFERSON

RC (DLC: TJ Papers, ser. 10); at foot of first page: "Mr Mazzei"; endorsed by Mazzei as answered 27 Sept. 1812 (this reply not recorded in SJL and not found). Tr (DLC: TJ Papers, ser. 10); in Mazzei's hand; in Italian; subjoined to RC. Tr (NhD); in English. Enclosed in TJ to David Bailie Warden, 9 July 1811.

On 1 Aug. 1811 the United States FRIGATE *Constitution* left Annapolis for France by way of Norfolk, carrying Joel Barlow and David Bailie Warden (*Alexandria Daily Gazette, Commercial & Political*, 7 Aug. 1811). Mazzei wrote letters of introduction for Frederick H. Wollaston (WOOLLASTON) to both TJ and James Madison on 13 Sept. 1807 (both at Archivio Filippo Mazzei, Pisa). Wollaston evidently paid his brief visit to TJ during the second half of 1808 or early in 1809 (Wollaston to TJ, 2 June 1808 [DLC]).

[1] Tr (NhD): "quite."

To David Bailie Warden

DEAR SIR Monticello July 9. 11.

The possibility that another post may still find you at Washington induces me to risk another letter's getting in time to have the benefit of your care. mr Mazzei, of Pisa, to whom it is addressed, is the intimate friend of mr Febroni, probably known to you as a man of letters, lately appointed by the Emperor a Maitre de requetes, charged with the care of roads and bridges South of the Alps, and passing most of his time at Paris. if put into his hands it will be sure of a safe conveyance, but in case of his absence, such other conveyance as you can find for it will oblige me. repeating my wishes for a pleasant voyage, I add the assurance of my great esteem and respect.

TH: JEFFERSON

RC (MdHi: Warden Papers); at foot of text: "M[r] Warden"; endorsed by Warden. PoC (DLC); endorsed by TJ. Enclosure: TJ to Philip Mazzei, 9 July 1811.

Giovanni Valentino Maria Fabbroni (FEBRONI) was the EMPEROR Napoleon's MAITRE DE REQUETES (master of petitions) for the portions of northwestern Italy that had been annexed by France.

To Lafayette

MY DEAR SIR Monticello July 10. 11.

Since writing my letter of the day before yesterday I have recieved by post the inclosed copy of the Review of Montesquieu which I hasten to forward thro' you to M. Tracy. had I another it should have been devoted to you. it is even doubtful whether this may reach Washington in time to find mr Warden still there. I am not without hopes he will have been able to get a copy & carry [it][1] with him. ever affectionately Yours TH: JEFFERSON

PoC (DLC); at foot of text: "M. de la Fayette"; endorsed by TJ. Enclosure: Destutt de Tracy, *Commentary and Review of Montesquieu's Spirit of Laws*. Enclosed in TJ to David Bailie Warden, 10 July 1811.

[1] Omitted word editorially supplied.

To David Bailie Warden

Monticello July 10. 11.

Th: Jefferson presents his friendly salutations to mr Warden and having recieved a single copy of the Review of Montesquieu he is anxious to have the benefit of the safe conveyance by mr Warden & the Essex to get it to France. he again therefore takes the chance of a letter still finding him at Washington & of asking his care of it with a repetition of his wishes for a happy voiage.

RC (ViU: TJP); dateline at foot of text; endorsed by Warden. PoC (DLC); endorsed by TJ. Enclosure: TJ to Lafayette, 10 July 1811, and enclosure.

From Benjamin Galloway

DEAR SIR, Hagers Town July 11th 1811

I have taken the liberty of troubling you with the inclosed Papers. I shall continue to animadvert on a Steady Patriot, from time to time. his grand object is to influence the approaching choice of Electors of the Senate of Maryland. our Citizens in Washington County are true to the principles of July 4th 76—but, an attempt is now making to debauch them. I have placed myself in their defence, and be assured, I will be constant, watchful and decided—In haste, permit me with best wishes for your health & happiness much respected Sir

yrs &a BEN GALLOWAY

RC (DLC); dateline at foot of text; endorsed by TJ as received 17 July 1811 and so recorded in SJL.

Benjamin Galloway (1752–1831), an attorney and planter who had been educated in England, represented his native Anne Arundel County in the Maryland House of Delegates in 1777 and served briefly as the state's attorney general the following year. In the 1780s he served as a county justice. About 1796 Galloway moved to what soon became Hagerstown in Washington County, and he later sat on the county court. He returned to the House of Delegates in 1822 for one term and was an outspoken Republican throughout his adulthood. At the time of his death Galloway owned about 1,300 acres in Washington County, 1,000 in Anne Arundel, and seven lots in Hagerstown (*BDML*, 1:338–9; *PTJ*, 29:566–7; Papenfuse, *Maryland Public Officials*, 1:265; Thomas J. C. Williams, *A History of Washington County Maryland* [1906; repr. 1968], 169–70, 198–200; *Maryland Herald, and Hagers-Town Weekly Advertiser*, 11 July, 16 Nov. 1804; *Hagers-Town Gazette*, 29 Aug. 1809, 18 Sept. 1810; Washington *Daily National Intelligencer*, 23 Aug. 1831).

The INCLOSED PAPERS probably included two letters written by A STEADY PATRIOT and printed in the *Hagers-Town Gazette* on 25 June and 2 July 1811, as well as Galloway's response published in the *Maryland Herald, and Hagers-Town Weekly Advertiser* on 26 June 1811. "Steady Patriot" argued that it was "more consistent with nature's laws, that the Americans should feel a greater regard for them [Great Britain] than for any other nation"; defended Britain's policy of impressment but not its excesses; condemned Napoleon's Berlin and Milan decrees; decried the pro-French course taken by the American government; and urged readers to "animadvert upon the general deportment of the present administration," which was leading the United States toward an "abyss," and to support Federalists in the upcoming senatorial election. Galloway's rebuttal, dated Hagerstown, 25 June 1811, and issued under the nom de plume of "July 4th, 1776," suggested that his opponent had "deliberately promulgated doctrines so fundamentally, so totally repugnant to, so altogether at war, with all that is praise worthy, and valuable in the estimation of a steady patriot," that he should henceforth publish as a "Steady (British) Patriot."

From James T. Austin

Boston 12. July 1811.

A citizen who holds in most exalted respect the illustrious character of the late President of the United States begs leave to enclose a pamphlet, written with a view of supporting the laws & constitution of the Country—and seizes this only occassion in his life of expressing the most devoted admiration of JAMES T AUSTIN.—

RC (DLC); dateline beneath signature; at foot of text: "Thomas Jefferson Esqr"; endorsed by TJ as received 28 July 1811 and so recorded in SJL. Enclosure: "Leolin" [Austin], *Resistance to Laws of the United States; considered in four letters to the Honorable Harrison Gray Otis, Esq. Late President of the Senate of Massachusetts* (Boston, 1811; Sowerby, no. 3404; with presentation copy at DLC containing Austin's inscription on title page: "Thomas Jefferson with the respects Of the Author"), denouncing resolutions made at a Federalist caucus held at Fanueil Hall in Boston on 31 Mar. 1811, including one which declared that the reimposition of commercial nonintercourse with Great Britain, its colonies, and its dependencies would lead "to the ruin or impoverishment of some of the most industrious and meritorious citizens of the United States—and that the only means short of an appeal to force to prevent such a calamity, (which heaven avert) *is the election of such men to the various offices in the State Government* as will OPPOSE by peaceable but firm measures THE EXECUTION OF LAWS which if persisted in, MUST AND WILL BE RESISTED!!" (p. 4); criticizing especially caucus leader Harrison Gray Otis for condoning this implicit threat of force; arguing that most Americans would dismiss as ludicrous the idea of resisting a federal statute through violence, yet insisting that any such threat tended to undermine the Constitution and the Union; and concluding (p. 24) that Otis had brought upon himself the "DISGRACE AND RUIN OF PREMEDITATED REBELLION."

James Trecothick Austin (1784–1870), attorney and author, received an A.B. degree from Harvard University in 1802, was admitted to the Massachusetts bar in 1805, and married a daughter of Elbridge Gerry the following year. He was attorney for Suffolk County, 1807–32, and state attorney general, 1832–43. Austin also saw service as a director of the state prison, a member of Harvard's governing board, an agent to report on the boundary disputes enumerated in the fourth article of the 1814 Treaty of Ghent, a delegate to a state constitutional convention in 1820, and a state senator. A strong Republican, he later became a Whig and opposed the antislavery movement. Austin edited a literary magazine, 1806–08, wrote articles for the *Boston Patriot* (in which the above enclosure first appeared), the *Christian Examiner*, and the *Law Reporter*, and composed a two-volume biography of his father-in-law, 1828–29. In 1860 Austin owned real estate worth $50,000 and personal property valued at $30,000 (*DAB*; *JEP*, 3:42, 43 [8, 11 Apr. 1816]; DNA: RG 29, CS, Watertown, Mass., 1860; *Boston Daily Journal*, 9 May 1870).

To Mary Lewis

July 12. 11.

Th: Jefferson presents his friendly salutations to mrs Lewis[1] and sends her[2] some figs, of the few which come forward at this season. if she has cucumbers to spare he will avail himself of her kind offer of them, his own being not yet advanced, and the drought of May & June having left him without lettuce.

RC (ViU: Peter Coolidge Deposit); dateline at foot of text. Not recorded in SJL.

[1] Preceding three words interlined.
[2] TJ here canceled "a few figs."

From John Milledge

Dear Sir, near Augusta, Georgia. 12th July 1811

I have received your esteemed favor of the 5th of last month—I was apprehensive that Monticello, and its nieghbourhood would be too cold for the bene, so as to make it a profitable article of cultivation for Market—If you can raise a sufficiency of seed for your own use, it will be, in my opinion, as much as can be done—accept my warmest thanks, for communicating your different essays at presses for making of the oil—I have made oil for my own use, and nieghbours, for two years past, it took me some time before I succeeded, and now with very little trouble, I can make about a gallon and a quart of pure cold drawn oil, to a bushel of seed—I took a block of sweet gum, 4 feet by 2½, a mortise in the centre, 12 inches long, 8 wide, and 9 inches deep, an inch Auger was passed obliquely through, so as to hit the centre of one side of the mortise at the bottom, into which I introduced a piece of gun barrel as a tube—at the bottom of the mortise, grooves were cut, with a chisel, in different directions, gradually made deeper as they inclined to the tube—strips of sheet Iron about an inch wide, and nearly the length of the mortise, was placed over the grooves, about 3–8th of an inch apart—In my first essay I had no grooves, a considerable part of the oil was forced up, little ran out at the tube, I have the seed bruised in a mortar, then put into a bag knitted of coarse yarn the bag with seed is placed in the mortise, a piece of sweet gum, about 3 inches thick, made exactly to occupy the mortise, is put on the bag, a block of the size of the mortise follows next—a large wooden screw, which I have for compressing cotton into square bales, is made to act on the block, the lever is of considerable length, and of course the power great, your method of the beam must answer equally as well as the screw, perhaps better, as the pressure is more gradual—I was impressed with the belief, that the beam would answer, and recommended it last winter to Mr Willis Alston of North Carolina—The way I have hitherto taken to clear the seed of the refuse particles is by wenches riddling the seed in small baskets, in the same manner that is done with corn, to take the husk from it, after being beat for hommony—I some times cleanse the seed by wind, putting a bench on a sheet for a person to stand on, and lowering and raising the seed, according to the force of the wind—I once used a wheat fanner, the only objection, the sieve was too coarse—Colo Few informs me, that a fanner has been invented for the bene seed, and in use at an oil mill on second river, New Jersey, which separates the seed remarkably well—The rice which you sent me, I distributed among some of our best rice planters near savannah, one of the aquatic kind, is said to be equal if not superior, to the rice now generally cultivated—The bearded rice grows well on high land, and requires only the usual seasons for bringing Indian corn to perfection—I will have the result of the experiments published—

I intend sending to our friend Gen[l] smith of Baltimore, a rice barrel of bene seed for you, with a request that he send it to Richmond. I think you will find a difference in the weight of the seed, raised in Georgia, and that with you—I should like to know the method which is used in the old Country to clarify oil. I find a sediment after the oil remains some time bottled, and it retains a vegetable scent which ought to be removed—as we appear to have somewhat of an intercourse with France, would you be desirous of making a second attempt of cotton seed? it is only to inform me, and it shall be sent to whatever port you may direct—The Sheep of south Carolina, and Georgia, I believe to be little inferior to the best of that Species, either for the wool, or table—our mutton has been long admired, and it has been but a few years since we have noticed the texture of the wool—I think I informed you, that I sent to Col[o] Humphreys manufactory, some wool from a place I have near the sea, to have its quality ascertained, in return I had cloth sent me, made of the wool, which I am now wearing, very little inferior to the best broad cloth—A late arrival from Lisbon, has brought us upwards of 100 Merino sheep—The unjust measures towards us of the two great Belligerent Powers, has certainly openned the eyes of our Countrymen, and turned their attention to their true interest—The mechanical genius is exerting itself throughout our extended nation—we already see it in many things [e]qual, and in some superior to the old Country.

The deplorable situation of M[rs] Milledge, now nearly three years confined to her bed laying on her back not able to turn, to the right, or left—her legs and thighs swelled to an enormous Size, her Body a perfect skeleton—never moved but on a sheet raised by three persons on each side, and in constant excruciating pain—It is the wonder of every one who has seen her, that her existance has been prolonged to this day—She unites with me in our sincere respect and best wishes for yourself M[r] and M[rs] Randolph—I will thank you to remember me to my young friend Jefferson—

Accept the assurances of my high, and great esteem.—

JN[O] MILLEDGE.

RC (DLC); edge frayed; endorsed by TJ as received 4 Aug. 1811 and so recorded in SJL.

WENCHES: winches.

From Philip Turpin

DEAR SIR Salisbury, July 13th 1811.

Mr William Harris has inform'd me of his intention of making a tender of his services to his country in the naval line, and has requested a letter of recommendation to you: this request I have cheerfully complied with, as I have known Mr Harris from his infancy, and think him a young gentleman of merit and respectability, and doubt not his inclination or ability to deserve well of his country, should his services be accepted.

To you, dear sir, no apology I presume is necessary for the liberty I have taken; persuaded as I am of the pleasure you receive from furthering the views, and promoting the interests of young men of worth and respectability.

I am happy to hear by Mr Harris that you continue to enjoy a good share of health, which I sincerely wish the continuance of, not only on your own account, but also on that of your country: for I cannot but hope that if that blessing be continued, your activity of mind, and philanthropy will induce you to add to the number of your literary productions.

I have in a great measure declin'd the practice of physic; but I have not the happiness, like you, to retire with the applause of millions; nor have I your consolation, of having either written what deserves to be read, or of having perform'd what will deserve to be recorded.

With my sincerest wishes for your health & happiness

I am, dear sir, your sincere friend and hble servt

PHILIP TURPIN

RC (MHi); endorsed by TJ as received 5 Sept. 1811 and so recorded in SJL.

Philip Turpin (1749–1828), physician and TJ's first cousin, received an M.D. degree from the University of Edinburgh in 1774 before traveling to Paris for additional medical training. The onset of the Revolutionary War left him destitute of funds and unable to return to America. Turpin was obliged to take a position as a surgeon in the British Navy in 1777 and returned to America in that capacity in 1781. After Lord Cornwallis denied his application to pass through the lines to the American side, he remained in the British service and was captured at Yorktown. Turpin was accordingly suspected of Loyalist sympathies and relied in part on TJ's intervention to regain his status as a Virginia citizen in December 1783. Late in the 1780s Turpin purchased a Chesterfield County estate called Salisbury from Thomas Mann Randolph (1741–93), and in 1789 he sold John Marshall the lot in Richmond on which the latter's house still stands. Turpin's medical practice periodically took him to the aid of TJ's relations at Eppington (Mary Denham Ackerly and Lula Eastman Jeter Parker, *"Our Kin": The Genealogies of Some of the Early Families who Made History in the Founding and Development of Bedford County Virginia* [1930], 372–3; *PTJ*, 1:23–4, 6:324–33, 31:389; *MB*, 2:936–7; Madison, *Papers,*

Congress. Ser., 7:232–3; Marshall, *Papers*, 2:28–9; Jeffrey M. O'Dell, *Chesterfield County: Early Architecture and Historic Sites* [1983], 287–8; *Richmond Enquirer*, 16 May 1828).

From Burwell Bassett

DEAR SIR July 20th 1811.

Your letter of the 17th ult has been received and the answering of it thus long delaid. to procure the desired information—. I have this day seen Mr Ratcliffe the person named in the letter of Monsr Beauvois. He is a man I have long been acquainted with, and I know him to be deserving of confidence. He states that he was sent for to write Mr Piernetz will and that at the time he began to write the will there were many of the neighbours in the store but that before he could finish it they had all gone home that Piernetz then in his perfect senses approved the will and as there were no persons to witness it he said to Mr Ratcliffe that if he would ride down in the morning that he Piernetz would send for some of his neighbours and get the will witnessed but the next morning was too late and the paper not signed. The court of new Kent admited the paper to record as a noncupative will and Lacy has petitioned the Legislature and a law has passed at the last session, in what form I can not say most probable only relinquishing the right[1] of the commonwealth. This is the substance of Mr Ratcliffe,s information. I am not informed whether an escheat was ever taken out, nor can I say any thing certain as to Ruelle's having made himself a citizen but I am disposed from my knowledge of the man to believe he did acquire the right of citizenship & I am the more induced to think so because the first thing he did almost was to purchase land, he would not[2] have been so unadvised as to neglect the means of securing it. whether Mrs Ruelle made herself a citizen would then be a question. If it be material to your views of this subject to know whether Ruelle became a citizen I can have the record[3] examined and inform you. I could if desired send copies of the will &c. There being opposition made to the recording the will I should suppose that it would be difficult to set aside that decision. I am not apprised of the strength of testimony besides that of Mr Ratcliffe which may be aduced but as he observed that were many persons at the house when he went to write the will it is probable some were privy to the circumstances. This is the sum of the information that have as yet been able to gather on this subject should any other come to my knowledge they shall be communicated.

I cannot doubt that any thing connected with the natural history of our country will be highly interesting to you and that you will receive with pleasure the information of the bones of the Mamouth have been[4] found on the shores of York River. This discovery was made at Mr Gowin Corbins between the mouths of King & of Queens creek and between high & low water mark. The teeth which I have seen are as perfect as those sent you by Mr Clarke, Two of them were connected in their socket and there was more or less bone connected with all the teeth. The pelvis which I did not see is said to be five across. The place of this deposite tho now covered at high tide it would seem had not been always so for in diging for these bones many roots of trees were discovered. As yet all the place where the carcass was suppose'd to ly has not been explored. The head & tail had been most exposed by the washing of the tide and those parts have as yet only been found. The teeth with the bones attached to them have been lodged in College as I presume the other parts will be as found.

with the assurance of much esteem[5] and respect your obt. Ser

BURWELL BASSETT

RC (DLC); endorsed by TJ as received 28 July 1811 and so recorded in SJL.

NONCUPATIVE (nuncupative): "oral." On 8 Jan. 1811 the Virginia General Assembly PASSED a law relinquishing in favor of Stephen H. Lacy "the Commonwealth's right to the real Estate whereof Peter Piernet died seized," but explicitly leaving unchanged all other claims to this property (*Acts of Assembly*, 1810–11 sess., 99). The fossilized teeth were taken to the COLLEGE of William and Mary, and its president, Bishop James Madison, wrote a paper on the subject (Richmond *Enquirer*, 26 July 1811; *Medical Repository of Original Essays and Intelligence* 3 [1812]: 388–90).

[1] Word interlined in place of "title."
[2] Manuscript: "not not."
[3] Manuscript: "recorn."
[4] Manuscript: "be."
[5] Manuscript: "exteem."

From Jacob Franklin Heston

SIR, [before 20 July 1811]

IN dedicating this book to you, I have many reasons to expect, that I shall escape the censures, which the authors of dedicatory addresses so generally, and so justly, deserve. If you had not retired from office into the peace of private life, this address might have afforded some pretext, perhaps, to charge me with motives, very different from those by which I am actuated. But sir, you neither wear a crown, nor hold an office; and therefore, the base incentives by which dedicators are so often influenced, cannot with any plausibility be imputed to me. Indeed, if you were still in office, such reproaches could not be believed; because it could not be supposed that I am ignorant of a character, which is known to all the rest of my fellow citizens. It is[1] now obvious, I believe, that no eulogium could induce you to grant favours to the unworthy; nor the omission of it to withhold them from merit. Hence, sir, if you were still in office, it must be evident that I would not, if I were seeking promotion or gain, inscribe my productions to one, from whom no more could be obtained by that means, than could be obtained without. Besides, as so fit an occasion, for an address of this kind, has seldom, or perhaps never, occurred before, I ought not to be judged by common criterions.

I have addressed you, sir, on the present occasion, not only for the purpose of expressing my gratitude for the services which you have rendered to mankind; but for the honour of publicly declaring my intire approbation of your public and private life. I may not perhaps, be informed of all your private transactions; but I give them this approbation, with the fullest confidence; because your political and official conduct has given the most unequivocal proof, that your private life has been laudable and correct. He who preserves an unsullied virtue in the highest stations, and in the greatest prosperity, as well as under the pressure of the greatest difficulties, would certainly act with propriety in every sphere in which he could be placed; for whoever with virtuous firmness uniformly resists the stronger temptations, would surely not yield to the weaker.

You will observe, sir, that I do no more at present, than adopt the easiest method of participating in the honour of another's merit. For, by adopting the works and sentiments of others, we seem to share in their fame; though we have neither the wisdom with which their plans were devised, nor the prudence or fortitude by which they were executed. And it is thus, sir, by this approbation of Your policy, that I seem to share in the honour of it.

But, independent of the high gratification and honour, which I derive from this public acknowledgment of my approbation and regard; if the tendency of this book is consistent with the design of writing it, to whom could I offer the homage of its dedication, with that propriety with which it is now offered to you. For, you were not only the first to make a prompt and manly declaration of independence; but you have uniformly evinced, on all occasions since, the most incorruptible attachment to liberty, and the most disinterested desire to extend and preserve it for the benefit of the human race. Under your administration the most obvious defects of the constitution were removed; and its best principles strengthened and preserved. Under you, the friends of liberty, cheerfully and unanimously united for its defence; and by you it was protected from foreign and domestic foes. Under you, the diabolical spirit of despotism was suppressed; and by your firmness, some of the would be tyrants of our country, were driven from our shores.

In short, under your wise, lenient, and pacific administration, we enjoyed the most unexampled prosperity, and "witnessed the safety with which error of opinion may be tolerated, where reason is left free to combat it."

After so many heart saddening instances of the infamous and cruel success of monarchs; and amidst so many shocking examples of political turpitude and apostacy, it is peculiarly grateful to the mind, to behold, in this happy country, wisdom triumphing over folly, virtue over vice, and truth over falshood. It must, indeed, be the sweetest consolation, amidst these melancholy instances of political, immoral, and infernal deception; to behold a great and incorruptible statesman, scorning the baubles and temptations of ambition, trampling on the spirit of tyranny and oppression, and, with a firm heart and capacious mind, protecting his country from the evils which threaten it, and preserving its freedom, peace, and prosperity. At least, to a mind possessed of honest sensibility, I cannot imagine what could afford a higher gratification, than to see a good man always successful, when he is struggling with such glorious and invincible integrity, to discharge the most sacred of duties: especially, when he bears down before the tide of his good fortune, the extreme cruelty and depravity of a despotic or monarchical spirit: for as history proves that there is nothing more cruel than the success of that spirit; so nothing should give us more joy, than to see it successfully opposed. Hence, sir, while I have beheld your success, I have felt the liveliest gratification; and have imbibed the pleasing hope, that your great example would limit the ambition of others; and stimulate your successors to walk in your path.

But sir, if it is a pleasure to reflect on your services, it must also be a pleasure to know that they have met with a grateful reward. I do not, however, mean to insinuate that your reward is equal to your services; but I believe it is the greatest which a wise man can experience, and it arises from the happiness, gratitude and veneration of his fellow citizens. If it must afford pleasure even to an ordinary mind, to reflect on the happiness of this extensive country; what delight must it give to you to behold the felicity of so many millions; especially, if you consider that you were so greatly instrumental in procuring it.

With respect sir, to this book, whatever may be its effect, or its merit, it was written in favour of liberty: and therefore I think I could not offer the homage of this dedication to any one with as much consistency as it is now offered to you, to whom we are so much indebted for the liberty which we at present enjoy.

But, if I am acquainted with the sentiments of the public, it is not only your political discernment, services and integrity which have, in their judgment, entitled you to our respect; but, though I have addressed this book to you merely as to the great defender of liberty, yet, if it had possessed the greatest literary merit, I should, nevertheless, have thought it most proper to inscribe it to you: and the propriety of it would, I believe, be no less obvious to the public.

I have not, however, the vanity to expect that one who has been accustomed to write with the greatest elegance, perspicuity, and correctness, will find much, except truth, to esteem in this book: nor do I expect that one who possesses the finest taste, and is the most capable of perceiving the smallest shade or tincture of impropriety, can peruse it without meeting with many gloomy or unsavoury passages in his way. But I confidently hope, that, if it would be an atom in the scale of liberty, you will be cautious in animadverting on it's defects; for I cannot, be insensible that if this work has any merit, the sanction of your name would give it currency, and notwithstanding its defects, make it in some degree useful to the public.

If, in making this address without your knowledge or consent, I have committed an error, I know that there are none more likely to pardon errors, than those who know how to avoid them; and the hope of impunity encouraged me to gratify my inclination, by a more free communication of sentiment, than may, perhaps, be proper on the present occasion. I have not however mentioned facts and opinions, because I thought that it would be agreeable to you to hear even the truth in your own praise, but because I thought that it would be honourable to me, and in some other respects proper, to mention them. I have not said enough to do justice to my own feelings, although I have said more than can be agreeable to yours: but, if I have derived a gratification at your expence, I hope you will pardon this freedom when you reflect, that I consider this as the only opportunity which I can ever have of publishing sentiments so honourable to myself. I hope also that you will pardon the manner of publishing them, when you reflect on the plainness of my understanding, and the difficulty of attaining the object which I desire on the one hand, without violating the strict rules of decorum on the other. This is a difficulty to which I fear I am unequal: and I should make the experiment with the greatest apprehension if it could occasion any serious injury. But, for particular reasons, I have determined to express the truth in this address; and when all other apologies fail, I will plainly appeal for my justification to the right, which every man has of declaring his approbation of another's conduct. This is a right which you cannot deny. I do not, however, wish to appear in the high road of venal dedicators: and, lest I should seem to be treading in the same path, I will only recapitulate what I have, before observed, that I wish this address to be considered, merely as the sincere declaration of the gratitude which I feel, and of the sentiments which I am proud to proclaim: and that, to consider it in any other light would indeed be an act of injustice: for as to the assertions which it contains, they are notoriously true; and as to the expression of my regard, there is no reason to believe that it is not, what it really is, the purest homage of my soul, uninfluenced by the body or its concerns.

I will now conclude, without venturing to trouble you with any other remark, except, that I fear the length and prolixity of this address will admit of no excuse; permit me however, in taking my leave to reiterate the warmest assurances of my sincerity and of the great veneration, with which

I have the honour to be, Sir, your most devoted friend and Fellow Citizen, JACOB FRANKLIN HESTON

Printed in Heston, *Moral & Political Truth; or Reflections Suggested by reading History and Biography* (Philadelphia, 1811; Sowerby, no. 3542), 1–8; undated; at head of text: "Dedication. To Thomas Jefferson, Esq. Late President of the United States, &c. &c."

Jacob Franklin Heston (ca. 1779–1845), attorney, was born in Philadelphia County and admitted to the bar in 1804. The following year he became an associate judge of the Court of Common Pleas of the City and County of Philadelphia. In 1824 Heston was elected as a Democrat to represent Philadelphia County in the lower house of the Pennsylvania legislature (John Hill Martin, *Martin's Bench and Bar of Philadelphia* [1883], 55, 277; John A. Paxton, *The Philadelphia Directory and Register, for 1813* [Philadelphia, 1813], 203; J. Thomas Scharf and Thompson Westcott, *History of Philadelphia, 1609–1884* [1884], 1:611; Philadelphia *Public Ledger*, 8 Dec. 1845).

Heston's *Moral & Political Truth* was advertised for sale in the Philadelphia *Poulson's American Daily Advertiser*, 24 May 1811, and sent by Heston to Secretary of State James Monroe for copyright deposit on 20 July 1811 (DNA: RG 59, MLR).

THE SAFETY . . . FREE TO COMBAT IT: a quotation from TJ's first inaugural address (*PTJ*, 33:149).

[1] Printed text: "It it."

From Benjamin Morgan

D SIR New Orleans July 20th 1811

Your favour of the 11th Ult° reached me a few days ago covering the papers asked for in my letter of the 22d March and it appears a further delay is to take place with this unfortunate business—Lieut Peyton is stationed at Fort Stoddard a considerable distance from hence and could not be got here before the Adjournment of our Superior Court which takes place to day

The Court opens again on the first Monday in November by which time I will endeavour to have Mr Peyton here and terminate this longstanding Affair

I am with much respect & esteem your most Obt Hble servant

BENJA MORGAN

RC (MHi); between dateline and salutation: "Thomas Jefferson Esquire"; endorsed by TJ as received 25 Aug. 1811 and so recorded in SJL.

To Robert Rives

DEAR SIR Monticello July 20. 11.

The failure of the postmaster of Charlottesville to forward your favor of the 3d to Milton, to which place I send every post day for my letters, has delayed my reciept of it till this moment. I hasten therefore to inclose you by tomorrow's post an order on Gibson & Jefferson for the amount of the disbursements[1] which I make 91. D 34 c; altho' it is probable that my ignorance may have omitted articles of charge, which, not being stated in the papers, are unknown to me. I shall cheerfully supply any deficiency on it's being intimated to me. I return you many thanks for the trouble this commission has given you. I had asked it of your son only in the event of your writing for books for him, in which case, making a part of the order for him, it would have scarcely increased the trouble.

As a separate business it has enlarged my trespass on your convenience as well as my obligations for your kindness I pray you, with the assurances of my thankfulness, to accept those of my perfect esteem & respect TH: JEFFERSON

PoC (MHi); at foot of text: "Mr Rives"; endorsed by TJ. Enclosure not found.

The POSTMASTER OF CHARLOTTESVILLE was John Winn.

[1] Preceding three words interlined.

From Joel Barlow

[received 21 July 1811]

Mammoth Rye. I recieved it last year from France. it is lately from Asia. I sowed 70 grains in my garden. it produced 7483 grains. but they are not so plump as those I sowed. It is heavier than wheat & gives a flour as white. The stalk being more solid than that of common rye it will probably resist the fly. Sow in Sep^r—

Caspian wheat. recieved with the rye. was extremely plump & heavy, has somewhat degenerated in my garden, possibly owing to the season & the exposure uncommonly dry & warm. Having a solid stalk it will give more fodder than common wheat & may escape the fly. it has a cluster head. Sow in Sep^r—

Persian Barley, recieved with the rye & wheat. has degenerated less with me. It was much heavier than common barley, with a thinner & softer coat. Sow in Spring.

I pray Mr Jefferson to accept the samples herewith sent as above described. After one or two years trial he will be able to appreciate them, & if he finds them valuable he will impart them to others for public benefit. The names I have given them are somewhat arbitrary, but not entirely so. They came I understand from regions that are well enough indicated by the names of the two latter. the first will speak for itself.

As the president is soon to quit the city I suppose I shall soon embark, but the prospect of doing good is not very brilliant.

I recieved two packets from you Some time ago, each containing enclosures for France. To each I returned an answer, & in one of mine I mentioned the disposition I had made of your books &c at my house. They are deposited at the presidents house to your order, & in the Same boxes they came to me in.—

with the greatest possible attachment & respect, including wishes for your long life & happiness—I remain y^rs ob^t St J. Barlow

RC (DLC: TJ Papers, 193:34314); undated; notation by TJ beneath signature: "May 2. 15." (the dates of Barlow's most recent letters to TJ); endorsed by TJ as received 21 July 1811 and so recorded in SJL.

From James Walker

DEAR SIR Hardware Mills July 21st 1811.

I have taken a second consideration on the calculation of the running gears intended for your saw Mill. both for a 10.½ feet water-wheel &. a 15 feet wheel—&. am most in favour of the latter. more particularly as you intend using the small branch the 15 feet wheel will with the same quantity of water drawn on it produce the greatest effect as there will be so many more[1] buckets to act at the same time. should you have a 15 foot wheel it may work by the side of the saw Mill and if the top of the wheel projects above the floore of the mill house it will not be in the way of any thing. the water from the river may act on the same perpendicular descent & more buckets than on the 10.½ foot wheel=&. the water from the branch will act on a much greater perpendicular descent consiquently the wheel of 15 feet damr[2] with the same quantity of water must act with most power—as you can obtain sufficient fall in the branch—I should clearly recommend the 15 feet wheel=we can also give the saw 10 or 12 strokes in a minute more than with the 10.½ foot wheel, as it will bear gearing reather higher—but in either case it will be difficult with only single gearing to give the saw sufficient motion without having the cogwheel too large & wallower too[3] small=in case you should have a 15 foot water wheel I have added at the bottom of the former Bill=a little to the length and sizes of some of the timbers—

I am Sir your obt servt JAMES WALKER

RC (DLC); at foot of text: "mr. Thos Jefferson"; endorsed by TJ as received 25 Aug. 1811 and so recorded in SJL.

WALLOWER: trundle, or lantern-wheel (*OED*).

[1] Word interlined.

[2] Abbreviation for "diameter."

[3] Manuscript: "to."

ENCLOSURE

James Walker's Timber List for Thomas Jefferson's Sawmill Wheels

Timber	Length in feet & parts—	Breadth in Inches	Thickness in Inches—		
6	10	16	4.½	Back Cants for Cogwheels white oak or heart pine	Coggwheel, &c. To be season[d]
6	10	15	3.¼	Face Cants for ditto.	
6	9.½	12	3.¼	Arms for ditto.	
150	1–2	4	3.¼	Coggs for ditto good Locust	
8	10	14	2	Plank for wallowers &c white oak.	
3	10	12	4.¼	For Ragwheel of heart pine	
For water wheel					
6	14	21	3.¼	Shrouding of good white oak or heart pine	Not seasoned
6	10.½	8.½	3.½	Arms.	
60	6	8	1.⅛	Soling. of pine—	
24	5	18	1	Buckets ditto	
24	6	2.½	1.¾	Elboes— ditto	
6	12	16	5	back cants	Cogwheel for 15 feet water wheel
6	10	15	3.¼	Face ditto	
6	13	14	3.¾	arms	
8	14½	18	3.¼	Shrouding	Water wheel 15 feet diam[r]
8	15.½	9	3.½	arms	
60	6	9	1.⅛	Soling	
40	4.½	18	1—	buckets	
40	4.½	2.½	1.½	Elboes	

J WALKER

20th July 1811—

MS (DLC); in Walker's hand; endorsed by Walker: "Bill of wheel Timbers for Mr. Jeffersons Saw mill."

A RAGWHEEL has projections that allow it to catch the links of a chain passing overhead. SHROUDING: the annular rims on the buckets of a waterwheel (*OED*).

To Joel Barlow

DEAR SIR Monticello July 22. 11.

I had not supposed a letter would still find you at Washington. yours by last post tells me otherwise. those of May 2. & 15 had been recieved in due time. with respect to my books, lodged at the President's house, if you should see mr Coles, the President's Secretary, and be so good as to mention it, he will be so kind as to have them put on board some vessel bound to Richmond, addressed to the care of Gibson & Jefferson there, whom he knows. your doubts whether any good can be effected with the Emperor of France are too well grounded. he has understanding enough, but it is confined to particular lines. of the principles and advantages of commerce he appears ignorant, and his domineering temper deafens him moreover[1] to the dictates of interest, of honor & of morality. a nation like ours, recognising no arrogance of language or conduct can never enjoy the favor of such a character. the impression too which our public has been made to recieve from the different stiles of correspondence used by two of our foreign agents, has increased the difficulties of steering between the bristling pride of the two parties. it seems to point out the Quaker stile of plain reason, void of offence: the suppression of all passion, & chaste language of good sense.

heaven prosper your endeavors for our good, and preserve you in health and happiness. TH: JEFFERSON

the grains recieved shall be duly attended to

RC (DLC: Breckenridge Long Papers); addressed: "Joel Barlow esquire Kalorama near Washington Col."; franked; endorsed by Barlow. PoC (DLC); lacks postscript.

[1] Word interlined.

From John L. Thomas

DEAR SIR Richmond July 23^{d} 1811

My Brother Norborn & myself having Commenced a Commission buisiness in this place any encouragement You may be disposed to give to young & dependent beginners will be thankfully received by

Y^{r} most obt J. L. THOMAS

RC (MHi); addressed: "Thomas Jefferson esqr. Monticello"; endorsed by TJ as received 1 Aug. 1811 and so recorded in SJL.

John L. Thomas (1785–1846) worked as a commission merchant in Richmond with a firm that changed its name from J. L. & N. K. Thomas to N. K. Thomas & Company in 1815. He returned to Albemarle County in 1818. Himself a bachelor, Thomas farmed land owned by his family and used the proceeds to support his parents and unmarried sisters. Unsuccessful in an attempt to become the librarian of the nascent University of Virginia in 1825, he served for a time as a collector for that institution and became a county magistrate in 1838 (Woods, *Albemarle*, 327–8; Richmond *Enquirer*, 26 Apr. 1815; Thomas to TJ, 5 Jan., 1 Mar., 17 Sept. 1825; TJ to Thomas, 9 Jan. 1825; Albemarle Co. Will Book, 17:454; *Albemarle County Cemeteries*, 7:245).

From Robert Wash

D^R^ SIR St Louis July 23^ird^ 1811.

Mr John T Mason, intends to pass thro' your part of the Country on his return to Loudon; and having expressed[1] a desire to see Monticello &C, I have ventured to give him a pretext for calling. Should he deliver the Nos. of the Louisiana Gazette in person, you will be able to obtain from conversations with him, information more useful, interesting & authentic than they can possibly afford.

Mr Mason, is the son of Stephen Thompson Mason of Virg. deceased, & the brother-in-law of Governor Howard. From him, you may learn the News, condition &C of the Territory in detail.

Beleive me with sincere esteem y^r^ &C R: WASH

RC (DLC); endorsed by TJ as received 18 Sept. 1811 and so recorded in SJL.

John Thomson Mason (1787–1850), attorney, was born in Loudoun County and probably attended the College of William and Mary in about 1808. He practiced law in Leesburg before moving his family to Kentucky around 1812. On the recommendation of Henry Clay, President James Monroe appointed Mason federal marshal for the Kentucky district in 1817, and he served in that capacity until 1823. Having fallen on hard times, he accepted Andrew Jackson's nomination as secretary of Michigan Territory in 1830. Mason relinquished this post the following year to become an agent of the Galveston Bay and Texas Land Company. In 1836 he strongly supported the successful Texan bid for independence from Mexico. Although Mason spent much of the final decade of his life in New York City, he returned to Texas on a number of occasions and died in Galveston (Pamela C. Copeland and Richard K. Macmaster, *The Five George Masons* [1975], genealogical table opp. p. 268; *William and Mary Provisional List*, 27; *DAB*, 6:375; Mason to TJ, 4 May 1823; Clay, *Papers*, 2:351; *JEP*, 3:96, 98, 318, 4:100, 178 [12, 17 Dec. 1817, 3 Jan. 1823, 8 May 1830, 7 Dec. 1831]; Kate Mason Rowland, "General John Thompson Mason: An Early Friend of Texas," *Quarterly of the Texas State Historical Association* 11 [1908]: 163–98; Washington *Daily National Intelligencer*, 3 May 1850).

[1] Manuscript: "expessed."

From Benjamin Franklin Thompson

SIR. Setauket (Long-Island New york) July 24–1811.

A sincere and ardent veneration for your person and character, has induced me, to transmit you an Oration of mine, lately delivered in this place, at the request of the Tammany Society N° 1 of the Island of Nassau & N° 4 of the State, of which I have the honor to be Grand Sachem.

The publication has no particular merit to recommend it to your notice; but as I have taken the liberty to mention your many virtues, perhaps it will not prove an unwelcome present.

Should you ever contemplate a Tour thro' this State, your presence on Long Island, would excite inexpressible satisfaction to a very numerous majority of Republicans and especially to your

Obedient Humble Servant

BENJAMIN FRANKLIN THOMPSON.

RC (MHi); between dateline and salutation: "Thomas Jefferson Esq[r] LLD, &c[o]"; endorsed by TJ as received 4 Aug. 1811 and so recorded in SJL. Enclosure: Thompson, *An Oration, delivered before the Tammany Society, or, Columbian Order, of Brookhaven, (L.I.) and a numerous assemblage of citizens, on . . . July 4, 1811* (Brooklyn, 1811), praising the Jefferson and Madison administrations for thwarting the enemies of republican government; summarizing TJ's political career; exhorting the retired TJ to "bequeath to future ages those nicer principles of republican liberty which have been so successfully inculcated and vigorously pursued thro the whole course of thy active life" (p. 7); detailing TJ's success as president in meeting the challenges of public debt, a depleted treasury, party strife, and pro-British elements intent on involving the United States in a war with France; praising the repeal of the Judiciary Act and the acquisition of Louisiana; and arguing that the Embargo would have succeeded "had not the malignant spirit of faction and foreign influence raised its hydra head" (p. 9).

Benjamin Franklin Thompson (1784–1849), physician, lawyer, and author, was born in Setauket, New York, and attended Yale College for a year in 1802. He practiced medicine for a decade and served as an assistant clerk for Suffolk County in 1811, as an army surgeon during the War of 1812, and as a justice of the peace, revenue collector, and member of the lower house of the state legislature for several terms during the 1810s. Thompson was also Setauket's postmaster, 1816–24, and the district attorney for Queens County, 1826–36. He published a *History of Long Island* in one volume in 1839 and two volumes in 1843. It appeared posthumously in four volumes in 1918 (Charles J. Werner's brief biography of the author in Thompson, *History of Long Island*, 3d ed. [1918], 1:xxv–l; *Brooklyn Daily Eagle and Kings County Democrat*, 22 Mar. 1849; gravestone in Old Town Burying Ground, Hempstead, N.Y.).

From David Bailie Warden

SIR, Washington, 24 July, 1811—

I beg leave to inform you, that I have received the volume for general La Fayette. I shall set out tomorrow, for annapolis, where I expect to embark for France, with mr Barlow, in the course of a few days—the French Minister has received dispatches from France announcing the Emperors' decision to admit into the ports of his Empire, the productions of the United States—It is stated, that the duties, on american articles, with the exception of tobacco, will be but one half of the late tariff—I am, Sir, with great respect, your ever obliged Servt

D. B. WARDEN

RC (DLC); at foot of text: "Thomas Jefferson Esquire"; endorsed by TJ as received 28 July 1811 and so recorded in SJL.

On 23 July 1811 the FRENCH MINISTER, Louis Barbé Charles Sérurier, advised Secretary of State James Monroe of Napoleon's decision to release all sequestered American vessels and to admit into French ports ships "coming from the United States, and loaded with merchandise the growth of the country" (*ASP, Foreign Relations*, 3:508–9).

To Edmund M. Blunt

SIR Monticello July 25. 11.

I have duly recieved your favor of June 28. accompanied by a copy of your edition of the Nautical Almanac for the next year. for this be pleased to recieve my thanks. the present is acceptable, the book being in the form to which I have been the most accustomed. I have, for 3. or 4. years, been in the habit of using Garnet's edition, without observing the errors you ascribe to it. the misfortunes to which such errors may expose the mariner are certainly serious, but their entire avoidance is all but impracticable. we are obliged to take those things on trust, and run the risks attending them. yet he undoubtedly who avoids most of them, deserves best of the public. the British Requisite tables have two pages of Errata closely printed. their Ephemeris is probably nearer being correct. I think you have done wisely in adhering strictly to it's form. seamen are taught to use it mechanically, and what may be real improvements of form[1] to men of science, are, with them, obstacles to it's use. as so much of the merit of your edition depends on the accuracy of the copy, you are sensible I can say nothing on that head. even an habitual use[2] furnishes but accidental detections of figures. nothing less than the literal examination which should be used by the corrector of the press, can authorise a recommendation on that head. I shall be glad to be an annual customer for your edition, & presume the deposit you propose to make at Norfolk will enable me to obtain a copy annually. wishing you an encoraging remuneration of your undertaking I tender you the assurance of my respect

TH: JEFFERSON

PoC (DLC); at foot of text: "Mr Edmund M. Blunt"; endorsed by TJ.

BRITISH REQUISITE TABLES: Nevil Maskelyne, *Tables requisite to be used with the Nautical Ephemeris for finding the Latitude and Longitude at Sea*, 2d ed. (London, 1781; Sowerby, no. 3811).

Bonsal, Conrad & Company, booksellers in NORFOLK, were listed on the cover of Blunt's nautical almanac as among those stocking the work.

[1] Preceding two words interlined.

[2] TJ here canceled "is not sufficient to."

To William Duane

DEAR SIR Monticello July 25. 11.

Your letter of the 5th with the volume of Montesquieu accompanying it, came to hand in due time; the latter indeed in lucky time as, inclosing it by the return of post, I was enabled to get it into mr Warden's hands before his departure, for a friend abroad to whom it will be a most acceptable offering. of the residue of the copies I asked, I would wish to recieve one well bound for my own library, the others in boards as that before sent. one of these in boards may come to me by post, for use until the others are recieved, which I would prefer having sent by water, as vessels depart almost daily from Philadelphia for Richmond. Messrs Gibson & Jefferson of that place will recieve & forward the packet to me. add to it if you please a copy of Franklin's works, bound, and send me by post a note of the amount of the whole, and of my newspaper account, which has been suffered to run in arrear by the difficulty of remitting small & fractional sums to a distance, from a canton having only it's local money, & little commercial intercourse beyond it's own limits.

I learnt with sincere regret that my former letters had given you pain. nothing could be further from their intention. what I had said and done was from the most friendly dispositions towards yourself, and from a zeal for maintaining the republican ascendancy. federalism, stripped as it now nearly is, of it's landed and labouring support, is Monarchism & Anglicism, and whenever our own dissensions shall let these in upon us, the last ray of free government closes on the horizon of the world. I have been lately reading Komarzewski's Coup d'oeil on the history of Poland. tho' without any charms of stile or composition, it gives a lesson, which all our countrymen should study; the example of a country erased from the map of the world by the dissensions of it's own citizens. the papers of every day read them the counter lesson of the impossibility of subduing a people acting with an undivided will. Spain, under all her disadvantages, physical and mental, is an encouraging example of this. she proves too another truth, not less valuable, that a people having no king to sell them for a mess of pottage for himself, no shackles to restrain their powers of self defence, find resources within themselves equal to every trial. this we did during the revolutionary war and this we can do again, let who will attack us, if we act heartily with one another. this is my creed. to the principle of union I sacrifice all minor differences of opinion. these, like differences of face, are a law of our nature, and should be viewed with the same tolerance. the clouds which have appeared for some time to be gathering around us, have given me anxiety, lest an enemy always on the watch, always prompt & firm, & acting in well disciplined phalanx, should find an opening to dissipate hopes, with the loss of which, I would wish that of life itself. to myself personally the sufferings would be short. the powers of life have declined with me more in the last six months, than in as many preceding years. a rheumatic indisposition, under which your letter found me, has caused this delay in acknoleging it's reciept, and in the expressions of regret that I had inadvertently said or done any thing which had given you uneasiness. I pray you to be assured that no unkind motive directed me, and that my sentiments of friendship and respect continue the same. TH: JEFFERSON

PoC (DLC); at foot of first page: "Col° Duane."

TJ's FRIEND ABROAD was Destutt de Tracy, the author of the *Commentary and Review of Montesquieu's Spirit of Laws* mentioned above. In the Bible, Esau sold his birthright to Jacob for a MESS OF POTTAGE (Genesis 25.29–34).

From George Jefferson

DEAR SIR Richmond 25th July 1811

I inclose as you direct 200$.—I likewise inclose an account of the sale of your last 54 barrels of flour, the net proceeds as you will observe, being $:429.$\frac{17}{100}$.—This should have been forwarded some time ago, had I not received a letter from you informing me there was more to come down, which induced me to keep it back, with the view of including the whole in one account. As however no more has yet arrived, I conclude that you must have been mistaken as to the quantity. I yesterday sent up by Johnson, some nail rod & iron lately received, together with a small box received some time ago.—I will endeavour to sell your Tobacco seperately as you suggest, but fear the chance is bad, as the demand even for the very finest quality has greatly subsided.

I am Dear Sir Your Very humble servt GEO. JEFFERSON

RC (MHi); at foot of text: "Thomas Jefferson esq^{r}"; endorsed by TJ as received 28 July 1811 and so recorded in SJL.

SJL records missing letters from TJ to Jefferson of 21 and 22 July 1811. On the earlier day, TJ completed the payment of Tufton overseer William McGehee's 1810 wages by drawing on Gibson & Jefferson for $180 in McGehee's favor (*MB*, 2:1267).

ENCLOSURE

Account from Sale of Thomas Jefferson's Flour

Sales of 54 Barrels flour made on account of Thomas Jefferson Esqr June 24th 1811 To Wm Mackenzie for Jno Leslies note at 60 days vz^{t}

49 Barrels Superfine	at 9$ 441.—	
5 " fine	8½ 42 50	
		$483.50
Charges		
toll on 54 B^{bls}	$5.62½	
Storage	4.50	
Coop^{g} 105 Inspection 108	2.13	
freight 45 Barrels	30.—	
Commission on 483.50 at 2½ ℘C^{t}	12. 8	54.33½
		$429.17

EE[1]

Richmond 2nd July 1811

MS (MHi); in James Ligon's hand.

[1] Abbreviation for "errors excepted."

From Wilson J. Cary

Dear Sir Carysbrook. July 26. 1811.

I ask the favor of you to deliver to the bearer (who is directed to receive and take charge of him) the Merino Ram lamb we are entitled to, out of the produce of our ewes. An apology is due to you for having given you the trouble of keeping him so long; but the distance from hence to Monticello and the variety of pressing business always on hand upon a large and complicated farm must plead our excuse for having delayed removing him untill now.

I am with great respect and regard &c Wilson J. Cary—

RC (ViU: TJP-CC); endorsed by TJ as received 27 July 1811 and so recorded in SJL.

Wilson Jefferson Cary (1784–1823), the son of Wilson Cary and TJ's niece Jane Barbara Carr Cary, attended the College of William and Mary in about 1803, studied law in Richmond under Edmund Randolph, and was admitted to the Virginia bar. He married Thomas Mann Randolph's sister Virginia at Monticello in 1805, moved to Carysbrook in Fluvanna County by 1809, and represented that county in the Virginia House of Delegates, 1821–23, where he supported the establishment of the University of Virginia. Cary was also active in the Agricultural Society of Albemarle. He was buried in the Monticello graveyard (*PTJ*, 7:302; *MB*, 2:1248n, 1399; Fairfax Harrison, *The Virginia Carys: An Essay in Genealogy* [1919], 112–3; *William and Mary Provisional List*, 12; Leonard, *General Assembly*, 308, 313; Joseph C. Cabell to TJ, 30 Dec. 1822; Shackelford, *Descendants*, 253; *Richmond Enquirer*, 3 Oct. 1823; Fluvanna Co. Will Book, 3:6–7, 9–12).

From John H. Cocke

SIR, Carysbrook July 26th 1811

Be so good as to deliver my Merino Lamb to the Bearer hereof.—

Some time ago, I would gladly have taken back the Ewes which I sent to Monticello on Colonel Fontaines account cou'd I have obtain'd permission of his Executors—but it is no longer desirable to me as I have purchased some full blood'd Merino's

I am sir Yours most respectfully JOHN H. COCKE

RC (CSmH: JF); at foot of text: "Mr Jefferson"; endorsed by TJ as received 27 July 1811 and so recorded in SJL.

To William Short

DEAR SIR Monticello July 6. [26] 11.

On the reciept of your letters of May 29. & June 18. I wrote to mr Bankhead, then with his family in Port-royal, offering your lands to him at 12.D. for altho I had seen no reason for a great sudden rise in the price of our lands, yet two sales had been made as I formerly wrote you, far above what had been deemed the neighborhood price. himself had been one of the purchasers. I therefore thought this advance not out of proportion. but his father has declined the plan of removing from Portroyal. but a mr Thresly from that neighborhood, came, on his recommendation, to see the lands. in the mean time I had seen Price & recieved from him the information that the leases of the tenants were for three years, & he said he had consulted me. in this I think he is mistaken, because I have not the smallest trace of it in my memory, and because I am conscious I should not have undertaken to approve, but have left him to his instructions. from the time I informed you that my residence at Washington would render my further attentions to that place impracticable, & unprofitable to you, I never meddled at all. Price generally called to see me, whenever I came home, & of course would tell me what he was doing, and I may have said Yea or Nay as any other neighbor would in the way of conversation. this has perhaps taken place, & he may have construed something of this kind into an approbation, & I have no doubt he did so, being persuaded of his entire honesty & truth. on mr Threshly's arrival, I told him of the leases, and that if he should like the land, he should recieve the rents as owner, in compensation of the interest, or he might be clear of interest, leaving us the profit of rents. after visiting the land, he declined the purchase, objecting both to the price & the want of possession. Col° Lindsay, some time ago, expressed a wish to purchase this land. I shall make him the offer at 12.D. but if, getting over the objection of possession, he should decline on the point of price alone, I shall fall to your price. if he buys, he will pay the cash, in Richmond to your order. but I fear the leases will stand much in the way of the sale. I have been confined to the house for three weeks by rheumatism, and this is among the first fruits of my return to my writing table, or I should on reciept of your last favor of June 23. have no longer delayed writing to you in the expectation of doing it with more information. as soon as I am able to ride, I will go to Indian camp, to learn the state of things, and make the best arrangements the case will admit of, either for the surrender of the leases in the event of sale, or for the care of the land if they continue.

Absorbed by the principal object of your letters, the sale of the land, the article respecting the settlement of your accounts, ment[d] in that of June 18. had escaped me. there will be no difficulty in the case, mr Upham's folly & malignity notwithstanding. the constitution, & ten thousand instances of practice make the appointment good to the end of the next session following it. you have only to inclose your account to the Secretary of state, who will refer you for the production of your vouchers to the Auditor, stating to him the principles on which it is to be settled.

Should Col° Monroe propose to purchase Indian camp, as I have heard said, and as you also mention, it will be a transaction to be settled of course between yourselves. my relation to you both would make me an improper & unwilling mediator. we expect him daily. would not the season, as well as the occasion, joined to our wishes, tempt you to come and look to this matter yourself? I need not tell you the pleasure it would give us to recieve you here: but in that and all other events I repeat with sincerity the assurances of my affectionate esteem & respect.

TH: JEFFERSON

RC (ViW: TJP); misdated; at foot of first page: "M[r] Short"; endorsed by Short as a letter of 6 July 1811 received 8 Aug. 1811 at "P." [Portsmouth, N.H.]. Recorded in SJL as a letter of 26 July 1811 dated "July 6. by mistake."

Missing letters from Short to TJ of

MAY 29, JUNE 18, and June 23 are recorded in SJL as received from Philadelphia on 2, 23, and 30 June 1811. They are also listed in Short's epistolary record for 1811 (DLC: Short Papers, 34:6346). Short's PRICE for Indian Camp was $10 an acre (TJ to Short, 17 May 1811).

THRESLY (Threshly): Robert B. Sthreshly. In TJ's view, Federalist congressman Jabez Upham displayed FOLLY & MALIGNITY by successfully moving on 23 Apr. 1810 that Secretary of the Treasury Albert Gallatin be ordered "to lay before this House a statement of any sum or sums of money for outfit or compensation to William Short, as Minister or agent from the United States to the Court of St. Petersburg . . . together with a statement of the authority or authorities under which the same may have been received." The Federalists believed that Short had been "secretly and unconstitutionally appointed" and that any money advanced to him should be returned to the treasury (*JHR*, 7:388–9; *Trenton Federalist*, 30 Apr. 1810).

To Wilson J. Cary

DEAR SIR Monticello July 28. 11.

Your servant, with 4. lambs for mr Cocke, will recieve a 5th for yourself. it is the second best of the 5. mr Cocke's are from his own ewes, the one destined for you is from mine, the best I had except one. one of your ewes proved to be with lamb when she came; the other missed altogether. the two last merino ewes I recieved brought the scab into my flock, & I lost several. I tried mercurial ointment with no effect. repeated anointings with brimstone & fat have eradicated it, except in a single subject, now separated. none of the lambs have ever had a symptom of it. still you should be on the look out, because of the possibility. the falling off of the wool and scabs in it's place is the indication, & the ointment immediately rubbed in effects the cure at once.

I was on the eve of setting out for Bedford 3. weeks ago, & mr Randolph's family had consequently gone to Edgehill to pass the harvest, when I was taken with the rheumatism which confined me to the house & mostly to the bed for a fortnight. I am on the recovery, able to ride into the plantation, and to walk with less pain. I only await the return of strength enough to commence my intended journey. Patsy has been unwell also, and is just getting about. I heard from Dunlora yesterday. my sister is extremely low. I did not know till then that your mother had gone there, nor that Colo Cary and his lady had got up to Carysbrook. if I find my strength will permit me to pay him a visit either as I go or return from Bedford, I shall certainly do it. I intended it the last year, but various matters of business procrastinated it until I learnt he was gone. be so good as to present my friendly respects to himself & mrs Cary the elder & younger & be assured I am ever affectionately Your's TH: JEFFERSON

PoC (ViU: TJP-CC); at foot of text: "Wilson J. Cary"; endorsed by TJ.

PATSY: Martha Jefferson Randolph. TJ's ailing SISTER was Martha Jefferson Carr, Cary's maternal grandmother. COL^{o} CARY AND HIS LADY: Cary's paternal grandparents, Wilson Miles Cary and Rebecca Dawson Cary.

To John H. Cocke

DEAR SIR Monticello July 28. 11.

The servant who delivered your letter will recieve 4. ram lambs, 3 of them from the half dozen ewes you sent, the other in commutation for 2. ewes sent by Col^{o} Fontaine, but which I am sure he never saw, as they were such miserable half grown, diminutive animals that I could not permit them to run with my flock, and sent them to another place. I send a lamb from my own ewes however in exchange for them, & in sending it to you I comply with the request of Col^{o} Fontaine to mr Randolph. I had a Merino ram & 3. ewes of the three different races, selected by mr Jarvis of Lisbon. the two last of them recieved brought the scab into my flock. I lost one of the ewes by it, and two of them from their ill state of health lost their lambs immediately. I now have therefore but the ram, which is a very fine animal, 2. ewes and one ram lamb. the wool of one of the ewes was considered at Washington as superior to any of the samples ever shewn there. we have, with a great deal of trouble extirpated the scab, except in a single individual which I have separated from the flock. none of the lambs have ever had a symptom of it. yet the possibility of it's coming on them renders attention adviseable. the loss of their wool is the first visible indication, & then the scabs appearing on the naked part. a mixture of sulphur & fat rubbed on at once, cures the disease effectually. in mine however it had become so inveterate as to need a 3^{d} & 4th anointment, having previously bid defiance to mercurial ointment. Accept the assurances of my great esteem & respect

TH: JEFFERSON

PoC (DLC); at foot of text: "John H. Cocke esq."; endorsed by TJ.

To Joel Barlow

DEAR SIR Monticello July 29. 11.

I fear I shall overload yourself, if not your ship, with my accumulated commissions. the inclosed publications will, I think be acceptable to men of mind in any country. will you be so good as to deliver them according to their respective addresses, and accept renewed assurances of my great esteem and respect Th: Jefferson

PoC (DLC); at foot of text: "Mr Barlow"; endorsed by TJ. Enclosures not identified.

From George Jefferson

Dear Sir Richmond 1st Augt 1811

Mr Thomas Taylor an acquaintance of mine having lately purchased some land near the West-ham ferry, it occurred to me that he would probably purchase the lots which I recollected to have heard you say you owned there.—On mentioning it to him, I found him very anxious to purchase. As the place can never more be of any value as a landing, unless we suppose the Canal to be abandoned, I conclude that you would be willing to sell the lots, since the trifle they would bring would be better saved than lost: if so, be so obliging as to inform Mr Taylor or myself[1] of the number you have, and of their numbers.

I have not been able to do any thing with your Tobacco, not even by dividing it as you proposed.

I am Dear Sir Your Very humble servt Geo. Jefferson

RC (MHi); at foot of text: "Thomas Jefferson esqr"; endorsed by TJ as received 4 Aug. 1811 and so recorded in SJL.

The town of Beverley was located at Westham (WEST-HAM) on the James River, six miles upstream from Richmond (*MB*, 1:391n, 2:1326n). TJ inherited from his father "4. lots in Beverley town, Henrico. viz. No 57. at the foot of the hill, 107. & 108. on the public road, and 151. includes the ferry landing, being the uppermost lot of the town on the river" (Betts, *Farm Book*, pt. 1, 127; TJ to Thomas Taylor, 28 Dec. 1814). The nearby CANAL around the falls of the James River was completed in 1800 (*MB*, 2:1326n).

[1] Preceding two words interlined.

From Benjamin Henry Latrobe

Dear Sir Washington, Augt 1st 1811

Having received your very acceptable letter of the 14th of[1] April in the midst of the hurry & anxiety of my departure for Philadelphia, I did not acknowledge its receipt untill after my arrival in that city; and then only cursorily, and with a wish that my silence might not appear to have been the effect of insensibility to your kindness. I remained in Philadelphia more than six weeks, detained by the designs of two

private houses which I made.—I transmitted to you from thence my oration on opening the first exhibition of pictures & Sculpture which has been held, of native production, since the commencement of the settlement of Europaeans on this side of the Atlantic.—On the 13th of June I returned to this city, and have since then been so incessantly employed in attending to the Works in the Navy yard & to the Canal, unassisted, that it has been impossible for me to find an hour of mental & corporeal leisure, in which I could again write to You.
For the very full & honorable testimony which you have been so good as to bear to the zeal and integrity with which I conducted the public works during your presidency I cannot express the satisfaction & gratitude I feel.—If it were in my power to remove from your mind the impression, that the excess which occurred of expenditure beyond the appropriation was owing to some neglect of duty[2] which it was in my power to perform, I should be exceedingly happy;—altho' it is perhaps more than I ought to expect.—Indeed, unless I could prove that I was always ignorant of the exhausted state of the funds I should fail in proving that I had not wilfully exceeded them.—But there are situations in which the necessity of acting so as to risk the imputation of wrong and to incur actually the blame of acting against orders is unavoidable, and that has always been my situation. I have never been free to act so as to avoid expenditure beyond the appropriation, without taking the outrageous step of dismissing all my workmen[3] about Septr and then measuring the work, collecting & certifying the accounts and waiting with whatever balance might be in hand untill congress should please to make a new appropriation.[4] One Year indeed,—namely in Jany 1805 an appropriation was made which was not expended in that year. I had asked by a letter written in answer to one from the Chairman of the Committee of the house for 139.500.$ But by a most unaccountable propensity to curtail my estimates I received only 110.000. The consequence was that I was obliged to omit the staircases & entrance to the house, to build up the North Wall of the S. Wing independently of all support, &, to prevent its warping or falling, to make it 1f 6 thicker than necessary; & afterwards in 1807 when further provision was made for the access to the house, to expend ten thousand dollars at least in work to support what I had done before, because that immense Wall 120 feet long, 126 feet high & only 3f 10 thick carried up without support had settled eight inches into the vacant space between the wings. But my principal embarrassment was always my total ignorance of the state of the accounts. For Mr Munroe personally I have the highest respect. The U States have not a more faithful & honest Officer in their serv-

ice, but certainly he was not, either by our relative situations, or from the acknowledged operation upon his mind by others, inclined to give me a compleat command of his books, without which, (as all the accounts did not for the first 4 or 5 Years pass through my hands) it was impossible for me to know anything about them. At last I was allowed a Clerk of accts.[5] I took into the office a young man recommended by Mr Munroe. I was very unfortunate, not in the choise of the young man, but in the course of adventures that happened to him. A week after his appointment he was thrown against a tree from his horse, struck his head & wholly lost his memory for many months, so as to be useless to me. When he a little[6] recovered he had the misfortune accidentally to lodge a load of small shot in the body of a young lady, the friend of his Sister, & for a long time, he was almost distracted. The books which were opened could not be kept up, & when I pressed for the means of recovering them, I received the enclosed[7] letter, from McIntire the Clerk, who during the winter had assisted Mr Munroe in the Post office.—

On a full explanation which I have had with Mr Munroe on all the circumstances of our connexion, he frankly owned, that he heard of me from many quarters such accounts as to my avowed hostility to him, of my declared contempt of his person & authority, & of my determination to act independently of him, that it is not to be wondered at, that he should do nothing but what his strict duty required.—On my part, I can assure you with truth and in the most solemn manner, that untill the late friendly explanation with him I had not the remotest idea, that his distance and inequality of conduct towards me, arose from any cause but from the temper of a sedentary man: and especially from the impossibility that our separate provinces could, in the very nature of things mutually be assisting to each other. I therefore, excepting perhaps in indulging sometimes the ebullitions of my own temper, when harrassed beyond bearing by public calumny, and private vexations in the performance of my duty, am not conscious of ever[8] having done or said anything that ought to have been cause of offence. I am sure I never intended it. The hasty expression of a moment may perhaps have struck all concerned with me; even of yourself I may have complained in respect to the unfortunate Skylights, but I am certain that I never intended to convey a settled opinion derogatory to Mr Munroe's much less to your character or conduct. Even such hasty[9] expressions are not on my memory. I have said all this to show you, that in a great measure, my sin was a sin of ignorance: but in a much greater it was a sin of necessity.—I had responsibility,—in fact <u>all</u> the responsibility,—without power, but such as was granted me by courtesy, & forced into my hands from necessity. The estimates were mine, & congress curtailed them, and which was quite as bad, granted in March or May, what ought, (to have been adequate), to have been given in December. With curtailed estimates I was expected to do fully the business reported, & with diminished time, to be ready for the Session. By being made 3 to[10] 6 Months later than they were required, even[11] the appropriations which reached my estimates were rendered insufficient. I never could lay in a stock of Materials beforehand, or buy them at the best market;—and altho' responsible for its expenditure, I never knew its state untill the emptiness of the Treasury was announced to me. Then indeed I might have discharged all the workmen, left the buildings to go to wreck in the winter, measured and settled all the accounts, and getting rid of a charge, light in comparison, that of exceeding the appropriation have incurred that of distressing 30 or 40 families, or of driving them from the city,—and of wasting the public property by so illmanaged a conduct of the Work.—It would however have been my best policy no doubt, but with my feelings I could not pursue it.—

The great cause of all this however arose in the arrangement itself. Your idea that Mr Munroe stood relatively to me in the situation of Captn Tingey to the Master workmen of the navy Yard, on which you desired me to arrange my operations had this inconvenience, that Mr Munroe was not a professional man; & if he had been one he must have devoted his whole time to the subject.—The Captn (of the Navy Yard)[12] is a judge of all that is done in the Yard, as to price quality & quantity of Materials, and as to goodness price and necessity of Workmanship. Therefore in passing accounts, he sanctions only the cost of what himself has directed to be done, and probably agreed for. I need not point out the difference of the cases more distinctly, because it will at once strike you in all its bearings.—

I am so anxious that I should be approved by you in all my conduct, that I trespass most unreasonably on your patience. I have done and beg you to excuse me, and to consider what I have said as to Mr Munroe[13] as confidential, a perfect explanation having taken [place],[14] & mutual kindness prevailing between us.—

I have sent you by the President the stone brought to you by Mr Lewis from the west of the Mississippi Our Italians have labored it most minutely at their spare hours. I could not get it sooner out of their hands. There is still another slab, which Andrei cut off, in my possession. Andrei is a most admirable Man He has less Genius, but much more dignity & moral worth of character than Franzoni. But the latter is also a good man. He has now 4 American children. A Letter from you to each of them would be more honored than any other compensation. The figure is Franzoni's, the rest of the piece Andrei's.—

I am with the highest esteem

Yours faithfully B HENRY LATROBE

My polygraph has become so loose that I write indifferently with it. It will be easily repaired.

RC (DLC); at head of text: "Thomas Jefferson Esq[re] Monticello"; endorsed by TJ as received 4 Aug. 1811 and so recorded in SJL. PoC (MdHi: Latrobe Letterbook); lacks postscript. Enclosure: Alexander McIntire to Latrobe, Post Office, Washington, 12 Mar. [1811?], stating that he had been too busy to "devote five minutes" to "bringing up the books to that state which I intended"; that in the absence of city superintendent Thomas Munroe he had looked for the accounts and discovered that almost all of them had been returned to the treasury; that when he asked to copy them, Munroe replied that "our books were nothing to him, & as he was not to [be] governed by them, it was of no consequence"; that Munroe would not answer questions about the accounts; and that those of the last quarter had presumably already gone to the treasury (RC in DLC: TJ Papers, 192:34239; partially dated; omitted word editorially supplied; addressed: "B H Latrobe Esq[r]").

On 30 Dec. 1804 Latrobe wrote Philip R. Thompson, the CHAIRMAN OF THE COMMITTEE OF THE HOUSE overseeing the appropriation of money for public building in the nation's capital, asking for $134,300, not $139,500. The reduction that Congress imposed in this instance was actually quite small. In January 1805 Congress granted $110,000 for the south wing of the United States Capitol and $20,000 for repairs to the north wing and other federal structures nearby (Latrobe, *Papers*, 1:586–8; *Annals*, 8th Cong., 2d sess., 41, 985, 1662 [15, 23, 25 Jan. 1805]). By the summer of 1807 the UNFORTUNATE SKYLIGHTS on top of the United States Capitol were leaking so badly "that Congress could not sit under them" (Latrobe, *Papers*, 2:471).

[1] Manuscript: "14 of[th]."

[2] Reworked from "to my neglect of any duty."

[3] PoC here adds "annually."

[4] Manuscript: "appropiation."

[5] Preceding two words interlined.

[6] Preceding three words interlined.

[7] Word interlined in place of "following."

[8] Manuscript: "every."

[9] Preceding two words interlined in place of "those."

[10] Word interlined in place of "or."

[11] Word interlined.

[12] Omitted closing parenthesis editorially supplied.

[13] Manuscript: "Monroe."

[14] Word, omitted in RC, supplied from PoC.

To James T. Austin

SIR Monticello Aug. 2. 11.

I have duly recieved your favor of July 12. with the pamphlet inclosed for which be pleased to accept my thanks. I had before read the papers separately in the newspapers with great satisfaction, but without knowing to whom we were indebted for so just a censure of the act which is the subject of it. this was certainly the grossest insult which any organised society ever recieved from it's own members, and I have no doubt it will enlighten the more faithful citizens of Massachusets as to the dangers to which they may[1] be exposed from such citizens within their own bosoms, under circumstances which at present appear to threaten us. I have never doubted that in the appeal to arms which has been threatened by some intemperate persons, the sound parts of your state would be sufficient to take care of the unsound. I am particularly thankful for the kind expressions of your letter towards myself, and tender you the assurances of my esteem & respect TH: JEFFERSON

RC (CtY: Franklin Collection); addressed: "Mr James T. Austin Boston"; franked; endorsed by Austin. PoC (DLC); endorsed by TJ.

Austin's PAMPHLET, described in note to Austin to TJ, 12 July 1811, had been reprinted widely in THE NEWSPAPERS, including the Washington *National Intelligencer*, 20, 25 Apr., 4, 11 May, and 25 June 1811. TJ perceived the GROSSEST INSULT to ORGANISED SOCIETY in the resolutions of a Federalist caucus condemned by Austin in this essay.

[1] Word interlined in place of "will."

To Burwell Bassett

DEAR SIR Monticello Aug. 2. 11.

I have duly recieved your favor of July 20th and thank you [for] the trouble you have been so good as to take in the case of M. Beauvois. to this I will not add by troubling you with the further enquiries you so kindly offer to make if necessary. it will be the duty of M. Beauvois' agent to give me any further information necessary, as I am only requested to advise him in his proceedings. this I shall do on motives of common duty, that if M. de Beauvois has any rights, his being a foreigner & absent may be no obstacle to his recovery of them. I pray you to be assured of my esteem & respect. TH: JEFFERSON

PoC (DLC); one word faint; at foot of text: "Burwell Basset esq."; endorsed by TJ.

Palisot de BEAUVOIS' AGENT was Lewis A. Pauly.

To John Bracken

SIR Monticello Aug. 2. 11.

I have lately recieved a letter from mr Mazzei in which he sais 'I have several times mentioned to you the unhappy state of the poor old sisters of our deceased friend Bellini. referring you to former letters,

I will only add to what I have before said, my prayers for your aid to the interests of these poor & distressed old women.'

On recurring to our former correspondence on this subject I observe you had sent me a letter containing a bill of exchange for these ladies, but on information of the failure of the merchant on whom the bill was drawn, you had desired me to return the letter. entirely unacquainted with any transactions in the case since that, I take the liberty, in compliance with the request of mr Mazzei, of only saying that if I can be useful in conveying either letters or remittances to the representatives of mr Bellini, I shall do it with pleasure, and pray you to accept the assurances of my great respect. TH: JEFFERSON

PoC (DLC); at foot of text: "The rev[d] M[r] Bracken"; endorsed by TJ.

John Bracken (1747–1818) immigrated to Virginia from his native England by the summer of 1769 and was ordained a minister of the Church of England in 1772. The following year he was elected rector of Bruton Parish in Williamsburg, a position he held until his death. In 1775 Bracken became the master of the grammar school at the College of William and Mary and, two years later, he attained the associated position of professor of humanity. He lost this post with the abolition of the grammar school in 1779, taught privately for more than a decade, and was reinstated by William and Mary at his former rank in 1792. Bracken served as Williamsburg's mayor on several occasions and was president of the board of the Public Hospital. He succeeded James Madison as bishop of Virginia and president of William and Mary at the latter's death in 1812. In poor health and lacking the vigor to revive either struggling institution, Bracken gave up his diocese in May 1813 without being consecrated, and he resigned the college's presidency at the request of its board of visitors in June of the following year (*DVB*; Rutherfoord Goodwin, "The Reverend John Bracken [1745–1818], Rector of Bruton Parish and President of William and Mary College in Virginia," *Historical Magazine of the Protestant Episcopal Church* 10 [1941]: 354–89; Bracken to TJ, 6 Aug. 1805 [DLC]; *Richmond Enquirer*, 24 July 1818).

Bracken sent TJ a BILL OF EXCHANGE for the Bellini sisters on 6 Feb. 1807 but asked him to RETURN it on 3 Mar. of that year (both letters in DLC).

To Benjamin Galloway

Monticello Aug. 2. 11.

Th: Jefferson presents his compliments to mr Galloway and his thanks for the papers he inclosed. they furnish proofs of his firm perseverance in the principles of sound patriotism. retired himself to scenes of tranquility and repose, he trusts with entire confidence to the vigilance of his republican fellow citizens to render harmless all designs against our happy constitution. he prays mr Galloway to be assured of his esteem & respect.

PoC (MHi); dateline at foot of text; endorsed by TJ.

To Martin Oster

SIR Monticello Aug. 2. 11.

I have lately recieved a letter from M. de Beauvois of Paris stating the claims of Madame Beauvois to the property of her brother M. Piernetz, in the county of New Kent, claimed & held by a mr Ratcliffe of that county, under a supposed will of Piernetz. mr Beauvois requests me to counsel his friend and agent M. Pauly how to proceed in maintaining his claims, and says he lives in Louisa near Staunton. this error in our geography renders it impossible for me to find M. Pauly, in order to assure him of my dispositions to be useful to M. de Beauvois, & with that view to offer any services I can render. as I find by M. de Beauvois' letter that you have been so kind as to give him information on this subject, I have presumed you would do the further favor to us both to furnish me with the address of M. Pauly, to enable me to make him a tender of my assistance in this case. I pray you to excuse this trouble on behalf of M. de Beauvois and to accept the assurances of my esteem & respect. TH: JEFFERSON

PoC (MHi); at foot of text: "M. Oster Consul of France"; endorsed by TJ.

Martin Oster (ca. 1741–1827) studied law before serving in the French quartermaster's corps during the Seven Years' War, 1760–63. He then worked settling army accounts before obtaining employment at the Hôtel Royale des Invalides in 1765, where he eventually rose to be first secretary. Oster sailed for America late in 1777 at the behest of the French monarchy. He was named vice-consul at Philadelphia in 1778, transferred to Richmond in 1783, and later resided in Norfolk. The revolutionary government in Paris recalled Oster in 1792, but he remained in Virginia. He held a post as French commissary for commercial relations at Norfolk until the returning Bourbon monarchy retired him with a pension about 1815 (J. Rives Childs, "French Consul Martin Oster Reports on Virginia, 1784–1796," *VMHB* 76 [1968]: 27–40, esp. 28–9, 38–9; Abraham P. Nasatir and Gary Elwyn Monell, *French Consuls in the United States: A Calendar of their Correspondence in the Archives Nationales* [1967], 566–7; Worthington C. Ford and others, eds., *Journals of the Continental Congress, 1774–1789* [1904–37], 12:948; *PTJ*, esp. 10:544; Washington *Daily National Intelligencer*, 8 Dec. 1827).

STAUNTON is in Augusta, not Louisa County.

Certificate of Henry Cassidy

I do Certify that I can make oath if required that in the year 1805 when I came to s[t] Louis to enter the Titles Papers of Elisha Winters & Gabriel Winters Lands at the Arkansas that I advised with General Wilkinson on the subject and that he advised me to Employ Rufus Easton Esqr as agent for the claim Saying at the time that he was a man of honor & abilities and would do me Justice in attending to the Interest of the Claimants Given under my hand at St Louis the 4th Augt 1811 HENRY CASSIDY

The above named Gentleman has been and is appointed a judge of the Courts of Arkansas District by Governor Howard—

MS (MHi); certificate and signature in Cassidy's hand, with postscript and address in an unidentified hand; addressed: "The Honorable Thomas Jefferson Monticello Virginia"; franked; postmarked Saint Louis, 8 Aug.; endorsed by TJ as a letter from Cassidy received 5 Sept. 1811 and so recorded in SJL.

Henry Cassidy, attorney and real-estate investor, was appointed a justice of the peace in the Cape Girardeau district of the Louisiana Territory in 1806, a deputy surveyor in 1807, a judge of the Arkansas District courts in 1811, and a township justice in the newly created Missouri Territory in 1813. He was given a full four-year term as township justice in 1814, and he briefly represented Arkansas County in the Missouri legislature. In addition, Cassidy was named attorney of the second judicial circuit of the new Arkansas Territory in August 1819, lost a bid to become Arkansas's first delegate to Congress that November, and was clerk of the Arkansas House of Representatives in the autumn of 1820. Thirteen members of the territorial legislature unsuccessfully recommended him for a seat on the superior court the same year. According to Arkansas's executive register, Cassidy "decamped in the dark" from his position as public attorney during the spring of 1821 (*Terr. Papers*, 13:546, 14:150–1, 650, 795, 19:118–9, 170–1, 789; Lynn Foster, "Courts and Lawyers on the Arkansas Frontier: The First Years of American Justice," *Arkansas Historical Quarterly* 62 [2003]: 307, 311–7; *Arkansas Gazette*, 1 Jan., 7 Oct. 1820).

On 6 Aug. 1811 Cassidy swore before Justice of the Peace Thomas F. Riddick to an affidavit of which the opening paragaph was substantially the same as the above certificate, with an added assertion that James WILKINSON had indicated that Rufus Easton's work for Cassidy "would not be in any manner inconsistent with the station of the said Easton as a judge of the Territory." The concluding paragraph affirmed that Wilkinson had recommended his namesake son to transact Cassidy's legal business even though he was "attached to the army." Cassidy sent the affidavit to Postmaster General Gideon Granger late in December 1811 (*Terr. Papers*, 14:463–4). He seems to have been accusing General Wilkinson of encouraging Easton and the younger Wilkinson to engage in conflicts of interest.

To Nicolas G. Dufief

SIR Monticello Aug. 4. 11.

I recieved some time ago your valuable dictionary, and have now had time & trial enough to pronounce it the very best French & English dictionary which has ever been published. it's handy size too increases it's convenience. the 3d volume is a treasure. I only wish it's numerous alphabets had been digested into a single one to save the double research first for the proper alphabet, & then for the article wanted from it. will you be so good as to note to me the price which I will take care to remit you as soon as known. I am anxious to get a copy of La Croix's Cours de Mathematiques, (I believe it is in 7. vols 8[vo]) but I think I have learnt that you have ceased to act in the bookselling line. I formerly had some dealings with Mess[rs] Roches, freres, booksellers of Philadelphia. if my information as to yourself is right, perhaps they would be so kind as to send me a copy with a note of it's amount which should be promptly remitted them. it might come any week by vessels bound to Richmond, & if addressed to Messrs Gibson & Jefferson there would come safely to me. Accept the assurances of my esteem & respect. TH: JEFFERSON

PoC (DLC); at foot of text: "M. Dufief"; endorsed by TJ.

Sylvestre François Lacroix's (LA CROIX'S) *Cours de Mathematiques à l'usage de l'École Centrale des Quatres-Nations*, 7 vols. (Paris, 1802–07; Poor, *Jefferson's Library*, 8 [no. 391]), reissued separate works on geometry, arithmetic, trigonometry, algebra, education, and differential and integral calculus (*DSB*). Between 1805 and 1807 TJ purchased a number of works from P. & C. Roche, BOOKSELLERS in Philadelphia, a partnership of Peter Roche and his brother Christian Roche (*MB*, 2:1155, 1177, 1206, 1214; James Robinson, *The Philadelphia Directory for 1807* [Philadelphia, 1807]).

To James Ogilvie

DEAR SIR Monticello Aug. 4. 11.

Your favor of May 24. was very long on it's passage to me. it gave us all pleasure to learn from yourself the progress of your peregrination, and your prospect of approaching rest, for a while, among our Western brethren. of 'rest for the body, some, none for the mind.' to that, action is said to be all it's joy: and we have no more remarkeable proof of it than in yourself. the newspapers have kept us informed of the splendid course you have run, and of the flattering impressions made on the public mind, & which must have been so grateful to yourself. the new intellectual feast you are preparing for them in your Western retirement, will excite new appetites, and will be hailed like the returning sun, when he reappears in the East. your peripatetic enterprise, when first made known to us, alarmed our apprehensions for you, lest the taste of the times, and of our country, should not be up to the revival of this classical experiment. much to their credit however, unshackled by the prejudices which chain down the minds of the common mass of Europe, the experiment has proved that, where thought is free in it's range, we need never fear to hazard what is good in itself. this sample of the American mind is an additional item for the flattering picture your letter presents of our situation, and our prospects. I firmly believe in them all; and that human nature has never looked forward, under circumstances so auspicious, either for the sum of happiness, or the spread of surface provided to recieve it. very contrary opinions are inculcated in Europe, and in England especially, where I much doubt if you would be tolerated in presenting the views you propose. the English have been a wise, a virtuous & truly estimable people. but commerce and a corrupt government have rotted them to the core. every generous, nay every just sentiment, is absorbed in the thirst for gold. I speak of their cities, which we may certainly pronounce to be ripe for despotism, and fitted to no other government. whether the leaven of the agricultural body is sufficient to regenerate the residuary mass, and maintain it in a sound state, under any reformation of government, may well be doubted. nations, like individuals, wish to enjoy a fair reputation. it is therefore desireable for us that the slanders on our country, disseminated by hired or prejudiced travellers, should be corrected. but politics, like religion, hold up the torches of martyrdom to the reformers of error. nor is it in the theatre of Ephesus alone that tumults have been excited when the crafts were in danger. you must be cautious therefore in telling unacceptable truths beyond the water. You wish me to suggest any subject which occurs to myself as fit for the rostrum. but your own selection has proved you would have been aided by no counsel, and that you can best judge of the topics which open to your own mind a field for developement, and promise to your hearers instruction better adapted to the useful purposes of society, than the weekly disquisitions of their hired instructors. all the efforts of these people are directed to the maintenance of the artificial structure of their craft, viewing but as a subordinate concern the inculcation of morality. if we will but be Christians according to their schemes of Christianity, they will compound good naturedly with our immoralities.

Cannot your circuit be so shaped as to lead you through our neighborhood on your return? it would give us all pleasure to see you, if it be only en passant, for after such a survey of varied country, we cannot flatter ourselves that ours would be the selected residence. but whether you can visit us or not, I shall always be happy to hear from you, & to know that you succeed in whatever you undertake. with these assurances accept those of great esteem & respect from myself & all the members of my family. TH: JEFFERSON

P.S. since writing the above, an interesting subject occurs. what would you think of a discourse on the benefits of the union, and the miseries which would follow a separation of the states, to be exemplified in the eternal & wasting wars of Europe, in the pillage & profligacy to which these lead, and the abject oppression and degradation to which they reduce it's inhabitants? painted by your vivid pencil, what could make deeper impressions and what impressions could come more home to our concern or kindle a livelier sense of our present blessings?

PoC (DLC); at foot of first page: "Mr Ogilvie." Enclosed in TJ to John Jordan, 5 Aug. 1811.

REST FOR THE BODY, SOME, NONE FOR THE MIND: in John Milton's *Samson Agonistes*, line 18, the blinded Samson observes that a break from his labors for the Philistines provides "Ease to the body some, none to the mind" (Frank Allen Patterson, ed., *The Works of John Milton* [1931], vol. 1, pt. 2, p. 337). In the biblical New Testament, several followers of the apostle Paul were dragged into the THEATRE OF EPHESUS for teachings that threatened the livelihoods of local craftsmen who manufactured objects pertaining to the goddess Diana (Acts 19.23–41).

From Robert Rives

SIR Oak Ridge Augt 4th 1811

I have just got home after an absence of 10 days and found your fav of the 20th Ult: covering a drft on G & J for $91.34 which is $12.34 over the cost of the books as ℔ statd below—for which I enclose you a drft on M D & Co of Milton—

For your kind services towards my Son I am with inexpressible gratitude very respectfully

Your m^{t} ob sert RO RIVES

Paid in London 26th Dec 1810	=£17. 0.3	
Int: to 26th Oct allow^{g} 3 months to place the money in London	14.2	
	17.14.5	
Exchange 115 ℔Cent (the present rate at which we sell bills)—	2.13.3	
	20. 7.8 is	$67.94
Duty		11. 6
		$79

RC (MHi); endorsed by TJ as received 25 Aug. 1811 and so recorded in SJL. Enclosure not found.

G & J: Gibson & Jefferson. M D & CO: Martin Dawson & Company.

To John Jordan

SIR Monticello Aug. 5. 1811.

M[r] Ogilvie, to whom the inclosed letter is addressed, was about the latter end of May at Columbia S.C. on his way to Lexington in Kentucky. presuming him to be still there I have so addressed the Letter. should he not be there, will you be so good as to superscribe the proper address, & forward it by post. if in that country, I presume his position known to you, because being engaged in giving lectures in public which deservedly draw great attention from the public, the newspapers generally announce where he is. excuse the trouble thus proposed to you by a stranger and accept the assurances of my respect TH: JEFFERSON

PoC (MoSHi: TJC-BC); at foot of text: "M[r] Jordan"; endorsed by TJ as a letter to "Jordan postmaster Frankfort" and so recorded (under 4 Aug. 1811) in SJL. Enclosure: TJ to James Ogilvie, 4 Aug. 1811.

John Jordan (d. 1813), a merchant born in Great Britain, was the postmaster of Lexington, Kentucky, 1802–13. He also served on the town's board of trustees, sat on the board of directors of the Kentucky Insurance Company, and in 1805 was a manager of the Indiana Canal Company. With his brother William, Jordan gave Aaron Burr promissory notes for $2,000 in 1806, and that same year he testified at Burr's trial in Kentucky (Charles R. Staples, *The History of Pioneer Lexington [Kentucky] 1779–1806* [1939]; Mary-Jo Kline and others, eds., *Political Correspondence and Public Papers of Aaron Burr* [1983], 2:955–6; Lexington *Kentucky Gazette*, 14 Sept. 1813).

From James Lyle

DEAR SIR Manchester Aug[t] 5. 1811

This is to acknowledge the receipt of your favor, enclosing an order on Mess[rs] Gibson & Jefferson for $1000 which was punctually paid. This you will please observe, as by the enclosed statement, is not enterd to your credit on our Companys book,[1] but to your credit on my private books where you stood debetor for the debt due Rich[rd] Harvie & C[o]

The enclosed State, is made from your Letter to me on that subject. I would have been glad you could have made it convenient to have p[d] the Whole of D Harvies that I might have balanced his Acc[t] on my private books The bal[e] appears to be £94.12.4 Sterling with interest from July 6th last past. I continue very blind, although I write this with difficulty, I cannot see to read it over. I am with great Regard

Your Most hu[le] serv[t] JAMES LYLE

In your next I am honord with please mention if the enclosed State be correct
JL

RC (MHi); at head of text: "Thomas Jefferson Esquire"; endorsed by TJ as received 25 Aug. 1811 and so recorded in SJL. FC (ViHi: Lyle Letterbook).

OUR COMPANYS BOOK refers to the financial records of Henderson, McCaul, & Company. Lyle based the enclosed statement on information TJ provided him in his LETTER of 17 Sept. 1803 (MHi).

[1] FC: "Books."

ENCLOSURE

Account with James Lyle

Thomas Jefferson Esqr on acct of Richd Harvie

In acct. with James Lyle

	To This sum, ꝑ Col: Jefferson's letter, due with interest from the 19th of April 1783 at 5 ꝑC^t ꝑ Ann:—Sterling Money		£132.12.0
	To Interest on the same till July the 6th 1811 being 28 years 2½ Months		187. 0.4
1811			319.12.4
July 6.	By Cash of Gibson & Jefferson ꝑ order $1000	£300.0.0	
	Deduct Exchange at 133⅓	75.	225. 0.0
	Bal: due JL. July 6th 1811		£94.12.4

Errors Excepted

JAMES LYLE

MS (MHi); in a clerk's hand, with signature and line above it by Lyle.

To Benjamin Franklin Thompson

Monticello Aug. 5. 1811.

Th Jefferson returns his thanks to Doct^r Benjamin Franklin Thompson for the pamphlet he has been so kind as to send him, and owes him special acknolegements for the indulgence with which he has been pleased to view the general tenor of his political life. the sentiments of the pamphlet bespeak through the whole a glow of genuine republicanism, which it is ever delightful to him to percieve, and which strengthen his confidence in the duration of our happy form of government. he salutes Dr Thompson with esteem & respect.

PoC (MHi); dateline at foot of text; endorsed by TJ.

From Joshua Simmons

Rowe—Massachusetts—AD 1811
Dear Sir Hampshire county Aug 7th

I am about to request a favor that will appear verry extraordinary from an entire stranger but I am under the necesity of doing it to some person who is not acquainted with [me] for I know of no one with whom I [am] personally acquainted that is in a situation [to do?] me the favor I am in absolute need of which is the lone of one hundred dollars for the term of one year—And then I will be punctual in refunding it—with interest.[1] I reside in the town of Rowe Farming is my profession now Setting up a gin still on a small scale and have not quite money sufficient to go through with it without being verry much embarrassed—If you will Send me the hundred dollars I shall ever consider you as my benefactor—It is not becuse my credit is so low that I am under the necesity of applying to a stranger I can be credited any thing among my acquaintance they have to Sell but money is so scarce it is not to be obtained I have tried to conjecture what reception this will meet with I think could I now be placed in your circumstances after experienceing the want of a little money I should send it but had I never known[2] the want of money I cannot determine what I should do under like Situation—The hearts of millions attend you

And among them that of your real friend and Humble Servt—

Joshua Simmons

RC (MHi); torn at seal; between dateline and salutation: "Thomas Jefferson Esqr"; endorsed by TJ as a "begging" letter received 25 Aug. 1811 and so recorded in SJL.

[1] Preceding two words interlined.
[2] Manuscript: "know."

To Archibald Stuart

Dear Sir Monticello Aug. 8. 11.

I ask the favor of you to purchase for me as much fresh timothy seed as the inclosed bill will pay for, pack & forward, and that you will have the goodness to direct it to be lodged at mr Leitch's store in Charlottesville by the waggoner who brings it. you see how bold your indulgencies make me in intruding on your kindness.

I do not know that the government means to make known what has passed between them & Foster before the meeting of Congress;

but in the mean time individuals, who are in the way, think they have a right to fish it out, and in this way the sum of it has become known. Great Britain has certainly come forward and declared to our government by an official paper that the conduct of France towards her during this war has obliged her to take possession of the ocean, and to determine that no commerce shall be carried on with the nations connected with France. that however she is disposed to relax in this determination so far as to permit the commerce which may be carried on thro the British ports. I have, for 3 or 4. years been confident, that knowing that her own resources were not adequate to the maintenance of her present navy, she meant with it to claim the conquest of the ocean, and to permit no nation to navigate it, but on paiment of a tribute for the maintenance of the fleet necessary to secure that dominion. a thousand circumstances brought together left me without a doubt that that policy directed all her conduct, altho' not avowed. this is the first time she has thrown off the mask. the answer & conduct of the government have been what they ought to have been, & Congress is called[1] a little earlier, to be ready to act on the reciept of the reply, for which time has been given. God bless you

from yours affectionately Th Jefferson

RC (ViHi: Stuart Papers); addressed: "The honble Judge Stewart Staunton Virg[a]"; franking signature clipped; stamped; postmarked Charlottesville, 11 Aug. PoC (DLC).

The INCLOSED BILL was for $10 (*MB*, 2:1268).

On 3 July 1811 Augustus John FOSTER, the new British minister plenipotentiary, declared to Secretary of State James Monroe that Napoleon's Continental System, as a "violation of the established law of civilized nations in war, would have justified Great Britain in retaliating upon the enemy by a similar interdiction of all commerce with France and with such other countries as might co-operate with France in her system of commercial hostility against Great Britain. The object of Great Britain was not, however, the destruction of trade, but its preservation, under such regulations as might be compatible with her own security, at the same time that she extended an indulgence to foreign commerce which strict principles would have entitled her to withhold. The retaliation of Great Britain was not, therefore, urged to the full extent of her right; our prohibition of French trade was not absolute, but modified; and in return for the absolute prohibition of all trade with Great Britain, we prohibited not all commerce with France, but all such commerce with France as should not be carried on through Great Britain. It was evident that this system must prove prejudicial to neutral nations: this calamity was foreseen and deeply regretted. But the injury to the neutral nation arose from the aggression of France, which had compelled Great Britain, in her own defence, to resort to adequate retaliatory measures of war" (*ASP, Foreign Relations*, 3:435).

On 24 July President James Madison ordered Congress to convene on 4 Nov. 1811, about a month EARLIER than the date originally set, to consider "great and weighty matters . . . receive such communications as may then be made to them, and to consult and determine on such measures as in their wisdom may be deemed meet for the welfare of the United States" (Madison, *Papers, Pres. Ser.*, 3:392–3; *New-York Herald*, 30 Nov. 1811).

[1] Manuscript: "is called is called."

From Nicolas G. Dufief

MONSIEUR, A Philadelphie ce 9 Août, 1811

Je m'empresse d'accuser réception de votre lettre du 4 courant & de vous remercier de l'opinion favorable que vous avez eue la bonté de manifester au Sujet du nouveau dictionnaire dont un exemplaire vous fut envoyé par L'Auteur, qui vous priait de l'agréer comme une bien faible marque de la vive reconnaissance & du profond respect qu'il conservera toujours pour vous.

Je ne puis, en ce moment, trouver ici que 2 volumes des œuvres de la Croix, savoir L'Algèbre & la Trigonométrie à laquelle on a joint les sections coniques & l'Application de l'Algèbre à la Géométrie. Comme je compte vous procurer bientôt le cours complet, je ne retiendrai point pour vous ces deux ouvrages détachés.

Les Frères Roche dont vous parlez ont quitté Philadelphie, depuis à-peu-près deux ans, pour aller s'établir à la N[lle] Orléans—Je me propose, Sous peu de jours, de remplir leur place, en ouvrant un magazin de livres Français, Anglais, Espagnols, &c[a] & de Stationery. Je me flatte par mes correspondances dans les Etats-Unis & en Europe de pouvoir réunir tous les ouvrages curieux & récherchés dans tous les genres, & J'ose Espérer, Monsieur, que vous continuerez à m'honorer de vos ordres & que vous voudrez bien me recommander à ceux de vos amis à qui Je pourrais être utile pour les objets du ressort de la librairie

Je Suis avec la plus haute considération, votre très-respectueux Serviteur N. G. DUFIEF

EDITORS' TRANSLATION

SIR, Philadelphia 9 August, 1811

I hasten to acknowledge the receipt of your letter of the 4th of this month and to thank you for the favorable opinion that you had the kindness to express regarding the new dictionary, a copy of which was sent to you by the author, who asked you to accept it as a small token of the deep gratitude and profound respect that he will always have for you.

I can only find two volumes of Lacroix's works here at present, namely algebra and trigonometry, the latter of which includes conic sections and the application of algebra to geometry. As I intend to procure the complete *Cours de Mathematiques* for you shortly, I will not retain these two works for you.

The Roche brothers, whom you mentioned, left Philadelphia nearly two years ago and went to New Orleans to set up business. In a few days I plan to take their place by opening a store selling French, English, and Spanish titles, etc., and stationery. I am confident that through my contacts in the United States and Europe, I will be able to assemble all the rare and sought-after books in every genre. I dare to hope, Sir, that you will continue to honor me with your orders and that you will be willing to recommend me to those of your friends to whom I could be of use regarding the objects commonly found in a bookstore.

I am with the highest consideration, your very respectful servant

N. G. Dufief

RC (DLC); at foot of text: "A Monsieur Jefferson"; endorsed by TJ as received 25 Aug. 1811 and so recorded in SJL. Translation by Dr. Roland H. Simon.

The 2 VOLUMES by Sylvestre François Lacroix were *Complément des élémens d'algèbre* (Paris, 1800; and later eds.) and *Traité élémentaire de trigonométrie rectiligne et sphérique et d'application de l'algèbre à la géométrie* (Paris, 1798; and later eds.).

From John Bracken

Sir, Wmsburg Aug 13. 1811

Two days ago I received your letter of Aug. 2. & have to observe, in answer thereto, that in compliance with Mr Mazzei's request, I remitted to him by one of U.S. Ships bound up the Mediterranean a bill purchased of Mr Rutherfoord on London Jan. 1807. I sent some time after a duplicate by another national Vessel, & I enclosed a triplicate to my friend Mr Munroe then in London to present for acceptance, which he obtained & left the Bill with his Merchant Mr John Rennolds. Not knowing whether to attribute the want of application for payment to death or the circumstances of Europe, I two years ago requested Mr Rennolds to apply for payment in my name, which was refused without an indemnification against Mazzei, as the bill was made payable to him. This cou'd not be expected from Mr Rennolds, to whom I was a stranger, but has lately been complied with by Mr Saml Gist, who authorizes me to receive the amount from his Dividend in the Dismal Swamp Land Company. If you can point out to me any safe opportunity of remittance by which I may be exonerated, I will with readiness embrace it; or if you will yourself receive the Money on behalf of Mr Mazzei, & the two old Ladies, I will deposit it in your hands.

With respect & due consideration,
I am your most obed[t] Serv[t] JOHN BRACKEN

P[s] I shall in a few days set off for Frederic with my daughter whose state of health requires a change of climate & not return before the 15. Oct.

RC (DLC); dateline adjacent to signature; endorsed by TJ as received 5 Sept. 1811 and so recorded in SJL.

From Nathaniel H. Hooe

D[R] SIR King George C[t] August 13th 11.

Your having passed the usual time of year of remiting the hire's of M[rs] Daingerfields & my Negroes has Caused her with me to make application to you for the last years hire as well as the balance for the time before, Our wants has compelled this measure or I should not have Call on you untill about the first of january Next & hope sir you will make the deposit as soon as Convenient in the Bank of Fredericksburgh and inform me of the same

Yours with Very great Respect NATH[L] H. HOOE

RC (MHi); at foot of text: "Mr Thos Jefferson"; endorsed by TJ as received 5 Sept. 1811 and so recorded in SJL.

From Martin Oster

MONSIEUR ET TRÈS VÉNÉRABLE ANCIEN PRÉSIDENT, Norfolk Le 13. Aoust 1811.

J'ai reçu la lettre dont vous m'avez honnoré le 2 Courant, par laquélle vous paraissez desirer l'adresse de Mr Pauly, ami de Mr de Beauvois. La voici telle qu'il me l'a donnée.

M[r] L[is] Abraham Pauly,
at Calfpasture
Staunton,
Augusta County Virginia.

J'aurois eu l'honneur de repondre 3 jours plustôt à Votre Excellence, Si je n'avois point espéré pouvoir recevoir de New-Kent et vous adresser avec la présente, tant copie du prétendu testament de feu Piernet, que du jugement de la Cour de New Kent, Sur les dispositions étranges qu'il Comporte en faveur du nommé Stewen Lacy, storekeeper du dit Piernet. J'aprends à l'instant, que Ces piéces ne me seront envoyées que dans 8. Jours dès quelles me Seront parvenues, je m'empresserai de vous les acheminer, pour Servir à fixer vôtre opinion sur la nature des réclamations de Mad[e] de Beauvois dans la Succession de M[r] son frére.

Salut et Respect

EDITORS' TRANSLATION

Sir and very Venerable former president, Norfolk 13. August 1811.

I have received the letter with which you honored me dated the 2d of this month, which appears to request the address of Mr. Pauly, a friend of Mr. de Beauvois. Here it is as he gave it to me.

Mr. L[is] Abraham Pauly,
at Calfpasture
Staunton,
Augusta County Virginia.

I would have had the honor of answering Your Excellency three days ago if I had not hoped to be able to receive from New Kent County, and to enclose in the present letter, copies of the alleged will of the late Piernet and the ruling of the court in New Kent County regarding the strange clauses in favor of a certain Stephen Lacy, the storekeeper of the aforesaid Piernet. I have now learned that these papers will not be sent to me for another eight days. As soon as they arrive, I will hasten to forward them to you, so that you may come to your own conclusions about the nature of Madame de Beauvois's claim to her brother's estate.

Greetings and Respect

RC (MHi); endorsed by TJ as a letter from "Oster" received 25 Aug. 1811 and so recorded in SJL. Translation by Dr. Roland H. Simon.

To Henry Dearborn

Dear General and friend Poplar Forest Aug. 14. 11.

I write from a place which I visit occasionally, near the New London of this state, 90. miles from Monticello, and where I have not the means of examining whether I have let the annual period pass over of saying 'all's well' and 'how d'ye do'? your letter of came in due time. I had learned by the newspapers the afflicting event it announced, had felt it as your friend, and as the friend of the inestimable character which had left us. but I said nothing, and I say nothing; well knowing that condolances renew the grief they would assuage, & that time and silence are the only medecines for that affliction.

I am happy to learn that your own health is good, and I hope it will long continue so. the friends we left behind us have fallen out by the way. I sincerely lament it, because I sincerely esteem them all, & because it multiplies schisms where harmony is safety. as far as I have been able to judge however, it has made no sensible impression against the government. those who were murmuring before are a little louder now; but the mass of our citizens is firm and unshaken. it furnishes, as an incident, another proof that they are perfectly equal to the purposes of self-government, and that we have nothing to fear for it's stability. the spirit indeed which manifests itself among the tories of your quarter, altho' I believe there is a majority there sufficient to keep it down in peaceable times, leaves me not without some disquietude. should the determination of England, now formally expressed, to take possession of the ocean, & to suffer no commerce on it but thro' her ports, force a war upon us, I foresee a possibility of a separate treaty between her & your Essex men, on the principles of neutrality & commerce. Pickering here, & his nephew Williams there, can easily negotiate this. such a lure to the quietists in our ranks with you might recruit theirs to a majority. yet, excluded as they would be, from intercourse with the rest of the union and of Europe, I scarcely see the gain they would propose to themselves, even for the moment. the defection would certainly disconcert the other states, but it could not ultimately endanger their safety. they are adequate in all points to a defensive war. however I hope your majority, with the aid it is entitled to, will save us from this trial, to which I think it possible we are advancing. the death of George may come to our relief; but I fear the dominion of the sea is the insanity of the nation itself also. perhaps, if some stroke of fortune were to rid us at the same time from the Mammoth of the land as well as the Leviathan of the ocean, the people of England might lose their fears, & recover their sober senses again. tell my old friend, Governor Gerry that I give him glory for the rasping with which he rubbed down his herd of traitors. let them have justice, and protection against personal violence, but no favor. powers & preeminences[1] conferred on them are daggers put into the hands of assassins, to be plunged into our own bosoms in the moment the thrust can go home to the heart. moderation can never reclaim them. they deem it timidity, & despise without fearing the tameness from which it flows. backed by England, they never lose the hope that their day is to come, when the terrorism of their earlier power is to be merged in the more gratifying "system of deportation & the guillotine."[2] being now hors de combat myself, I resign to others these cares. a long attack of rheumatism has greatly enfeebled me, & warns me that they will not very long be within my ken. but you may have to meet the trial, & in the focus of it's fury. God send you a safe deliverance, a happy issue out of all afflictions, personal & public, with long life, long health, & friends as sincerely attached as

yours affectionately TH: JEFFERSON

RC (Joseph Rubinfine, West Palm Beach, Florida, 2002); addressed: "General Henry Dearborne Boston"; franked; endorsed as "Private" by Henry A. S. Dearborn. PoC (DLC).

TJ regarded ESSEX County, Massachusetts, as a hotbed of extreme Federalist sentiment. The MAMMOTH OF THE LAND was Napoleon.

After Dearborn forwarded TJ's letter to Elbridge GERRY, the latter asked Dearborn to assure TJ "that his sentiments in regard to the implacable tories of this State & of the Union, perfectly coincide with my own; as well in respect to the malady, as to the cure. my policy is directed to this point, a discrimination & as far as it can be effected, a seperation, between the revolutional, & antirevolutional federalists. the former, altho some of them may pant for a monarchy, in order to be nobles, are generally disposed to preserve our Union & independence; the latter, with some disappointed expectants, & visionary Burrites, are decidedly for a secession of the northern states, & the erection over them of an Hanoverian monarchy. This at least is my decided opinion, & as the laconic scotch General said to his army of 3000, when his enemy consisting of 5000 were in sight, 'if we do not kill them, they will kill us.' The conduct of the 'Boston assemblage,' left me no alternative, but that of a decided opposition to them, or an abandonment of the General Government, of our Union & Independence. I have entered the list with them, & will never retreat, or yeild, before my last breath" (Gerry to Dearborn, 2 Sept. 1811, MeHi).

[1] Manuscript: "preeminces."

[2] Quotation marks missing from PoC.

From John Dortic

SIR New York Aug[t] 14th 1811

He who forwarded you the Small Seed box through me Could not, indeed, believe that Such an introduction to you, would be more troublesome than the invoice agreeable. I hope, whoever, that the Subject on which I now take the liberty of entertaining you with, being in behalf of the country will carry My excuse with it.

I am not acquainted, in your State, with any one So well delighted with agriculture as you are and, of course, none cannot be as good Judge as you, Sir, of the qualities of the Soil Suitable for Vines. That is the question I am about to lay under your eyes

Circumstanced as this country is, in regard to Europe, we must try of every thing to free ourselves from being tributaries of foreign produces.

The Eastern powers Wish to annihilate the trade of nations in getting into their own dominions those produces refused, I dare Say, by nature and so wisely distributed, over the globe, as to make of them the tied of the civilised nations

If the Europeans endeavour to enrich their own Soil with cotton, sugar, Indigo, &c &c Why the Americans Should not adorn their country with Such a tree as to have Wine oil, Silk &c Such an advantage belongs to a Government that includes under his laws the 30th & 45th degree of latitude; Such a Situation offers better change to any kind of culture than Europe for their desig. The Soil of the U.S. may provide the inhabitants with any Sort of French and Italian produce.

I think of Vine as of a culture deserving the best encouragement and to which any one acquainted with must be bound to make it Succeed

The Eastern and northen States are to cold; the frequent and Sudden change of the weather forbids that experiment

I consider Virginia and the Western States back better than any other part throughout the union

Therefore I take the liberty, Sir, to beg of Your kindness to favour me with your opinion on that Subject, and with some notice on the Soil, and how deep the ground can be digged and what quality is to be found at 2 or 3 feet down.

Excuse me, Sir, for troubling you, but your country life brings into my mind, the idea that you cannot be desagreed with a question, when the prosperity of the country is in the Scope of it. you know what Said a celebrated author on the grapes of Burgundy transported[1] to the cape of Good Hope.

I have the Honour to be Respectfully Sir Your most obedient Servant

John Dortic

RC (DLC); dateline at foot of text; at foot of first page: "Thomas Jefferson Esqr"; endorsed by TJ as received 25 Aug. 1811 and so recorded in SJL.

Earlier this year Dortic forwarded TJ a small seed box from André Thoüin (Dortic to TJ, 24 Apr. 1811, and note).

Laurence Sterne alluded to grapes of burgundy transported to the cape of good hope in *A Sentimental Journey through France and Italy* (London, 1768; Sowerby, no. 4335), 29.

[1] Manuscript: "transproted."

To Charles Clay

Dear Sir P.F. Aug. 16. 11.

I thank you for the contents of your basket and was just about writing to you when your boy came. I find I shall not have strength enough to ride as far as your house: but I should be very glad if you could meet me at the Double branches in the road, the day after tomorrow (Sunday) and that you may not have to wait, I will be sure to be there before 11. aclock. I have had some measures made which, in event, puzzle me not a little. you will excuse this trouble which has been encouraged by your own kindness. I will propose to mr Steptoe to meet you here at dinner. I salute you with friendship & respect

Th: Jefferson

RC (Mr. C. A. Mallory, Richmond, 1956; photocopy in ViU: TJP); addressed: "M[r] Clay"; endorsed by Clay. Not recorded in SJL.

A 21 July 1811 letter from Clay to TJ, not found, is recorded in SJL as a "recomdn Moorman & Pemberton" received 24 July 1811.

Preliminary Agreement with William & Reuben Mitchell

[ca. 16 Aug. 1811]

We will purchase M[r] Jeffersons crop Wheat & will give him Within 2/3[1] of the Richm[d] price at the time of delivery Payable in a 60 day bill on Richm[d], or will grind it on the usual terms & deliver the Flour 60 days after the delivery of the Wheat— W. & R M

[*Notation by TJ on verso:*]

M[r] Mitchell agrees to give within 2/ a bushel of the best price which shall be given in Richm[d] from this day for 40. day to come (Aug. 17. to Sep. 26.) the wheat[2] to be delivered at Lynchbg as fast as one team can carry it in & the money[3] payable in Richmond within 60. days after the 6th of Sep.

MS (MHi); written on a small scrap by a representative of William & Reuben Mitchell; undated, with notation added by TJ on 17 Aug. 1811.

The Lynchburg firm of William & Reuben Mitchell bought wheat from and ground flour for TJ's Poplar Forest plantation on various occasions between 1810 and 1819. William Mitchell (d. 1824) subscribed $50 to the nascent University of Virginia in 1821 and paid it the following year. He retired to Amherst County and declared bankruptcy shortly before his death. Reuben Mitchell (d. 1828) resided in Richmond for some years (*MB*, 2:1270, 1277, 1380, 1389; TJ's account with William Mitchell,

Apr. 1817; Amherst Co. Will Book, 6:596; Lynchburg *Virginian*, 18 June 1824; *Richmond Commercial Compiler*, 31 Oct. 1828).

[1] Amount interlined in place of "two shillings."

[2] Preceding two words interlined.

[3] Preceding three words interlined.

Final Agreement with William & Reuben Mitchell

We have purchased of Mr Thomas Jefferson the whole of his present Crop of Wheat at the Poplar Forest to be delivered in the Black Water Mills as soon as one Waggon can conveniently haul it—the price to be within two shillings of that of Richmond; to be fixed at any time within forty days from this time; and payable in a Bill on Richmond at 60 days from the 5th of September next—

Witness — W & R MITCHELL

OWEN OWENS — Lynchburg 16th Augst 1811

MS (MHi); in the hand of a representative of William & Reuben Mitchell, signed as witness by Owens; endorsed by TJ: "Mitchell W. & R. agreement."

To Benjamin Rush

DEAR SIR — Poplar Forest Aug. 17. 11.

I write to you from a place, 90. miles from Monticello, near the New London of this state, which I visit three or four times a year, & stay from a fortnight to a month at a time. I have fixed myself comfortably, keep some books here, bring others occasionally, am in the solitude of a hermit, and quite at leisure to attend to my absent friends. I note this to shew that I am not in a situation to examine the dates of our letters, whether I have overgone the annual period of asking how you do? I know that within that time I have recieved one or more letters from you, accompanied by a volume of your introductory lectures,[1] for which accept my thanks. I have read them with pleasure and edification, for I acknolege facts in medecine, as far as they go, distrusting only their extension by theory. having to conduct my grandson through his course of Mathematics, I have resumed that study with great avidity. it was ever my favorite one. we have no theories there, no uncertainties remain on the mind; all is demonstration & satisfaction. I have forgotten much, and recover it with more difficulty than, when in the vigor of my mind, I originally acquired it. it is wonderful to me that old men should not be sensible that their minds keep pace with their bodies in the progress of decay. our old revolutionary friend, Clinton, for example, who was a hero, but never a man of mind, is wonderfully jealous on this head. he tells eternally the stories of his younger days, to prove his memory. as if memory and reason were the same faculty. nothing betrays imbecility so much as the being insensible of it. had not a conviction of the danger to which an unlimited occupation of the Executive chair would expose the republican constitution of our government made it conscientiously a duty to retire when I did, the fear of becoming a dotard and of being insensible of it, would of itself have resisted all solicitations to remain.—I have had a long attack of rheumatism, without fever, & without pain while I kept myself still. a total prostration of the muscles of the back, hips, & thighs deprived me of the power of walking, and leaves it still in a very impaired state. a pain, when I walk, seems to have fixed itself in the hip, and to threaten permanence. I take moderate rides without much fatigue: but my journey to this place, in a hard-going gig, gave me great sufferings, which I expect will be renewed on my return, as soon as I am able. the loss of the power of[2] taking exercise would be a sore affliction to me. it has been the delight of my retirement to be in constant bodily activity, looking after my affairs. it was never damped, as the pleasures of reading are, by the question of cui bono? for what object? I hope your health of body continues firm. your works shew that of your mind. the habits of exercise, which your calling has given to both, will tend long to preserve them. the sedentary character of my public occupations sapped a constitution naturally sound and vigorous, and draws it to an earlier close. but it will still last quite as long as I wish it. there is a fulness of time when men should go, & not occupy too long the ground to which others have a right to advance.—we must continue, while here, to exchange occasionally our mutual good wishes. I find friendship to be like wine, raw when new, ripened with age, the true old man's milk, & restorative cordial. god bless you & preserve you through a long & healthy old age. TH: JEFFERSON

RC (NNGL, on deposit NHi); addressed: "Doct[r] Benjamin Rush Philadelphia"; franked; postmarked Lynchburg, 19 Aug.; endorsed by Rush. PoC (DLC).

Thomas Jefferson Randolph was the GRANDSON.

[1] Word interlined in place of "letters."
[2] TJ here canceled "walking."

From Palisot de Beauvois

Monsieur et cher Confrère, Paris 18 aoust 1811.

Le 19 Mars dernier j'ai eu L'honneur de vous ecrire pour reclamer vos bontés et vous prier de me faire rendre, dans Votre païs la justice, qui nous est dus. Ma Lettre tres detaillée Se trouve jointe par duplicata, a celle-ci. La Certitude que j'ai de L'arrivée du Navire chargé de Cette dépêche Me rassure Sur Sa destination. je ne doute donc pas qu'elle ne vous Soit parvenue, et je compte assez Sur vos bontés et Sur Votre amour pour Ce qui est juste. j'ai donc lieu de croire que vous aurez eu L'obligeance de vous mêler de Cette affaire de maniere a conserver mes droits.

j'adresse par Cette occasion a M.M. oster et Teterel, Ce dernier Negociant à Williams bourg, toutes les pieces necessaires a L'appui de ma reclamation; Tels que Extraits Baptistaires, et Mortuaires, acte de notorieté &c. procuration et tout, document[1] Legalisé, propre a justifier mon droit. un point essentiel est de Savoir que dans la Succession d'un Americain mort en france, notre gouvernement a Laissé Ses heritiers jouir de tous les biens de la Succession. M. Maclure, qui Sans doute vous est connu, etait interressé dans Cet heritage. de plus M. M'raie votre Consul, et actuellement En Amerique, a Connaissance de Ce fait. je dois donc esperer que les francais, qui, d'apres tous les traités, doivent jouir des memes prérogatives que les citoyens des Nations les plus favorisées, auront le Meme avantage et que les biens delaissés par mon beau frere Seront rendus a Ses heritiers Naturels.

Nous ne donnons pas notre procuration a M. Pauly, Notre Ami, par Ce que devant comparaitre Comme temoin dans la procedure, il ne pourrait pas etre en Même temps temoin et réclamant.

j'ai L'honneur d'etre avec la plus haute Consideration, Monsieur et cher Confrere Votre tres humble et tres obeissant

Serviteur Palisot de Beauvois

membre de l'institut, rue de Turenne n° 58.

EDITORS' TRANSLATION

Sir and dear colleague, Paris 18 August 1811.

Last 19 March I had the honor of writing you to ask for your assistance in obtaining the justice that is due to us in your country. A duplicate of my very detailed letter is subjoined to this one. My certainty of the arrival of the ship that carried it reassures me as to the delivery of that dispatch. I do not doubt that it reached you, and I count on your kindness and love of all that is just. I have, therefore, every reason to believe that you have been so good as to involve yourself in this affair in such a way as to protect my rights.

At this time I also send Mr. Oster and Mr. Teterel, the latter a Williamsburg merchant, all the papers necessary to support my claim, such as birth and death certificates, the deed, etc., power of attorney, and all of the appropriate notarized documents to justify my rights. An essential point with regard to the inheritance of an American dying in France is whether our government has allowed his heirs to dispose of his estate freely. Mr. Maclure, whom you probably know, had an interest in such an inheritance. Moreover, your consul, Mr. McRae, who is in America at this time, is aware of that fact. I hope, therefore, that French citizens, who, according to treaty, should enjoy the same prerogatives as citizens of the most favored nations, will have the same advantage, and that the possessions left by my brother-in-law will be returned to his lawful heirs.

We have not given the power of attorney to our friend Mr. Pauly, because he will appear in court as a witness, and he cannot be both a witness and a claimant at the same time.

I have the honor to be, with the highest consideration, Sir and dear colleague, your very humble and very obedient

servant PALISOT DE BEAUVOIS

member of the Institut, Rue de Turenne Number 58.

RC (DLC); endorsed by TJ as received 1 Mar. 1812 and so recorded in SJL; conjoined with Dupl of Palisot de Beauvois to TJ, 19 Mar. 1811. Translation by Dr. Roland H. Simon.

French citizens were accorded most-favored-nation status (DES NATIONS LES PLUS FAVORISÉES) in Franco-American treaties and conventions signed in 1778, 1800, and 1803 (*U.S. Statutes at Large*, 8:14, 180, 182, 204 [6 Feb. 1778, 30 Sept. 1800, 30 Apr. 1803]).

[1] Manuscript: "ducment."

To William A. Burwell

DEAR SIR Poplar Forest Aug. 19. 11.

I am here after a long absence, having been confined at home a month by rheumatism. I thought myself equal to the journey when I sat out, but I have suffered much coming, staying, & shall returning. if I am not better after a little rest at home, I shall set out for the warm springs. the object of this letter is to inform mrs Burwell that a ring which she left where she washed the morning of leaving Fludd's is safe & will be delivered to her order or to herself when she passes. I have not seen the President since he came home, nor do I know what has passed with Foster from the fountain head: but thro' a channel in which I have confidence I learn he has delivered a formal Note in the name of his government declaring that the circumstances of the war oblige them to take possession of the ocean and permit no commerce on it but thro' their ports. thus their purpose is at length avowed. they cannot from their own resources maintain the navy necessary to retain the dominion of the ocean, and mean that other nations shall be assessed to maintain their own chains. should the king die, as is probable, altho the ministry which would come in, stand so committed to repeal the orders of Council, I doubt if the nation will permit it. for the usurpation of the sea has become a national disease. this state of things annihilates the culture of Tob° except of about 15,000 hhds on the prime lands. wheat & flour keep up. wheat was @ 9/6 at Richmond ten days ago. I have sold mine here at the Richmond price, abating[1] 2/. but 8/ a bushel has been offered for machined wheat. present me respectfully to mrs Burwell, and accept assurances of affectionate respect & esteem. TH: JEFFERSON

RC (CSmH: JF-BA); at foot of text: "Wm A. Burwell esq." PoC (DLC).

[1] Manuscript: "abeting."

From William J. Harris

SIR Powhatan August 19. 1811.

I have the honour to transmit to you, the Enclosed letters which you advised me to get, and I am in hopes you will forward them on as soon as possible

I am with great and esteem[1] Sir yours &c

WILLIAM J. HARRIS

RC (DLC); endorsed by TJ as received 5 Sept. 1811 and so recorded in SJL. Enclosures: (1) Thomas Turpin to [John Wayles Eppes and William B. Giles], Powhatan, 9 July 1811, recommending Harris, a distant relation he has known from birth as "a young Gentleman of good character and respectable connexions"; mentioning Harris's father's Revolutionary War service; and asking for help in getting the younger Harris a naval appointment. (2) Philip Turpin to [Eppes and Giles], Salisbury, 13 July 1811, recommending Harris, whom he has known from infancy and regards as "a young gentleman of merit and respectability." (3) James Pleasants to [Giles], Goochland County, 23 July 1811, recommending Harris, whom he has known from infancy, and commenting on "his general good character" and the respectability of his parents and relations. (4) Eppes to Paul Hamilton, Buckingham, 7 Aug. 1811, enclosing nos. 1–2, also mentioning a supportive letter by Pleasants and indicating that he does not know Harris, but describing his relations favorably and advising his appointment as a midshipman. (5) Giles to Hamilton, Wigwam, 7 Aug. 1811, enclosing nos. 1–3 and indicating that he does not know Harris but emphasizing the good character of his father, relatives, and those recommending him (two RCs of nos. 1–2 and one of nos. 3–5 in DNA: RG 45, MLRSN).

William Jordan Harris (b. 1791), the great-grandson of TJ's aunt Mary Jefferson Turpin, was appointed a midshipman in the United States Navy on 1 Sept. 1811 but resigned his commission later that year for health reasons (*VMHB*

38 [1930]: 178; William D. Ligon Jr., *The Ligon Family and Connections* [1947], 846–7; Edward W. Callahan, *List of Officers of the Navy of the United States and of the Marine Corps from 1775 to 1900* [1901; repr. 1969], 249; Harris to Hamilton, 12 Dec. 1811 [DNA: RG 45, MLRSN]).

[1] Thus in manuscript.

From James L. Edwards

RESPECTED SIR, Boston, 20th August 1811

I presume an apology is unnecessary on the present occasion; and shall therefore proceed to the subject of this communication without. It may not probably have escaped your recollection, that for certain services performd by Mr. James Lyon and mr. Samuel Morse, formerly Editors of the Savannah Republican, you promised them the sum of $1000—a promise from so distinguished a character as the President of the U. S. was considered in the light of a debt, as much so as if it had been "for value received": at any rate, so it was considered by them: and as such it was transferred with the establishment of the paper above mentioned, to Mr. Norman McLean; he informed me a short time previous to his death, that he had some expectation of getting the money, as he had the honor of receiving a letter from you on the subject. Mr. McLean was in debt to me, and on my leaving Savannah I gave up his note which I held, in consequence of his promise that I should be paid as soon as he received the money from you—So much confidence did I repose in him, that I acted in the way I have stated—it was perhaps impolitic. I trust, Sir, that you will take this into serious consideration, and that you will be disposed to grant me some relief, as I at present labor under the distresses peculiar to the times, and to the republicans of this Town.

If you doubt that what I have stated is[1] true, I would refer you to David Everett, Esq. Editor of the Boston Patriot for my character, as well as to Benjamin Homans, Esq. Secretary of this Commonwealth; Major Daniel Parker and Lewis Edwards, of the War Department; Hon. Ezekiel Bacon, a member of Congress from Pittsfield in this State; Colonel Peterson Goodwyn, a member of Congress from Dinwiddie, Virg. (the county where I was born.) and many other gentlemen of respectability with some of whom you have probably a personal acquaintance—

An early answer will greatly oblige me. That you may enjoy in your retirement all the happiness which your public Services certainly entitle you to, is the desire of your

most humble Servant— JAMES L. EDWARDS

RC (DLC); between dateline and salutation: "Hon. Thomas Jefferson"; endorsed by TJ as received 30 Aug. 1811 and so recorded in SJL. Enclosed in TJ to James Lyon, 5 Sept. 1811.

James L. Edwards, printer, was associated with at least four short-lived newspapers between 1805 and 1812: the Halifax *North-Carolina Journal* (1805–06), the Petersburg *Virginia Mercury* (1807–08), the Boston *Scourge* (1811), and the Boston *Satirist* (1812) (Brigham, *American Newspapers*, 1:345, 346, 2:765, 1135; Salem, Mass., *Essex Register*, 12 Sept. 1810; Raleigh *Star*, 1 Nov. 1810).

[1] Edwards here canceled "not."

To Charles Willson Peale

Pop. Forest. Aug. 20.[1]

It is long, my dear Sir, since we have exchanged a letter. our former correspondence had always some little matter of business interspersed; but this being at an end, I shall still be anxious to hear from you sometimes, and to know that you are well & happy. I know indeed that your system is that of contentment under any situation.[2] I have heard that you have retired from the city to a farm, & that you give your whole time to that. does not the Museum suffer? and is the farm as interesting? here, as you know, we are all farmers, but not in a pleasing stile. we have so little labor in proportion to our land, that altho' perhaps we make more profit from the same labor we cannot give to our grounds that stile of beauty which satisfies the eye of the amateur. our rotations are Corn, wheat & clover, or corn wheat, clover & clover, or wheat, corn, wheat, clover & clover; preceding the clover by a plaistering. but some, instead of clover, substitute mere rest, and all are slovenly enough. we are adding the care of Merino sheep. I have often thought that if heaven had given me choice of my position & calling, it should have been on a rich spot of earth, well watered, and near a good market for the productions of the garden. no occupation is so delightful to me as the culture of the earth, & no culture comparable to that of the garden. such a variety of subjects, some one always coming to perfection, the failure of one thing repaired by the success of another, & instead of one harvest a continued one thro' the year. under a total want of demand except for our family table I am still devoted to the garden. but tho' an old man, I am but a young gardener.[3] your application to whatever you are engaged in I know to be incessant. but Sundays and rainy days are always days of writing for the farmer. think of me sometimes when you have your pen in hand, & give me information of your health and occupations; and be always assured of my great esteem & respect

TH: JEFFERSON

PoC (DLC: TJ Papers, 193:34408); partially dated; at foot of text: "M[r] Peale." Tr (PPAmP: Peale Letterbook); extracts in Peale to Rembrandt Peale, 9 Sept. 1811 (letter printed in full in Peale, *Papers*, 3:103–9). Recorded in SJL as a letter of 20 Aug. 1811 written at Poplar Forest.

[1] Dateline added above "<*Monticello Aug. 25. 11.*> qu. date? & if any." Both datelines are in an ink different from that of remainder of PoC.

[2] Preceding two sentences included in Tr.

[3] Text from "I have often thought" to this point included in Tr.

To Brown & Robertson

MESS[RS] BROWN & ROBERTSON Pop. Forest Aug. 21. 11.

The accounts handed me by mr Garland have been examined. those from the autumn of 1809. are as I expected; because at that time I directed mr Griffin to have his whole dealings at your store. those preceding that period were unknown to me. it is possible they may have been mentioned to me, altho' I have no such recollection. but my memory is not sufficiently faithful to enable me to speak positively. but, if mentioned at all, it must have been before that period, while mr Griffin had the disposal of my wheat crops, and every thing except the tobacco, with which, I had taken for granted, all his accounts were kept even. this is mentioned only to apologize for my apparent inattention to these accounts, which would not have taken place had I been aware of them. as it is, provision must be made for their paiment. this cannot suddenly be done. I have sold my wheat of the present year, & am now delivering it to mr Mitchell. the quantity is as yet unknown, and the price depending on that at Richmond within a given time, payable in 60. days from the 5th of September. these uncertainties prevent my knowing the amount of what I may count on from this fund, or being more precise at present than naming some general limits. I shall not, for instance, be able out of it to pay up the whole of the bond, but certainly may more than the half of it. I shall be as anxious as yourselves to go as far into it as possible; and what I cannot pay this year, I must trust to your having the goodness to wait for till the next; and these accounts once brought even, it will certainly be my care to pay the dealings of every year out of the produce of the year. Accept the assurances of my esteem & respect.

TH: JEFFERSON

PoC (ViU: TJP); endorsed by TJ.

William Brown (d. 1811), the owner of Lynchburg's first dry-goods store, was a prominent banker, agent, and merchant until his death in the Richmond Theatre fire of 26 Dec. 1811. His partner, Archibald Robertson (d. 1835), continued to do business with TJ into the 1820s, acting as his commission agent in the Lynchburg area and becoming one of his largest creditors. At the time of his death in 1826, TJ owed Robertson almost $6,200. Robertson retired to Amherst County and left a personal estate valued in excess of $17,000, including more than thirty slaves (William Asbury Christian, *Lynchburg and Its People* [1900], 46–7; Chambers, *Poplar Forest*, esp. 67; Richmond *Enquirer*, 31 Dec. 1811; *MB*, esp. 2:1273–4n, 1386, 1407; Malone, *Jefferson*, 6:511; *Richmond Enquirer*, 30 June 1835; Amherst Co. Will Book, 9:137, 140–3).

SJL records letters from TJ to Burgess Griffin of 22 June and 20 July 1811, not found, as well as Griffin's missing letter to TJ of 3 July 1811, received from Poplar Forest on 11 July 1811.

To George Jefferson

DEAR SIR Poplar Forest Aug. 21. 11.

I have sold my wheat crop of this place at what shall be given in Richmond from the 16th of the present, to the 25th of the ensuing month, deducting 2/ for carriage & all other expences. I must rely on your friendship to be on the watch for this maximum, and to be furnished at the close of the period with a certificate by which I may settle with the purchaser. that of Albemarle I shall have ground and sent down as flour, in the fall or winter, according to the prospect of prices.

We have here a more promising crop of tobacco than that of the last year. the quality of that was admitted to have been equal, or superior to any brought to Lynchburg,[1] & as well handled. it brought, as I am told 13½ D. in Richmond, while I got here but 7.D. I had been persuaded to believe that the prices here were quite equal, & sometimes superior to those of Richmond, deducting carriage. this I find is a mere puff, and that buyers have a different gage. four of the capital purchasers offered me 7.D. for that crop of tob° and not one would go a cent beyond that. this coincidence imposed on me for the moment, and lost me 2000.D. which would have counted pleasingly to us all at the bank. but it proves the ratio of the profits aimed at here, & that they are immoderate. I set out for Monticello tomorrow. accept assurances of my constant affection. TH: JEFFERSON

PoC (Forbes Magazine Collection, New York City, 2003); at foot of text: "Mr Jefferson"; endorsed by TJ.

[1] Manuscript: "Lyncburg."

Calculations for a Horizontal Sundial at Poplar Forest

[ca. 23 Aug. 1811]

Hour lines of horizont^l dial for Lat 37°–22′–26″[1]

Hour H ′	horary angle ° ′	Logarithm Tang^t	Hourline[2] ° ′ ″
0 – 5.	1–15	8.1220547	0–45–32
10	2–30	8.4232915	1–31– 5
15	3–45	8.5997278	2–16–41
20	5– 0	8.7251502	3– 2–24
25.	6–15.	8.8226832	3–48–12
30.	7–30	8.9026275	4–34– 8
35	8–45	8.9704786	5–20–15
40	10– 0	9.0295171	6– 6–33
45	11–15	9.0818602	6–53– 5
50	12–30	9.1289536	7–39–52
55.	13–45	9.1718296	8–26–55
I. XI.	15– 0	9.2112508	9–14–18
5.	16–15	9.2477974	10– 2– 0
10.	17–30	9.2819207	10–50– 5
15.	18–45	9.3139797	11–38–35
20.	20– 0	9.3442643	12–27–31
25.	21–15	9.3730126	13–16–54
30.	22–30	9.4004227	14– 6–48
35.	23–45	9.4266615	14–57–15
40.	25– 0	9.4518709	15–48–15
45.	26–15–	9.4761734	16–39–53
50.	27–30	9.4996751	17–32–10
55.	28–45.	9.5224691	18–25– 7
II. X.	30– 0	9.5446378	19–18–49
5.	31–15.	9.5662546	20–13–15
10.	32–30	9.5873857	21– 8–31
15.	33–45	9.6080910	22– 4–38
20.	35– 0	9.6286940	23– 2–24
25.	36–15	9.6484388	23–59–34
30.	37–30	9.6681789	24–58–30
35.	38–45	9.6876894	25–58–28
40.	40– 0	9.7070119	26–59–30
45.	41–15	9.7261863	28– 1–41
50.	42–30	9.7452509	29– 5– 8

55.	43–45	9.7642427	30– 9–37
III. IX.	45– 0	9.7831984	31–15–30
5.	46–15.	9.8021541	32–22–49
10.	47–30.	9.8211459	33–31–19
15.	48–45	9.8402105	34–41–23
20.	50– 0	9.8593849	35–52–57
25.	51–15	9.8787074	37– 6– 4
30.	52–30	9.8982179	38–20–48
35.	53–45	9.9179580	39–37–12
40.	55– 0	9.9379716	40–55–20
45.	56–15	9.9583058	42–15–14
50.	57–30	9.9790111	43–36–58
55.	58–45	10.0001414	45– 0–33
IV. VIII.	60– 0	10.0217590	46–26– 5
5.	61–15	10.0439277	47–53–34
10.	62–30	10.0667217	49–23– 3
15.	63–45	10.0902234	50–54–33
20.	65– 0	10.1145259	52–28– 7
25.	66–15	10.1397353	54– 3–45
30.	67–30	10.1659741	55–41–28
35.	68–45	10.1[ ]35842	57–21–17
40.	70– 0	10.2221325	59– 3–10
45.	71–15	10.2524171	60–47– 7
50.	72–30	10.2844761	62–33– 5
55.	73–45	10.3185994	64–21– 3
V. VII.	75– 0	10.3551459	66–10–56
5.	76–15	10.3945672	68– 2–41
10.	77–30	10.4374432	69–56–12
15.	78–45	10.4845366	71–51–24
20.	80– 0	10.5368796	73–48– 8
25.	81–15	10.5959182	75–46–19
30.	82–30	10.6637693	77–45–46
35.	83–45	10.7437136	79–46–22
40.	85– 0	10.8412466	81–47–56
45.	86–15	10.9666690	83–50–14
50.	87–30	11.1431053	85–53– 9
55.	88–45	11.4443421	87–56–29
VI.	90– 0	infinite	90– 0– 0[3]

As Radius :
to the Sine of the latitude ::
so is the tang^t of the horary angle :
to the tang^t of ∠ of hourline with ye merid^n

MS (MHi); entirely in TJ's hand; undated; written on both sides of a small scrap; one number illegible. Tr (ViU: TJP); entirely in TJ's hand; undated; written on one side of a small scrap; lacking heading, middle two columns, and concluding section; with TJ's notation perpendicular to text: "Hour lines for an horizontal dial for Lat. 37.°–22′–26″"; enclosed in TJ to Charles Clay, 23 Aug. 1811.

[1] MS: "37″–22′–26″."
[2] Tr: "horizont[l] angle."
[3] Tr ends here, as does recto of MS.

To Charles Clay

Dear Sir — Poplar Forest Aug. 23. 11.

While here, & much confined to the house by my rheumatism, I have amused myself with calculating the hour lines of a horisontal dial for the latitude of this place which I find to be 37°–22′–26″. the calculations are for every 5. minutes of time, and are always exact to within less than half a second of a degree. as I do not know that any body here has taken this trouble before, I have supposed a copy would be acceptable to you. it may be a good exercise for master Cyrus to make you a dial by them. he will need nothing but a protractor, or a line of chords & dividers. a dial of size, say of from 12.I. to 2.f. square, is the cheapest & most accurate measure of time for general use, & would, I suppose, be more common if every one possessed the proper horary lines for his own latitude. Williamsburg being very nearly in the parallel of Poplar Forest, the calculations now sent would serve for all the counties in the line between that place & this, for your own place, New London, & Lynchburg in this neighborhood. slate, as being less affected by the sun, is preferable to wood or metal, & needs but a saw & plane to prepare it, and a knife point to mark the lines and figures. if worth the trouble, you will of course use the paper inclosed; if not, some of your neighbors may wish to do it, & the effort to be of some use to you will strengthen the assurances of my great esteem & respect.

Th: Jefferson

RC (ViU: TJP); addressed: "Charles Clay esq."; endorsed by Clay: "Th. Jefferson. 1811 of a Dial." PoC (DLC). Enclosure: Tr of Calculations for a Horizontal Sundial at Poplar Forest, [ca. 23 Aug. 1811].

From Levett Harris

SIR, St. Petersburg 11/23. August 1811.

I received, a few days Since, from the department of State, two letters recommended by You to my care for Professor Vater at Konigsberg & Count John Potocki, both of which I have forwarded to their respective addresses.

I have now the pleasure of inclosing You a little work which I am Sure will interest You; it is from the Same Mr Adelung, whom I have already several times named to you. The Success of this enlightened man in assimilating the Sanscrit[1] language with that of Russia has certainly been happy, and will undoubtedly obtain him praises from the world of letters.

I have the honor to remain, with the highest Consideration & respect, Sir, Your most obedient humble Servant

LEVETT HARRIS.

RC (DLC); at foot of text: "The honorable Thomas Jefferson Monticello"; endorsed by TJ as received 14 Nov. 1811 and so recorded in SJL. Enclosure: Friedrich Adelung, *Rapports entre la langue sanscrit et la langue Russe présentés à l'Académie Impériale Russe* (Saint Petersburg, 1811; probably Poor, *Jefferson's Library*, 14 [no. 913]).

Friedrich ADELUNG became the director of the Oriental Institute at Saint Petersburg in 1823 (Raymond Schwab, *The Oriental Renaissance: Europe's Rediscovery of India and the East, 1680–1880* [1984], 450).

[1] Manuscript: "Transcrit."

From George Jefferson

DEAR SIR Richmond 23^d Augt 1811

As it is very seldom that I see Mr Randolph's Harry, I must ask the favor of you to direct him to call for the negroes blankets.—They should have been sent up sooner, but the person of whom I bought them did not like to open a bale, for fear of the moth: he has lately been opening some, and called upon me to take yours away.—I had them baled up again, but not so securely perhaps that the moth cannot get at them.—the sooner the negroes have them therefore, the better, as each can take care of his own.

I inclose you a note for renewal in the bank, and am

Dear Sir Your Very humble serv^t GEO. JEFFERSON

RC (MHi); at foot of text: "Thomas Jefferson esq^r"; endorsed by TJ as received 25 Aug. 1811 and so recorded in SJL. Enclosure not found, but see note to Jefferson to TJ, 29 Aug. 1811.

To Levi Lincoln

Monticello Aug. 25. 11.

It is long, my good friend, since we have exchanged a letter. and yet I demur to all prescription against it. I cannot relinquish the right of correspondence with those I have learnt to esteem. if the extension of common acquaintance in public life be an inconvenience, that with select worth is more than a counterpoise. be assured your place is high among those whose remembrance I have brought with me into retirement, and cherish with warmth. I was overjoyed when I heard you were appointed to the supreme bench of national justice, and as much mortified when I heard you had declined it. you are too young to be entitled to withdraw your services from your country. you cannot yet number the quadraginta stipendia of the veteran. our friends, whom we left behind, have ceased to be friends among themselves. I am sorry for it, on their account, and on my own, for I have sincere affection for them all. I hope it will produce no schisms among us, no desertions from our ranks: that no Essexman will find matter of triumph in it. the secret treasons of his heart, and open rebellions on his tongue, will still be punished, while in fieri by the detestation of his country, and by it's vengeance in the overt act. what a pity that history furnishes so many abuses of the punishment by exile, the most rational of all punishments for meditated treason. their great king beyond the water would doubtless recieve them as kindly as his Asiatic prototype did the fugitive aristocracy of Greece.—but let us turn to good-humored things. how do you do? what are you doing? does the farm or the study occupy your time, or each by turns? do you read law or divinity? and which affords the most curious and cunning learning? which is most disinterested? and which was it that crucified it's Savior? or were the two professions united among the Jews? in that case what must their Caiaphases have been? answer me these questions, or any others you like better, but let me hear from you and know that you are well and happy. that you may long continue so is the prayer of your's affectionately Th: Jefferson

RC (John Herron, Dobbs Ferry, New York, 2002, on deposit MWA); dateline added separately to RC and PoC; at foot of text: "Levi Lincoln esq." PoC (DLC).

QUADRAGINTA STIPENDIA: "forty years' service." IN FIERI: "pending" (*Black's Law Dictionary*).

From Brown & Robertson

Sir Lynchburg 26 Aug[t] 1811

Yours of 21st Ins[t] is at hand and observe the contents we make no doubt but that you will do us impartial Justice and make such payments towards our claims as justice requires—I take the liberty in behalf of M[r] Robertson who is absent to return our thanks for your past custom and hope to merit a continuance of your favours—with due resp[t] we remain[1] Yo mo obt

hm ser[t]

B & Robertson
℔ [. . .] Garland

RC (MHi); entirely in Garland's hand; initial in signature illegible; between dateline and salutation: "M[r] Jefferson"; endorsed by TJ as a letter from "Garland P. A." received 5 Sept. 1811 and so recorded in SJL.

[1] Manuscript: "remai."

To Thomas Mann Randolph

Dear Sir Mont[o] Aug. 26–11—

I told Newby that I should refer to yourself entirely the choice of an overseer, but that before the evening I would write to you on the subject. I was just going over to Goodman's, to make some enquiry about his brother, Tomlins, E[t]c. he tells me it is a brother whose name I have forgot who drinks. I think it began with an F., but that Nathan is perfectly sober, good humored towards the negroes; & he thinks him equal as a manager to any man in the county. if he will come at all to Tufton, he will take 200. Dollars. Tomlins, he says, has been brought up in the school of the Garths, & is excessively severe; otherwise a very good manager; but his severity puts him out of the question. he is to go tomorrow, to engage for me at Lego, a man of the name of Ham: who has lived long at mr Durrett's, and is of the best qualifications & dispositions. between Nathan Goodman, Newby & their competitors for Tufton, you must be so good as to decide as you think best.

Your's affectionately Th: Jefferson

RC (CtY: Franklin Collection); addressed: "Col[o] Tho[s] M. Randolph"; endorsed by Randolph. Not recorded in SJL.

A letter from TJ to Randolph of 15 July 1811, not found, is recorded in SJL, as are missing letters from Randolph to TJ of 22 Sept. 1811 and 17 Mar. 1812, both received on the date they were written.

From Benjamin Rush

MY DEAR OLD FRIEND Philadelphia Augst 26. 1811

I sit down thus early to answer your pleasant and friendly letter from your Forest, with a desire to administer to your relief from your present indisposition. There shall not be single theory in my prescriptions, & what will be more grateful to you, all of them Shall be derived from the resources of empiricism.—The following remedies have been found useful in similar Cases. I shall begin with the most simple, & apparently the most feeble, and Afterwards mention such as are of a more Active nature.

1 A peice of Calico, or small bodies of Cotton worn Constantly upon the Affected parts.

2 Bruised rolls of Sulphur quilted into peices of muslin and used in like manner.

3 Friction upon the parts affected, with a <u>dry</u> hand. or 4 with a flesh brush, or a peice of Coarse linnen or Woolen Cloath. or 5 drawing an iron Comb, or three or four forks over the parts affected so as gently to irritate the Skin. This is not a Substitute for Perkins's points, but preferable to them. 6. Bathing the affected parts twice a day with a Linament composed by adding two ounces of scraped Castile or Venice Soap, an ounce of Camphor—half an Ounce of opium, and two drams of solid volative Salt to a quart[1] of Spirit of any kind, or 7 with a pint of Spirit of any kind in which a table Spoonful of Cayenne pepper has been mixed. or 8 with equal parts of the Spirit of Hartshorn & Sweet Oil, or 9: equal parts of the Spirit of Turpentine and Sweet oil. 10 the Warm Bath. These applications may All be used with Safety in the order in which they are mentioned.

The famous Admiral Wager was once indisposed with a fever. His naval Surgeon prescribed bathing his feet in warm water, & some other <u>external</u> remedies, and then proposed sending him a dose of physic. "No—no (said the Admiral) Doctor—You may batter my hulk as much as you please, but you shan't board me."—If you have no objection to being "boarded" by medicine, I will add to the remedies that have been mentioned, two or three to be taken internally. 1 From ten to thirty drops of the Spirit of Turpentine three times a day in a little syrup or molasses. Encrease them gradually. 2 From one to three teaspoonsful of the volatile tincture of gum guajacum in the same Vehicle as the Turpentine 3 a Quart of a tea made of the Sassafras root taken in the Course of a day.—They may be taken in Succession & rotation.

I fully agree with you in your opinions upon the Subject of[2] the coincidence of decay in the mental faculties with the bodily organs. It is to be lamented that the former is not as perceptible as the latter, and that we are so apt to mistake the Continuance of early memory for correct reason.—I wait only for the Arrival of my 3rd Son whom I expect with every tide from Europe where he has spent two years in completing his studies in medicine, to retire to the back ground of my profession. I have two beacons constantly before my eyes to warn me to quicken my steps to the Shade of life. These were two physicians of this city[3] who lived to a great age, and who made[4] the ears of thier patients sore with thier details of the exploits of thier Children & grand Children. I think I have observed that the infirmities of old age do not unfit[5] a man so much for Study, as for company or business. There is time in writing for the tardy[6] powers of the mind to act with thier usual Vigor and correctness, which is not the case in the former situations. Under the influence of this beleif, I have began to prepare my lectures for publication.—I have several motives for leaving a Copy of these lectures to the public. One of them is to justify myself from the imputations which have been so liberally cast upon me from partial and imperfect views of my System of medicine. When read in toto,—they will I hope vindicate my name from the Calumnies which the malice of my brethren and the revenge of the tories have heaped upon it. "The Whigs have done too much, suffered too much, sacrificed too much, and succeeded too well (says Mr Jno Adams in a letter I lately received from him) ever to be forgiven."—hence the revenge of the tories to which I have alluded.

Our Country has twice declared itself independant of Great Britain,—once in 1776, & again 1800. In the former year, the legislatures—the bench—the bar—and the Clergy were nearly all united in producing that event. In the latter year—the legislatures—the bench—the bar, and the Clergy were nearly all opposed to it. It was effected chiefly by the people without concert,—without System, and in many places, without leaders. Are we upon the eve of a declaration of our independance upon G Britain being repeated a third time, not by the pen, or by a general Suffrage but by the mouths of our Cannon?—But whith[er] am I hurried?—Away—away with the loathsom[e] Subject of politicks! I was surprised into it by mentioning One of the motives for spending the old age which it has pleased God to give me in preparing my lectures for the press.—

ADieu! my dear old friend of 1775—may health and peace be your portions during the resid[ue] of your life!—and Heaven, your happiness to all eternity.—

From Yours truly and Affectionately BENJN RUSH

PS: Recollect—all the remedies I have prescribed for your Rheumatism are founded upon your saying it is <u>without</u> fever.

RC (DLC); margin of last page chipped; beneath signature: "Thos Jefferson Esqr"; endorsed by TJ as received 1 Sept. 1811 and so recorded in SJL.

Elisha Perkins, a physician from Connecticut, won wide acclaim for his metallic tractors, pieces of metal that supposedly had a galvanic effect capable of removing pain when drawn over or rubbed against the afflicted part of a person's body. Although he received a United States patent in 1796, the Connecticut Medical Society expelled him shortly thereafter, and PERKINS'S POINTS came to be regarded as quack devices (*ANB*; *List of Patents*, 10). THE WHIGS HAVE DONE TOO MUCH . . . EVER TO BE FORGIVEN quotes from John Adams to Rush, 31 July 1811 (MHi: Adams Papers).

[1] Word interlined in place of "pint."

[2] Rush here canceled "Old."

[3] Preceding three words interlined.

[4] Word interlined in place of "tired."

[5] Word interlined in place of "disqualif."

[6] Word interlined in place of "enfeebled."

From George Jefferson

DEAR SIR Richmond 29th Augt 1811

I have duly received your favors of the 21st and 26th with the inclosure mentioned in the last.

Wheat having fallen as you were informed by Mr Coles on Monday the 19th—that is, no sales having been made at 9/. <u>after</u> saturday the 17th I concluded as it came so near your time, it was best to procure a Certificate at once, whilst the circumstance was recollected: indeed on enquiring of Mr Gallego he informed me that the price on the 17th was 8/6; but on my telling him I understood it had not fallen until monday, he said that he had reduced the price in the afternoon of saturday.—so that you will observe Certificates might possibly be procured against us, of the price being only 8/6 on the 17th—and it might be contended perhaps that <u>from</u> the 16th did not include that day.—I am thus particular lest some difficulty should be raised, and <u>my</u> recollection should fail me.—I would have gotten a Certificate from Gallego, but he refuses to give any, for fear of being carried to distant parts of the Country as a witness.—the one I procured I now inclose.—should wheat rise previous to the 25th of next month, I can easily get another.—but of that I fear there is but little,[1] the price being now down to 7/6.

You may observe perhaps that it is quoted in the Enquirer at \$:1.66.$\frac{2}{3}$, which must have been occasioned by an error in extending shillings into dollars & cents.

A few sales were made some time ago at 9/6 as you heard, but they were on credit.—Randolph Harrison I know sold his crop at that price, but it is not to be paid for until Christmas.

You certainly have lost considerably by the sale of your last crop of Tobacco in Lynchburg, and would continue to lose by making sales there, unless by mere accident you might happen to make an advantageous one: as purchases there are almost invariably made with the view of sales being effected to the shippers here, and of course on the calculation of a profit. Your last crop however was not sold at the price you have heard, having been sold to Mr Rutherfoord at $:9. only.—it should be observed though, that it was included in a parcel of 300 Hhds of Mr Harrisons, which, although the best of his selection during the year, was still I have no doubt an advantage to the sale of it.—Mutter & Stewart took one third of the purchase of M^r^ R— and shipped it, so that I know it could not have been resold at the price you mention.

I am Dear Sir Your Very humble serv^t^ GEO. JEFFERSON

RC (MHi); addressed: "Thomas Jefferson esquire Monticello"; franked; postmarked Richmond, 29 Aug.; endorsed by TJ as received 1 Sept. 1811 and so recorded in SJL. Enclosure not found.

TJ's letter to Jefferson of 26TH Aug. 1811 is recorded in SJL but has not been found. Its INCLOSURE was probably TJ's 3 Sept. 1811 renewal of his $3,000 note on the Bank of Virginia, which he signed on 25 Aug. 1811 (*MB*, 2:1268). The table of local prices periodically published in the Richmond ENQUIRER listed the price of wheat at $1.50, not $1.66⅔, throughout the month of August 1811.

[1] Thus in manuscript.

From the Seventy-Six Association

SIR, Charleston South Carolina August 29th 1811—

In obedience to a regulation of the "Seventy Six" Association, we as their Standing Committee have transmitted a Copy of an Oration delivered on the 4th of July by Benjamin A. Markley Esquire, A member of that Institution, for your perusal—

We remain Sir, with respect and esteem Your obedient and humble servants—

JO^S^ JOHNSON
J.B. WHITE
WILLIAM LANCE
JOSEPH KIRKLAND
MYER MOSES

RC (Christian S. Hutter Jr., on deposit ViU: TJP); in Johnson's hand except for the other signatures; at foot of text: "To Thomas Jefferson Esquire"; endorsed by

TJ as received from "Johnson Joseph et al." on 15 Sept. 1811 and so recorded in SJL; with unrelated calculations by TJ on verso. Enclosure: Benjamin A. Markley, *An Oration Delivered on 4th July, 1811, in commemoration of American Independence, before The '76 Association* (Charleston, S.C., 1811), declaring that the benefits of freedom make Americans "the only happy people on earth" (pp. 3–4); arguing that the United States has a right to a share of world commerce and has shown remarkable forbearance in the face of British and French provocations; linking the Fourth of July to the growing independence of South America; praising George Washington; and calling on God to preserve the republic.

Joseph Johnson (1776–1862), physician and author, was born at Mount Pleasant, near Charleston, South Carolina. He graduated from the College of Charleston in 1793 and received an M.D. from the University of Pennsylvania four years later. Having returned to Charleston to practice medicine and operate an apothecary shop, Johnson was president of the Medical Society of South Carolina, 1808–09, and wrote and spoke on influenza, smallpox, and yellow fever. He may be best known for his *Traditions and Reminiscences chiefly of the American Revolution in the South* (1851). Johnson was also president of the Charleston branch of the Bank of the United States, 1818–25, intendant (mayor) of Charleston in 1826, and a longtime public school commissioner and steward of the South Carolina Society. He opposed nullification in 1832 (*DAB*; Joseph I. Waring, *A History of Medicine in South Carolina* [1964–71], 1:248–51, 347; *Charleston Daily Courier*, 8 Oct. 1862).

John Blake White (1781–1859), painter, attorney, and author, was born near Eutaw Springs, South Carolina. He studied painting in London under Benjamin West but failed to establish himself as an artist after his return to America in 1803. White moved to Charleston a year later, studied law, was admitted to the bar in 1808, and earned his living as an attorney thereafter. However, he continued to paint and began to compose and publish plays. Four of White's paintings depicting events from the Revolutionary War now hang in the United States Capitol. He also represented Saint Philip and Saint Michael parishes in the South Carolina House of Representatives, 1818–19, served as a local magistrate, 1820–22, and was inspector of the Charleston customhouse, 1840–59 (*DAB*; *BDSCHR*, 5:280–1; Anna Wells Rutledge, *Artists in the Life of Charleston: Through Colony and State From Restoration to Reconstruction* [1949], 136; *Charleston Daily Courier*, 25 Aug. 1859).

William Lance (1791–1840), attorney, was a native of Charleston who was admitted to the South Carolina bar in 1811. He represented Saint Philip and Saint Michael parishes in the state House of Representatives, 1812–13 and 1816–19, and served as a commissioner of the poor in 1815. Lance was also a solicitor for the Union Bank of Charleston from about 1821 to 1836, a longtime member of the Charleston Library Society and the Hibernian Society, a ranking Masonic officer, and the author of several short works, including a partially completed biography of George Washington in Latin (*BDSCHR*, 4:337–9; Joseph Folker, *A Directory of the City and District of Charleston . . . for the year 1813* [Charleston, 1813], 44; Lance to John C. Calhoun, 16 Sept. 1820 [DNA: RG 59, LAR, 1817–25]; Lance, *Georgii Washingtonis vita* [1836]; Charleston *Southern Patriot*, 18 Mar. 1840).

Joseph Kirkland (1770–1817), physician, was a native of Fairfield County, near Columbia, South Carolina. He opened an office and pharmaceutical dispensary in Charleston by 1801. Kirkland owned nineteen slaves in 1800 and represented Saint Philip and Saint Michael parishes in the state House of Representatives, 1810–15. He was also a commissioner of the local free schools, 1811, and a member of the Charleston Library Society and the Medical Society of South Carolina (*BDSCHR*, 4:334–5; DNA: RG 29, CS, Charleston, 1800; John Dixon Nelson, *Nelson's Charleston Directory, and Strangers Guide, for . . . 1801* [Charleston,

1801], 89; Eleazer Elizer, *A Directory for 1803* [Charleston, 1803], 32; Charleston *Times*, 27 Nov. 1817).

Myer Moses (ca. 1780–1833) was a merchant and auctioneer in his native Charleston. He served as a militia captain, 1809–11, and represented Saint Philip and Saint Michael parishes in the South Carolina House of Representatives, 1810–12. During the War of 1812 Moses raised the Charleston Volunteers, a company composed entirely of his Jewish coreligionists, which he commanded with the rank of major. Although he suffered severe financial reverses thereafter, in 1820 he still owned nine slaves. Moses moved to New York City in 1825 and there authored works on American commercial law and on the 1830 revolution in France (*BDSCHR*, 4:417; James William Hagy, *This Happy Land: The Jews of Colonial and Antebellum Charleston* [1993], 120n, 134, 136, 376; DNA: RG 29, CS, Charleston, 1820; *Charleston Courier*, 1 Apr. 1833).

Charleston's Seventy-Six Association was organized in July 1809 to commemorate "the most interesting events in the history of the United States." United States Supreme Court justice William Johnson was its first president (Charleston *Carolina Gazette*, 28 July 1809).

SJL records TJ's missing 30 Sept. 1811 reply to "Johnson Joseph et al."

From William C. Rives

MY DEAR SIR, Oak-Ridge August 30th, 11.—

Since I had the pleasure of being at Monticello, the unsettled state of my health has totally disqualified me for intellectual exertion. Indeed, for the last two years, either the incapacity resulting from this cause, or the avocations of business have materially obstructed my desire of knowledge, by taking away the physical power of obtaining it.—The former evil being now partially removed by a recent visit to the Springs, I am determined, in spite of the latter, to renew my studies with energy & zeal.—But finding myself deficient in those elementary parts of learning which serve as a scaffolding for higher attainments, & having always meditated a recurrence to them when circumstances should favour my design, I must adopt some new arrangement for the purpose of comprehending them in my future course. The subjects to which I allude, are Mathematics, Physics, the antient, & some of the modern, languages, all of which will become subservient, either directly or indirectly, to my ultimate profession.—In order to incorporate these with my other studies, it will be necessary, however, to make the reading of Law for some time a secondary object; nor will the temporary abridgement of my legal researches be at all inconvenient, as I am not anxious to precipitate the period of active employment. It will be necessary likewise, to change the scene of my literary labours, for the difficulties of Mathematics cannot be easily overcome without the aid of an instructor or the co-operation of a fellow-student, the principles of Natural philosophy cannot be distinctly understood without experimental proofs, and the dull exercise of committing grammars & vocabularies to memory cannot be patiently endured without sharing it with a companion. Possessing none of these advantages at home, I have been induced to look abroad for a more favourable situation, and bounding my view by the limits of the State, I have at length selected Williamsburg as the best. I have not extended my view to other states, because it appears desirable that every person should receive his education in the particular state which is destined to be the theatre of his future life, as he is thereby better enabled to accommodate himself to the tone of feelings & manners which prevail among his fellow-citizens.—In Wms-burg there are able professors in all the departments I have mentioned. As a Mathematician, Mr. Blackburn is supposed to be inferior to no man in Virginia, and the original simplicity of his method of instruction entitles him to the first rank as a teacher. Bishop Madison, I believe, has acted a distinguished part in the Philosophical transactions of his own country, and in Europe, his name is highly respected. The professor of modern languages, also, is said to be a man of considerable erudition, & possesses a critical & complete[1] knowledge of the French, which is his vernacular tongue.—To these advantages, I may superadd the edifying society of studious & enlightened young-men of whom there are at least six or seven at that place, in years of the greatest scarcity.—

The very friendly disposition which you have manifested towards me, together with your experience in matters of this kind particularly & the rectitude of your judgement on all, has emboldened me to solicit your remarks & advice on the subject of my future course. Will you do me the favour, sir, to say whether you consider Wms-burg an eligible[2] situation for the objects I propose, and if not, what other you would recommend? I desire to be most respectfully presented to Mr. & Mrs. Randolph & their family, and with zealous prayers for the continuance of your health & happiness,

I have the honour to be your mo. obt. serv. WM C RIVES

RC (MHi); addressed: "Thomas Jefferson late President of U.S. Monticello. pr. mail to Milton"; franked; postmarked Lovingston, 30 Aug., and Nelson Court House, 31 Aug. 1811; endorsed by TJ as received 5 Sept. 1811 and so recorded in SJL.

In 1812 Rives returned to the College of William and Mary, from which he had been expelled in 1809 (*William and Mary Provisional List*, 34). He may be referring to its former PROFESSOR OF MODERN LANGUAGES, Louis H. Girardin.

[1] Preceding two words interlined.

[2] Reworked from "a proper."

From "A Bond Street Lounger"

SIR

Augt 31st 1811

The letter of Mr Sec^{y} Smith (lately published) has fully exposed the diabolical views, & Strange fallacy of the democrats of America in fine the above letter will do more for the Cause of Federalism than all their own writers Combined could have done—to use a Cant & Vulgar phrase "when theives fall out, honest Men Come by their own"—the above speaks more than volumes—in fine you must Shrink from the present high tone towards us or your demo. gov^{t} will fall—mark these words—a few Lectures from Sir Joseph will settle the business—You will find that you have Neither energy nor Strength to support your [. . .].

Y^{r} fr^{d}

A BOND STREET LOUNGER

My Comp^{ts} to the official Lyar. or liar. the gallant Commodore/ The Nelson of America—

RC (DLC); one word illegible; addressed: "The Honble Thos Jefferson Esqr Monticello Virginia"; franked; postmarked New York, 20 Sept.; endorsed by TJ as an anonymous letter "(from Engl^{d})" received 26 Sept. 1811 and so recorded in SJL.

SIR JOSEPH Yorke commanded a British squadron that was wrongly thought to be bound for American waters (Philadelphia *Poulson's American Daily Advertiser*, 30 Aug., 21 Oct. 1811). BOND STREET: part of the fashionable shopping district located in London's West End. The GALLANT COMMODORE was John Rodgers (note to James Madison to TJ, 7 June 1811).

From Peter Carr

MY DEAR SIR

Carr's-brook. Aug. 31st 1811.

You will receive by James, a very fine boar-pig of the Chinese or Parkinson breed; he is just eight weeks old, and as the sow is in heat again, I thought it best, to seperate them. If they Should answer the character given of them, they will certainly be, a valuable acquisition. Judge Holmes and Genl Smith of Winchester, speak of their being made fit for the table, on a third or even a fourth of the corn, used for the common hog.

Our dear mother is yeilding at length to the unconquerable force of her disease—she is perfectly helpless, knows no person, and is insensible to every thing. I did not think, she could have lived through the last night—She cannot possibly survive many days. Adieu affectionately.

P^{R} CARR

RC (ViU: TJP-CC); addressed: "Thomas Jefferson esq[r] Monticello"; endorsed by TJ as received 31 Aug. 1811 and so recorded in SJL.

Richard PARKINSON described his breeding of Chinese pigs (*Sus indicus*) in *The Experienced Farmer, an entire new work, in which the whole system of Agriculture, Husbandry, and Breeding of Cattle, is explained and copiously enlarged upon* (London, 1798), 1:298–9. For an American ed., see Sowerby, no. 703.

To George Hay

DEAR SIR Monticello Aug. 31. 11.

M[r] Bolling Robertson proposing to return shortly to N. Orleans to resume the practice of the law there, I have thought it best to engage him to conduct the examination of witnesses there when we get to that stage of Livingston's suit. and in order that he might understand the points which are likely to be made in the cause, I have communicated to him my view of it. a great proportion of the facts on which it rests, are such as both parties will probably readily admit, differing only as to the law arising on those facts. would it not be better for him to propose to Livingston to agree these facts in writing, in order to curtail the trouble as well as the volume of evidence? the most material facts on which we shall differ are those respecting the injury already done and likely to ensue from Livingston's works. the approbation by the Spanish govmt of Gravier's fauxbourg, that the batture was not included in the Inventory of sale, the perseverance of the former government in keeping it clear of intruders E[t]c E[t]c on which testimony will be to be taken. for this purpose would it be best for us to communicate to E.L. our statement of facts & let him strike out from it those he does not admit, or require a statement from him also, have it collated with ours by mr Robertson & himself, and those facts selected in which both agree? the latter is probably best but I leave this to you gentlemen of the law. mr Robertson will suggest to you proper names to insert for Commissioners, to wit, Benjamin Morgan, Moreau de Lislet, Derbigny E[t]c he can also give you interesting information as to the facility with which our adversary may obtain there proof of any thing he pleases. Accept the assurances of my great esteem & respect TH: JEFFERSON

PoC (DLC); at foot of text: "M[r] Hay"; endorsed by TJ.

TJ must have communicated his VIEW of Edward Livingston's suit on the batture to Thomas B. Robertson during the latter's visit to Monticello (TJ to Robertson, 20 Apr. 1812). By INVENTORY OF SALE TJ probably meant the 1797 inventory of Bertrand Gravier's estate, not Jean Gravier's 1804 sale of the batture to Peter Delabigarre. TJ's STATEMENT OF FACTS is printed above at 23 Mar. 1811.

From Josef Yznardy

EXMÔ. SENÔR Rota 31. de Agosto de 1811

Muy Senôr mio y de mi mayor veneracion y respeto: Mucho tíempo hace caresco de la complacencía de savér de la salud de V.E. q^e celebraré sea la mas robusta, la mía es bien endeble, despues de haver pasado, tantas fatígas, desvelos, y perdídas desde la entrada de las tropas Imperiales en este Pais, q^e si no me hallase tan cargado de años y familia, y de propiedad fincal, me trasladaría á esa, á finalizár mis dias con algun descanso.

Para q^e V.E. se convenza de la míseria en q^e deve estár la España, se exîgen 72. p% de contribucion sobre las fincas ùrbanas, y 90. sre. las rùsticas, y sobre lo industrial y Comercio, por requisiciones forzadas á los tenedores de la especie, reduciendo los Pueblos á imponderable miseria, agregandosele á esto, q^e las Cosechas del año pasado y $pres^{te}$ han sido tan escàsas de granos y liquidos, q^e la libra de pan vale díez cientos, y el quartillo de vino lo mismo, la libra de Carne treinta, y á proporcion todo comestible.

En mi particular hasta aqui he ido pasando, teniendo q^e pagar $diariam^{te}$ diez fuertes de $contribuc^n$ q^e si dura mucho, no será posible soportarla, y no hay otra felicidad, q^e la de no haver enfermedades, pero és indispensable haya hambre el año proxîmo, si no se verifica importacíon.

En medio de estas calamidades, yò no me he olvidado de la amistad de V.E. y p^r cuya felicidad anhelo, suplicandole tenga la bondad de q^e reciva yó la satisfaccion de vèr letra suya, pues desde el 5. de Febrero del año pasado, q^e vine de Cadiz á esta á visitár mi familia, se me privò oficialmente de toda comunicacion con dha. Cíudad, ignorando quanto à pasado y pasa en ella, teniendo la pena de hallarme una hora distante de navegacion, sín tener noticias verdaderas de ella, hasta q^e Díos quiera, pues crèo està muy distante, y sin otro motivo tengo el honor de repetír á V.E. la sinceridad de mi respeto, rogando á Díos gue. su vida m^s a^s.

Exmo. Señor B.S.M. de V.E. su mas atento y Seg^{ro} Servidor.

JOSEF YZNARDI

EDITORS' TRANSLATION

DEAR SIR Rota 31. August 1811

My dear Sir and with my greatest veneration and respect: it has been a while since I have had the pleasure to learn of your health, which I pray is very robust; mine is very weak, having suffered so much fatigue, sleeplessness, and so many losses since the imperial troops entered this country, that if I did not feel so tied down by old age, family, and property, I would move and end my days in peace.

To convince you of the misery that exists in Spain, they are demanding 72 percent in taxes on urban properties and 90 percent on rural ones, and on industry and trade; because of forced requisitions in kind, the villages are reduced to incalculable misery and, in addition, the harvests of last year and this year have been so scanty in grains and liquids that a pound of bread costs ten cents, and a quart of wine the same, a pound of meat thirty, and so on for all the other foodstuffs.

This situation, having to pay taxes of ten fuertes a day, if it goes on for very long, will be untenable, and there is no happiness, other than that of not being sick; but famine next year is certain if we do not import food.

In the midst of these calamities, I have not forgotten your friendship and I long for your happiness, begging you to have the goodness to provide me with the satisfaction of receiving a letter from you, because since 5 February of last year, when I came here from Cádiz to visit my family, I have been officially deprived of all communication with that city; not knowing what has happened and is happening there, suffering in finding myself an hour away, without having real news of it, until God wishes it, which I think is very far off in the future, and with no other motive I have the honor to repeat to you the sincerity of my respect, praying that God preserves your life for many years.

Dear Sir I kiss your hand. Your most attentive and loyal servant.

JOSEF YZNARDI

RC (CSmH: JF-BA); in a clerk's hand, signed by Yznardy; dateline above closing; at foot of text: "Exmô. Senôr D[n] Tomàs Jeffersson"; endorsed by TJ as received 22 Dec. 1811 and so recorded in SJL. Translation by Dr. David T. Gies and Dr. Jennifer McCune.

The French army (TROPAS IMPERIALES) besieged CADIZ from February 1810 until August 1812 (Ian C. Robertson, *Wellington at War in the Peninsula, 1808–1814* [2000], 10, 217).

To Gideon Granger

DEAR SIR Monticello Sep. 1. 11.

Will you be so good as to inform me to what place I should address a letter to James Lyon, son of Col° Matthew Lyon. it is so long since I have heard any thing of him, that I am quite uninformed of his residence, and have occasion to write to him. Let me take this occasion of thanking you for the new, post book, which is a daily convenience to me, and of renewing the assurances of my constant esteem & respect. Th: Jefferson

RC (ViU: TJP); at foot of text: "Gideon Granger esq." PoC (DLC); endorsed by TJ.

From John Jordan

Sir, Lexington K. Sep[r] 1st 1811.

I had the honor to receive[1] your favor of the 5th Ul[t] covering one for M[r] Ogilvie, which I enveloped and forwarded him at Bairdstown Kentucky by the same Mail—having taken up his residence at that place to be near a literary friend of his (M[r] M[c]Alister)

M[r] Ogilvie diliverd several Lectures during his stay at this place, they were received with the most unbounded applause.

It affords me a real & sincere pleasure to have it in my power to render you so small a service—Particularly when I reflect on the many benefits our State has derived during your, and our Present Presidents administration

We have encreased in Population, and for our age no State has excelled us in Agriculture and Manufactures—and happy am I to say that Republicanism keeps pace.

We have been some what agitated in our late elections as to State Legislatures Instructing their Senators in Congress—should time present itself to you I shoud deem it a most singular favor for your opinion on this head—for this query I trust you will have the goodness to pardon me—as I may have form'd an eronious opinion, particularly as our Senators as related to the U.S. Bank question have differed—

I again repeat the pleasure that twill at all times afford me to prove serviceable to you or any of your Friends

That you may enjoy health—And that Posterity justly appreciate what you have done for your Country is the fervent & sincere Wish of

Your Most ob[t] Sert. John Jordan J[r]

RC (MoSHi: TJC-BC); between dateline and salutation: "His Excellency Thomas Jefferson Monticello. V[a]"; endorsed by TJ as received 2 Oct. 1811 and so recorded in SJL.

bairdstown: Bardstown. On 31 Jan. 1811 Kentucky's legislature passed a resolution instructing its congressional delegation to oppose the rechartering of the bank of the United States. Its senators at the time were Henry Clay, who complied, and John Pope, who gave a lengthy speech supporting rechartering on 15 Feb. 1811. The Senate defeated renewal of the charter five days later (*Acts Passed at the First Session of the Nineteenth General Assembly for the Commonwealth of Kentucky* [Frankfort, 1811], 159; *Annals*, 11th Cong., 3d sess.,

219–40, 346–7). After Clay's term expired in March, George M. Bibb replaced him (*Biog. Dir. Cong.*).

[1] Manuscript: "receive receive."

Mutual Assurance Society Account for Insuring Milton Warehouses

[ca. 1 Sept. 1811]

The Honble Thos Jefferson
To ye Ml A Society Dr

1809 Apl 1	To Quota on Warehouses in Milton Insured by J Henderson that is on those standing at that date	
	Vizt **A** a Scale House valued	at 400
	B a Transfer house	at 250
	C W House[1] 11.2 x 30	at 360
		1110[2]
	as 1510 $ is to 9.11 $ so is 1110	6.69
	Interest to 1st Septr 1811 is 2 yrs 5 Mos	0.97
1810 Apl 1	To same Quota for this yr	6.69
	Interest to 1 Septr 1811 is 17 Moss	0.57
1811 Apl 1	To do this year	6.69
	Interest to 1 Septr is 5 Mos	0.17[3]
″	To ye Quota for this Year ℔ Decln No 389	12.84
	Intst to 1st Sept 5 Mos	0.32
		34.94
	To Attorys Comsn thereon 5 ℔Ct	1.74
	Amot	$35.68[4]

Recd the above $35.68 but it is understood to be without prejudice to any other or further legal claim which the Society may have on Account of those Warehouses which may have been destroyed by time or otherwise

MS (MHi); in Benjamin Brown's hand; undated; notation by Brown on verso: "Ml A. Society vs T. Jefferson"; endorsed by TJ: "Mutual assurce 35.68 rendd by Benj Brown 1809.10.11."

John HENDERSON had taken out a policy on the Milton warehouses on 4 May 1799 (Vi: Business Records Collection, Mutual Assurance Society Declarations, no. 337). Brown's failure to sign the receipt above shows that TJ did not settle the account at this time. On 7 Aug. 1813 TJ calculated that the society's claim "for the scalehouse, transfer & warehouse Milton 1809–13" ought to be $38.30 plus commission, but he chose not to pay, noting that the society had then omitted it in its account and concluding that these buildings had been, "if I recollect rightly, withdrawn from insurance by me heretofore" (*MB*, 2:1292).

On 8 Apr. 1812 Brown reported to Samuel Greenhow, the principal agent of the society, that "Mr Jefferson does not consider himself bound to pay the arrearages for Hendersons mill, the ground of his opinion I stated to you some time ago. Jno Henderson the Guard^n^ of the Legatees of B^t^ Henderson is insolvent & the legatees all without the State. I shall wait your instructions in this case. Can a purchaser be made personally answerable for what is due at the time of the purchase, unless the property be transfered to him in the manner prescribed by the rules of the Society? I should be glad of advice upon this point as it frequently occurs" (Vi: Mutual Assurance Society, Incoming Correspondence).

1 Manuscript: "Huse."

2 Sum should be 1010.

3 Beneath this line an unidentified hand penciled the numbers 21.68 and 13.16, the first being ten cents less than the total for the preceding six lines and the second the sum of the two following lines.

4 Total should be 36.68.

From Francis Eppes

DEAR GRANDPAPA — Mill brook Sep 2 1811

I wish to see you very much I am very sorry that you did not answer my letter give my love to aunt Randolph and all the children—believe me to be your most affectionnate Grandson

FRANCIS EPPES

RC (ViU: TJP-ER); endorsed by TJ as received 5 Sept. 1811 and so recorded in SJL.

Francis Wayles Eppes (1801–81) was the only surviving child of TJ's daughter Maria Jefferson Eppes and his wife's nephew John Wayles Eppes. After the death of his mother in 1804, Eppes spent much of his time at Monticello, where TJ sought to inspire in him a love of learning. Eppes was educated at various private schools, including New London Academy near Poplar Forest, Georgetown College (later Georgetown University), and South Carolina College (later the University of South Carolina). He began to read law but was never admitted to the bar. TJ turned over his Poplar Forest plantation to Eppes at the time of the latter's marriage in 1822 to Mary Cleland Randolph, the daughter of Thomas Eston Randolph, and he promised to bequeath the estate to his grandson. On learning of the magnitude of TJ's financial difficulties, Eppes offered to return the property, but was refused. In 1828 Eppes sold Poplar Forest and moved his family to Florida, where he was a planter, a justice of the peace, and served several terms as intendant (mayor) of Tallahassee. He also sat on the board of West Florida Seminary (later Florida State University), 1857–68, including eight years as president. Late in the 1860s Eppes moved to Orange County, Florida, near present-day Orlando (Shackelford, *Descendants*, 167–78; Mrs. Nicholas Ware Eppes, "Francis Eppes [1801–1881], Pioneer of Florida," *Florida Historical Society Quarterly* 5 [1926]: 94–102; Chambers, *Poplar Forest*; *MB*, esp. 2:1051; Francis Eppes Memorandum Book [Corporation for Jefferson's Poplar Forest]; *Terr. Papers*, 24:815, 25:105, 375; William George Dodd, *History of West Florida Seminary* [1952], 109–10).

For Eppes's previous LETTER, see note to TJ to Eppes, 6 Sept. 1811. The current letter was probably enclosed in John Wayles Eppes to TJ, 2 Sept. 1811, not found, but recorded in SJL as received from Mill Brook on 5 Sept. 1811.

From James S. Gaines

Dear Sir Patrick County September 3rd 1811

The State of Virginia which was foremost in her contest for Liberty appear to be the last to enjoy it. for at the close of the war it seems as if she was quite exhausted, and Just nestled herself down under some of the most Corrupt principles of the old regal Government. principles Sir, if persisted in will finally eventuate in the downfall of all that have been atchieved the last hope of the Philanthrophist. you sir predicted thirty years ago "that the time would arrive when our rulers would forget right and make interested uses of power and that patriotism would no longer be a shield sufficient for the protection of the Liberties of the people." the time have I presume already arrived, and your predictions are but too fully verrified. Laws are now passed with impunity, infringing some of the dearest rights of freemen, and there is a most shameful waste of the public money. I am now Sir, fully prepared, to subscribe to the opinion of my venerable great uncle (the Late Edmund Pendleton) who said "of men advanced to power there is more who would try to destroy Liberty than preserve it." hence then the necessity of a well organized Government, with suitable checks on the rulers to secure the Liberties of the ruled, with powers so well defined, that public agents will not be able by any forced construction of expediency or implied right to overleap the barriers of the Constitution. I take the Liberty Sir, of enclosing to you what in my opinion are the most important defects of the Constitution of this State together with a new plan or form of Government which I conceive to be well adapted to the genius of Republicanism in this new place. I have endeavored as much as possible to keep the departments of the Government seperate and independant in such manner that they shall be as so many checks one on the other. 2. that each section of the state shall be equally represented which will include wealth and population, and ballance betwixt the commercial and agricultural parts of the Community. 3. Responsibility the Soul. 4. Economy the Body of a representative Government.

Be so good Sir, as to give the enclosed a perusal, and write me the result of your deliberations on the subject. I am Just about to remove myself to Madison County Bent of Tennessee please to direct your letter to the care of Gabriel Moore attorney at Law of that place with sentiments of the most perfect esteem and respect I subscribe myself yours &c JAMES S. GAINES

Octr 14th 1811

It grieves me Sir, that I have to trouble you in your Retirement but you must yet Continue to Illumine our political[1] Hemisphere, as the Sun is to the solar Systam, so are you to the political world, altho the Emperor of France Occupy[2] the highest place in the Temple of Mars, as [a] Statesman & Philanthropist, you sir stand unrivaled, and will Occupy the highest place in the Temple of Liberty.

Embargo War or submision again present themselves, your measures must again be resorted to, & may now I flatter myself be enforced,—

if you should think propper to answer me please to direct the same to Knoxville I shall give the Postmaster at that place the necessary directions,—your most Obediant servt JAMES S GAINES

RC (DLC: TJ Papers, 193:34426, 34475); damaged at seal; postscript on verso of address cover; addressed: "Thomas Jefferson Esqr Albemarle County V.a."; stamped; endorsed by TJ as received 22 Dec. 1811 and so recorded in SJL.

James Strother Gaines (1769–1823) was the grandson of Isabella Pendleton Gaines, a sister of the Virginia statesman Edmund Pendleton (1721–1803). Gaines lived in Patrick County, 1797–1811, and later moved to Tennessee, where he helped to run the boundary with Georgia in 1817. A noted mathematician, he composed but did not publish a lengthy manuscript proposing "a totally different and entirely new" theory of astronomy. Late in life he moved to Dallas County, Alabama (Calvin E. Sutherd, *A Compilation of Gaines Family Data, with special emphasis on the lineage of William and Isabella (Pendleton) Gaines*, 2d ed. [1972], 227, 229; John Trotwood Moore and Austin P. Foster, eds., *Tennessee the Volunteer State, 1769–1923* [1923], 1:371; *Baltimore Patriot & Mercantile Advertiser*, 14 Nov. 1826).

No precise match has been found for TJ's quote from THIRTY YEARS AGO, but he made a similar statement about the same time in his *Notes on the State of Virginia*: "the spirit of the times may alter, will alter. Our rulers will become corrupt, our people careless. . . . From the conclusion of this war we shall be going down hill. It will not then be necessary to resort every moment to the people for support. They will be forgotten, therefore, and their rights disregarded. They will forget themselves, but in the sole faculty of making money, and will never think of uniting to effect a due respect for their rights" (*Notes*, ed. Peden, 161). In "The Danger Not Over," a widely reprinted 1801 essay, Edmund Pendleton proposed eight amendments to the United States Constitution intended to strengthen the separation of powers among the three branches of government and gave THE OPINION that "of men advanced to power, more are inclined to destroy *liberty*, than to defend it" (David John Mays, *The Letters and Papers of Edmund Pendleton, 1734–1803* [1967], 2:699).

MADISON COUNTY, located in the Big or Great Bend (BENT) of the TENNESSEE River, was then in Mississippi Territory but later became part of Alabama.

[1] Manuscript: "poloticol."
[2] Manuscript: "Occcupy."

ENCLOSURE

James S. Gaines's Plan for a New Virginia Constitution and Revised Legal Code

A New plan or form of Government—
Divisions of the State

1. The state of Virginia shall as follows be laid off into three departments the first thirty Counties lying along the atlantic ocean shall be called the Eastern department the next thirty two Counties lying parallel with the Eastern department shall be denominated the middle department and the thirty Counties lying North & West of the middle department shall be called the Western department. 2. each department shall be again laid off into Senatorial districts of eight Counties each and each senatorial district shall be subdivided into representative districts of two counties each—

Article 1. Sec. 1. all legislative powers herein granted shall be vested in a General assembly of the State of Virginia. which shall consist of a Senate and house of Representatives. 2. There shall be but one senator from each Senatorial district and one representative from each representative district who shall receive for their services while serving on the General assembly a compensation that shall neither be increased or diminished[1] during the time for which they shall have been Elected. 3. No foreigner emigrating to this State after the adoption of this constitution shall be elected to serve in the General assembly or appointed to fill any office civil or military of trust or emolument under the authority of this State 4. no person shall be elected to serve on the General assembly who is a practitioner of the law, or preacher belonging to any religious sect of people, or who shall be licensed to sell goods wares and merchandize by wholesale or retail, or to keep a public house or who shall be appointed to fill any office civil or military under the authority of this State or of the United States 5. No senator or representative shall during the time for which he shall have been Elected be appointed to any civil office under the authority of this State

6 Elections to elect members to the General assembly shall be held on the fourth monday in august to be continued from day to day if by any casualty it cannot be concluded on the first day: 7. The sheriffs of Counties shall on the tenth day subsequent to the day of election convene at some convenient place in each senatorial district and from the poll so taken in their respective Counties return as senator the person having the highest number of votes in the whole district and also as representative the person having the highest number of votes in each representative district. 8. all free white persons enrolled on a muster list or the list of a tax gatherer (except those who shall hereafter be excepted) shall be entitled to vote for a member of the house of representatives who shall vote by ballot and not otherwise. 9. all persons possessed of a freehold Estate of fifty acres of land which shall be in the occupency of himself or a tenant at will shall be entitled to vote for a senator and shall give his vote viva voice and not otherwise. 10. No person holding any lucrative office under the authority of this State shall be entitled to the right of suffrage no person born after the adoption of this Constitution who cannot read & write and who does not understand arithmatic as far as the rule of Three shall be entitled to vote for members of the General assembly.

No person shall be entitled to the right of suffrage who have been guilty of a breach of any of the penal laws of this State which thereby shall have subjected him to infamous punishment untill restored to such forfeited privilege by the Judge of the superior court where such offence shall have been committed No foreigner emigrating to this State after the adoption of this constitution shall be entitled to the right of suffrage. 11. The Legislative shall assemble at the Capitol in the City of Richmond once in each year & Such meeting shall be on the first monday in December except they shall by law appoint a different day. 12. The attendance of three Senators and twelve members of the house of Representatives from each department shall constitute a quoram to do business but a smaller number[2] may adjourn from day to day untill such quoram shall have been completed. 13. Each house shall be the sole Judges of the elections, returns, and qualifications of its own members may compel the attendance of absent members in such manner and under such penalties as the General assembly shall by Law provide may determine the rules of its own proceedings punish its members for disorderly behavior and with the concurrence of two thirds of both houses expel a member. 14. all Bills shall originate in the house of representatives and when having passed thru several readings shall before it become a law be sent to the Senate for their concurrence if they concur the speaker shall sign the bill if they do not concur the bill shall be returned with their objections to the house of representatives who shall enter the same at large on their Journals and proceed to reconsidder if after such reconsideration two thirds of that house shall again pass the Bill the speaker of the senate shall sign the same which shall become a Law any thing to the contrary notwithstanding. But in all such cases the votes of both houses shall be determined by yeas and nays and the names of the persons voting for and against the bill shall be entered on the Journals of both houses respectively. If any bill shall not be returned by the Senate within six days sundays excepted after it shall have been presented to them the same shall become a Law in like manner as if they had concurred except the house of representatives by their adjournment prevent its return in which case the bill shall be Lost. 15. The Journals of both houses respectively shall be published anually together with a regular Statement and account of the receipts and expenditures of all public money one for each member of the General assembly and one for each magistrate throughout the state 16. No money shall be drawn from the Treasury but in consequence of appropriations made by Law and all monies appropriated to the Establishment of Seminaries of Learning or public improvements of any description shall be levied exclusively on the inhabitants of senatorial districts where such seminaries may be established or such public improvements shall have been so made 17. Taxes shall be uniform throughout the State and the like tax shall be paid on every hundred dollars in any of the Chartered Banks of this State as on a Hundred dollars worth of land according to the equalizing Law. 18. at the first session of the General assembly after the adoption of this Constitution the Judges of the superior courts shall convene at the Capitol in the City of Richmond for the purpose of revising and simplifying the whole body of the laws of this State now in force and such Laws when so revised and made conformable to the principles of this constitution shall by the General assembly be made permanent and shall not thereafter be repealed or revised untill two thirds of the Judges of said superior courts shall petition to the General assembly to that effect. 19. The General assembly shall pass no Laws subjecting Lands whereon the owner resides Household and Kitchen furniture plantation tools or provisions necessary for the support of his or her families to the payment of any debts which shall be contracted after the adoption of this Constitution. 20. all Laws which shall be passed by the General assembly contravening the principles of this constitution or of the constitution of the united States or infringing any of the fundamental rights apertaining to freemen shall be null and void from and after the passing thereof. 21. The yeas and nays shall be taken in the house of representatives on all questions that shall be decided on of a public and general nature which shall be inserted in their Journals. 22. The seats of the members of both houses of the General assembly from the Eastern department shall be vacated at the expiration of the first session the seats of those from the Western department at the expiration of the second session and the seats of those from the middle department at the expiration of the third Session and so to continue alternately—

Article 2. sec. 1. The executive powers shall be exercised by a Governor under the regulation of such Laws as the General assembly shall think expedient to pass 2. at the first meeting of the General assembly the senate shall proceed to Elect by ballot a Governor and Lieutenant Governor for three years who shall be ineligible three years after having been twice Elected they shall be allowed by the house of representatives a compensation for their services quarter yearly which shall neither be increased or diminished[3] during their continuance in office they shall not during such time receive any other emolument under the authority of this State or of the united states they shall be natural born Citizens of this State but shall not both be Elected from the same department. 3. The Lieutenant Governor shall be speaker of the Senate and shall have the casting vote whenever they shall be equally divided. 4. In case of the removal by impeachment of the Governor from office or of his death, resignation, or inability to discharge the duties thereof the same shall devolve on the Lieutenant Governor and the General assembly shall by Law provide for the case of removal, death, resignation or inability both of the Governor and Lieutenant Governor declaring by what mode such vacancies shall be supplied untill the disability be removed or regular Elections shall have taken place 5. In case of the death resignation or inability to act of any of the members of the General assembly the Governor shall issue writs of Election to supply any such vacancy that may so happen. 6. The Governor shall by and with the advice and consent of the senate two thirds concurring therein nominate and appoint the Judges of the court of appeals and of the superior courts the attorney General the public Treasurer the register of the Land office and clerks of both houses of the General assembly. but their salaries shall severally be allowed them by the house of representatives 7. The Governor shall appoint the military field officers and they shall appoint the other commissioned officers but the appointment of the noncommissioned officers shall devolve on the companies severally. 8. he shall at the commencement of each session report to the General Assembly the state of the commonwealth and exhibit a regular statement of her finances which shall be entered at large on the Journals of the house of representatives he shall recommend to their consideration such measures as he may Judge necessary and expedient and may on extraordinary occasions convene both houses of the General assembly. 9. The Governor Lieutenant Governor and all civil officers of the State shall be removed from office on impeachment for and conviction of Treason bribery or other high crimes and misdemeanors

Article 3. Sec. 1. The Judicial power of this State shall be vested in one Supreme Court or Court of Appeals and superior Courts to be held in each County together with such other County Courts as the General assembly shall think expedient to Establish. 2. The Judges of both the supreme and Superior Courts shall hold their offices during good behavior and shall quarter yearly receive for their services a compensation which shall not be increased or diminished[4] during their continuance in office. 3. The Judges of the superior courts of common Law shall give relief in equity as well as in Law. 4. no appeal from these courts to the Court of appeals shall be had of right but on application being made to the Judges of the court of appeals they may grant a supersidius if in their opinion a wrong Judgement has been given in the superior Court where such decision was had—

Article 4. Sec. 1. The magistrates in each Captains district shall by rotation take in a List of all taxable property in said districts shall be furnished by the public printer with blank books for that purpose and in consequence of such services be exempted from working on roads or performing military duty in time of peace 2. The office of Sheriff shall by the County Court be let to the highest bidder and the money arising therefrom converted to the use of the Poor Establishment and County Charges—

Article 5. Sec 1. There shall be erected at or near the centre of each senatorial district a house for the reception of the poor a foundling Hospital and work house to be under such regulations as the General assembly shall from time to time adopt

Article 6. Sec. 1 There shall be erected on some eligible spot over ten and not to exceed twenty miles from the City of Richmond an arsenal and military academy at which place all the arms implements of war and military Stores shall be deposited 2. The Governor shall by and with the advice and consent of the senate select from each department a certain number of young men not to exceed ten to be taught at the military academy in the most approved arts and sciences of modern warfare[5] 3. The General assembly shall pass such Laws and make such regulations as they shall think necessary and expedient for carrying the foregoing article into operation 4. In case of an Invasion by a foreign foe the militia from the Eastern department shall be called out in the months of June, July, august, and September those from the Western department in the months of October, November, December, and January and those from the middle department in the months of February, March, april and May, under such other regulations as the General assembly shall from time to time adopt—

Article 7. Sec 1. whenever one third of the members of the house of representatives shall deem it expedient to call a convention for the purpose of revising this Constitution the General assembly shall without delay pass a Law directing the Sheriffs of Counties and sergeants of Corporations to open a poll at the next Election thereafter for the purpose of taking the sense of the people if two thirds of the whole number of voters in the State shall be in favor of a revision a Law shall be passed at the next General assembly for the purpose of calling a convention—

Article 8. Sec. 1. The Senators and members of the house of representatives shall in all cases except treason felony and breeches of the peace be privileged from arrest during their attendance at the General assembly and in going to and returning from the same and for any speech or debate in either house they shall not be questioned in any other place—

Article 9. sec. 1. The senators and Representatives before mentioned and all executive Judicial and military officers of the Government shall be bound by oath (or affirmation) to support this Constitution but no religious test shall be required as a qualification to any office or public trust under the authority of this State—

A criminal Code of Laws—

Rape in the first degree Murder in the first degree bigamy in the 1. degree[6] robbing on the highway and the burning a house at that time the residence of some person shall constitute the first grade of offences and if committed in the first degree of malignancy shall be punished with hard Labor and solitary confinement in the Penitentiary House during Life, and if in the second degree of malignancy for a term of years, over 25. and not to exceed 30. years. Treason, Manslaughter, Treason[7] Perjury, Forgery or Counterfeiting, Horse stealing or the wilfully Stabbing or wounding any person with the appearance of an intent to kill, shall constitute the second grade of offences and shall be punished with hard Labor and solitary confinement for a term of years, over 15. and not to exceed 25. years; The publishing any thing Hostile to this Government by speaking, writing, or printing whilst a negociation is pending betwixt this Country and any foreign Court, that may thereby impede such negotiation[8] shall Constitute the third grade of offences, and shall be punished with hard Labor &c for a term of years, over 10. and not to exceed 15. years. the offences that comes under the description of Petty Larceny shall be punished by making restoration of four times the value of the thing stolen by standing in the Pillory from three to six hours, and by being deprived of all the rights of a free white person while residing in this State, untill restored to such forfeited privilege by the Grand Jury, and assented to by the Judge of the superior Court, where such conviction was had. Drunkeness, fighting, Cursing and swearing[9] or making use of such indecent Language as may have a tendency to Corrupt the morals of the people, shall constitute the fourth grade of offences, and be punished with a fine over twenty and [not][10] to exceed thirty dollars, or a deprivation for twelve months of all the rights of a free white person[11]

The defects of the Constitution of this State are 1. The want of Responsibility in the Legislative and executive[12] branches of the Government the senate by being Elected for four years and from Large districts are scarcely directly or indirectly accountable to their constituents and by having an unqualified negative on the acts of the house of delegates greatly lessens the responsibility of that branch of the Government and in the executive branch by the Governor having a Council and by having no vote at the council board. 2. The General assembly are too numerous there being two members from each County the means of Corruption may become too General Candidates have it too much in their power to influence some and overawe others especially since their votes are given viva voice. 3. The General assembly by having the appointment of the Governor and Council and all other important officers of the Government and the giving them their Salaries acquire thereby an undue influence over the other departments the Government is too much blended and all power result exclusively to the Legislature. 4. The inequality of the representation of the people both in the Senate and house of delegates arising from the great difference in the extent and population of the senatorial districts and of the Counties. 5. The right of Suffrage as it respects the state and federal Legislature being withheld from nearly one half of the Citizens of this Commonwealth who contribute to the protection and support of the Government 6. The Bill of Rights not being recognized by the Constitution is therefore no part of the Constitution and of course of no validity. 7. The defects of the Judiciary first the multitude of Courts which occasion useless delays and expences Second the wrong organization of the Courts. 1. by being a useless number of County Courts in a year 2. The want of responsibility in the magistrates. 3. The power of increasing their number without limitation and 4. Their chosing a sheriff from among themselves—

MS (DLC: TJ Papers, 193:34427–31); entirely in Gaines's hand; undated.

[1] Manuscript: "dimished."
[2] Manuscript: "mumber."
[3] Manuscript: "dimished."
[4] Manuscript: "dimished."
[5] Manuscript: "warefare."
[6] Preceding five words interlined.
[7] Word interlined.
[8] Manuscript: "nogotiation."
[9] Gaines here canceled "the singing vulgar songs."
[10] Omitted word editorially supplied.
[11] Remainder of text on a separate sheet.
[12] Manuscript: "exective."

From Paul Hamilton

DEAR SIR Washington Sept[er] 3[d] 1811

My Son who has lately returned from Europe with public dispatches, and goes with them to M[r] Monroe, will not fail to gratify himself by calling on you: and although I am not[1] favored with a personal acquaintance with you, I cannot consistently with justice to him hesitate to announce him to you: respect for you having been a part of his education; and I do it the more readily as it affords me an opportunity to offer to you the assurance of my cordial respect & veneration. I beg your acceptance of my sincere wishes for your health & happiness, and am, Sir, truly y[rs] PAUL HAMILTON

RC (DLC); at foot of text: "M[r] Jefferson"; endorsed by TJ as a letter of 1 Sept. 1811 received seven days later and so recorded in SJL.

Hamilton's SON, Paul Hamilton (1788–1817), arrived in Washington, D.C., from Boston on 2 Sept. 1811. He set out the following day to deliver the PUBLIC DISPATCHES he brought from Europe to James Madison at Montpellier and James Monroe at his Highland estate in Albemarle County (Madison, *Papers, Pres. Ser.*, 3:441, 443, 451).

[1] Word added in left margin.

From Joseph Dougherty

Dear Sir City of Washington Septr 4th—11

I now solicit you on a cause of great importance to me, and one too in which you can make more interest for me than I can Suppose, Mr Mathers, the Door keeper for the Senate was buried the other day, and no doubt but there will be one hundred applicants for his place, my friends advise me to try for it,

Now Sir, you best know what will be the best mode to pursue, would a few lines from you to each of the Senators (or at least) those that are your friends answer a good purpose for the present as there is supposed to be several letters already sent to them

I am sir, Sorry, and should be more so, to give you so much trouble:—if I had the smallest idea that you would do it reluctantly: I can perhaps make some intercession with the federalists through my old friend Mr Otis. but you sir is my only dependant. please to advise me what will be best to do would [a][1] few words from you, to Messrs. Madison & Muroe be necessary

Sir I do not know that I ever have;—and hopes I never shall disgrace any recommendation that you in your goodness may give me

I am sir your humble Servant Jo^s Dougherty

RC (DLC); at foot of text: "Mr Thos Jefferson"; endorsed by TJ as received 8 Sept. 1811 and so recorded in SJL.

muroe: James Monroe.

[1] Omitted word editorially supplied.

From Pierre Samuel Du Pont de Nemours

Mon respectable Ami, 5 Septembre 1811.

J'envoie en Amérique trois bons Précurseurs, ma Belle Fille Madame de Pusy que vous y avez déja vue; Sa Fille très aimable qui a eu l'honneur de diner chez vous à Washington quand elle était encore enfant, et qui ne dément point ce qu'elle promettait alors; et enfin Maurice de Pusy qui n'avait que trois mois la premiere fois qu'il S'est embarqué pour les Etats-Unis, et qui est devenu l'espérance de cette branche de ma Famille.—Il a eu un commencement d'instruction dans le meilleur de nos Lycées, y était toujours parmi les premiers de Sa Classe, et y a obtenu plusieurs Prix. J'espere qu'il ne fera pas moins bien dans le College Américain où il sera placé; et je vous Serai bien obligé d'indiquer à Sa Mere auquel elle devra donner la préférence.

Ce n'est point Sans regret que je vois qu'on n'a pas encore beaucoup avancé les Etablissemens d'Instruction publique dont Votre Excellence avait eu la bonté de me demander le Plan, auquel elle avait donné Son approbation.

Ce qui pressait et ce qui presse encore le plus est la confection des livres classiques pour les petites Ecoles, c'est-à-dire pour les plus importantes de toutes: Car c'est dans les Colleges, les Universités, les Académies que Se forme le petit nombre des Savans; mais c'est dans les Ecoles primaires que la Nation entiere est élevée. C'est de là qu'elle doit Sortir pour vue de raison, de Courage, de lumieres et de Vertu.

Vous avez à présent du loisir, mon respectable ami; vous avez du génie et une grande élevation de vue, vous êtes très bon et très éclairé, faites le plan et le prospectus des quatre ou cinq livres qui Sont nécessaires pour les trois classes dont les plus petites écoles doivent être composées; pour les enfans de Sept à huit ans; de huit à neuf; de neuf à dix. Obtenez de votre Gouvernement ou d'une Souscription généreuse les douze mille dollars qui devront être distribués en prix à leurs auteurs; et voyez dans vingt ou trente ans d'ici les hommes, les citoyens qu'ils auront formés. Je n'espere pas être au milieu d'eux, mais je les vois et les admire comme Si j'y étais.

Je vous envoie la vie d'un Grand Homme Sur lequel ce genre d'idées avait beaucoup de pouvoir, et que j'ai vu attendri jusqu'aux larmes en parlant du degré de bonté que l'espece humaine est capable d'acquerir, qu'elle acquerra un jour: mais seulement après qu'elle aura joui pendant trente ou quarante années d'une bonne éducation publique et particuliere, dont de bons livres classiques pour la petite enfance sont le premier et le principal élément.

Je vous Supplie de faire en sorte que, lorsque je pourrai d'Eleutherian-Mill aller passer un mois à Monticello, je trouve ce travail ou fait ou prêt à être terminé.

Si l'on vous rappellait à la Présidence, ne la refusez pas.

Les hommes capables d'être grandement utiles à leur Patrie et à toutes les Nations, Sont aujourd'hui Si rares que pour eux la vieillesse et même les infirmités doivent être comme rien. Il est indispensable qu'ils meurent à l'ouvrage et debout.

Je vous salue avec tendresse, espérance, et respect.

DUPONT (DE NEMOURS)

EDITORS' TRANSLATION

My respectable Friend, 5 September 1811.

I am sending to America three fine precursors, my stepdaughter Madame de Pusy, whom you have already seen; her very charming daughter, who had the honor of dining at your house in Washington when she was still a child, and who does not fail to live up to all that she then promised to be; and lastly Maurice de Pusy, who was only three months old the first time he boarded a ship for the United States, and who has become the best hope of this branch of my family—He began his education at our finest secondary school, was always among the best students in his class, and received many prizes. I hope that he will do as well in the American college where he will be enrolled, and I would be much obliged if you would tell his mother which one she should choose.

I see with regret that little progress has been made toward the creation of public schools, a subject on which Your Excellency kindly asked me to draft a plan that received your approbation.

What was urgent and remains even more so is the preparation of textbooks for the primary schools, that is to say for the most important schools. Secondary schools, universities, and academies train a few learned people, but in primary schools the entire nation is educated. From them people will graduate with courage, wisdom, virtue, and the ability to reason.

You have at present some leisure, my esteemed friend; you have genius and lofty thoughts; you are a very good and wise man. Draft and design the four or five books that are needed for the three levels that comprise the primary schools: for children between the ages of seven and eight, eight and nine, and nine and ten. Obtain from the government or through a generous subscription the twelve thousand dollars that will be given to the authors in prizes, and twenty or thirty years from now look at the men, the citizens, they will have produced. I do not expect to be among them, but I can see and admire them as if I were there.

I am sending you the life of a great man on whom this sort of idea had great influence. I saw him moved to tears when speaking of the degree of goodness of which the human species is capable, and which it will someday acquire. But this will come only after mankind has enjoyed for thirty or forty years a good private and public education, whose first and principal component is good textbooks for little children.

I beg you to see to it so that I find this work done or close to completion when I am able to leave the Eleutherian Mills for a month at Monticello.

If you are called back to the presidency, do not refuse to go.

Men capable of being greatly useful to their country and to all nations are so rare these days that old age and even frailty count as nothing. Such people must die on the job and on their feet.

I salute you with affection, hope, and respect.

Dupont (de Nemours)

RC (DLC); dateline at foot of text; at head of text: "a Monsieur Jefferson"; endorsed by TJ as received 22 Dec. 1812 and so recorded in SJL. Dft (DeGH: Pierre Samuel Du Pont de Nemours Papers, Winterthur Manuscripts); in a clerk's hand, with minor emendations by Du Pont; unsigned. Translation by Dr. Roland H. Simon. Enclosure: Du Pont de Nemours, ed., *Oeuvres de Mr Turgot, mi-*

nistre d'état, précédées et accompagnées de mémoires et de notes sur sa vie, son administration et ses ouvrages (Paris, 1808–11; Sowerby, no. 2436; Poor, *Jefferson's Library*, 11 [no. 702]), vol. 1.

Du Pont published his PLAN to reform education in the United States as *Sur l'éducation nationale dans les États-Unis d'Amérique* (Paris, 1812; Poor, *Jefferson's Library*, 5 [nos. 207, 209–10]).

To James L. Edwards

SIR Monticello Sep. 5. 11.

Your letter of Aug. 20. has truly surprised me. in this it is said that for certain services performed by mr James Lyon and mr Samuel Morse, formerly editors of the Savanna Republican, I promised them the sum of 1000.D. this, Sir, is totally unfounded. I never promised to any printer on earth the sum of 1000.D. nor any other sum, for certain services performed, or for any services which that expression would imply. I have had no accounts with printers but for their newspapers, for which I have paid always the ordinary price & no more. I have occasionally joined in moderate contributions, to printers, as I have done to other descriptions of persons, distressed or persecuted, not by promise, but the actual paiment of what I contributed. When mr Morse went to Savanna, he called on me & told me he meant to publish a paper there, for which I subscribed, and paid him the year in advance. I continued to take it from his successors Everitt & M^c^lean, & Everett and Evans, and paid for it, at different epochs, up to Dec. 31. 1808. when I withdrew my subscription. you say M^c^lean informed you 'he had some expectation of getting the money, as he had recieved a letter from me on the subject.' if such a letter exists under my name, it is a forgery. I never wrote but a single letter to him; that was of the 28th of Jan. 1810. and was on the subject of the last paiment made for his newspaper, & on no other subject: and I have two reciepts of his, (the last dated Mar. 9. 1809.)[1] of paiments for his paper, both stating to be in full of all demands, and a letter of the 17th of Apr. 1810. in reply to mine, manifestly shewing he had no demand against me of any other nature. the promise is said to have been made to Morse & Lyon. were mr Morse living, I should appeal to him with confidence, as I believe him to have been a very honest man. mr Lyon I suppose to be living, and will, I am sure acquit me of any such transaction as that alledged. the truth then being that I never made the promise suggested, nor any one of a like nature to any printer or other person whatever, every principle of justice and of self respect requires that I should not listen to any such demand.

TH: JEFFERSON

RC (William Reese Company, New Haven, Conn., 2004); addressed: "James L. Edwards Boston"; franked. PoC (DLC); endorsed by TJ.

TJ first SUBSCRIBED to Samuel Morse's and James Lyon's Savannah *Georgia Republican* in June 1802. He closed his account and canceled his subscription in February 1809 (*MB*, 2:1074, 1240; TJ to John Milledge, 6 Feb. 1809 [DLC]). SJL records TJ's letter to Norman McLean of the 28TH OF JAN. 1810, but neither it nor the TWO RECIEPTS in TJ's possession have been found. SJL also records missing letters from McLean of 1 Jan. and of the 17TH OF APR. 1810, received respectively from Augusta on 17 Jan. and Savannah on 2 May 1810.

[1] Period moved inside parenthesis by Editors.

From Ralph Granger

RESPECTED SIR, Washington City Sep: 5: 1811.

My Father being absent on a journey to N England, the pleasing office of answering your's of the 1'st devolves on me—

It is reported, on what grounds I know not, that Mr James Lyon dares not be seen at his usual place of residence, but a letter directed to him at Carthage, Smith County, Tennessee, where his family resides, by their conveyance would doubtless find him—

With the greatest Respect and Esteem, Sir, I have the honour to be Your's &C. RALPH GRANGER

RC (DLC); between dateline and salutation: "Thomas Jefferson Esqr"; endorsed by TJ as received 8 Sept. 1811 and so recorded in SJL.

Ralph Granger (1790–1843), the eldest son of Postmaster General Gideon Granger, graduated from Yale University in 1810. He became an attorney and settled in Ohio, where he sat in the state senate, 1835–36, served as president of Willoughby University of Lake Erie during his last years, and became the first mayor of Fairport (Arthur S. Hamlin, *Gideon Granger* [1982], vi; *Catalogue of the Officers and Graduates of Yale University . . . 1701–1910* [1910], 86; William W. Williams, *History of Ashtabula County, Ohio* [1878], 30; Granger, *Introductory Lecture, delivered at the Willoughby Medical College of the Willoughby University of Lake Erie* [1837]; *Circular and Catalogue of the Officers, Professors and Students of Willoughby University* [1842], 7; William Ganson Rose, *Cleveland: The Making of a City* [1950], 1075; *Cleveland Herald*, 9 Dec. 1843).

From Robert Johnson

DR SIR, Great Crossings Septr. 5 1811

The right of instruction by state Legislatures has become a subject of controversy in Kentucky Perhaps on account of the state Legislature having passed a resolution to the following effect Resolved[1] That our Senators & Representatives in Congress are requested to oppose a renewal of the Charter[2] of the Bank of the United States. Two members in the lower house voted against the resolution. A request was Sent by Petition from some of the Inhabitants of Lexington to our members of Congress in favour of renewing the Charter of said Bank The resolution was also sent requesting our members to oppose the renewal. Mr Clay voted against the renewal and Mr. Pope in favour of it. It is said by the party in opposition to instructions: That it is a Dangerous and alarming usurpation of the Peoples right for state Legislatures to instruct; That the constitution has not vested any such power in the state Legislatures. Some of them agree that the people have a right to instruct & others that they have not: on the other hand it is observed:[3] that the national government possess all power given by the federal constitution and no more. That the state governments possess all powers except those prohibited or reserved[4] to the people: That the state governments are parties to the federal compact and have a right to speak their sentiments on any infraction on the Constitution: That the state Legislatures are the people by representation and are accountable to them for improper conduct: That they have a right to offer instructions on political Subjects on important occasions and if right; it is proper but ought not to do it on trivial or Doubtful occasions If instructions are disregarded the corrective will be at next election. That the Bank Charter not being confined within the ten miles square was unconstitutional and created unconstitutional criminal Jurisdiction in the federal Courts (over Counterfeiters of notes) not given by the constitution. They refer to the virginia resolutions in 1798 and their reconsideration at their next session. That the Institution admitted Brittish Subjects to hold the greater part of the stock in this great monied institution and It was as impolitic as to permit aliens to hold land and have influence on the great landed interest. It seems the right of instruction to members in Parliament of G. B. by the people was not questioned for 150 years That Judge Blackstone was the first who oppose[d] it in England Since that time the Brittish government has become more corrup[t] having hinted some points in controversy and being desirous to have your opinion on state Legislative instructions to their Senators and representatives in Congress on Subjects not included within the powers given to them by the constitution also on the Doctrine[5] of instruction in cases of policy which are included in those powers Delegated to them If it be not Disagreable or inconvenient you will very much oblige me in sending a letter on the Subject directed to me at the Post office at the Great Crossings, Scott County Kentucky or to my son Richard M. Johnson at Congress who will forward it to me. If I have made too free in addressing this letter to you I hope you will forgive your friend and obedient Servant Robert Johnson

RC (DLC); edge trimmed; originally endorsed by TJ as a letter of 25 Sept. 1811 received 2 Oct. 1811 and so recorded in SJL; TJ later corrected the date of the letter in his endorsement but not in SJL.

Robert Johnson (1745–1815) was a native of Orange County who first traveled to what is now Kentucky in 1779, moved there with his family the following year, settled about 1783 at Great Crossing in Scott County, and amassed an estate totaling more than 100,000 acres. He established a reputation as an Indian fighter in 1780 and 1782, and in the latter year he represented Fayette County in the Virginia House of Delegates. Johnson took part in conventions to draft constitutions for Kentucky in 1792 and 1799. He was also a state senator from Woodford County, 1792–95, represented Scott County eight times in the Kentucky House of Representatives between 1796 and 1813, and helped to establish the boundary between Kentucky and Virginia. His son Richard Mentor Johnson became the ninth vice president of the United States (John E. Kleber and others, eds., *The Kentucky Encyclopedia* [1992], 76, 102–3, 475–6; Clay, *Papers*, 1:183; Leonard, *General Assembly*, 145; John D. Barnhart, "Frontiersmen and Planters in the Formation of Kentucky," *Journal of Southern History* 7 [1941]: 26; Lexington [Ky.] *Western Monitor*, 27 Oct. 1815).

For the Kentucky legislature's RESOLUTION instructing its congressional delegation to oppose RENEWAL of the charter of the Bank of the United States, see John Jordan to TJ, 1 Sept. 1811, and note. William BLACKSTONE argued that every member of Parliament, "though chosen by one particular district, when elected and returned serves for the whole realm. . . . And therefore he is not bound, like a deputy in the united provinces, to consult with, or take the advice, of his constituents upon any particular point, unless he himself thinks it proper or prudent so to do" (*Commentaries on the Laws of England* [Oxford, 1765–69; Sowerby, nos. 1806–7], 1:155).

[1] Manuscript: "Resolred."
[2] Manuscript: "Chater."
[3] Manuscript: "obseved."
[4] Manuscript: "reseved."
[5] Manuscript: "Doctrime."

To James Lyon

Sir Monticello Sep. 5. 1811.

I inclose you the copy of a letter I have recieved from a James L. Edwards of Boston. you will percieve at once it's swindling object. it appeals to two dead men, and one (yourself) whom he supposes I cannot get at. I have written him an answer which may perhaps prevent his persevering in the attempt, for the whole face of his letter betrays a consciousness of it's guilt. but perhaps he may expect that I would sacrifice a sum of money rather than be disturbed with encountering a bold falsehood. in this he is mistaken; and to prepare to meet him, should he repeat his demand, and considering that he has presumed to implicate your name in this attempt, I take the liberty of requesting a letter from you bearing testimony to the truth of my never having made to you, or within your knolege or information, any such promise to yourself, your partner Morse, or any other. my confidence in your character leaves me without a doubt of your honest aid in repelling this base & bold attempt to fix on me practices to which no honors, or powers in this world would ever have induced me to stoop. I have sollicited none, intrigued for none. those which my country has thought proper to confide to me, have been of their own mere motion, unasked by me. such practices as this letter-writer imputes to me, would have proved me unworthy of their confidence.

It is long since I have known any thing of your situation or pursuits. I hope they have been succesful, and tender you my best wishes that they may continue so, & for your own health & happiness.

TH: JEFFERSON

PoC (DLC); at foot of text: "Mr James Lyon." Enclosure: James L. Edwards to TJ, 20 Aug. 1811.

James Lyon (1776–1824), journalist, shared the Republican politics of his father, Congressman Matthew Lyon. He founded fourteen newspapers in his native Vermont, Virginia, five other southern states, and the District of Columbia during a thirty-year career. TJ and James Madison both subscribed to his newspapers. Lyon died in Cheraw, South Carolina, where he had established the *Pee Dee Gazette* in 1820 (*PTJ*, esp. 32:261–2, 329; *MB*; Aleine Austin, *Matthew Lyon: "New Man" of the Democratic Revolution, 1749–1822* [1981], 17, 76–7, 121; Brigham, *American Newspapers*, esp. 2:1447; Washington *Daily National Intelligencer*, 28 Apr. 1824).

To Francis Eppes

DEAR FRANCIS Monticello Sep. 6. 11.

Your letter of Aug. 19. came to hand only 4. or 5. days ago. I should have answered it by post had not Martin arrived with your second. I am glad to learn you are becoming a Roman, which a familiarity with their history will certainly make you. the putting you into qui, quae, quod, was only to strengthen your memory, which you may do quite as well by getting pieces of poetry by heart. Jefferson & myself intend you a visit in November, and it will then be a question for the consideration of your papa and yourself whether you shall not return with us & visit your cousins. this will be acceptable to us all, and only deprecated by the partridges & snowbirds against which you may commence hostilities. adieu my dear Francis, be industrious in advancing yourself in knolege, which with your good dispositions, will ensure the love of others, & your own happiness, & the love & happiness of none more than of

Yours affectionately Th: Jefferson

RC (NcU: Southern Historical Collection, Hubard Family Papers); addressed: "Francis Eppes Millbrook." PoC (CSmH: JF); endorsed by TJ.

Eppes's letter to TJ of aug. 19, not found, is recorded in SJL as received from "Millbrook (near Ça ira)" on 1 Sept. 1811. qui, quae, quod: declension of the Latin pronoun for who, which, and what. jefferson: Thomas Jefferson Randolph.

To John Wayles Eppes

Dear Sir Monticello Sep. 6. 11.

I had before learned with great concern your affliction with the rheumatism. your remedy of the cold bath is new to me, except a single instance of the wife of an overseer of mine who uses the cold bath every day of her life, and the day she omits it, has a return of Rheumatic symptoms. I have had an attack of it myself for two months past, confined a part of the time, without fever, and without pain except when I attempted to walk. I rode with little inconvenience, and took a journey to Bedford in the time, but am still unable to walk a hundred or two yards, & that with pain & great feebleness. a sensible degree of amendment latterly has diverted my determination to go to the warm springs, which you ought to do. they are the only infallible remedy in the world. My sister Carr has at length yielded to a course of gradual debility of two years, & so gradual that it could not be said from one week, or even one month to another that she was sensibly worse, and died in the same way. I am obliged to be at Poplar Forest on the 25th of Nov. on a change of managers. Jefferson is to go with me, and we propose calling on you, either going or returning. he has been intending a visit to you for some time, but has been prevented by different casualties. when I come it will be an object to go to the top of Willis's mountain to take it's latitude from the highest point which constitutes my meridian here, and to repeat the observations afterwards from any place in it's neighborhood due East or West from it. but I can go to the top only in the case of it's being accessible on horseback,[1] for I could not walk a hundred yards up it. Patsy is well & her family. they went to Edgehill at the beginning of harvest, at the close of which my trip to Bedford occasioned their continuance there, & other accidents have still detained them. a part of the family is now come, and the rest will be here within 2. or 3. days. we expect within a few days a visit from mr & mrs Madison, the Secretaries at War & of the Navy and their families. Monroe is now at his seat. however the visit of the two Secretaries may be prevented by the incident of a British frigate and sloop of war stationing themselves in the Delaware & refusing to withdraw. a person of perfect truth direct from Washington told me he had it from the Secretary of the Navy himself who said he should remove them by force if practicable. Foster has explicitly and officially stated in writing that his government finds it necessary to take possession of the ocean, and permit no commerce on it but thro the ports of Great Britain. unable to maintain their navy, in it's present gigantic state, from their own resources, I have been confident for 4. or 5. years they meant this. you will see by the papers that they are acting on this principle. in fact war seems determined on their part, & inevitable on ours if the old king lives. if he dies there is some chance that a change of administration may produce a change of disposition; and I consider the expectation of the king's death as the only circumstance which ought to delay the calling of Congress and taking immediate possession [of][2] Canada, before the Indians commence open hostilities. this will put an everlasting end to their aggressions. Orleans will fall for want of a force within itself capable of defending it. no militia more distant than that of the Misipi territory will ever be prevailed on to go to it's defence or recovery. regular troops alone can be depended on for that & the raising a number superior to what the British may place there will be slow & difficult. Accept the assurances of my constant and affectionate esteem and respect. TH: JEFFERSON

P.S. the removal of vines would now be entirely desperate the proper time for them & the figs will be in the spring when you can have any number.

PoC (DLC); at foot of first page: "M[r] Eppes"; endorsed by TJ.

In the CHANGE OF MANAGERS at Poplar Forest, Jeremiah A. Goodman replaced Burgess Griffin. JEFFERSON: Thomas Jefferson Randolph. PATSY: Martha Jefferson Randolph. Highland was James Monroe's Albemarle County SEAT. The FRIGATE *Belvidere* and the SLOOP OF WAR *Emulous* were among the British ships patrolling in and near the Delaware River late in August 1811 (Wilkes-Barre *Gleaner, and Luzerne Advertiser*, 20 Sept. 1811).

[1] Preceding two words interlined.
[2] Omitted word editorially supplied.

To Randolph Jefferson

Dear brother Monticello Sep. 6. 11.

Our worthy[1] sister Carr has at length yielded to the wasting complaint which has for two or three years been gaining upon her. without any increase of pain, or any other than her gradual decay, she expired three days ago, and was yesterday deposited here by the side of the companion who had been taken from her 38. years before. she had the happiness, and it is a great one, of seeing all her children become worthy & respectable members of society & enjoying the esteem of all. present my best respects to my sister and be assured of my constant affection. Th: Jefferson

PoC (ViU: TJP-CC); endorsed by TJ.

my sister: TJ's sister-in-law Mitchie Pryor Jefferson.

SJL records a missing letter of this date from TJ to his sister Anne Scott Marks.

[1] Word reworked from "sis."

From David Campbell

Dear Sir, Abingdon V[a] 7th September 1811.

Without a personal acquaintance I beg leave to ask of you an answer to the following enquiries. In October 1780 a volunteer expedition was fitted out from the County of Washington under the command of Colonel William Campbell, which with extraordinary promptitude marched to the State of South Carolina and in conjunction with other militia from the Carolinas defeated and made prisoners, the forces under Colonel Furguson posted on the hights of Kings-mountain. The signal advantages which resulted to the American cause from this achievement are well known to you, and will always be remembered with the most lively emotions by the Southern people.

In a notice of the Council of May last which has appeared for some time in the different Newspapers I observe that it was the intention of Virginia to grant a bounty in Lands to her Officers and Soldiers on the Continental and State establishments; to those who were employed in the marine service of the Commonwealth and "to those meritorious persons to whom special donations of Land were intended to have been made."

Your knowledge of the transactions of those times will enable you to say who those meritorious persons were. Was it not intended to include such as had rendered essential services to the country, and were not on the continental or State establishments or in the marine service; and were not the volunteers of Kings-mountain of this description?

I have been informed that Colonel Campbell for those extraordinary services received a military warrant of 5.000 acres, but no application has yet been made by the soldiers or any other of the Officers, some of whom acted a most distinguished part, particularly the Edmistons three of whom fell. The Virginia Legislature at their Session immediately afterwards acknowledged the services of the militia on this occasion, in the most grateful manner.

Excuse the liberty I have taken and beleive to be With the highest esteem Your Ob[t] serv[t] DAVID CAMPBELL

RC (DLC); endorsed by TJ as received 18 Sept. 1811 and so recorded in SJL.

David Campbell (1779–1859) studied law as a young man but made his living in Abingdon as a merchant and investor in land. He held a commission in the United States Army from 1812 to 1814, rising from major to lieutenant colonel and serving in infantry regiments on the Canadian frontier. Campbell sat in the Senate of Virginia, 1820–24, and then succeeded his father as clerk of Washington County. Initially a Jeffersonian, he eventually migrated from the Democratic to the Whig Party. The Virginia legislature elected Campbell a major general of militia in 1834 and governor in 1837. Following his three-year term, he returned to his Montcalm estate near Abingdon (*DVB*; Heitman, *U.S. Army*, 277; Leonard, *General Assembly*, 306, 311, 316, 321; *Daily Richmond Enquirer*, 24 Mar. 1859).

On 23 May 1811 the Virginia COUNCIL of State ordered that in the interest of determining "the amount of the unsatisfied claims for land" dating from the Revolutionary War, "all persons having such claims are required to present them to the executive of this state on or before the 20th day of November next, authenticated by such evidence as the law now requires" (Richmond *Enquirer*, 31 May 1811). The EDMISTONS: Ensign Andrew Edmondson and Lieutenant Robert Edmondson Sr. were killed and Lieutenant Robert Edmondson Jr. and Major William Edmondson were wounded on 7 Oct. 1780 at the Battle of Kings Mountain (Heitman, *Continental Army*, 212). On 10 and 15 Nov. 1780 the lower and upper houses of the VIRGINIA LEGISLATURE separately voted their unanimous thanks to "colonel William Campbell, of the county of Washington, and the officers and soldiers of the militia under his command" for their recent victory over "a party of the enemy commanded by major Ferguson, consisting of about eleven hundred and five men (British and Tories) strongly posted on King's Mountain" (Philadelphia *Pennsylvania Packet or the General Advertiser*, 30 Dec. 1780).

To Charles Wingfield

DEAR SIR Monticello Sep. 8. 11.

The death of mrs Carr, my sister, which took place a few days ago, and the desire that she should be buried here by the side of her husband, induce me to trouble you with a request that you would be so kind as to come and officiate on the occasion of her funeral. it is proposed that it shall take place on Wednesday the 11th at 12 aclock. it will be private, her near connections only proposing to attend, and our desire is to have the ceremony performed in a simple way, with prayers Etc as you shall think proper. I defer inviting her friends until I can recieve an answer from you by the bearer, whether we may hope the favor of your attendance. accept the assurance of my great esteem & respect. Th: Jefferson

RC (Kate Joyner Bailey, Keswick, Virginia, 2004; photocopy in ViU: TJP); addressed: "Charles Wingfield." PoC (MHi); at foot of text: "Revd Charles Wingfield"; endorsed by TJ.

Charles Wingfield (1752–1819) may have been the man of that name who attended Hampden-Sydney College and served as a tutor there in 1778. He lived on the Hardware River at Bell-air fourteen miles southwest of Monticello. Wingfield served as an Albemarle County magistrate in 1794 and had been sheriff briefly at the time of his death. He was licensed as a Presbyterian minister in 1808 and officiated at least twice at Monticello funerals (Woods, *Albemarle*, 345; *MB*, 2:959, 1268, 1279; Herbert C. Bradshaw, *History of Hampden-Sydney College* [1976], 45, 77; Richard Wingfield Quarles, "The Wingfields of Albemarle County, Virginia: A Correction," *Magazine of Virginia Genealogy* 26 [1988]: 83; Hanover Presbytery Minutes, 4:230, 241, 242 [21 Oct. 1807, 7 May 1808]; Albemarle Co. Order Book [1808–10], 294; Albemarle Co. Will Book, 7:7–9, 27–9).

From Charles Wingfield

Dear Sir, Bell-air September the 8th 1811.

I received yours, of the date abovementioned, have observed the contents; shall attend at Monticello on wednesday the eleventh, at 12 OClock, to officiate on the occasion of the funeral Solemnities. Accept the assurance of my great esteem & respect.

Charles Wingfield

RC (MHi); addressed: "Mr Thomas Jefferson Monticello"; endorsed by TJ as received 8 Sept. 1811 and so recorded in SJL.

From Charles Willson Peale

My good friend Farm Persevere Sepr 9th 1811.

I most chearfully accept your kind invitation of a renewal of corispondance; tho' with very [little][1] expectation that I shall be able to add to your stock of Information in your favorite occupations, however with this pleasing hope, that as my subjects must necessarily be on the culture of the Earth, I shall[2] get instruction in my new occupation, that of a farmer, which thus may be difused to others, as I am willing to put into practice every[3] thing that promisses to melorate the condition of Man. To produce the best effect of labour with ease how vastly important! Your Mould-board ought to be studied by every Man that makes a Plow, if the form of it was given to every Plow, the land would be infinitely better plowed; greater products consequently, withall less labour to Horses. I have lately sought for one of the best Plow-makers in the vicinity of Germantown, and made a model of your invention in his shop, and required of him to make me a plow & give the mould-board that form. He thought he could do it with one of his slabs which had in part some of the natural twist, such as wheel-rights generally provide for mould-boards, after my Plow was made I found it had not the 4½ Inches hanging over, therefore insufficient to turn the sod completely over. This mechanicks excuse, was, that his slab was not quite thick enough to form the angle. I have been examining all those of Cast Iron that I could find in Stores, none of them please me, & therefore I am now making an experiment of twisting a white-oak board by means of Steam. I cut down a sound White-oak, split the But into several slabs of sufficient thickness &c I intend to prepare the following means to give the proper twist—Mortice of the size of the end of the slab in a log fixed in the ground, placing the slab perpendicular into the Mortice, to the upper end of the slab fix two pieces of Scantlin, thus:

To steam the slab, take a Hogshead, taking out the head & putting within the slab, place the head on the top of the cask with sufficient weight on it to confine the steam, from my Steam-kettle insert its tube at the bung-hole. After the slab has got a full proportion of twist, secure the long lever-arms untill the slab is completely seasoned, which perhaps will take 2 or 3 weeks, when all its sides are exposed to the air. It will I expect then keep its form, more especially if well secured in the framing of the Plow. one thing may opperate against such Mould-boards—Farmers too frequently leave their Plows in the field, exposed to Sun & Rain, which may possibly injure the twist, therefore a well formed casting must be preferable—will wear better & smoother. yet they are not unfrequently broken on our Stony Lands. The well formed mould-board is very easily covered with steel Saw blades; they can be twisted, if not very thick, without heat.

you ask whether the Museum will not suffer by my retiring to the farm. I thought it necessary to satisfy public men that the Museum could be well conducted without my presence, it was also necessary to give my Son Rubens a profession that would engage him to a good work, finding he was fond of Natural history and liked to arrange & dress the Museum, I addressed him thus, I am growing Old and may be taken away soon, it will be a satisfaction to me to see the Museum well managed without my attention to it—I have gained much credit for my exertions in forming, and more honour than I expected, or have deserved, I wish you to receive all the honour of it in future, I wish to be out of sight, by retiring to the Country, to muse away the remainder of my life—you must give me a certain sum yearly and all you can gain more shall be for the improvement of the Museum and a surpluss for your emolument, and in proportion to your good management[4] so will your profits be encreased, & the higher your reputation will be exalted. he accepted my offer, and I can very truely say that I have very great satisfaction in finding that he has improved the Museum far beyond my expectation and I think you will frequently hear from those who visit it, how neat and handsomely it is arranged, and withall how very instructing, and, how very[5] beneficial to the Public. You ask whether "the farm is interresting?" my answer is that it is exactly what you would wish, "a rich spot of Earth, well watered, and near a good market for the produce of the Garden." I am situated $\frac{1}{2}$ a mile from Germantown and have the same distance to the old-york turnpike road—two Streams run through my land, who's sourses are within 3 miles, on each there are 3 mills above me, from the east stream I can have 23 feet head of water, and on the other 10 feet within my own land, and liberty from my neighbours land below to add 5 feet more—This stream is the nearest to my dwelling. It is my intention as soon as I can conveniently have it executed, to Build the End of a Mill-house, which may be extended if wanted in future, my object at present is only to apply it to the saving of labour of the farm, such as churning of Butter, Grinding our tools, beating of Homony, washing of Linnen, a turn bench &c &c all of which may be performed by bands, thus expence of wheels is avoided. on the other Stream I intend to Build a Grist Mill, after my farm is put into compleat order, if I am able to make it so. I began with putting out the farm on shares, and I thought I had engaged a good farmer, for he had served his apprenteship with Joseph Cooper, opposite Philad[a] a noted good farmer. But my farmer was too lazy a man, and too poor to hire men to do the work for him, consequently every thing was put too late into the ground, my crops fell short, corn untoped & all the fodder lost, and all my Cattle half starved throughout the winter. my only consolation was that I had no repugnance in putting my farmer away, And taking the whole charge on myself. It is a fact, that this year I have had less trouble than the last, my Crops plentiful, and every thing looks as well as I should wish, except the extended part of my Garden; a part which I had proposed to make an early market Garden, with a SE aspect; side of a Hill, promising to produce early crops—my first planting of Strawberry beds succeeded, and every thing was promising when our harvest came on, I thought that a few days neglect of the Garden might be soon repaired by giving assistance to the Gardiner, Rain succeeding a long drought, made the weeds grow so fast that the loss of labour could not be recovered, great part of my new Garden became a wilderness I am now taught to know that a garden must be constantly attended to—This is not the only mistake I have committed, even with the best intentions, I have laughed at my folly in thinking I could do wonders by my steady perseverance. I see my farm, and those of all my neighbours around having an abundance of weeds, I thought that if I cut off those weeds while in Blossom that I should prevent them from seeding, and by a persevering labour of cuting them off, I should at last have my place free of weeds—I procured bryer hooks, and set to work in my destruction of the S[t] Johnsworth, wild Carrots & plantain, it was my daily work for a long time, and I conceived that I was doing wonders, I made the muscels of my right arm sore, I then began with my left hand as I thought that I must go on. But after some time visiting those parts where my Herculian labour began, I found that where I had cut off one head, Hydra-like a half dozen had sprouted up in its place, and, then I found that I ought to have rooted them up, as I had done with the Docks, to do any good. It then recured to me that I had seen an experiment of planting Guinea & brown corn and cutting it down when it was 3 or 4 feet high for fodder, each plant then gave 4 or 5 sprouts, this was also cut down and a third crop of encreased sprouts[6] was obtained for food, to his cattle, that was not suffered to graise on his fields.—This Gentleman is a speculative farmer about 3 miles distant from me, when I have time to pay him some more visits I may be furnished with subjects for another letter. As I have every thing to learn about farming, I gain all the knowledge[7] I can from my neighbours as well as from Books. Pray Sir do you find the french work entitled <u>Maison Rustic</u> contains useful knowledge for the American farmer and Gardiner? I once had that work, and taking a thought that keeping a library which I did not use, was a folly, I therefore sent it & all those which I thought I should not want, and made a sacrifise of them at auction. But the important reason I have for liking the farmers life, is yet to be told, For many years before I came to this place, my lungs was not sound; salt phlegm troubled me, and I seldom could get into sound sleep before I had thrown off that Phlegm—By using a great deal of exercise in the open air; with hilly grounds, fine Water and temperate eating I am more than paid for the cost of the farm, by strong health. It is true that I had experienced considerable benefit by an abridgment of my Solid food, before I left the City, I had been relieved from Colicks and head-achs; from the time I had read Sr John Sinclears code of Longevity, about the time my Son Rembrandt went to France.

Milk food may also have contributed to cure my Lunges; it serves for drink as well as food, and we have it in perfection in the Country but shamefully spoiled by the retailers of it in the City.

10th The last line gives me the thought of a Machine to carry milk to Market, like one I contrived to take my milk from the Cow-pen to the Spring-House, which saves a great deal of labour—a short description of it may be acceptable, I got a large ceder Tub of an Oval form made with a cover to it, a little below the top are 4 pegs to rest a strainer on, a wire of N° 1. make to fit its place, a broad hem to run the wire through. To prevent the wire from rusting, I varnished it. A

frame to let the Tub[8] moove freely in, with pivots in opposite direction to those in the Tub, and thus it swings like the mariners compass— The carriage has 3 wheels, the hind wheels with a crook'd axle-Tree to let the carriage be low. The strainer prevents the splashing of the Milk from perpendicular jolts.

The pivots of the Tub so as admit it to be tilted to pour into a pan set on the forepart of the Carriage, having a lip to the Tub to prevent the spilling of Milk. The fore wheel with a swivel, and the tongue imbraces the axle tree to turn the wheel to the right or left—

altho' my drawing is[9] very slight, yet with the description sufficient for your comprehension, Such a Carriage on a larger Scale to be drawn by a Horse would be good to carry milk to the City, and the profits will pay for the trouble. in the hot weather this Summer, they could not get milk at any price, at least for a few days. A Grass farm gives the least trouble, and most profit near to the City—I shall endeavor to make mine such, but time is necessary for this as well as perfectioning of Fruit Tree's. I dont want fruit Tree's to make Cyder,

I consider it a pernicious liquor, as causing Stone and Gout &c. I have further observed that the time of making Cyder, is in a busey season with the farmer, and much very necessary business is neglected through their love of Cyder. some of my friends tell me that I ought to make Cyder for Sale, I know that where[10] it is made it[11] will be drank, and the profit of making it is, small, the apples sent to market is more profitable in[12] every point of view—last year being a plentiful year for apples, I dryed a great many of them, I made sliding stages, so that on the appearance of Rain, they were drawn in, under cover, with very little trouble. the failure of Apples this year, I am thus supplied for another year. I am endeavoring to have fruit of every kind near my dwelling Trees at a distance we cannot keep from pillagers. Peach trees ought to be planted with us every year, however I cannot help thinking that the owners of Peach trees neglect attending to the roots at the proper seasons to distroy the worms. I have thought if our Peach trees could be preserved untill they become large & strong, that they would be less liable to be injured by worms. I am told that the Chinease put casses round the[13] lower part of their tree's filled with sand. Mr Richard Wistar, a brother of the Doctor, is trying the chinease method of preserving[14] them. I dont recollect that the people of maryland had any difficulty to preserve their Tree's, and I presume that in Virginia, being still further South, that Peach tree's are equally lasting?

I wish to know the best construction of a Kiln for drying of fruit which I contemplate building, after I have done with some other more necessary works. I find my hands & head[15] full of business, even rainey days, I contrive to give my Men full imployment in my workshop. because we are learning to make all our farming Utensils. my present labourers are all young men, and teaching them the use of Carpenters tools, may be of some importance to them hereafter. I am fond of such work, more especially as by it I can fill up all vacant hours and thus drive away ennui. yet I do not entirely neglect the Brush, I have painted a few portraits with encaustic Colours from my son Rembrandt's instruction, and hope to produce some pictures of Value on[16] account of their colouring.

Some of my friends told me that I would soon be tired of a country life, as others of their acquaintance had been. I believe my fondness for the farmers life is becoming daily stronger.

I have been making some experiments to know whether Plaster or ashes answers best on my land, also different modes of producing Potatoes. After my Crops are gathered, I will give you the result, if it is deserving of notice. I wish you health & long life, & am with due respect[17] your friend C W Peale

RC (DLC); at foot of text: "Thomas Jefferson Esqr"; endorsed by TJ as received 22 Sept. 1811 and so recorded in SJL. PoC (PPAmP: Peale Letterbook).

a rich spot of earth . . . produce of the garden: Peale is quoting from TJ's letter of 20 Aug. 1811. docks: *Rumex*, a weedy plant of the buckwheat family. guinea corn is a variety of millet or grain sorghum. Job Roberts was probably the nearby speculative farmer (Peale, *Papers*, 3:49, 60n). maison rustique: Charles Estienne and Jean Liebault, *Maison Rustique, or the Covntrie Farme*, trans. Richard Surflet (London, 1600; Sowerby, no. 694; and later eds.). Sir John Sinclair's work on longevity was *An Essay on Longevity* (London, 1802; Sowerby, no. 985).

1 Omitted word editorially supplied.
2 Word interlined in place of "must."
3 Manuscript: "very."
4 Manuscript: "managenent."
5 Manuscript: "every."
6 Manuscript: "spouts."
7 Preceding two words interlined.
8 Manuscript: "Tup."
9 Manuscript: "it."
10 Manuscript: "were."
11 Manuscript: "is."
12 Manuscript: "is."
13 Manuscript: "round the <*roots*> the."
14 Manuscript: "perseving."
15 Preceding two words interlined.
16 Manuscript: "or."
17 Manuscript: "respespect."

From Nathaniel H. Hooe

Dr Sir King George ct Sept 10th 11

I received a letter from Mr John Daingerfield of the 2nd Inst who says he was authorised by Mrs Mary Daingerfield to make a request of me whether I had written to you relative to the Balance of money due her & whether I had herd from you & if I had to be informed of the prospect of her geting the money due her Viz the full hire of Edmund with some balances of Intirest that is due her from the times that her moneys became due & not punctually paid, I informed Mr Daingerfield that I had written to you on the subject of a payment that I had reced no answer to the letter I had written to you, but expected one on the 5th Inst at the post office at King George Ct House, & if I received one I would send her a copy, be assurred sir that a speedy payment to Mrs Daingerfield & myself would be a very great accommodation to us Yours Very Respectfuly

Nathl H. Hooe

RC (MHi); addressed: "Mr Thos Jefferson Albemarl Ct Monticello"; franked; endorsed by TJ as received 2 Oct. 1811 and so recorded in SJL; with TJ's Notes on a Conversation with Nathaniel H. Hooe, 6 Jan. 1812, on address leaf.

To William McClure

SIR Monticello Sep. 10. 1811.

In order to commence the establishment for family manufacture in our neighborhood, on which we conversed the other day, I will, for myself, engage of you a spinning Jenny, and a loom with a flying shuttle, doing towards them myself whatever my workmen can do; I will furnish six women or girls to work for myself on them under your direction, build a house for them to lodge in, contribute to a common manufacturing room, & dwelling house for yourself, all of logs, furnish subsistence for my own people, contribute a quota of corn & pork for that of your family, furnish the materials for my own people to work up, giving you, for your trouble, such proportion of what shall be woven as shall be agreed on: all however on the conditions that the numbers to be employed in the factory shall not exceed a limit to be agreed on, and that the establishment shall be at a distance to be agreed on from the two[1] towns in the neighborhood, & on the opposite side of the river from them: and I should suggest as a convenient position some spot in the woods near the Edgehill and Lego line, where a spring may be found. these propositions are submitted to you for consideration, with my best wishes for the success of the establishment, & for your own welfare.

TH: JEFFERSON

PoC (MHi); at foot of text: "Mr Mclure"; endorsed by TJ.

William McClure (McLure), weaver, successfully petitioned the South Carolina legislature in 1795 to authorize a lottery to help him establish a cotton factory in that state. After acquiring a reputation as a skilled manufacturer of spinning machines, he relocated to North Carolina in the winter of 1808–09. McClure moved to Albemarle County in 1811 at the behest of TJ, Thomas Mann Randolph, James Monroe, and eight of their neighbors, each of whom pledged $50 toward the liquidation of his North Carolina debts. In that year TJ and Randolph also hired McClure to superintend their small cloth factory and instruct slaves assigned to learn the art of spinning there. He gave up the position two years later, after his charges were sufficiently skilled to carry on without him (*Acts and Resolutions of the General Assembly of the state of South Carolina passed in Nov. and Dec. 1795* [Charleston, S.C., 1796], 19–20; Raleigh *Star*, 16 Feb., 6 Apr. 1809; *MB*, esp. 2:1278, 1279, 1286; TJ to Nathaniel Macon, 24 Sept. 1811; TJ to McClure, 16 Oct. 1813; McClure's signature as witness to Will of Anne Scott Marks, 26 Mar. 1813; Letter of Recommendation for McClure by TJ and Randolph, 12 Mar. 1814).

The TWO TOWNS IN THE NEIGHBORHOOD, Charlottesville and Milton, were both situated on the southern side of the Rivanna River.

[1] Word interlined.

From James Walker

Dear Sir Hardware, sept[r] 10th 1811.

I send the bill of scantling for your sawmill which you gave to me the other day=as also a bill for the pitt gears of the same=the bill you gave me was not the sam that I supposed—I sent you a 2[d] bill whilst you ware at Beadford which I suppose your servant has not delivered to you, however you may destroy that as the two which I now send will be sufficient=please have them filled up as soon as may be convenient=I wish you to refer putting up the pittwalls untill I come again which will be in two or three weeks—

I am with respect your Ob[t] serv[t] Ja[s] Walker

RC (DLC); addressed: "Monticello ℘ stephen"; endorsed by TJ as received 12 Sept. 1811 and so recorded in SJL.

Neither the bill that TJ gave Walker THE OTHER DAY nor Walker's 2[D] BILL has been found. REFER can mean the reserving of a subject for later consideration (*OED*).

ENCLOSURES

I

James Walker's Timber List for Thomas Jefferson's Sawmill

Nomber	Length in ft &. Inches	Breadth in inches	Thickness in Inches—	Terms for the different pieces of Timber
2	50	14	12	Main sills pine or poplar
2	50	9	9	Plates ditto
3	11.½	18	12	Cross sills—
8	9.¼	9	9	Posts—
2	9.¼	11	9	ditto—
2	11.½	11	11	Fender posts pine or oak
1	12	11	11	Enterties—
2	12	9	9	ditto—
24	11.½	8	6	sleepers—
2	14	8	6	ditto—
1	30	8.½	6.½	for Carriage pine to be very straight
1	30	7.½	6½	ditto ditto ditto
2	4.¼	11	3.¾	ditto—
2	5.¾	16	8—	Headblocks—oak
2	9.¼	4.½	3.½	saw frame pine or oak
2	6.½	12	3.½	ditto ditto

10	7.½	7	4	Braces—
3	9.½	7	4	ditto—
8	13	10	1.½	way plank pine or oak—
8	13	8.½	1.¼	oak to shoe the carriage—
3	11	13	4.¼	pine or oak for Rag wheel
3	5.½	6	2.¼	pine for ditto—
[1]00	1	3	3	good hickory or white oak for coggs
8	1	2.½	2.½	dogwood for rounds—
[3]0	1	4.½	3.½	way coggs white oak
[3]0	1	3.½	3.½	ditto ditto

MS (DLC: TJ Papers, 194:34447); edges trimmed; entirely in Walker's hand; undated; endorsed by Walker: "Bill of Timbers for Mr. Jeffersons Sawmill 1811."

ENTERTIES (obsolete form of interdice) are horizontal pieces of timber used to connect two vertical pieces. HEADBLOCKS hold the log on the carriage while it is being sawed (*OED*).

II

James Walker's Timber List for Thomas Jefferson's Sawmill Pit Gears

Nomber	Length in feet &. parts	Breadth in Inches &. parts	Thickness in Inches &. parts	Terms for different pieces—	
18	8	19.½	3¼	shrouding for Water wheel heart pine	Clear of cracks
8	20.½	9.½	3.¾	arms for ditto ditto	
50	3.½	18	.⅞	Buckets for ditto ditto	
50	3.½	3	1.½	Elboes for ditto pine	
76	3.¾	10	.⅞	Soling for ditto heart pine	
16	9.½	19	5.½	Back cants for 2 cogwheels of the spurr kind &. heart pine	*<Cogwheels>*
16	7.½	17	3	Face ditto for ditto ditto	
8	18.½	16	3.¾	arms for ditto ditto	
2	18	9	3.¾	Locks for the arms ditto	
350	1.¼	3.½	3.½	good Locust for spurr cogs	
12	18.I.[1]	2.½	2.½	dogwood for rounds	
2	5	16	13	Main headblocks oak or pine heart	
4	3.½	6	6	spurrs for the headblocks to rest on ditto	
6	12	13	2	white oak for wallowers &.C.	

MS (DLC: TJ Papers, 194:34448); in Walker's hand, with one insertion by TJ; undated; endorsed by Walker: "Bill scantling for the pitt gears of Mr. Jeffersons Saw Mill—Septr 1811."

[1] Abbreviation inserted by TJ.

To Benjamin Smith Barton

Dear Sir Monticello Sep. 11. 11.

Mr Oemler, not having found me here, delivered me your letter of May 1. on the 19th Ult. at a place 90. miles Southwestwardly near the New London of this state, which I visit frequently, & with considerable stay. this absence & the date of delivery will account for this late answer. We are in no hurry for Persoone, and I am happy in it's emploiment to a good purpose. for altho' I do not know exactly the extent of the work you are engaged in, I am sure it will be useful & add instruction to the public.

The river Hardware, after which you enquire, passes within 10. miles of me. it's name is pronounced as the same term when applied to the merchandize called hardware. I think the name undoubtedly English, and given when this part of the country was first settled, which was only 80. years ago; the earliest grant of land I have seen or heard of being of 1730. & bordering on that river, which is in fact but a creek. I conclude it English, as well from it's idiom, as from the fact that every other name, in the country roundabout, is English: and it is a singular circumstance that while the waters of the neighboring rivers, York, Rappahanoc & Patomac, North, and Appamattox & Roanoke in the South, have retained abundance of Indian names, there does not remain a single one, as far as I can recollect, to the waters of James river, covering one third of the state below the Alleghany ridge. all is English. you may observe that in New England, the next oldest settlement, the names are almost wholly English. the names in the neighborhood of Hardware are Willis's river, Slate river, Rockfish, Buffalo, Tye river, Piney river, Fluvanna, Rivanna, Moreman's river, Mechum's river E^tc

You will have seen the name of a mr Bradbury among the adventurers from St Louis up the Missouri, & lately returned thence to St Louis. he is an English Artisan from Liverpool, who being desirous to move his family to this country, and not free, by their regulations, to come under that character, was employed by the Botanical society of Liverpool to come out as their herboriser. he is an estimable man and really learned in the vegetable, animal and mineral departments of science. he is indefatigable in his researches, and before that journey, had already discovered a great number of new articles, which he has communicated from time to time, to his employers: and has returned to S[t] Louis fraught, without doubt, with a great mass of information, which will immediately pass the Atlantic, to appear first there. he was recommended to me by mr Roscoe, & staid here three weeks, passing every day in the woods from morning to night. he found, even on this mountain, many inedited articles. with respect therefore to your work, as well as Gov[r] Lewis's, I am anxious that, whatever you do, should be done quickly.

Accept the assurance of my great esteem & respect.

TH: JEFFERSON

PoC (DLC); at foot of first page: "D[r] Barton"; endorsed by TJ.

HERBORISER: a gatherer of plants or herbs. INEDITED: unknown, described in no printed source (*OED*).

To Robert Patterson

DEAR SIR Monticello Sep. 11. 11.

The inclosed work came to me without a scrip of a pen other than what you see in the title page. 'A Monsr le president de la societé.' from this I conclude it intended for the Philosophical society, & for them I now inclose it to you. you will find the notes really of value. they embody and ascertain to us all the scraps of new discoveries which we have learnt in detached articles, from less authentic publications. M. Gudin has generally expressed his measures according to the old, as well as the new standard, which is a convenience to me, as I do not make a point of retaining the last in my memory. I confess indeed, I do not like the new system of French measures, because not the best, and adapted to a standard accessible to themselves exclusively, and to be obtained by other nations only from them. for, on examining the map of the earth, you will find no meridian on it, but the one passing thro' their country, offering the extent of land on both sides of the 45th degree, and terminating at both ends in a portion of the ocean, which the conditions of the problem for an universal standard of measures require. were all nations to agree therefore to adopt this standard, they must go to Paris to ask it; and they might as well, long ago, have all agreed to adopt the French foot, the standard of which they could equally have obtained from Paris. whereas the Pendulum is equally fixed by the laws of nature, is in possession of every nation, may be verified every where, & by every person, and at an expence within every one's means. I am not therefore without a hope that the other nations of the world will still concur, some day, in making the pendulum the basis of a common system of measures, weights & coins, which applied to the present metrical systems of France and of other countries will render them all intelligible to one another. England and this country may give it a beginning, notwithstanding the war they are entering into. the republic of letters is unaffected by the wars of geographical divisions of the earth. France, by her power & science, now bears down every thing. but that power has it's measure in time by the life of one man. the day cannot be distant, in the history of human revolutions, when the indignation of mankind will burst forth, and an insurrection of the universe against the political tyranny of France will overwhelm all her arrogations. whatever is most opposite to them will be most popular, and what is reasonable therefore in itself cannot fail to be adopted the sooner from that motive. but why leave this adoption to the tardy will of governments, who are always, in their stock of information, a century or two behind the intelligent part of mankind? and who have interests against touching antient institutions? why should not the College of the literary societies of the world adopt the second pendulum as the unit of measure, on the authorities of reason, convenience, & common consent? and why should not our society open the proposition by a circular letter to the other learned institutions of the earth? if men of science, in their publications, would express measures always in multiples & decimals of the pendulum, annexing their value in municipal measures, as botanists add the popular to the botanical names of plants, they would soon become familiar to all men of instruction, and prepare the way for legal adoptions. at any rate it would render the writers of every nation intelligible to the readers of every other, when expressing the measures of things.   the French, I believe have given up their Decadary Calendar,[1] but it does not appear that they retire from the centesimal division of the quadrant. on the contrary M. Borda has calculated, according to that division, new trigonometrical tables, not yet I believe printed. in the excellent tables of Callet, lately published by Didot in stereotype, he has given a table of Logarithmic Sines & Tangents for the hundred degrees of the quadrant, abridged from Borda's manuscript. but he has given others for the sexagesimal division, which being for every 10″ thro' the whole table, are more convenient than Hutton's, Scherwin's or any of their predecessors. it cannot be denied that the Centesimal division would facilitate our arithmetic, and that it might have been preferable, had it been originally adopted; as a numeration by eights would have been more convenient than by tens. but the advantages would not now compensate the embarrasments of a change.

I extremely regret the not being provided with a time piece equal to the observation of the approaching eclipse of the sun. can you tell me what would be the cost in Philadelphia of a clock, the time-keeping part of which should be perfect? and what the difference of cost between a wooden & gridiron pendulum? to be of course without a striking apparatus, as it would be wanted for astronomical purposes only. Accept assurances of affectionate esteem & respect.

TH: JEFFERSON

PoC (DLC); at foot of first page: "Doct[r] Patterson." Enclosure: Paul Philippe Gudin de la Brenellerie, *L'Astronomie, Poëme en Quatre Chants* (Paris, 1810; Sowerby, no. 4495).

TJ proposed the oscillation of a rod pendulum as the BASIS OF A COMMON SYSTEM OF MEASURES, WEIGHTS & COINS in his Report on Weights and Measures, 4 July 1790 (*PTJ*, 16:602–75). He believed that France's hegemony and THE LIFE OF ONE MAN, Napoleon, would end at the same time. In 1806 that ruler abolished the DECADARY CALENDAR in use in France since early in the 1790s, which had assigned three ten-day weeks called décades to every month, and returned the nation to the traditional Gregorian calendar (Connelly, *Napoleonic France*, 93–4). TJ alluded to Charles HUTTON'S *Mathematical Tables: containing Common, Hyperbolic, and Logistic Logarithms* (London, 1785; Sowerby, no. 3697), and Henry SCHERWIN'S (Sherwin's) *Mathematical Tables, contrived after a most comprehensive method* (London, 1705, and later editions).

[1] Reworked from "decimal Calendar, of months."

From Littleton W. Tazewell

DEAR SIR; Norfolk. September 11. 1811.

I have been flattering myself during the whole summer, with the hope of having it in my power to pay a visit to the Mountain Country, and in the course of my projected tour I contemplated calling upon you; but the situation of my family, and some perplexing business which I have found great difficulty in adjusting, has protracted my stay here to so late a period, that I find myself now compelled to abandon my intended journey—Being thus disappointed in the pleasure I anticipated from a personal interview with you, I am compelled to write to you upon the subject of business, which has heretofore frequently engaged our attention, I allude to the claim of Welch against you—On the first of October annually I remit to that Gentleman my account, shewing the transactions of the preceding year, to which by his directions I always subjoin a statement of the debts due him yet uncollected, with notes of the times when payment of all or any part of such debts may be expected—In my last years statement I remarked upon your debt, that I had received your assurances, that you would make provision for its payment out of the proceeds of your crops as they accrued, and your other engagements would permit; so that he might expect to receive a part if not the whole of this claim during the course of the then next year—That year is now about expiring, and I have therefore to request of you to inform me, if you can conveniently enable me to make a remittance to Mr Welch about the period I have mentioned, or if not, to say to me when I may inform him he may expect such remittance, and how much.

I am very respectfully Sir your mo: obd^t^ serv^t^

LITT^N^: W TAZEWELL

RC (MHi); endorsed by TJ as received 22 Sept. 1811 and so recorded in SJL.

From Benjamin Galloway

SIR, Hagers Town Washington County M^d^ Septr 12th 1811—

The recent appearance, in a public paper, of a letter reported to have been written and transmitted by you to the Earl of Buchan, some years ago, has it may with truth be affirmed, astounded your political adversaries in this quarter; nor are they of the most[1] scrupulous Cast. It has compleatly thrown them on their Beam Ends: nor will their shattered Barques from present appearances, be speedily refitted for active service—The shot was a most unexpected one: judiciously aimed, and struck first between wind and water—The character of that <u>noble</u> Lord, by whose instrumentality, friendship and love of justice, the important fact was communicated, is too firmly established in the judgment and knowledge of impartial men, to be shaken, by any of the vile means so generally employed to effect party purposes. An attempt was made by <u>a few</u>, to deny the authenticity of said letter: but, soon discovering that such assertion obtained no credit with the generality of citizens; they now content themselves by admitting said letter to be authentic, and gratify their evil disposition towards you, by declaring it to be an additional proof of your want of sincerity—I am disposed to indulge a fond hope, that the lately published address of the House Holders of the City of Westminster, to the Prince Regent, will have the effect of darting the rays of political illumination into the mind and heart of the nation, with a rapidity like unto an <u>Electric Shock</u>—I learn by a letter lately received from my much valued friend, M^r^ G Duval, that, a British Fleet is daily expected on our Coast, commanded by Sir Joseph Yorke, and, report announces the arrival of considerable reinforcement of British Regulars in Canada: headed by a distinguished military character—Prominent appearances, I much lament, justify suspicion, that common sense and common honesty being at variance with British Claims and Pretensions the "ultima ratio regum" is determined on. Indeed, Mr Foster is generally reported and believed to *have thrown out such an hint*: If so: it furnishes another proof of the verity and soundness of the observation in your first communication as P US, to wit "feel power, and forget right." I pray, that their present provokingly offensive attitude, may be intended, *in terrorem* only: but, should it prove otherwise: (their *tender* mercies have so often eventuated in *cruelty*) one of two events will probably follow: The subjugation of Great Britain by France: or a Civil War, among themselves, may reasonably be expected to happen. The condition of the British Empire is most unquestionably at this moment *portentous indeed*! and may involve the European world in incalculable distress. That, we have among us a band of desperate, worthless *non-Contents*, *who stand prepared* to aid and assist in any mad project, designed against our happy constitution, I am thorough convinced: *Vigilance*, Therefore, is the *indispensable* duty of all good citizens—

Your esteemed favour of the second of last month, was duly received: in return for which, permit me to make an offering of my sincere acknowledgments. It was indeed *short*: but, *to the point*, and *highly consolatory* to *my feelings*—

We have just passed through[2] an *hard* struggle for Electors of State Senators. we have as you will have been informed, ere this reaches your hands, been *succesful*. The calculation as to the Strength of parties in the Electoral Body, is *twenty two* to *eighteen* Electors. so far, so good: but, the *Magnum Opus*, is *yet* to be accomplished: Will the Electors, in Truth, select for that important branch of our State Legislature, Men of *wisdom*, *virtue* and *experience*? or will (procul, O,) party rage, or the "civium ardor prava jubentium" *be again triumphant*? I must confess, I have *my fears alive*: That the Electoral Body will select fifteen *Zealous* characters, I *doubt not*! but, I am apprehensive, that the *qualifications* enumerated in our State Constitution, vid^t^ Wisdom, Virtue & Experience will most probably be viewed and held by *too many* of that body, as mere secondary objects, when they make the *selection* of characters. I hope, I may have taken up and given entertainment to an *enormous* Idea *quo ad hoc*: but, I have, Sir, seen so many instances in our State, where *passion* was not so unequivocally substituted for reason, as it now seems to be in the choice of public agents; that I much question, whether we shall be blessed with such a body of Men in our Senate, as the party who have the choice, could easily furnish. The Times most indubitably call for Zeal: but, that quality may be pernicious, if not associated with Wisdom, Virtue and Experience.—But "De republicâ nil desperandum est!"[3] The Electors meet at Annapolis on Monday next—

"Pax bello potior," was the leading Star by whose guiding influence, you, Sir, you strenuously endeavoured, to steer the good ship United States, so long as you were honoured with the direction of the governmental Helm: It was my good fortune, most heartily to cooperate with you in that work, as far as the wishes of a very uninfluential citizen could extend, and his feeble efforts, checque the too frequent disposition of some honest, but thoughtless men in one circle, to go to war with a foreign nation.—The ways I have so acted, I have sometimes thought may be owing to the following: my progenitors, both male & female, were members of the religious society of Friends, vulgarly called Quakers: and, my good Father, who though never very closely attached to the forms observed by Friends,[4] having in early life been educated in their Tenets, most strictly adhered to their principles! While, with his children, He instilled into them with parental sollicitude, a firm[5] conviction, that offensive war, so [. . .], is not justifiable in the eye of God: But, defensive war, he advocated: and, therefore, was not permitted by the Broad Brim Gentry to continue within the pale of their religious society. my maternal Grand-Father, was the Father of Old Benjamin Chew late of 3d Street Philadelphia: who, I presume, you may have had some acquaintance with. Said Samuel, was the Chief Justice of the Three lower counties on Delaware, as may be more authentically known by a perusal of his excellent speech, delivered from the Bench to a Grand Jury of the County of New-Castle, Novr 21. 1741—The speech alluded to, was republished at the commencement of our revolutionary war, and may be seen in a work of that period, entitled "The Pennsilvania Magazine, or American Museum"[6] for August 1775—It attracted public attention at that eventful crisis; and, if, Sir, you have it not, and the possession of it, would not be disagreeable to you, I will do myself the pleasure of transmitting to you a copy of it. The republication of it was judged adviseable in 1775—may hap it may soon be equally so. The doctrine attempted and, in my opinion, most ably maintained in said charge, is "The lawfulness of defence against an armed enemy"—in which, he detects, and exposes the assistors and abettors of the negative side of said doctrine, (The great Apologist Barklay

&c) by incontestably shewing, and proving "it not only to be without warrant, or colour, either from reason, or revelation; but, in its consequences pernicious to society, and destructive to all civil government" I shall in a few days pass below the Mountains. Mrs Galloway will accompany me: we shall be absent from Hagers Town about four weeks; shall probably visit the City of Washington as we return home: when, I hope Mrs Madison will have reached the Seat of Government: This is only mentioned, in consequence, of that Lady having expressed a wish to see Mrs G last Winter, when I was last at the City—

I am with perfect Esteem & Regard Yours &c

BENJAMIN GALLOWAY

RC (DLC); one word illegible; addressed: "Thomas Jefferson Esqr Monticello Virginia"; postmarked Washington, 18 Sept.; endorsed by TJ as received 22 Sept. 1811 and so recorded in SJL.

David Steuart Erskine, 11th Earl of BUCHAN, quoted TJ's 10 July 1803 letter to him (DLC) in an address the earl delivered to a group of Americans at Edinburgh on George Washington's birthday, 22 Feb. 1811. The letter, which appeared in numerous American newspapers during the summer of 1811, expressed disillusionment with the outcome of the French Revolution: "I expect your lordship has been disappointed as I acknowledge I have been in the issue of the convulsions on the other side of the channel (in France). This has certainly lessened the interest which the philanthropist warmly felt in those struggles. *Without befriending human liberty, a gigantic force has risen up which seems to threaten the world*" (Washington *National Intelligencer*, 9 July 1811).

The householders of WESTMINSTER had recently issued an address decrying political corruption and imploring the British prince regent (later George IV) to support the cause of parliamentary reform (New York *Public Advertiser*, 3 June 1811). ULTIMA RATIO REGUM: "The last argument of kings"; force as the final arbiter of disagreements. Galloway quoted from TJ's FIRST COMMUNICATION as president, his 1801 inaugural address (*PTJ*, 33:148). IN TERROREM: as a warning or deterrent.

Galloway's CALCULATION of the Republican vote in the newly elected forty-man electoral college that chose Maryland's state senators was correct. It returned fifteen Republican senators and no Federalists, with all the winners receiving twenty-two or twenty-one votes (*Hagers-Town Gazette*, 24 Sept. 1811).

PROCUL, O: "begone, oh." CIVIUM ARDOR PRAVA JUBENTIUM: "hot-headed citizens urging him to do wrong" (Horace, *Odes*, III.3.2, in *Horace: Odes and Epodes*, trans. Niall Rudd, Loeb Classical Library [2004], 146–7). QUO AD HOC: "with respect to this" (*Black's Law Dictionary*). DE REPUBLICÂ NIL DESPERANDUM EST!: "one must in no respect despair of the republic!" PAX BELLO POTIOR: "peace is preferable to war."

Samuel Chew endorsed self-defense against an armed enemy in a 21 Nov. 1741 speech to the GRAND JURY of New Castle County, Delaware. It was published by Benjamin Franklin as *The Speech of Samuel Chew, Esq; . . .* (Philadelphia, 1741), reissued in pamphlet form in 1742 and 1775, and printed in the *Pennsylvania Magazine; or, American Monthly Museum* 1 [1775]: 346–53.

1 Reworked from "least."

2 Manuscript: "thorough."

3 Omitted closing quotation mark editorially supplied.

4 Galloway here canceled "through life."

5 Manuscript: "frim."

6 Omitted closing quotation mark editorially supplied.

To David Higginbotham

Sir Monticello Sep. 12. 11

The lot in Richmond which is the subject of your enquiry, mr Jefferson was some time ago authorised to sell whenever he could get what I gave for it, and a fair interest on it, that is to say, adding interest to principal at every doubling of the latter at 6. percent. I gave Col° Byrd for the lot £25. Jan. 8. 1774. in that period there would be two consolidations of interest with the principal, so that on the 8th of this month it would amount to £132.[1] it is lot N° 335. open on one side to the road or street, on another to the beach or common shore of the river, on a third bounded by N° 334. formerly the property of Patrick Coutts, & on the fourth side by the remaining part of 335. formerly the property of R. C. Nicholas, & afterwards of mr Ambler. it contains 825. square yards, which brings the price to not quite[2] 6. cents a square foot, at this time, but increasing with the interest. I have also 4. or 5 lots at Beverley town, Westham, on one of which is the ferry landing. they cost £4–6 a piece about 60. years ago. the ferry is probably now of value, but must become so with the increase of the country, as there cannot be another nearer than Richmond. as land, they would sell probably at £25. the acre, at which price I would sell them. the paiments would be a present credit in my account with you. I wish it may suit you to take the whole. accept my respects Th: Jefferson

RC (ViU: TJP); addressed: "Mr David Higginbotham Milton"; endorsed by Higginbotham.

David Higginbotham (1775–1853) first became acquainted with TJ while working as a factor for Robert Rives & Company late in the 1790s. Later he became a prosperous merchant in the town of Milton and a man to whom TJ was perpetually indebted. TJ considered him to be "of very fair character, steady application to business, sound in his circumstances, and perfectly correct in all his conduct," but also "uninformed & unlettered, & so much so as to be entirely insensible of it himself." In 1813 Higginbotham purchased through TJ's agency William Short's Indian Camp plantation a few miles south of Monticello. He changed its name to Morven and built a fine Federal-style brick house there in 1821. At his death Higginbotham left a personal estate worth more than $100,000, including fifty-six slaves (David Higginbotham Papers, ViHi; William Montgomery Sweeny, "Higginbotham Family of Virginia," *WMQ*, 1st ser., 27 [1918]: 124; Woods, *Albemarle*, 58, 222; *PTJ*, 30:27, 29n; *MB*, esp. 2:988; George Green Shackelford, "William Short and Albemarle," *MACH* 15 [1955/56]: 21; Lay, *Architecture*, 133–4; Malone, *Jefferson*, 6:82–3; TJ to James Madison, 10 Aug. 1812 [two letters]; Albemarle Co. Will Book, 22:135–6, 209–14; *Richmond Enquirer*, 25 Jan. 1853).

Higginbotham probably made his ENQUIRY in a missing letter to TJ of 10 Sept. 1811, recorded in SJL as received from Milton the following day. SJL also records a letter from Higginbotham to

TJ of 26 Sept. 1811, received on that date from Milton, and a letter of 5 Oct. 1811 from TJ to Higginbotham, neither of which has been found.

[1] Sum interlined in place of "D209."

[2] Preceding two words interlined in place of "about."

From Lafayette

My dear friend La grange 12^h 7^ber 1811

Altho' my Letters to you Have for a very Long time Remained unanswered, I Cannot let madame de puzy Go to America without these lines from me—Not that she is in Need of a Recommendation to the friend upon whose Sentiments for Herself and Her parents she and Her children are chiefly to depend. she abandons the prospects to which the Distinguished Services of Her Husband, not only in our times, But under the present Government did Entitle them. Her daughter, the little Sara you Have known, is now an Accomplished young Lady—Her Son is very promising and will do Honour to Any profession He Embraces—your good advice and kind offices will not Be wanting to them. to Entreat would be on my part Superfluous—But to Enjoy the testimonies of your kindness to that family will Be Equally proper and pleasing.

mr Barlow is Every day Expected—we Have Long been without Any particular intelligences. those from mexico and South Spain give us the prospect of an independance which I did Early and more than Ever do wish to See Extended to Every part of America. most affectionately, tho' very Angrily at your Silence, I am Your friend

Lafayette

RC (DLC); endorsed by TJ as received 3 June 1812 and so recorded in SJL. Enclosed in Madame Bureaux de Pusy to TJ, 23 May 1812.

south spain probably refers to the Spanish colonial possessions in Central and South America.

From Charles Wingfield

Dear Sir, Bell-air Thursday Sep. 12. 1811.—

I received yours of the twelfth instant, shall attend agreeably to request, tomorrow at 12 OClock, unless the rain should be very excessive. with the assurance of my esteem & respect.

Charles Wingfield

RC (MHi); addressed: "M[r] Thomas Jefferson Monticello"; endorsed by TJ as received 13 Sept. 1811.

TJ's note to Wingfield OF THE TWELFTH INSTANT is not recorded in SJL and has not been found. On 13 Sept. 1811 TJ paid Wingfield $20 for "officiating at my sister Carr's funeral" (*MB*, 2:1268).

To George Divers

DEAR SIR Monticello Sep. 14. 11.

The advance of the season makes me uneasy about your timothy seed. on the 8th of Aug. I inclosed a 10.D. bill t[o] Judge Stewart requesting him to procure the amount of it in timothy seed, fresh, & forward it to mr Leitch's in Charlottesville. as I have not heard from him I have this day written to him by post. when it arrives at mr Leitch's, call for it without waiting for communication with me on the subject, lest it should occasion a delay which the season forbids.

Your's affectionately TH: JEFFERSON

PoC (MHi); one word illegible due to fault in the polygraph; at foot of text: "M[r] Divers"; endorsed by TJ.

To Archibald Stuart

DEAR SIR Monticello Sep. 14. 11.

In a letter to you of Aug. 8. I took the liberty of requesting you to procure for me some timothy seed to the amount of a 10. Dollar bill then inclosed. this being to replace some seed I borrowed in the spring from mr Divers, and the season now approaching for sowing it, I am induced to mention it again merely by the fear that perhaps my letter (which went by post) might not have got safely to you, and the season might slip over without my knowing that & mr Divers be thus disappointed.

War is, I think, inevitable. indeed it is commenced already by Great Britain as far as she can wage any war against us, that is by the capture of all our vessels bound elsewhere than to England. the death of the king can alone change their measures. this event may be hoped for every hour. but the present ministry are endeavoring to have it so far committed that their successors cannot stop it. every circumstance which delays our closing in the appeal to arms may have the happy effect of preventing the war, by giving time for another ministry to come in and stop these mad measures. so far it is fortunate that the meeting of Congress is at some distance

Affectionately yours Th: Jefferson

PoC (MoSHi: TJC-BC); at foot of text: "Judge Stewart"; endorsed by TJ.

TJ had borrowed $1\frac{1}{2}$ bushels of timothy seed from George Divers the preceding March (Divers to TJ, 17 Mar. 1811).

Stuart's reply to TJ of 22 Sept. 1811, not found, is recorded in SJL as received from Staunton on 26 Sept. 1811.

To Clement Caines

Sir Monticello in Virginia. Sep. 16. 1811.

Your favor of Apr. 2. was not recieved till the 23[d] of June last with the volume accompanying it, for which be pleased to accept my thanks. I have read it with great satisfaction, & recieved from it information, the more acceptable as coming from a source which could be relied on. the retort, on European Censors, of their own practices on the liberties of man, the inculcation on the master of the moral duties which he owes to the slave, in return for the benefits of his service, that is to say, of food, cloathing, care in sickness, & maintenance under age & disability, so as to make him in fact as comfortable, & more secure than the laboring man in most[1] parts of the world, and the idea suggested of substituting free whites in all houshold occupations, & manual arts, thus lessening the call for the other kind of labor, while it would increase the public security, give great merit to the work, and will, I have no doubt, produce wholsome impressions. the habitual violation of the equal rights of the colonist by the dominant (for I will not call them the mother) countries of Europe, the invariable sacrifice of their highest interests to the minor advantages of any individual trade or calling at home, are as immoral in principle, as the continuance of them is unwise in practice, after the lessons they have recieved. what in short is the whole system of Europe, towards America, but an atrocious & insulting tyranny? one hemisphere of the earth,[2] separated from the other by wide seas on both sides, having a different system of interests flowing from different climates, different soils, different productions, different modes of existence, & it's own local relations and duties, is made subservient to all the petty interests of the other, to their laws, their regulations, their passions and wars, and interdicted from social intercourse, from the interchange of mutual duties & comforts with their neighbors, enjoined on all men by the laws of nature. happily these abuses of human rights are drawing to a close on both our continents, and are not likely to survive the present mad contest of the lions and tygers of the other. nor does it seem certain that the insular colonies will not soon have to take care of themselves, and to enter into the general system of independance & free intercourse with their neighboring & natural friends. the acknoleged depreciation of the paper circulation of England, with the known laws of it's rapid progression to bankruptcy, will leave that nation shortly without revenue, & without the means of supporting the naval power necessary to maintain dominion over the rights & interests of distant nations. the intention too, which they now formally avow, of taking possession of the ocean as their exclusive domain, & of suffering no commerce on it, but thro' their ports, makes it the interest of all mankind to contribute their efforts to bring such usurpations to an end. we have hitherto been able to avoid professed war, & to continue to our industry a more salutary direction. but the determination to take all our vessels bound to any other than her ports, amounting to all the war she can make (for we fear no invasion) it would be folly in us to let that war be all on one side only, & to make no effort towards indemnification & retaliation by reprisal. that a contest thus forced on us by a nation a thousand leagues from us both, should place your country & mine in relations of hostility, who have not a single motive or interest, but of mutual friendship & interchange of comforts, shews the monstrous character of the system under which we live. but, however, in the event of war, greedy individuals on both sides, availing themselves of it's laws, may commit depredations on each other. I trust that our quiet inhabitants, conscious that no cause exists but for neighborly good will, & the furtherance of common interests, will feel only those brotherly affections which nature has ordained to be those of our situation.

A letter of thanks for a good book has thus run away from it's subject into fields of speculation into which discretion perhaps should have forbidden me to enter, & for which an apology is due. I trust that the reflections I hasard will be considered as no more than what they really are, those of a private individual, withdrawn from the councils of his country, uncommunicating with them, & responsible alone for any errors of fact or opinion expressed; as the reveries in short of an old man, who, looking beyond the present day, looks into times not his own, and as evidences of confidence in the liberal mind of the person to whom they are so freely addressed. permit me however to add to them best wishes for his personal happiness, & assurances of the highest consideration & respect Th: Jefferson

PoC (DLC); at foot of first page: "Clement Caine esq."

[1] Word interlined in place of "many."
[2] Word interlined in place of "globe."

From John Chambers

SIR New york, 16th sepr 1811

When my friend Mr D. B. Warden was last here, he communicated to me a Letter of yours on the subject of the Fiorin Grass mentioned in the Belfast Ag. Society's papers, & requested me to endeavour to procure some of it for you

I have very great pleasure in now informing you, that in consequence of having written to a Botanical friend in Belfast, I have just received a small parcel in excellent preservation, & have put it into the care of Mr Weightman, Bookseller, of Washington City who is now on his Return, & expects to be in that City in about a Week, & will then, search for the safest conveyance of it to you:—but it is possible you may be able to point out one to him, upon which you may have more perfect reliance. The parcel is too large to convey by Post, & I was unwilling to divide & put it into so small a compass, from a fear of injury

This Grass has been chosen by a Gentleman of much Botanical knowledge, who has put it up in the manner directed by you in your Letter to Mr Warden; & I hope it will reach you in perfect safety, & fully answer the expectations you entertain of it

Permit me to express the satisfaction I feel, in having an opportunity of paying you even this small mark of Attention, & believe me, sir, with great respect, your obedient servt J: CHAMBERS

RC (DLC); at foot of text: "Ths Jefferson, Esqr"; endorsed by TJ as received 22 Sept. 1811 and so recorded in SJL.

John Chambers (1754–1837), a printer and bookseller in Dublin and a member of the United Irishmen, was incarcerated in Scotland for three years following a failed 1798 Irish rebellion against English rule. He was released in 1802 and deported to Germany, moved to France the same year, and immigrated to the United States in 1805. Chambers operated a stationer's shop in New York City by 1807, retired in about 1819, and devoted himself to philanthropic pursuits thereafter (Mary Pollard, *A Dictionary of Members of the Dublin Book Trade, 1550–1800* [2000], 99–101; Pollard, "John Chambers, Printer and United Irishman," *Irish Book* 3 [1964]: 1–22; *Longworth's New York Directory* [1807], 140; [1819], 104; Washington *Daily National Intelligencer*, 13 Feb. 1837).

TJ wrote David Bailie Warden about FIORIN GRASS on 12 Jan. 1811.

From Charles G. Paleske

SIR Philadelphia September 16th 1811

Equally convinced with You of the incalculable benefit, which would result to the United States,—a country enjoying all climates and productions of the earth,—and particularly in its present situation in regard to external commerce, equally hazardous and unproductive in future—from well constructed canals—am induced to inclose the law passed the 2d April last, the proclamation of our Governor and the byelaws, also the terms of the intended Loan for $100,000, and the address to the citizens, which were intended (perhaps with some alterations) to be printed and annexed to the printed Laws. But the many failures during last forthnight and the number apprehended during this autumn have induced the board to postpone the application for the present. And we further apprehend, that the revolution it will create in all mony transactions will be felt sufficiently long to prevent any attempt of making surveys next Year, unless the United States will make the said Loan to our corporation free of Interest for seven Years, on condition of our paying the Surveys and estimates to Lake Erie,—to which effect it is intended to make application to the next Congress as early as may be adviseable, hoping it will meet Your approbation and countenance.

Inclosed blank certificate for the new Stock hope will be found a good specimen of the improvements made in the art of engraving.—

I have the honor to be with great respect and consideration Sir Your obedient Servt CHARLES G: PALESKE

RC (MHi); dateline adjacent to closing; at foot of text: "Thomas Jefferson Esquire Late President of the United States of America"; endorsed by TJ as received 22 Sept. 1811 and so recorded in SJL.

Charles Gottfried Paleske (1758–1816), a native of Gdánsk, immigrated in 1783 to Philadelphia, where he became a merchant and served as Prussia's consul-general, 1792–1802. He was elected one of the managers of the Schuylkill and Susquehanna Navigation Company in 1806. When it merged in 1811 with the Delaware and Schuylkill Canal, Paleske became president of the resulting Union Canal Company and served until his death. He was also a notary public, 1814–16 (*PTJ*, 24:99–101, 285; Paleske to Benjamin Franklin, 7 Mar., 27 May 1783 [PPAmP: Franklin Papers]; Philadelphia *Pennsylvania Packet, and Daily Advertiser*, 11 Aug. 1785, 16 May 1786; Madison, *Papers, Sec. of State Ser.*, 2:351; Paleske, *Substance of an Address Intended to be delivered on the 25th of January, 1812* [Lancaster, Pa., 1812]; Philadelphia *Poulson's American Daily Advertiser*, 5 Aug. 1812, 27 Mar., 4 Nov. 1816; Boston *New-England Palladium*, 6 Sept. 1814; Philadelphia Will Book, 6:271 [PHi]).

The act of incorporation for the Union Canal Company, which the Pennsylvania legislature passed on the 2D APRIL 1811, Simon Snyder's 30 May 1811 gubernatorial PROCLAMATION putting the law into effect, and the company's 24 July 1811 BYELAWS were subsequently printed as pp. 3–18, 19–20, and 21–4 of the enclosure to Paleske to TJ, 7 Dec. 1811. Other enclosures not found. The act authorized the company to improve navigation on and between the Delaware, Schuylkill, and Susquehanna rivers; supply Philadelphia with water; and construct a canal linking Pennsylvania rivers to LAKE ERIE.

From Peter Minor

D[R] SIR Ridgway Sep[t] 17. 1811

I have taken the liberty of sending You the enclosed "Projet of a Law to encourage the raising of Sheep" in the hope that you will lend your attention to the Subject, improve upon, or modify the Scheme, & assist us in trying to obtain its passage by the next legislature. The principal features I have taken from the Pensylvania Dog Law, as it is mentioned by Judge Peters in the Memoirs of the Philadelphia Agricultural Society—I have subjoined some calculations, which I think will not be found extravagant.

Since the introduction of the Merino & other valuable breeds of Sheep, I think it particularly behoves us to guard against their destruction by dogs. But Independent of their propensity to destroy Sheep, why should we not endeavour to diminish a race of Animals, which to make the best of them, are a nuisance, but when considered in a state of madness are certainly as great a curse as can visit us?

Y[rs] with the highest respect & Esteem P. MINOR.

RC (MHi); endorsed by TJ as received 18 Sept. 1811 and so recorded in SJL. Enclosures not found.

The PROJET (project) was probably an early version of the Petition of Albemarle County Residents to the Virginia General Assembly, [before 19 Dec. 1811], which Minor and TJ both signed. In relaying information about a canine attack on his flock, Richard PETERS complained that the "flagitious sagacity of dogs is almost incredible, when they are addicted to sheep-killing. They often kill both in the day and night; but more commonly in the grey of the morning, as do the human savages of our wilderness. Of this vice, when it is once fixed, they are never cured while living: death is the only effectual remedy" (Peters, "On Sheep-killing Dogs," *Memoirs of the Philadelphia Society for Promoting Agriculture* 2 [1811]: 247–53). Peters also hailed Pennsylvania's 1809 dog law, a version of which was enclosed in James Ronaldson to TJ, 20 Mar. 1809.

To William C. Rives

DEAR SIR Monticello Sep. 18. 11.

Company & particular occupations have prevented my sooner acknoleging the reciept of your letter of Aug. 30. which delay however should not have been yielded to, but that I considered the season as forbidding your immediate departure for the lower country.

Nothing can be sounder than your view of the importance of laying a broad foundation in other branches of knolege whereon to raise the superstructure of any particular science which one would chuse[1] to profess with credit & usefulness. the lamentable disregard of this, since the revolution has filled our country with Blackstone lawyers, Sangrado physicians, a ranting clergy, & a lounging gentry, who render neither honor nor service to mankind, and when their country has occasion for scientific services, it looks for them in vain over it's wide extended surface. the particular sciences[2] too which you propose to yourself are certainly well allied to that of the lawyer, who has many occasions at the bar for mathematical knolege, and cannot, without disreputation, be ignorant of the physical constitution[3] of the subjects which surround him. history, the closest adjunct of law, can be acquired in our cabinet; but mathematics & Natural philosophy require academical aid: & I know no place where this can be had to greater profit than at William and Mary. it possesses the double advantage of as able professors, & a better apparatus than any other institution I know. inasmuch therefore as you are not pressed in time to begin the practice of your profession, I entirely approve your idea of going there to perfect yourself in these sciences. I would not however, while there, lose time in attending to branches which can be as well acquired by reading in retirement, as by listening to lectures. such are history beforementioned, ethics, politics, political economy, belles-lettres E^t^c. considering the progress you have already made in the law, and that it's greatest difficulties are now surmounted, the habit of reflection in that line should not be lost by an entire disuse. I would devote an hour or two of the four & twenty to maintain the ground gained, & even to advance it. this would be done by reading the reporters, which may really be considered as but the light reading of that science. but you should common place them as you go; and, in doing that, take great pains to acquire the habit of condensing your matter, and of couching ideas in the fewest & most correct words possible. they will thus occupy less space in the mind and leave more room in it for other aphorisms.[4] Among the modern languages to be attended to the Spanish is important. within your day, our country will have more communication with that than with any other language but it's own. all our antient history too is written in that language. Spanish English & French cover the whole face of our continents & islands; & the last, as the language of science & of general conversation, is an universal passport. they are therefore the languages exclusively which every American of education ought to possess. I think it useless to lose time on Italian, German E^t^c which tho' abounding with works of science & taste, are rather beyond the limits of utility for us. I have thus hasarded my thoughts to you frankly, because you desired it, believing at the same time that your own judgment and appetite for science would be sure guides for you. be assured in all situations of my friendship & respect.

TH: JEFFERSON

RC (DLC: Rives Papers); addressed: "Mr William Rives Oakridge"; franked; postmarked Milton, 22 Sept.; endorsed by Rives. PoC (DLC); endorsed by TJ. Tr (DLC: Rives Papers); in Rives's hand; extract in Rives to Hugh B. Grigsby, 6 Apr. 1866.

The fictional SANGRADO, a quack doctor whose ministrations often led to the demise of his patients, appears in Alain-René Le Sage's *Histoire de Gil Blas de Santillane*, 4 vols. (Paris, 1715–35; repr. London, 1769; Sowerby, no. 4346).

[1] Tr: "desire."
[2] Word interlined in place of "services."
[3] Tr: "condition."
[4] Tr, which begins with the start of the second paragraph, ends here.

To Joseph Dougherty

DEAR JOSEPH Monticello Sep. 19. 11.

Your letter of the 4th came to hand on the 8 inst. but it was not till I could get a list of the Senate that I could do any thing in it. mr E. Coles accompanying the President on a visit here has furnished me one, and I have immediately written to those members of the present Senate to whom I felt myself at liberty to apply. with some of the others I am not acquainted, and a recommendation from me to the federalists would be a sufficient condemnation of you. my letters to Genl Smith of Balt. Doct^r^ Leib, mr Giles & mr Brent I have forwarded by this post, because I knew their address. but those to Messrs Varnum, J. Smith of N.Y. Gregg, Condit, Lambert, Worthington, Pope, Anderson, Franklin, Turner & Crawford, not knowing their post offices, I now inclose to you to superscribe the place of their abode, or to retain till you see them as you think best. I sincerely wish they may have the effect you wish for. the thing to be apprehended is that some revolutionary officer or souldier may be a competitor, & rendered formidable by the favor shewn to them. I leave one of the letters open, for your perusal, all of them being the same. seal it before you send it off. I wish you every possible success. TH: JEFFERSON

PoC (DLC); at foot of text: "Mr Joseph Dougherty"; endorsed by TJ. Enclosure: eleven copies of TJ's Circular to Certain Republican Senators, 19 Sept. 1811.

TJ's apprehensions were justified, for a former REVOLUTIONARY OFFICER from Maryland, Mountjoy Bayly, was appointed doorkeeper and sergeant at arms of the United States Senate on 5 Nov. 1811 (Heitman, *Continental Army*, 81; *JS*, 5:4).

Circular to Certain Republican Senators

DEAR SIR Monticello Sep. 19. 11.

The death of mr Mathers, Serjeant at arms to the Senate, is likely, I understand, to overwhelm you with sollicitations. each candidate will doubtless put into motion every lever he can employ. one of them, Joseph Dougherty, whom perhaps[1] you knew while he lived with me in Washington, where he did my riding business, imagines I may serve him, by bearing testimony to his character. during the eight years he lived with me, I found him sober, honest, diligent & uncommonly intelligent in business: and I verily believe he will[2] carry all these good qualities into the service of the Senate, without a single one that I know of to lessen their value. his political principles too, which are perfectly correct,[3] are not a matter of indifference in the choice of that officer. I know that your justice will weigh him in a fair balance with his competitors, and if you find him nothing wanting, it will give me real satisfaction that the lot should fall on him. the religious duty I feel of being useful to the future fortunes of one who was so long a faithful member of my family must apologise for the trouble I give you in[4] reading this, and it is quickened by the occasion it presents of tendering you assurances of my continued esteem & respect. TH: JEFFERSON

RC (CSmH: JF); addressed: "The honble Gen[l] John Smith of the Senate of the US."; franked. RC (ViHi); addressed: "The honble Thomas Worthington of the Senate of the US."; endorsed by Worthington, in part, as "recomme[n]ding Doherty as doorke[e]per." FC (DLC); entirely in TJ's hand, with his list of addressees in left margin: "M[r] Varnum J. Smith N.Y. Gregg, Leib. Condit Lambert S. Smith Mar. Giles Brent Worthington Pope Anderson Franklin Turner Crawford"; endorsed by TJ as a letter to "Varnum et al." and so recorded in SJL. TJ prepared this circular for William H. Crawford (Georgia), Jesse Franklin and James Turner (North Carolina), Joseph Anderson (Tennessee), Richard Brent and William Branch Giles (Virginia), John Pope (Kentucky), Samuel Smith (Maryland), Thomas Worthington (Ohio), Andrew Gregg and Michael Leib (Pennsylvania), John Condit and John Lambert (New Jersey), John Smith (New York), and Joseph Varnum (Massachusetts). Eleven copies enclosed in TJ to Joseph Dougherty, 19 Sept. 1811.

[1] RC to Worthington and FC: "possibly."

[2] FC: "would."

[3] RC to Worthington: "perfectly sound." FC: "sound."

[4] RC to Worthington and FC: "of."

To George Callaway

SIR Monticello Sep. 21. 11.

My wheat made at Poplar forest the last year was delivered at your mill under a contract made by yourself with mr Griffin to give me a barrel of flour warranted superfine at the Richmond inspection for every five bushels. when your milldam was carried away, I pressed for a relinquishment[1] of the bargain, and redelivery of the wheat, making reasonable allowance for diminution of quantity. you declined doing it. when the dam was carried away a second time I pressed the same thing again, but you again refused it, & the bargain was thus doubly and trebly insisted on, on your part. the quantity delivered you was 1397. bushels, which, at 5. bushels to the barrel, entitled me to recieve $279\frac{2}{5}$ barrels of superfine flour. I have recieved however but 232. barrels (some of which was not superfine) so that $47\frac{2}{5}$ barrels are still due to me. I sold what I recieved at an average of $9\frac{1}{4}$ Dollars in Richmond, which netted me $7\frac{3}{4}$ D a barrel. this on $47\frac{2}{5}$ barrels amounts to 367. D 35 c M[r] Griffin informs me that on application for what is due you referred him to mr Mitchell. but be pleased to observe, Sir, that I did not make the contract with mr Mitchell, and cannot of right be turned over to him; altho' I shall willingly accept his assumpsit, if he will give it: but this he declines. I am not without a due consideration of your misfortune in the loss of your dam, and not disposed therefore to an overrigorous adherence to all the rights which the bargain gives me. but you must be sensible that 367. D 35 c would be a greater sacrifice than could in reason be expected from a mere stranger. I have desired mr Griffin to call on you personally & to ask your final answer; which I hope will be so reasonable as to relieve me from any adversary proceedings, which it would be painful for me to engage in. Accept the assurances of my respect. TH: JEFFERSON

PoC (MHi); at foot of text: "Doct[r] Callaway"; endorsed by TJ.

George Callaway (ca. 1786–1822), farmer and physician, lived in Bedford County near Lynchburg on an estate inherited from his father in 1809. He operated a mill on land between the fork of Blackwater Creek and the James River. In 1818 Callaway moved to Nelson County. When he died he owned personal property valued at just over \$10,000, including twenty-five slaves and numerous debts owed to him (Ruth H. Early, *Campbell Chronicles and Family Sketches, Embracing the History of Campbell County, Virginia, 1782–1926* [1927], 363; Alexander Brown, *The Cabells and their Kin*, 2d ed., rev. [1939, repr. 1994], 397–8; Bedford Co. Will Book, 3:214–7; DNA: RG 29, CS, Nelson Co., 1820; *Richmond Enquirer*, 8 Oct. 1822; Nelson Co. Superior Court Will Book, A:11–2, 13–20, 21).

TJ's earlier understanding of their BARGAIN had Callaway producing one barrel of superfine flour per $5\frac{1}{2}$ rather than 5 bushels of wheat (TJ to Charles A.

Scott, 9 Feb. 1811). For payment Callaway had REFERRED TJ's overseer to William or Reuben Mitchell.

Letters from TJ to Burgess Griffin of 9 and 21 Sept. 1811, not found, are recorded in SJL, as is a missing letter from Griffin to TJ of 14 Sept. 1811, received from Poplar Forest on 17 Sept. 1811.

[1] Preceding two words interlined in place of "an annulment."

From Martin Oster

MONSIEUR ET TRÈS VÉNÉRABLE ANCIEN PRÉSIDENT, Norfolk, le 22 Septembre 1811.

Le 13 du passé, J'ai eû lhonneur de Vous accuser reception de la lettre que vous m'avez fait celui de m'adresser le 2. concernant la Succession reclamée par Mr de Beauvois et à l'occasion de Mr Pauly qui fait La résidence at Calf Pasture Augusta-County, près Staunton.

Aujourd'hui, Je m'emprêsse d'acheminer à Vôtre Excellence, copie du prétendu testament de defunt Pierre Piernet, Frère de Madme de Beauvois, décèdé à Potney, près New-Kent-Court-house en Virginie; elle Servira à asseoir vôtre opinion Sur Sa validité, et Sur celle des dispositions y contenues.

Salut et Respect OSTER

EDITORS' TRANSLATION

SIR AND VERY VENERABLE FORMER PRESIDENT, Norfolk, 22 September 1811.

On the 13th of last month, I had the honor to acknowledge to you the receipt of the letter that you had written me on the 2d concerning the inheritance claimed by Mr. de Beauvois and, by that opportunity, to send the address of Mr. Pauly, who lives at Calf Pasture, Augusta County, near Staunton.

Today I hasten to send Your Excellency a copy of the so-called final will of the deceased, Pierre Piernet, brother of Madame de Beauvois, who passed away at Putney, near New Kent Court House in Virginia; it will help you to decide on its validity and the legality of the dispositions contained therein.

Salutations and Respects OSTER

RC (MHi); addressed: "Á Son Excellence Monsieur Th. Jefferson, ancien Président des Etats-Vnis Monticello above Richmond Virginia"; franked; postmarked Norfolk, 25 Sept.; endorsed by TJ as received 29 Sept. 1811 and so recorded in SJL. Translation by Dr. Roland H. Simon. Enclosure: Will of Pierre (Peter) Piernet, 2 Feb. 1810, with subjoined deposition by Thomas Ratcliffe in New Kent County Court, 8 Feb. 1810; attested the same day by county clerk William B. Clayton (Tr in MHi, in Oster's hand; Tr filed with Stephen H. Lacy, Petition to the Virginia General Assembly, [ca. 7 Dec. 1810] [Vi: RG 78, Legislative Petitions, New Kent Co.]; described in note to Palisot de Beauvois to TJ, 19 Mar. 1811).

From Robert Patterson

SIR Philadelphia Sepr 23^d^ 1811

Some days ago, I received your favour of the 11, with the French poem on Astronomy. The Society had rec^d^ a copy of the same work from the Author, & therefore they wish me to return your copy.

They have eagerly embraced your proposal respecting the universal standard of weights and measures, and have referred the subject to a Committee who earnestly solicit, not merely your co-operation, but your detailed instructions on this important point.

Mr Thos Voigt, a very ingenious mechanic, a son of our chief coiner at the mint, would very cheerfully undertake to make you such an astronomical clock as you desire; the price 65 dollars, without any case. He prefers, both to the wooden & grid-iron pendulum, one with a simple steel rod, to which is attached a mercurial tube which acts as a compensating thermometer. This is the pendulum which Mr Rittenhouse used, & is still in use in his very accurate astronomical clock now in the custody of our Society—You will please to signify your pleasure on this subject

Along with the Poem I send you a Nautical Almanac for the year 13, which is as far as Mr Garnett has yet published. I am ashamed to apologise for my delay in sending you the improved artificial horizon I so long ago promised. It has been long made and only waits for a spirit-level to accompany it which I spoke for to a lazy mechanic three months ago—

With Sentiments of the very greatest respect & esteem I have the honour to be Your most obed^t^ Servant R. PATTERSON

RC (MHi); endorsed by TJ as received 29 Sept. 1811 and so recorded in SJL. Enclosure: John Garnett, *The Nautical Almanac and Astronomical Ephemeris for the year 1813* (New Brunswick, N.J., 1811; Sowerby, no. 3810).

On 19 July 1811 the American Philosophical Society received its own copy of the FRENCH POEM that Patterson now returned to TJ, Paul Philippe Gudin de la Brenellerie, *L'Astronomie, Poëme en Quatre Chants* (Paris, 1810; Sowerby, no. 4495). The society read TJ's 11 Sept. 1811 letter to Patterson on 20 Sept. 1811 and appointed a committee composed of Patterson, John R. Smith, and Burgess Allison to take his "important remarks" relative to a UNIVERSAL STANDARD OF WEIGHTS AND MEASURES "& the subject generally into consideration" and report thereon (APS, Minutes [MS in PPAmP]). Although TJ and Patterson exchanged further letters on the subject, the committee did not report back to the society. An ARTIFICIAL HORIZON is an instrument that takes altitude readings using a small plate-glass mirror affixed to a quadrant or sextant, half of which is left unsilvered so that the horizon line or other objects can be seen through it (*OED*; Patterson to TJ, 12 Mar. 1811).

From Jonathan Brunt

HONOURED SIR, Wythe Court-h^{e} Septr 24, 1811.

Last December but one, soon after I had left your seat at Monticello, I was very unfortunate in being poisoned two or three times; I believe all the masters of the different families were innocent, except one.—I parted with clear blood, three or four days together, except the intermission of one day.—This was within 60 miles of Winchester.—It is evident, that Divine Providence fought for me; for if I had been such an evil-disposed person, as those intriguing miscreants represented, I should have positively died, in two weeks, or less.—After the above misfortune, I seemed as well as ever in a month.—I am now returning from the Western country, but I shall come by way of Raleigh in North Carolina;—except I alter my route.—As I have not had two month's work, since I went to the Western country, last June but one, I am under the necessity of asking, pecuniary, personal aid.—The present coat that I have is more than 2½ years old; also, have only one good shirt left.—This is therefore, to request your Excellency to be pleased to give me a new suit of clothes, and small clothes; for I humbly presume, that you will not treat me in this respect, as if I was a miserable dram drinker, excited thereto by aged female intrigues. I hope the said speculative corruption will not have any weight with your honour, in granting the said necessaries of cloathing.—In your extensive library, perhaps, you have got Agrarian Law, &c. stated.—Sir, when I was once at your house, you asked, indirectly, for a great Thing.—I know, very well, that the Supreme Deity could change the heart of any rich man in a moment, for that sacred purpose.—If ruin awaits my native land, I do not charge myself with being an accomplice therein.—I am, Sir, your obed^{t} serv^{t}

JONATHAN BRUNT, PRINTER.

RC (MHi); dateline at foot of text; endorsed by TJ as received 2 Oct. 1811 and so recorded in SJL.

The work on AGRARIAN LAW Brunt had in mind may have been Thomas Paine, *Agrarian Justice, opposed to Agrarian Law, and to Agrarian Monopoly* (Philadelphia, 1797; Sowerby, no. 3187), which called for an annuity of ten pounds for people over fifty years old.

To Nathaniel Macon

DEAR SIR Monticello Sep. 24. 11.

M[r] M[c]lure, the bearer of this, has been employed in this neighborhood for some time in making spinning machines, and we are anxious to get him removed here. to this he consents, but says candidly that he owes some money, about 500.D. in your neighborhood, his present residence, which he must pay or secure before he comes away. we have therefore, a number of us, subscribed 50.D. apiece to be paid within one month after his establishment here, and it is made payable in the bank of Richmond to facilitate the transfer of it to those to whom he may assign our engagements. he has requested me to write to you, in the belief that from your personal knolege of Col[o] Monroe, mr Randolph, myself, & perhaps some others who are subscribers, you might strengthen the confidence of those to whom he might wish to assign our engagements, that we will perform what we have promised, by paying our quotas into the bank of Richmond to the order of the assignee on notice of the assignment: and should they be at a loss for the means of giving the notice, I will notify the subscribers for them, on their addressing a letter to me and return them information when the money shall have been deposited in the bank for their order. I have relied on your goodness for the doing this act of kindness for mr M[c]lure, and for us also, who are anxious to get him here, and I do it with the more pleasure as it furnishes an occasion of renewing to you the assurances of my continued and great esteem & respect. TH: JEFFERSON

PoC (MHi); at foot of text: "M[r] Macon"; endorsed by TJ.

Nathaniel Macon (1758–1837), planter and political leader, was a native of North Carolina who studied at the College of New Jersey (later Princeton University) in the mid-1770s and then served intermittently in the militia during the Revolutionary War. He served in the North Carolina senate in 1781, 1782, and 1784, and he was elected to a seat in the Confederation Congress in 1785 but never attended. Macon represented North Carolina in the United States House of Representatives, 1791–1815, and in the Senate, 1815–28. He was Speaker of the House, 1801–07, and president pro tempore of the Senate, 1826–28. In addition, he received Virginia's electoral votes for vice president in 1824 and presided over North Carolina's 1835 constitutional convention. During his long political career, Macon was a consistent states' rights Republican who opposed the new federal Constitution, Alexander Hamilton's funding system, the Jay Treaty, the construction of a navy, the Bank of the United States, and high tariffs. However, he also opposed nullification in 1832. Macon favored the Louisiana Purchase, the Embargo, the institution of slavery, the right of states to secede, and, reluctantly, the War of 1812. Initially supportive of TJ's political efforts, Macon associated himself with the Tertium Quids during the latter years of his administration. He nonetheless maintained a friendly but sporadic correspondence with TJ during the latter's retirement (*ANB*; *DAB*; William S. Powell, ed., *Dictionary of North Carolina Biography* [1979–96], 4:185–7; *Princetonians, 1776–83*, pp. 230–6; *PTJ*, 23:410–1; TJ to Macon, 21 Feb., 24 Mar. 1826; *Richmond Enquirer*, 4, 11 July 1837).

To Peter Minor

Dear Sir Monticello Sep. 24. 11.

I participate in all your hostility to dogs, and would readily join in any plan for exterminating the whole race. I consider them as the most afflicting of all the follies for which men tax themselves. but as total extirpation cannot be hoped for, let it be partial. I like well your outlines of a law for this purpose: but should we not add a provision for making the owner of a dog liable for all the mischeif done by him, and requiring that every dog shall wear a collar with the name of the person inscribed who shall be security for his honest demeanor? I believe your calculation of their numbers & cost is far within bounds; & I am satisfied that taking the whole mass of dogs in the state into consideration, the average of what they get fairly & unfairly of the food fit for man, would[1] feed a man. are there not as many sheep and hogs annually lost to the owners, by dogs, or with their aid, as there are dogs in the state? the petition to the legislature should I think refer to the wisdom of the legislature whether the law should be general, or confined to the counties below the ridge, or local to such counties only as shall chuse to be named in it, but should pray ultimately that if no other county concurs, it may yet be made the law for the county of Albemarle. I know of no service I can render in this business, unless perhaps to write to some friends in the legislature to interest themselves in promoting it. accept assurances of my esteem & respect. Th: Jefferson

PoC (MHi); at foot of text: "P. Minor esq."; endorsed by TJ.

below the ridge: east of the Blue Ridge Mountains.

[1] TJ here canceled "main."

From William & Reuben Mitchell

Sir Lynchburg 25th sept. 1811

Mr Griffin call'd on us yesterday for a settlement of the Crop of Wheat purchased of you, and we lament to find our understanding upon the subject at variance. we thought we had been expressive, and that Mr Griffin had understood our bargain; to give a specific price and the rise for forty days was what we never thought of or intended. Our offer, and[1] what we supposed to have been accepted by Mr Griffin, was for him to price at any time within the forty days, but not that he should look back at the end of forty days and make choice of the highest price. we proposed to Mr Griffin to submit the Memo: expressive of our bargain to any Gentlemen either here or in Richmond and their construction of the matter as expressed should be decisive—

We beg leave to apologise for troubleing you on this subject; the indefinite manner of Mr Griffin and our wish for an immediate adjustment, appears to make it necessary.

your instructions to Mr Griffin or an answer to this will greatly oblige.—

yr. obt: Servants W^M & REUBIN MITCHELL

RC (MHi); in an unidentified hand; endorsed by TJ as received 2 Oct. 1811 and so recorded in SJL.

[1] Manuscript: "and and."

From Samuel Smith (of Maryland)

DEAR SIR Baltimore 27 sept^r 1811

I am honored with your letter of 19^t P. Mark 23^d Ins^t, recommending J. Dougherty as Door Keeper to the Senate. I remember him and have no doubt but he is every way qualified—he will have many Competitors. Some of them very respectable—I observe that his political principles are Sound. they however will not long be thought an important recommendation Accept assurances[1] of my high respect & Sincere friendship— S. SMITH

RC (DLC); endorsed by TJ as received 2 Oct. 1811 and so recorded in SJL.

[1] Manuscript: "assuranes."

To Paul Hamilton

SIR Monticello Sep. 28. 11

Mr William Jordan Harris, a young gentleman of a neighboring county, being desirous of entering into the navy of the US. as a Midshipman, has requested me to be the channel of conveyance for his application. an antient connection with his family, and an intimate knolege of it's great worth & respectability, make it a duty in me to decline no opportunity of doing what is their desire. with the young gentleman himself I am not personally acquainted otherwise than by a single visit from him. but those who know him speak highly of him as of the most correct deportment, and one who, in the hour of danger, will certainly fulfill the duties of a brave soldier. mr Pleasant's letter particularly (among those inclosed) is worthy of entire confidence, because he has had great opportunities of knowing the young man, and because he is himself a character of the first order, lately elected to Congress by a neighboring district; and, speaking of him, permit me to observe to you that that body will not possess an abler or more amiable member. I avail myself of this occasion of marking him for your notice, because, if he can conquer an aversion to contest, allied to some indolence, his excellent dispositions & sound principles, may make him precious to the administration.

I was unfortunate in not recieving, from the hands of mr Hamilton, your son, the letter with which you honored me by him. an absence of an hour only lost me the pleasure of seeing him. I had been flattered by the President with the hope that, on an intended visit by yourself and family, to Monpelier, you might have been induced to lengthen your excursion as far as this place. it would have given me great pleasure to have recieved you here, and to have testified to you personally my great esteem for your character. I cherish the hope that another season may repair our loss, and pray you to accept assurances of my high consideration and respect. TH: JEFFERSON

RC (DNA: RG 45, MLRSN); addressed: "The Hnbl Secretary of the Navy." PoC (DLC); endorsed by TJ. Enclosures: enclosures to William J. Harris to TJ, 19 Aug. 1811.

To John Wayles Eppes

DEAR SIR Monticello Sep. 29. 11.

The inclosed letter came under cover to me without any indication from what quarter it came.

Our latest arrival brings information of the death of the king of England. it's coming from Ireland & not direct from England would make it little worthy of notice, were not the event so probable. on the 26th of July the English papers say he was expected hourly to expire. this vessel sailed from Ireland the 4th of August, and says an express brought notice the day before to the government that he died on the 1st. but whether on that day or not, we may be certain he is dead and entertain therefore a hope that a change of ministers will produce that revocation of the orders of council for which they stand so committed. in this event we may still remain at peace, and that probably concluded between the other powers. I am so far, in that case, from believing that our reputation will be tarnished by our not having mixed in the mad contests of the rest of the world that, setting aside the ravings of pepper pot politicians, of whom there are enough in every age and country, I believe it will place us high in the scale of wisdom, to have preserved our country[1] tranquil & prosperous during a contest which prostrated the honor, & power, independance, laws & property of every country on the other side of the Atlantic. which of them have better preserved their honor?[2] has Spain, has Portugal, Italy, Switzerland, Holland, Prussia, Austria, the other German powers, Sweden, Denmark, or even Russia? and would we accept of the infamy of France & England in exchange for our honest reputation, or of the result of their enormities, despotism to the one, & bankruptcy & prostration to the other in exchange for the prosperity, the freedom & independance which we have preserved safely thro' the wreck? the bottom of my page warns me it is time to present my homage to mrs Eppes, and to yourself & Francis my affectionate adieux

Th: Jefferson

PoC (DLC); at foot of text: "Mr Eppes." Enclosure not found.

Late in July 1811 the ENGLISH PAPERS stated that George III was suffering from "a swelling in the throat, which not only prevents his swallowing any aliment, but also renders his breathing extremely difficult," as a result of which "his dissolution was daily expected" (Washington *National Intelligencer*, 14, 21 Sept. 1811). The brig *Sarah Maria* brought word from Dublin, IRELAND, that the king had expired, a report that turned out to be untrue (Philadelphia *Poulson's American Daily Advertiser* and Richmond *Enquirer*, both 20 Sept. 1811).

Eppes's reply to TJ of 8 Oct. 1811, not found, is recorded in SJL as received from Mill Brook on 20 Oct. 1811.

[1] Word interlined in place of "selves."

[2] Word interlined in place of "power."

From Michael Leib

Dear Sir, Philadelphia Septr 29th 1811

Your recommendation would at all times be a sufficient inducement to me to patronize any one who was favord with it; and the extension of your good opinion to Joseph Dougherty has secured mine. It will add much to my gratification to be in any manner instrumental in the promotion of any wish of yours whether public or private.

The times are inauspicious, not only to the nation, but to some meritorious individuals—My friend Col. Duane seems to be the devoted victim of persecution at various seasons—For a paragraph published in the Aurora, furnished by the late D[r] Reynolds, whilst a member of the board of health, and therefore, in some sort official, he has been mulcted, under the direction of a tory judge, Yates, and a federal jury, in the sum of eight hundred dollars and costs of suit. This, with the pressure of the U.S. Bank influence upon his affairs and other party causes, bear very heavy upon him, and call for the interposition of the friends of the freedom of the press and of the able and useful editor of the Aurora. I have not forgotten your offer of kind offices on a former occasion, and therefore, feel free to suggest to you, that they will be useful and acceptable on this occasion; more especially as he is to defend himself in the next Circuit court of the U.S. against the charge of a libel on D[r] Romayne, for his connection in the conspiracy of Blount

Accept, dear Sir the assurance of my sincere regard and respect

M LEIB

RC (MoSHi: TJC-BC); at foot of text: "Thomas Jefferson Esq[r]"; mistakenly endorsed by TJ as a letter from Matthew Leib received 6 Oct. 1811 and so recorded in SJL.

Michael Leib (1760–1822), physician and politician, received medical training from Benjamin Rush and as a surgeon attached to the Pennsylvania militia during the Revolutionary War. Later he became associated with the College of Physicians of Philadelphia and the Philadelphia almshouse and dispensary. Leib sat in the Pennsylvania House of Representatives, 1795–98, 1806–08, and 1817–18, in the United States House of Representatives, 1799–1806, in the United States Senate, 1809–14, and in the Pennsylvania Senate, 1818–21. He also served as Philadelphia's postmaster, 1814–15. Initially an outspoken Jeffersonian, Leib remained fiercely loyal to William Duane and joined him in strident opposition to James Madison's administration as part of the steadily weakening Pennsylvania faction of Old School Democrats (*ANB*; *DAB*; Leib to TJ, 6 Apr. 1801 [DNA: RG 59, LAR, 1801–09; *PTJ*, 33:543]; Philadelphia *Poulson's American Daily Advertiser*, 30 Dec. 1822).

Duane had been convicted of libel seven years after publishing a PARAGRAPH that accused James E. Smith of corrupt practices as "steward of the Lazaretto" quarantine hospital near Philadelphia. James Reynolds served on the BOARD OF HEALTH that ousted Smith. Jasper Yeates (YATES) was a justice of the Pennsylvania Supreme Court (*Relfs Philadelphia Gazette. And Daily Advertiser*, 19 July 1804; Philadelphia *Aurora General Advertiser*, 20 July 1804; New York *Commercial Advertiser*, 3 Aug. 1811; John Hill Martin, *Martin's Bench and Bar of Philadelphia* [1883], 23, 326).

On a FORMER OCCASION TJ advised Leib that he "would do any thing in my power to assuage & reconcile" the warring branches of Pennsylvania Republicans (TJ to Leib, 12 Aug. 1805 [DLC]).

William Blount, a former governor of the Southwest Territory, briefly represented the new state of Tennessee in the United States Senate before that body expelled him in 1797 for involvement in a conspiracy to transfer possession of Florida and Louisiana from Spain to Great Britain (*DAB*). In 1797 Duane charged that the New York physician Nicholas ROMAYNE was a British agent promoting the plot. When Romayne departed for

England three years later, Duane commented that "where such characters are on *the move* there cannot be much good *brewing*" (New York *Diary and Mercantile Advertiser*, 14 July 1797; Alexandria *Times: and District of Columbia Daily Advertiser*, 7 July 1800).

To John Chambers

Sir Monticello Sep. 30. 11.

Your favor of Sep. 16. has been duly recieved, and I pray you to accept my thanks for the trouble you have been so kind as to take in fulfilling my request to mr Warden. I had been impressed with the value of the fiorin grass described in the papers of the Belfast Agricultural society, and hoped it might answer good purposes here. I have ever considered the addition of an useful plant to the agriculture of a country as an essential service rendered to it, the merit of which in this case will be entirely yours. M[r] Weightman, to whom you have been so kind as to confide the grass, will, I doubt not, forward it safely. the stage passing weekly between Washington & Charlottesville will furnish a safe conveyance. with the repetition of my thanks, be pleased to accept the assurance of my consideration & respect

Th: Jefferson

PoC (DLC); at foot of text: "M[r] Chambers"; endorsed by TJ.

To Charles G. Paleske

Sir Monticello Sep. 30. 11.

I thank you for the communication of the papers respecting the Union canal company of Pensylvania. no one is more anxious to see enterprises of that nature carried into execution, and especially to see them formed into a general system, and the public contributions, which other nations employ in war, applied by us to the improvement of our country. retired now from all intermedling with public things, I can only contribute my good wishes to the success of the company adding for yourself the assurance of my great esteem & respect

Th: Jefferson

PoC (MHi); at foot of text: "Charles G. Paleske esq."; endorsed by TJ.

To David Campbell

SIR Monticello Oct. 1. 11.

Your favor of Sep. 11 has been duly recieved, but I am sorry it is in my power to give no information on the subject of your enquiries. 30. years of general absence from the state, an entire occupation in other scenes of business, to which must be added the effect of years, have erased from my mind nearly all particular knolege of the affairs of the state. no time, nor circumstances indeed can erase from my memory the inappreciable services rendered by Col° Wm Campbell and his brave companions: but I am quite a stranger to the remunerations provided for them by the legislature. I have never seen the laws on that subject, nor do I possess a copy of them. I am therefore quite unable to inform you what line of distinction they have found it proper & practicable to draw between the officers of different grades, and privates of the various corps of militia who were called into service on different occasions. I presume that information could be obtained from some of the public officers at Richmond, but I do not know to which of them the application should be made. Accept the expressions of my regret that I am so little able to give the information you desire, and the assurances of my respect. TH: JEFFERSON

PoC (DLC); at foot of text: "Mr David Campbell"; endorsed by TJ.

Campbell's FAVOR was actually dated 7 Sept. 1811.

To John Dortic

SIR Monticello Oct. 1. 11.

Your favor of Aug. 14. was recieved after an unusual delay of the post. I formerly believed it was best for every country to make what it could make to best advantage, and to exchange it with others for those articles which it could not so well make. I did not then suppose that a whole quarter of the globe could within the short space of a dozen years, from being the most civilized, become the most savage portion of the human race. I am come over therefore to your opinion that, abandoning to a certain degree those agricultural pursuits, which best suited our situation, we must endeavor to make every thing we want within ourselves, and have as little intercourse as possible with Europe in it's present demoralised state. wine being among the earliest luxuries in which we indulge ourselves, it is desirable it should be made here, and we have every soil, aspect & climate of the best wine countries, and I have myself drank wines[1] made in this state & in Maryland, of the quality of the best Burgundy. in answer to your enquiries respecting soils & their depth, in this state, I can only say in general that any character, & any depth of soil required may be found in the different parts of the state. I am best acquainted with James river, and may therefore affirm this fact more certainly as to that. the low grounds of that river are a deep vegetable mould, the same for 20. F^t depth. I live in a mountainous country, the vegetable mould of which is from 6. to 12. inches deep, &, below that, many feet of fertile loam without any sand in it. but these soils are probably too rich to make fine wine. the Italian, Mazzei, who came here to make wine, fixed on these South West mountains, having a S.E. aspect, and abundance of lean & meagre spots of stony & red soil, without sand, resembling extremely the Cote of Burgundy from Chambertin to Monrachet where the famous wines of Burgundy are made. I am inclined to believe he was right in preferring[2] the South Eastern face of this ridge of mountains. it is the first ridge, from the sea, begins on the North side of James river, & extends North Eastwardly thro' the state under the different names, in different parts of it, of the Green mountain, the Southwest mountains, and Bull run mountains. doubtless however, other parts of the state furnish the proper soil & climate. beyond the blue ridge the climate becomes severe, & I should suppose less favorable. this, Sir, is as much as my scanty knolege of this subject will permit me to say, and with my best wishes for the success of your enterprize, if you engage in it I tender you the assurance of my respects TH: JEFFERSON

PoC (DLC); at foot of first page: "Mr Dortic"; endorsed by TJ.

The COTE OF BURGUNDY, or Côte d'Or ("golden slope"), is located just southwest of Dijon, France. The name is an abbreviation of Côte d'Orient ("eastern slope").

[1] Reworked from "a wine."

[2] Word interlined in place of "considering."

From Hezekiah Niles

[1 Oct. 1811]

[*Ed. Note*: In SJL on 6 Oct. 1811 TJ recorded receipt of a letter written five days earlier in Baltimore by "R. Niles." TJ's reply to Niles of 14 Oct. 1811 is also recorded in SJL. While neither of these letters has come to light, their contents can be conjectured. On 29 Oct. 1813 TJ sent Hezekiah Niles, the editor of the Baltimore *Weekly Register*, $15 for a "3. years subscription" to his journal. On 22 Mar. 1815 he forwarded a further $10, which, as he noted in his memorandum book, "pays up" his account "to Sep. 1816." The letters covering these payments are recorded in SJL but have not been found. Neither has Niles's reply to TJ of 17 Nov. 1813, which is recorded in SJL as received from Baltimore on 13 Dec. 1813. However, TJ's record of these payments and his subsequent acknowledgment that he owned a complete set (TJ to Niles, 26 June 1815) proves that he had been taking Niles's journal from its inception in September 1811. Furthermore, "H. Niles" can easily be mistaken for "R. Niles" in the editor's signature. The extant evidence therefore suggests that Niles's letter of 1 Oct. 1811 asked TJ to subscribe to his new journal and that TJ agreed to do so in his 14 Oct. 1811 response (*MB*, 2:1294, 1307).]

Hezekiah Niles (1777–1839), journalist, was a native of Chester County, Pennsylvania. At age seventeen he was apprenticed to Benjamin Johnson, a printer, bookbinder, and bookseller in Philadelphia. Niles soon established a reputation as an efficient typesetter in Philadelphia and Wilmington, Delaware. He moved to Baltimore in 1805 and there edited the *Baltimore Evening Post*, 1805–11, and the *Weekly Register*, 1811–36 (*Niles' Weekly Register* from 1814). The *Register* rejected advertising and undertook to be less a periodical than a national reference work on politics and current events. It had a wide circulation and counted TJ, James Madison, and Andrew Jackson among its patrons, with TJ maintaining his subscription until his death. A passionate nationalist, Niles favored political isolationism, economic protectionism, and gradual emancipation and opposed states' rights and nullification, although he scrupulously accorded space to opposing viewpoints in his papers. He also served as Wilmington's town clerk, sat on the Baltimore city council, and was a leader of the Baltimore Typographical Society (*ANB*; *DAB*; Brigham, *American Newspapers*, 1:81, 230–1; TJ to Niles, 22 Aug. 1817, 6 May 1826; *Niles' National Register*, 6, 13 Apr. 1839; *Baltimore Sun*, 3 Apr. 1839).

From Paul Hamilton

SIR City of Washington October 2[d] 1811

I am honored by the receipt of your letter of the 28th ult. I have not seen M[r] Harris, who left his letters at my office while I was absent from it, but I have not hesitated to make out his appointment, and when he calls I shall with particular satisfaction deliver him his papers. It is very pleasing to observe young men of his respectability offering themselves to the public service, and in that respect, this Department has been very fortunate of late—My Son returned to me much mortified at not having had the good fortune to find you at home when he called at Monticello; and such was the chagrin which I felt at the disappointment, that I was much disposed to censure him on the occasion, but he pleaded that he understood that you were to be absent all day; and further urged in his vindication the nature of his Orders which he construed as requiring his speedy return to this place, and although his construction was too rigid I could but acknowledge that he was not without excuse—For your kind invitation to your house I am very thankful, and beg you will be assured that I shall rank amongst the happy incidents of my life the commencement of a personal acquaintance with you. Disappointed as I have been this season in this hope, I promise myself recompense the next.

With sentiments of sincere respect & regard I have the honor, Sir, to be y^{rs} PAUL HAMILTON

RC (DLC); at foot of first page: "Mr Jefferson"; endorsed by TJ as received 6 Oct. 1811 and so recorded in SJL.

From Charles Willson Peale

DEAR SIR Farm Persevere Aug^{t} [Oct.] 3^{d} 1811.

Since writing my last letter to you, I have visited a small farm in my neigbourhood, belonging to Doct^{r} Beneville, the culture of which, has pleased me much. part of the land had been swampy, so much so, as to mire his Cattle, and often times put them to the trouble of draging them out—it is a flat rich bottom of a good many acres extent. The Doct^{r} has now reclaimed it, or rather has made it fine arrable land producing Wheat and Indian Corn &^{ca}

There are hills bordering it within his tract, between the hills in the desending Vallies, he has made french drains, which drains he has continued round the hills and dug the trenches so deep as to cut off the land springs, in many places the ditches to make his french drains are upwards of 10 feet deep, I am not doubting that you know what is called a french drain, however a few words will explain it; a drawing better.  after forming the hollow way by stones resting against each other, he threw all the small stones upon it & then his dirt. and in making these drains has cleared all his fields of stones; which in this part of the Country abound on most farms. a considerable part of my time with the aid of my children was employed last year[1] in clearing two fields of Stones—and I beleive that none of the Possessors of this land, had done any such work on it. But to return to the Docters drains of land springs[2]—he shewed me where they ended near the common stream of the Valley, there is a constant stream, runing out of his french drains. The bottom land is so rich that they will scarcely ever want manure, and are now firm & good walking on them, his present Indian Corn & Buckwheat are luxurient. He says that his labour of making these drains will very soon be richly paid for, by the product of the land.

Another observation I made, was, that I did not see a weed in our walk over his farm, he told that he always pulled them up by the roots & obliged his men to do the same as they passed backward & forward to their work. Also, that he did not cut down Tree's, but dug round the roots and cut them off, and when the Tree was fallen, the Stump was sawed off, and the stump was then split to pieces with Gunpowder. A part of the sides of his hills he had watered, by making dam that stoped a small stream from the neighbouring lands, & by a trench carried it round the hills that bordered his rich bottom.

I have but one thing more to note about the Doct^r^, which is that he works hard, has a rudy complection, 60 years old, and so active, that coming to a fence does not climb it, but puting his hands on the top rail he leaps over it. He told me that he was in a bad state of health when he lived in the City, fast approaching to his grave, but coming to this farm and working daily recovered his health. He is much animated, & very communicative.

I can make as yet very little observations on gardening, being a novice in that art. but it appears to me that Selery planted with one or two rows in a trench is better than making the beds 4 feet wide as McMahon directs in p. 423. they are easier managed as he directs for early use (June). My Selery in single or narrow beds looks better [than][3] that I have planted in larger beds.

I suppose you cultivate okra Doct^r^ Ramsey of South Carolina thinks it the most nutritive of vegetables. and Major Butler my neighbour says Okra and Tomaters with a shin of Beef makes the most delicious soop. Some years past I strung okra with a Needle & thread in bunches & dryed them for Winter use, I dont remember the effect, but do not doubt that thus dryed they will answer for Soops. By the neglect of my Market Garden I have lost the greater part of my Okra's, therefore I cannot this year make the tryal of drying them again.

Since my last letter I have made a tryal of my Potatoes, & find that those which we planted with Stable Manure is not so good as another feild in which we used long straw only—the Potatoes of the latter is not so strong in taste, more mealy, and I believe will give as plentiful a crop as that done with Stable manure

Robert Morris (Miller) near frankford has made more experiments with Plaster of Paris than any other person I have heard off and the product of his farm for the size of it, appeared to me much greater than any farm in this neighbourhood. I make some tryal of Plaster this year, & finding it answers with my land I mean to use it more freely on some of the feilds sowed with Timothy & Clover.

I have found it very easey to twist the mould board, but instead of using 2 pieces of Scantling, I made use of a small tree, by making a mortice, I have found it necessary to wedge each end of the board at its edges, which will prevent it from spliting, and the mortices ought also to fit close to the board. I also made tryal of heating a board over a fire weting & turning it often, And find it sufficient I was induced to make this tryal because it is not convenient for every workman to get the apparatus for steaming.

14th Some business called me to the City—I found the Museum in the most complete order it could well be made in those Rooms, I hope the Public will feel the benefit of the Institution, and thinking part of the Community will take an active part with the Legislature to get fire-proof offices built for the safe keeping of the records, and over them to extend rooms for extending the Museum, agreable to a design which I laid before the Legislature last session. My plan of giving my Son Rubens the opportunity of exerting his talents in the arrangement; in management of it, fully answers my expectation, and the continuing the system of giving the manager an Interest in promoting its reputation, and thereby invite visitors by a small payment at entrance, it will be keept in good order, and continually increase its public utility.

My Son Rembrandt took the portrait of a noted Indian Chief called the Bastard, of a tribe from the upper lakes—he is 70 years old, a fine head, but what lead me to mention him, is a striking trait of the Indian Character As is usial the visiting Indians are shewn every thing that is esteemed curious in the City—A Painting by Vertmullier, Dana & the Shower of Gold now exhibiting for pay—The Indians was led to see it, while the Conductor was arranging matters at the door, the Indian Chief & his Son was sent forward to the room of Exhibition, when the conductor came to the Room he found the old man & his Son setting with thier backs towards the picture conversing togather, he then pointed to the piece which they were brought to see, The old man replied, "that was not[4] fit to be seen" and they would not[5] look at[6] it. This exactly corrisponded with another instance of Indian modesty, that I noticed before the revolution War, In one [of][7] my visits to Philad[a], to paint some portraits, I had my brother James with me and for his improvement I sett him to Copy a Venus coppyed from Titian by West, I finished it & put it in a private room at my lodging, some Indians was brought to see my paintings, this Venus was shewn them, one of the Indians by the Intreperter asked me, "for what I painted this picture," he did not think it proper to make such pictures— However well I love the art of Painting, In my present Idea's I think that we should guard against familiarising our Citizens to sights which may excite a blush in the most modest. The artist may always find subjects to shew his excellence of Colouring &c without choosing such as may offend Modesty. Therefore at our last Exhibition at the Academy of arts, I advised & procured some old pictures of Nudities, to be put out of sight.

When I can find anything worth noticing I shall communicate again, but you will be so good as excuse my incorrectness[8] of stile, or other faults of writing, enterlining &c. I make no Copies but what my Polygraph gives, which I annually give a slight binding, these will give my Children my Idea's on a variety of Subjects, which I sometimes enlarge, in order to be more profitable to them in some future day. farewell—accept[9] the best wishes of your friend

C W PEALE

RC (DLC: TJ Papers, 196:34394–5); misdated; holed in manuscript and torn at seal, with missing text supplied from PoC; addressed: "The Honorable Thomas Jefferson Esq[r] Monticello Virginia ℔ Posts"; franked and postmarked; endorsed by TJ as a letter of "Aug. for Oct. 3. 11." received 24 Oct. 1811 and so recorded in SJL. PoC (PPAmP: Peale Letterbook).

Bernard McMahon described the planting of celery on P. 423–4 of his *Gardener's Calendar*. Peale's efforts to lobby the Pennsylvania LEGISLATURE ultimately failed (Peale, *Papers*, 3:xl, 1–2, 20–4, 76, 420). THE BASTARD was an Ottawa chief from Michilimackinack (*Massachusetts Spy, or Worcester Gazette*, 9 Oct. 1811); Adolf Ulrich Wertmüller (VERTMULLIER), a Swedish artist who settled permanently in the United States in the mid-1790s, painted *Danäe and the Shower of Gold* in 1787 and first exhibited it in Philadelphia in 1806 (Peale, *Papers*, vol. 2, pt. 2, p. 834n; Philadelphia *Poulson's American Daily Advertiser*, 15 Apr. 1811).

[1] Preceding two words interlined.
[2] Manuscript: "spings."
[3] Omitted word editorially supplied.
[4] Word interlined.
[5] Word interlined.
[6] Manuscript: "took at."
[7] Omitted word editorially supplied.
[8] Manuscript: "incorretness."
[9] Manuscript: "except."

To James Leitch

Oct. 4. 11.

2 canteens of French brandy

TH:J.

RC (NN: Liebmann Collection); dateline beneath signature; written on a small scrap; at foot of text: "M[r] Leitch." Not recorded in SJL.

This is one of a series of terse notes with which TJ ordered goods from Charlottesville merchant James Leitch.

To Nathaniel H. Hooe

SIR Monticello Oct. 6. 11.

Your letters of Aug. 13. and Sep. 10. were each of them 23. days getting to this place. the former came while I was in Bedford during an absence of between 2. & 3. weeks. I did not write an immediate answer because a very little delay, added to what had preceded would enable me to do it with effect. within the course of 3. weeks I am to recieve a quarter's rent of my mill (now in more punctual hands) in flour, from the proceeds of which I intended, to make a remittance of the negro hire now due. a few days of delay may occur in making sale, but they will be very few, which I mention lest such a delay might occasion an apprehension of disappointment, which shall not take place. with respect to the article of interest, I will settle it with you when you come up at Christmas, as I do not know that I could do it of myself to the satisfaction of mrs Dangerfield. at that time too I propose to cease hiring Tom; as the want of punctuality in others towards myself, renders punctuality on my part so uncertain. Accept the assurances of my esteem & respect TH: JEFFERSON

PoC (MHi); at foot of text: "Nathaniel H. Hooe esq."; endorsed by TJ.

The MORE PUNCTUAL HANDS now in charge at TJ's Shadwell mill were James McKinney and Thomas Mann Randolph.

From Randolph Jefferson

DEAR BROTHER Octr 6: 11

I Received yours of the twenty six of last month and am extremly sorry to hear of my sisters death and would of bin over but it was not raly in my power but it is what we may all expect to come to either later or sooner I Got mr pryor to call and leave this letter for me as he was Going to albemarle court and recomended it to him to make montocello his first days stage I intend coming over some time next month which I expect will be towards the last of the month as I shall be very busy a Getting my crop of wheat down to Richmond and sowing my present[1] crop you will not forget to take care of my puppy if you have not Given him a way to any one I expect by this time he must be large I have Just Got over a very severe tack of the Gravil I could not of survived many ours had I not Got releaf from a physician immidately: my wife and family prsents there respects to you and family I am yrs

affectionately RH; JEFFERSON

RC (ViU: TJP-CC); endorsed by TJ as received 7 Oct. 1811 and so recorded in SJL.

TJ had written his brother on 6 Sept. 1811, not THE TWENTY SIX OF LAST MONTH. Several of Randolph Jefferson's PRYOR brothers-in-law lived in Buckingham County at this time.

[1] Word interlined.

To William & Reuben Mitchell

MESS[RS] W[M] & REUBEN MITCHELL Monticello Oct. 6. 11.

Your letter of Sep. 25. was brought me by our last post I was certainly not aware that any question could arise on the terms of our agreement. mr Griffin had brought me your first proposition of 2/6 less than the Richmond price, which I declined, but told him that if you would give within 2/ of the Richmond price, the best which should be given within a reasonable number of days, you should have the wheat. when he returned he informed me he had sold to you on those terms allowing a space of 40. days, and within 2/ of the best price within them, and handed me your paper. I barely read it, and considered it's import to be as he explained it: and on a careful revisal of it now, it clearly bears that construction. however, no difficulty can occur where neither party desires no more than what is right.[1] be so good as to give your note paiable in Richmond on the 5th of the next month, for the sum you consider as due, without prejudice to my ulterior right, and when I come up, which will be towards the middle or last of the ensuing month, if we cannot bring our minds to the same understanding of the agreement, let honest and disinterested men decide for us what it really was. I have desired mr Griffin to transmit your note to mess[rs] Gibson & Jefferson of Richmond who will recieve it's contents, & apply them agreeably to engagements I had entered into for the 5th of Nov. in expectation of recieving this money then. Accept the assurances of my respect.

TH: JEFFERSON

PoC (MHi); endorsed by TJ.

Letters from Burgess Griffin to TJ of 25 Sept. and 20 Oct. 1811, not found, are recorded in SJL as received from Poplar Forest on 2 Oct. and 7 Nov. 1811. SJL also records a missing letter from TJ to Griffin of 8 Oct. 1811.

[1] Thus in manuscript.

To John Bracken

SIR Monticello Oct. 9. 11.

I duly recieved your favor of Aug. 13. stating the ineffectual effort you had made to remit to the sisters of Bellini the amount of their claim on his effects. they are very old, said to be in great poverty & distress, and therefore entitled in charity to our good offices in conveying their money to them. a remittance thro' England to the continent of Europe is now impracticable, & a direct one to Italy scarcely to be expected. a fortunate medium happens however now to occur. mr George Jefferson of the house of Gibson & Jefferson in Richmond, is going, within a month or two, to Lisbon, as Consul of the US. and can readily make any remittance from thence to Leghorn. any sum of money therefore which you will be pleased to deposit in his hands for these old ladies, I hereby make myself responsible to yourself & them for his faithful care in conveying or remitting to them. if you think it safer for yourself to deposit it in the bank of Richmond "on[1] account of the sisters of Bellini," subject to the order of either mr Jefferson or myself, our agency for remitting it to them shall still be exerted. Accept the assurances of my great respect. TH: JEFFERSON

PoC (DLC); at foot of text: "The rev[d] John Bracken"; endorsed by TJ.

A letter from GEORGE JEFFERSON to TJ of 3 Oct. 1811, not found, is recorded in SJL as received from Richmond on 6 Oct. 1811.

[1] Mismatched opening single quotation mark editorially changed to double quotation mark.

To William J. Harris

SIR Monticello Oct. 9. 11.

On the reciept of the letters of mr Eppes, mr Giles & others in your behalf, I wrote to mr Hamilton, Secretary of the navy inclosin[g] them, and have just recieved his answer expressing his readiness to make out your appointment as midshipman whenever you will call for it. you have now therefore only to go to Washington, there recieve your appointment, and the instructions of mr Hamilton relative to your new duties. not doubting you will so fulfill them as to do honor to your friends & service to your country, I tender you my best wishes for your success & happiness. TH: JEFFERSON

PoC (DLC); one word faint; at foot of text: "M[r] William Jordan Harris"; endorsed by TJ.

From Benjamin & Thomas Kite

RESPECTED FRIEND, TH. JEFFERSON, Philad[a] 10th mo 9–1811

We forward 'The Picture of Philadelphia,'[1] for which thou art a Subscriber,—The price is One Dollar, which thou wilt be pleased to send us when convenient.—

We are thy friends BENJ. & THO. KITE

RC (MoSHi: TJC-BC); endorsed by TJ as received 31 Oct. 1811 and so recorded in SJL; notations by TJ on verso: "1.D. to be remitted" and "June 17. 12. remitted thro' Benj. Jones." Enclosure: James Mease, *The Picture of Philadelphia, giving an account of its origin, increase and improvements in Arts, Sciences, Manufactures, Commerce and Revenue* (Philadelphia, 1811; Sowerby, no. 4027).

Benjamin Kite (ca. 1754–1838) worked as a schoolmaster in Philadelphia from about 1797 until 1807. In 1806 he entered the bookselling and stationery trade in partnership with his son Thomas Kite (1785–1845). The Kites published books, almanacs, and directories. They also involved themselves in various philanthropic enterprises. Benjamin Kite supported charity schooling and was an officer of the Pennsylvania Society for Promoting the Abolition of Slavery. Thomas Kite, who was also a Quaker minister, became a manager of the Association of Friends for the Printing and Distribution of Tracts on Moral and Religious Subjects. The Kites initially housed the association in their bookstore after its inception in 1817. Thomas Kite continued the family firm under his own name after his father retired late in the 1820s (William Kite, *Memoirs and Letters of Thomas Kite* [1883], esp. 9, 36, 92, 232, 479; William Wade Hinshaw and others, *Encyclopedia of American Quaker Genealogy* [1936–], 2:386, 574; Cornelius William Stafford, *The Philadelphia Directory, for 1797* [Philadelphia, 1797], 106; James Robinson, *The Philadelphia Directory, for 1807* [Philadelphia, 1807]; James Robinson, *The Philadelphia Directory, for 1808* [Philadelphia, 1808]; Robert Desilver, *Desilver's Philadelphia Directory and Stranger's Guide, 1829* [Philadelphia, 1829], 104; Edwin B. Bronner, "Distributing the Printed Word: The Tract Association of Friends, 1816–1966," *PMHB* 91 [1967]: 346–7; William C. Kashatus III, "The Inner Light and Popular Enlightenment: Philadelphia Quakers and Charity Schooling, 1790–1820," *PMHB* 118 [1994]: 103; Philadelphia *Poulson's American Daily Advertiser*, 16 Jan. 1801, 3 Oct. 1811, 17 Sept. 1838; *The Friend; a Religious and Literary Journal*, 8 Feb. 1845).

[1] Omitted closing quotation mark editorially supplied.

To James Madison

DEAR SIR Monticello Oct. 10. 11.

M[rs] Lewis, the widow of Col[o] Nich Lewis, has requested me to mention to yourself the name of a mr Wood, an applicant for a commission in the army. on recieving the request I rode to her house to ask something about him, observing to her that something more than his name would be necessary. she candidly told me at once that he was a very capable young man, connected with her only as being a brother to one of her sons in law, that he had married a respectable girl in Louisa, but became so dissipated and disorderly in his conduct that his father in law drove him off and procured an act of divorce from his wife, who is now married to another husband. this affected him so that he went off to the Western country, and, as she has been informed, became quite a new man: but had no knolege of it herself. she was inclined to suppose it true as her son Nicholas had written to her pressingly on his behalf and had particularly urged her to get me to mention him to you. to this neighbor I can refuse nothing, and I therefore comply with her request, stating the grounds on which we are both[1] put into motion, and adding some information which perhaps may not be conveyed by others. the old king dies hard; but he will die. I wish we were as sure that his successor would give us justice and peace. I think it a little more than barely possible, relying on his former habits of connection, not on his principles, for he has none worthy of reliance. ever affectionately your's

TH: JEFFERSON

RC (DLC: Madison Papers); at foot of text: "The President of the US." PoC (DLC); endorsed by TJ.

[1] Word interlined.

From Samuel M. Stephenson

HON^D SIR — Belfast the 10 October 1811

At the Request of our friend D: B. Warden; I herewith send you a small Box, containing 2 Roots of the agrostis Stolonifera in Irish, Fiorin Grass: with printed Directions for the Culture of it. It is often transported in a dry state, I have sent it with the Roots in a little Earth, supposing this the most Successful mode.

As I wish to hear of your Success, in the Culture of our Indigenous Grass; I request a line from you, in Spring. & I am Hon^d Sir your most obed^t Servant

S: M: STEPHENSON M.D.

RC (MHi); dateline at foot of text; endorsed by TJ as received 22 Dec. 1811 and so recorded in SJL. Enclosed in William & Samuel Craig to TJ, 29 Nov. 1811. Enclosure not found.

Samuel Martin Stephenson (1742–1833), physician and Presbyterian clergyman, was a native of County Antrim in northern Ireland. He attended Glasgow University, was licensed for the ministry in 1767 and ordained a minister in 1774, and received an M.D. from Edinburgh University in 1776. Stephenson preached and practiced medicine in Greyabbey, County Down, until he relocated to Belfast in 1785. There he became a noted specialist in the treatment of fevers and helped found a dispensary in 1792 and a fever hospital in 1797. Stephenson was also active in the Belfast Literary Society, serving as its vice president, 1802–03, president, 1803–04 and 1811–12, and secretary and treasurer, 1805–06. He presented seventeen papers before the society on topics ranging from lightning to lyric poetry, and he published a number of religious, medical, historical, and antiquarian works. Stephenson served as vice president of Belfast's Linen Hall Library, 1814–17, and as its president, 1817–28. He gave up the practice of medicine in 1821 and took up farming (*DNB*; *ODNB*; *Belfast Literary Society, 1801–1901: Historical Sketch* [1902], 151, 185).

To John Payne Todd

DEAR SIR Monticello Oct. 10. 11.

According to promise I send you our observations of the solar eclipse of Sep. 17. we had, you know, a perfect observation of the passage of the sun over the meridian, and the eclipse began so soon after as to leave little room for error from the time piece. her rate of going however was ascertained by 10. days subsequent observation and comparison with the sun, and the times, as I now give them to you are corrected by these. I have no confidence in the times of the 1st & ultimate contacts, because you know we were not early enough on the watch, decieved by our time piece which was too slow. the impression on the sun was too sensible when we first observed it, to be considered as the moment of commencement, and the largeness of our conjectural correction (18″) shews that that part of the observation should be considered as nothing. the last contact was well enough observed, but it is on the forming and breaking of the annulus that I rely with entire confidence. I am certain there was not an error of an instant of time in either. I would be governed therefore solely by them, and not suffer their result to be affected by the others. I have not yet entered on the calculation of our longitude from them. they will enable you to do it as a college exercise. affectionately yours

TH: JEFFERSON

	H ′ ″		H ′ ″		H ′ ″
1st contact	0–13–54			central time of the two contacts (1st and ultimate)	1–51–28
annulus formed	1–53– 0	central time of annulus (formed and broken)	1–56–12½		
annulus broken	1–59–25				
ultimate contact	3–29– 2				

Latitude of Monticello 38°–8′

RC (NjMoHP: Lloyd W. Smith Collection); at foot of text: "Mr Paine Todd." PoC (DLC).

John Payne Todd (1792–1852) was the only child to survive infancy of Dolley Payne Todd Madison and her first husband, John Todd. He attended Saint Mary's College in Baltimore from 1805 until 1812. Todd served briefly as his stepfather James Madison's secretary early in 1813, and in the spring of that year he joined Albert Gallatin's diplomatic mission to Russia. During his European travels Todd began a lifelong pattern of dissipation. He drank and gambled heavily and amassed huge debts after returning to the United States in 1815. Madison paid Todd's creditors some $40,000 between 1813 and his own death in 1836, but Todd was still imprisoned for debt on several occasions. In his will the unmarried Todd directed that his slaves be freed and given $200 each, and he left the residue of his estate to the American Colonization Society. Given the extent of his debts, the bequests were probably not honored (Dolley Madison, *Selected Letters*, esp. 219–20, 325–6, 414; Ralph Ketcham, *James Madison: A Biography* [1971; repr. 1990], 552, 601, 615–6; Madison, *Papers, Pres. Ser.*, 2:370–2, 4:444; Orange Co. Will Book, 11:476–8, 12:18–20).

During an annular eclipse the moon passes directly in front of the sun, leaving a ring of light, the ANNULUS (*OED*).

From Peter Walsh

SIR Cête 10. October 1811

Your much respected Letter of the 27th March has been just forwarded to me by Mr Warden from Paris. I am not unknown to you Sir as you Suppose, having had the honour of your acquaintance in New York in 1789., being then Established in Cadiz. a disorder which I got in America obliged me to come to this Place and circumstances have made me remain in it, but it's climate is changed much for the worse within these 30. or 40 years, which the Celebrated Doctor Fouquet attributes to the Earthquake of Lisbon and Calabria. That Great Man Died four years ago, as did during the Revolution all the other Physicians who were the chief Ornament of this renowned College, to which the present race is far inferior. We however still possess the reputed Botanical Professor Mr Gouan, who often enquires for you. at the age of 76, he enjoys very good health and often reminds me of the Virginia Plants which your Neighbour Mr Joseph C. Cabell, when he was here, promised to send him.

Your order for Wine is duly noted, but our Vessels being for a long time excluded by the English from these Seas, obliges me to try the means of geting it Ship't from Bordeaux, for which purpose I have written to Mr Lee our Consul there. You may be assured sir that nothing shall be omitted by me to have said wine Conveyed safely to you and of it's being of the best quality, and that your's and your Friends Commands shall be always carefully Complied with

I am with great respect Your very obt hble Servt

PETER WALSH

I beg leave to be remembered to Mr Cole

RC (MoSHi: TJC-BC); below postscript: "Thomas Jefferson Esquir^{e} Monticello"; endorsed by TJ as received 26 Feb. 1812 and so recorded in SJL. Enclosed in David Bailie Warden to TJ, 10 Dec. 1811.

Walsh presented a letter of introduction to TJ in NEW YORK in May 1790, not in 1789 (*PTJ,* 15:539, 545). An earthquake destroyed most of LISBON on 1 Nov. 1755, while a number of sizable tremors shook the Italian province of CALABRIA between 1783 and 1786 (Judite Nozes, ed., *The Lisbon earthquake of 1755: some British eye-witness accounts* [1987]; Demetrio De Stefano, *I terremoti in Calabria e nel Messinese* [ca. 1987]). The RENOWNED COLLEGE was the University of Medicine at Montpellier.

To Dudley Burwell

SIR — Monticello Oct. 11. 11.

Mr Burwell of Franklin, your relation, has requested me to send you a letter of introduction to Doct^{r} Wistar whose lectures you are attending. I comply with pleasure with this request, and shall be happy if I can serve you in your useful pursuits, or gratify you by obtaining the more particular attentions of so estimable a character as Doct^{r} Wistar. with this view I ask the favor of you to call on Doct^{r} Wistar yourself with the inclosed letter, and to accept the assurance of my best wishes & respect.

TH: JEFFERSON

PoC (MHi); at foot of text: "Mr Dudley Burwell"; endorsed by TJ. Enclosure: TJ to Caspar Wistar, 11 Oct. 1811.

Dudley Burwell (d. 1832), a medical student at the University of Pennsylvania, later practiced medicine at Middletown in Frederick County. His personal estate at his death was appraised at $1,227.70, including surgical instruments and two slaves so elderly that they were assigned no monetary value (Archibald Alexander, *A Discourse occasioned By the Burning of the Theatre in the City of Richmond, Virginia, on the twenty-sixth of December, 1811* [Philadelphia, 1812], iv; DNA: RG 29, CS, Middletown, Frederick Co., 1820 [giving his age as between twenty and thirty]; Frederick Co. Will Book, 17:241–2).

To Caspar Wistar

DEAR SIR — Monticello Oct. 11. 11.

The inclosed letter is from mr Wm A. Burwell, one of the members of Congress from our state. he lived with me at Washington as Secretary, perhaps at the time you paid us a visit there, or perhaps he may be known to you thro' the medium of his speeches in Congress, where he distinguishes himself by his good sense, his devotion to his country united with the most conciliatory conduct towards all. he has a relation, Dudley Burwell, an attendant on your lectures, who from gratitude and attachment for the benefits of the instruction he is recieving from you, wishes to be somewhat known to you, and to have opportunities of proving his devotion to you. if you can by any little marks of attention make him sensible of your notice in the croud of hearers, you will encourage him, oblige me, and gratify his worthy relation who is one of my most intimate friends. my grandson retains all his affections and gratitude to you, which his expressions on all occasions testify. he passed a twelvemonth in the academy of Richmond in Mathematical pursuits, which he is now continuing under my direction. once tolerably strong myself in that branch, always attached to it, but covered with a rust of fifty years entire occupation in other pursuits, I return to this with pleasure, am furbishing myself up, and accompany & encourage him in conquering it's difficulties. I am in hopes the establishment of your health has relieved you from the necessity of pursuing it by long rides. were that necessity continued, while regretting the cause, it would be a great gratification, if, directing them to this quarter, I should ever have the pleasure of recieving you here. we could promise you every benefit[1] which climate and affectionate attentions could render. of these be assured as well as of my high respect & attachment.

TH: JEFFERSON

PoC (DLC); at foot of text: "Dr Wistar"; endorsed by TJ. Enclosed in TJ to Dudley Burwell, 11 Oct. 1811.

Although the body of the INCLOSED LETTER from William A. Burwell to TJ of 2 Oct. 1811 has not been found, TJ retained the address cover in his papers (RC at MHi; addressed: "Thomas Jefferson Esq Monticello fav'd Harmer Gilmer"; endorsed by TJ as received 8 Oct. 1811 and so recorded in SJL; notation by TJ below endorsement: "sent the letter to Dr Wistar. 129. arch str.").

MY GRANDSON: Thomas Jefferson Randolph.

[1] Word interlined in place of "thing."

From Henry Foxall

RESPECTED SIR George Town Octr 12–1811

The time that has Elaps^d^ since you last wrote me, and my silence on the Subject of the Stove, of which you sent me the moddal[1] must have caused you to suppose that I had neglected it all together—However I have made a pattren[2] therefrom and have cast two Stoves from the same—I have no doubt but your very high Opinion of their Utility will be fully realized—I have put one of them up in my Blacksmiths Shop—and Connected thereto a small length of pipe without its being attatched to a chimney—I find that a few Minuits with a small quantity of wood is Sufficient to give it a considerable heat, fare greater, with the same quantity of wood, then anything of the stove kind, I have ever been acquainted with—I have no doubt but the flue which I have connected to it, will be of great utility if properly used, but this must never be used untill the wood is intirely burned down to a Coal, and the smoke compleatly gone of—

I have made the pattern for the Stove (the outsides thereof) of Square pannel work, I think it looks Neat tho plain—M[r] Whann Cashier of the Bank of Columbia has purchased one of them, and is now puting it up in the office of Pay and Deposite, in the Treasurey office—he says it is neater then it would be, were it ornamented with figures—However my object was first to assertain its usefulness, and whether I had hit, on the best size to make them, and what alteration on the pattern would be Necessary if any was required—These perticulars I thought it best first to assertain, before I went to too great expence in the pattern in as much as the Expence as it now stands was considerable, but I am much pleased to find that on trial I at present see no Necessity to make any chaing or alteration, except one of a larger Size Might be preferable for a very large Room and in that case, I presume two of the present, would be better then one much larger—

The price I charge for them is $40—They amount to this sum at the common price of Castings of the same kind, adding the expence of Smith work in fitting them up,—thereto,—I will thank you to say if you wish one sent on to you; and if so, in what way would you like to have it sent—whether you have pipe suitable or can obtain it, or whether you would wish me to obtain it here if so, what length of straight pipe, and whether any Elbow pipe would be wanting—Your wishes in the above perticulars shall be promptly Complied with by

Respected Sir Your Obliged & very humble Serv[t]

HEN:[Y] FOXALL

RC (MHi); between dateline and salutation: "Thomas Jefferson Esquire"; endorsed by TJ as received 16 Oct. 1811 and so recorded in SJL.

[1] Word interlined in place of "pattern."

[2] Word interlined in place of "<*pattern*> modal."

From Roger C. Weightman

SIR, Washington, Oct 12. 1811

M Chambers of N York put into my charge a parcel of Fiorin grass recently received from Ireland, with directions to take the earliest and safest mode of conveyance to Monticello. Since my return home I have had it boxed and directed to the care of the post master at Fredericksburg. Mr Wm B. Randolph did me the favor to take charge of the box and will deliver it safely into the hands of the Post master.

I am Sir Very respectfully Yours R. C. WEIGHTMAN

RC (MHi); endorsed by TJ as received 16 Oct. 1811 and so recorded in SJL; notation on verso by TJ relating to his 19 Oct. 1811 reply: "Scott's works 5.v. miniature edn."

Roger Chew Weightman (1787–1876) was born in Alexandria and moved in 1801 to Washington, D.C. There he learned the printing business under Andrew Way and William Duane, acquiring the latter's bookstore and printing office in 1807. Weightman printed the journals of the United States Senate, 1807–14, and TJ purchased books and stationery from him on several occasions. After serving in the cavalry during the War of 1812, he accepted a commission in the militia. Weightman was a brigadier general at the time of Lafayette's visit in 1824, and in 1861 he rose to major general in charge of the District of Columbia's militia. Although his health had begun to fail, he served in that capacity throughout the Civil War. Weightman was also a justice of the peace, 1816–42, mayor of Washington, 1824–27, cashier of the Bank of Washington, 1827–34, and a clerk and librarian at the United States Patent Office, 1851–70. In his capacity as mayor, he invited TJ to Washington's celebration of the fiftieth anniversary of the Declaration of Independence, eliciting TJ's last public letter (*MB*, 2:1208, 1239, 1274; Washington *National Intelligencer*, 27 May 1807; Washington *Daily National Intelligencer*, 7 May 1814; *JEP*; Weightman to TJ, 14 June 1826; TJ to Weightman, 24 June 1826; Washington *Evening Star*, 1 July 1872, 2 Feb. 1876).

The Fredericksburg POST MASTER was John Benson.

To Edward Coles

DEAR SIR Monticello Oct. 13. 11

I lent to mr Barlow a great collection of newspapers pamphlets E^t^c in several large boxes, which on his departure he informed me he had deposited in the President's house. I have therefore to request the favor of you to assist me in getting them back again. vessels are so constantly passing from Washington to Richmond that I presume there can be no difficulty in finding one which will take them & deliver them to Messrs Gibson & Jefferson of Richmond who will pay the freight. mr Barnes I am sure will readily inform you of a conveyance. any little expences of drayage E^t^c shall be repaid on a knolege of their amount. I am anxious they should come on immediately that they may be brought up the river in the dry season of autumn, our boats being without cover. Accept the assurances of my great esteem and respect. TH: JEFFERSON

RC (NjP: Coles Papers); addressed: "Edward Coles esq. Secretary to the Pr. US. Washington"; TJ's franking signature clipped; postmarked Milton, 14 Oct. 1811; endorsed by Coles. PoC (MHi); endorsed by TJ.

From Archibald Stuart

DEAR SIR Staunton 13th Octr 1811

On my return home I found that three bushels and eight quts[1] of Timothy seed of the price of 10$ had been forwarded to Mr Leitch in Mr Harnests waggon—By the same conveyance was sent a smal Ferkin of butter made at my dairy which I beg you will accept as a present—I directed it to be made & packed in this month in expectation that the weather would have proved more favorable than it has been for its conveyance

I am Dr Sir yours most sincerely ARCHD STUART

RC (MHi); at foot of text: "The Honble Thos Jefferson"; endorsed by TJ as received 16 Oct. 1811 and so recorded in SJL.

[1] Probably an abbreviation for the word "quarts."

To Littleton W. Tazewell

DEAR SIR Monticello Oct. 13. [11.]

Your favor of Sep. 11. was recieved after a considerable delay on the road. on the subject of my debt to mr Welsh, if you will have the goodness to recur to my letter of June 5. 10. you will find a candid statement of the circumstances which have, of necessity, suspended my attention to it for a while. in winding up my affairs at Washington, an accumulation of outstanding accounts, which had been unknown to me, or witheld till I had forgotten them, came upon me in the moment of my departure, and obliged me to have recourse to the bank of Richmond for 8000.D. of this I repaid 2000. from the crop of the preceding[1] year (9.[2]) 3000 from that of the same year (10.) and the crop of 11. now in the house, ensures my clearing off the remaining 3000.D. when sold, which will be in the spring, if no new events disturb our prices. in the same letter therefore I asked a continuance of the money of mr Welch in my hands some time longer, which your answer of July 3. induced me to hope would not be inadmissible. I had been led to proceed less steadily, than in the other debts of mr Wayles, in the paiment of this, the last of them now unpaid, from a conversation with mr Welch, when I was in London, as well as from the circumstances which have since prevailed in Europe, & which I had believed would strengthen a willingness to keep some funds here independant of events on that side the Atlantic. however it is enough for me to know that mr Welch wishes to call home his funds to command my early attention. for the reasons above explained, this cannot be begun but with the crop of the ensuing year. thenceforward I will make such paiments of interest & principal, regularly, as shall close the transaction within a short period. I am afraid to fix the amount at this moment of crisis as to circumstances which might so much affect prices. the state of things the ensuing year will enable me to do it with that kind of certainty which will exclude disappointment on either side.

I am sorry you were prevented from your projected tour through the upper country. I should have been happy to have recieved you here, and to have had an opportunity of testifying to you[3] in person my esteem. the particulars respecting mr Welch's debt might have been more fully explained in conversation, and some further thoughts might perhaps have been exchanged on Livingston's affair. some future season may be more favorable, and indemnify us for the loss of the last. be this when it may I shall be happy to see you, and pray you to be assured of my great esteem & respect. TH: JEFFERSON

RC (NjMoHP: Lloyd W. Smith Collection); partially dated, with year supplied from PoC; addressed: "Littleton W. Tazewell esq. Norfolk"; franked; postmarked Milton, 14 Oct. 1811; endorsed by Tazewell. PoC (MHi); endorsed by TJ.

TJ's CONVERSATION with Wakelin Welch took place while the former was in London helping John Adams negotiate commercial treaties with Portugal and Tripoli in the spring of 1786 (*PTJ*, 9:364n, 396, 465).

[1] Reworked from "of that."
[2] Date reworked from "10."
[3] Preceding two words interlined.

From Henry A. S. Dearborn

MUCH RESPECTED SIR, Boston Octo 14. 1811

A fiew days [ago][1] I spent the afternoon at Salem with my friend Nath. Bowditch to consult him on the observations which he hade made on the Comet which now blazes in the nothern regions of the sky. He had attentively observed it since its first appearance & had nearly finished his calculations of its Elements.

Yesterday I received a letter from him, requesting me to forward to you, the enclosed succinct result of his calculations of its orbit, with a note thereto attatched, desiring that you would do him the favor, of furnishing such observations, as you may have made, or can procure, on the recent Solar Eclipse. I have known him for a number of years & so far as I am capable of judging, have no doubt, of his being, by far the ablest astronomical mathematician in this country & equal to any in Europe. He is entirely self educated & who from early youth, discovered a great taste for the mathematics. By constant study & practical observation, he has become famillier with all the varios authors both ancient & modern, who have made great advances in the most sublime science of Astronomy. He is modest & unassuming—preeminantly distinguished for his amiable virtues & extensive researches & by unceasing study & observation elevated his fame in the minds of those who have the pleasure of knowing him, to that honorable station, where stand the greatest geniouses of Phylosophy. Unattatched to any of our seminaries of learning, his mathematical researches & character have not been greatly extended. He has for some years corresponded with the celebrated La Place. The government of Harvard University have offered him the professorship of mathematics & Astronomy, but not having received a Collegiate education, he did not think himself adequate, thus modesty has deprived our literary institution of an inestimable treasure. In the early part of life he went to sea & was master of a ship, when he was chosen President of an Insureance Office, where he remains. He is not 40 years of age. It is unnecessary to observe that a communication from a gentleman of your distinction, relative to the subjects contained in the enclosed Paper, would be received with peculiar pleasure

He is preparing at length[2] two communications for the A. of A. S. of this state, which will contain his calculations on the Comet & Eclipse. When the number is published I shall do myself the pleasure of forwarding it to you.—

You will excuse the liberty I have taken in thus trespassing on your time, but knowing your fondness for scientific discoveries & pleased at the rising fame of the U.S., I hope this particular detail relative to Mr. Bowditch will not be unwelcome.

While my father was at the head of the war Department, my youth & short residence[3] at Washington did not admit of my being much known to you.

However my respect is that, of an American citizen, for the most distinguished of her worthies.

With the highest esteem I am with respect Your Obt. Sevt.

H,A,S, Dearborn

RC (DLC); at foot of text: "Hon. Th. Jefferson"; endorsed by TJ as received 24 Oct. 1811 and so recorded in SJL. Enclosure: Nathaniel Bowditch, *The Comet: Elements of the Orbit of the Comet, now visible*, calculating the perihelion of a comet hitherto unknown to astronomers, based on observations taken between 6 and 23 Sept. 1811, and estimating its previous and future course; reporting that he had observed the annular solar eclipse of 17 Sept. 1811 in Salem, Massachusetts ("about 300 feet s.s.w. of the Rev. Dr. BARNARD's meeting house"), aided by "a four feet achromatic telescope and a well regulated time-keeper. The beginning was at 0H. 55M. 14.3S. and the end at 3H. 59M. 00.1S. apparent time. Latitude of the place of observation 42 deg. 33 min. 30 sec. N.; longitude 70 deg. 53 min. w. from Greenwich"; and concluding that he "*wishes to make a complete collection of the observations of the Eclipse (viz. the beginning and end of the eclipse, and the beginning and end of the annular appearance) that were carefully made with a well regulated clock or watch. The gentleman to whom this is addressed is respectfully requested to furnish any observations that may be depended upon in the district where he resides, with the latitudes and estimated longitudes of the places of observation. These observations may be communicated in a letter directed to Nathaniel Bowditch, Salem, Massachusetts*" (broadside in DLC: TJ Papers, 194:34459; undated; endorsed by TJ: "Astronomy. Solar eclipse of Sept. 17. 1811. by Bowditch").

Henry Alexander Scammell Dearborn (1783–1851) was the son of Henry Dearborn, the secretary of war during TJ's presidency. A native of Exeter, New Hampshire, he graduated from the College of William and Mary in 1803. After further study under William Wirt and Joseph Story, he established a legal practice in Salem, Massachusetts. Soon tiring of the law, Dearborn served as a deputy customs collector for three years, succeeded his father as collector at Boston in 1812, and retained this position until 1829. He was also appointed a brigadier general of militia during the War of 1812 and placed in command of the American defenses around Boston's harbor. Dearborn was a member of the state house of representatives in 1829, the state senate the following year, and the United States House of Representatives, 1831–33. He served as state adjutant general, 1835–43, and as mayor of Roxbury, Massachusetts, from 1847 until his death. A prolific author and speaker, Dearborn was the first president of the Massachusetts Horticultural Society (*DAB*; George Putnam, *An Address, delivered before the City Government and Citizens of Roxbury, on the Life and Character of the late Henry A. S. Dearborn, Mayor of the City, September 3d, 1851* [1851]; *JEP*, 2:278, 279, 4:46 [22, 26 June 1812, 14 Jan. 1830]; Madison, *Papers, Pres. Ser.*, 4:476–7; *Boston Daily Advertiser*, 30, 31 July 1851).

A. OF A. S.: the American Academy of Arts and Sciences in Boston.

On this day Dearborn also sent Bowditch's broadside to James Madison (Madison, *Papers, Pres. Ser.*, 3:487–8).

[1] Omitted word editorially supplied.
[2] Preceding two words interlined.
[3] Manuscript: "resdidence."

To William Short

DEAR SIR Monticello Oct. 15. 11.

Your letter of Aug. 10. from Portsmouth[1] came duly to hand. according to promise I have made exact research into the situation of your land. I rode to Price's and enquired of him with respect to the leases, to whom, on what conditions, and for what terms they were made?

I found them to be as follows.

Richard Shackleford	100. a^s^ rent 50.D.	written[2] leases for 3. years from the beginning of the year 1811. recorded.
Curtis Johnson	100. a^s^ rent 50.D.	
Charles Lively	100. a^s^ rent 50.D.	

Richard Gamble.	200. a^{s} rent 100.D.	on a written lease for the same term not recorded.
William Gamble.	100. a^{s} rent 50.[3] D.	holding from year to year only without writing.
Joseph Price	100. a^{s} rent 50.D.	
d^{o}	100. a^{s} rent 20.D.	lease written & recorded for his own and his wife's life.

I told Price that you did not think you had authorised him to lease for such a term, and asked him if he had such authority in writing. he answered, certainly not, but that from his agency under your former instructions, in laying off[4] the original hundred acre lots & leasing them, he thought it your intention & wish to continue that system, which enabled him to get better tenants and enforce better a proper rotation, which he found impossible with those who were for a year only: that the tenants now on the land were honest, careful of the land, & paid their rent without trouble. that they were to tend their farm in corn one year only, in small grain one year, & to rest a year, under which course the land was improving. I got him to go with me thro' all the farms (which I had not seen for 11. years) and I found with great pleasure that they had really improved since I knew them, the whole in excellent heart, and manifesting proofs of it by the crops on the ground. I did not see a single gully on the land, nor a single galled spot, which are so common on all our mountain lands. the principal disadvantage which I observed was from the openings being so numerous & small, separated by intervals of wood: but this was a necessary consequence of the system of small farms. one of the farms is now without a tenant. finding the footing on which the written leases had placed 5. of the lots, and believing that, if legally tried, they would be confirmed by a jury of the peers of the tenant, I thought it best to say nothing which should disturb them. Price thinks some of them might give up for a consideration, and the others seeing that they will not be continued on the same tenure after their leases are out, will probably begin after the ensuing year to look out for other places. some think of going to the Western country. I am afraid that their occupation may hinder the sale for a year more, but not[5] after that, as no purchaser expects possession till the end of the year of the purchase: and indeed I think the land so excellent a bargain at your price of 10.D. that I cannot believe it will be long unsold, even with it's present incumbrances. I have made it known that it is for sale at 10.D. but have had no offer since the one I formerly mentioned.

We are all a tip-toe for the death of the old Maniac king, believing that no other event can save us from war, & doubtful whether even[6] his successor may not continue the same maniac purpose of taking possession of the ocean, & requiring, for the privilege of using it, a tribute for the maintenance of their navy. on this point the nation itself seems maniacal & may not perhaps permit their king or ministry to give it up, even if so disposed. misfortunes however in the peninsula,[7] or their rapid progress to bankruptcy, may chop them about and offer another chance of peace for us. accept assurances of my constant & affectionate attachment & respect TH: JEFFERSON

RC (ViW: TJP); at foot of first page: "Mr Short"; endorsed by Short as received by an agent at Philadelphia on 22 Oct., forwarded to New York, and received by him there on 1 Nov. 1811.

Short's letter to TJ OF AUG. 10., not found, is recorded in SJL as received from Portsmouth, New Hampshire, on 25 Aug. 1811. It is also recorded in Short's epistolary record for 1811 (DLC: Short Papers, 34:6346). The OLD MANIAC KING was George III of Great Britain.

[1] Reworked from "Portland."
[2] Word interlined.
[3] Number interlined in place of "100."
[4] Preceding two words interlined.
[5] TJ here canceled "during."
[6] Word interlined.
[7] Manuscript: "peninsul."

From David Gelston

DEAR SIR, New York 17th Oct: 1811

Being sensible of the interest You feel in all useful discoveries and improvements in our country,—I take the liberty of enclosing the amount of the tonnage of the Steam boats now in actual employment—

very truly & sincerely your's DAVID GELSTON

RC (MHi); at foot of text: "Mr Jefferson"; endorsed by TJ as received 24 Oct. 1811 and so recorded in SJL.

ENCLOSURE

David Gelston's List of Steamboats

List of Steam Boats

Between		Length	Breadth	Depth	Tonnage
New York & Albany	Paragon	167.6	26.10	7.9	331.39
	Car of Neptune	169.0	25.2	7.3	295.55
	North river	149.0	17.11	7.0	182.48
	Hope	149.0	20.8	7.7	225.33
	Perseverance	147.0	20.6	7.6	218.00
					1252.80[1]
N York & Brunswick	Raritan[2]	129.0	21.0	6.8	163.93
					1416.78[3]

MS (MHi); in an unidentified hand; undated.

[1] The correct figure is 1252.75.
[2] Manuscript: "Rariton."
[3] The correct figure is 1416.68.

From Joseph Dougherty

DEAR SIR Washington City Oct[r] 18th–11

I observe in a late paper that M[r] G: W: Campbell is elected to the Senate of the U:S: in the place of M[r] Whiteside resigned, as he is an active man, and a warm friend to the republican cause, I expect he will be here at the commencement of the session, I believe him to be your friend: however that is best known to your Self

To say any thing of the trouble you have already taken would be useless; you know my disposition well. and all that I have to say is that you have only fulfil[d] my expectation and should the lot fall on me, I will exert myself to cherish that recommendation which you were so kind as to give me.

I hope M[r] & M[rs] Randolph & the family is well:

our city is verry sickly at present, and many sudden deaths has been leatly. Thank God myself and family is healthy

I am sir your Humble Servant JO[S] DOUGHERTY

RC (DLC); at foot of text: "M[r] Th. Jefferson"; endorsed by TJ as received 24 Oct. 1811 and so recorded in SJL.

Washington was SICKLY with a bilious fever that Dolley Madison blamed on standing water from an unfinished canal (Dolley Madison, *Selected Letters*, 150–1).

From James Walker

DEAR SIR Hardware 18th Oct[r] 1811.

I suppose you are getting impatient for me to come on to commence your S. Mill. as the time appointed for me to come is elapsed, some parts of mr. Cockes mill has given out. so that he cant go on to manufactor to advantage. he is pressing me to fix him before I remove down to work for you. we have a large cogwheel to make[1] and some other small jobs to do before I can come which will take 2 or 3 weeks longer—after which shall come on with double the nomber of hands that I now have the command of, as a job of work in nelson county will be finished where some of my best workmen are—it has not been convenient to me to come as I promised when I last wrote you. & am in hopes it will make no material difference— I am your obt. servt JAS WALKER.

RC (DLC); addressed: "Thomas Jefferson Esqr"; endorsed by TJ as received 20 Oct. 1811 and so recorded in SJL.

[1] Preceding two words added in margin.

To Joseph Milligan

SIR Monticello Oct. 19. 11

I have at two or three different dates written to ask the favor of you to let me know how much I am in your debt, but have received no answer. if you will be so good as to inform me, it shall be promptly remitted, as it should have been long ago, had the amount been known to me. should you in the mean time have been able to get the 7th & 8th vols of the Scientific dialogues I shall be glad to recieve them by post. the whole of the 8. vols would be well worthy of reprinting, there being no book on the same subject equal to it for general use. accept my best wishes & respects TH: JEFFERSON

PoC (DLC); at foot of text: "Mr Milligan"; endorsed by TJ.

To Roger C. Weightman

SIR Monticello Oct. 19. 11.

I have duly recieved your favor of the 12th and also the parcel of fiorin grass of which you were so kind as to take charge, and for your care of which I pray you to accept my thanks. it has been immediately planted, and every care will be taken to add it to the useful grasses of our country.

I observe in the National Intelligencer you mention having for sale among other books, a miniature edition of Scott's works in 5. vols. I will pray you to send it to me by the mail, carefully done up, with a note of the price which I will take care to remit you. if I can recieve it by the first return of post, it will be the more acceptable. I tender you my best wishes & respects TH: JEFFERSON

PoC (MoSHi: TJC-BC); at foot of text: "Mr Weightman"; endorsed by TJ.

Weightman advertised "an assortment of late and VALUABLE WORKS," including a five-volume MINIATURE EDITION of Sir Walter Scott's poetry, in the Washington *National Intelligencer*, 12 Oct. 1811.

From Edmund M. Blunt

SIR, New-York. Oct. 21, 1811

Permit me respectfully to beg your acceptance of Nautical Almanac for 1813—If consistent with rule of propriety may I beg your influence with Secretary of the Navy for his order for my Edition, to be used by the Officers—Mr Garnetts Edition for 1813, contains no less than 45 errors, all of may[1] I have pointed out.

With respect your obt. hum sert EDM M BLUNT

RC (DLC); between dateline and salutation: "Hon Thos Jefferson"; endorsed by TJ as received 27 Oct. 1811 and so recorded in SJL. Enclosure: Blunt, *The Nautical Almanac and Astronomical Ephemeris for the year 1813* (New York, 1811; Sowerby, no. 3810).

[1] Thus in manuscript.

From Destutt de Tracy

MONSIEUR a paris ce 21 8bre 1811.

je ne vous dissimulerai pas que j'attendois une reponse de vous a ma lettre du 12 juin 1809., avec une impatience extreme et une inquietude proportionnée au prix infini que j'attache a l'honneur de votre Suffrage. vos bontés ont passé toutes mes esperances.

Mr Warden, a Son arrivée ici, a remis de votre part a M^r le G^al la fayette un exemplaire de la traduction du commentaire Sur Montesquieu qui venoit de parôitre au moment de Son depart. il m'a dit a moi meme, Sans Savoir tout le plaisir qu'il me faisoit, que vous estimiez cet ouvrage et que vous aviez mis beaucoup d'interest a Sa publication; et en meme tems il m'a donné votre lettre du 26 janvier 1811. qui a mis le comble a ma Satisfaction et a ma reconnoissance.

vous me parlez de gloire, Monsieur; j'ai toujours cru qu'elle etoit placée trop haut pour que je puisse[1] jamais y atteindre, et je m'en consolois facilement. c'est le Sincere desir d'etre utile tost ou tard et non la vaine esperance d'etre celebre, qui m'a fait travailler. mais j'obtiens aujourdhuy la gloire la plus Solide et la Seule qui je desirasse réelement. c'est l'aprobation de l'homme d'etat le plus vertueux et le plus veritablement eclairé qui ait jamais presidé aux destinées d'un grand peuple.

je Sens tout ce que je dois a votre indulgence et a votre aimable desir d'encourager quelqu'un a qui vous voyez de bonnes intentions. mais enfin meme en retranchant beaucoup des eloges que vous voulez bien me donner, il me reste la douce certitude que vous aprouvez mes vues, et que par consequent elles Sont Saines. vous les avez preservées de l'oubli au quel elles Sembloient condamnées. vous les avez publiées et repandues dans un Vaste pays qui est l'esperance et l'exemple de l'univers. je Suis plus que content. le destin des verités est de faire le tour du monde, une fois qu'elles Sont connues; et je me console trés bien que celles-cy ne reviennent en europe qu'aprés ma mort, puisqu'elles y troubleroient ma vie. je vous remercie infiniment d'avoir protegé mon Secret.

je ne vous dois pas moins de remerciments, Monsieur, pour le desir que vous me marquez, que je reprenne le plan entier de Montesquieu, et que je refasse moi meme un traité des loix. ce Souhait de votre part est Si flatteur qu'il me donne la confiance de vous avouer que j'avois osé tenter cette grande entreprise, et que je la regardois comme une consequence et une Suitte de mon travail Sur nos facultés intellectuelles. pour vous expliquer mes idées a cet egard, permettez moi de vous rappeller qu'en 1804. j'eus l'honneur de vous envoyer mes deux premiers volumes, l'un intitulé idéologie, l'autre Grammaire. ne Sachant pas Si ces recherches pouvoient meriter votre attention, je n'ai jamais osé vous envoyer la troisieme partie intitulée logique. aujourdhuy vous me donnez plus d'assurance, et je prends la liberté de vous envoyer cy joint un exemplaire de ces trois volumes tels qu'ils Sont maintenant. ils traitent de la formation, de l'expression, et de la combinaison de nos idées. ils composent, Suivant ma maniere de voir, l'histoire de nos moyens de connoitre, ou Si vous voulez, un traité de notre entendement.

Si vous daignez jetter les yeux Sur le tableau qui termine le neuvieme chapitre du troisieme volume, vous verrez que je ne considere ce traité de l'entendement que comme la premiere Section d'un plus grand ouvrage dont la Seconde Section devroit etre un traité de la volonté et de Ses effets; et que ce traité de la volonté devroit aussi etre composé de trois parties traitant de nos actions, de nos Sentiments, et de la maniere de diriger les unes et les autres, et intitulées economie, morale, et gouvernement ou plustot legislation. c'est a dire que la premiere auroit été destinée a bien faire connoitre nos veritables interests physiques et economiques, la Seconde a developper nos interets et nos affections morales; et c'est la troisieme Seule dont j'aurois taché de faire un traité des loix civiles et politiques, et de l'esprit dans le quel elles doivent etre faites. mais je n'aurois jamais voulu aborder ce grand Sujet qu'aprés tous ces préliminaires, parcequ'il me Semble qu'eux Seuls pouvoient assurer ma marche et m'empecher de tomber dans ces divagations et ces incoherences dont Montesquieu n'a pu Se preserver malgrés Son genie. en effet en procedant ainsi on pourroit arriver par une Suitte de consequences rigoureuses et non interompues, depuis l'examen de notre premier acte intellectuel jusqu'a la derniere de nos dispositions legislatives; et il n'y auroit aucun principe etabli dont on ne trouvat la cause et la demonstration dans les observations anterieures, ou plustot ils Sortiroient d'eux memes des faits bien observés.

mes remarques Sur Montesquieu n'avoient d'autre objet que d'eclaircir quelques unes de mes idées et de me fournir des materiaux pour l'execution de ce projet. les encouragements que vous avez la bonté de me prodiguer me donnent un bien vif desir de m'y livrer. mais malheureusement les chagrins et les Souffrances m'amenant a une vieillesse prematurée, ont deja bien diminué le peu de capacité que j'avois. cependant je ferai tous mes efforts puisque vous voulez bien vous y interesser. je vous confierai meme que le discours préliminaire de ce traité de la volonté, et toute la premiere partie qui traite de l'économie politique, Sont a peu prés terminés. Si je puis y mettre la derniere main, j'aurai l'honneur de vous en envoyer une copie manuscripte, dans l'esperance de recevoir vos avis et vos critiques. l'idée Seule que vous voulez bien vous en occuper me Soustiendra et me donnera de nouvelles forces que je n'aurois pas trouvées en moi.

A l'egard des observations que vous voulez bien me faire Sur la necessité d'un president du conseil executif, je vous dirai, Monsieur, qu'elles m'ont beaucoup interessé, beaucoup eclairé, mais je vous avouerai que loin de me rassurer elles m'inquietent beaucoup; et vous devinez aisément pourquoy. en effet vous m'aprenez des faits trés curieux, et qui en eux memes ou par l'issue qu'ils ont eu, Sont tous trés honorables pour votre nation, et vous me prouvez trés bien que la voix préponderante d'un president est trés utile, vous ne me montrez meme que trop qu'elle est presque necessaire. il est vrai que vous me prouvez trés bien aussi qu'elle est Sans danger. mais vous convenez que votre plus grand motif de Securité est dans l'excellence de votre constitution fédérative; et vous me permettrez d'ajouter qu'il ne peut pas y avoir de vrais dangers pour la liberté d'un pays dont les gouvernants, quand ils Sont le plus divisés par l'esprit de faction, (comme votre comité des etats en 1784) prennent le parti de S'en aller chacun chez eux et d'attendre tranquillement que la volonté nationale Se manifeste légalement, d'un pays dont les habitants laissent ecouler paisiblement cette espece d'interregne de prés de Six mois, et Surtout d'un pays dont le premier citoyen m'ecrit cette phrase admirable que je n'ose traduire, tant elle me paroit etrangere a toute langue européenne: nor have I ever been able to conceive how any rational being could propose happiness to himself from the exercise[2] of power over others.

Vraiment, Monsieur, avec de telles garanties je n'en demanderois pas d'autres et je Serois aussi tranquille que vous. mais vous Savez mieux que moi que ce n'est que bien a la longue que les meilleures institutions parviennent a former de grands citoyens et un caractere national Solide et Sage. le Seul des avantages de votre pays que l'on puisse Se donner promptement, c'est donc une constitution federative. or cette ressource lá meme n'est pas a l'usage d'un peuple environné de gouvernements ennemis et puissants. Si notre france avoit été partagée en un certain nombre d'etats bien Separés, bien indépendants les uns des autres, et reunis Seulement par un foible lien fédératif, jamais nous n'aurions pu faire venir ceux du midi au Secours de ceux du nord, ny ceux de l'ouest au Secours de ceux de l'est; jamais nous n'aurions pu Soutenir la terrible lutte dont nous ne Sommes Sortis vainqueurs que par l'effet du pouvoir central le plus energique qui ait jamais existé; immanquablement notre pays eut été Subjugué ou dechiré; c'est ce que vous assureront tous ceux qui l'ont vu dans ces tems de crise et de calamité. Si donc une constitution fédérative est impossible quand on est entouré de voisins dangereux, Si en meme tems l'unité du pouvoir éxécutif n'est Sans danger que dans une constitution federative, et Si pourtant cette unité est indispensable pour qu'un gouvernement libre puisse Se Soutenir, il faudroit en tirer cette triste consequence que dans notre vieille europe et Surtout dans les pays mediterranés, tout gouvernement moderé et legal est impossible a la longue. permettez moi, Monsieur, d'esperer qu'il n'est que difficile, et que par d'habiles combinaisons on peut Supléer aux avantages de la fédération. toutes fois (j'en conviens et je crois l'avoir dit) la fédération resoud le probléme de la maniere la plus facile et la plus Sure. j'en Suis Si persuadé que je crois encor que quand un peuple S'est donné un gouvernement representatif fondé Sur le principe de l'unité et de l'indivisibilité, il n'est bien Sur de le conserver que quand il [S'est] formé autour de lui des gouvernements Semblables avec les quels il puisse former une Confédératio[n] plus ou moins etroite. car je Suis convaincu qu'une reunion de cette espece est necessaire pour donne[r] de la Solidité a chacune des parties qui la composent, les quelles demeurant isolées resteroient toujou[rs] bien plus exposées a des revolutions frequentes, ne fut-ce que parcequ'elles Seroient plus exposées a [des] guerres etrangeres; car la guerre est la Source de la tirannie, comme la paix est le plus ferme apu[y] de la liberté: j'aime donc bien, Monsieur, le Sisteme fédératif; j'en Sens vivement tous les avantages; ainsi j'espere m'eloigner bien peu de votre façon de penser. Seulement vous me force[z à] croire que la liberté est encor un peu plus difficile a conserver que je ne l'avois imaginé. Si malgr[é] tant de difficultés elle parvient, comme je l'espere, a S'etablir un jour parmi les hommes, ce Sera a [votre] pays qu'on en aura l'obligation, et par consequent a vous plus qu'a personne au monde. jugez, Monsieur, de ma veneration pour votre personne, et veuillez bien en agréer les assurances ain[si] que celles de ma reconnoissance et de mon respect. DESTUTT-TRACY

EDITORS' TRANSLATION

SIR Paris 21 October 1811.

I will not conceal from you that I awaited an answer to my letter of 12 June 1809 with extreme impatience and an anxiety proportional to the infinite value that I attach to your opinion. Your kindnesses have exceeded all my hopes.

On his arrival Mr. Warden gave General Lafayette on your behalf a copy of the translation of the commentary on Montesquieu, which had just come out at the time of his departure. Without fully realizing the pleasure he was giving me, he told me that you liked the work and had shown a great deal of interest in its publication. At the same time he gave me your letter of 26 January 1811, which brought my satisfaction and gratitude to a peak.

You speak of glory, Sir. I always thought it too lofty a goal for me ever to attain, or so I easily consoled myself. I worked from a sincere desire to be useful sooner or later rather than with the vain hope of being famous. Today, I receive the surest and only glory that I really desire: the approval of the most virtuous and truly enlightened statesman ever to preside over the destiny of a great people.

I am conscious of all that I owe you for your indulgence and your kind desire to encourage someone in whom you recognize good intentions, but even after discounting much of the praise you so willingly give me, I am left with the sweet certainty that you approve of my views and that, in consequence, they are sound. You have saved them from the oblivion to which they seemed doomed. You have published and spread them in a vast country that is the hope and example of the universe. I am more than satisfied. Truths are destined to circle the globe, once they are known, and I am quite reconciled to the thought that mine will return to Europe only after my death, as they would, if known, only disturb my life. I am immensely grateful that you have kept my secret.

Sir, I also owe you thanks for your desire that I take up all of Montesquieu and write my own treatise on law. This very flattering suggestion emboldens me to confess that I have dared to attempt so large an undertaking and that I looked on it as a consequence and continuation of my work on our intellectual faculties. So as to explain my ideas in this regard, allow me to remind you that in 1804 I had the honor of sending you my first two volumes, one entitled Ideology and the other Grammar. Not knowing whether these works merited your attention, I never sent you the third part entitled Logic. You have today bolstered my confidence on this score, and I take the liberty of sending you herewith the three volumes as they now stand. They deal with the formation, expression, and combination of our ideas. In my view, they constitute the history of our means to know or, if you will, a treatise on our understanding.

If you would be so good as to examine the table that concludes the ninth chapter of the third volume, you will see that I consider the treatise on understanding as only the first part of a bigger project, the second part of which concerns the will and its effects. This treatise should likewise be comprised of three parts, entitled economy, morals, and government or, rather, legislation, and deal with our actions and feelings, and the ways in which we control them. That is to say, the first part will be devoted to learning what our true physical and economic interests are; the second to exposing our interests and moral affections; and only in the third part will I try to write a treatise on civil and political law and the spirit in which laws must be made. I would never have wanted to approach this subject before completing all of those preliminary works, because in so doing I can steady my course and avoid the ramblings and incoherencies from which Montesquieu, despite his genius, could not safeguard himself. Indeed in this way one could proceed, through a series of rigorous and uninterrupted inferences, from the examination of our first intellectual act to our most recent legislative measures. We could find the cause and proof in previous observations for every established principle, or rather they would come to light by themselves through well-observed facts.

In commenting on Montesquieu my only object was to clarify some of my ideas and provide myself with materials to carry out this project. Your kind encouragement makes me want to devote myself to it. Unfortunately, sorrows and sufferings are aging me prematurely and have already diminished my small means. Nevertheless, because you are so kind as to take an interest, I will make great efforts. I will even share with you the fact that the preliminary discourse of this treatise on the will and all of the first part dealing with political economy are nearly finished. Once I have put the finishing touches on them, I will give myself the honor of sending you a handwritten copy with the hope of receiving your comments and criticisms. Your interest in it will sustain me and give me renewed strength that I would not have found in myself.

I found your observations on the need for a president of the executive council quite interesting and thought-provoking, but I must confess that, far from reassuring me, they worry me a lot, and you can easily guess why. You apprise me of some very curious facts which, in and of themselves or because of their outcome, are very honorable for your nation. You prove to me that giving the deciding vote to a president is very useful; you show all too well that it is almost a necessity and is not dangerous. You acknowledge, however, that your main reason for feeling safe is the excellence of your federal constitution. You will allow me to add that the freedom of a country can be in no real danger when those in power during a time of the deepest party divisions (as with your confederation of states in 1784), make up their minds to go home and patiently wait for the national will to express itself legally; where people let this sort of interregnum go on peacefully for close to six months; and especially where its first citizen writes an admirable sentence that I dare not translate, as it seems to me so foreign to every European language: nor have I ever been able to conceive how any rational being could propose happiness to himself from the exercise of power over others.

Truly, Sir, such guarantees would keep me from seeking any other and I would be as unworried as you are, but you know better than I that the best institutions succeed in shaping good citizens and a strong and wise national character only in the long run. Of all your country's advantages, another nation could only make quick use of a federal constitution. But this resource is no help to a people surrounded by powerful enemy governments. If our own France had been divided into a certain number of separate states, quite independent from one another, and united only by a feeble federal bond, we would never have been able to summon aid from the South for those of the North, nor help from the West for those of the East. Never could we have sustained the terrific struggle from which we have emerged victorious only because of the most energetic central power that ever existed. Our country would inevitably have been crushed or torn apart. All observers of those days of crisis and calamity will earnestly tell you this. Therefore, if a federal constitution is impossible whilst dangerous neighbors surround a country, if at the same time a unified executive is only safe within the confines of a federal constitution, and if this unity is nevertheless indispensable for a free government to assert itself, we must sadly conclude that in our old Europe, and especially in Mediterranean countries, all moderate and legal government is impossible in the short run. Allow me to hope, Sir, that it is only difficult, and that through skillful combinations we can supply some of the advantages of the federal system. However (I admit and believe I have already said), a federal system solves the problem in the easiest and surest way. I am so convinced of this that I still believe that, when a people has given itself a unified and indivisible representative government, its preservation can only be assured by creating around it similar governments with which it can federate more or less closely. I am convinced that such a union is needed to give solidity to each of its component parts. If they remained isolated, they will always be much more exposed to frequent revolutions, if only because they will be more exposed to foreign wars. War is the source of tyranny, just as peace is the firmest support of freedom. Therefore, Sir, I like the federal system very much. I clearly see its advantages, and so I hope to avoid moving too far from your way of thinking. You induce me, however, to recognize that freedom is even harder to preserve than I had imagined. If, in spite of all these difficulties, it manages some day to be established among men, as I hope it will, we will owe it to your country and consequently to yourself more than to anyone else. Sir, witness my profound esteem for your person and rest assured that it is sincere, as are my gratitude and respect.

DESTUTT-TRACY

RC (DLC); right margin of last page cropped, with gaps supplied from Gilbert Chinard, *Jefferson et les Idéologues* [1925], 90–1; endorsed by TJ as received 26 Feb. 1812 and so recorded in SJL. Translation by Dr. Roland H. Simon. Enclosures: (1) Destutt de Tracy, *Élémens d'Idéologie: Idéologie proprement dite* (Paris, 1804; Sowerby, no. 1239). (2) Destutt de Tracy, *Grammaire* (Paris, 1803; Sowerby, no. 1239). (3) Destutt de Tracy, *Logique* (Paris, 1805). Enclosed in David Bailie Warden to TJ, 10 Dec. 1811.

Destutt de Tracy also sent TJ the first two enclosures in a letter dated 21 Feb. 1804 (DLC). NOR HAVE I EVER BEEN ABLE TO CONCEIVE . . . THE EXERCISE OF POWER OVER OTHERS: Destutt de Tracy here quotes from TJ's letter of 26 Jan. 1811.

[1] Manuscript: "pusse."
[2] Manuscript: "exercice."

From Nathaniel Macon

SIR Buck Spring 21 Oc^tr^ 1811

By M^r^ M^c^lure I yesterday received the letter, which you wrote to me on the 24, of last month, and have written at his request, to two of his principal creditors, in each letter I gave an extract from yours; one of the creditors lives in Franklin, the other in Granville, each about 40. miles from me; I was not acquainted with M^r^ M^c^Lure till he came here with your letter, I would have seen his chief creditor, had I not have been preparing to start for Washington

I am with the most perfect respect & esteem
sir y^r^ ob^t^ ser^t^ NATH^L^ MACON

RC (MHi); endorsed by TJ as received 14 Nov. 1811 and so recorded in SJL.

James Hamilton, of GRANVILLE County, North Carolina, seems to have been William McClure's CHIEF CREDITOR (Hamilton to TJ, 16 Apr. 1812; TJ to Hamilton, 25 June 1812).

Notes on Household Consumption

1809.

June 3. a beef purchased Apr. 15. weighing the 4. quarters 637 ℔
and another supposed to weigh about
have lasted to this day, to wit 7. weeks. this is about 20.℔ of beef a day.

Aug. 27. the two Canteens of brandy from Leitch.

Aug. 29. 25.℔ brown sugar rec^d^ from Leitch Aug. 22. now out. there has been much company. this is 3½ ℔ a day

29. rec^d^ 25.℔ from Leitch.

Sep. 7.[1] groceries from Gordon & Trokes opened. see their lre of Aug. 29.

Nov. 30. the wood box in my bedroom holds $\frac{1}{10}$ of a cord, and in 9 days, partly excessive cold, partly very moderate was used twice full, which is a cord in 45 days = $6\frac{1}{2}$ weeks the box was filled Nov. 22. 26. 30

Dec. 5. 12. 15. 18. 23. 28. 31.
Jan. 5. 13. 19. 22. 25. 27. 29.
Feb $\frac{2}{2.}$ 3. 5. 8. 13. 20. 28.
Mar. 10. 16. $\frac{22}{2.}$

Dec. 4. agreed to take of mrs Lewis 16. young geese @ .5. and 12. Turkies @ $.66\frac{2}{3}$ also fresh butter thro' the winter

1810.

Apr. 22. statement of cyder made in November last.
1. cask of Taliaferro cyder was bottled & served thro' the winter to this day.
in March we bottled 460. bottles more of Taliaferro
72. of red Hughes
532
making in the whole about 175. gallons.

May 2. recieved from Richmond 4. quant quart bottles of olive oil; being entirely without. they probably contain about three real quarts. June 12. it was out. which is at the rate of a pint a week.

June. 15. rec[d] 12. similar bottles of d[o] of $1\frac{1}{2}$ pint each = 18. pints: will of course last till about the last of Sep.

July 16. rec[d] from Leitch 35.℔ brown sugar & 3. gall[s] Fr. brandy

Aug 2. rec[d] from d[o] 25.℔ coffee

3. rec[d] from Leitch 25 ℔ brown sugar.
℔ cotton

18. 50.℔ brown sugar & 3. gall[s] brandy from Leitch 2 gall[s] whisky

Sep. 28. 2 loaves sugar from Higginb.

29. 25.℔ brown d[o] from d[o]

Oct. 13. 2. loaves sugar from Higginb.

20. 20 ℔ coffee D. Hig

23. 25.℔ brown sugar } from d[o]
2.℔ tea }

Nov. 7. 50.℔ brown sugar. 20.℔ coffee from Hig

12. 2 loaves sugar Hig

24. 2. canteens Fr. brandy.

Dec. 10. 2. loaves sugar
25.℔ coffee

1.℔ black pepper[2]

1811.

Jan.	10.	50.℔ brown[3] sugar. this proved full of sand 2. loaves white sugar 25.℔ coffee	Higginb.
	23.	4.[4] loaves white sugar. Hig.	
	27.	50.℔ brown sugar. Watson and Vest.[5]	
Mar.	5.	2.℔ tea 2. loaves white sugar 50.℔ brown d°	D.H.
	6.	50.℔ brown sugar 4. cheeses 96.℔	Watson & Vest
	13.	50.℔ coffee 2. loaves sugar	D.H.
	23.	a hhd molasses D.H. @ 3/ + carriage. 90 gallons. 200.℔ cotton.	
	28.	2.℔ tea 4. loaves sugar 1.℔ black pepper	D.H.
May.	26.	2. loaves sugar. D.H.	
	30.	50.℔ brown sugar 20 ℔ coffee	D.H.
June	22.	2. loaves sugar 50.℔ brown d°	D H.
	25.	2.℔ tea	
July	7.	2 loaves sugar. D.H.	
	28	2 d° d°	
Aug.	3.	20 ℔ coffee. d°	
	26.	50.℔ br. sugar 2. loaves white 2.℔ tea.	
Sep.	10.	50.℔ brown sugar 2. loaves white 1.℔ race ginger. 1 oz. mace. 2. oz. cloves	
	15.	2.℔ tea 2. loaves sugar 20.℔ coffee.	
Oct.	4.	2 canteens Fr. brandy from Leitch	
	23.	2 ℔ tea. 2 loaves sugar 50.℔ brown d°	

MS (MHi); written entirely in TJ's hand on both sides of a single sheet; with Notes on Household Consumption, 21 Feb. 1815, subjoined.

RACE GINGER: ginger root (*OED*).

1 Reworked from "6."
2 Recto ends here.
3 Reworked from "coffee."
4 Reworked from "3."
5 Manuscript: "Velt."

From George Jefferson

DEAR SIR — Richmond 24th Octr 1811

I have received of Mr Griffin W. & R. Mitchell's dft on Robert Gamble for 600$ due the 5th of next month, which is accepted.

I now inclose a note for your signature, to renew with at the Bank.—I also inclose 3 blanks, which, if you think proper, you can[1] fill up and return, as it will save you the trouble of frequent applications.

I am Dear Sir Your Very humble servt — GEO. JEFFERSON

RC (MHi); at foot of text: "Thomas Jefferson esqr"; endorsed by TJ as received 26 Oct. 1811 and so recorded in SJL. Enclosures not found.

SJL records a missing letter from TJ to Jefferson of 20 Oct. 1811.

1 Manuscript: "call."

From George Jefferson

DEAR SIR — Richmond 24th Octr 1811

Will you have the goodness to inform me if it will not be necessary, previous to my departure to Lisbon, to go to Washington? It occurs to me that verbal as well as written instructions may be desirable. As yet I have received none, not even an intimation as to the bond which I observe the law requires.

I would ask this information of Mr Monroe, but I have been too decidedly hostile to what I conceived to be his new politics, to ask any thing of him; unless I thought my official situation absolutely required it.

even then it would be unpleasant.

I am Dear Sir Your Mt faithful friend & servt

GEO. JEFFERSON

RC (MHi); at foot of text: "Thomas Jefferson esqr"; endorsed by TJ as received 26 Oct. 1811 and so recorded in SJL.

"An Act concerning Consuls and Vice-Consuls," 14 Apr. 1792, required every newly appointed consul and vice-consul to provide the secretary of state with a

BOND for between $2,000 and $10,000 before entering upon their duties (*U.S. Statutes at Large*, 1:256). Jefferson had apparently been angered by James Monroe's NEW POLITICS, particularly his flirtation with the Richmond Junto and the Tertium Quids and his opposition to TJ's chosen successor, James Madison, during the 1808 presidential election.

From Melatiah Nash

DEAR SIR, New York Oct. 24th 1811

having frequently observed the small degree of knowledge which prevails amongst mankind in general respecting the solar system and the Stars, and believing a general dissemination of astronomical knowledge would be of great utility, I am preparing for the press a small work, which, it is presumed, will lay a foundation for general improvement in that important science. But before its publication I deem it necessary to have the opinion of gentlemen, eminent in science, on its probable utility, and request the aid [o]f their recommendations.—The title of the work is [t]o be, "The Columbian Ephemeris and Astronomical Diary"—There will be four pages to each month. The first page will be a transcript of the Nautical Almanac with the addition of Chronological events; chiefly such as relate to our own country. Also phenomena of the Heavenly bodies, principally, conjunctions of the moon with Stars near her orbit, and conjunctions of the Planets with Stars and with one another. These, expressed in astronomical terms, will afterwards be explained in language intelligible to every capacity. The second page will shew the time of the rising and setting of the Sun, the rising, setting, and culminating of the moon and planets.[1] The third page will shew the time of the rising, setting, and culminating of the principal fixed stars. The fourth page will give the time of high water at sixteen principal ports, harbours, and headlands of the United States. These calculations are made on astronomical principles. For the angular distance of the Sun and Moon, and for the distance of the moon from the Earth at the time of high water allowance is made. A brief compendium of Astronomy will be prefixed, and a tide table for the whole coast of the Union will be inserted. Though the tides are sometimes affected by winds and other circumstances, yet, it is presumed this part of the work will be of great service to persons employed in the coasting trade. All the calculations in the Ephemeris are made to apparent, and adapted, to civil time. The principal design of the publication bei[ng] to enable all readers to know the Planets, and many of the fixed Stars, it is thought the work will serve this purpose throughout the United States. This first number which is made for the year 1812 will contain one hundred or more pages octavo, and if due encouragement is given one will be published for several succeeding years, with annual additions and improvements. I have no apology to offer for the trouble I have given you Sir, except the desire of obtaining your ideas on my humble attempt. Your opinion is considered of great importance, and by communicating it, You[2] will receive my grateful acknowledgements.—

I am, Sir, with the greatest respect your Humble Servant.

MELATIAH NASH.

RC (MiU-C); dateline beneath signature; mutilated at seal; at foot of text: "Thomas Jefferson Esq[r]"; endorsed by TJ as received 31 Oct. 1811 and so recorded in SJL.

Melatiah Nash (ca. 1768–1830) kept what was variously described as a select academy, select seminary, mathematical and philosophical academy, and commercial school in New York City from about 1803 until his death. He also operated a circulating library and grocery during the first decade of the nineteenth century. Nash published a translation of Jean Baptiste Louvet de Couvray's French novel, *Emilia de Varmont, or the Necessary Divorce; and Memoirs of Curate Sevin* (New York, 1799), *The Columbian Ephemeris and Astronomical Diary, for the year 1812* (New York, 1812), and three annual numbers of *The Ladies' and Gentlemen's Diary, or, United States Almanac, and Repository of Science and Amusement* (New York, 1819–21). He also prepared a revised edition of a textbook by S. Treeby, *The Elements of Astronomy* (New York, 1823), and a short essay on methods of determining latitude and longitude ashore for the New York *American Monthly Magazine and Critical Review* 2 (1817): 92–5 (*Longworth's New York Directory* [1803], 224; [1806], 273; [1830], 454; New York *Weekly Museum*, 5 Mar. 1803, 23 May 1807; *New-York Columbian*, 29 Nov. 1811, 21 Oct. 1817; *New-York Evening Post*, 5 Aug. 1813, 24 July 1830).

[1] For use in his 15 Nov. 1811 reply, TJ here keyed the marginal note "eqn time" (equation of time) with a caret.

[2] Nash here canceled "Sir."

From John Bracken

SIR, W[ms]burg 25. Oct. 1811

I thank you for the information given in your letter of Oct. 9 of the opportunity afforded by M[r] George Jefferson of making a remittance to the poor sisters of Bellini. I intend to make use of that fair opportunity, & with that view will wait on M[r] G. Jefferson in Rich[d] in the course of next Month.

With great respect & regard
I am Your most obed[t] Serv[t] JOHN BRACKEN.

RC (DLC); dateline at foot of text; endorsed by TJ as received 7 Nov. 1811 and so recorded in SJL.

From Edward Coles

Dear Sir Washington Oct. 25th 1811

I shiped yesterday on board the schooner Goodintent, Elliott Kirwan, Master, bound for Richmond, the seven Boxes left here by Mr Barlow containing your Papers &c, and shall this day forward the Bill of Lading to Messrs Gibson & Jefferson, to whose care I have directed them. You desired me to return you an estimate of the expences[1] that might be incured before they were shiped, but as they were conveyed to the wharf by Mr Oneale, who is the owner of the Vessel, he has charged the Drayage, with the freight, in the bill of lading, which will be paid in Richmond by Messrs Gibson & Jefferson.

with the greatest respect & esteem I am your friend

Edward Coles

RC (DLC); at foot of text: "Th: Jefferson"; endorsed by TJ as received 29 Oct. 1811, but recorded in SJL as received two days earlier.

[1] Manuscript: "expencces."

From Edward Coles

Oct. 30th 1811

E. Coles presents his respectful compliments to Mr Jefferson, and takes the liberty of informing him, that he received information a few days ago from Mr Lee, the Collector at Salem, that he had received from Mr Baker, our consul at Palma, "the following articles addressed to Th: Jefferson, One Cask of wine, one Box Marble, one Box of olives, and one Bag of Almonds," and that he shipped them on the 19th. of October on board the schooner Jachin, William Silver master for Alexandria to the care of the Collector

RC (DLC); dateline at foot of text; endorsed by TJ as received 3 Nov. 1811 and so recorded in SJL.

To Henry Foxall

Dear Sir Monticello Oct. 31. 11.

Your favor of the 12th has been duly recieved, and I am glad to learn that you have made the Swedish stove. I have no doubt it will repay your expences well after it shall become known. it's high estimation in Europe authorises the same here, & to presume it will become general. I do expect that the stile of plain panneled work in which you have executed it, is probably neater than more complicated ornaments. I shall be glad to have one of them sent to me, by the way of Richmond, & to the address of my correspondents there, Gibson & Jefferson. I shall need about 20. feet of pipe, and three elbows, these cannot be obtained here, & must therefore come with the stove. I would wish the whole packed in boxes not too heavy to be handled by two men. the expence of boxes is less than the risk of loss & injury passing thro' so many hands by the way. the advancing season will make the early reciept the more acceptable. I salute you with assurances of my great esteem & respect.

TH: JEFFERSON

P.S. where the pipe passes thro' an upper floor what has been found the best way of securing the floor against taking fire from the heat of the pipe?

PoC (MHi); above postscript: "Mr Foxall"; endorsed by TJ.

From George Jefferson

DEAR SIR Richmond 31st Octr 1811

I apprehend from your favor of the 27th that I must have expressed my meaning very badly, respecting my future correspondence with M^r M—. I retained no copy of my letter, not having wished to leave any trace behind me upon such a subject.—I was perfectly aware of the absolute necessity of a regular correspondence with him.—I merely meant to say, that I should not like to ask any thing of him out of the strict line of our official duties: and that even that would be unpleasant to me.—I could say any thing, to any person, which I thought my official situation required; but it would be unpleasant to me to correspond with a person, even officially, when my feelings towards him had undergone a very great change to his prejudice: yet although unpleasant, when duty required it, submission would be easy.

Nothing of a personal nature, in the smallest degree unpleasant, has ever occurred between M^r M— and myself.

I have said harsh things of his public conduct, even to his warmest friend—which, that I may not be thought to have acted with indelicacy, I will say were forced from me, by harsh and indelicate observations from that friend.

Having said such things of him, and even still retaining the same opinion, notwithstanding the obviously different one of the two persons on earth of whom I think most highly, I should be unwilling to make an offer of personal services, unless you should still think that from my official situation, common civility,[1] rendered it necessary: if so, I will submit—but if otherwise, I would gladly forego the apparent duplicity and meanness of making a tender of such services: which might even be construed into a change of tone produced by his change of situation—and perhaps too, to the base motive, of looking forward to him hereafter, for a continuance of my preferment.—but for these considerations, I should certainly be perfectly willing to render any reasonable services to Mr M—, as I hope from my contemplated situation I should be, to any other of my Countrymen.

I repeat my willingness however, after this explanation, to be governed wholly by you.— Should no public measure take place to render my immediate departure unnecessary,[2] I contemplate going at furthest by the last[3] of next month.

Mr Gibson's health will not permit of his return so soon as he expected, but after experiencing such long indulgence, I ought not to ask it to be extended.

Your four notes for renewal in the bank, to last until the 5th of May; & for 60 days thereafter, are received.

I am Dear Sir Your constant friend & servt

GEO. JEFFERSON

Your flour has not yet arrived—some sales have been made at 7$.

RC (MHi); postscript on verso of address leaf; addressed: "Thomas Jefferson esquire Monticello"; franked; postmarked Richmond, 31 Oct.; endorsed by TJ as received 3 Nov. 1811 and so recorded in SJL.

SJL records TJ's missing letter to Jefferson of October THE 27TH. MR M—: James Monroe. The TWO PERSONS ON EARTH OF WHOM I THINK MOST HIGHLY were probably TJ and James Madison.

[1] Jefferson interlined "<*or*> common civility."

[2] Thus in manuscript.

[3] Word interlined in place of "middle."

To Nathaniel H. Hooe

DEAR SIR Monticello Nov. 3.[1] 11.

I have this day desired messrs Gibson & Jefferson to remit to the bank of Fredericksburg subject to your order 131.D. for the hire of Tom & Edmund the last year, to wit, 74.D. for Tom, and 57.D. for Edmund. his death taking place on the 18th of Oct. from Dec. 25. to that time, @ 70.D. a year comes to 57.D. the other matters which are the subject of your last letter, may be arranged when you come into our neighborhood the next month. we hope you will make this your head quarters. Accept the assurance of my esteem & respect.

Th: Jefferson

PoC (MHi); at foot of text: "Nathan[1] H. Hooe esq."; endorsed by TJ.

SJL records the letter from TJ to George Jefferson of THIS DAY, not found, by which he "Desired G. Jefferson to remit to Nathl. H. Hooe 131.D." (*MB*, 2:1270).

[1] Number reworked from "1" or "2."

To Eleuthère I. du Pont de Nemours

Dear Sir Monticello Nov. 4. 11.

I recieved, some time since, the keg of powder, you forwarded for me, and I have been daily expecting you would be so kind as to send on the note of the cost that I might remit it to you. the object of the present is to pray you to forward me another quarter of a hundred, comprehending half a doz: cannisters of shooting powder as before, & the rest proper for blowing rock, of which I have much to do, & to send a note of the cost of both parcels, which shall be immediately remitted you. both qualities have been found of very superior kind, and having distributed the cannisters among the merchants & gentlemen of this quarter, I presume it will occasion calls on you from them. Accept the assurance of my great esteem & respect.

Th: Jefferson

RC (DeGH: DuPont Company Documents); addressed: "Mr E. I. Dupont at the Eleutherian mills near Wilmington. Del."; franked; postmarked Milton, 7 Nov. 1811. PoC (MHi); endorsed by TJ.

To George Jefferson

Dear Sir Monticello Nov. 4. 11.

I recieved by yesterday's post your favor of Oct. 31. and I hasten, by it's return to say in answer to your enquiry that it is not necessary that you should make any particular tender of services to Colo Monroe, altho you may be assured he knows you too well to ascribe it to any unworthy motive, for I know from himself that he holds you in high respect.

My experience in the affairs of the government enables me to make observations on the office you are to enter on which may be useful to you; age renders us prone to assume the office of advice, and my affection for you, while it urges, will at the same time excuse what I say. the Consuls of France recieve salaries & are not permitted to trade. some of the English consuls are on the same footing. these particular gentlemen think themselves obliged to live splendidly, fully up to their salaries, and affect a diplomatic character, to which they are not at all entitled by the law of nations. all other nations chuse for their consuls persons who are in trade, allow them no salary, and expect them to incur no expence as to their office, but to live merely as merchants do, according to their private circumstances. our government places it's consuls on this footing, & expects no display from them: nor do I know that our Consuls any where have thought themselves bound to incur any expence, extraordinary, except mr Hackley. he, I am told, lives at an expence of 12,000.D. a year. this is perfect insanity; it marks him at least to be equally vain, weak, & improvident. it is true, it is said, he recieves 4 or 5000.D. a month. but he misapplies them not the less unwisely. all our other consuls live economically as merchants, & according to their circumstances, and so I am sure you will do, on being apprised that no duty to the government requires you to do otherwise. the President, when here in August, observed you were losing a rich harvest. I suppose the peculiar situation of Cadiz & Lisbon throws much into the hand of the Consul, and that this harvest may end if the French get possession. you should hasten therefore to gather as much as you can of it; & to store it up in your barn.

I am told the ploughs, called Peacock ploughs are to be had in Richmond. I think they are sold by Fitzwhylson & co. will you be so good as to send me one of the larger & one of the smaller size. be careful to distinguish them from the Cary or the Pease plough. they have a cast iron mould board and a coulter on their point. these, and some boxes of books expected from Washington, may come either by mr Randolph's boatmen, or by the William Johnson who carried my flour down, & is quite trustworthy. the same may be trusted with a cask of wine & 3. boxes which will be forwarded to you by the Collector of Alexandria. mrs Hackley sets out in a few days for Richmond. I have requested her to chuse a piece of cotton shirting for me,[1] and to send the bill to you for paiment. affectionately Yours

TH: JEFFERSON

PoC (CtY: Franklin Collection); at foot of first page: "Mr Jefferson"; endorsed by TJ.

David PEACOCK, of Burlington County, New Jersey, patented his cast-iron plow on 1 Apr. 1807 (*List of Patents*, 59;

Philadelphia *United States' Gazette*, 9 June 1807). The CARY plow, characterized by its pyramidal share, was also known as the Dagen or Connecticut plow (Lucia Stanton, "'A Little Matter': Jefferson's Moldboard of Least Resistance," *Chronicle of the Early American Industries Association* 58 [2005]: 3–11, 36). Horace PEASE, of Hartford County, Connecticut, patented his cast-iron plow on 7 Aug. 1813 but sold it locally two years earlier (*List of Patents*, 128; Greenfield, Mass., *Traveller*, 9 July 1811).

[1] Preceding two words interlined.

To William R. Lee

SIR Monticello Nov. 4. 11.

I have just recieved information that there came addressed to you, for me, from mr Baker, our Consul at Palma, a cask of wine, a box, of marble, one of olives & one of almonds, which you have been so good as to forward on to Alexandria. the object of this letter is to thank you for your attention & trouble with these articles, and to pray you to forward to me a note of any expences they may have incurred at your port, under an assurance that they shall be promptly remitted. Accept the tender of my best respects. TH: JEFFERSON

PoC (MHi); at foot of text: "M[r] Lee"; endorsed by TJ.

William Raymond Lee (1745–1824), a native of Manchester, Massachusetts, rose from captain to colonel while serving in the Continental army, 1775–78. After the war he worked as a merchant in Marblehead and Salem. TJ appointed him customs collector for Salem and Beverly in 1802, and he held the post until his death (*Vital Records of Manchester, Massachusetts, to the end of 1849* [1903], 84; Heitman, *Continental Army*, 346; *Salem Gazette*, 26 Dec. 1782, 29 Oct. 1824; Lee to TJ, 28 Sept. 1801 [DNA: RG 59, LAR, 1801–09]; *JEP*, 1:432, 437 [11, 17 Jan. 1803]; Boston *Independent Chronicle*, 7 May 1807).

To Charles Simms

SIR Monticello Nov. 4. 11.

I have just recieved information that mr Lee, the Collector of Salem has forwarded for me to Alexandria by the Schooner Jachin, W[m] Silver a cask of wine, a box of marble, a box of olives, & a bag of almonds. the wine is of the growth of the island of Majorca. can I get the favor of you to have them transhipped on board some vessel bound to Richmond, addressing them to Mess[rs] Gibson & Jefferson? and if the paiment of duties & other charges can be transferred to the same place, that house will discharge them more conveniently for me. but any expences you may incur for the articles at Alexandria if you will have the goodness to drop me a note of them, I will remit them to you without delay. Accept the assurance of my respect.

TH: JEFFERSON

RC (ViU: TJP); at foot of text: "Col° Charles Simms." PoC (MHi); endorsed by TJ.

Charles Simms (1755–1819) rose from major to lieutenant colonel in Virginia regiments of the Continental army, 1776–79. He later opened a law office in Alexandria and represented Fairfax County in the Virginia House of Delegates, 1785–86, 1792, and 1796, and at the Virginia ratification convention of 1788, where he supported the new United States Constitution. President John Adams appointed Simms customs collector for the Alexandria district in 1799, and he held the post until his death. In that capacity he occasionally had dealings with TJ. Simms also served as mayor of Alexandria, one of the directors of the Bank of Alexandria, and president of the Potomac Company (Heitman, *Continental Army*, 497; Leonard, *General Assembly*, 156, 172, 187, 203; Merrill Jensen, John P. Kaminski, and others, eds., *The Documentary History of the Ratification of the Constitution* [1976–], 8:168–9, 10:1585; T. Michael Miller, comp., *Artisans and Merchants of Alexandria, Virginia 1780–1820* [1991–92], 1:20, 2:44–5; *JEP*, 1:325–6, 327 [5, 10 Dec. 1799]; *PTJ*, 29:193–6; *MB*, 2:1325, 1341, 1348; Washington *National Intelligencer*, 12 Mar. 1812; Washington *Daily National Intelligencer*, 1 Sept. 1819; Alexandria Co. Account Book, 4:139–40, 158–9; Alexandria Co. Will Book, 2:358–61).

From George Jefferson

MY DEAR SIR Richmond 7th Novr 1811.

I have duly received your much esteemed favor of the 4th, for which, if any words were adequate, I would thank you:—From your experience, and from every other consideration which ought to govern[1] me, I should have taken the liberty of asking the favor of your advice; but feared I had already taken up too much of your time: upon this subject therefore, I will occupy no more.

I have remitted Mr Hooe 131$, and now inclose you $:350—, agreeably to your direction.

I have bought two of Peacock's ploughs for you, one of the smallest size, & one of the largest now here.—he makes some larger, but has sent only a very few of them to this place, most people being of opinion that they are too large for two horses.

The boxes of books from Washington (7) are here.

I am my dear Sir Your Mt humble servt GEO. JEFFERSON

RC (MHi); at foot of text: "Thomas Jefferson esqr"; endorsed by TJ as received 10 Nov. 1811 and so recorded in SJL.

[1] Word interlined in place of "influence."

To Robert Patterson

Dear Sir Monticello. Nov. 10. 1811.

Your favor of Sep. 23. came to hand in due time, and I thank you for the Nautical almanac it covered for the year 1813. I learn with pleasure that the Philosophical society has concluded to take into consideration the subject of a fixed standard of measures weights and coins; and you ask my ideas on it; insulated as my situation is, I am sure I can offer nothing but what will occur to the Committee engaged in it, with the advantage, on their part, of correction by an interchange of sentiments and observations among themselves. I will however hazard some general ideas, because you desire it, and if a single one be useful, the labor will not be lost.

The subject to be referred to as a standard, whether it be matter or motion, should be fixed by nature, invariable, & accessible to all nations, independantly of others, and with a convenience not disproportioned to it's utility. what subject in nature fulfills best these conditions? what system shall we propose on this, embracing measures, weights & coins? and in what form shall we present it to the world? these are the questions before the Committee.

Some other subjects have, at different times, been proposed as standards, but two only have divided the opinions of men. 1. a direct admeasurement of a line on the earth's surface. or 2. a measure derived from it's motion on it's axis. To measure directly such a portion of the earth as would furnish an element of measure, which might be found again with certainty in all future times, would be too far beyond the competence of our means to be taken into consideration. I am free, at the same time, to say that, if these were within our power, in the most ample degree, this element would not meet my preference. the admeasurement would of course be of a portion of some great circle of the earth. if of the Equator, the countries over which that passes, their character and remoteness, render the undertaking arduous, and we may say, impracticable for most nations. if of some meridian, the varying measures of it's degrees, from the Equator to the pole, require a mean to be sought,[1] of which some equal part may[2] furnish what is desired. for this purpose the 45th degree has been recurred to, and such a length of line on both sides of it terminating at each end in the ocean, as may furnish a satisfactory law for a deduction of the unmeasured part of the Quadrant. the portion resorted to by the French philosophers, (and there is no other on the globe under circumstances equally satisfactory) is the meridian passing through their country and a portion of Spain, from Dunkirk to

Barcelona. the objections to such an admeasurement, as an element of measure, are the labor, the time, the number of highly qualified agents, and the great expence required. all this too is to be repeated whenever any accident shall have destroyed the standard derived from it, or impaired it's dimensions. this portion of that particular meridian is accessible of right to no one nation on earth. France indeed, availing herself of a moment of peculiar relation between Spain and herself, has executed such an admeasurement. but how would it be, at this moment, as to either France or Spain? and how is it at all times, as to other nations, in point either of right, or of practice? must these go through the same operation, or take their measures from the standard prepared by France? neither case bears that character of independance which the problem requires, and which neither the equality nor convenience of nations can dispense with. how would it now be, were England the deposit of a standard for the world? at war with all the world, the standard would be inaccessible to all other nations. against this too are the inaccuracies of admeasurements over hills & vallies, mountains & waters, inaccuracies often unobserved by the agent himself, & always unknown to the world. the various results of the different measures heretofore attempted sufficiently prove the inadequacy of human means to make such an admeasurement with the exactness requisite.

Let us now see under what circumstances the pendulum offers itself as an element of measure. the motion of the earth on it's axis from noon to noon[3] of a mean solar day has been divided from time immemorial, and by very general consent, into 86400. portions of time called seconds. the length of a pendulum, vibrating in one of these portions, is determined by the laws of nature, is invariable under the same parallel, and accessible independantly to all men. like a degree of the meridian indeed it varies in it's length from the Equator to the pole: and like that too requires to be reduced to a mean. in seeking a mean in the first case, the 45th degree occurs with unrivalled preferences. it is the midway of the celestial ark from the Equator to the pole. it is a mean between the two extreme degrees of the terrestrial ark, or between any two equidistant from it. and it is also a mean value of all it's degrees. in like manner, when seeking a mean for the pendulum, the same 45th degree offers itself on the same grounds; it's increments being governed by the same laws which determine those of the different degrees of the meridian.

In a pendulum loaded with a Bob, some difficulty occurs in finding the center of oscillation; & consequently the distance between that and the point of suspension. to lessen this, it has been proposed to substitute, for the pendulum, a cylindrical rod of small diameter, in which the displacement of the center of oscillation would be lessened. it has also been proposed to prolong the suspending wire of the pendulum below the Bob, until their centers of oscillation shall coincide. but these propositions not appearing to have recieved general approbation, we recur to the pendulum, suspended and charged as has been usual. and the rather as the laws which determine the center of oscillation leave no room for error in finding it, other than that minimum in practice to which all operations are subject in their execution.[4] the other sources of inaccu[ra]cy in the length of the pendulum need not be mentioned, because easily guarded against. but the great and decisive superiority of the pendulum, as a standard of measure, is in it's accessibility to all men, at all times, & in all places. to obtain the second pendulum for 45.° it is not necessary to go actually to that latitude. having ascertained it's length in our own parallel, both theory & observation give us a law for ascertaining the difference between that and the pendulum of any other. to make a new measure therefore, or verify an old one, nothing is necessary in any place but a well regulated[5] time piece, or a good meridian, and such a knolege of the subject as is common in all civilized nations.

Those indeed who have preferred the other element, do justice to the certainty, as well as superior facilities of the pendulum, by proposing to recur to one, of the length of their standard, and to ascertain it's number of vibrations in a day. these being once known, if any accident impair their standard, it is to be recovered by means of a pendulum which shall make the requisite number of vibrations in a day. and among the several commissions established by the academy of sciences for the execution of the several branches of their work on measures and weights, that respecting the pendulum was assigned to Messrs Borda, Coulomb, & Cassini, the result of whose labours however I have not learned.

Let our Unit of measures then be a pendulum of such length, as in the Lat. of 45.° in the level of the ocean, and in a given temperature, shall perform it's vibrations, in small & equal arcs, in one second of mean time.

what ratio shall we adopt for the parts and multiples of this Unit? the decimal without a doubt. our arithmetic being founded in a decimal numeration, the same numeration in a system of measures, weights & coins, tallies at once with that. on this question, I believe, there has been no difference of opinion.

In measures of length then the pendulum is our unit. it is a little more than our yard, & less than the ell. it's 10th or dime will be not quite 4. inches. it's hundredth, or cent not quite .4 of an inch; it's thousandth, or Mill not quite .04 of an inch, and so on. the traveller will count his road by a longer measure. 1000 Units, or a Kiliad will be not quite $\frac{2}{3}$ of our present mile, and more nearly a thousand paces than that.

For measures of surface, the square unit, equal to about 10 square feet, or $\frac{1}{9}$ more than a square yard, will be generally convenient. but for those of lands a larger measure will be wanted. a Kiliad would be not quite a Rood, or quarter of an acre; a Myriad not quite $2\frac{1}{2}$ acres.

For measures of capacity, wet and dry, the

Cubic Unit =	1. would be about	35. cub. feet,	28. bushels dry, or $\frac{7}{8}$ of a ton liquid.
dime =	.1	3.5 cub. f.	2.8 bush. or about $\frac{7}{8}$ of a barrel liquid.
cent =	.01. about 50. cubic inches, or $\frac{7}{8}$ of a quart.		
mill =	.001 = .5 of a cubic inch, or $\frac{2}{3}$ of a gill.		

To incorporate into the same system our weights and coins, we must recur to some natural substance, to be found every where, and of a composition sufficiently uniform. water has been generally considered as the most eligible substance, and rainwater more nearly uniform than any other kind found in nature. that circumstance renders it preferable to distilled water, and it's variations in weight may be called insensible.

The cubic Unit of this	=	1. would weigh about 2165℔ or a ton between the long & short
the dime	=	.1 a little more than 2. kentals.
cent	=	.01 a little more than 20.℔.
mill	=	.001 a little more than 2.℔.
decimmil	=	.0001 about $3\frac{1}{2}$. oz. avoirdupoise
centimmil	=	.00001 a little more than 6. dwt
millionth	=	.000001 about 15. grains
decimmillionth	=	.0000001 about $1\frac{1}{2}$ grain
centimmillionth	=	.00000001 about .14 of a grain.
billionth	=	.000000001 about .014 of a grain.

With respect to our coins, the pure silver in a Dollar being fixed by law at $347\frac{1}{4}$ grains, and all debts and contracts being bottomed on that value, we can only state the pure silver in the dollar, which would be very nearly 23. millionths.

I have used loose & round numbers (the exact Unit being yet undetermined) merely to give a general idea of the measures & weights proposed, when compared with those we now use. and in the names of the subdivisions I have followed the metrology of the Ordinance of

Congress of 1786. which, for their series below Unit adopted the Roman numerals. for that above unit the Grecian is convenient, and has been adopted in the new French system.

We come now to our last question, in what form shall we offer this metrical system to the world? in some one which shall be altogether unassuming; which shall not have the appearance of taking the lead among our sister institutions in making a general proposition. so jealous is the spirit of equality in the republic of letters, that the smallest excitement of that would marr our views, however salutary for all. we are in habits of correspondence with some of these institutions, and identity of character, & of object authorise our entering into correspondence with all. let us then mature our system as far as can be done at present, by ascertaining the length of the second pendulum of 45.° by forming two tables, one of which shall give the equivalent of every different denomination of measures weights and coins in these states, in the Unit of that pendulum, it's decimals and multiples: and the other stating the equivalent of all the decimal parts and multiples of that pendulum, in the several denominations of measures, weights and coins of our existing system. this done, we might communicate to one or more of these institutions in every civilised country a copy of these tables, stating, as our motive, the difficulty we had experienced, & often the impossibility, of ascertaining the value of the measures, weights & coins of other countries, expressed in any standard which we possess; that desirous of being relieved from this, and of obtaining information which could be relied on for the purposes of science, as well as of business, we had concluded to ask it from the learned societies of other nations, who are especially qualified to give it, with the requisite accuracy; that in making this request, we had thought it our duty first to do ourselves, and to offer to others, what we meant to ask from them, by stating the value of our own measures, weights, and coins, in some Unit of measure already possessed, or easily obtainable, by all nations: that the pendulum vibrating seconds of mean time, presents itself as such an Unit; it's length being determined by the laws of nature, and easily ascertainable at all times & places: that we have thought that of 45.° would be the most unexceptionable, as being a mean of all other parallels, and open to actual trial in both hemispheres. in this therefore, as an Unit, and in it's parts & multiples, in the decimal ratio, we have expressed, in the tables communicated, the values of all the measures, weights and coins used in the United States, and we ask in return from their body a table of the weights, measures & coins in use within their country, expressed in the parts and multiples of the same Unit. having requested the same favor from the learned societies of other nations, our object is with their assistance, to place within the reach of our fellow citizens at large a perfect knolege of the measures, weights, and coins, of the countries with which they have commercial or friendly intercourse: and should the societies of other countries interchange their respective tables, the learned will be in possession of an uniform language in measures, weights, and coins, which may with time become useful to other descriptions of their citizens, and even to their governments. this however will rest with their pleasure, not presuming, in the present proposition, to extend our views beyond the limits of our own nation. I offer this sketch merely as the outline of the kind of communication which I should hope would excite no jealousy or repugnance.

Peculiar circumstances however would require letters of a more special character to the Institute of France, and the Royal society of England. the magnificent work which France has executed in the admeasurement of so large a portion of a meridian, has a claim to great respect, in our reference to it. we should only ask a communication of their metrical system, expressed in equivalent values of the second pendulum of 45.° as ascertained by Mess[rs] Borda, Coulomb & Cassini, adding perhaps the request of an actual rod of the length of that pendulum.

With England, our explanations will be much more delicate. they are the older country, the mother country, more advanced in the arts and sciences possessing more wealth and leisure for their improvement, and animated by a pride more than laudable.† it is their measures too which we undertake to ascertain and communicate to themselves. the subject should therefore be opened to them with infinite tenderness and respect, and in some way which might give them due place in it's agency. the parallel of 45.° being within our latitude and not within theirs, the actual experiments under that would be of course assignable to us. but as a corrective, I would propose that they should ascertain the length of the pendulum vibrating seconds in the city of London or at the Observatory of Greenwich,[6] while we should do the same in an equidistant parallel to the South of 45.° suppose in 38°–29′. we might ask of them too, as they are in possession of the standards of Guildhall, of which we can have but an unauthentic

† we are all occupied in industrious pursuits. they abound with persons living on the industry of their fathers, or on the earnings of their fellow citizens, given away by their rulers in sinecures and pensions. some of these, desirous of laudable distinction, devote their time and means to the pursuits of science, and become profitable members of society by an industry of a higher order.

account, to make the actual application of those standards to the pendulum when ascertained.   the operation we should undertake under the 45th parallel, (about Passimaquoddy) would give us a happy occasion too of engaging our sister-society of Boston in our views, by referring to them the execution of that part of the work. for that of 38°–29′ we should be at a loss. it crosses the tidewaters of the Patomac about Dumfries, and I do not know what our resources there would be, unless we borrow them from Washington, where there are competent persons.

Altho' I have not mentioned Philadelphia in these operations, I by no means propose to relinquish the benefit of observations to be made there. her science & perfection in the arts would be a valuable corrective to the less perfect state of them in the other places of observation. indeed it is to be wished that Philadelphia could be made the point of observation South of 45.° and that the Royal society would undertake the counterpoint on the North, which would be somewhere between the Lizard & Falmouth. the actual pendulums, from both of our points of observation, & not merely the measures of them, should be delivered to the Philosophical society to be measured under their eye & direction.

As this is really a work of common & equal interest to England and the US. perhaps it would be still more respectful to make our proposition to her Royal society in the outset, and to agree with them on a partition of the re-work.[7] in this case any commencement of actual experiments, on our part should be provisional only, and preparatory to the ultimate results. we might in the mean time, provisionally also, form a table adapted to the length of the pendulum of 45.° according to the most approved estimates, including those of the French Commissioners. this would serve to introduce the subject to the foreign societies, in the way before proposed, reserving to ourselves the charge of communicating to them a more perfect one, when that shall have been compleated.

We may even go a step further, and make a general table of the measures weights & coins of all nations, taking their value, hypothetically for the present, from the tables in the Commercial dictionary of the Encyclopedie Methodique, which are very extensive, and have the appearance of being made with great labour & exactness. to these I expect we must, in the end, recur, as a supplement, for the measures which we may fail to obtain from other countries directly. their reference is to the foot & inch of Paris as a standard, which we may convert into parts of the second pendulum of 45.°

I have thus, my dear Sir, committed to writing my general ideas on this subject; the more freely, as they are intended merely as suggestions for consideration. it is not probable they offer any thing which would not have occurred to the committee itself. my apology on offering them must be found in your request. my confidence in the committee, of which I take for granted you are one is too entire to have intruded a single idea but on that ground.

Be assured of my affectionate & high esteem & respect.

TH: JEFFERSON

PoC (DLC); edge torn; at foot of first page: "Doctor Robert Patterson."

KENTALS: quintals, or hundredweight. The Confederation Congress resolved on 8 Aug. 1786 that "the Money of Account" in the United States should "proceed in a decimal ratio" from mills to cents to dimes to dollars. On 16 Oct. 1786 it passed an ORDINANCE establishing a mint and "regulating the value and alloy of Coin" using the same monetary subdivisions (Worthington C. Ford and others, eds., *Journals of the Continental Congress, 1774–1789* [1904–37], 31:503–4, 876–8). The SISTER-SOCIETY OF BOSTON was the American Academy of Arts and Sciences.

[1] TJ here canceled "from which a quadrant."

[2] TJ here canceled "answer."

[3] Reworked from "meridian to meridian."

[4] TJ placed an unexplained asterisk here.

[5] TJ here canceled "clock."

[6] Manuscript: "Greewich."

[7] Prefix interlined.

To Robert Patterson

DEAR SIR Monticello Nov. 10. 1811.

I write this letter separate, because you may perhaps think something in the other of the same date, worth communicating to the Committee.

I accept willingly mr Voigt's offer to make me a timepeice, & with the kind of pendulum he proposes. I wish it to be as good as hands can make it, in every thing useful; but no unnecessary labour to be spent on mere ornament. a plain, but neat mahogany case will be preferred.

I have a curiosity to try the length of the pendulum vibrating seconds here: and would wish mr Voigt to prepare one which could be substituted for that of the clock occasionally, without requiring any thing more than unhanging the one and hanging the other, in it's place. the bob should be spherical, of lead, and it's radius, I presume, about one inch. as I should not have the convenience of a room of uniform temperature, the suspending rod should be such as not to be affected by heat or cold, nor yet so heavy as to affect too[1] sensibly the center of oscillation. would not a rod of wood, not larger than a large wire, answer this double view? I remember mr Rittenhouse told me he had made experiments, on some occasion on the expansibility of wood lengthwise by heat, which satisfied him it was as good as the gridiron for a suspender of the bob. by the experiments on the strength of wood & iron in supporting weights appended to them, iron has been found but about six times as strong as wood, while it's specific gravity is eight times as great. consequently a rod of it, of equal strength, will weigh but $\frac{3}{4}$ of one of iron, and disturb the center of oscillation less in proportion. a rod of wood of white oak e.g.[2] not larger than a seine twine would probably support a spherical bob of lead of 1.I. radius. it might be worked down to that size, I suppose, by the cabinet makers, who are in the practice of preparing smaller threads of wood for inlaying. the difficulty would be in making it fast to the bob at one end, and scapement at the other, so as to regulate the length with ease & accuracy. this mr Voigt's ingenuity can supply, and in all things I would[3] submit the whole matter to your direction to him, and be thankful to you to give it.

Your's affectionately TH: JEFFERSON

PoC (DLC); at foot of text: "Doct: Robert Patterson." SJL records only one 10 Nov. 1811 letter to Patterson.

[1] Word interlined.
[2] Preceding four words interlined.
[3] TJ here canceled "wish."

From Robert Patterson

SIR Philadelphia Novr 11th 1811

Presuming that you may not as yet have seen a little tract, by Doctor Buchanan, on "Christian Researches in Asia," lately republished in Boston; and not doubting that you would find it highly interesting, I have taken the liberty of sending you a copy, of which I most respectfully request your acceptance.

Some time ago, inclosed I believe in A Nautical Almanack for the year 1813, I returned an answer to some queries you had made in your letter of Sepr 11, 11. respecting an Astronomical clock, and informed you that young Mr Voigt, an ingenious artist, would make such a one as you had described for sixty five dollars. If you should think this a reasonable price, & will please to give orders for having it made, Mr Voigt will immediately undertake it—

I have the honour to be with the greatest respect & esteem Your most obed^t Servt R^T PATTERSON

RC (MHi); at foot of text: "Thomas Jefferson"; endorsed by TJ as received 17 Nov. 1811 and so recorded in SJL. Enclosure: Claudius Buchanan, *Two Discourses preached before the University of Cambridge, on Commencement Sunday, July 1, 1810. And a Sermon preached before the Society for Missions to Africa and the East; at their tenth anniversary, July 12, 1810. To which are added Christian Researches in Asia* (Boston, 1811; Sowerby, no. 1711).

From William Mann

DEAR SIR Madison County 12th Novr 1811

I have in my possession a Spa in Chay[1] at The Suit of Randolphs executiors[2] againest Randolph and others—among the Parties you are named as a defendant and I have other Business to call me another way you I am told are nothing more Than a nominal Party. will you Give me leave to returne It Executed as to yourself. If So be pleased to take the Trouble to Drope me a line I have enclosed[3] you a rough copy of The Spa With much Respt. I Remain your Hbls. servt

WM MANN

P.s. my residence is in Richmond

RC (MHi); endorsed by TJ as a letter of 11 Nov. 1811 received 22 Dec. 1811 and so recorded in SJL. Enclosure not found.

William Mann (ca. 1778–1852) resided in Richmond as deputy federal marshal for the Virginia district from at least 1806 until about 1820, when he became a farmer in King and Queen County. He owned twenty-eight slaves in 1840 and real estate worth $7,000 a decade later (Richmond *Enquirer*, 11 Feb. 1806; *The Richmond Directory, Register and Almanac, for the year 1819* [Richmond, 1819], 57; Marshall, *Papers*, 9:232–6; DNA: RG 29, CS, King and Queen Co., 1840, 1850; *Richmond Enquirer*, 23 Mar. 1852; *Richmond Whig and Public Advertiser*, 30 Mar. 1852).

Robert Gourley, the executor of the will of Edmund Randolph's mother, Ariana Jenings Randolph, had applied earlier in the year to the United States Court for the Virginia District, in Richmond, for "an order restraining and enjoining the above named Edmund Randolph from disposing of or conveying away the following property conveyed by the said Randolph to Thomas Jefferson William Foushee Daniel L Hylton William DuVal Samuel McCraw Lewis Nicholas & Phillip Norborne Nicholas by Deed bearing date the Nineteenth day of May one Thousand eight hundred in Trust for the payment of a debt due by him to the said Robert Gourleys Testatrix & others towit the following Slaves towit Dick, Judy and their Children Sucky & Lucy & Sam Aggy and their children, Succordy, Mourning, Edmonia Lewis Blenheim & his wife, Phillis & children, Charles & Moses, Harry and Nanny his wife Watt & Billy & Jemmy & his wife Dolly and Child Lydia & Jenny Willard Lewis and their encrease present and future all the said Randolphs library of Books and especially the Law Books all his furniture whether Beds Blanketts Sheets House linnen or standing or other furniture or moveables the plate of the said Randolph consisting of a Silver Cup, Chased, a Silver Coffee pot fluted five silver waiters of different sizes Six dozen large and small Silver Spoons also carpets bedsteads China of every description one Coach one Phaeton two old Bay Horses Silver Teapot Silver Sugar dish" (Bond for payment of costs and damages by Gourley, Robert West, and Thomas West to Edmund Randolph if injunction is dissolved, 23 Feb. 1811 [TJ Editorial Files, photocopy of MS received from ViU in 1965; in a clerk's hand, signed by both Wests, witnessed by Francis Thornton Jr., with subjoined signed statement by William Harwood, magistrate, that Thomas West had appeared before him at the Gloucester County Court and sworn that his estate was worth more than the $4,500 bond, 23 Feb. 1811; endorsed as filed 9 Mar. 1811]).

TJ was named in the SUIT in his capacity as a trustee for the payment of Ariana Randolph's annuity by her son, an obligation that was one of the debts for which the increasingly impecunious Edmund Randolph mortgaged his estate on 19 May 1800 (*PTJ*, 31:583–5).

[1] Abbreviation for "Subpoena in Chancery."

[2] Manuscript: "Randolps ecutiors."

[3] Manuscript: "encosed."

From Henry Foxall

SIR George Town Nov[r] 13th 1811

Your favor of the 31st Ulto came [to][1] hand in due course—Two[2] Days ago I was fortunate enough to find a Vessel bound from this place Direct to Richmond on which I have put your Stove, pipes &c the bill of lading is sent on to your Corrospondents Gibson & Jefferson Richmond I have put the whole in cases but not Exactly as[3] you requested, I have put the Intire Stove in case, without taking it apart—I was afraid it would be difficult to find the right places for the interior plates, not only so, but it goes together considerably hard on account of so many inward plates—It will not be so portable as it would have been had it been sent in two or more boxes agreeable to your request, but upon the whole I judged it the best way of sending it—I have Sent a cast Iron Square Stand, on which it is to be placed—It may be necessary to get a little <u>very</u> fine Morter to putty up the joints when it is fixt in its place—a little black lead put on with a brush, and afterwards rubed with a dry Brush, will make it look well and I flatter myself if it dose not exceed, it will come up to your Expectation in point of utility—Before I sent away I had as large a fire made in it, as ever will be required, to prove the plates, and to satisfy myself that they would stand a great heat without Injury, which they did to my satisfaction

I Enclose you the Bills of Stove &a but not in order that you might at present send me the am[t], for that I do not wish you to do, till Such time you have got the Stove home and made trial of it, nor even then if it dose not answer your expectation

The best mode of secureing a floor from fire through which a stove pipe passes, that I Am acquainted with, is to have a Short peice of pipe made of Tin the depth of [Joist?] and ceiling with a small flange turned down at one end, to nail to the floor—the hole in the floor to be somwhat larger then the tin pipe, and the tin pipe to be about half an Inch larger then the stove pipe, so that the air can pass round the outside of the tin pipe up to the floor; and also all round the inside of tin pipe between that and the Stove pipe at the place it passes through the floor—If it is fixt in that way the Tin will remain cool alltho the Stove pipe is considerably hot—It will be found on trial, that the pipes of those Stoves will never get so hot as the pipes of those made in the usual way, in as much as the heat which is contained in the flame & smoke, is greatly exausted before it leaves the body of the Stove—I am with great Respect

Sir your Obed^t Sev^t HEN:^Y FOXALL

RC (MHi); one word illegible; between dateline and salutation: "Thomas Jefferson Esqr"; endorsed by TJ as received 22 Dec. 1811 and so recorded in SJL. Enclosures not found.

[1] Omitted word editorially supplied.
[2] Manuscript: "Tow."
[3] Manuscript: "has."

To George Jefferson

DEAR SIR Monticello Nov. 13. 11

M^r M^ckinney tells me I misunderstood him when I considered a part of the flour formerly shipped as destined to pay me a quarter's rent: but he yesterday sent off Johnson's boat with 50. barrels to be delivered to you on my account. it will probably arrive before this letter. be pleased to recieve and sell it for the best price you can, as I do not know the state of the market, I fix no limit: and the rather because a number of neighborhood debts have been waiting for this remittance, and have obliged me to draw on it this day as follows

	D c
in favour of D. Higginbotham	74.17
Isham Chisolm	35.
Watson &. Vest	44.57

to these I must pray you to add for mrs Hackley 85.D. which I owe her. she will be in Richmond when you recieve this and for a day or two after, and I will thank you to send the money to her, as I have not given her an order. I mentioned before that she would send one or two small bills to you for things she was to purchase for me. ever affectionately yours TH: JEFFERSON

P.S. any articles of mine may be trusted to Johnson to bring up.

PoC (DLC: TJ Papers, ser. 10); above postscript: "M[r] G. Jefferson"; endorsed by TJ.

SJL records a missing letter from TJ to Jefferson of 16 Nov. 1811. On 21 Nov. 1811 Gibson & Jefferson indicated that the firm had "received of Thomas Jefferson Esq[r] ℔ mr W[m] Johnson Forty Seven Barrels Superfine & three Barrels fine flour," and that the tolls paid on the 50. BARRELS came to $5.21 (MS in DLC; in James Ligon's hand; endorsed in an unidentified hand as Gibson & Jefferson's "Rec[t]" of that date). TJ was reimbursing Harriet Randolph HACKLEY for "a set of Liverpool china" she had bought for him (*MB*, 2:1271).

From Thomas Law

DEAR SIR— Philadelphia Nov[r] 13–1811—

For several months I did not think the Baltimore printers "family anecdote" of consequence enough to send home, but in May I forwarded it, & my B[r] Lord Ellenborough says that "Fox never did or would have used the expressions quoted as his,—it was not his manner of acting"[1]— I am induced to intrude with this, out of justice to so worthy a man, & not to convince you that the Federal republican has published a calumny—

The Presidents Message, M[r] Monroes correspondence with M[r] Foster[2] & Mr Pinkneys last Letter to the Marquis of Wellesley have impressed all descriptions of men with a conviction that the Government has been sported with & the nation wronged—as an Englishman I sincerely hope, that our Ministers[3] will no longer be deluded by an idea mischievously inculcated that this Government dare not assert its rights by the last appeal, the ultima ratio—it would have been gratifying to me if my Government had voluntarily preceded Bonaparte in revokations, & assumed the character of Defender of neutral rights—Peace between this Country & my own has always been the object of my wishes, & I have made a last effort for this purpose in my yesterdays Letters—by the Packet—

It is a satisfaction to me in reading publications from India, to learn that my system has made millions secure in their possessions & prosperous; you must enjoy the retrospect of your countrys rapid advancement during peace—Had 30000 men been employed in armies & navies, & 20000 in building Ships, making tents, ammunition arms &c[a] the labor of 50000 men would have been lost annually for 12 Years—which at a Dollar per diem amounts to 50000

300 days

15000,000

12 years.

180.000000

Your former obliging invitation to Mount Vernon, is too flattering for me not to avail myself of it, I am here attending to my daughters education

I remain With unfeigned respect & esteem THOS LAW

RC (DLC); addressed: "Thomas Jefferson Esqr Monticello"; franked; postmarked Philadelphia, 15 Nov.; endorsed by TJ as received 22 Dec. 1811 and so recorded in SJL.

For the FAMILY ANECDOTE, see Law to TJ, 22 Dec. 1810. Law considered the introduction of his SYSTEM of regular, predictable taxation in India as one of his greatest accomplishments as an employee of the East India Company. On 15 Jan. 1811 TJ had invited Law to visit Monticello, not MOUNT VERNON.

[1] Superfluous quotation marks editorially omitted.

[2] Preceding three words interlined. Manuscript: "Forster."

[3] Preceding two words interlined in place of "they."

To David Gelston

Monticello Nov. 14. 1811.

Th: Jefferson presents his salutations to mr Gelston, & his thanks for his statement of the tonnage of steamboats now actually employed. he has no doubt that this invention will materially improve the condition of our country. he avails himself of this occasion of assuring mr Gelston of his constant esteem & respect.

RC (NNGL, on deposit NHi); dateline at foot of text; lacks address cover. RC (Mrs. F. deLancy Robinson, Greenport, N.Y., 1947); address cover only; addressed: "David Gelston esq. New York"; franked; postmarked Milton, 18 Nov. 1811; endorsed by Gelston. PoC (MHi); endorsed by TJ.

From William Lambert

SIR, City of Washington, November 14th 1811.

The President of William and Mary college having lately sent me the result of your observations of the solar eclipse of Septr 17th at Monticello, I have calculated the longitude from Greenwich, using the first and last contacts, which will always give a near approximation to the truth, if the apparent times and latitude of the place have been correctly ascertained. I have taken great pains to find all the elements accurately by various rules, and have never, in any previous computation, discovered so great a variance in the time of true conjunction, found from the beginning and End of an eclipse or occultation. It will readily occur to you, that if there be an error in the apparent times, the Moon's parallaxes, and consequently the true difference of longitude of Sun and Moon, will be proportionably affected. Permit me to remark, that a repetition of the process, using the longitude found, instead of the estimated longitude, would be advisable, in which case, the altitude and longitude of the nonagesimal, and the parallaxes in longitude and latitude would be obtained with greater certainty, and one, among the rules I have given, might be sufficient for each. If it be contemplated to find the longitude from the internal contacts, the difference of the Sun and Moon's semidiameters instead of the sum, must be used for the purpose, and the difference of apparent longitude of Sun and Moon computed for those times, respectively; but I do not suppose it necessary, as the result already obtained, is believed to be near the truth.

From the data afforded by the same eclipse, the longitude of the

	° ′ ″
capitol in this city, is found to be	76. 57. 51. 907.
Monticello	78. 35. 10. 950.
difference of longitude	1. 37. 19. 043.

I am, Sir, with great respect, Your most obedient servant,

William Lambert.

RC (DLC); addressed: "Thomas Jefferson, late President of the United States, Monticello, Virginia"; notation by TJ on verso: "Long. Monticello 78°–35′–11″"; endorsed by TJ as received 22 Dec. 1811 and so recorded in SJL.

Bishop James Madison was PRESIDENT of the College of William and Mary. The NONAGESIMAL is the point of an ecliptic highest above the horizon (*OED*).

To Archibald Stuart

Dear Sir Monticello Nov. 14. 11.

We have safely recieved the cask of timothy seed, as[1] also the very excellent parcel of butter which you have been so kind as to send us; for which be pleased to accept my thanks, or perhaps I should more properly request you to tender them with my respects to mrs Stuart.

You have, days since, seen the most excellent, rational & dignified message of the president, & the documents accompanying it. in these you see the British government have openly avowed that they will enforce their orders of council, that is, will keep exclusive possession of the ocean, until France will allow her manufactures to go in the ships of other nations into the continent of Europe & France herself, altho she does not permit, even in time of peace, the manufactures of any nation to be brought to England in other ships but of the nation manufacturing them. in the mean time she is taking all our vessels, which is all the war she can make on her side. and indeed the style of Foster's correspondence is altogether a style of defiance. always affectionately yours Th: Jefferson

RC (ViHi: Stuart Papers); at foot of text: "Judge Stuart." PoC (CSmH: JF-BA); endorsed by TJ.

James Madison's MESSAGE to Congress of 5 Nov. 1811 covered nearly one hundred DOCUMENTS relating to American relations with Denmark, France, and Great Britain (Madison, *Papers, Pres. Ser.*, 4:1–6; *ASP, Foreign Relations*, 3:435–51, 500–12, 521–36; *Documents accompanying the Message of the President of the United States to the Two Houses of Congress, at the Commencement of the First Session of the Twelfth Congress* (Washington, D.C., 1811).

[1] PoC: "and."

To Henry A. S. Dearborn

Sir Monticello Nov. 15. 11.

Your favor of Oct. 14. was duly recieved, and with it mr Bowditch's observations on the comet, for which I pray you to accept my thanks, and to be so good as to present them to mr Bowditch also. I am much pleased to find that we have so able a person engaged in observing the path of this great phaenomenon; and hope that from his observations & those of others of our philosophical citizens on it's orbit we shall have ascertained, on this side of the Atlantic, whether it be one of those which have heretofore visited us. on the other side of the water they have great advantages in their well established Observatories, the magnificent instruments provided for them, and the leisure & information of their scientific men. the acquirements of mr Bowditch in solitude & unaided by these advantages do him great honor:

With respect to the eclipse of Sep. 17. I know of no observations made in this state but my own, altho' I have no doubt that others have observed it. I used myself an Equatorial telescope, & was aided by a friend, who happened to be with me, and observed thro' an achromatic telescope of Dollond's. two others attended the timepieces.[1] I had a perfect observation of the passage of the sun over the meridian, and the eclipse commencing but a few minutes after, left little room for error in our time. this little was corrected by the known rate of going of the clock. but we as good as lost the first appulse by a want of sufficiently early attention to be at our places, & composed. I have no confidence therefore, by several seconds, in the time noted.

the last osculation of the two luminaries was better observed.[2] yet even there was a certain term of uncertainty as to the precise moment at which the indenture on the limb of the sun entirely[3] evanished. it is therefore the forming of the annulus, & it's breaking, which alone possess my entire & compleat confidence. I am certain there was not an error of an instant of time in the observation of either of them. their result therefore should not be suffered to be affected by either of the others. the four observations were as follows.[4]

	H ′ ″		
The 1st appulse	0–13–54		central time of the two[5] contacts 1 H–51′–28″
annulus formed	1–53– 0	central time of annulus 1 H–56′–12½″	
annulus broken	1–59–25		
last osculation	3–29– 2[6]		

Latitude[7] of Monticello 38°–8′

I have thus given you, Sir, my observations, with a candid statement of their imperfections. if they can be of any use to mr Bowditch, it will be more than was in view when they were made; and should I hear of any other observations made in this state, I shall not fail to procure & send him a copy of them. be so good as to present me affectionately to your much esteemed father, & to accept the tender of my respect.

TH: JEFFERSON

RC (Mrs. Henry I. Bowditch, Jamaica Plain, Mass., 1946); addressed: "Mr H. A. S. Dearborn Boston"; franked; postmarked Milton, 18 Nov. 1811. PoC (DLC). PoC of 1st Tr (DLC: TJ Papers, 194:34537); undated extract in TJ's hand enclosed in TJ to William Lambert, 29 Dec. 1811. 2d Tr (DLC: TJ Papers, ser. 7, Weather Record, 1776–1818); undated extract in TJ's hand; at head of text: "Observation of the Annular eclipse of the ☉ Sep. 17. 1811. at Monticello."

Nathaniel Bowditch made use of TJ's observations in his article "On the Eclipse of the Sun of Sept. 17, 1811, with the longitudes of several places in this country," *Memoirs of the American Academy of Arts and Sciences* 3 (1815): 255–304, esp. 268–9, 297, 299. See also TJ to Bowditch, 2 May 1815.

In 1805 TJ attached a twelve-inch telescope to his Universal EQUATORIAL Instrument, a sophisticated device manufactured by London instrument-maker Jesse Ramsden. It used clockwork settings to track celestial bodies across the sky. In 1793 TJ acquired his equatorial, for a time the only one in the United States (*MB*, 2:888, 1170; *PTJ*, 24:287–9; Silvio A. Bedini, *Thomas Jefferson: Statesman of Science* [1990], 228–30). The FRIEND and others who attended the observation of the annular solar eclipse at Monticello on 17 Sept. 1811 may have included President James Madison and his secretary Edward Coles (Madison, *Papers, Pres. Ser.*, 3:460; TJ to Joseph Dougherty, 19 Sept. 1811). TJ purchased his ACHROMATIC TELESCOPE from the London opticians Peter & John Dollond in March 1786 (*MB*, 1:614). An APPULSE is the coming into conjunction of two heavenly bodies (*OED*).

[1] Both Trs begin here.

[2] Both Trs: "in the time noted for the 1st external contact. the last was better observed."

[3] Both Trs: "exactly."

[4] Preceding six words omitted from both Trs. The PoC of 1st Tr gives the

table of observations above the explanatory paragraph.

[5] PoC of 1st Tr here adds "external."

[6] 2d Tr provides only the first column of the table, but adds to the right of it: "by the calculations of Wm Lambert, a calculator of the first order in point of accuracy the outer contacts give the Long. of Mont^o^ 78°–35′–10.95″ the inner (West from Greenwich) 78–50–18.877 which last is to be considered as the true longitude" (see Lambert to TJ, 14 Nov. 1811, 8 Jan. 1812). 2d Tr concludes with TJ's later notation that "Mr Bowditch of Salem makes the Longitude of Mont^o^ from the same elements 78–47–36."

[7] PoC of 1st Tr ends immediately before this word.

From Destutt de Tracy

MONSIEUR a paris le 15 novembre 1811.

j'ai eu l'honneur de vous ecrire le 21 du mois dernier une lettre qui vous parviendra en meme tems que celle-cy. j'espere qu'elle vous aura montré combien je Suis reconnoissant de vos bontés, et combien je Suis heureux de l'indulgence avec la quelle vous avez acceuilli mon petit ecrit Sur Montesquieu. elle vous aura meme prouvé que cette indulgence me donne une bien grande confiance, puisque j'ai pris la liberté de vous envoyer un exemplaire complet de mon traité de l'entendement en trois volumes, dont vous n'aviez que les deux premiers; et puisque j'ai osé vous avouer que j'avois conçu l'idée de faire un traité de la volonté aussi en trois volumes, dont le dernier Seroit un traité des loix et de l'esprit dans le quel elles doivent etre faites, en consequence des faits etablis auparavant par une observation exacte de nos facultés.

je crains bien que vous ne trouviez aujourdhuy que ma confiance va jusqu'a la temerité. car j'ai l'honneur de vous envoyer cy joint le manuscript du premier volume de ce traité de la volonté, qui doit etre en meme tems le quatrieme de l'ouvrage entier. ce manuscript contient premierement un Suplément a mon traité de l'entendement que j'ai cru necessaire pour en rendre les resultats plus pratiques et plus faciles a Saisir: Secondement une introduction au traité de la volonté qui apartient egalement aux trois parties dont il doit etre composé: troisiemement enfin la premiere partie de ce traité de la volonté qui traite Spécialement de nos actions ou de nos moyens de pouvoir a nos besoins, la quelle je viens de terminer tout a l'heure.

je Sens, Monsieur, combien il y a d'inconsequence a vous avouer que ma foible capacité est beaucoup diminuée, et a vous Soumettre le moment d'aprés des productions qui par consequent ne doivent pas en valoir la peine. mais ce qui m'excuse c'est que les deux premiers des morceaux dont il S'agit, le Suplément et l'introduction, Sont faits depuis longtems et anterieurement aux malheurs qui ont pesé Sur ma tete; et que le troisieme n'est qu'une exposition plus methodique et plus detaillée des principes que vous avez déja aprouvés dans le commentaire Sur Montesquieu, nommement a propos des livres 7e 13e 20e 21e 22e et 23e, qui traitent du luxe, de l'impot, du commerce, de la monnaye, et de la population.

j'ose donc, Monsieur, desirer que vous vouliez bien jetter un coup d'oeuil Sur les trois ecrits qui composent ce volume. aucun des trois ne Sera publié dans ce pays cy de mon vivant. les deux premiers Sont trop metaphysiques; et ce n'est plus la mode ici de S'occuper de ces objets, ou moins ostensiblement. le troisieme est au contraire trop pratique. il contient beaucoup d'idées qui me paroissent opposées a ce que j'entends dire journellement. je crois qu'on n'en permettroit pas la publication; et quand on la permettroit je ne la voudrois pas, non Seulement parceque je craindrois qu'on ne m'en Sut mauvais gré, mais encor parce que je pense qu'un bon citoyen ne doit dire que ce qu'il croit la verité, mais doit etre trés reservé a la dire quand elle peut passer pour la critique d'un gouvernement Sur le quel il n'a point de moyen legal d'agir. vous Seul, Monsieur, me tiendrez lieu du public; et comme je Suis trés persuadé qu'on doit peser les Suffrages et non pas les compter, je Serai beaucoup plus content Si j'obtiens le votre, que Si j'avois l'aplaudissement universel au quel vous refuseriez de vous joindre.

d'ailleurs je pense que Si jamais dans votre pays on me faisoit l'honneur de traduire mes premiers volumes, on pourroit Si vous le trouviez bon, traduire aussi celui-cy: et par là l'edition traduite Seroit plus complette et par consequent plus recherchée que l'edition originale qui au reste est bien prés d'etre epuisée. quant a ma personne je n'y verrois aucun inconvenient, quand meme cette edition traduitte reviendroit ici meme avec mon nom en tete, premierement parcequ'etant en langue etrangere elle ne Seroit jamais extremement repandue et ne pourroit pas passer pour avoir été faitte par mes Soins, Secondement parcequ'enfin ce que contient ce quatrieme volume ne pourroit pas deplaire a un certain point vu qu'il n'y est question que d'economie politique, et non pas de l'organisation Sociale et des bases fondamentales des gouvernements comme dans le commentaire Sur Montesquieu.

de tout cela, ce que je crains le plus c'est que l'ouvrage tout entier dans Son ensemble et dans Ses details ne merite gueres votre attention, et que vous ne jugiez que je n'ai pas Suivi le fameux precepte: quid valeant humeri, quid ferre recusent. j'ai bien impatience de Savoir ce que vous en penserez. en attendant, Si je puis un peu rassembles mes idées et ranimer ma faculté de penser, je ferai tous mes efforts pour continuer l'execution de mon plan. car le desir de vous plaire et celui d'etre utile me donnent bien du courage. il n'y a que le manque de forces qui puisse m'arreter. mais malheureusement il est bien difficile de juger Soi meme quand on ne fait plus rien de bon, et bien difficile encor de trouver des amis asséz Sinceres pour vous en avertir franchement.

Recevez, je vous prie Monsieur, les assurances de ma trés grande consideration, de mon attachement, de mon respect, et de tous les Sentiments qui vous Sont dus et dont je Suis penetré pour vous.

DESTUTT-TRACY

P.S. en collationant mon manuscript, je m'apercois Monsieur, que j'ai osé parler Souvent des etats unis que peut-etre je connois mal, car malheureusement les communications Sont bien difficiles. ou je me Serai trompé je vous prie de corriger Sans menagements. je vous aurois une double obligation Si vous vouliez prendre la peine de rectifier mes idées, en me disant ou Sont les fautes.

EDITORS' TRANSLATION

SIR Paris 15 November 1811.

I had the honor of writing you a letter on the 21st of last month that will reach you with this one. I hope it will have shown you how grateful I am for your kindness and how happy I am for the generosity with which you greeted my little piece on Montesquieu. It will also have demonstrated the great confidence your indulgence inspires, in that I took the liberty of sending you a complete set of my three-volume treatise on understanding, of which you had only the first two volumes, and I dared to confess that I had conceived of writing a three-volume work on the will, the first of which would study the law and the spirit in which laws must be made, in keeping with facts ascertained beforehand through an exact observation of our faculties.

I fear that you will now find my confidence extended to temerity, as I have the honor of sending you herewith the manuscript of the first volume of the aforesaid treatise on the will, which is at the same time the fourth volume of the entire work. This manuscript contains first, a supplement to my work on understanding that I thought necessary in order to make it more practical and easily understood; secondly, an introduction to my discussion of the will and its three component parts; thirdly and lastly, the first part of my treatise on the will, dealing specifically with our actions or our means of providing for our needs and finished only a moment ago.

Sir, I sense the great contradiction between my assertion that my feeble capabilities are greatly diminished and my submission to you immediately thereafter of works that, in consequence, cannot merit your attention. My excuse is that the first two pieces in question, the supplement and the introduction, were done long ago, before the misfortunes that have since weighed on my mind, and the third is only a more methodical and detailed exposition of principles that you already approved in my commentary on Montesquieu, namely those concerning books 7, 13, 20, 21, 22, and 23, dealing with luxury, taxation, commerce, money, and population.

Thereafter, Sir, I venture to hope that you will glance at the three texts comprising this volume. None of them will be published in this country while I am alive. The first two are too metaphysical, and it is not now fashionable to take an interest in such things, at least openly. The third is, on the contrary, too practical. It contains many ideas that to me seem contradictory to what I hear people say daily. I think that its publication would not be permitted. If it should be, I would not desire it, not only because I would be afraid that it would be held against me, but also because I think that a good citizen must say only what he knows to be true. He must, however, have strong reservations about telling the truth when it might be construed as criticizing a government in which he plays no legal part. You alone, Sir, will be my audience, and because I am quite convinced that votes should be weighed and not counted, yours would make me happier than universal applause in which you refused to join.

Moreover, I think that if I could have my first volumes translated in your country, this one might also be translated, if you found it worthwhile. The translated edition would then be more complete and therefore more sought after than the original, which, by the way, is nearly out of print. I can see no drawbacks, even if this translated edition were to make its way back here with my name on the title page. First, being in a foreign language, it would never be widely read and its publication could not be attributed to me. Secondly, this fourth volume could not cause much displeasure, because it deals with political economy rather than the organization of society and the fundamental basis of government, as did my commentary on Montesquieu.

My greatest fear is that the work as a whole and in detail scarcely merits your attention, and that you will end up thinking that I have ignored the famous precept: quid valeant humeri, quid ferre recusent. I am very impatient for your reaction. Meanwhile, if I can gather my ideas and rekindle my ability to think, I will make great efforts to go on with the execution of my plan, emboldened by the desire to please you and be useful. Only weakness could stop me, but unfortunately it is difficult to judge when one can no longer do anything right, and friends are very rarely sincere enough to inform you frankly of that fact.

Sir, I beg you to accept the assurance of my very high consideration, attachment, respect, and all the other sentiments that I deservedly feel for you.

DESTUTT-TRACY

P.S. Sir, in collating my manuscript I realized that I had dared to speak often of the United States, which I do not know well because, unfortunately, communications are so difficult. Where I am mistaken, please feel free to correct me. I would be doubly obliged if you would take the trouble to tell me where I have gone wrong.

RC (DLC); endorsed by TJ as received 26 Feb. 1812 and so recorded in SJL. Translation by Dr. Roland H. Simon. Enclosed in David Bailie Warden to TJ, 10 Dec. 1811.

TJ expended a great deal of energy over the next seven years getting the enclosed French-language draft of the fourth volume of Destutt de Tracy's *Élémens d'Idéologie* (MS in ViU: TJP, in a clerk's hand; Poor, *Jefferson's Library*, 11 [no. 699]) translated into English and published in America. First, he submitted the MANUSCRIPT to William Duane, who hired a translator but otherwise did little to bring it into print. For various reasons, by the summer of 1814 Duane admitted that he could not complete the project. TJ then turned to Thomas Ritchie, editor of the Richmond *Enquirer*, who declined the commission, and, ultimately, to the Georgetown publisher Joseph Milligan. Although TJ revised the completed translation during the spring of 1816 and began correcting batches of page proofs as they appeared, lengthy delays in the printing process led him to despair of the work ever being published. Milligan finally completed the job in the autumn of 1818, despite the earlier publication date of *A Treatise on Political Economy; to which is prefixed a supplement to a preceding work on the understanding, or Elements of Ideology* (Georgetown, 1817; Poor, *Jefferson's Library*, 11 [no. 700]). Contrary to Destutt de Tracy's predictions, a French version of this work entitled *Traité de la volonté et de ses effets* (Paris, 1818) was published during his lifetime (Duane to TJ, 14 Feb. 1813; TJ to Ritchie, 27 Sept. 1814; Ritchie to TJ, 9 Oct. 1814; TJ to Milligan, 17 Oct. 1814, 18 May 1816, 3 Jan., 25 Oct. 1818; Milligan to TJ, 16 Nov. 1814, 17 Oct. 1818; TJ to Duane, 24 Nov. 1814).

QUID VALEANT HUMERI, QUID FERRE RECUSENT: to consider "what the shoulders refuse, and what they have the strength to bear," from Horace, *Ars Poetica*, 39–40 (*Horace: Satires, Epistles and Ars Poetica*, trans. H. Rushton Fairclough, Loeb Classical Library [1926; repr. 1970], 452–3).

To Melatiah Nash

SIR Monticello Nov. 15. 11.

I duly recieved your letter of Oct. 24. on the publication of an Ephemeris. I have long thought it desirable that something of that kind should be published in the US holding a middle station between the Nautical, & the common popular almanacs. it would certainly be acceptable to a numerous & respectable description of our fellow citizens, who, without undertaking the higher astronomical operations, for which the former is calculated, yet occasionally wish for information beyond the scope of the common almanacs. what you propose to insert in your Ephemeris is very well so far. but I think you might give it more of the character desired, by the addition of some other articles, which would not enlarge it more than a leaf or two. for instance, the Equation of time is essential to the regulation of our clocks & watches, and would only add a narrow column to your 2[d] page. the Sun's declination is often desirable, and would add but another narrow column to the same page. this last would be the more useful as an element for obtaining the rising and setting of the sun, in every part of the US. for your Ephemeris will, I suppose, give it only for a particular parallel, as of N. York, which would in a great measure restrain it's circulation to that parallel. but the ☉'s declination would enable every one to calculate sunrise for himself, with scarcely more trouble than taking it from an Almanac. if you would add, at the end of the work, a formula for that calculation; as, for example, that of Delalande §.1026. a little altered. thus. to the Logarithmic tangent of the latitude (a constant number)

add the Log. tangent of the ☉'s declination:
taking 10. from the Index, the remainder is the Sine of an arch which, turned into time & added to **VI**. Hours
gives Sunrise for the Winter half } of the year.
and Sunset for the Summer half }

to which may be added 3. lines only from the table of refractions §. 1028. or, to save even this trouble, & give the calculation ready made for every parallel, print a table of semidiurnal arches, ranging the latitudes from 30. to 45.° in a line at top, & the degrees of declination in a vertical line on the left, and stating, in the line of the declination, the semidiurnal arch for each degree of latitude. so that every one knowing the latitude of his place, & the declination of the day, would find his sunrise or sunset where their horizontal and vertical lines meet. this table is to be found in many astronomical books, as, for instance, in Wakeley's Mariner's compass rectified, and more accurately in the Connoissance des tems for 1788. it would not occupy more than two pages at the end of the work, & would render it an Almanac for every part of the US.

To give novelty, and increase the appetite for continuing to buy your Ephemeris annually, you might every year select some one or two useful tables which many would wish to possess & preserve. these are to be found in the Requisite tables, the Connoissance des tems of different years, and many in Pike's arithmetic.

I have given these hints because you requested my opinion. they may extend the plan of your Ephemeris beyond your view, which will be sufficient reason for not regarding them. in any event I shall willingly become a subscriber to it, if you should have any place of deposit for them in Virginia where the price can be paid. Accept the tender of my respects TH: JEFFERSON

PoC (DLC); at foot of first page (trimmed): "[Me]latiah Nash."

DELALANDE: Joseph Jérôme Le Français de Lalande, *Astronomie*, 2d ed., 4 vols. (Paris, 1771–81; Sowerby, no. 3796; Poor, *Jefferson's Library*, 7 [no. 373]). WAKELEY's work was Andrew Wakely, *The Mariner's Compass Rectified* (London, 1787; Sowerby, no. 3788). CONNOISSANCE DES TEMS: at this time TJ owned twenty-three annual issues, ranging from 1777 to 1808, of the *Connoissance des Temps: ou, Des Mouvements célestes à l'usage des astronomes et des navigations* (Paris; Sowerby, no. 3808; see also Poor, *Jefferson's Library*, 8 [no. 383]). REQUISITE TABLES: Nevil Maskelyne, *Tables requisite to be used with the Nautical Ephemeris for finding the Latitude and Longitude at Sea*, 2d ed. (London, 1781; Sowerby, no. 3811; Poor,

Jefferson's Library, 8 [no. 381]), or John Garnett's American edition (New Brunswick, N.J., 1806; Sowerby, no. 3809). Nicolas PIKE's text was *A New and Complete System of Arithmetic. Composed for the Use of the Citizens of the United States*, 2d ed. (Worcester, Mass., 1797; Sowerby, no. 3666). Nash took TJ's HINTS to heart and included in his *Columbian Ephemeris and Astronomical Diary, for the year 1812* (New York, 1812) both a "Table of the Sun's Declination" and a "Table of the Equation of Time" (pp. 85–6).

Notes on Joseph Fossett's Account for Plating Saddle Trees

1811.	Saddle trees plated for M[r] Burnley	D
	the former acc[t] given me by Joe was for 32. trees	32.
Nov. 18.	now given in by him	
	4. mens trees common @ 1.D.	
	17. d[o] plated round the Cantle @ 7/	
	1. Woman's tree common	
	3. d[o] plated round the Cantle	

MS (MHi); entirely in TJ's hand; endorsed by TJ: "Burnley."

Joseph (Joe) Fossett (1780–1858), blacksmith, was TJ's slave from his birth until TJ's death. He was the son of Betty Hemings's daughter Mary and, presumably, William Fosset, who worked as a carpenter's apprentice at Monticello late in the 1770s. Although his mother and two of his siblings were freed in 1792 after her sale to Thomas Bell, her common-law husband in Charlottesville, Fossett remained at Monticello. There he worked in the nailery (becoming foreman in 1800), ran errands, and helped to serve meals in the main house. In 1801 he began an apprenticeship with blacksmith William Stewart, and Fossett operated the Monticello blacksmith shop from 1807. He made an unauthorized journey in 1806 to Washington, D.C., to be with his wife Edith Hern, who was being trained as a cook at the President's House. He was captured soon thereafter and returned to Monticello. The couple were not reunited until TJ's retirement from politics in 1809, but they ultimately had ten children together. TJ freed Fossett in his will and gave him his blacksmithing tools. His family was, however, sold at the auction that disposed of most of TJ's estate. Within a few years Fossett had set up shop in Charlottesville, and in 1837 he engineered the emancipation of his wife, five of his children, and four grandchildren. The Fossetts eventually relocated to Cincinnati (Betts, *Farm Book*, pt. 1, p. 31; *MB*, 1:390, 2:1186; Lucia Stanton, *Slavery at Monticello* [1996]; Stanton, *Free Some Day*, 131–3, 149–51; TJ's will and codicil, 16–17 Mar. 1826; Albemarle Co. Deed Book, 35:219–20; Fossett's tombstone inscription, Union Baptist Cemetery, Cincinnati).

The FORMER ACC[T] had been for $34.50, not $32. On 13 Apr. 1811 TJ gave Fossett "1/ in every dollar of the work done," which in that case came to $6 (*MB*, 2:1265). For a change in the rules governing Fossett's plating work, see William Watson to TJ, 9 Mar. 1812.

From Bishop James Madison

DEAR SIR, Nov[r] 19[h] 1811 W[g]

Having seen your Observations upon the late solar Eclipse, I took the Liberty to transmit a Copy of them to M[r] W. Lambert, in Washington, & to request him to favour me with a Calculation of the Longitude of Monticello founded upon them. I now transmit his Paper, & hope it will prove agreable to you. The Facility & Accuracy of M[r] L. in astronomical Calculation is very remarkable. This I have known for some Time past; & upon that Ground the application was made to him. Mr Blackburn, the Math[l] Professor, is also a good Calculator; but he is so engaged that I know not when he will attempt a similar Deduction.

M[r] Lambert's Paper is drawn up more fully than may appear necessary; but it serves to test the Accuracy of the apparently different Rules given by celebrated Astronomers.

By my Observation upon the solar Eclipse of 1806, the End of which was accurately noted, & the Time well ascertained, Williamsburg is 5^{H} 17′ 4″ from Paris 9′ 20″ by Greenwich,[1] which compared with the Long. of Monticello, gives the strait-lined Distance, I beleive, very accurately, or rather nearly.

I am, D[r] Sir, Yrs with sincere Respect & Esteem

J MADISON

	° ′ ″
Monticello	78.35.10
W[m] & M C.	76.56
	1:39:10

RC (DLC); dateline beneath signature; postscript to left of closing; endorsed by TJ as received 22 Dec. 1811 and so recorded in SJL.

[1] Preceding two words and coordinates interlined.

ENCLOSURE

William Lambert's Calculation of Monticello's Longitude from Greenwich

Calculation of the longitude from Greenwich, of Monticello, in Virginia, from the solar eclipse of the 17th of September, 1811.

Latitude 38.° 8′ Estimated Longitude, 5. h. 14. m. 0. sec = 78.° 30.′ 0.″ West.
Ratio of the equatorial diameter to the polar axis of the earth, 320 to 319.

Constant Log. to reduce the latitude (320 to 319)		9.9972814.
Lat. of the place 38.° 8.′ 0″	log. tangent	9.8948918.
Lat. of Monticello, reduced, 37.° 57.′ 33.″ 341. dec	log. tangent	9.8921732.
Constant log. to reduce the Moon's equat. hor. parallax, for lat. and ratio,		9.9994827.

		° ′ ″ dec.
Apparent time of beginning of the eclipse, 0. h. 13. m. 54.0 sec.	=	3.28.30.000
Corresponding time at Greenwich 5. h. 27. m. 54. Sec.		
Sun's right ascension,		174.23.10.067.
Right ascension of the meridian from the beginning of ♈,		177.51.40.067
d° d° from the beginning of ♑,		92. 8.19.933

The operation at large, with several rules to find the altitude and longitude of the nonagesimal.

Rule 1.

	° ′ ″ dec.		
Log. versed sine R.A. meridian from ♑,	92. 8.19.933		10.0159134
" cosine lat. place, reduced,	37.57.33.341		9.8967732.
" Sine obliquity of the ecliptic	23.27.42.690		9.6000342
corresponding natural number, **A.**	3256273.	(−3 from index)	6.5127208.

	° ′ ″		
Lat. red.	37.57.33.341		
obliq. ecl.	23.27.42.690.		
	61.25.16.031	Natural sine	8781593.
Nat. cosine alt. nonag. 56.° 27.′ 32″ 783 dec.			5525320.

	° ′ ″	
Log. cosecant R.A. meridian from ♑,	92. 8.19.933	10.0003027.
" Secant lat. place, reduced,	37.57.33.341	10.1032268.
" Sine altitude of the nonagesimal	56.27.32.783	9.9209013.
" Secant, long. of the nonag. from ♎, west,	19. 2.19.000	10.0244308.
	180. 0. 0 −	
Long. nonag. from beginning of ♈,	160.57.41.000	

Rule 2.

	° ′ ″					
Log. cotangent lat. reduced,	37.57.33.341	10.1078268				
" sine R.A. meridian from ♈.	177.51.40.067	8.5719609	tangent	8.5722636.		
" tangent arch **A.**	2.44.20.111	8.6797877	cosecant,	11.3207087.		
obliq. ecliptic	+23.27.42.690.		Sine	9.6449484.	tang.	9.6920338
arch **B.**	26.12. 2.801.	° ′ ″ dec		9.5379207.	cosecant,	10.4865100.
Longitude nonag. from ♎, West,		19. 2.18.840		° ′ ″	tang.	10.1785438.
d° from beg. of ♈,		160.57.41.160	alt. nonag.	56.27.32.733.		

☞ R.A. meridian less than 180°, the sum of arch **A**, and obliq: eclip = arch **B**, otherwise, their difference. The supplement of R.A. meridian might have been used, as producing the same result.

Rule 3.

° ° ′ ″ ° ′ ″		° ′ ″		° ′ ″ dec	
90,−37.57.33.341.−23.27.42.690.	=	28.34.43.969	half,	14.17.21.9845.	**(B)**
90,−37.57.33.341.+23.27.42.690.	=	75.30. 9.349.	half	37.45. 4.6745	**(C)**
Right ascension meridian from ♑,	=	92. 8.19.933.	half	46. 4. 9.9665	**(D)**

	° ′ ″			
Sine of **C**,	37.45. 4.6745. ar. comp.	0.2130817	ar. comp. cosine.	0.1020016.
Sine **B**,	14.17.21.9845	9.3923811	Cosine	9.9863512.
Cotangent **D**,	46. 4. 9.9665	9.9837838.	cotangent	9.9837838.
tangent **E**,	21.13.28.984	9.5892466.	tangent **F**, =	10.0721366
				° ′ ″ 49.44.12.139
			E,	+21.13.28.984.
			from [...], East,	70.57.41.123.
				+90 − − −
			Longitude of the nonag. from beginning of ♈,	160.57.41.123

	° ′ ″		
Log. sine **E**,	21.13.28.984.	arith. comp.	0.4412594.
" Sine **F**,	49.44.12.139		9.8825715.
" tang. **D**,	14.17.21.9845		9.4060298
" tang. **C**,	23.13.46.392		9.7298607.
	2		
	56.27.32.784	altitude of the nonagesimal.	

Rule 4. (M[r] Brinkley's.)

	° ′ ″ dec			
Log. cosine lat. place, reduced,	37.57.33.341.	9.8967732	Cotangent,	10.1078268.
" cosine R.A. meridian from ♈,	177.51.40.067.	9.9996973	Sine,	8.5719609.
" cosine arch **I**,	141.59.22.529.	9.8964705	Cotangent,	8.6797877.
			Arch **II**,	87.15.39.889.
			Ob. Ecl.	−23.27.42.690
			Arch **III**	63.47.57.199

	° ′ ″ dec.			
Log. sine arch **I**	141.59.22.529	9.7894430	tangent	9.8929724.
" Sine arch **III.**	63.47.57.199	9.9529146	Cosine,	9.6449485
" cosine alt. nonagesimal,		9.7423576	tangent,	9.5379209
				° ′ ″
° ′ ″ dec				−19. 2.18.869
= 56.27.32.742.				180. 0. 0. −
Longitude nonag. from ♈,				160.57.41.131

		Alt. nonagesimal.		Longitude nonagesimal.
		° ′ ″		° ′ ″
By Rule	1	56.27.32.783		160.57.41.000
	2	56.27.32.783		160.57.41.160.
	3	56.27.32.784		160.57.41.123
	4	56.27.32.742		160.57.41.131
Mean,		56.27.32.773.	Mean,	160.57.41.103.

	° ′ ″ dec.
Moon's true longitude	173.12.40.980
Longitude of the nonagesimal,	160.57.41.103.
Moon's true distance from the nonagesimal. (East)	12.14.59.877

Moon's equatorial horizontal parallax,		54′. 9.366″ = 3249.366″	log.		3.5117986
Constant log. for latitude and ratio					9.9994827.
Moon's hor. parallax, reduced		54. 5.498. 3245.498			3.5112813.
Sun's hor. parallax, Sept. 17		−8.700			
hor. parallax ☽ à ☉,		53.56.798 = 3236.798.	log.		3.5101156
Log sine altitude of the nonag.		56°.27′.32″.773			9.9209013
Moon's true lat. north, asc		0.32.47.332	ar. comp. cosine,		0.0000197
				(a)	3.4310366
Moon's true dist. à nonag. (East)		12.14.59.877		(b)	9.3266985
1st approximation,	a + b,	9.32.447	log.	(c)	2.7577351
Sine	b + c,	12.24.32.324		(d)	9.3322129
2d approximation,	a + d,	9.39.761	log.	(e)	2.7632495
Sine	b + e,	12.24.39.638		(f)	9.3322829
3d approximation,	a + f,	9.39.855	log.	(g)	2.7633195.
Sine	b + g,	12.24.39.732		(h)	9.3322838
4th approximation,	a + h	9.39.856	log.	(i)	2.7633204
Sine	b + i,	12.24.39.733		(k)	9.3322838
Parallax in long:	a + k	9.39.856	log.	(l)	2.7633204.

Other rules to find the parallax in longitude.

	° ′ ″				
Log. cosine ☽'s true latitude.	0.32.47.332		9.9999803.		
" cosine true dist à nonag.	12.14.59.877		+9.9899974		
	Log. (**A**)		9.9899777	natural number,	9771870.
hor. parallax ☽ à ☉,	0.53.56.798	Sine	8.1956726		
altitude of the nonag.	56.27.32.773	Sine,	9.9209013		
	(**B**)		8.1165739.	natural num.	–0130790.
Corresponding log. of **C**			9.9841257	(**C**)	9641080.
arith. comp.			0.0158743		
Cosine Moon's true latitude			9.9999803.		
Sine Moon's true dist. à nonag			9.3266985		
tang. ☽'s apparent dist. à nonag.	12.24.39.710.		9.3425531		
true dist d°	12.14.59.877.				
Parallax in longitude,	9.39.833.				
Log. sine hor. parallax ☽ à ☉,	0.53.56.798.	Sine	8.1956726.		
" Sine alt. nonagesimal.	56.27.32.773.	Sine,	9.9209013.		
		(x)	8.1165739.		
" cosine ☽'s true dist. à nonag.			9.9899974.		
		(y)	8.1065713	nat: number,	0127812
Natural cosine Moon's true latitude					9999546.
Corresponding log. (z)			9.9943931	(z)	9871734.
ar. comp.			0.0056069		
log. (x)			8.1165739.		
Log. sine ☽'s true dist. à nonagesimal,			9.3266985		
tangent parallax in longitude 9.′ 39.″ 834			7.4488793		

	Parallax in long.		apparent dist. ☽ à nonag.
	′ ″		° ′ ″
Rule 1	9.39.856		12.24.39.733
2	9.39.833		12.24.39.710
3	9.39.834		12.24.39.711
Mean	9.39.841.	Mean	12.24.39.718.

For the Moon's parallax in latitude.
Rule 1. (M. de la Lande's.)

	° ′ ″		
hor. parallax ☽ à ⊙,	0.53.56.798	Sine,	8.1956726.
altitude of the nonagesimal	56.27.32.773.	Cosine,	9.7423575
Moon's true dist. à nonag	12.14.59.877.	ar. comp. sine	0.6733015
" apparent distance d°	12.24.39.718	Sine	9.3322837
first part parallax in lat.	0.30.11.532	Sine,	7.9436153
Moon's true latitude	0.32.47.332.	Sine	7.9794460.
" true dist. à nonag	12.14.59.877.	ar. co. sine	0.6733045.
" parallax in long.	0. 9.39.841	sine	7.4487832
true dist. à nonag. + $\frac{\text{par. in long}}{2}$	12.19.49.797.	cosine	9.9898644
Second part	–0. 0.25.464	sine	–6.0914951
First part	0.30.11.532		
Parallax in lat. approximated	29.46.068	Sine	7.9374675.
Moon's true latitude	32.47.332		
" apparent lat. approxim	3. 1.264.	Cosine	9.9999998
Parallax in latitude, (correct)	0.29.46.067	Sine	7.9374673

2. Dr Maskelyne's rule

	° ′ ″		
hor. parallax ☽ à ⊙,	0.53.56.798	Sine,	8.1956726.
altitude nonagesimal	56.27.32.773	cosine	9.7423575.
☽'s apparent lat. (found above)	0. 3. 1.265	cosine	9.9999998
1st part parallax in lat.	0.29.48.383	Sine	7.9380299
hor. parallax ☽ à ⊙,	0.53.56.798	Sine	8.1956726.
altitude of nonagesimal	56.27.32.773	Sine	9.9209023
Moon's apparent lat.	0. 3. 1.265	Sine	6.9438888
true dist. à nonag + $\frac{\text{par. in long.}}{2}$	12.19.49.797	cosine	9.9898644
Second part	0. 0. 2.316	Sine	5.0503271.
Arst part	0.29.48.383		
Parallax in latitude	0.29.46.067		

Rule 3. (Mr Seth Pease's.)

	° ′ ″			
hor. parallax ☽ à ⊙	0.53.56.798	Sine	8.1956726.	
altitude nonagesimal	56.27.32.773	Cosine	9.7423575	Nat. number[1]
	0.32.47.332		7.9380301.	0086702.
Natural Sine Moon's true lat.				0095377
Corresponding log		6.9382695.	Nat. n°	0008675.
Moon's true dist. à nonag	cosecant,	10.6733015.		
" apparent distance	Sine	9.3322837.		
" true latitude	Secant	10.0000197		
" apparent lat. 3′. 1″.259.	tangent	6.9438744		
true lat 32.47.332				
Parallax in lat 29.46.073				

		° ′ ″
By rule	1.	0.29.46.067.
	2	0.29.46.067.
	3.	0.29.46.073.
Mean,		0.29.46.069.

	° ′ ″ dec.
Moon's true longitude	173.12.40.980
" Parallax in longitude, (mean result)	+9.39.841.
" apparent longitude d°	173.22.20.821.
Sun's longitude	173.53. 1.967.
difference of apparent longitude ☉ and ☽,	30.41.146.
Moon's true latitude, North,	0.32.47.332.
" Parallax in latitude (mean result)	– 0.29.46.069
" apparent latitude, north,	0. 3. 1.263.

	° ′ ″ dec
Apparent time of the end of the eclipse, 3. h 29. m. 4. sec. 4 d	= 52.16. 6.000
Corresponding time at Green[wch] 8. h. 43. m 4.4 Sec Sun's Right ascension,	174.30.28.191
Right ascension of the meridian from beginning of ♈,	226.46.34.191.
ditto from the beginning of ♑, (west)	43.13.25.809

Rule 1.

	° ′ ″		
Log. versed sine R.A. meridian from ♑.	43.13.25.809.	(– 3 from index)	6.4334758.
" Cosine latitude place, reduced,	37.57.33.341		9.8967732.
" Sine obliquity of the ecliptic,	23.27.42.690		9.6000342
corresponding natural number	– 851693	**(A)**	5.9302832.

	° ′ ″		
Lat. reduced	37.57.33.341		
Obliq: eclip	23.27.42.690.		
Sum,	61.25.16.031	Natural sine	8781593.
Nat. cosine altitude nonag.	37.32.3.047.		7929900.

	° ′ ″	
Log. cosant R.A. meridian from ♑	43.13.25.809	10.1644044.
" Secant lat. place, reduced,	37.57.33.341	10.1032268
" Sine altitude of the nonagesimal	37.32. 3.047	9.7847845
" Secant long. nonag. from ♎, (East)	27.35.13.818	10.0524157
	+180. 0. 0 –	
Longitude of the nonag. from ♈	207.35.13.818.	

Rule 2.

	° ′ ″ dec.				
Lat. place, reduced,	37.57.33.341	cotangent	10.1078268.		
R.A. meridian from ♎,	46.46.34.191	sine	9.8625391	tang.	10.0269434
arch **A**	43. 2.48.214.	tang.	9.9703659	cosec.	10.1658372.
obliq. eclip.	–23.27.42.690.				
(**B**)	19.35. 5.524	Sine			9.5253076.
			° ′ ″ 27.35.13.823.	tang.	9.7180882
			180. 0. 0		
Longitude of the nonag.			207.35.13.823.		

	° ′ ″		
arch **B**	19.35. 5.524	tangent	9.5511894.
	27.35.13.823	cosecant,	10.3343274.
altitude of the nonag.	37.32. 3.046	tangent	9.8855168.

Rule 3.

Sine of **C**,	ar. comp.	0.2130817	cosine, ar. co.	0.1020016.
Sine **B**,		9.3923811	cosine	9.9863512.
Cotangent **D**,= 21.° 36.′ 42.″ 9045		10.4021199	cotangent	10.4021199.
	tang.	10.0075827	tang.	10.4904727.
		E. 45.30. 0.571.		**E.** 72. 5.13.222
				E. 45.30. 0.571
				90 – –
			Long. nonag.	207.35.13.793

E, ar. comp. sine	0.1467568	
F, Sine	9.9784201	
B tangent	9.4060298	
G. tang. 18.° 46.′ 1.″ 522	9.5312067	G × 2 = 37.° 32.′ 3.″ 044. altitude nonag.

Rule 4.

	° ′ ″			
Log. cosine lat. reduced,	37.57.33.341	9.8967732	co-tangent	10.1078268
" cosine R.A. mer. from ♎,	46.46.34.191	9.8355957	Sine	9.8625391.
" cosine arch **I**	57.19. 6.484	9.7323689	cotang	9.9703659
			Arch **II.**	46.57.11.786.
			obl. ecl.	+23.27.42.690
			Arch **III**,	70.24.54.476

	° ′ ″				
arch **I**	57.19. 6.484.	Sine	9.9256695.	tangent	10.1927806
arch **III**	70.24.54.476.	Sine	9.9741183	cosine	9.5253076
alt. nonag.	37.32. 3.000		9.8992678	tang	9.7180882

	27.35.13.823
	+180
Long. nonag.	207.35.13.823

	Altitude nonag.	Longitude nonag.
By rule 1	37.32.3.047	207.35.13.818.
2	37.32.3.046	207.35.13.823
	37.32.3.046	
3		207.35.13.793
4		207.35.13.823
Mean result		207.35.13.814.

Longitude of the nonagesimal	207.35.13.814.		
Moon's true longitude	174.49.20.531.		
☽'s true distance à nonagesimal, (west)	32.45.53.283.		
Moon's equatorial horizontal parallax 54.′ 10.″ 179 = 3250.″ 179. log.			3.5119073.
Constant logarithm for latitude and ratio			9.9994827
Moon's horizontal parallax, reduced		3246.310	3.5113900.
Sun's horizontal parallax		−8.700	
horizontal parallax, ☽ à ☉,		3237.610 log.	3.5102245.

Sine altitude of the nonagesimal		37°.32′. 3″.046		9.7847845
ar. comp. cosine Moon's true lat. north		0.41.38.115		0.0000318
			(a)	3.2950408.
Sine Moon's true distance à nonagesimal,		32.45.53.283	(b)	9.7333511
1st approximation,	a + b,	17.47.559	(c)	3.0283919.
Sine	b + c,	33.3.40.842	(d)	9.7368240
2d approximation,	a + d	17.56.130	(e)	3.0318648
Sine	b + e	33.3.49.413	(f)	9.7368517.
3d approximation	a + f,	17.56.199	(g)	3.0318925.
Sine	b + g	33.3.49.482	(h)	9.7368519
4th approximation,	a + h	17.56.200	(i)	3.0318527.
Sine	b + i,	33.3.49.483	(k)	9.7368519
Parallax in long.	a + k	17.56.200	(l)	3.0318527.

Rule 2.

	° ′ ″			
Log. cosine Moon's true latitude,	0.41.38.115	9.9999682.		
" cosine ☽'s true dist. à nonag.	32.45.53.283	9.9247439.		
		9.9247121.	Nat. num.	8408375.
Sine, hor. parallax ☽ à ⊙,	0.53.57.610	8.1957816.		
Sine altitude of the nonagesimal,	37.32. 3.046	9.7847845		
		7.9805661.	nat. num.	0095624.
corresponding log.		9.9197448		8312751.
arith. comp.		0.0802552		
Cosine Moon's true latitude		9.9999682.		
Sine Moon's true dist. à nonagesimal	° ′ ″	9.7333511.		
tangent ☽'s apparent dist.	33. 3.49.457.	9.8135745.		
true dist.	32.45.53.283.			
Parallax in longitude	– 17.56.174			

Rule 3.

	° ′ ″				
hor. parallax ☽ à ⊙,	0.53.57.610,	Sine	8.1957816.		
Altitude nonagesimal	37.32. 3.046.	Sine	9.7847845		
		(x)	7.9805661		
Moon's true distance à nonag.	32.45.53.283	Cosine,	9.9247439		
		(y)	7.9053100	nat: number,	0080410
Natural cosine Moon's true latitude					9999267.
corresponding log.		(z)	9.9961656.	nat num.	9918857.
arith. comp			0.0035354		
		(x)	7.9805661.		
Moon's true distance à nonagesimal		Sine	9.7333511.		
tangent parallax in longitude	′ ″ 17.56.160		7.7174556.		

	Parallax in longitude		☽'s apparent dist. à nonagesimal.
	′ ″		° ′ ″ dec
Rule 1	17.56.200		33.3.49.483.
2	17.56.174		33.3.49.457.
3	17.56.160		33.3.49.443.
Mean,	17.56.178	Mean,	33.3.49.461

	° ′ ″
Moon's true longitude	174.49.20.531.
Parallax in longitude, (☽ West of nonag.)	− 0.17.56.178.
Moon's apparent longitude	174.31.24.353.
Sun's longitude	174. 0.58.817.
difference of apparent longitude, ☽ East of ☉,	30.25.536

For the Moon's parallax in latitude.

Rule 1. (M. de la Lande's)

	° ′ ″		
hor. parallax ☽ à ☉,	0.53.57.610	sine	8.1957816.
altitude of the nonagesimal	37.32. 3.046	cosine	9.8992677
☽'s true dist. à nonagesimal	32.45.53.283	ar. comp. sine	0.2666489.
" apparent dist. d°	33. 3.49.461	Sine	9.7368518.
1st part parallax in latitude,	0.43. 8.133	Sine	8.0985500.

Moon's true latitude	0.41.38.115	Sine	8.0831707.
" true dist. à nonag.	32.45.53.283	ar. comp. sine	0.2666489.
" Parallax in longitude	0.17.56.178	Sine	7.7174570
" true dist. à nonag. + $\frac{\text{par. in long}}{2}$	32.54.51.372	cosine	9.9240127
Second part parallax	– 0. 0.20.217	Sine	5.9912953
First part d°	0.43. 8.133		
Parallax in lat. approximated	0.42.47.916		
Moon's true latitude, north	0.41.38.115		
" apparent lat. south,	1. 9.801.	(co-sine nearly equal to radius.)	

The approximated parallax and apparent lat. in this case, may be considered as correct.

Rule 2. (Dr Maskelyne's)

	° ′ ″ dec		
hor. parallax ☽ à ⊙	0.53.57.610	Sine	8.1957816.
altitude of the nonagesimal	37.32. 3.046	Cosine	9.8992677
Moon's apparent lat. S (as above)	0. 1. 9.801	ar. comp. cosine,	0.0000000
1st part parallax in latitude,	0.42.47.353	Sine	8.0950493.
hor. parallax ☽ à ⊙	0.53.57.610	Sine	8.1957816.
altitude of the nonagesimal	37.32. 3.046	Sine	9.7847845
☽'s apparent lat. South (as above)	0. 1. 9.801	Sine	6.5294365.
true dist. à nonag + $\frac{\text{par. in long.}}{2}$	32.54.51.372	Cosine	9.9240127
Second part parallax	0. 0. 0.560	Sine	4.4340153.
First part (☽'s apparent lat. S.)	+0.42.47.353.		
Parallax in latitude,	0.42.47.913.		

Rule 3. (Mr Seth Pease's.)

	° ′ ″				
hor. parallax ☽ à ☉,	0.53.57.610	Sine	8.1957816.		nat. number
altitude of the nonagesimal,	37.32. 3.046.	cosine	9.8992677		
			8.0950493.		0124465.6
Moon's true latitude, north	0.41.38.115	Natural sine			–0121109.1
	corresponding log.	6.5258867		(South)	0003356.5.
Moon's true dist. à nonag.	co-secant	10.2666489			
" apparent dist. d°	Sine	9.7368518.			
" true latitude	Secant	10.0000318.			
	′ ″				
tangent, ☽'s apparent lat. south,	1. 9.798	6.5294192.			
☽'s true latitude, north	+41.38.115				
Parallax in latitude	42.47.913.				

Parallax in latitude

	° ′ ″ dec.
Rule 1	0.42.47.916
2	0.42.47.913.
3	0.42.47.913
Mean	0.42.47.914

	° ′ ″ dec
Mean Moon's apparent S.	0. 1. 9.799
at the beginning of the eclipse north,	+0. 3. 1.263.
Moon's motion in apparent lat. during the transit,	4.11.062.

	′ ″
difference of apparent longitude, at the beginning	30.41.146
ditto d° at end of eclipse	+30.25.536
☽'s motion in apparent longitude à ☉, during the transit	61. 6.682.

The Moon's distance from the meridian at the beginning of the eclipse was 3.° 52.′ 35.″ 344 dec declination north 3.° 11.′ 56.″ 974 dec at the end, the Moon's horary angle was 51.° 15.′ 38.″ 415 dec declination, north, 2.° 41.′ 53.″ 065 hence, by calculation allowing for the spheroidal figure of the Earth, according to the ratio 320 to 319.—

	° ′ ″ dec.
The Moon's true altitude at the beginning, was	55. 3.33.493
Parallax in altitude	0.31.22.998.
apparent altitude, exclusive of refraction	54.32.10.495.
" true altitude, at the end of the eclipse	31.27.31.269.
Parallax in altitude	0.46.31.833.
apparent altitude, exclusive of refraction,	30.40.59.436.

An allowance of –1.623.″ dec. for irradiation of the Sun's light, and –2.977,″ for inflexion of the Moon's light, as stated by M[r] Ferrer, in his calculation of the longitude of Kinderhook, in the State of New-York, from the solar eclipse of June 16th 1806, will be made in the present case.

At the beginning.	′ ″	′ ″
Sun's semidiameter,	15.57.227.	
Irradiation of light	– 1.623.	
		15.55.604
☽'s horiz. semidiam.	14.45.455.	
augment^{n} for altitude,	+11.533.	
Inflexion of light	– 2.977	
		14.54.011.
Sum of ☉ and ☽'s semidiameters, corrected.		30.49.615.

End of the Eclipse.	′ ″	
Sun's semid.	15.57.250	
Irrad: of light	– 1.623	
		15.55.627
☽'s hor. sem.	14.45.726	
augment.	+ 7.253	
Inflexion,	– 2.977	
		14.50.002
Sum of semidiameters, corrected.		30.45.629.

Moon's motion in apparent lat.	251.062″	log. + 10. =	12.3997810.
" motion in apparent long.	3666.682	log.	3.5642733
angle of inclination	tangent, 3.° 55.′ 1.″ 181.		8.8355077.
Moon's motion in apparent longitude	3666.682″.	log	3.5642733.
angle of inclination	3.° 55.′ 1.″ 181	ar. comp. cos.	0.0010156
chord of transit, or line of ☽'s path in the apparent orbit.	61.′ 15.″ 267. = 3675.267″		3.5652889.
chord of transit	3675.267″.	ar. co. log.	6.4347111.
Sum of semidiameters	3695.244	log	3.5676432
difference of ditto	3.986	log	0.6005373.
(x)	4.007	log	0.6028916.

3675.267 + 4.007 = 3679.274 half = 1839.637″.
3675.267 − 4.007 = 3671.260. half = 1835.630

1839.637″	log	3.2647321.
1849.615. (Sum of Sem^{rs} at beg.)	ar. co. log.	6.7329187.
cosine angle of conjunction	5.° 57.′ 14.″ 500	9.9976508

			° ′ ″ dec
Angle of conjunction, at the beginning of the eclipse,			5.57.14.500.
Angle of inclination of the ☽, in the apparent orbit,			−3.55. 1.181.
Central angle, at the beginning			2. 2.13.319.

1835.630		log.	3.2637851
1845.629.		ar. co. log.	6.7338556.
Cosine angle of conjunction, at the end	° ′ ″ 5.58. 0.500		9.9976407.
Angle of inclination,	+3.55. 1.181		
	9.53. 1.681.		

Sum of Semidiameters at beginning	1849.″ 615. dec	log.	3.2670813.
Central angle	2.° 2.′ 13.″ 319.	cosine,	9.9997255
diff. apparent long. ⊙ & ☽, 30.′ 48.″ 446 =	1848.″ 446		3.2668068.
Sum of Semidiameters at the end of eclipse,	1845.″ 629.	log.	3.2661444.
Central angle, at end of the eclipse,	9.° 53.′ 1.″ 681.	cosine	9.9935062
diff. apparent long. ⊙ and ☽, 30.′ 18.″ 237 =	1818.″ 237		3.2596506.

	′ ″
diff. of apparent long. at the beginning,	+30.48.446.
Parallax in longitude,	+ 9.39.841
True difference long. ⊙ and ☽, at the beginning	+40.28.287
diff. of apparent longitude at the end	−30.18.237
Parallax in longitude,	−17.56.178
True difference longitude ⊙ and ☽, at the end,	−48.14.415.

The hourly velocity in longitude ☽ à ☉, at a middle time between the beginning of the eclipse and the estimated time of true conjunction at Monticello, was 27.′ 5.″ 7572 dec, and between the end and true conjunction, 27.′ 6.″ 3006. dec

---

As 27.′ 5.″ 7572 dec. to one hour or 60 minutes, so is 40.′ 28.″ 287 to 1. h. 29. m. 37. Sec. 084. dec. which added to 0. h. 13. m. 54. sec the apparent time of beginning, gives 1. h. 43. m 31. Sec. 084 dec., the time of <u>true</u> conjunction at Monticello, by the beginning of the eclipse.

As 27.′ 6.″ 3006 dec., to one hour or 60 minutes, so is 48.′ 14.″ 415. to 1. h. 46. m. 47. Sec. 114. dec which subtracted from 3. h. 29. m. 4. Sec. 400. dec., gives 1. h. 42. m. 17. sec. 286. dec., the time of true conjunction, by the end of the eclipse.

		h. m. Sec. dec		° ′ ″ dec.
	By the beginning	1.43.31.084		
	" the end,	1.42.17.286		
Mean,	True conjunction at Monticello,	1.42.54.185.		
	D° at Greenwich,	6.57.14.915		
	Longitude in time, west,	5.14.20.730.	=	78.35.10.950.

City of Washington,
November 14th 1811.

William Lambert.

MS (DLC); written entirely in Lambert's hand on five folio sheets; with one small hole.

[1] Manuscript: "numbe."

From Oliver Pollock

SIR, Richmond 19th November 1811

I had the honor of receiving your letter dated on the 4th of may, some time back and delayed making an acknowledgement until I could do it fully to my own Satisfaction.

I find to my regret that you do not retain as particular a recollection of the transactions of the Government of Virginia as I had hoped, this indeed is not surprising considering the numerous and important offices which you have since filled and the lapse of thirty two years—but yet I am confident that you will remember what was a matter of much notoriety both then and afterwards, first. that I acted as the official public Agent of Virginia at New orleans—secondly—that I incurred large Debts in that Character—thirdly—that my agency resulted in great benefits to the Public, not only in the destruction of a dangerous Enemy—but in the acquisition of a Valuable Country to the United States.

I am of opinion that a testimonial under your hand clearly ascertaining these facts will be of service to me and Will be highly gratifying to my feelings to have such co-operating testimony from a name so high and respectable, by that means additional Validity will be given to what has been stated by others, and particularly by the late Col. William Heth, in his Character as Agent for settling the Accounts relating to the Conquest of the Isilinois. Col. Heth's letter is the last document in a pamphlet now sent, and I refer you to it to refresh your memory as to some particulars which may not be at once recollected.

I cannot doubt that it will afford you pleasure to comply with a request which has for its object nothing more than the exhibition of truth, to which may be added the gratification of the feelings of an old and very Zealous, but unfortunate public Servant—and likewise

Your friend and very Hble. Servt. OLR POLLOCK.

Please to direct to me here as soon as possible

RC (DLC); adjacent to signature: "Thomas Jefferson Esq."; endorsed by TJ as received 22 Dec. 1811 and so recorded in SJL. Enclosure: Pollock, *To the Honourable the Legislature of Virginia. The Memorial of Oliver Pollock, of the State of Maryland* (1811).

In his 12 Mar. 1806 letter to Pollock, WILLIAM HETH confirmed Pollock's important role in supplying George Rogers Clark's expedition, admitted that in his capacity as an agent to settle Pollock's accounts he had originally doubted but ultimately fully accepted his claims and his veracity, and affirmed that Pollock's fortunes were ruined by his "zeal to discharge the trust and confidence reposed in him" (Pollock, *Memorial*, 12). Clark's CONQUEST OF THE ISILINOIS (Illinois) region secured to the United States what would become known as the Northwest Territory.

From William Short

Dear sir New-York Nov. 19–11

I was exploring the Jersey mountains in search of a farm when your favor of the 15th Oct. was forwarded here, agreeably to directions left with my agent at Philadelphia, as to my letters. I did not succeed in my search but hope to be more successful next year.—

Let me now express all my thanks for your kindness as to Ind. Camp—I am indeed truly obliged by it, & prefer much the plan of allowing the leases to remain quietly as they are—should an offer be made, it will then be time to see what arrangement can be made, or what will be best to be done. I am glad to see you think the land cheap at 10.d.—I shall be satisfied perfectly with the price, & particularly if the purchaser will pay the interest with punctuality—In that case it will be a kind of property which will suit one in my situation much better than land—although if I had a family I should be of a very different opinion & should prefer land to any thing.

Some time ago having occasion to write to Mr Wickham on my law business with my worthy friend & relation Colo S.—I mentioned to him my wish to sell this land—I had hope it might suit him, as I know he is a land purchaser—He told me he did not wish it himself, but would aid me in the sale as far as he could—& that he would direct the land to be viewed by the father of his manager, who lived near it—This was I think more than a year ago—I believe indeed on my return to this country—& if I am not mistaken I mentioned the price of 10 dols to him—I have found here on my return from the Jersey a letter on Colo S.'s business from Mr Wickham[1] & in it he tells me that his manager Mr Sampson has visited the lands, & that his father in law Mr Rogers, who lives near them & is well acquainted with the price & value of lands has also viewed them & is to give an opinion which he daily expects—Mr W. adds—"from what I can learn they would command from 10 to 12 dols ℔ acre, on the usual terms of sale."—Still as I have said above I shall be perfectly satisfied with 10 dols as being a more convenient arrangement for me than holding lands. should Mr W. find a purchaser he will of course inform me of it, & I shall do nothing without first communicating with you.

I have a letter from Mde de Tessé of March last of which this is an extract—"presentez mes plus tendres & plus respectueux hommages à Mr Jefferson, dans toutes les occasions ou cela vous sera possible—Je ne suis pas encore consoleé de ne plus trouver de ses beaux discours dans les gazettes. Si vous etes assez heureux pour aller a Monticello il seroit bon de vous mettre pour un petit moment à genoux devant mon autel—j'aimerais bien a scavoir si vos ennemis ont conservè leur credit—si votre Gouvernement s'obstine a ignorer qu'on reconnait jamais bien les moeurs d'un pays dont on ne parle pas la langue, & que le patriotisme ne supplie pas aux lumières &c."—I endeavored to explain to her &[2] others the state of my case—but it was telling the fabulam surdo.—And she is on this a proof in point of her own maxim above, as to not knowing les moeurs d'un pays, &[3] the Government, administration & views of a country, may be included as well as the moeurs.

I am now inclined to believe that it is necessary not only to have the language, but to be personally present to possess a knowlege of a foreign country, in this century of unceasing changes—On my return to France I found such a perfect revolution in every thing, that it was quite a new country & to be studied once again—Notwithstanding I had kept up a correspondence with my friends there, yet events had succeeded with so much rapidity that I was totally in arrear—And the first month it was a matter of great amusement to my friends & myself to be learning from them at every moment, events of real importance & still operating their effect, of which I had never heard or dreamed. I was like La Peyrouse in the little comedy which was written in the year 1790—in which he is made to arrive at Paris; where of course he finds nothing as he left it in 85.—& had to ask the explanation of every thing.— I had an opportunity by going from France to England, of verifying the perfect state of ignorance in which these two countries are with respect to each other—When you consider that they are separated by only seven leagues of water, & that there is much communication, it really passes all comprehension—It is not always safe to endeavor to rectify errors of this kind—because it is necessary to begin by telling people that they are mistaken, & that you know better than they do.—They will very certainly not believe you in the first place—& in the second, they will probably be displeased by you; & particularly if you enter as a volunteer. Chance gave me whilst in France an opportunity of being admitted further into the secret cabinet of the leader or rather the driver there, than can possibly happen to any one but by chance—& I can aver that the real feelings & views, particularly the former, as to this country, are considered there as very different from what they are here. I do not think it right to commit[4] to paper the source through which this came to me, but I will do so when I have the pleasure of seeing you.— In England I met with an old acquaintance formed a great many years ago on the continent, who is a thoroughgoing Ministerialist—By his situation, by the places he has held & by his connexions he is in fact one of them, although he has no department. I saw a few of the opposition, who however were not the leaders—These were all Englishmen & I had a good deal of conversation with them, & in a way in which there could be no disguise or disposition to deceive—They were men of information as to their own country—they had all been on the continent & in France particularly, & yet I can assure you that however well they may have been acquainted with France "as it was," they were totally mistaken in their ideas of France "as it is." And I observed that they had not only different, but opposite, ideas—just as they would have had on a question in the house of commons. They had each mixed up all they had formerly known with all they were daily learning, & made a dish according to the taste of their palates, but really not at all according to the nature of the thing.

I saw also three foreigners who have so long resided in London that they are much better informed of the true state, & real interests, of England in its foreign relations, than any Englishman I saw—for it seems as if that kind of knowlege was more difficult to be attained by an Englishman than any other—Dumouriez & Count d'Antraigues (the last you will recollect as having been of the constituent assembly, having written a pamphlet in which he went far ahead of his peers in favor of the revolution & then taking the steed & emigrating either with or before Mourriez) have with the active industry & intelligence of Frenchmen acquired a most intimate knowlege of the state of things & parties as regards England in its interior—Being foreigners, & employed & paid (at least Dumouriez) by the government, they see with the same freedom each succeeding ministry—They have become acquainted with them as they have come into power, & shewed respect for them & retained an intimacy with the influential when they have lost their power, not knowing how soon they may come up again—Being thus free of the fogs of party spirit, it appeared to me that they had a clearer & more distinct view of the present, as well as what would probably be the future, in England than any one I saw there.

Dumouriez is consulted on all military operations in Europe—he forms plans for them—of which they never take more than a part—just enough to incur all the expense, & never enough to give a chance of success.—or if they adopt the whole of his plan, they then begin it some months later than agreed on so as to insure its failure in that way. It is clear from the opinion of both Dumouriez & d'Antraigues—that the present is the weakest ministry they have yet been able to collect—The Marquis of Wellesley they say is a man of enterprize & extensive views, proper for a first Minister, but totally incapable of the details of a department—He came in under the full expectation of being premier, of which he had the assurance, but was outwitted completely by Perceval, who was when at the bar an Avocat sans cause, & who always will be a ministre sans talent. The details of this manoeuvre are really curious, as I had it from d'An— —& the main spring of the intrigue & what secured Perceval's success, was his representing to the King that he was really without talents or influence himself—& of course could be nothing but by the King, whereas those who had talents & influence, would always endeavour to make themselves independent of the King & control him.—

The opinion of many was, that it would be a piece of good fortune for England if the Ministry were baffled at once & the armies driven out of the Peninsula, so as to have necessity for the excuse of abandoning their mode of carrying on the war there—It would be too long to go into detail on this subject at the end of so long a letter—So far as we may judge from what took place in Gallicia, during the campaign of Sir John Moore & after the expulsion of his army, the resistance would not be diminished by such an event. This is the opinion of the famous Savary, Duke de Rovigo, now Minister of Police, the same who brought off the Prince of Asturias—Whilst I was at Paris he told a Lady of my acquaintance, who repeated it to me the same day—"As to conquering Spain, if by dispersing its armies, a conquest is meant, that is already done—but if a quiet possession is meant, that cannot be effected but by a permanent garrison of 600,000 men—& considering the Peninsula as a place forte."

Instead of disasters in the peninsula & the expulsion of the British from thence, making them more tractable as to our affairs, might it not on the contrary remove one of the principal inducements which they have to peace with us in the present state of things, the necessity of their armies deriving supplies from hence? The effect of a bankruptcy on their internal state & foreign relations, or the probability of such an event would require the going into a longer investigation of the interior of England than you would perhaps think worthy of the time—It was evident to me whilst in England, although no Englishman that I saw would then[5] admit it, that they were verging towards a paper money—Huskisson however has since shewn that in its true light Have you seen his pamphlet?[6]—In time, paper money (which however is different from paper currency) if continued, inevitably produces one kind of bankruptcy—But whilst this money can hold out it adds strength instead of taking it away—And after it can hold out no longer we have seen one instance at least, that of France, of a country immediately arising like a phenix from its ashes. I do not pretend to decide that this would be the same with every other—but it is worthy of being taken into consideration. Indeed there are so many things to be taken into consideration in examining, & more especially in deciding, on this vast subject the war with England[7] & which must of course[8] have occupied the mind of the administration for some time back, that I have been imprudent perhaps in thus touching on it, as I can only do it in a contracted way. I think with you that it is very uncertain whether the nation itself will not soon force the Prince, or King, & Ministry into a war with us. Perceval would not perhaps be sorry to be thus forced, but most others would be sorry for it. The present course of the two governments, however it seems to me, tends towards war—& although I do not believe that either government does or can wish for it, yet in their present attitudes, some event, or some succession of events may take place which will render it still more probable, if not inevitable.—I should like much to have been at Monticello last summer with M & M, & have heard them discuss some points, which must, I should imagine, have been discussed; such as whether this be the most favorable time for engaging in a war in favor of neutral rights, seeing that all the world is belligerent except ourselves—& that each belligerent is equally hostile to these rights.—*what would be the probable effect on ourselves, of a war undertaken at this time—whether there be no means of evading for the present (if the moment be unfavorable for war) & of postponing war without renouncing any principle & with a determination of preparing for the assertion & maintenance of every principle on the first favorable occasion which may present a good chance of success.—If there be no such means, then of course war at present is necessary & inevitable, & removes the trouble of every other consideration, except as to carrying it on with the greatest effect.

A person situated as I am & who of course can have only a part of the subject under his view, is so exposed to form half starved incorrect opinions that he should not perhaps trouble other people with them: but where we feel very much interested it is almost impossible not to form an opinion, & difficult not to communicate it when speaking confidentially. I take it for granted that since the length of time

* I have travelled a great deal this summer—& seen many of all parties—& this point I have heard particularly conversed & ideas thrown out as to the certainty of its changing the administration after the first election. Whether that w[d] really be the case I do not pretend to say.

that our commercial difficulties have begun with the belligerent powers, Government must, in its various views of that subject, have examined the alternative of leaving commerce to its own protection, when carried beyond our own limits—or inviting the citizens of the U.S. to remain at home & employ their capitals here; but at the same time leaving them free to manage their affairs in their own way, & at their own risk & peril, if they will persist in placing themselves between Scylla & Charybdis.—I suppose, as this plan has never (I believe) been brought forward, that there must be some objection to it arising out of circumstances unknown to me. I had a good deal of conversation on this subject with Daniel Parker, as to its commercial effects. No person that I know, carries more analysis into commercial questions than he does—He has established his reputation as a clear & combining head on these matters, as well at London as at Amsterdam—& his long residence abroad has not diminished his attachment to his own country—Indeed I believe that residence abroad, free from the asperities one sees at home, & the injustice & abuse to which one is exposed, increases & exalts one's attachment instead of diminishing it. Parker has more than once developed the commercial bearings that this measure would have, in so satisfactory a manner that I requested he would give me a memoir with these developements, that I might send it to you—He promised this with pleasure & would have executed it with zeal, but before he had done intelligence was recieved from America which shewed it was then unnecessary.

As far as we can judge from what has transpired from Washington, there appears no symptom of the Executive contemplating such a measure—How would they like its coming from the legislature?—I have no reason to suppose that such a plan exists there—but a gentleman here told me that a Republican member of the house who came down the North River with him, said outright on board of the steam boat, that should be his plan.

The Hornet is here under sailing orders for Europe—The report is that a new Minister to London[9] is to go out in that vessel—& that Dr Eustis is the person intended. This may perhaps merely proceed from the affair of the Chesapeake being arranged—Perhaps also this arrangement may act as an entering wedge—& to use an Irish phrase, draw things closer together—but I am not sufficiently instructed, to see how it will do it.

On looking back at this long letter, I am really, bona fide, sans phrase, frightened at it—& almost tempted to suppress it altogether, & write another merely as to Ind: Camp—but hoping & taking for granted you will only read as much of it as you please, I let it go, with the repeated assurance of all my gratitude for your kindness as to Ind: Camp, & of my being ever your friend & servant

W SHORT

RC (MHi); endorsed by TJ as received 22 Dec. 1811 and so recorded in SJL.

COLO S.: Henry Skipwith.

PRESENTEZ MES PLUS TENDRES ... AUX LUMIÈRES &C.: "present my most tender and respectful regards to Mr. Jefferson every chance you get—I am disconsolate that I can no longer find his wonderful speeches in the gazettes. If you are so fortunate as to go to Monticello, you should kneel in front of my altar for a moment—I would very much like to know whether your enemies have retained their influence—and if your government still fails to recognize that one never knows the customs of a country well when one does not speak its language, and that patriotism does not provide enlightenment, etc."

FABULAM SURDO: "story to the deaf." August Friedrich Ferdinand von Kotzebue's comedy LA PEYROUSE was translated into English in 1799 and went through many editions. Emmanuel Henri Louis Alexandre de Launay, comte D'ANTRAIGUES, wrote a *Mémoire sur les Etats-généraux, leurs droits, et la maniere de les convoquer* (Paris, 1788). AVOCAT SANS CAUSE: "lawyer without cases." MINISTRE SANS TALENT: "minister without talent." Ferdinand VII of Spain used the PRINCE OF ASTURIAS as his title while he was crown prince, 1789–1808 (Connelly, *Napoleonic France*, 175). PLACE FORTE: "fortified place." William Huskisson's PAMPHLET was *The Question concerning the Depreciation of our Currency Stated and Examined* (London, 1810). M & M: James Madison and James Monroe. BONA FIDE, SANS PHRASE: "truly, without mincing words."

[1] Preceding three words interlined.
[2] Preceding two words interlined.
[3] Short here canceled "I might add the."
[4] Reworked from the first two letters of "admit."
[5] Preceding five words interlined in place of "would."
[6] Preceding five words interlined.
[7] Preceding four words interlined.
[8] Manuscript: "couse."
[9] Preceding two words interlined.

From Sylvanus Bourne

SIR

Amsterdam Novr 20 1811

As you are acquainted with the embarrassing situation in which I have laboured for some years & which has now reached a point bordering on distress, I take the liberty most respectfully to mention to you that I have made an application to the President of the U States to be named to fill the Consular vacancy in London when the State of our relations with that Country may render this appointment proper & expedient, & I have most earnestly to solicit the favr of your interest with the President for obtaining said appointment—There will be doubtless many Competitors which will tend greatly to enhance the value of your friendship towards me of which I shall ever entertain a most gratefull Sense, & my Children shall be taught to reverence the name of their Protector & friend

I have the honor Dr Sir with the greatest Respect Yr Ob Servt

S Bourne

RC (DLC); at foot of text: "The Hon^r-ble Thos Jefferson Esqr at his Seat Monticello Virginia"; endorsed by TJ as received 1 Mar. 1812 and so recorded in SJL.

In a letter to President James Madison of 3 July 1812 (Madison, *Papers, Pres. Ser.*, 4:552), Bourne reiterated his initial APPLICATION, not found, for a transfer to London.

From William Lambert

Sir, City of Washington, November 22^d 1811.

The observations relating to the solar eclipse of the 17th September last, were made in this city opposite Rhodes's hotel, North 71.° West, 1.$\frac{3}{8}$. m American measure, from the Capitol. The apparent times of the principal appearances, to the nearest second, are as follow:—

	h.	m.	s.
Beginning of the Eclipse,	0.	22.	9.
Annulus formed,	2.	2.	6.
d^o broken,	2.	6.	53.
End of the Eclipse,	3.	36.	53.

	° ′ ″ dec.
Latitude of the place of observation, (assumed)	38.53.25.
d^o reduced, (320 to 319)	38.42.54.465.
Constant log. to reduce the ☽'s equat. hor. parallax[1] for lat. and ratio	9.9994653.

An allowance of –1.″ 623. dec for irradiation of the Sun's, and –2.″ 977. dec for inflexion of the Moon's light, has been made in the calculation.

From the foregoing data, and the elements connected, which have been computed to great exactness, the solar time of true conjunction—

	h. m. Sec. dec.
By the beginning of the Eclipse, is	1.49.17.635.
" the End	1.49.17.678.
Mean True Conjunction at Washington,	1.49.17.656
Ditto at Greenwich	6.57.14.915
Longitude in time, of the place of observation,	5. 7.57.259.
	° ′ ″
Equal to	76.59.18.885.
difference of longitude West of the Capitol,	– 1.26.978.
Longitude of the Capitol, by the external contacts,	76.57.51.907.

Say 76.° 57.′ 52.″

If we connect this result with that obtained from the occultation of n Pleiadum (Alcyone) by the Moon, on the 20th of October 1804, a mean of the two will be, nearly 76.° 55.′ 45.″, or 5. h. 7. m. 43. Sec. in time, being an approximation which will not, perhaps vary much from the truth, when it shall be tested by future observations.

Before this comes to hand, you will, probably, have received from bishop Madison, my calculation of the longitude of Monticello, from the external contacts of the same Eclipse.

I am, Sir, with great respect, Your most obedient servant,

William Lambert.

RC (DLC); at foot of text: "Thomas Jefferson, late President U.S."; endorsed by TJ as received 22 Dec. 1811 and so recorded in SJL.

[1] Abbreviation for "equatorial horizontal parallax."

From James Ogilvie

Dear Sir Cameleon Springs Novr 24th

I have to thank you for a letter, which had I wanted any additional motives to stimulate my exertions during my temporary seclusion from the world, would have supplied them.—Accept my cordial thanks for the benevolent interest in my future welfare & usefulness you have done me the honour to express, coupled with an assurance, that I shall endeavour to deserve a continuance of your friendly regard.—

The subject you suggested as well calculated for illustration from the Rostrum, will be included in an oration I am now composing "On the situation condition & Prospects of the American People."—Finding total solitude necessary to call forth the concentrated & persevering exertion of my faculties, I have retired to a sequestered spot in the bosom of the woods:—There exists not a human being within several miles of the place: I reside in a log-house situated in a deep glen & encircled by hills, which I climb twice a day for exercise—Here I am determined to remain until I can accomplish the purpose of my temporary seclusion—

I take the liberty to enclose for your perusal[1] a copy of proposals, recently issued by James Mcallister, for publishing a weekly paper in Bards town Ky.

I am warranted by intimate knowlege of this truly great man, in saying, that his capacity and qualifications to execute, with fidelity & ability the design he has commenced, are probably preeminent; Assuredly his paper will be characterised by an accuracy in the statement of facts, an impartiality & profoundness in the discussion of political questions, a variety of useful information & an elegance of stile, unequalled in any American News-paper.—

Should you do him the honour to take his paper, it will perhaps be necessary to intimate your wish by addressing a few lines to him at Bards' Town.—

It is my intention after finishing the orations I am now composing, to revisit Virginia for the purpose of delivering them in Richmond. During this visit, it will afford me peculiar satisfaction to make an excursion to Albemarle—

With best wishes to all around you, believe me to be,

Dear Sir, with profound respects, yours &c James Ogilvie

RC (MHi); partially dated; addressed: "Thomas Jefferson Esqr Monticello Albemarle Virginia"; franked; postmarked Bowling Green, Kentucky, 27 Nov. 1811; endorsed by TJ as received 25 Dec. 1811 and so recorded in SJL.

The enclosed prospectus, not found, was for a new WEEKLY PAPER, the *Bardstown Repository*, which began publication in about February 1812 (Brigham, *American Newspapers*, 1:146–7).

[1] Preceding three words interlined.

From George Jefferson

Dear Sir Richmond 25th Novr 1811

Having received the form of the bond which I am to execute previous to entering upon the duties of my office, I avail myself of your kind offer of joining me in it, and now inclose it for your signature.

I have not inserted the third name, as I wish to take the chance (small as it is) of Mr Gibson's return previous to my departure: there being but very few persons to whom I like to lay myself under such an obligation, which greatly enhances the favor you have done me—for which, to say nothing of your many other kindnesses, I can never sufficiently thank you.

Have the goodness to inclose the bond to Gibson & Jefferson, as, should there be any delay in the mail, I may possibly be gone before it is returned, in which case I shall leave a letter in which for it to be inclosed, with orders for it to be forwarded.

I am Dear Sir Your ever faithful friend Geo. Jefferson

RC (MHi); at foot of text: "Thomas Jefferson esq^r"; endorsed by TJ as received 28 Nov. 1811, but mistakenly recorded in SJL as received on the day it was written. Enclosure: George Jefferson's consular bond, 25 Nov. 1811, obligating him, TJ, and William Wardlaw to pay $2,000 to the United States if

Jefferson did not "truly and faithfully discharge the duties of his said office, according to law," and "truly account for all monies, goods and effects, which may come into his possession by virtue of the laws of the United States, or of his said office" (printed form in DNA: RG 39, SB; with names, date, and title of appointment filled in by Jefferson and signed by him, TJ, and Wardlaw; with Jefferson's signature witnessed by James Ligon and William S. Warwick, TJ's signature witnessed by Thomas Jefferson Randolph and Charles L. Bankhead, and Wardlaw's signature witnessed by Corbin Warwick and Ligon; with signed approval by James Monroe at the State Department, 3 Apr. 1812; endorsed in an unidentified hand: "Bond George Jefferson Consul 1811").

From Nicolas G. Dufief

MONSIEUR A Philadelphie ce 26 Novembre 1811

Je m'empresse de vous faire l'hommage de mon catalogue avant que Sa publication ait été encore annoncé. Je dois vous prévenir que la difficulté qu'on éprouve à Se procurer des Livres Francais est cause qu'une partie de ceux qui composent ma Bibliothèque est de rencontre, mais les prix ont été fixés en conséquence.

Agreez, Je vous prie, les assurances du profond respect avec lequel, J'ai l'honneur d'être Monsieur votre très-dévoué Serviteur

N. G. DUFIEF

P.S Je reçois à l'instant un grand nombre de livres dont je vous enverrai la note par la première occasion

EDITORS' TRANSLATION

SIR Philadelphia 26 November 1811

I eagerly compliment you with my catalogue before its publication has been announced. I must caution you that procuring French books is so difficult that some of those making up my bookstall are secondhand, but their prices have been set accordingly.

I pray you to accept the assurances of the profound respect with which I have the honor to be Sir your most devoted Servant N. G. DUFIEF

P.S. I am receiving many books at present. I will describe them to you at the first opportunity

RC (DLC); dateline adjacent to signature; at foot of text: "Th: Jefferson, Esq[re] Monticello"; endorsed by TJ as received 22 Dec. 1811 and so recorded in SJL. Translation by Dr. Roland H. Simon. Enclosure not found.

Survey of Bear Creek Lands

11. Nov. 26.

beginning on Bear creek on the E. side of the road.

√ N. 34½ E. 50. po. leaving the branch on the E.
√ at 10. po. further the branch is 4.6 po. on the E.
√ at 80. po. from the Beginning, branch 4.8 E.
√ at 92. from d° touched it.
√ at 100. branch 4. po. E.
√ at 132. cross the branch
√ at 150. recross d°
√ at 160. cross a 3d time.
√ at 210. to the edge of the branch
√ N. 54½ E. 58. po. along the side of the branch. to a poplar in the field.
√ N. 22 E. 22. po. touching the branch.
√ sa. co. contind 14. po. branch 8. po. W.
√ sa. co. 12. po. to a poplar on the branch in the woods.
√ N. 52½ E. 8. po. along the branch.
√ sa. co. 52. po. going off from the branch.
√ N. 70. E. 140. po.
√ S. 20. E. 16. po
√ N. 25. W. 26. po.
√ N. varying from 72. to 78. W. 218. po. [N. 77. W.
S. 26. W. 332. po. to the road[1]

Nov. 27.

S. 85½ E. 88 po. to the beginning[2]

Nov. 28.[3]

Beginning at the Poplar in the woods on Bear branch.

√ N. 38. E. 24.[4] po. branch on the E. to a wh. oak
√ N. 2. E. 20. crossing branch to a poplar
√ N. 5. E. 16. branch 6. W. after recrossing it
sa. co. 6. to intersection of the branch & line at an elm

---

again beginning at Robinson's corner.

√ N. 25½ W. 50. po.
√ S. 77. W. 80. po. to Bear branch. on Gill's line.
√ sa. co. 148 po.
S. 26. W. 338[5] po. on C. Bankhead's line to it's intersection with Liberty road[6]

MS (ViU: TJP, TB [Thurlow-Berkeley no.] 1136 [532j-3]); entirely in TJ's hand; unmatched bracket in original; with Thomas Jefferson Randolph's survey notes (532j-2) on verso.

TJ and his grandson Thomas Jefferson Randolph apparently surveyed the Bear Creek section of TJ's Poplar Forest property together, with notes taken by Randolph on separate scraps of paper serving as the basis for and now filed with the above document. Randolph's notes and the completed survey differ primarily in his use of chains and links, as opposed to the poles (PO.) TJ favored as a unit of measure. SA. CO.: "same course."

[1] Text to this point reworked from Randolph's manuscript notes in ViU: TJP, TB 1136 (532j-2).

[2] Line repeated from Randolph's notes in ViU: TJP, TB 1136 (532j-14).

[3] Remainder of survey adapted from Randolph's survey notes in ViU: TJP, TB 1136 (532j-7, 532j-9, and 532j-12).

[4] Reworked from "22."

[5] Beneath this number TJ erased "332."

[6] Beneath this line TJ erased "S. 85. E. 83 po. to hiccory."

Account with Reuben Perry

[ca. 28 Nov. 1811]

Mr Thomas Jefferson

In Account with R. Perry

Sept 1810	To 2 Treessels Bedsteads @ $3	£1.16.
	one apple mill @ $12—	3.12.
	11 Days work @ 4/6	2. 9.6
Feby 10th 1811	Altering doors 12/	.12.
	one bookcase Lock @ 3/	. 3.
Auggust 20th	To 9 Days work @ 4/6	2. 0.6
	Mending wheat[1] machene @ 12/	.12.
Novm 28th	To one Level	. 6.
		£11.11.0

MS (ViW: TC-JP); entirely in Perry's hand; undated; attached at some point to a separate sheet containing Account with Reuben Perry, [ca. May 1813].

TJ acknowledged this debt in his Account with Reuben Perry, 10 Dec. 1813.

[1] Word interlined.

From William & Samuel Craig

SIR New York 29 Novem^r^ 1811

We[1] have the honor to inclose a Letter for you, received by a Ship of ours from Belfast; accompanied by a small Box, which We have taken in charge; & will be happy to forward it agreeably to such instructions as you may please to honor Us with.—We have the honor to subscribe ourselves

Sir Your M^t Ob ser W^M & SAM^L CRAIG

RC (MHi); dateline beneath signature; at foot of text: "Thomas Jefferson Esqu^e"; endorsed by TJ as received 22 Dec. 1811 and so recorded in SJL. Enclosure: Samuel M. Stephenson to TJ, 10 Oct. 1811.

William Craig (ca. 1775–1826) joined his uncle in business as Henry Sadler & Company in 1794. After Sadler's death, Craig went into business with his younger brother Samuel Craig (ca. 1780–1830) under the name of William & Samuel Craig. The firm survived until Samuel Craig's death (New York *Daily Advertiser*, 13 Sept. 1794; *New-York Commercial Advertiser*, 6 Aug. 1805; *Longworth's New York Directory* [1806], 145; [1830], 207; *New-York Evening Post*, 5 Sept. 1826, 9, 15 July 1830).

[1] Manuscript: "The."

From John Low

HON^D SIR Washington City, Novr 29th 1811

I have sent you by mail, a Sett of the New Encyclopædia, published in Newyork, which a few years ago you did the honor to Subscribe to.—His Excellency Mr Madison, has also rec^d his sett for which he subscribed, at about the same time—I hope, Sir, the Books and Binding will meet your approbation.—Be pleased, Sir, to order a draft for the amount, on this city, which is $75.—I have carefully done them up, and hope they will arrive Safe.—With Sentiments of the deepest respect for your dignified character and Virtuous life, and with the principles of true Republicanism,

Believe me to be yours respectfully JN^O LOW.

P.S. I expect to be in town for 8 or 10 days yet, and a letter directed to me, at the Post Office, will come Safe.—

RC (DLC); endorsed by TJ as received 22 Dec. 1811 and so recorded in SJL. Enclosure: *The New and Complete American Encyclopædia: or, Universal Dictionary of Arts and Sciences . . . from the Encyclopaedia Perthensis, with Improvements*, 7 vols. (New York, 1805–11); the first five volumes of which were published by the elder John Low, and the final two by his widow and successor, Esther Prentiss Low.

John Low (ca. 1790–1829), printer, was born in London, the son of John Low (1763–1809) and his wife Esther Prentiss Low, all of whom immigrated to America shortly after his birth. By 1796–97 the elder Low had established himself as a printer and bookseller in New York City. Upon his death his wife ran their printing establishment. The younger John Low worked in the family business until 1812 and then operated his own printing enterprise and bookstore (Sanford A. Moss, *The Low Family of New York City Publishers, 1795–1829* [1943], 1–4; George J. McKay, *A Register of Artists, Engravers, Booksellers, Bookbinders, Printers &*

Publishers in New York City, 1633–1820 [1942], 45; New York *Public Advertiser*, 25 May 1809; *Longworth's New York Directory* [1812], 190; [1813], 207; [1828], 380).

From Valentín de Foronda

Coruña Noviembre 30 de 1811.

Philosofo respetable, tengo la honra de remitir á Vm un exemplar de un folleto, que viene á ser una copia de los apuntes que imprimi en Philadelphia sobre la nueva constitucion en que aconsejaba á las Cortes la senda, que creia debia seguir, y que no ha seguido de lo que ha resultado una perdida de tiempo inmensa, lo que no podia menos de succeder, no habiendo fixado las vases sobre las que se debia edificar: asi tan pronto se ha tocado un punto como otro enteramente inconexo. Se ha hecho cosas buenas, y se han dexado en pie grandes absurdos.

La parte primera de la Constitucion está aprobada. En el mismo dia, que me llegó el proyecto presentado por la comision hice rapidamente las observaciones que lerá Vm. Se resiente de ideas goticas, de librazos viejos; de nuestras rancias préocupaciones.

Va tambien una carta contra Claros, nombre supuesto, que se aplicó su Autor el Obispo celebre de Orense, que huele á santidad, que ha sido Regente, que no quiso por el pronto hacer el juramento al Pueblo Soberano; pero al cabo lo hizo. En este papel trato varios puntos del Derecho-publico. Aunque me firme Claro y franco todos saben, que soy el Autor.

Celebraria tener la coleccion de Cartas, que he insertado en el diario de S^{n} Tiago en los 6 meses que me hallo en Galicia; pero no teniendo sino un exemplar no puedo desprenderme de él. He hablado á lo Philosofo me he opuesto a que se gritara en los Escritos viva el Rey; sino que fuese viva el pueblo Español : y me explicaba así. Lo que deviera ser es viva el Soberano, que nunca he oido: pero esta grandiosa idea moral no se concive por el pueblo: está mas a su alcance, Viva la Nacion y aun mas (por lo que le doy la preferencia) viva el pueblo Español. Me he opuesto á que se llamen Reales Exercitos, sino Exercitos Nacionales. No es cosa de molestar á Vm.

Habiendo tocado en un papel varios puntos en que se creia interesada la Clerecia, y Frayleria se han sublevado: me han escrito varios anonimos, han impreso algunos, y han predicado contra mi. Yo contesté y pulvericé á los dos primeros, anunciando que no gastaria el tiempo en contestar á necedades que ya[1] han salido otros anonimos, que han ridiculizado á mis antagonistas. Es menester confesar, que hay todavia muchas preocupaciones, que sobstienen varias gentes, y con las que no pueden los Sabios, los Philosofos de que hay algunos. Si, Philantropo Jefferson son de tanto merito, que los pondria á luchar con los primeros sabios de Europa.

Remito tambien 6 cartas que escribi en Lisboa en el mes de Julio de 1810. En la 6ª verá Vm un dialogo sobre la Nobleza.

Envio igualmente un papelito que gustará á Vm por el solo merito de haberlo publicado en favor de un Ciudadano, y contra un Juez.

No remito exemplares para su amigo de Vm el Philosofo, el sabio Madisson porque seria exponerme á que los ignorantes, los interpretes iniqüos de las acciones humanas, incapaces de distinguir lo que es un acto de Cortesania, de respeto á las luces lo atribuieran, á que tenia correspondencia con un enemigo declarado de la España.

No hablo del Estado Guerrero, porque me he propuesto no hablar de estas cosas con los estrangeros, y espero que no llevara á mal semejante conducta.

Deseo á Vm la mas perfecta salud en compañia de sus apreciables hijas, á cuyos pies se servirá ponerme disponiendo de su admirador, y atento Servidor que SMB. VALENTIN DE FORONDA

EDITORS' TRANSLATION

Coruña November 30, 1811.

Respectable philosopher, I have the honor of sending you a copy of a pamphlet which is itself a reproduction of the notes that I printed in Philadelphia about the new constitution. In it, I advised the Cortes of the path that I thought should be taken, but which has not been pursued resulting in an immense waste of time, which was unavoidable, as it had not established the necessary foundations on which to build: in consequence, as soon as it touched on one point another became entirely unconnected. It has done good things, but it has left standing huge absurdities.

The first part of the constitution is approved. On the same day that the plan presented by the commission arrived, I quickly made the enclosed observations. It is weakened by gothic ideas, outdated books, and our antiquated preoccupations.

I am also sending a letter attacking Claros, an assumed name used by the celebrated bishop of Orense, who reeks of saintliness, who was regent, and who refused for a time to take the oath to the sovereign people, but who finally did it. In this paper I address various points of public law. Although I sign myself Claro y franco, everyone knows that I am the author.

I would be delighted to transmit the collection of letters that I inserted in the Santiago newspaper during the six months I have been in Galicia; but having only one copy, I cannot detach myself from it. I have spoken like a philosopher. In my writings I have opposed shouting long live the king; on the contrary it should be long live the Spanish people: I explained myself in this way: it should be long live the Sovereign, which I have never heard; but this grandiose moral idea is not understood by the people: it is more within their grasp to say long live the Nation and even more so (that which I prefer) to say long live the Spanish people. I have opposed the idea of calling our forces royal armies, but prefer national armies instead. This is not something to bother yourself about, however.

Having touched in one paper on various points in which the clergy has a vested interest, the monks have risen in insurrection: several anonymous authors have written to me, others have been published, and some have preached against me. I answered and crushed the first two, announcing that I would not waste my time answering stupidities; other anonymous writings have appeared to ridicule my antagonists. People admittedly still have many concerns that wise men cannot resolve, even philosophers, of whom there are a few. Yes, philanthropic Jefferson, their merit is such that I would set them against the wisest men in Europe.

I also send six letters that I wrote in Lisbon in the month of July 1810. In the last you will see a dialogue on the nobility.

In addition, I am forwarding a little essay that you will like solely because I published it in favor of a citizen, and against a judge.

I am not sending copies to your friend the wise philosopher Madison, because that would mean exposing myself to the ignorant, with their iniquitous interpretations of human actions. Incapable of recognizing it as an act of courtesy and respect to the enlightened, they would instead interpret it as correspondence by me with a declared enemy of Spain.

I do not speak of the progress of the war, because I have decided to avoid such topics with foreigners, but I hope you do not take this the wrong way.

I wish you the best of health in the company of your fine daughters, at whose feet I place myself at your disposal, your admirer, and attentive servant who kisses your hand. VALENTIN DE FORONDA

RC (DLC); one word illegible; at head of text: "S[r] D[n] Tomas de Jefferson"; endorsed by TJ as received 15 Feb. 1812 and so recorded in SJL. Translation by Dr. David T. Gies and Dr. Jennifer McCune. Enclosures not found. Enclosed in TJ to James Madison, 19 Feb. 1812, and Madison to TJ, 6 Mar. 1812.

Foronda's observations on the new Spanish constitution, *Apuntes Ligeros sobre la Nueva Constitucion, proyectada por la Magestad de la Junta Suprema Española, y reformas que intenta hacer en las leyes*, had been published in PHILADELPHIA in 1809. CLARO Y FRANCO: "clear and frank." President James Madison (MADISSON) was thought to be an enemy of Spain because of his refusal to recognize the minister sent to America by the Supreme Junta, his decision to order the occupation of West Florida in 1811, and his belief that East Florida should also be added to the United States if its local authorities requested assistance or any foreign nation threatened to invade it (Madison, *Papers, Pres. Ser.*, 2:26–7n, 193–4, 3:55n; Ralph Ketcham, *James Madison* [1971; repr. 1990], 501–2).

[1] Manuscript: "yo."

From John Fowler

SIR Lexington. State of Kentucky Novem 30. 1811

The bearer Mr William W Worsley a resident of this Town contemplates in a few days commenceing a journey to Richmond Virginia, and will pass thro' your neighbourhood. he has expressed a desire of being made acquainted with you; It is with much pleasure I embrace the oppertunity of introduceing an amiable intelligent person to your acquaintance, as an Editor of a paper (the reporter) he is not equalled in this State, and will rank with the first any where, He no doubt will be gratified by a personal conversation with you, and I flatter myself you will be pleased by the oppertunity of an Acquaintance with him. There is not a more stanch republican any where.

I have the honour to be respectfully
Yr. Mo. Ob servant JOHN FOWLER

RC (MHi); endorsed by TJ as received 1 Jan. 1812 and so recorded in SJL.

John Fowler (1756–1840) was a native of Chesterfield County who was wounded and captured during service as a lieutenant in that county's militia during the Revolutionary War. He moved his family to what is now Kentucky at the conclusion of hostilities and eventually settled in Lexington. Fowler represented Fayette County in the Virginia House of Delegates, 1786–88, and at the 1788 state ratification convention, where he opposed the new United States Constitution. He returned to the General Assembly as a delegate from Woodford County in 1791. A strong advocate of Kentucky statehood, Fowler served his adopted state as a Republican member of the United States House of Representatives, 1797–1807. Having amassed large landholdings, his economic interests also included farming, wagoning, racetracks, and pleasure gardens. Fowler sat on Lexington's town council, was its postmaster, 1814–22, and served as a trustee and treasurer of Transylvania University (Ila Earle Fowler, *Captain John Fowler of Virginia and Kentucky* [1942]; *The Pension Roll of 1835* [1835; indexed ed., 1992], 3:275; Leonard, *General Assembly*, 160, 164, 172, 185; Merrill Jensen, John P. Kaminski, and others, eds., *The Documentary History of the Ratification of the Constitution* [1976–], 9:907; Clay, *Papers*; Lexington *Kentucky Gazette*, 27 Aug. 1840).

William W. WORSLEY (ca. 1782–1852) edited the Norfolk *Commercial Register*, 1802–03, the Richmond *Examiner*, 1804, and (with Thomas Ritchie) the Richmond *Enquirer*, 1804–05, before relocating to Lexington, Kentucky. In 1808 he established the Lexington *Reporter* and managed it, alone or with a partner, for eleven years. Worsley later moved to Louisville, where he operated a bookstore and owned another journal, the *Focus of Politics, Commerce, and Literature*, 1826–32. He was a longtime correspondent and political supporter of Henry Clay (Brigham, *American Newspapers*, 1:166, 2:1124, 1138–9, 1507; Clay, *Papers*, esp. 5:861–2, 10:503–5; DNA: RG 29, CS, Louisville, Ky, 1850; gravestone in Cave Hill Cemetery, Louisville).

From Thomas Erskine Birch

Most Respectable sir. [Nov. 1811]

The inclosed volume was committed to the press near the close of your Excellency's administration. The author saw with superlative pleasure the efforts that you were making to preserve that precious boon, for which, he when but a youth of 19 years of age was contending for with a naval lieutenant's commission. From 15 to 20 years of age, he was incessantly traversing the seas in search of the enemy, and was assisting at the capture of no less than 47 of their vessels.

The Ode which is dedicated to your Excellency is the only laurel that the author can offer, to your administration

Such as it is—ah might it worthier be,
Its scanty foliage all is due to thee.

With sentiments of high regard and all due consideration, I beg leave to style my self, Sir, Your most obedient and very humble Servant

Thos Erskine Birch
Preceptor of "Anchor & Hope" Acady, Wythe County, Virga

RC (MHi); undated, with partial date given in Birch to TJ, 1 Jan. 1812; endorsed by TJ as received 22 Dec. 1811 and so recorded in SJL. Enclosure: Birch, comp., *The Virginian Orator: being a variety of Original and Selected Poems, Orations and Dramatic Scenes; to Improve the American Youth in the Ornamental and Useful Art of Eloquence & Gesture* (Richmond, 1808; Sowerby, no. 4680).

Thomas Erskine Birch (1763–1821), educator, was born in Saint Christopher in the British West Indies. He served for five years as a midshipman in the Royal Navy, including three years under Horatio Nelson. Failing to obtain further preferment, Birch resigned, joined a British privateer, and soon found himself in captivity in Spain. There he joined the American cause and sailed under Alexander Gillon, among other commanders. After the Revolutionary War, Birch was a merchant seaman until about 1793, when he settled in Virginia. In England he also became a Congregationalist minister, and he subsequently officiated as a Presbyterian and a Lutheran. Having taught oratory and belles-lettres near Richmond for a time, Birch ran the Anchor and Hope Academy in Wythe County in the early years of the nineteenth century. While there, he called for the abolition of the property qualification for voting in Virginia. Following stints at Abingdon Academy in Washington County and Amity Hall Academy in Russell County, Birch moved about 1817 to Cynthiana, Kentucky, where he founded the short-lived Washington College (*DVB*; Bernerd L. O'Neil, *The Birch Family History* [1998], 51–72 [including dates of birth and baptism from parish registers]; Mary B. Kegley and Frederick B. Kegley, *Early Adventurers on the Western Waters* [1980–], 2:143, 249–50; Lexington Presbytery Minutes, 4:155–6 [9 Nov. 1804]; Birch to Samuel Smith, 17 Mar. 1809 [with variant birth year of 1760], and Birch to Paul Hamilton, 17 Apr. 1809 [DNA: RG 45, MLRSN]).

Birch's claim to have been involved in the capture of forty-seven British vessels probably grew out of his participation with Gillon in the successful Spanish expedition against the Bahamas in 1782.

Birch's ODE, entitled "His Excellency Thomas Jefferson, Esq.," celebrates TJ's triumph over opposition as president and declares a readiness to fight any power that threatens American naval interests, especially while "Jefferson trims all the sails, With helm in his hand." The same volume includes two orations by unidentified authors celebrating TJ as he entered retirement (Birch, *Virginian Orator*, 15–22, 64–6). The lines SUCH AS IT IS—AH MIGHT IT WORTHIER BE,/ ITS SCANTY FOLIAGE ALL IS DUE TO THEE were written in 1750 by St. George Molesworth (James Hervey, *Meditations and Contemplations* [London, 1753], 1:xxv).

Conveyance of Thomas Jefferson's Lot in Richmond to David Higginbotham

This indenture made on the day of Nov[r] one Thousand eight hundred [and] eleven between Thomas Jefferson of the one part and David Higginbotham of the other; both of the County of Albermarle witnesseth that the said Thomas in consideration of the sum of one hundred and thirty pounds currant money of Virginia to him in hand paid by the said David, hath given granted bargained & sold unto the said David one certain parcel of land in the city of Richmond adjacent to James [River] containing by estimation eight hundred & twenty five square yards, be the [abovementioned lot included within?] four right lines, whereof one on the South Eas[tern side] bounding on the [lot with?] Number 334 formerly the property of Patrick Cout[ts] is 36 yrds long[.] one other on the southwestern side bounding on the common towards the River is twenty four yards long[.] one other on the North Western side bounding on the common laid off as a road from Shockoe warehouse to the wharf is thirty nine yards long & the other on the Northeastern side bounding on the lands formerly the property of Robert Carter Nicholas dec[d] is twenty two yards long which line [before]mentioned forms right angles with the first and third lines beforementioned[. The] parcel of land meant to be conveyed by these presents is part of t[he lot] designated in the plan of the said city by the number three hundred and thirty five[.] the other part thereof having[1] belonged to Robert Carter Ni[cholas] aforesaid dec[d]. To have and to hold the said parcel of land with its appurtenanc[es] to the said David and his heirs. and the said Thomas his heirs executors and administrators, the said parcel of land to the said David and his heirs against all persons claiming under the said Thomas, will forever warrant and defend entirely and against all lawful claims prior to the date of these presents he will warrant and defend to the amount of the sum of one hundred & thirty pounds [before]mentioned & no further. in testimony whereof the said Thomas hath herewith subscribed and affixed his seal on the day and year above mentioned

Signed sealed and delivered in presence of } Signed THOMAS JEFFERSON

COLEMAN ESTES
CHARLES VEST
DAVID HUCKSTEP
JOHN BURKS

Tr (ViU: TJP); faint, with portions of right margin damaged; unrelated calculations in an unidentified hand on verso; endorsed (in part): "Thomas Jefferson to David Higginbotham" and "A true Copy."

On 20 Oct. 1811 TJ noted that he had sold his "lot in Richmond" to Higginbotham, with the proceeds "to be credited in my account with him" (*MB*, 2:1270). William Mayo and James Wood had drawn the first PLAN of Richmond in the winter of 1736–37 at the behest of its pioneering owner, William Byrd (1674–1744). Lot 335 is shown in city plans of 1804 and 1809 (Richard W. Stephenson and Marianne M. McKee, *Virginia in Maps: Four Centuries of Settlement, Growth, and Development* [2000], 70–1; Richmond city plans, 1737, 1804, 1809 [Vi]). Higginbotham subsequently sold the lot to John G. Gamble (Gamble to TJ, 20 July 1813; TJ to Gamble, 10 Aug. 1813).

A 20 Oct. 1811 letter from TJ to Higginbotham is recorded in SJL. Higginbotham's letters to TJ of 20 Oct. and 2 Nov. 1811 are recorded in SJL as received from Milton on 20 Oct. and 3 Nov. 1811, and an undated letter and one of 23 Dec. 1811 are both recorded as received on 24 Dec. 1811. None of these letters has been found.

[1] Manuscript: "having having."

From Joseph Milligan

DEAR SIR Georgetown December 2nd 1811

Your esteemed favour of the 19th October was duly received and Should have been regularly attended[1] to but I was at that time much engaged in the business of the Potomac and Shenandoah Navigation Lottery which is Since finished, indeed this lottery has taken up much of my time the past summer but I am happy to say that I have now got through it and am able to attend to my bookselling concern which I will prosecute with all the vigour that I am master of

The first edition of Jeffersons Manual is now out of print I should be happy to have your permission to print a second edition I believe that 200 Copies would be wanted for the Senate & House of Representatives—

I have repeatedly tried to procure a complete Copy of Scientific

Dialogues or the 7th & 8th volumes but have always failed in the attempt—a few days ago I was Shewn a sett in nine Volumes with about 35 plates I am strongly tempted to reprint them in four duodecimo volumes to cost about Six Dollars a Sett that which I seen belongs to a Revd Mr Grassi of Georgetown College he is an Italian but last from england where he resided some months he brought his sett with him he is highly pleased with it I believe[2] it to be the only complete Copy that is to come at in the united States he will let me have it to print from If you say that you would recommend it as a useful book I will go on with it immediatly

I have at your request enclosed your account please accept my best wishes for your health and happiness

With respect & Esteem Your obedient Servant

JOSEPH MILLIGAN

RC (DLC); at foot of text: "Thomas Jefferson Esqr Monticello"; endorsed by TJ as received 22 Dec. 1811 and so recorded in SJL.

For JEFFERSONS MANUAL, see *PW*.

[1] Manuscript: "attend."
[2] Manuscript: "bellieve."

ENCLOSURE

Account with Joseph Milligan

Thomas Jefferson Esqr
In a/c with Joseph Milligan

1809 June	17 To Binding 2 Oc State papers	1.25		
	Half ditto Journal House Rep	.50		
	Ditto Ditto senate	50		
	Ditto 1 folio Vol state papers	1.50		
	Binding 2 Volume A Gardener	1		
			4.75	
July	5 To 2 Nautical Almanacs		2.50	
	28 To 1 Ream H Pres'd paper & expences		8.12½	
1810 February	3 To 1 Sett Parents Assistant		3 00	
1811 May	14 To 1 Edgeworths Moral Tales (Ex)		4 —	
	1 Modern Griselda		1 75	
	1 Humboldts New spain		5[1]	
	To 3 Volumes American Ornithology		36 —	
			$65.12½	

MS (DLC: TJ Papers, 195:34736); in Milligan's hand; undated; endorsed by TJ: "Milligan Joseph pd Mar. 15. 12."

A GARDENER: either John Gardiner and David Hepburn, *The American Gardener, containing ample directions for working a Kitchen Garden, Every Month in the Year* (Washington, 1804; Sowerby, no. 809), or McMahon, *Gardener's Calendar*.

[1] Reworked from "2."

From George Jefferson

Dear Sir Richmond 3d Decr 1811

I have long delayed saying any thing to you respecting the situation of Mr Mazzie's property here, in the hope of being enabled to inform you of the receipt of the rent at the same time.—I have not received any however, since that which appeared in[1] our acct which was rendered to the 30th of June 1810, except merely 20$ received of Mrs Taylor some time ago, & of that only $:2.79 will appear at your credit, as ℘ memorandum at foot.—I did not wish to interfere with the Clerks ticket, as Mr McCraw had the direction of that business: he however refused to pay it, & as I thought it ought to be paid, I took it in on the sheriffs application to me.—The City tax you will observe is enormous, which is owing to the paving of our Streets, now going on.—Mrs Taylor still owes 40$, which she promises to pay as soon as she can, but I doubt if that time will ever arrive.—The present tenant is a Mrs[2] Richardson, whose year expires the 6th of this month.—She gives the same rent of 120$ ℘ annum, but there were some repairs required to the house & inclosure, without doing which I could not have gotten a tenant, & the whole would certainly have gone to ruin.—I concluded it best therefore to allow those repairs to be made, & for the amount to be deducted from the rent.—I informed her some time ago that I should leave the Country about this time, and that I should wish to come to a settlement before my departure: on calling on her some days ago however, she informed me that her Son who kept the acct was out of Town in ill health, & that she could not ascertain the amount.
she promises shortly to settle with Mr Gibson, & I have no doubt she will do so, being a very respectable woman. She has taken the house for another year, if a sale of it should not previously be directed: in that case, I have promised to give her 3 months notice, before she shall be compelled to leave it.—for the present year I fear there will be but little coming from her.

Your own lot I think I informed you I had allowed an old negro to put a small[3] house on—he was to remove it whenever called upon by us to do so.—The poor fellow was to inclose the lot as soon as it was in his power, but he soon became entirely blind, & was removed to the Country. Mr Saml Paine has in some way become the owner of the house, & of course holds it on the same condition.

As I shall certainly set off in a few days, I have concluded it will be best for me to write as things occur, and as I can snatch the time, without regard to the post day. You may therefore perhaps receive several letters from me by the same mail.

I am Dear Sir Your Very humble serv[t] GEO. JEFFERSON

rec[d] of M[rs] Taylor in part of Rent from the 21st of April to the 21st of Oct[r] 1810		$:20—
deduct		
Clerks ticket in the suit Mazzie vs Taylor	$:4. 1	
& City taxes on M[r] M's lots for 1811	13.20	–17.21
bal[a] to M[r] J's credit the 30th Nov[r] 1811.		$:2.79

RC (MHi); addressed: "Thomas Jefferson esquire Monticello"; franked; postmarked Richmond, 5 Dec.; endorsed by TJ as received 22 Dec. 1811 and so recorded in SJL.

The ACC[T] through THE 30TH OF JUNE 1810 has not been found.

[1] Preceding four words interlined.
[2] Jefferson here canceled "Whitlock."
[3] Word interlined.

The Dismissal of *Livingston v. Jefferson*

I. JOHN TYLER'S OPINION IN LIVINGSTON V. JEFFERSON, [4 DEC. 1811]

II. JOHN MARSHALL'S OPINION IN LIVINGSTON V. JEFFERSON, [4 DEC. 1811]

III. LITTLETON W. TAZEWELL TO THOMAS JEFFERSON, 4 DEC. 1811

IV. DECISION OF UNITED STATES CIRCUIT COURT IN LIVINGSTON V. JEFFERSON, 5 DEC. 1811

EDITORIAL NOTE

The material printed below documents the failure of Edward Livingston's attempt to make Jefferson personally liable for the loss Livingston had sustained when the president ordered him expelled from the Batture Sainte Marie in New Orleans in 1807. Ever since Livingston had filed a lawuit in May 1810 claiming $100,000 in damages, Jefferson had been anxiously gathering evidence and legal precedents, advising his counsel, and drafting a statement defending his conduct. The case was argued on 2 and 3 Dec. 1811 and decided on 4 Dec. 1811 by a United States Circuit Court consisting of John Tyler, the federal judge for the District of Virginia, and Chief Justice John Marshall, whose duties included sitting on that district's circuit court. Tyler found for Jefferson on jurisdictional grounds. After failing to convince Tyler that the case should be moved to the Supreme Court, John Marshall added a concurring opinion in which he strongly hinted that Jefferson would not have fared so well had the actual merits of the case been considered. As one of the ex-president's counsel, Littleton W. Tazewell wrote Jefferson with news of the lawsuit's termination even before the court formally recorded the decision the next day.

The dismissal of the suit on procedural grounds did not end the controversy. George Hay, another of Jefferson's counsel, immediately urged him to make his case publicly, and both contestants eventually issued pamphlets justifying their conduct. Jefferson's statement of *The Proceedings of the Government of the United States, in maintaining the Public Right to the beach of the Missisipi, adjacent to New-Orleans, against the intrusion of Edward Livingston* (New York, 1812; Sowerby, nos. 3501, 3509; Poor, *Jefferson's Library*, 10 [no. 604]) and Livingston's rebuttal, *An Answer to Mr. Jefferson's Justification of His Conduct in the Case of the New Orleans Batture* (Philadelphia, 1813; Sowerby, no. 3507) laid out their legal arguments in excruciating detail (both works will appear in an upcoming volume of the *Papers of Thomas Jefferson*: Second Series, dealing with the batture controversy). On 4 Aug. 1813 the federal district court at New Orleans ruled in Livingston's favor, stating that his dispossession had been illegal and ordering the batture restored to him. Further litigation, the exigencies of wartime Louisiana, and the emergence of other claimants prevented Livingston from enjoying any of the fruits of his victory until the mid-1820s. Eventually, however, it did enable him to satisfy his large debts to the federal government, which resulted from the embezzlement of public funds in 1803 by a clerk for whom he was responsible.

The contentiousness of the dispute notwithstanding, Livingston and Jefferson were eventually able to end hostilities. In 1824 Jefferson wrote President James Monroe of his former antagonist that he "may be assured I have not a spark of unfriendly feeling towards him . . . mr Livingston would now be recieved at Monticello with as hearty a welcome as he would have been in 1800." Livingston did not visit Monticello, but the two men exchanged several friendly letters during Jefferson's final years (John Wickham to TJ, 16 May 1810; George Hay to TJ, 20 July 1810, and enclosure, and 5 Dec. 1811; Jefferson's Statement on the Batture Case, 31 July 1810; Jefferson's pleas published above at 28 Feb. 1811; Tyler to TJ, 17 May 1812; William C. C. Claiborne to TJ, 14 Aug. 1813; TJ to Monroe, 27 Mar. 1824; Malone, *Jefferson*, 6:67–73; William B. Hatcher, *Edward Livingston: Jeffersonian Republican and Jacksonian Democrat* [1940], 162–89; George Dargo, *Jefferson's Louisiana: Politics and the Clash of Legal Traditions* [1975], 98–101, 217–8).

I. John Tyler's Opinion in *Livingston v. Jefferson*

[4 Dec. 1811]

FEDERAL CIRCUIT COURT
LIVINGSTON VS JEFFERSON
IN TRESPASS QUARE CLAUSUM FREGIT.
Demurrer on a plea to this jurisdiction. } TYLER, J.

OPINION.—This case, although so ably and elaborately argued on both sides, affords but a single question; and that may be drawn within a narrow compass; and while I freely acknowledge how much I was pleased with the ingenuity and eloquence of the Plaintiff's Counsel, I cannot do so much injustice to plain truth as to say, that any conviction was wrought on my mind of the soundness of the arguments they exhibited in a legal acceptation. It is the happy talent of some professional gentlemen, and particularly of the Plaintiff's Counsel often to make the worse appear the better "cause," but it is the duty of the Judge to guard against the effects intended to be produced, by selecting those arguments & principles from the mass afforded as will enable him to give such an opinion, at least, as may satisfy himself, if not others—These arguments and this eloquence, however, have been met by an Herculean strength of forensic ability, which I take pride in saying sheds a lustre over the bar of Virginia.

But to proceed in the examination of the single[1] point before us; and that is, to enquire, whether this court has Jurisdiction over this cause? And how it comes to be made a question at this day, I confess myself entirely at a loss to say; but as it is made, we must determine it.

By the Common Law which was adopted by an Act of Convention of this State, so far as it applied to our Constitution, then formed, this point has been settled uninterruptedly for Centuries past, and recognized by uniform opinion & decisions both in England & America. It is true the great Luminary of the judicial department of G.B. did make an effort to shake the principle they had established, but the Judges in that country would not suffer it to be unsettled, it having been so long acknowledged as the indubitable law of the land. Nor was it for them—nor is it for us, to be over-scrupulous in enquiring for the reasons on which the opinion was originally given, why an action of *Trespass* should be deemed a *local* Action.

Time may have cast a shade over the reasons of many maxims and principles; & yet they are principles and maxims much to be respected.—But to me some appear to be evident; for instance; in this action the title and bounds of land may come in question; & who so proper to decide on them as one's Neighbors who are so much better acquainted with each other's lines and every thing else which may lead to[2] fair decision? In an action of this kind it may be necessary to direct a Survey and lay down the pretensions of both parties; for the defendant has a right to show in himself a better title and defend himself on that title. He calls for a direction from the court for this purpose; & if it goes at all, it must go to an Officer to carry his Posse to remove force, if any should be offered. And suppose the Sheriff and Jury should deny the power of the Court, can[3] they be coerced? And is not this an undeniable proof of the want of jurisdiction; since although we should sustain the cause in court by a sort of violence against principle, we should not be able to compleat what was begun?[4] The law never sanctions a vain thing—How vain therefore to begin what we cannot end! Is not this enough to show the locality of the action & the consequent want of jurisdiction?

I shall not attempt to travel up to the time when both real and personal actions were local. This has been sufficiently done (though perhaps not necessary,) by the Gentlemen at[5] bar, nor shall I enquire when the distinction took place between local and transitory actions. It is enough to say that notwithstanding this distinction, the action for Trespass *Quare Clausum Fregit* still remained local & is so held to this day. The Jury of the Vicinage was & still is a valuable privilege in both cases—May it not be true that when G.B. had emancipated herself from her insulated state, figuratively speaking, by spreading her canvass & carrying her commerce over every clime and every region, this change, this distinction soon followed after it, so as to give greater energy to the transactions between man and man; therefore, by a fiction in law, suffer a transitory action to be maintained any where and every where in which a contract could be made.

But some how or other the Court must have jurisdiction of every cause it attempts to sustain; and I can conceive no better scheme than that which is pursued, of giving the Court jurisdiction by a fiction in transitory actions in this way; that a contract, for instance, was entered into in New-Orleans, to wit, in the City of Richmond, between the parties (not traversable but in case of jurisdiction,) from which City or the County in which the City is, the Jury must come. I say must be supposed to come, notwithstanding the Act of Assembly which requires the by-standers to be summoned, for they are of the County or Vicinage;[6] and this Act saves the necessity of a *Venire facias* in every case. The Venire therefore is indispensible in my opinion to show Jurisdiction.

Again; I well recollect a case of Waste brought in the Petersburg District Court, when the County of Greensville was supposed[7] to make one which composed that District. The cause went on to trial, & a Verdict passed for the Plaintiff, without its being observed that Greensville belonged to Brunswick District; but at length the Defendant's Counsel found it out and moved in arrest of Judgment; but the Verdict was sustained, an Appeal was taken and the High Court of Appeals reversed the Judgment, because, it being a local action, it ought to have been instituted in the District where the Trespass was committed over which that Court alone had jurisdiction—Notwithstanding a Verdict had passed, upon the general issue, & it often has been determined that no consent of the parties by their pleadings could give[8] jurisdiction—Various are the causes which have been determined in this country in support of the doctrine laid down in this cause, & not one to the contrary[9] I venture to affirm can be reverted[10] to. Why then attempt to alter this settled principle? Has any statute been passed in this country that in the slightest manner disturbs the uniform decisions? The case I have referred to was between Galt[11] and Thweatt; & I own is a strong one, as the place wasted and recovered was to have been delivered up and the Court had no power to enforce the judgment.—But I have given reasons enough to shew how inadequate would be the power of this Court to carry on the cause before us and enforce the Judgment.

It seems clear then, that where title of land is in question, the action must be local, notwithstanding, what may be and has been said of a contract to convey land—I well know there is a legal and moral obligation on every man to perform what he contracts to perform: and this among others is a reason why an action personal should follow a person wherever he might be found and there rise in judgment against him.

Upon the ground taken, so far then, the action cannot be maintained in this Court; but the ingenious Counsel, never at a loss for argument and new matter, has resorted to what he calls the General, the Universal law. Now, I want to see this undefined law, before I can sustain a principle under it. I suppose what is meant by the General or Universal law is the Law of Nature and Nations; and who yet has been able to find where the Law of Nature has defined what a civil action is, or directed the mode of proceeding in it, or in what court it should be brought;—These are high sounding words, indeed, but they only serve to round a period and fill up a vacuum in the argument. This is something like the last resort of Kings where every thing else fails: for I know of no other *actions* in that quarter but such as flow from that *source:* Neither do I know of any law that can change the locality of a man's land in New-Orleans to the City of Richmond. This mighty engine therefore fails; this undefined law as to the case before us ceases to be any thing more than empty sound.

But I will suppose for the sake of argument that we now were proceeding with the Trial of the cause, and the witnesses with the survey and plat were before us, which would show the Trespass, if any[12] had been committed, to have been committed in the Territory of New-Orleans; what could the court do but send the cause out of doors? For take notice, there is to be no fiction in a local action. Here the Venire is laid in Henrico, the evidence would come from a distant territorial government and would not agree with[13] the allegations in the Declaration; and here would end the struggle. Indeed taking the premises, which I have laid down, to be true, which cannot well be denied; and the question resolves itself into a self-evident proposition.

But there would be a failure of justice, unless we sustain this action; and to avoid this evil, we must enact a law, for, I know of no other way of answering the plaintiff's design—but this I cannot consent to do; neither can I fly in the face of my own decisions, until better taught.

But there is no failure of justice: there is a court of competent power to try the cause, if an actual Trespass has been committed; and there ought the suit to have been brought against the real Trespasser. I own there may be cases where a man might so manage his matters as to run through another's ground and lay waste his enclosures and even pull down his fences, and then flee from justice, like another criminal, and thus get out of the reach of the law; which is not uncommon.—There are cases that no law can well provide against, and these[14] may be considered as partial evils, and exceptions to a good general Rule.

I am too unwell to follow and pay respect to all the arguments which have been advanced in support of the jurisdiction of this court over the case before us; and therefore must conclude by giving my decided opinion in favor of the Plea to the jurisdiction. The cause must therefore go out of Court.

Printed in Richmond *Enquirer*, 19 Dec. 1811; undated. Reprinted in *American Law Journal* 4 (1813): 78–82, and *The Federal Cases: comprising Cases Argued and Determined in the Circuit and District Courts of the United States* (1894–97), 15:661–3 (case no. 8,411).

TRESPASS QUARE CLAUSUM FREGIT: unlawful entry onto land that is visibly enclosed (*Black's Law Dictionary*). The Virginia Convention of 1776 stipulated that the COMMON LAW "of *England*, all statutes or acts of parliament made in aid of the common law prior to the fourth year of the reign of king *James* the first, and which are of a general nature, not local to that kingdom . . . shall be considered as in full force, until the same shall be altered by the legislative power of this colony" (*Ordinances Passed at a General Convention of Delegates and Representatives, From the several Counties and Corporations of Virginia* [Williamsburg, 1776], 21). The GREAT LUMINARY OF THE JUDICIAL DEPARTMENT of Great Britain (G.B.) was William Murray, 1st Earl of Mansfield. Under Virginia law, sheriffs were authorized to choose jurors from the local pool of BY-STANDERS (Samuel Shepherd, *The Statutes at Large of Virginia, from October Session 1792, to December Session 1806, Inclusive* [1835, repr. 1970], 1:19).

[1] Word omitted in *American Law Journal*. Here and below, *Federal Cases* follows *American Law Journal*.
[2] *American Law Journal* here adds "a."
[3] *American Law Journal*: "could."
[4] *American Law Journal*: "what we begun."
[5] *American Law Journal* here adds "the."
[6] *American Law Journal*: "vicarage."
[7] *Enquirer*: "suppposed."
[8] *American Law Journal*: "prove."
[9] *Enquirer*: "contsary."
[10] *American Law Journal*: "adverted."
[11] *American Law Journal*: "Gall."
[12] *American Law Journal*: "if one."
[13] *American Law Journal*: "without."
[14] *American Law Journal*: "they."

II. John Marshall's Opinion in *Livingston v. Jefferson*

[4 Dec. 1811]

Livingstone
v.
Jefferson } demurrer on a[1] plea to the jurisdiction

The sole question now to be decided is this; Can this court take cognizance of a trespass committed on lands lying within the United States, & without the District[2] of Virginia in a case where the trespasser is a resident of[3] & is found within the District?

I concur with my brother Judge in the opinion that it cannot.

I regret that the inconvenience to which delay might expose at least one of the parties, together with the situation of the court, prevent me from bestowing on this question[4] that deliberate consideration which the very able discussion it has received from the bar would seem to require; but I have purposely avoided any investigation of the subject previous to the argument, & must now be content with a brief statement of the opinion I have formed, & a sketch of the course of reasoning which has led to it.

The doctrine of actions local & transitory has been traced up to its origin in the common law; &, as has been truely stated on both sides, it appears that originally all actions were local. That is that, according to the principles of the common law, every fact must be tried by a jury of the vicinage. The plain consequence of this principle was[5] that those courts only could take jurisdiction of a case who were capable of directing such a jury as must try the material facts on which their judgement would depend. The jurisdiction of the courts therefore necessarily became local with respect to every species of action.

But the superior courts of England having power to direct a jury to every part of the Kingdom, their jurisdiction could be restrained by this principle only to cases arising on transactions which occurred within the realm. Being able to direct a jury either to Surry or Middlesex, the necessity of averring in the declaration that the cause of action arose in either county, could not be produced in order to give the court jurisdiction, but to furnish a venue.[6] For the purpose of jurisdiction, it would unquestionably[7] be sufficient to aver that the transaction took place within the realm.[8]

This however being not a statutory regulation, but a principle of unwritten law, which is really human reason applied by courts, not capriciously but[9] in a regular train of decisions, to human affairs[10]—according to the circumstances of the nation, the necessity of the times, & the general state of things, was thought susceptible of modification, & Judges have modified it. They have not changed the old principle as to form. It is still necessary to give a venue; and where the contract exhibits on its face evidence of the place where it was made, the party is at liberty to aver that such place lies in any county in England.

This is known to be a fiction. Like an ejectment, it is the creature of the court, & is moulded to the purposes of justice according to the view which its inventors have taken of its capacity to effect those purposes. It is not[11] however of undefinable[12] extent. It has not absolutely prostrated all distinctions of place, but has certain limits prescribed to it founded in reasoning satisfactory to those who have gradually fixed these limits. It may well be doubted whether, at this day, they are to[13] be changed by a Judge not perfectly satisfied with their extent.

This fiction is so far protected by its inventors that the averment is not traversable for the purpose of defeating an action it was invented to sustain; but it is traversable whenever such traverse may be essential to the merits of the cause. It is always traversable[14] for the purpose of contesting a jurisdiction[15] not intended to be protected by the fiction.

In the case at bar it is traversed for that purpose, & the question is whether this be a case in which such traverse is sustainable; or, in other words, whether courts have so far extended their fiction as, by its aid, to take cognizance of trespasses on lands not lying within those limits which bound their process.

They have, without legislative aid, applied this fiction to all personal torts,[16] & to all contracts wherever executed. To this general rule contracts respecting lands form no exception. It is admitted that on a contract respecting lands[17] an action is sustainable wherever the defendent may be found. Yet in such a case, every difficulty may occur which presents itself in an action of trespass. An investigation of title may become necessary. A question of boundary may arise, & a survey may be essential to the full merits of the cause. Yet these difficulties have not prevailed against the jurisdiction of the court. They have been countervailed & more than countervailed by the opposing consideration that, if the action be disallowed, the injured party may have a clear right[18] without a remedy[19] in a case where the person who has done the wrong & who ought to make the compensation, is within the power of the court.

That this consideration should lose its influence where the action pursues a thing not within the reach of the court, is of inevitable necessity; but for the loss of its influence where the remedy is against the person & can be afforded by the court, I have not yet discerned a reason, other than a technical one, which can satisfy my judgement.

If however this technical distinction be firmly established, if all other Judges respect it, I cannot venture to disregard it.

The distinction taken is that actions are deemed transitory where the transactions on which they are founded might have taken place any where; but are local where their cause is in its nature necessarily local.

If this distinction be established: if Judges have determined to carry their innovation on the old rule no further; if, for a long course of time, under circumstances which have not changed, they have determined this to be the limit of their fiction, it would require a hardihood which[20] I do not possess, to pass this limit.

This distinction has been repeatedly taken in the books, & is recognized by the best[21] elementary writers, especially by Judge Blackstone, from whose authority no man will lightly dissent He expressly classes an action[22] for a trespass on lands with those actions which demand their possession, &[23] which are local, & makes only those actions transitory which are brought on occurrences that might happen in any place. From the cases which support this distinction no exception I beleive is to be found among those that have been decided in court on solemn argument.

One of the greatest Judges who ever sat on any bench, & who has done more than any other to remove those technical impediments which grew out of a different state of society, & too long continued to obstruct the course of substantial justice, was so struck with the weakness of the distinction between taking jurisdiction in cases of contract respecting lands, & of torts committed on the same lands, that he attempted to abolish it. In the case of Mostyn[24] v Fabrigas Lord Mansfield stated the true[25] distinction to be between proceedings which are in rem, in which the effect of a judgement can not be had[26] unless the thing ly within the reach of the court, & proceedings against the person where damages only are demanded. But this opinion was given in an action for a personal wrong which is admitted to be transitory. It has not therefore the authority to which it would be entitled had this distinction been laid down in an action deemed local. It may be termed an obiter dictum. He recites in that opinion two cases decided by himself in which an action was sustained for trespass on lands lying in the foreign dominions of his Britannic Majesty;[27] but both those decisions were at nisi prius: And though the overbearing influence of Lord Mansfield might have sustained them[28] on a motion for a new trial, that motion never was made, & the principle did not obtain the sanction of the court. In a subsequent case reported in 4th D & E. these decisions are expressly referred to &[29] overruled, and the old distinction is affirmed.

It has been said that the decisions of British courts made since the revolution are not authority in this country. I admit it. But they are entitled to that respect which is due to the opinions of wise men who have maturely studied the subject they decide. Had the regular course of decisions previous to the revolution been against the distinction now asserted, and had the old rule been overthrown by adjudications made subsequent to that event, this court might have felt itself bound to disregard them; but where the distinction is of[30] antient date, has been long preserved, & a modern attempt to overrule it has itself been overruled since the revolution, I can consider the last adjudication in no other light than as the true declaration of the antient rule.

According to the common law of England then, the distinction taken by the defendents counsel between actions local & transitory is the true distinction,[31] & an action of trespass[32] quare clausum fregit is a local action.

This common law has been adopted by the legislature of Virginia. Had it not been adopted I should have thought it in force. When our ancestors migrated to America they brought with them the common law of their native country so far as it was applicable to their new situation, & I do not concieve that the revolution would in any degree have changed the relations of man to man, or the law which regulated those relations. In breaking our political connection[33] with the parent state,[34] we did not break our connections with each other. It remained subject[35] to the antient rules until those rules should be changed by the competent authority.

But it has been said that this rule of the common law is impliedly changed by the act of assembly which directs that a jury shall be summoned from the by standers.

Were I to discuss the effect of this act in the courts of the State,[36] the enquiry whether the fiction already noticed was not equivalent to it in giving jurisdiction, would present itself. There are also other regulations, as that the jurors should be citizens, which would deserve to be taken into view. But I pass over these considerations because I am decidedly of opinion that the jurisdiction of the courts of the United States depends exclusively on the constitution & laws of the United States.[37]

In considering the jurisdiction of the circuit courts[38] as defined in the judicial act, & in the constitution which that act carries into execution, it is worthy of observation that the jurisdiction of the court depends on the character of the parties, & that only the court of that district in which the defendent resides or is found can take jurisdiction of the cause. In a court so constituted, the argument drawn from the total failure of justice should a trespasser[39] be declared to be only amenable to the court of that District in which the land lies & in which he will never be found appeared to me to be entitled to peculiar weight. But according to the course of the common law the process of the court must be executed in order to give it the[40] right to try the cause, & consequently the same defect of justice might occur. Other Judges have felt the weight of this argument, & have struggled ineffectually against the distinction which produces the inconvenience of a clear right without a remedy. I must submit to it.

The law upon the demurrer is in favor of the defendent.

2d Dft (PPAmP: Marshall Judicial Opinions); in Marshall's hand; undated; endorsed by Marshall: "Livingstone v Jefferson opinion." 1st Dft (PPAmP: Marshall Judicial Opinions); in Marshall's hand; undated; endorsed by Marshall: "Livingstone v Jefferson." Only the most important textual differences between the drafts are noted below; each is printed separately in Marshall, *Papers*, 7:276–88. Printed in Richmond *Enquirer*, 19 Dec. 1811, *American Law Journal* 4 (1813): 82–7, and *The Federal Cases: comprising Cases Argued and Determined in the Circuit and District Courts of the United States* (1894–97), 15:663–5 (case no. 8,411).

John Marshall (1755–1835), fourth chief justice of the United States, 1801–35, was born in Prince William County (in a section that became Fauquier County in 1759), rose from lieutenant to captain in the Continental army, 1776–81, and studied law under George Wythe at the College of William and Mary. He successively represented Fauquier and Henrico counties and the city of Richmond during eight terms in the Virginia House of Delegates between 1782 and 1797. Marshall supported the new United States Constitution at the state ratification convention of 1788 and was soon widely regarded as one of Virginia's leading Federalists. He defended the Jay Treaty, took part in the ill-fated diplomatic mission to France of 1797–98, won election to the United States House of Representatives in 1799, and served as John Adams's secretary of state from May 1800 until his appointment as chief justice in January 1801. Marshall's long tenure on the United States Supreme Court was defined by his vigorous and largely successful attempt to keep the judiciary independent of politics, establish the Constitution as the supreme law of the land, and make the Supreme Court the final interpreter and arbiter of matters constitutional. With *Marbury v. Madison* (1803), the high court declared an act of Congress unconstitutional for the first time, and it struck down state laws and the decisions of state courts on other occasions. Service on the Supreme Court also entailed Marshall's sitting on the federal circuit courts in Virginia and North Carolina. In this capacity he crafted a narrow, precedent-setting definition of treason while presiding over Aaron Burr's 1807 Richmond trial, which ended in an acquittal. The popularity of Marshall's five-volume *Life of George Washington* (Philadelphia, 1804–07; Sowerby, no. 496; Poor, *Jefferson's Library*, 4 [no. 133]) caused TJ to fear that a Federalist interpretation of the early national period would take hold in America. Marshall also participated in the Virginia state constitutional convention of 1829–30 (*ANB*; *DAB*; Marshall, *Papers*; Albert J. Beveridge, *The Life of John Marshall*, 4 vols. [1916–19]; Heitman, *Continental Army*, 381; Leonard, *General Assembly*; *PTJ*, 29:278–9; Washington *Daily National Intelligencer*, 9 July 1835).

In his *Commentaries on the Laws of England* (Oxford, 1765–69; Sowerby, nos. 1806–7), 3:294, William BLACKSTONE stipulated that "In *local* actions, where possession of land is to be recovered, or damages for an actual trespass, or for waste, &*c*, affecting land, the plaintiff must lay his declaration or declare his injury to have happened in the very county and place that it really did happen; but in *transitory* actions, for injuries that might have happened any where, as debt, detinue, slander, and the like, the plaintiff may declare in what county he pleases, and then the trial must be in that county in which the declaration is laid." In MOSTYN V FABRIGAS, which involved an accusation of assault and false imprisonment brought by a native of Minorca against the governor of that island, Lord Mansfield ruled that the case could be tried in England (Henry Cowper, *Reports of Cases Adjudged in the Court of King's Bench* [London, 1783], 161, 176; *The English Reports*, 98:1021, 1029). He based his decision on TWO CASES: one involving an English naval captain who pulled down alehouses in Nova Scotia and the other regarding an admiral who destroyed fishing huts on the coast of Labrador (Cowper, *Reports*, 180–1; *English Reports*, 98:1032). NISI PRIUS: a civil trial decided by a jury (*Black's Law Dictionary*). In the 1792 case of *Doulson v. Matthews and Another*, Judge Francis Buller OVERRULED Mansfield by remarking that "It is now too late for us to enquire whether it were wise or politic to make a distinction being transitory and local actions: it is sufficient for the courts that the law has settled the distinction, and that an action *quare clausum fregit* is local" (Charles Durnford and Edward Hyde East, *Reports of Cases argued and determined in the Court of King's Bench* [London, 1785–1800; Sowerby, no. 2087], 4:503–4; *English Reports*, 100:1144). Article III, section 1 of the

United States CONSTITUTION gave Congress the authority to "ordain and establish" a supreme court and such inferior courts as it saw fit. The CIRCUIT COURTS were duly created on 24 Sept. 1789 by "An Act to establish the Judicial Courts of the United States" (*U.S. Statutes at Large*, 1:73–93).

[1] Preceding three words omitted in 1st Dft.

[2] 1st Dft: "Commonwealth."

[3] Remainder of sentence in 1st Dft reads "this commonwealth?"

[4] Word interlined in place of "subject."

[5] *American Law Journal*: "is." Here and below, *Federal Cases* follows *American Law Journal* unless otherwise indicated.

[6] *American Law Journal*: "venire."

[7] Word not in 1st Dft.

[8] 1st Dft here adds "& the averment of a county could have no object but to <*direct*> furnish a guide for a venue."

[9] Preceding three words not in 1st Dft.

[10] In place of preceding two words the 1st Dft reads "the cases of individuals for the purposes of justice."

[11] Word omitted in *American Law Journal.*

[12] *American Law Journal*: "undeniable."

[13] In place of preceding two words the 1st Dft reads "might."

[14] 2d Dft: "traverable." 1st Dft: "traversable."

[15] Remainder of sentence in 1st Dft reads "of the court."

[16] 1st Dft here adds "wherever the wrong may have been committed."

[17] Preceding two words expanded in 1st Dft to read "executed in one place respecting lands lying in another."

[18] 2d Dft: "righ." 1st Dft: "right."

[19] Remainder of sentence not in 1st Dft.

[20] Marshall here canceled "in this place I cannot venture." Sentence from this point in 1st Dft reads "sitting in this place, I cannot venture on, to pass this limit."

[21] Preceding two words not in 1st Dft.

[22] Marshall here canceled "quare."

[23] 1st Dft here adds "with the action of waste."

[24] *Enquirer* and *American Law Journal*: "Mortyn." *Federal Cases*: "Mostyn."

[25] 1st Dft: "substantial."

[26] Remainder of sentence in 1st Dft reads "if given by the court, & where the remedy sounds in damages."

[27] 1st Dft reads "without the realm" instead of preceding eight words.

[28] Preceding two words, obscured in 2d Dft, supplied from 1st Dft.

[29] Preceding three words not in 1st Dft.

[30] Preceding three words omitted in *American Law Journal.*

[31] Remainder of sentence not in 1st Dft.

[32] Word omitted in *American Law Journal.*

[33] Reworked from "breaking off our connection."

[34] 1st Dft: "mother country."

[35] *Enquirer* and *American Law Journal*: "subsequent."

[36] Remainder of sentence not in 1st Dft, with sentence to this point positioned at conclusion of following sentence.

[37] 1st Dft ends here.

[38] Reworked from "of this court."

[39] Preceding two words interlined in place of "the court of that defendent in cases of trespass."

[40] Marshall here canceled "power."

III. Littleton W. Tazewell to Thomas Jefferson

DEAR SIR; Richmond Decr 4. 1811.

I am this moment returned from the Capitol where your suit with Livingston has been finally decided—It is dismissed, by reason of the

Courts sustaining the plea to its jurisdiction upon the ground of the locality of the Action—The decision was pronounced unanimously—The opinion of the Chief Justice was clear able and most satisfactory—I hasten to communicate the result as I presume it will give you some satisfaction—I have not time to say more, than that I am in great haste

yours truly LITT[N]: W TAZEWELL

RC (MHi); dateline at foot of text; endorsed by TJ as received 22 Dec. 1811 and so recorded in SJL.

IV. Decision of United States Circuit Court in *Livingston v. Jefferson*

Thursday—December the 5th 1811.

Present John Marshall esq[r]—chief Justice of the united States.

Edward Livingston plt }
against } In Trespass
Thomas Jefferson Deft }

This day came the parties by their attornies, and thereupon the defts demurrer to the plts replication to the defts plea to the Jurisdiction of the Court, being argued and adjudged good; It is considered by the Court that the plt take nothing by his bill but for his false clamour be in mercy &[a] and that the deft go thereof without day and recover against the plt his costs by him about his defence in this behalf expended.

MS (Vi: USCC-OB, 9:44); in the hand of William Marshall, the court's clerk; with John Marshall's signature approving the record of the day's proceedings. Tr (DLC); in William Marshall's hand and attested by him; top of page chipped; noted by William Marshall: "Defendants costs $22.44" and "John Wickham esq[r] of this City is the security for costs"; endorsed by William Marshall: "Livingston vs. Jefferson } Co. order"; enclosed in Alexander Lithgow (for William Marshall) to TJ, 27 July 1812, noted below at TJ to Marshall, 13 July 1812.

For the DEMURRER, REPLICATION, and PLEA, see Plea in *Livingston v. Jefferson* on Ground of Jurisdiction, [ca. 28 Feb. 1811], and note. By ruling that TJ as defendant could depart WITHOUT DAY, the court was dismissing the case against him (*Black's Law Dictionary*).

From Donald Fraser

REVERED SIR New York Dec[r] 4. 1811

Permit me to present, for the honour of your acceptance, a copy of a "Compendium"; which I lately published—As a Small testimony of respect, & regard for your talents & Patriotic Character—

I have the honor to be, very respectfully, Sir, Your obd[t] humble Servant D. FRASER

RC (MHi); dateline at foot of text; at head of text: "Thomas Jefferson L.L.D."; endorsed by TJ as received 25 Dec. 1811 and so recorded in SJL. Enclosure: Fraser, *A Compendium of the History of All Nations: exhibiting a Concise View of the Origin, Progress, Decline and Fall of the most Considerable Empires, Kingdoms, and States in the World* (New York, 1809).

Donald Fraser (ca. 1753–1820), schoolmaster and author, immigrated to the United States about 1774, probably from Scotland. He supported himself by teaching and occasionally preaching in New England and Virginia, including three years as an educator in Manchester, New Hampshire, before moving to New York City in the 1780s. After teaching there for some twenty years, Fraser became a bookseller and proprietor of a circulating library. He authored numerous educational, literary, historical, and political works during his long career, but struggled financially (*The New-York Directory, and Register, for 1789* [New York, 1789], 84; William Duncan, *The New-York Directory, and Register, for the year 1791* [New York, 1791], 45; New York *American Citizen*, 3 Dec. 1803; Fraser to TJ, 9 July 1805 [DLC], 10 Mar. 1812, 24 Sept. 1813, 14 Sept. 1814, 4 Oct. 1820; Sowerby, no. 426, 1396; *Longworth's New York Directory* [1811], 104; Fraser to James Monroe, 2 May 1812 [DNA: RG 59, LAR, 1809–17]; New York *Columbian*, 2 Nov. 1816; *New-York Daily Advertiser*, 18 Dec. 1820).

From John Pitman

HON[D] SIR, Providence December 4th 1811.

Suffer me to gratify the vanity of an author, and the pride of an American, by presenting the enclosed, for acceptance and perusal, to one, no less distinguished for his literary taste, than political wisdom. It will afford me much pleasure if, without diverting your attention from matters of more excellence and importance, I can procure you a momentary gratification, [in] the perusal of those effusions which, so far as it respects [my?] republican sentiments, your writings and example [have?] [h]ad no little agency in producing. In the avocations of party politics and professional life I have not had much time to devote to the cultivation of my muse—and indeed so fastidious has the taste of our country become with respect to native poetry, that there is but little encouragement for those who might otherwise emulate "the bards of other times."

Were I not persuaded that every American, whose heart is warmed with patriotism, is welcome to your retirement I would ask you to pardon this intrusion of one, who, though a stranger to you, is not a stranger to those deeds and virtues, which encircle you with a glory, that flings into shade the imperial and consuming splendors of Napoleon.

With every sentiment of esteem & reverence

I am Yours, &C JOHN PITMAN JUN[R]

RC (ViW: TC-JP); torn at seal; at foot of text: "The Hon: Thomas Jefferson Esq[r]"; endorsed by TJ as received 25 Dec. 1811 and so recorded in SJL.

John Pitman (1785–1864), attorney, was a native of Providence, Rhode Island, who graduated in 1799 from Rhode Island College (Brown University from 1804) and was admitted to the New York bar in 1806. He practiced law in Kentucky, 1807–08, Providence, 1808–12, Salem, Massachusetts, 1812–16, and Portsmouth, New Hampshire, 1816–20. Pitman returned to Providence for good in 1820. He was United States district attorney for Rhode Island, 1820–24, and served as federal district court judge from 1824 until his death. Pitman was also a trustee of Brown University, 1828–34, a fellow of that institution, 1834–64, and president of the Providence Athenæum, 1839–57 (*Historical Catalogue of Brown University, Providence, Rhode Island, 1764–1894* [1895], 43; Madison, *Papers, Pres. Ser.*, 3:45; *JEP*, 3:218, 226, 399, 402 [27 Nov., 9 Dec. 1820, 28 Dec. 1824, 3 Jan. 1825]; *Providence Daily Journal*, 18 Nov. 1864; gravestone inscription at North Burial Ground, Providence).

The enclosed EFFUSIONS were Pitman's pamphlets, *A Long Talk, delivered before the Tammany Society, or Columbian Order, on their anniversary, A. D. 1810: in Providence* (Providence, 1810), praising republicanism and the members of the Tammany Society for their defense of republican principles, and *A Poem on the Social State and its Future Progress: delivered before the Philermenian Society Brown University, on its Anniversary, September 3d, A. D. 1811* (Providence, [1811]), lamenting the violent tendencies of mankind and arguing that the diffusion of knowledge and the example set by a free and prosperous America will further the cause of peace. James Macpherson repeatedly used the phrase BARDS OF OTHER TIMES in his poems purportedly translated from the alleged ancient Gaelic author Ossian (*Fingal, an Ancient Epic Poem* [London, 1762], 81, 194; *Temora, an Ancient Epic Poem* [London, 1763], 17).

To Edmund Bacon

SIR Poplar Forest Dec. 5. 11.

I find I can drive from hence 4. or 5 beeves and as many muttons as we can want; all as fat as they can be; and having to drive these I conclude to drive the hogs also, and kill them at Monticello. the whole will start therefore as soon as the hogs are fat enough. of course we need buy no more beeves. I shall be glad if you will see mr Darnell and tell him that the business here is suffering unspeakably for want of him. we have been obliged to suspend prizing the tobacco at his place for want of somebody to overlook it, the places being too far apart & too much to do for mr Goodman to be able to attend to the whole. as soon therefore as mr Randolph's affairs can permit him to come I wish him to set out without losing an hour. it would be very important that he should arrive while I am here, which will be to about the 13th or 14th. tell Johnny Hemings to finish off immediately the frame for the round table for this place that it may come by the waggon which will go with the hogs. I promised to let mr Claxton know of the safe arrival of mr Goodman's family. they did not get to Lynchburg till Thursday night: but had fine weather and were quite comfortable in the boat. Accept my best wishes

TH: JEFFERSON

PoC (DLC); at foot of text: "Mr E. Bacon"; endorsed by TJ.

DARNELL: Nimrod Darnil. An image of the ROUND TABLE with a revolving top, completed about this time at the Monticello joinery for use at Poplar Forest, is reproduced elsewhere in this volume.

To George Callaway

SIR Poplar Forest Dec. 5. 11

I wrote you on the 21st of Sep. stating my claim on you for 47⅖ barrels of Superfine flour, or 367. D. 55 c their value, at the rate netted me by the 232. barrels recieved from you. this letter was delivered you by mr Griffin, and I have no answer but verbally thro' him that you decline acknoleging your liability. on my part it is insisted on, being myself perfectly satisfied of it's justice. as the question must therefore be decided for us by others, I presume it would be more agreeable to us both to have it amicably done by persons of our own chusing, who will certainly be as likely as a jury to give us a satisfactory decision, & save to us both the perplexity and expences of adversary proceedings. I propose therefore that we shall name two persons, and these two chuse a third to settle this matter for us, by arbitration. as my stay here can be but short, and I must have it settled before I leave the county, an early day in next week will be most agreeable to me. I will add further that whether the settlement had been by compromise between ourselves, or be by arbitration, it is not my intention to make the paiment inconvenient to you in point of time: being willing to admit any reasonable delay of that. I must request a definitive answer by the bearer for my government. Accept the assurances of my respect. TH: JEFFERSON

PoC (MHi); at foot of text: "Doct^r Callaway"; endorsed by TJ.

From George Callaway

Decr 5. 1811—

your note of this morning[1] I have rec^d & I am to express my utter astonishment at the claim you have therein set forth—such a claim was suggested to me by capt— Mitchell at the time you wished to sell him your wheat, but as to its validity I have never for a moment tho^t of it—However that you may be yourself satisfied I will see you to-morow at your own house where the boy tells Mr Griffen will also be—The present is the first line I have rec^d from you

GE^O CALLAWAY

RC (MHi); dateline beneath signature; at foot of text: "Mr. Thomas Jefferson"; endorsed by TJ as received 6 Dec. 1811 and so recorded in SJL.

William MITCHELL was a merchant in Lynchburg.

[1] Manuscript: "mornig."

To Samuel J. Harrison

SIR Poplar Forest Dec. 5. 11

I had left the inclosed papers with mr Griffin in case Scott should have given any further trouble. on his departure he returned them to me, and I think it proper they should be delivered up to you. I state the list of them below. accept the assurance of my respects.

TH: JEFFERSON

1771. Mar. 16 Richard Tullos's patent for 374. acres
1797. May 22. Thomas Jefferson's patent for 100. a^s
1795. Dec. 23. Wm P. Martin's copy of the survey of the 100. a^s
same date. Richard Stith's[1] certificate of the entry & survey
1803. Dec. 26. Edmund Tate's survey of 54¾ a^s of the same land.

1809. Nov. 15. Wm P. Martin's resurvey of the patent lines a plat of the 374 & 100. a^s shewing their contiguity.

PoC (ViU: TJP); adjacent to signature: "Mr Saml J. Harrison"; endorsed by TJ. Enclosures: (1) Land Grant to TJ, Richmond, 22 May 1797, signed by Governor James Wood by virtue of treasury warrant no. 1724, issued 5 Dec. 1795, and based on a 23 Dec. 1795 survey describing the land as containing 100 acres in Campbell County "on the South branches of Ivy Creek and bounded as followeth to wit Beginning at Wilkersons and Johnsons Corner pointers thence along Wilkersons lines North 60 degrees East 8 poles to his Corner red oak South 52 degrees East 94 poles to his Corner pointers, thence off North 76 degrees East 36 poles to a Hickory North 40 degrees East 130 poles to pointers on Tullos's line, thence along his lines North 60 degrees West 55 poles to his corner white oak, West 84 poles to his Corner pointers on Johnsons line at a small branch and along Johnsons South 38 degrees West 100 poles to the beginning" (MS in ViU: TJP, printed form with blanks filled and description of land entered in a clerk's hand, signed and sealed by Wood, with certification by William Price, register, Virginia Land Office, that "Thomas Jefferson hath title to the within," endorsed by Price as executed and recorded in "Book N° 39 page 303"; FC in Vi: RG 4, Virginia Land Office Grant Book, 39:303–4). (2) Survey for Edmund Tate, Campbell County, 26 Dec. 1803, consisting of a plat (illust. below) and accompanying description of "54$\frac{3}{4}$ Acres of Land bounded as follows viz begining at A Corner to Wilkerson Couch and Johnson N40 E 144 poles along Couches line to a hicory Corner at B then E—t 84 pole white Oak at C Corner to Tillis [i.e., Tullos] N 62 E 62 pole to white Oak at D Corner to Tillis & Saml Scott S 30 W 30 poles to E S 70 W 184 poles to hicory Corner to said Scott at F & then N 76 E 58 poles to the begining" (Tr in ViU: TJP, in William P. Martin's hand, at foot of text: "transfered to Saml Scott," endorsed: "Scotts plat 54$\frac{3}{4}$ Acres"; Trs of this and preceding enclosure in ViU: TJP, entirely in TJ's hand, attested by Martin and Blagrove, respectively, and by TJ, forming part of a set of exhibits submitted by TJ with his 11 July 1812 answer to Scott's bill of complaint in *Scott v. Jefferson and Harrison*; Trs of this and preceding enclosure in Campbell Co. Record of Surveys [1781–1827], 76, 103, with variant wording indicating that the latter was based on a 26 Apr. 1803 entry).

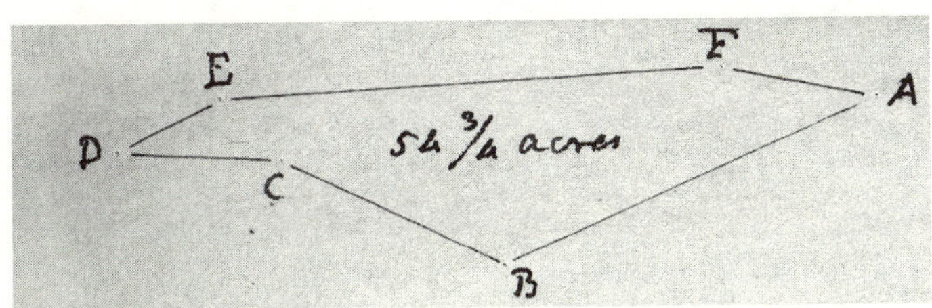

All of the enclosed documents, with the exception of RICHARD TULLOS's missing patent and the plat discussed below, were used as exhibits the following year in TJ's litigation with Samuel Scott (TJ's Answer to Samuel Scott's Bill of Complaint in *Scott v. Jefferson and Harrison*, 11 July 1812). For the DEC. 23. 1795 survey, see TJ to James Martin, 18 Feb. 1810, and note. William

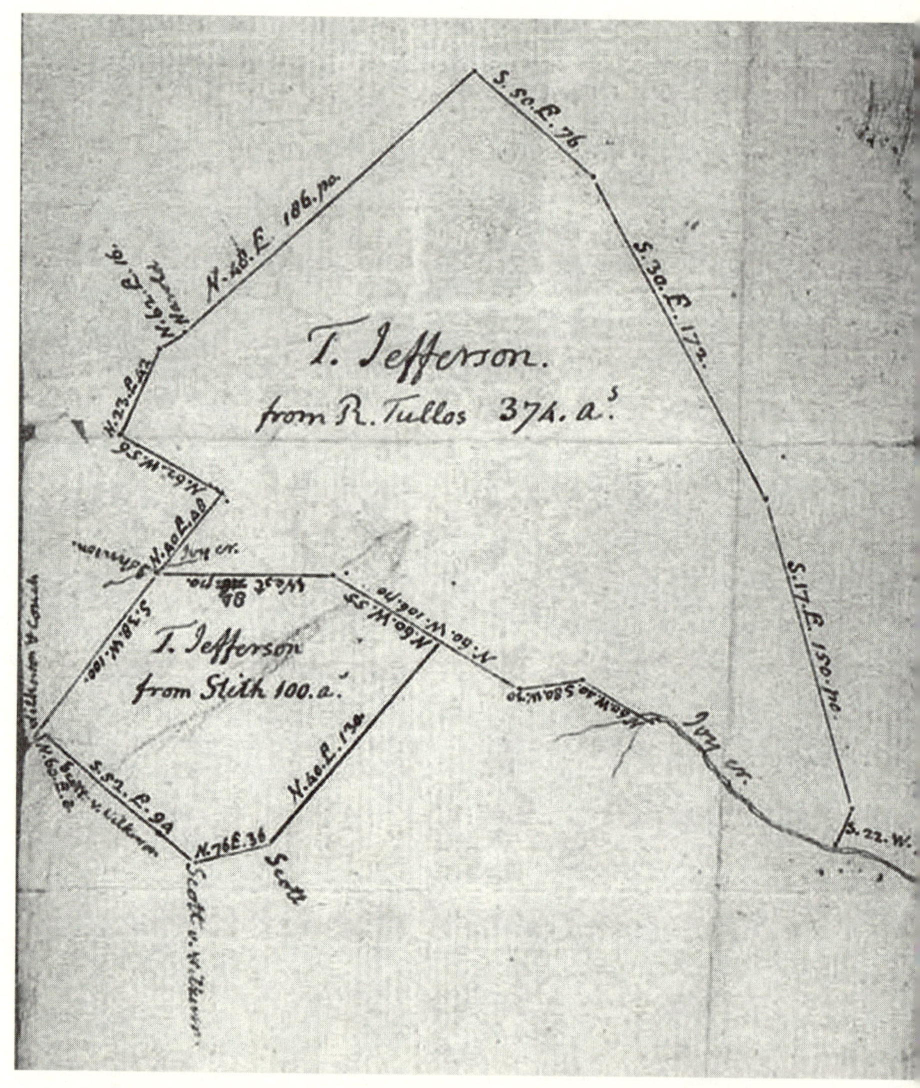

P. Martin's 15 Nov. 1809 RESURVEY is printed in note to TJ to Christopher Clark, 1 Apr. 1810. The plat showing the CONTIGUITY of the 374- and 100-acre tracts was probably a copy of the version illustrated above that TJ evidently retained in his papers (MS in ViU: TJP, Thurlow-Berkeley no. 1136 [532a]; entirely in TJ's hand; undated).

[1] Manuscript: "Smith's."

From George Hay

Sir, Richmond Decr 5. 1811

I have the pleasure to inform you that on monday last, the discussion of the question of Jurisdiction in Livingstons case Commenced. It was closed on tuesday: and on yesterday the two judges, concurring over-ruled the replication to the plea of jurisdiction.

You will pardon me for Suggesting to you, that as the Suit has gone off on a collateral point, it would afford great Satisfaction to the public[1] to See that its fate would have been no better if it had been tried on the merits. This they will See, if the defence which you entrusted to my hands Shall be made known. You will be So good as to Say what shall be done with it, and with the books and documents belonging to the Cause.—

I am, with very great respect y^r mo: ob: Sert Geo: Hay.

RC (DLC); endorsed by TJ as received 25 Dec. 1811 and so recorded in SJL.

The defence was TJ's Statement on the Batture Case, 31 July 1810.

[1] Preceding three words interlined.

From Robert McDermut

Richd Dec: 5th 1811

Having fortuitously met with Doctor Young's translation, from the french, of "D'Anville's complete body of Ancient Geography," in the hands of a near relation to whom he had presented the copy, it imediately occured to me that an Edition of it might be very acceptable in our schools and Colleges, as an useful key to Ancient History &c.

The work might, perhaps, be better adapted to use of schools by omitting most of the notes, which turn on Philosophical subjects; and by curtailing the elaborate enquiries into the extent of Ancient discoveries in Asia & Africa, and such other dilatations as swell the work without increasing the stock of information.

Should such an undertaking meet your approbation, with that of the Presidents of some of our Principal Colleges, it will be immediately commenced in Philadelphia, whither[1] the Editor will be compelled to resort for the convenience of employing an engraver for the maps.

I presume that the price of the book will not be more than two dollars.

Your correspondent is a native of Virginia, but thinks it prudent to withhold his name for the present. He will thank you for any thing that you may suggest on this subject, addressed R. M. to the care of Samuel Pleasants j[r] Printer, Rich[d]—and will ever be, with sentiments of the highest consideration

y[r] most ob[t] S[t] R. M.

RC (MHi); dateline beneath author's initials; at foot of text: "M[r] Jefferson"; endorsed by TJ as a letter from "Anon. Richm[d]" pertaining to "Danville's geography" received 22 Dec. 1811 and so recorded in SJL.

Robert McDermut (ca. 1764–1841) was a native Virginian who worked as a carpenter in New York City before opening a bookstore there in about 1803. He continued as a bookseller and printer, both alone and with various partners, until his death. McDermut was a Federalist who lost a bid for a seat in the lower house of the state legislature in 1815 by just two votes (William Duncan, *The New-York Directory, and Register, for the year 1791* [New York, 1791], 79; *Longworth's New York Directory* [1803], 203; [1813], 56, 213; [1841], 460; Ballston Spa, N.Y., *Independent American*, 10 May 1815; *New York City Hall Recorder* 4 [1819]: 12–25; New York *Evening Post*, 20 Aug. 1841).

During a partnership that lasted from about 1813 until 1817, McDermut joined Daniel D. Arden in publishing the first American edition of Jean Baptiste Bourguignon d'Anville's *Compendium of Ancient Geography . . . Calculated for Private Libraries, as well as for the Use of Schools* (New York, 1814). This work, which had originally appeared as *Géographie Ancienne Abrégée* (Paris, 1768), had already gone through several London editions.

[1] Manuscript: "whiter."

To Benjamin Rush

Dear Sir Poplar Forest Dec. 5. 11.

While at Monticello I am so much engrossed by business or society that I can only write on matters of strong urgency. here I have leisure, as I have every where the disposition to think of my friends. I recur therefore to the subject of your kind letters relating to mr Adams and myself, which a late occurrence has again presented to me. I communicated to you the correspondence which had parted mrs Adams and myself, in proof that I could not give friendship in exchange for such sentiments as she had recently taken up towards myself, and avowed & maintained in her letters to me. nothing but a total renunciation of these could admit a reconciliation, and that could be cordial only in proportion as the return to antient opinions was believed sincere. in these jaundiced sentiments of hers I had associated mr Adams, knowing the weight which her opinions had with him, and notwithstanding she declared in her letters that they were not communicated to him. a late incident has satisfied me that I wronged him as well as her in not yielding entire confidence to this assurance on her part. two of the mr Coles, my neighbors and friends, brothers to the one who lived with me as Secretary at Washington, took a tour to the Northward during the last summer. in Boston they fell into company with mr Adams, & by his invitation passed a day with him at Braintree. he spoke out to them every thing which came uppermost, & as it occurred to his mind, without any reserve; and seemed most disposed to dwell on those things which happened during his own administration. he spoke of his masters, as he called his heads of departments, as acting above his controul, & often against his opinions.[1] among many other topics, he adverted to the unprincipled licenciousness of the press against myself, adding 'I always loved Jefferson, and still love him'—this is enough for me. I only needed this knolege to revive towards him all the affections of the most cordial moments of our lives. changing a single word only in Dr Franklin's character of him, I knew him to be always an honest man, often a great one, but sometimes incorrect & precipitate in his judgments: and[2] it is known to those who have ever heard me speak of mr Adams, that I have ever done him justice myself, and defended him when assailed by others, with the single exception as to his political opinions. but with a man possessing so many other estimable qualities, why should we be dissocialized[3] by mere differences of opinion in politics, in religion in philosophy, or any thing else. his opinions are as honestly formed as my own. our different views of the same subject are the result of a difference in our organisation & experience. I never withdrew from the society of[4] any man on this account, altho' many have done it from me; much less should I do it from one with whom I had gone thro', with hand & heart, so many trying scenes. I wish therefore but for an apposite occasion to express to mr Adams my unchanged affections[5] for him. there is an awkwardness which hangs over the resuming a correspondence so long discontinued, unless something could arise which should call for a letter. time and chance may perhaps generate such an occasion, of which I shall not be wanting in promptitude to avail myself.[6] from this fusion of mutual affections, mrs Adams is of course separated. it will only be necessary that I never name her. in your letters to mr Adams you can perhaps suggest my continued cordiality towards him, & knowing this, should an occasion of writing, first present itself to him, he will perhaps avail himself of it, as I certainly will should it first occur to me. no ground for jealousy now existing, he will certainly give fair play to the natural warmth of his heart. perhaps I may open the way in some letter to my old friend Gerry, who I know is in habits of the greatest intimacy with him.

I have thus, my friend, laid open my heart to you, because you were so kind as to take an interest in healing again revolutionary affections, which have ceased in expression only, but not in their existence. God ever bless you and preserve you in life & health.

TH: JEFFERSON

RC (NNPM: Heineman Collection); at foot of first page: "D[r] Rush." PoC (DLC). Tr (MHi: Adams Papers); extract quoted in Rush to John Adams, 16 Dec. 1811.

In May 1857 Edward COLES wrote TJ's biographer Henry S. Randall a detailed description of his visit to John Adams: "In the summer of 1811, while Secretary to President Madison, I, accompanied by my Brother John, made a tour through the northern States, and took letters of introduction from the President to many of the most distinguished men of that section of the Union—among others, to Ex President John Adams, with whom we spent the greater part of two days, and were treated by him and his Wife with great civility & kindness. M[r] Adams talked very freely of men and of things, and detailed many highly interesting facts in the history of our Country, and particularly of his own Administration, and of incidents connected with the Presidential election of 1800. This, and his knowledge of my being a neighbour, and intimate with M[r] Jefferson, led him to converse freely, and by the nature of his remarks to open the door to expose his grievences, and to invite explanations of the causes of them. He complained, and mentioned several instances in which he thought he had reason to complain, of M[r] Jeffersons treatment of him. I told him I could not reconcile what he had heard of M[r] Jeffersons language and conduct to him, with what I had heard him repeatedly say, and that too to friends who were political opponents of M[r] Adams. Upon repeating some of the complimentary remarks thus made by M[r] Jefferson, M[r] Adams not only seemed but expressed himself highly pleased." After describing their discussion of the first interview between Adams and Jefferson following the election of 1800, in which he attempted to show Adams that Jefferson had been sensitive to his friend's anger at being turned out of office, Coles continued: "In the course of the many long conversations I had with M[r] Adams, he displayed, in general, kind feelings to M[r] Jefferson, and an exalted admiration of his character, and appreciation of his services to his Country, as well during the Revolution as subsequently; frequently making complimentary allusions to them, and displaying friendly feelings for him, in such expressions as, I always loved Jefferson & still love him; expressing in strong terms his disapprobation and mortification at the course pursued by some of his (Adams) friends in their scurrilous abuse of M[r] Jefferson &c &c" (Coles to Randall, 11 May 1857 [NjP: Coles Papers]; printed in Randall, *Life*, 3:639–40).

According to Benjamin FRANKLIN'S characterization, Adams "means well for his Country, is always an honest Man, often a wise one, but sometimes, and in some things, absolutely out of his senses" (Franklin to Robert R. Livingston, 22 July 1783, Albert Henry Smyth, ed., *The Writings of Benjamin Franklin* [1907], 9:62).

[1] Tr begins here.

[2] Sentence to this point omitted in Tr.

[3] Tr: "seperated."

[4] Preceding three words omitted in Tr.

[5] Tr: "affection," with this and preceding word underscored.

[6] Tr ends here.

To Jones & Howell

MESSRS JONES & HOWELL Poplar Forest Dec. 6. 11.

Be pleased to send me, before the closing of your river, 1. ton of nail rod, in which let there be a single bundle of half-crown rod, and the rest assorted for from 20d down to 6d nails also a quarter of a ton of toughest Swedish iron in bars from the size of a gigg axletree down to the small sizes, and one hundred weight of hoop iron for cut 4d nails.

I am told there is a patent auger for boring holes in the ground for post & rail fencing, which may be had in Philadelphia you will oblige me by sending one of the largest, if they are made of different sizes. the remittance for the above will be made in 90. days from the shipment as has been our usage. Accept the assurances of my respect.

TH: JEFFERSON

consign to Gibson & Jefferson at Richmond as usual.

PoC (MHi); endorsed by TJ.

Missing letters from Benjamin Jones to TJ of 15 Dec. 1811 and 28 Jan. 1812, recorded in SJL as received from Philadelphia on 25 Dec. 1811 and 4 Feb. 1812, apparently informed TJ that Jones & Howell could not then supply him with NAIL ROD and SWEDISH IRON (TJ to Jones, 17 June 1812). On 7 Nov. 1811 Anthony Butler, of Vermont, patented an AUGER "for boring posts" (*List of Patents*, 102).

From Charles G. Paleske

SIR Washington City December 7th 1811

I duly received Your favor of the 30th of September, for which I return You many thanks.—

An active agency of any extent in public undertakings would improperly intrude upon the leisure and retirement, which You have sought after the labours, in which You have for so many Years acted a distinguished and highly useful part.—For Your good wishes for the success of the company I am greatly indebted, and knowing that amidst the literary avocations, which no doubt now employ Your hours, it will not be unacceptable to hear of our further progress—I take the liberty of enclosing a pamphlet from which You will perceive that further attempts are now in prosecution for enlisting in the most beneficial object we have in view, the support of the General Government, as well as that of the State through which our Canals are to pass.

Accept, Sir, my best wishes for a prolongation of Your life and health, and beleive me with the highest consideration

Your obed[t] Serv[t] CHARLES G: PALESKE

RC (MHi); dateline adjacent to signature; at foot of text: "Thomas Jefferson Esquire Late President of the United States of America"; endorsed by TJ as received 22 Dec. 1811 and so recorded in SJL. Enclosure: *An Act to Incorporate the Union Canal Company, of Pennsylvania, with the Bye-laws, Rules, Orders and Regulations, enacted at a meeting of the Stockholders, on the 24th July, 1811* (Philadelphia, 1811).

The enclosed work included memorials of 19 Nov. 1811 from the Union Canal Company seeking support in an unspecified form from the legislature of the GENERAL GOVERNMENT and a $100,000 loan from that of the STATE of Pennsylvania (pp. 27–32, 32–4).

Conveyance of Bear Branch Land to William Radford and Joel Yancey

This indenture made on the seventh[1] day of December one thousand eight hundred and eleven between Thomas Jefferson of the county of Albemarle on the one part and William Radford and Joel Yancey both[2] of the county of Campbell on the other part, witnesseth that, in consideration of the sum of one dollar to him the sd Thomas in hand paid, and in execution of certain covenants heretofore entered into by him with Charles L. Bankhead, & Anne C. his wife, grandaughter of the said Thomas, and of other covenants heretofore entered into by the sd Charles L. and Anne C. his wife by written articles[3] with the said William and Joel[4] the said Thomas has given granted bargained and sold unto the said William and Joel[5] a certain tract or parcel of land, with it's appurtenances, in the county of Bedford lying on Bear branch[6] bounded as follows, to wit,[7] Beginning at a hiccory sapling, marked as a corner on the Western side of the public road and of Bear branch 5. poles & 10. links from an Ash on the branch, and running N. 38° E. 12. poles 17. links, N. 2° E. 14. po. 20. li. N. 66.° E. 14. po. 3. l. N. 28. E. 26. po. 11. l. Bear branch distant 3. p. 20. l N. 54. E. 24–24. Bear br. distant 2–20. N. 22. E. 11–22. to a branch, Bear branch being distant 8. poles. N. 25. E. 17–15. Bear br. distant 6. po. N. 84½ E. 6–20. Bear br. distant 2–20. N. 30½ E. 23–5. Bear br. dist[t] 4–20 N. 5. W. 15–5. Bear br. dist[t] 6. po. N. 34. E. 16. po. to a branch; same course 11–15. Bear br. distant 9. poles N. 47. E. 18–15. Bear br. dist[t] 3–3. N. 29½ E. 23. po. to a remarkable point of rock within 2. po. of a branch from the West, & 8. po. from Bear br. N. 69. E. 10–20. Bear br. dist[t] 3–5. ~"~"~"~"~"~

N. 59. E. 14–20. Bear br. dist^{t} 2. po. N. 36$\frac{1}{2}$ E. 12–20 Bear br. dist^{t} 10. po. N. 71$\frac{1}{2}$ E. 20–3 Bear br. dist^{t} 1–5.[8] N. 2$\frac{1}{2}$ W. 10–20. Bear br. dist. 1–5. N. 24. E. 14–4. Bear br. dist^{t} 4. po. N. 8. W. 15. po. Bear br. dist. 2. po. N. 40. E. 11–5. Bear br. dist. 4–10. S. 85. E. 9–5 to a large Poplar in the woods on the Eastern edge of[9] Bear branch: which courses from the hiccory aforesaid on the public road to the said Poplar are marked by trees wherever they occurred on the courses[10] are always on the Western side of Bear branch, are, in their general course, parallel with it, leaving room for a road on firm ground between them and the branch, and are, by agreement of the parties to these presents, substituted as the boundary of the premisses hereby conveyed, so far, instead of the Bear branch itself before agreed on as a boundary in the written articles between the sd Charles L. and the sd William & Joel:[11] then running from the said Poplar S. 85.° E. 18. po. N. 43$\frac{1}{2}$ E. 62. po. S. 80. E. 52 po. to where Gill corners with the lands of the sd Thomas purchased from Robinson, N. 25$\frac{1}{2}$ W. 50. po. and S. 77 W. 80. along the old Poplar forest lines to Bear branch and the same last course continued on the same[12] line S. 77. W. 148. poles to the line of the lands of the said Charles L. on Wolf branch, formerly the property of the said Thomas, since conveyed to the sd Charles L. and now sold to the sd William & Joel[13] & thence along the said line of the sd Charles L. S. 26. W. 512.[14] poles crossing[15] the public road aforesaid to Watts's corner, thence S. 10. E. 11. po. S. 35 E. 19$\frac{1}{4}$ po. N. 26. E. 200. po. a new line to the same public road[16] & thence[17] along the said[18] road S. 85$\frac{1}{2}$ E. 65 po. 5 links[19] to the hiccory at the beginning: which parcel of land, when added to that on Wolf creek already conveyed by the sd Charles L. to the sd W^{m} & Joel, will make up, according to different estimates from 962. to 984. acres, & in considn of the quality & situation of certain parts of it, is intended & accepted in full satisfaction of the convenant of the sd Charles L. to convey to them 1000. acres. Provided nevertheless that if the two parcels aforesd shall be found to contain less than 962. acres, and due proof thereof shall be given[20] to the sd Thomas at any time within 6. months from the date of these presents then the said Thomas shall be bound to convey to the sd W^{m} & Joel of such lands of his own adjacent to those conveyed by these presents as he shall chuse, the quantity which the sd two parcels shall so fall short of 962. acres; otherwise this conveyance to be deemed to be in full satisfaction.[21] to have & to hold the said parcel of lands herein conveyed[22] with it's appurtenances, to them the said William & Joel & their[23] heirs as tenants in common[24] and the said Thomas, his heirs, executors & administrators, the said parcel of lands with it's appurtenances, to them the said William & Joel and their[25] heirs and to every of them severally[26] will for ever warrant and defend. In witness whereof the said Thomas hath hereto put his hand and seal on the day & year above written.

Signed, sealed
and delivered
in presence of }

Dft (ViU: TJP); on indented paper; entirely in TJ's hand. Tr (Bedford Co. Deed Book, 13:694); entirely in a clerk's hand, including signatures by TJ and witnesses Tamerlane W. W. Davies, E. P. Hughes, and Colin Buckner; at foot of text: "At a Court held for Bedford county at the courthouse the 23d of December 1811. This Indenture of bargain & sale between Thomas Jefferson of the one part and Wm Radford & Joel Yancey of the other was proven by the oath of Collin Buckner a subscribing witness—and afterwards at a Court held for said County at the Courthouse the 23d day of March 1812 The same was further proven by the oath of Tamerlane W. W. Davies & E. P. Hughes subscribing Witnesses and ordered to be recorded—Teste, J Steptoe."

William Radford (1787–1861), attorney and farmer, was a native of Goochland County. He was educated at Washington Academy (now Washington and Lee University) and moved to Lynchburg by 1808. His mother-in-law, Anne Moseley, purchased a portion of TJ's original Poplar Forest tract from the Randolphs in 1810. By the end of his life Radford owned seventy-five slaves and Woodbourne, an impressive house in Bedford County. Starting about 1819 he served for a time as president of the Farmers' Bank of Lynchburg (Robert Somerville Radford Yates Sr., *William Radford of Richmond, Virginia: His Ancestors and Descendants from 1700 to 1986* [1986], sect. 4, pp. 54, 62, 71; Chambers, *Poplar Forest*, 71, 101–2, 154; Richmond *Visitor*, 8 Apr. 1809; Thomas Mann Randolph and Martha Jefferson Randolph's Conveyance of Bedford County Land, [before 19 Feb. 1810], and note; Radford to John Preston, 20 Dec. 1818 [ViBlbV: Preston Family Papers]; DNA: RG 29, CS, Bedford Co., 1850, 1860 slave schedules; Bedford Co. Will Book, 18:252–3, 475–8, 488–92; gravestone inscription, Saint Stephen's Church, Forest, Va.).

Joel Yancey (d. 1833) was probably born in Louisa County but moved to Campbell County by 1796. He built his house, Rothsay, about a mile from Poplar Forest shortly after acquiring the property mentioned above. Yancey served as superintendent of TJ's Bedford County property from about the end of May 1815 until December 1821. In this capacity he corresponded frequently with TJ, who paid him $400 a year to hire and supervise the overseers and otherwise protect his interests. Yancey also donated funds to the nascent University of Virginia on several occasions (Chambers, *Poplar Forest*, esp. 71, 90; *MB*, esp. 2:1317, 1332, 1343; TJ to Archibald Robertson, and Robertson to TJ, both 1 June 1815; Bedford Co. Will Book, 8:273–4, 300–2).

The COVENANTS HERETOFORE ENTERED INTO were confirmed in a separate transaction on 7 Dec. 1811 by which Charles and Ann C. Bankhead sold Radford and Yancey between 719 and 741 acres on Wolf Creek in Bedford County, a portion of TJ's original Poplar Forest plantation, for $12,800 (Tr in Bedford Co. Deed Book, 13:862–3; recorded 26 July 1813). The PARCEL OF LAND . . . ON BEAR BRANCH sold by TJ to Radford and Yancey was surveyed by Thomas Jefferson Randolph and Joseph Slaughter this same month and found to contain 243 acres (ViU: TJP, TB [Thurlow-Berkeley no.] 1136 [532g, 532h, 532i]).

On 9 Dec. 1811 TJ attempted to survey the "256. acres called Dan. Robinson's adjoining Poplar Forest," which he had earlier acquired through his father-in-law, John Wayles (MS at ViU: TJP, TB 1136 [532f-1], in TJ's hand; Betts, *Farm*

Book, pt. 1, 127 [TJ's 1810 land roll giving acreage as 214 and surname as Robertson]).

[1] Word supplied later by TJ to fill blank space.

[2] Preceding four words interlined.

[3] Preceding three words interlined.

[4] Preceding two words interlined.

[5] Preceding two words interlined.

[6] TJ here canceled "containing by estimation one hundred and ninety eight acres and one half, and."

[7] Section down to "S. 85. E. 9–5" in the next paragraph reworked from Thomas Jefferson Randolph's field notes, which TJ altered so as to give the measurements in poles, not chains (MS at ViU: TJP, TB 1136 [532j-18], in Randolph's hand, with TJ's emendations; MS at ViU: TJP, TB 1136 [532j-13], in Randolph's hand). TJ totaled the poles and links "from the hiccory on the road" on a separate piece of paper (MS at ViU: TJP, TB 1136 [532j-22]; in TJ's hand).

[8] Tr: "5p 5l."

[9] Dft: "of of." Tr: "of."

[10] Preceding ten words interlined.

[11] Reworked from "Charles L. and William."

[12] Text from "S. 85.° E. 18." to this point interlined in place of "down the branch the following courses, N. 38. E. 24. poles, N. 2. E. 20. po. N. 5. E. 23. po. to the intersection of the branch with the line of the said Thomas at an Elm tree: then along the said." TJ based revisions from this note and note 14 below on Randolph's field notes (MS at ViU: TJP, TB 1136 [532j-7]; in Randolph's hand).

[13] Preceding two words interlined.

[14] Number interlined in place of "332."

[15] Word interlined in place of "to."

[16] Text from "to Watt's corner" to this point interlined, with "a new line" further interlined.

[17] TJ here canceled "S. 85½ E. [23.] poles [9] links."

[18] TJ here canceled "public."

[19] Preceding seven words interlined.

[20] Reworked from "and notice thereof shall be duly given."

[21] Text from "which parcel of land" to this point interlined in place of "which conveyance by these presents is towards a fulfilment, in part only, of the written articles before mentioned; between the sd Charles L. & William, the said Thomas acknoleging himself to continue bound to add, according to the stipulations in the sd written articles, to the premisses now conveyed, as much more of his lands adjacent to them, or to the said tract on Wolf branch, as these premisses with the said tract on Wolf branch shall want of being one thousand acres, whenever that deficiency shall be ascertained and made known to the said Thomas."

[22] Preceding two words interlined.

[23] Reworked from "to him the said William & his."

[24] Preceding four words interlined in place of "for ever."

[25] Reworked from "to him the said William and his."

[26] Preceding six words interlined.

From André Thoüin

Monsieur et
venerable correspondant — à Paris ce 7 Xbre 1811

Permettez moi d'avoir l'honneur de vous présenter M. Correa de Serra, naturaliste portugais, mon honorable collegue à la Societé d'agriculture de Paris, à l'Institut de France, aux annales du Museum et mon respectable ami. Entrainé par une passion irresistible vers l'étude de la nature, de Ses loix et Surtout de Ses productions, il a voyagé dans diverses parties de l'Europe et S'est lié avec la plupart des Savans qui Suivent la même carrière; mais avec cette difference qu'il ne fait pas Son metier de la Science; Il la revêre comme une divinité, cherche à en découvrir les mystères et ensuite il les developpe à Ses contemporains. Les annales du Museum, les mémoires de la Societé d'agriculture, ceux de l'Institut et de beaucoup de compagnies Savantes renferment un grand nombre de Ses découvertes.

En quittant l'Europe il laisse après lui des regrets à toutes les personnes qui ont eu l'avantage de le connoitre et elles ne Supportent Sa perte que dans la ferme persuasion où elles Sont que M. Correa de Serra, apprecié comme il doit l'être par les habitans du nouveau monde, ne tardera pas à trouver un grand nombre d'amis. Sa moralité douce, Sa tolerance affectueuse Sa probité integre et Sa politesse franche en Sont de Surs garrants.

En vous présentant, Monsieur, mon ami, je n'ai d'autre but que de mettre en contact deux hommes faits pour S'apprecier et d'éviter les longueurs d'une appreciation tardive. De Sa part la vôtre est faite depuis longtems Comme pour tous les amis de l'humanité. Quelques Conferences Suffiront pour établir la votre et je felicite votre pays de l'avantage qu'il a de posseder un nouvel habitant tel que M. Correa de Serra.

Veuillez recevoir, Je vous prie, de nouveau, Monsieur et venerable Correspondant l'expression de mon inviolable et respectueux attachem[ent] Thoüin

Je joins ici un opuscule dans lequel j'ai pris la liberté de placer votre nom, desirant le voir honorer le jardinage comme il honore depuis longtems les Sciences politiques. Veuillez le recevoir avec votre indulgence accoutumée; je vous en aurai la plus Sincere obligation.

EDITORS' TRANSLATION

Sir and venerable correspondent Paris 7 December 1811

Allow me the honor of introducing to you Mr. Corrêa da Serra, a Portuguese naturalist, my honorable colleague at the Société d'Agriculture in Paris, the Institut de France, and the Annales du Muséum, and my respectable friend. Driven by an irresistible passion to study nature, its laws, and especially its productions, he has traveled through the various parts of Europe and made friends with most of the scientists who follow the same career, but with this difference, he does not make science his trade. He reveres it as a divinity, seeking to discover its mysteries and then explain them to his contemporaries. The Annales du Muséum, the memoirs of the Société d'Agriculture, and those of the Institut and numerous other learned societies contain many of his discoveries.

In departing from Europe, he leaves all the people who have had the advantage of knowing him feeling regretful. They bear the thought of losing him only through their firm conviction that Mr. Corrêa da Serra, appreciated as he must be by the people of the New World, will soon make many friends. His gentle morality, affectionate tolerance, honest probity, and candid politeness surely warrant it.

In introducing my friend, Sir, my only goal is to bring into contact two men who are bound to appreciate each other, and to avoid delaying their recognition of each other's worth. He has, like all friends of humanity, long held you in high esteem. A few meetings will suffice for him to earn your respect, and I congratulate your country on the advantage it now has of possessing a new resident like Mr. Corrêa da Serra.

Please accept again, I pray you, Sir and venerable correspondent, my expression of inviolable and respectful attachment THOÜIN

I enclose an essay in which I took the liberty of placing your name, wishing to see it bestow honor on gardening, as it has long been doing in the political sciences. Please receive it with your customary indulgence; which will place me under the most sincere obligation.

RC (DLC); edge chipped; endorsed by TJ as received 31 July 1813 and so recorded in SJL, which adds that it was delivered "by Mr Correa de Serra." Translation by Dr. Roland H. Simon.

The enclosed OPUSCULE honoring TJ was probably Thoüin's "Suite De La Description Des Greffes," *Annales du Muséum D'Histoire Naturelle* 17 [1811]: 34–53, on p. 50 of which Thoüin wrote of a technique of grafting named for TJ: "*Dénomination.* En l'honneur de M. THOMAS JEFFERSON, ci-devant président des États-Unis de l'Amérique, savant agronome auquel l'agriculture doit l'un des plus utiles perfectionnemens de la charrue, dont il a repris le manche en quittant les rênes de l'état qu'il a gouverné avec tant de sagesse" ("*Name.* In honor of Mr. THOMAS JEFFERSON, president of the United States of America, learned agriculturist to whom agriculture owes one of the most useful improvements of the plow, who has again taken it up after relinquishing the reins of the state that he governed with such wisdom").

From George Jefferson

DEAR SIR Richmond 8th Dec[r] 1811

I find upon attending more particularly to the notes which you forwarded for renewal in the bank, that you have filled up the dates for every two months, without regard to the number of days in the month, & also without regard to the allowance of 3 days grace.—this in the absence both of M[r] Gibson & myself, might be attended with inconvenience, as the notes as filled up, would not fall due on the discount days, which are but once a week.—renewals to be regular, should be made once in 63 days.—In order to guard against accidents to M[r] G—, I must put you to the trouble of signing & forwarding the new notes which are inclosed.—the old ones are returned herewith, defaced.—We some days since sold 50 Bbls of your flour at $8.\frac{1}{8}$\$.—by the last acc[ts] from New York, some little advance in price may be expected here.—You will of course give directions respecting the sale of what you may yet have to come down.—I leave particular orders that no sale shall be made on credit previous to M[r] G—'s return.

I am Dear Sir Your Very humble serv[t] Geo. Jefferson

RC (MHi); at foot of text: "Thomas Jefferson esq[r]"; endorsed by TJ as received 25 Dec. 1811 and so recorded in SJL. Enclosures not found.

TJ's reply to Gibson & Jefferson of 27 Dec. 1811, not found, is recorded in SJL. On that date he noted that he had "Signed notes for renewal of mine in bank for 3000.D. dated Jan. 7. Mar. 10. May 12" (*MB*, 2:1272).

From Madame de Tessé

Aulnay 8 decembre 1811

jai Reçu, monsieur, votre lettre du 27 mars avec La Reconnoissance et la satisfaction que m'inspire tout ce que me vient de vous, et profite avec empressement de la confiance due au bâtiment de L'etat pour vous Repondre sur ce que concerne le Castanea sativa dont vous avès mangé le fruit a Paris.

vous serès sans doute fort surpris d'aprendre que nous ne pouvons nous le procurer ni aux environs de Paris ni dans nos departemens. les pepinistes pretendent le cultiver et en vendent qui ne donnent jamais que des fruits miserables. j'en ai fais L'experience ainsi que M[r] de La fayette et mille autres personnes. a quoi cela apartient il? je L'ignore.

on apelle communement les meilleurs marrons des marchés de Paris marrons de Lyon, et L'arbre qui les porte n'existe pas aux environs de Lyon. il est probable quon les tire du chablais ou de La Savoie d'ou ils sont envoiés a Lyon pour être ensuite transportés a Paris. pourquoi n'y sont ils pas semés dirés vous? ils L'ont eté mille fois et n'ont rien produit de passable. cet arbre veut être greffé et d'une maniere toute particuliere que je vous ferois connaitre si j'avois le bonheur de m'en procurer pour vous. le degout des tentatives infructueuses pour le naturaliser chés soi y a fais Renoncer et on se borne a en acheter le fruit quand on ne veut pas se contenter de chataignes ou d'une espece de marrons tres inferieure

votre desir a Reveillé en moi le courage depuis Longtems etient de faire des Recherches sur cet objet. si je n'obtiens Rien au moins je saurai pourquoi, car je suivrai une correspondance deja entamee pour vous servir avec un homme intelligent qui me veut beaucoup de bien et qui n'habite pas Loin du canton dou L'on croit que les meilleurs marrons nous viennent. je ne desespere pas d'en obtenir du plan et quil ne se multiplie en France. a cette occasion, ce ne seroit pas La premiere fois qu'une decouverte echapee aux Recherches des savans auroit ete le produit d'un sentiment

on me dispute L'esperance fondee de vous plaire en vous envoiant un ouvrage qui m'a singulierement amuseè. je conviens que vous perdrés une partie de mes jouissances faute d'avoir vecu avec La partie La plus vulgaire de notre nation dont La Princesse a constamment le Style. mais L'extravagance de ce Roy et de cette Reine, La bassesse de tous ces sentimens, La Grossiereté de ces moeurs, La Ridicule pompe de ces cours, et ce grand Frederic qui n'attend pas que son pere soit mort pour insulter sa soeur cherie et L'aventir quelle ne dois compter sur aucun des services qu'il en a Reçu, vous ne pouvés y être tout a fait indifferent, car L'ouvrage est bien authentique. M[r] de humbold L'a En manuscrit en Prusse.

je trouve sous ma main de quoi vous donner une idée des compositions de nos meilleurs Poètes. je L'ajoute a mon Paquet

Mr Short me parle de son etablissement a Philadelphie qui me paroit assés bon. je ne lui ai jamais parlé de sa fortune. je voudrais La savoir telle qu'il n'eut Rien dessentiel a desirer. je sais qu'il n'y attache qu'un prix très secondaire dans La composition de son bonheur. sa conduite parmi nous en a fourni La preuve, mais j'aurois peine a Le defendre contre ses ennemis américains s'ils croient quon ne peut être bon Patriote sans aimer a boire et a manger Longtems.

il me seroit impossible d'exprimer avec La dignité de mon âge ce que jai Ressenti en Lisant que vous ne Regardès pas comme impossible de voir—et quon na jamais pu—et que suivant toute apparence on ne verra jamais. ah! soiés assés curieux et assés necessaire a vos compatriotes, Monsieur, pour Recevoir ici les hommages de tous les gens de bien, ceux de Mr de Tessé particulierement enfin de votre trés sensiblement et devotement affectionneé NOAILLES-TESSÉ

EDITORS' TRANSLATION

Aulnay 8 December 1811

I received, Sir, your letter of 27 March with the gratitude and satisfaction that everything from you inspires, and I hurriedly take advantage of the trust accorded to a public ship to answer you regarding the Castanea sativa, the fruit of which you ate in Paris.

You will not be greatly surprised to learn that we can find it neither near Paris nor in the provinces. Nurseries claim to grow it, but what they sell gives only miserable fruit. I have tried it, and so have Mr. Lafayette and a thousand other people. Why is that so? I do not know.

The best chestnuts in the Parisian markets are commonly called Lyon chestnuts, but the tree that bears them does not exist near Lyon. We probably get them from Chablais or Savoy, whence they are sent to Lyon and later to Paris. You will ask why are they not sown there? They have been a thousand times, but they produced nothing passable. This tree likes to be grafted, and in a very special way that I would describe to you if I could get one. Fruitless attempts at domestic cultivation have resulted in hopeless frustration, and we content ourselves with buying them when we do not want to make do with a very inferior type of chestnut.

Your wish has awakened in me the long-extinguished courage to do some research on this subject. If I learn nothing, at least I will know why, because, in order to aid you, I will correspond with a very intelligent man who wishes me well and lives not far from the county that is believed to grow the best chestnuts. I do not despair of getting from the project that which does not grow in France. This would not be the first time that a discovery escaped the research of the learned, but came about as a result of feeling.

I am told not to count too much on delighting you with a book that amused me immensely. I admit that you lose part of my enjoyment, because you do not live among the most vulgar people in our nation, as the princess constantly styles it. But the extravagance of this king and that queen, the baseness of their sentiments, the coarseness of their ways, the ridiculous pomp of all these courts, and that great Frederick who does not wait for his father to die before insulting his darling sister and informing her that she can count on him for none of the services that he received from her. You cannot be completely indifferent, because the work is authentic. Mr. von Humboldt has the manuscript in Prussia.

Near to hand I find something that will give you an idea of the compositions of the best poets. I add it to my package.

Mr. Short tells me that his business in Philadelphia appears to be going rather well. I have never before talked to him of his finances. I would like to know that he would never lack anything essential. With regard to his own happiness, I know that he attaches only a secondary importance to wealth. His conduct among us proved this, but I would be hard put to defend him against his American enemies, who believe that a good patriot likes to drink and eat all the time.

I find it impossible to express with the dignity of my age what I felt upon reading that you consider it impossible to come for a visit—and that you will never be able to—and that, in all likelihood, we will never see each other again. Ah! Sir, be so curious and indispensable to your fellow countrymen as to receive here the tribute of all good people, that of Mr. de Tessé particularly, and lastly that of your very deeply and devotedly affectionate

NOAILLES-TESSÉ

RC (MoSHi: TJC-BC); endorsed by TJ as received 26 Feb. 1812, and so recorded in SJL. Enclosure not found. Translation by Dr. Roland H. Simon.

SJL records, and an endorsement leaf in TJ's hand filed with the above letter confirms, the receipt on 17 Apr. 1812 of a second letter, not found, sent by Tessé from Aulnay on 8 Dec. 1811. It enclosed the *Mémoires de Frédérique Sophie Wilhelmine de Prusse, Margrave de Bareith, Soeur de Frédéric-le-Grand; Ecrits de sa main*, 2 vols. (Paris, 1811; Sowerby, no. 271).

From George Jefferson

DEAR SIR Richmond 9th Decr 1811

I duly received your much esteemed favor of the 29th, and should greatly prefer the mode which you are so good as to propose respecting the bond, but I had previously ask'd the favor of Doctor Wardlaw to join in it, who consented so willingly, that I should not like now to leave him out.—I leave this tomorrow for Norfolk, and expect the vessel in which I am to embark, (the Elizabeth Wilson) will be ready to sail on my arrival.

I will pay particular attention to your direction respecting wines, but fear from what I have heard, that you ought not to calculate upon receiving your supplies from Lisbon shortly.

Wishing you all possible happiness, and hoping that I shall find you on my return in perfect health,

I am my dear Sir Your ever truly grateful friend

GEO. JEFFERSON

RC (MHi); at foot of text: "Thomas Jefferson esqr Monticello"; endorsed by TJ as received 25 Dec. 1811 and so recorded in SJL.

SJL records TJ's missing letter to Jefferson OF THE 29TH Nov. 1811.

From David Bailie Warden

DEAR SIR, Paris, 10 December, 1811—

I have the honor of informing you, that I forwarded, to their address, the letters which you were pleased to confide to my care. That, for Mr.[1] Mazzei, was forwarded to him by Mr. Cathalan, of Marseilles—I inclose a letter, from Mr Walsh, in reply to that you sent by me. General La Fayette says, that he will write to you by the frigate—Baron Humboldt did not receive the letter which was forwarded by the John adams. He hopes to hear from you soon. He is now in Germany, and will shortly return to Paris. I inclose a letter from Senator Tracy—He proposes to write to you soon; and He sends you a MS., which I put under cover to the President—He is much pleased with the Commentary on Montesquieu. He has presented you a copy of his works, which will be conveyed in a case,[2] by the frigate Constitution, addressed to the Philosophical Society—In the same case, I have forwarded, for your acceptance, a copy of Peuchets' Statistique—and I have inclosed a copy of the Atlas of Le Sage, for Mrs. Randolph—a work which will amuse, and instruct the young Ladies— I send, under cover, for[3] the President, a packet from Madame de Tessy— General O'Connor,[4] who lives near Fontainbleau, took charge of the letters for General Kosciusko—

I am, at present, much occupied with the duties of my office, but hope soon to have leisure to communicate to you some late[5] improvements, of this Country, in Science and the Arts—

I pray you, to present my respects to Mr. and Mrs. Randolph, and to accept the renewal of my thanks for the interest which you were pleased to employ in my welfare—

I am, Sir, with great esteem & respect, your most obliged Servant

D. B. WARDEN

RC (DLC); between dateline and salutation: "To Thomas Jefferson Esquire Monticello"; endorsed by TJ as received 26 Feb. 1812 and so recorded in SJL. FC (MdHi: Warden Letterbook). Enclosures: (1) Peter Walsh to TJ, 10 Oct. 1811. (2) Destutt de Tracy to TJ, 21 Oct., 15 Nov. 1811.

UNDER COVER TO THE PRESIDENT, Warden sent TJ the manuscript of Destutt de Tracy's *Elémens d'Idéologie*, originally enclosed in Destutt de Tracy to TJ, 15 Nov. 1811, and described there. A month after he received the above letter and its enclosures, TJ had not yet received Destutt de Tracy's manuscript (Warden to James Madison, 2 Dec. 1811, Madison, *Papers, Pres. Ser.*, 4:48; TJ to Madison, 26 Mar. 1812). Warden also CONVEYED separately copies of Jacques Peuchet, *Statistique élémentaire de la France* (Paris, 1805; Sowerby, no. 2682), and Emmanuel Auguste Dieudonné Marin Joseph, comte de Las Cases (writing under the pseudonym of A. LE SAGE), *Genealogical, chronological, historical, and geographical atlas* (London, 1801), or a later French edition of this work.

[1] FC: "Mrs."

[2] FC: "conveyed to You."

[3] Revised from "for" to "to" in FC.

[4] Reworked from what appears to be "La Fayette."

[5] FC: "new."

From Richard Barry

SIR December 11th 1811

I am now under the necessity of calling on you for the ballance of my account if convenient I would not trouble you now but I am building a House in front of F and 12th Street three Story which I find that it will exhaust my little resources Indeed, Sir if I thought it was putting you to an inconvenience I would not trouble

I remain Sir with Sincere Wishes for your Happiness a friend

RICHARD BARRY

RC (MHi); at foot of text: "Thomas Jefferson Esqr"; endorsed by TJ as received 25 Dec. 1811 and so recorded in SJL.

From Pierre Samuel Du Pont de Nemours

MON TRÈS RESPECTABLE AMI, 12 X[bre] 1811.

J'ai reçu par Mr Barlow, et avec bien de la reconnaissance, votre Lettre du 15 avril.

Un Homme comme vous peut être retiré des Places, jamais des affaires. Vous êtes un Magistrat du Genre-humain.

Tant mieux Si l'établissement des Manufactures dans votre Pays ne vous oblige pas de changer le Systême de vos Finances aussi promptement que l'on paraissait avoir lieu de le craindre.

Mais le cas doit arriver un jour: et il faut que les pensées du Gouvernement, et Surtout que l'opinion publique y Soient préparées—La Science de l'Economie politique ne doit pas être ignorée, ni négligée aux Etats-Unis.—Où traiterait-on Ses questions les plus importantes, Si ce n'était pas dans une République qui respecte la liberté de la presse, qui est aujourd'hui la derniere des Républiques qui aient existé, la derniere espérance de celles qui Sont à naitre, et qu'elle propagera comme une Mere Abeille?—comment des Souverains, dans un Siecle où les lumieres, quoique moins vives et moins générales qu'il y a trente ans, Sont loin cependant d'être éteintes, Se refuseraient-ils à discuter avec profondeur leurs interêts, leurs droits, leurs devoirs?

Je regrette beaucoup de ne pouvoir y contribuer directement. Il me Sera impossible de devenir en Anglais un bon écrivain. On ne Saurait apprendre après Soixante ans à Se bien exprimer dans une langue qui fut étrangere à notre jeunesse. Mais Mr Paterson, que vous m'aviez recommandé, m'a promis de traduire la dissertation Sur les Finances, et l'Essai Sur l'Education nationale: deux ouvrages dont vous m'avez inspiré l'idée et que je dois à vos bontés.—Il m'a même promis de traduire aussi la Table raisonnée des Principes de l'Economie politique.—Je le prierai de vous communiquer ces Traductions quand elles Seront faites, pour que votre admirable talent lui indique les corrections que vous croirez nécessaires. C'est un jeune homme d'une grande espérance.

Je vois avec plaisir que les Etats-Unis ont du tems devant eux pour prendre un parti Sur leurs Revenus publics;[1] que l'extinction de leurs dettes diminuera beaucoup et promptement leurs besoins politiques;[2] et que les consommations de vos riches en marchandises étrangeres Soutiendront encore quelques années le produit de vos douanes, Si vous pouvez éviter la guerre.

Si elle ne peut être éviteé, consolidez votre union avec les Florides et opérez celle du Canada: Fortifiez vos Ports, et Surtout New-York pour qui l'Isle du gouverneur est une défense insuffisante. Puis faites la paix.—Une guerre maritime donnerait[3] pendant la premiere annee à vos corsaires quelques bénéfices corrupteurs et du plus mauvais genre. Mais en très peu de tems elle vous ferait perdre beaucoup de capitaux et d'hommes précieux. Elle augmenterait considérablement et contre vous la Puissance relative de l'Angleterre, par la prise de vos matelots et leur incorporation dans la Marine anglaise. N'exposez pas vos Enfans à verser le Sang de leurs Peres.—La nécessité de nourrir les habitans de leurs Isles doit rendre les Anglais faciles Sur les conditions de la Paix avec vous.

Toutes ces circonstances éventuelles peuvent retarder, ou hâter Selon les événemens, le besoin de vous faire un nouveau Systême de Finances. Remerciez dieu S'il accorde à votre Gouvernement et à vos concitoyens le loisir[4] d'y Songer encore; car avec le caractere grave et réservé de votre Nation, vous Seriez le plus inexcusable Peuple du monde Si vous faisiez une étourderie, et en matiere d'une si haute importance.

Vous croyez avoir, dès le commencement de votre Sage Administration, donné le coup de la mort au systême des Excises, malheureusement tenté par le Général Hamilton. Vous avez fait une très bonne chose—. Cependant si la Contribution territoriale continue d'être odieuse dans l'Eastern Territory, la partie la mieux cultiveé des Etats-Unis et qui a le bonheur de n'avoir point d'Esclaves, le Succès peut n'être pas complet: la maladie peut avoir une rechute.

Les erreurs principales relativement à l'Impôt ont deux motifs, dont le premier est l'envie de faire contribuer tout le monde, particulierement les Ouvriers, les Commerçans, les Capitalistes. C'est à quoi l'on ne Saurait parvenir; puisqu'il n'est aucun moyen d'empêcher les uns de vendre leur travail, et les autres de louer l'usage de leur argent, de maniere à s'indemniser avec grande usure aux dépens des Propriétaires de la récolte.

L'autre cause d'erreur vient de plus haut. Elle est une conséquence du défaut d'idées justes Sur ce que sont dans les Societés politiques les Propriétaires du Sol, et les hommes industrieux non-Propriétaires, et Sur ce que la Société doit à chacun d'eux.

Les derniers Sont les membres d'une République universelle et Sans Magistratures, répandus dans tous les autres Etats; à qui les Gouvernemens, et les Citoyens de tous les autres Etats qui ont une constitution, doivent la liberté du travail, l'immunité de toute taxe, la participation gratuite au bon ordre qui résulte de toutes les magistratures, l'éligibilité en raison du mérite et S'il convient aux Electeurs.—quand ils Sont élus à quelque emploi, ou quand ils ont acheté des terres, ce qui doit toujours leur être permis, ils deviennent citoyens: jusques là ils n'êtaient et ne doivent être qu'Habitans.—La liberté, l'exemption de contributions, la Sureté de leurs personnes et de leurs biens, la protection des Loix dans tous leurs contracts: voila l'étendue et les bornes de leurs droits. Leur accorder davantage serait aussi déraisonnable que de vouloir dans l'intérieur de chaque famille donner aux valets le droit de régler les affaires de la maison conjointement avec les maitres.—vouloir leur faire payer l'exercice de ces droits naturels, ce Serait agir comme l'Avare qui volait l'avoine de Ses chevaux.[5] Leur service en deviendrait moins bon et plus cher.

Les droits de cité et de Souveraineté, celui de Siéger et de déliberer dans les Assemblées politiques, celui d'élire, celui de promulguer et de faire exécuter les Loix, appartiennent exclusivement aux Propriétaires des terres; parce qu'il n'y a que ceux ci qui Soient membres d'une République particuliere, ayant un territoire, et le devoir de l'administrer.

quand on s'écarte de ces bases de la Société civilisée et constituée, quand on croit, ou quand on laisse croire, que ceux qui n'ont que leurs bras ou des biens purement mobiliers, Sont autant citoyens que les Propriétaires du territoire et ont droit, ou d'en demander part Sans l'acquérir, ou de déliberer sur les loix de ces propriétés qu'ils ne possedent pas, on fomente les orages, on prépare les révolutions, on ouvre la voie aux Pisistrates, aux Marius, aux Césars, qui se font plus démocrates que ne le veulent la nature la justice et la raison, pour devenir Tyrans, violer tous les droits, Substituer aux loix leurs volontés arbitraires, offenser la morale, avilir l'humanité.

Dans une République qui veut être paisible, durable, exempte de troubles, il faut donc faire en sorte qu'il n'y ait pas une classe qui Soit ou puisse se croire opprimée, et qui veuille[6] des Protecteurs pour opprimer à son tour: car il s'en trouve, et c'est un Rôle très recherché.

Il faut que tout le monde y puisse travailler et acquerir Sans etre Sujet à aucune vexation. Il faut que tout le monde y puisse dire et publier son opinion sur les choses, à la charge de ne pas insulter, et encore plus de ne pas calomnier les Personnes; c'est en quoi consiste la liberté de la parole et celle de la presse. Mais exprimer la pensée officieusement, ou en déliberer officiellement et Voter, Sont deux choses très differentes.—Le Principe est que chacun a le droit de Se mêler de Ses affaires, et lorsqu'elles sont communes avec celles de quelques autres d'y prendre part en raison de son interêt; mais que personne n'a droit de se mêler des affaires d'autrui sans mission.—

Ainsi quand le travail ou le Commerce Sont gênés, tous les Travailleurs, tous les Négocians ont droit de réclamer, et de prouver que l'on attente contre l'interêt public à leur liberté naturelle; Et Si des Loix mal calculeés les contraignent à faire l'avance du payement de quelques impôts, ils ont le droit, qu'ils ne manquent jamais d'exercer, de s'en indemniser par un haussement au moins équivalent dans le prix de leurs Salaires ou de leurs marchandises.

Mais ils n'ont pas le droit de Se croire membres du Souverain, tant qu'ils n'ont point acheté de terres. Ils n'ont pas celui d'entrer dans les Assemblées de la commune où ils Sont domiciliés: Et ils ne peuvent être députés à une autre Assemblée que par le libre choix que les Electeurs de leur Commune ou de leur Canton auraient fait d'eux pour cela. Ils peuvent être nommés à toute fonction publique par les Electeurs, ou par le Gouvernement, et alors ils ont le droit de remplir cette fonction qui leur a été confiée. Rien de plus.

Ils jouissent, dira-t-on, de la protection des Loix et du secours de la force publique, pourquoi ne les payeraient-ils point?—Ils en jouissent parce que ce Sont des choses qui ne doivent être refusées à qui que ce Soit, qui Sont dues au premier et au plus inconnu des Etrangers qui mettent le pied dans le Pays. que serait un Gouvernement qui permettrait de voler, d'insulter, de frapper, d'assassiner ceux qui ne Seraient pas citoyens? ce serait un Gouvernement de barbares.

Il y a dans la Propriété fonciere un interêt permanent et une habitude de travaux utiles qui deviennent un gage de raison. Les Assemblées de Propriétaires ne Sont ni trop nombreuses, ni tumultueuses. Le Pays est à ceux qui peuvent le vendre; et ils ont de puissans motifs pour le conserver, pour le bien gouverner.

S'ils ne demandent rien aux autres, leur Souveraineté est utile à tous et ne peut opprimer personne. Elle protège tout et tous: Elle admet à ses honneurs tous ceux qui sont assez économes et assez Sages pour arriver à l'acquisition d'un bien fonds. Elle ne repousse que l'inconduite ou le brigandage. Le Peuple libre et exempt de taxes n'a rien a désirer: un bon esprit peut le conduire à tout

Les révoltes dans les Républiques Sont toujours venues de ce que les nobles, ou les citoyens, voulaient faire payer le bas Peuple, gêner son travail, en exiger des Services humilians.—Un Ambitieux Se met à la tête de ces pauvres gens dont le travail et la propriété mobiliaire nont pas été respectés. Il les fait Pillards, et ils le font Prince.

Le Prince ou Ses Successeurs Se font détestes, parce que leur place les corrompt, et que le Pouvoir arbitraire est naturellement odieux.

Quelques gens d'esprit et les Riches le détronent et Se partagent

Ses dépouilles. mais ils croient ordinairement avoir hérité de son pouvoir. Ils regardent la faculté de vexer les classes inférieures comme un droit de la République ou de la Souveraineté

Qu'arrive-t-il? Le Peuple se révolte de nouveau, et d'une démocratie exagerée retombe toujours Sous une Tyrannie insupportable

Voila le cercle que toutes les Nations ont parcouru jusqu'à présent, et dont il faut Sortir: dont on Sortira très aisément avec un faible degré de lumieres de plus que l'on n'en a.

Si l'on excepte les nations entierement abruties on trouvera partout des Sentimens républicains. Et même Sous un certain aspect tous les Etats Sont déja des Républiques, ou très prets à le devenir. Ceux qu'on appelle des Monarchies Sont des Républiques où le Pouvoir exécutif et le Pouvoir législatif sont mal constitués, dans lesquelles le veritable souverain est opprimé, ou peut l'être par Ses délegués. Son droit pourtant n'est pas tout à fait méconnu. Nul Prince n'ôse et ne peut Se regarder que comme le Représentant ou le délegué des Propriétaires du Sol.

Nul homme n'ôse ni ne peut dire une Nation m'appartient. Nul homme ne peut dire j'ai le droit arbitraire de faire tout ce qu'il me plait. Nul n'ôse[7] dire j'ai le droit de commettre des crimes et de faire des injustices. ce n'est que le droit de rendre justice que réclament les despotes les plus absolus.

Il faut donc avant tout Savoir ce qui est juste. Il faut que tout le monde sache et ce qui est juste, et ce qui est utile, et que ces deux choses là ne Sont pas Séparables. Il faut qu'on reconnaisse que toute Loi vient de dieu qui a pour Ministres le calcul, la raison, et la Compassion.

Ces notions Simples Sont tellement naturelles qu'elles Sont entrées dans tous les esprits et dans tous les coeurs dès le tems de la formation des Langues, qui fut certainement celui des premieres ébauches de la Société. Il n'y a pas une Langue qui nait le mot Législateur ou Son équivalent. Il n'en est pas une Seule qui ait employé celui de légisfacteur, ni aucun équivalent.—Pourquoi cela? C'est que l'on a Senti, au moins confusément, qu'il S'agissait de bien comprendre le principe de la Loi, qui doit toujours être dans la nature, dans la morale, dans l'équite; et que la Loi êtant ainsi conçue, il n'est plus question que de la montrer,[8] de la démontrer, de la porter, de la présenter brillante de Son[9] pur éclat, appuyée de l'assentiment général et de la force Sociale, à l'obeïssance des Citoyens. On a Senti qu'il n'etait donné à aucun Homme de la faire: car le juste et l'injuste ne dépendent pas de nous.—Loi injuste, contra jus, contre le droit ou Les droits, renferme un contresens grossier dans les mots et dans les choses. Ce qui est injuste peut être Ordonnance; mais cette Ordonnance ne Saurait être[10] obligatoire pour la conscience:[11] ce qui est injuste n'est pas loi. Nulle Autorité nulle force[12] ne peut lui en imprimer le caractere. Obéis ou je te tue, ne prouve rien, sinon que l'on commet un crime en me menasest.[13] Si l'ordre est injuste, et que Si dans ce cas, l'on me tuait, on en commettrait deux.

ce Sont vos maximes, Excellent Philosophe; et c'est pourquoi je vous aime et vous respecte tant. DUPONT (DE NEMOURS)

EDITORS' TRANSLATION

MY VERY RESPECTABLE FRIEND, 12 December 1811.

I received through Mr. Barlow your letter of 15 April with much gratitude. A man like you may retire from office but never from public affairs. You are a magistrate of mankind.

So much the better if the establishment of manufacturing in your country does not oblige you to change your financial system as quickly as one might have feared.

But it must happen some day, and your government and especially public opinion must be prepared for it. The science of political economy must not be ignored or neglected in the United States.—Where would the most important questions be debated if not in a republic that respects the freedom of the press, one that is now the last in existence and the last hope for all those that are yet to be born, which it will propagate like a queen bee?—How could sovereigns refuse to discuss their interests, rights, and duties in a century in which enlightenment, though less general and intense than thirty years ago, is nevertheless far from extinguished?

I regret very much not being able to contribute to the discussion directly. I will never be able to write fluently in English. One cannot learn, after sixty years, to express oneself well in a language that was foreign to one's youth. But Mr. Patterson, whom you recommended to me, has promised to translate my essay on finance and the Essay Sur l'éducation nationale dans les Etats-Unis d'Amérique: two works that you inspired and that I owe to your kindness.—He even promised to translate my Table raisonné des principes de l'economie politique as well.—I will ask him to give you the translations once they are completed, so that you may use your admirable talents to point out any corrections that you believe to be necessary. He is a very promising young man.

I see with pleasure that the United States has some time before it must make a decision regarding its public revenues, that the disappearance of its debts will greatly and promptly diminish its political needs, and that the consumption of foreign goods by the wealthy will provide customs revenues for a few more years, if you are able to stay out of the war.

If war cannot be avoided, consolidate your union with the Floridas and form one with Canada. Fortify your harbors, and especially New York, as Governor's Island is insufficient to defend it. Then make peace.—During the first year, a maritime war would give your privateers some corrupting advantages of the worst kind, but it would soon result in the loss of much of your capital and many precious men. The taking of your sailors and their being drafted into the English navy would considerably increase England's strength relative to the United States. Do not put your children at risk of killing their fathers.—The necessity of feeding the inhabitants of the British Isles will induce them to make their peace terms less objectionable.

Depending on events, these circumstances may either delay or hasten your need for a new financial system. Thank God that He grants your government and citizenry time to think about it at your leisure. Given your nation's serious and cautious nature, you would be the most inexcusable people on earth if you made a blunder in a matter of such high importance.

You assume that you have, since the start of your wise administration, given the deathblow to the excise system unhappily tried by General Hamilton. You have done a very good thing.—However, if the land tax continues to be disliked in your eastern territory, the part of the United States that is best cultivated and has the good fortune of not having slaves, your success cannot be complete. You might have a relapse.

The principal mistakes relative to taxation arise from two motives: first, the desire to have everyone contribute, especially workers, merchants, and entrepreneurs. That goal is unattainable, because there is no way to prevent workers from selling their labor dearly and merchants from loaning out their money at high interest, to the detriment of landed proprietors.

The other mistake comes from a higher motive. It results from a lack of sound ideas as to what makes up a political society and what society owes to landowners and nonlandholding entrepreneurs.

The latter are members of a universal republic without magistrates. They are found in every nation, and the governments and citizens of every country with a constitution owes them the freedom to work, immunity from taxation, free participation in the good order that results from all lawful societies, and eligibility for office if they are meritorious and the voters wish to elect them.—When they are elected to office or have bought land, which they must be allowed to do, they become citizens. Up to that point, they were only residents.—Freedom, exemption from taxation, personal safety, and legal protection of their possessions and contracts: these are the extent and limit of their rights. To give them more would be as unreasonable as to give servants the right to manage household affairs in conjunction with their masters.—To make them pay for the exercise of their natural rights would be to act like the miser who steals his horses' hay. Their services would become more expensive and of a lesser quality.

The rights of citizenship and sovereignty—to sit and deliberate in political assemblies, to vote, to promulgate laws and have them carried out—belong exclusively to landowners, because only they are members of a particular republic with a territory that must be administered.

When we move away from these bases of civilized society or when we believe, or pretend to believe, that those having only their two arms or movable property are citizens just like the proprietors of the soil and have the right to ask for a part of the nation's wealth without acquiring it, or to deliberate on laws regarding the ownership of land that they do not possess, we foment storms, set the stage for revolutions, and prepare the way for the likes of

Pisistratus, Marius, and Caesar, who made themselves *more democratic* than nature, justice, and reason require in order to become *tyrants*, and to violate every right, substitute their will for the law, offend morality, and debase mankind.

In a republic that wishes to remain peaceful, durable, and free from turmoil, no class must be, or think itself to be, oppressed and wish for protectors so that it can take its turn as the oppressor. The role of protector is much coveted, and candidates are always to be found.

Everyone must be allowed to work and acquire things without being harassed. All must be able to speak and publish their opinions, as long as no one is insulted or, even worse, slandered. That is what freedom of speech and of the press consists of. But expressing one's thoughts *informally*, or deliberating *officially* and *voting*, are two very different things.—Everyone has the right to watch over his own business and defend his personal interests, as long as this right is shared with other people. No one has the right to meddle in other people's business without cause.—Thus, when labor or commerce is hindered, all merchants have the right to complain and prove that the public has infringed their natural liberty. And if ill-conceived laws force them to pay some of their taxes in advance, they have the right (one that they never fail to exercise) to compensate for it by raising their salaries or the price of their merchandise in at least an equivalent proportion.

But they do not have the right to consider themselves to be full citizens until they have purchased land. Nor can they attend town assemblies in the district in which they live, and they can only become representatives of their town or county in another assembly through the free choice of the voters. If they are appointed to any public office by the electors or the government, then they have the right to fulfill the duties that have been entrusted to them. Nothing more.

The question will be asked: *Why should they not pay for the protection and assistance they receive from the laws and the public sector?*—They enjoy these benefits because they can be denied to no one, and because we owe them to the most unknown stranger that sets foot in the country. What kind of government would allow stealing from, insulting, hitting, or killing those who do not happen to be citizens? That would be a government of barbarians.

Through landownership one gains a permanent interest and a habit of useful work that becomes a guarantee of reasonableness. Landowners' assemblies are neither too numerous nor tumultuous. *The country belongs to those who can sell it*, and they have powerful motives to protect and govern it well.

If they ask nothing of others, their sovereignty is nevertheless useful to everyone and can oppress no one. It protects everyone and everything. It bestows honors on those who are thrifty and wise enough to acquire landed property. It repels only misconduct and thievery. The people, free and exempt from taxes, wish for nothing. A good disposition of mind can take them anywhere they desire.

Revolts in republics have always arisen from the attempts of nobles or full citizens to make the lower classes pay taxes, to hinder their labor, and to demand humiliating services.—An ambitious person puts himself at the helm and leads these poor people, whose labor and personal property have not been respected. He makes them pillage and plunder, and they make him a prince.

The prince or his successors come to be loathed, because their position corrupts them and arbitrary rule is odious by nature.

Some quick-witted people and the rich dethrone the prince and share the spoils, and they think they have inherited his power. They regard insulting the lower classes as a right of the republic or of sovereignty.

What happens? The people revolt again, and, from an excess of democracy, inevitably fall back into an unbearable tyranny.

This is the cycle that all nations have followed up to now: the one from which we must steer clear and from which we will free ourselves very easily with only slightly more wisdom than has been shown in the past.

If we set aside nations that are entirely bereft of reason, we will find republican sentiments everywhere. It can even be said that, from a certain point of view, all states are already republics or close to becoming one. Those that we call monarchies are republics in which the executive and the legislative branches of government are badly constituted and in which the true sovereign is, or may be, oppressed by his delegates. His rights, however, are not totally ignored. No prince dares to regard himself as other than the representative or delegate of the landowners.

No man dares to say, nor can he say, a nation belongs to me. No man can say, I have the arbitrary right to do everything I please. No one dares to say, I have the right to commit crimes and act unjustly. The most absolute do not claim any more than the right to dispense justice.

We must therefore first of all know what is just. Everyone must know what is just and what is useful, and all must see that these two things are inseparable. We need to recognize that all laws come from God, whose ministers are thoughtfulness, reason, and compassion.

These simple notions are so natural that they have made their way into every heart and mind ever since the time when languages, which were certainly some of the earliest sketches of society, were first formed. No language lacks the word legislator or its equivalent. None have ever used legisfactor or its equivalent.—Why is that? Because it was felt, at least vaguely, that it is important to understand clearly the principle behind all law, which is always to be found in nature, morality, and equity. Thus conceived, the law has only to be shown, demonstrated, circulated, and presented in its pure, shining light for the citizens to obey, supported as it is by general consent and society's will. It was felt that no man could make it, because the just and the unjust do not depend on us.—Unjust law, against the law, against right or rights is the veriest nonsense. An edict may be unjust, but it could not possibly be obligatory on one's conscience: that which is unjust is not law. No authority or force can change its character. Obey or I will kill you does not prove anything other than that a crime is being committed in threatening me. If the order is unjust, and I am, in this instance, killed, then two crimes have been perpetrated.

These are your maxims, excellent philosopher, and that is why I love and respect you so much.

DuPont de Nemours

RC (DLC); at head of text: "a Thomas Jefferson"; endorsed by TJ as received 26 Feb. 1812 and so recorded in SJL. Tr (DeGH: H. A. Du Pont Papers); posthumous copy. Translation by Dr. Roland H. Simon.

[1] Preceding ten words interlined.

[2] Word interlined in place of "publics."

[3] Sentence to this point and preceding two sentences interlined in place of "puis faites la paix.—Une guerre maritime

donnerait" ("then make peace—a maritime war would give").

[4] Preceding ten words interlined in place of "vous accorde le tems" ("grants you the time").

[5] Tr: "cheveux" ("hair").

[6] Word interlined in place of "cherche" ("look for").

[7] Tr: "Nul ne peut" ("No one can").

[8] Preceding eight words interlined in place of "il la montrer" ("to show it").

[9] Tr: "dans" ("in").

[10] Remainder of letter written perpendicularly in margin.

[11] Preceding three words interlined.

[12] Preceding two words interlined.

[13] RC and Tr: "menasest" (for "menacer" ["to threaten"]).

From John Low

Respected Sir — Washington City. Decr 15th 1811

About 2 weeks ago I sent you p^{r} mail a Sett of the Encyclopædia, accompanied[1] with a letter, which I hope you have received. Being doubtful however whither they might have arrived I have thought proper to write you a few more lines, on the subject.—As I shall return in a few days, for newyork, by way of Baltimore, I would be extremely glad if the amount, (which is 75$) could be forwarded on to the last mentioned place, within a week from this; or after that to Newyork, directed to me.—I remain yours with

the greatest respect — Jno Low.

P.S. Not being acquainted with any of your correspondents, I take this mode of conveyance.—

RC (DLC); endorsed by TJ as received 25 Dec. 1811 and so recorded in SJL.

[1] Manuscript: "accompained."

From John Crawford

Highly respected Sir! — Baltimore 17th Decr 1811

In 1808 I did myself the honour to forward to you a periodical paper, the Observer, then published here, in which I made some communications on the cause and seat of diseases. I have been engaged with that subject ever since, in composing Lectures which I hope to deliver this winter. I presume to think I have brought it to a considerable degree of perfection and trust I shall be able to offer what will prove generally useful. The inclosed is a copy of my first Lecture, which contains the plan I propose to pursue. If you should honour it with a perusal, you will not meet with any of the technical language which renders medical works so revolting to those who are not of the profession. You will perceive Sir! that I have experienced the fate of nearly all who have endeavoured to accomplish reformation, or direct the views of men from a path, to which they have been long accustomed. Although I have held situations highly lucrative, the disposition of my mind has not led me to profit by them. Had I possessed such a disposition, I should have been unfitted for my present undertaking. I am however, urged by a spirit of perseverance in pursuit of the course I have adopted, and if I am enabled to develop the truth, hitherto concealed, its irresistable influence must, in the end prevail.

When I did myself the honour to address you in 1803, on the state of public affairs, I took the liberty to suggest my views of the principles on which they were founded. The intervening period has presented nothing to invalidate those views. The catastrophe is hastening to completion; the fate of England can not remain long undecided. Her exclusion of foreign commerce is now retorted on her whilst her own is verging fast to destruction; and the war she is carrying on in Portugal and Spain, notwithstanding momentary appearances, affording not a shadow of ultimate success, must So exhaust her tottering resources that it certainly requires no great depth of wisdom to foresee an event which is advancing with so much rapidity.

My ideas also[1] respecting the fate we are to experience from our Slaves appears to be but too well founded. I find the expected crisis is now freely spoken of in Congress, and yet no attempt is made to obviate the storm. On the contrary, the steps pursued are directly calculated to accelerate its approach. The most worthless and the most audacious are daily sent from this and perhaps some of the states in the vicinity to the Southward, where the embers of conflagration, at present couvered by the slightest tissue, will probably, by these be quickly blown into a flame which will consume all to whom it can have access. I have been long satisfied we shall not have a war with any European power. We can not, if my conception of the present trans-atlantic conflict be correct: the seperation of the temporal from the ecclesiastical power; this has been effected here, I am therefore to presume we shall feel no other consequence of it than in our commerce: on this the finger of Heaven seems now to be placed, on account of the prostration of morals it has entrained. Retribution awaits us where we have been still more culpable—I fear with you Sir! there is not virtue enough in those who are the objects of suffering, to induce their resort to any measures which might have a tendency to mitigate or avert the threatened evil. These are truly awful prospects on which it is distressing to dwell; but they are so continually presented to our view that the reflecting mind can not resist the impulse they excite.

May you highly respected Sir! long live in safety, to enjoy the exulting reflection of having saved your country when threatened with desolation, and receive the final reward of the multiplied benefits you conferred on those over whom you So honourably presided. Accept this tribute from him who is, with veneration yours most faithfully

JOHN CRAWFORD

RC (MHi); endorsed by TJ as received 29 Dec. 1811 and so recorded in SJL. Enclosure: Crawford, *A Lecture, introductory to a Course of Lectures on the Cause, Seat and Cure of Diseases proposed to be Delivered in the City of Baltimore* (Baltimore, 1811; Poor, *Jefferson's Library*, 5 [no. 198]).

John Crawford (1746–1813), physician, was a native of northern Ireland. Educated at Trinity College, Dublin, he worked as a surgeon in Barbados and Demerara, the latter while it was still under Dutch rule. Crawford received medical degrees from the University of Saint Andrews in Scotland in 1791 and the University of Leiden in the Netherlands three years later. In 1796 he immigrated to Baltimore, where he soon established himself as an innovative medical practitioner. Crawford assembled a large reference library (acquired after his death by the University of Maryland in Baltimore), wrote on yellow fever and tropical diseases, doubted the efficacy of quarantines, and expounded the controversial belief that parasites and insects, some invisible to the naked eye, cause human diseases. He also helped to found the Maryland Society for Promoting Useful and Ornamental Knowledge and was heavily involved in the local dispensary, library, and penitentiary. Crawford was a consulting physician to the city hospital, a member of the board of health, an officer of the Medical and Chirurgical Faculty of the State of Maryland, and a prominent Freemason (*ANB*; *DAB*; Eugene Fauntleroy Cordell, *The Medical Annals of Maryland, 1799–1899* [1903], 758–70; Julia E. Wilson, "An Early Baltimore Physician and His Medical Library," *Annals of Medical History*, 3d ser., 4 [1942]: 63–80; Raymond N. Doetsch, "John Crawford and His Contribution to the Doctrine of *Contagium Vivum*," *Bacteriological Reviews* 28 [1964]: 87–96; *Baltimore Patriot*, 10 May 1813; Tobias Watkins, *An Eulogium on the Character of Brother John Crawford, M.D.* [Baltimore, 1813]).

In 1807, not 1808, Crawford sent TJ copies of the Baltimore *Observer* containing medical pieces he had written. His lengthy 1803 letter to TJ on the STATE OF PUBLIC AFFAIRS argued for gradual emancipation of OUR SLAVES (Crawford to TJ, 18 Oct. 1803, 18 Aug. 1807, 1 Dec. 1808 [DLC]).

[1] Manuscript: "also also."

From Benjamin Rush

MY DEAR OLD FRIEND Philadelphia Decem^r 17th 1811

Yours of Decem^r 5th came to hand yesterday. I was charmed with the Subject of it. In order to hasten the object you have suggested I sat down last evening, and selected such passages from your letter as contained the kindest expressions of regard for m^r Adams and transmitted them to him. my letter which contained them,[1] was concluded as nearly as I can recollect, for I kept no Copy of it, with the following words. "Fellow labourers in erecting the fabric of American liberty and independance!—fellow sufferers in the calumnies and falsehoods of party rage!—fellow heirs of the gratitude and Affection of posterity!—& fellow passengers in the same stage which must soon Convey you both into the presence of a Judge with whom the forgiveness and love of enemies is the only Condition of your acceptance!—embrace—embrace each Other. Bedew your letters of reconcilliation with tears of Affection and joy. Let there be no retrospect of your past differences. Explanations may be proper between contending lovers but they are never so between divided friends. were I near to you I would put a pen into your hand, and guide it while it wrote the following note to Mr Jefferson.

my dear old friend—and fellow labourer in the Cause of the liberties and independance of our Common Country, I salute you with the most Cordial good wishes for your health and happiness.

John Adams."

I sincerely hope this my second effort to revive a friendly intercourse[2] between you by letters will be successful. Patriotism—liberty—Science & Religion would all gain a triumph by it.

How cold the feelings! and how feeble!—The expressions of indignation in Congress against the outrages committed by G Britain[3] upon our rights, compared with what they were in 1774. and 1775, against outrages of a less degrading and insulting nature! Randolph seems to have composed his speeches from the fragments of the tory publications of those memorable years, with which his Opponents seem to be shamefully unacquainted. But All I hope will yet end well. Mr Madison has inflicted a sore blow upon my whole family by taking my son Richard from us. He has been my friend and Counsellor for many years, & he relinquishes great political as well as professional prospects in his native state by accepting the office lately given to him under the general Government. His talents and acquirements qualify him for active and professional pursuits, and his manners—for popular favor. They will all be lost to his Country and family in an Office in which the mind can have no employment, and in which a merchent, or the Cashier of a bank would be more respectable than even a Burke or a Fox.

I once said to Hamilton Roan whom I met in Company at the time when Porcupine was amusing and gratifying the tory[4] Citizens of Philadelphia with his publications against me,—that "I lived, like himself in a foreign Country." "no Sir you do not, (said he.) You live in an enemy's country;." This has been strictly true ever since the restoration of the tories to thier antirevolutionary rank by the officers of the general Government upon the removal of Congress from new

York to Philadelphia. Previously to that time, I was courted and employed by them, but it was with a View of protecting themselves by means of my influence,[5] from the rage of the insulted and triumphant party of which I was then a member—nor did they sue for my Services in Vain. I constantly advised forgiveness and Clemency to be exercised towards them. Often did I supplicate the Executive Council and Judges of our state in thier favor, and from my attempts to serve them, as Often incurred the censure of my whig friends. By One of them whom I was chiefly instrumental in saving from banishment, or perhaps a worse fate, I was publickly abused and betrayed in the year 1800. I need not name him to you. He has been called in one of our papers a "traitor by instinct." From this detail of my situation in Philad[a][6]—living only with my patients and pupils, judge how severely I feel the loss of the Society & the friendship[7] of my son Richard!—My 3rd son James who lately returned from Europe And who assists me in my business, is very amiable, and promising,—but what can eminence in the "mute Art" of medicine (as Ovid calls it)[8] do to protect a young and persecuted family, compared with eminence at the bar, and a popular political character?

These fireside Communications I am sure will be felt by you, for you are both a father, and a friend. All thier Sensibilities are familiar to you.

As my son has quitted professional, for Official life, and state, for national prospects, I hope he will be remembred in some future arrangements of office by M[r] Madison.—

Health, respect and friendship! from my Dear sir your Sincere old friend BENJ[N] RUSH

PS: a state of nature has been called a state of war. may not the same thing be said of civilized and even of the most polished Societies?[9] they fight only with different weapons.

Judge of the disposition to the Class of our Citizens which I have described, towards the old whigs by the following fact. an old tory in passing bye the public library room some time ago pointed to the statue of D[r] Franklin which is placed in a niche in the front part of it, and with an acrid Sneer said to a person who was walking with him "But for that old fellow, we never Should have had Independance."—

RC (DLC); endorsed by TJ as received 29 Dec. 1811 and so recorded in SJL.

Rush's LETTER to John Adams urging reconciliation with TJ is dated 16 Dec. 1811 (Rush, *Letters*, 2:1110–1). His SON RICHARD Rush was appointed United States comptroller general on 22 Nov. 1811 (*JEP*, 2:191). HAMILTON ROAN: Archibald Hamilton Rowan. Under the nom de plume of Peter PORCUPINE, William Cobbett published ferocious attacks on Rush's political views and medical theories (Rush, *Letters*, 2:1213–8). Rush intervened to save Tench Coxe from BANISHMENT, OR PERHAPS A WORSE FATE at his 1778 treason trial (*Philadelphia Gazette & Daily Advertiser*, 14 Oct. 1800). In 1800 Rush and Coxe became embroiled in a newspaper controversy over Coxe's assertion that President Adams had monarchical leanings (Jacob E. Cooke, *Tench Coxe and the Early Republic* [1978], 382–4).

[1] Reworked from "to him."

[2] Manuscript: "intercouse."

[3] Preceding three words interlined, with "by" substituted for "against" by Rush.

[4] Word interlined.

[5] Preceding four words interlined in place of "my whigs Connections."

[6] Preceding two words interlined.

[7] Manuscript: "frienship." Rush here canceled "& the perfection."

[8] Parenthetical phrase interlined.

[9] Manuscript: "Socities."

From Charles Clay

DEAR SIR, Dec. 18. 1811

your Servant yesterday met with me in the field where I was a little engaged & gave me your Note, I sent him to the house with the baskett & to wait till I Should return, he did not wait for me, he left the Compass & protractor, but no Chain nor Compass Staff.—that part of your note respecting the hearth Stones will be particularly attended to Should I see the Masons as well as any other Command with which Mr Jefferson may think fit to honor

his Friend & humble Ser^t^ C. CLAY

RC (MHi); addressed: "Tho. Jefferson Esquire"; twice endorsed by TJ as received 18 Dec. 1811 and so recorded in SJL.

TJ's NOTE to Clay is not recorded in SJL and has not been found.

To William or Reuben Mitchell

SIR Poplar Forest Dec. 18. 11.

I did not bring with me from home the papers respecting my wheat ground at your mill of the crop of 1810. but I have, in a letter written from home to Doct^r^ Callaway on that subject a very exact statement made out on a view of all the papers. I recieved (according to the accounts rendered me by Gibson & Jefferson) 232. barrels of flour. most of them were superfine; the number of fine I have no note of here, but I know they were very few, and therefore I shall take no notice of them. they sold for from 9. to 9¾ D. but averaged 9¼ D. the expences of carriage, toll, Comm^n^ E^t^c. were 1½ Dollar a barrel, so that they netted me $7\frac{3}{4}$. D. a barrel. considering the wheat retained as flour netting this much you will be able to settle the difference between that & the half dollar a barrel due for Superfine.

I have requested mr Griffin to agree with Col[o] Watts & yourself on a day when our other matter may be setled either at Col[o] Watts's or Lynchburg. Accept the assurances of my respect

TH: JEFFERSON

P.S. Dec. 19. since writing the above I have found that I was mistaken in supposing that mr Griffin had sent the overseers' share of the wheat to another mill. that was a transaction of the last year, which I had confounded with the present. he is entitled to 81. bushels & Roberts to 49. making 130. bushels of what was delivered you. he is consequently a party interested in the question between us.

PoC (MHi); adjacent to signature: "M[r] Mitchell"; endorsed by TJ.

On 19 May 1812 TJ settled his "wheat accounts for 1810. & 1811" with William & Reuben Mitchell. The OVERSEERS' SHARE of the wheat crop proved to be somewhat smaller than TJ had originally estimated, with Burgess Griffin receiving \$47.80 for $63\frac{1}{3}$ bushels and Thomas Roberts \$28.61 for $38\frac{1}{9}$ bushels. TJ's "part was 699. bushels which @ 4/6 as arbitrated = \$524.25" (*MB*, 2:1277).

Letters from Burgess Griffin to TJ of 8 Nov., 21 Dec. 1811, and 10 Jan. 1812, not found, are recorded in SJL as received on 22 Dec. (from Poplar Forest), 26 Dec. 1811 (from Lynchburg), and 22 Jan. 1812. SJL also records missing letters from TJ to Griffin of 17 and 30 Dec. 1811.

Although he did not mention it in his correspondence, TJ "Felt shock of an earthquake abt. 4. oclock of the 16th" (*MB*, 2:1272). This earthquake, discerned as far away as Georgia and Massachusetts, was the first of a series of tremors and aftershocks centered near New Madrid in what is now southeastern Missouri and continuing for months (James Madison to TJ, 7 Feb. 1812; Elizabeth Trist to TJ, 24 Mar. 1812; William Leigh Pierce, *An Account of the Great Earthquakes, in the Western States particularly on the Mississippi River; December 16–23, 1811* [Newburyport, Mass., 1812]; Samuel L. Mitchill, "A Detailed Narrative of the Earthquakes which occurred on the 16th day of December, 1811 . . . ," *Transactions of the Literary and Philosophical Society of New York* 1 [1815]: 281–307).

From Charles Pinckney

DEAR SIR December 18: 1811 In Columbia

It is sometime since I had the pleasure to write to you but as I know the pleasure you will feel in finding that the Spirit of our first revolutionary Years still exists I take the liberty of inclosing you a Report which at the request of a Committee I have drawn & submitted to this House & which has just unanimously passed without the alteration of a single word—

As the Post goes out in an hour & I am now writing in the midst of the House of Representatives I have only time to inclose it to you & to say that the Spirit of our state is fully up to it & are only waiting the Signal that Congress will unfurl the Standard of the Nation, to rally round it—

allthough less in a situation to promote manufactures than the Northern States for want of sufficient white hands & Wool yet we are beginning to emulate them—great numbers of our planters this Year clothe their own negros & all our planters nearly in the Upper & middle parts of the state ($\frac{3}{4}^{th}$ of our white population—) are now clothed in homespun—more than $\frac{1}{2}$ of the house of Representatives in which I now write are clothed in it & Mr Gibert a member for Abbeville is at this moment sitting close to me dressed in a suit made from a mixture of wool & silk, both the Growth of his own plantation so handsomely & finely woven & dyed that it would do honour to any manufacture in Europe—

with the most affectionate respect & Esteem I am dear sir always Your's Truly

CHARLES PINCKNEY

RC (DLC); dateline beneath signature; endorsed by TJ as received 14 Jan. 1812 and so recorded in SJL.

Pinckney chaired a committee of the South Carolina House of Representatives appointed to consider the portion of Gov. Henry Middleton's annual message relating to foreign relations. The enclosed REPORT stated that "they could not avoid being deeply impressed with a sense of the injuries and humiliations inflicted on our beloved country, by the unprecedented and violent conduct of the belligerents of Europe" and hoped "that such a stand will be taken by the general government, at the present session of its legislature, as will effectually tend to secure the free enjoyment of the rights we are entitled to by the laws of nations." It added that, "France having withdrawn her obnoxious decrees, its now to be expected that Great Britain will follow her example . . . if she does not, a vigorous and decisive resort will be had to those means of defence, with which a bountiful providence has so amply supplied us, and which, in the opinion of your committee, are the only alternatives for the consideration of a government, worthy of conducting the destinies of the republic." The report also included a similarly patriotic address to President James Madison (printed broadside in DNA: RG 59, MLR, filed at 18 Dec. 1811).

Pinckney sent similar letters to Madison and to James Monroe on 18 Dec. 1811, and the South Carolina House of Representatives unanimously approved the address the same day and sent it to Madison on 22 Dec. 1811 (Madison, *Papers, Pres. Ser.*, 4:75–6, 83–7; letter to Monroe in DNA: RG 59, MLR).

Notes on the Latitude of Willis's Mountain

[ca. 19 Dec. 1811]

Latitude of Willis's mountain by observations of the Sun's meridian altitude taken from the peak on the right side of the gap, & next adjacent to it, as seen from Monticello.

	° ′ ″
1811. Nov. 21. Meridian alt. of ☉ by observn*	32–37–20[1]
Dec. 18.	29– 2–50[2]
19	29– 4–50[3]

the 1st by Th:J. the 2. last by Th:J.R.

---

other elements for the calculation.

Willis's mountains being 62.′ E. of the South as seen from Mont° and 40.[5] common miles distant, it's meridian will be .72136 of a mile E. of yt of Monticello. a degree of longitude in Lat. 37°–30′ = 47.6 geogr. mi. = 54.74 com. miles then .72136 of a common mile = 47.4″[6] of longitude

	° ′ ″
which subtracted from ye long. of Mont°	78–50–18.877
gives diffce of long. betw Greenwich & W's M.	78–49–31.477

		° ′ ″
Nov. 21. ☉'s meridian altitude by observn		32–37–20[7]
	′ ″	
– refraction	1–29	
+ parallax	8	1–21
true Alt. of ☉'s center		32–35–59[8]
		90–
Zenith distance		57–24– 1[9]
	° ′ ″	
☉'s decln at Greenwich	19–48–13	
increase for 78°– 50′– 19″[10]	2–42.8	19–50–56
		37–33– 5

---

*

	° ′	
	65–18	
–	3–20	error of[4] instrument
	65–14–40	
÷ 2	32–37–20	

		° ′ ″
Dec.[11] 18. ⊙'s merid. alt. by observn	′ ″	*29– 2–50
– refraction	1–42	
+ parallax	8	1–34
true alt. of ⊙'s center		29– 1–16
		90–
Zenith distance		60–58–44
	° ′ ″	
⊙'s decln Greenwich	23–23–34	
increase for 78°– 50′– 19″[12]	–17	23–23–34
Lat. of Willis's Mount[n]		37–35–10[13]

Dec. 19. Merid. Alt. of ⊙ by observn	′ ″	† 29– 4–50[14]
– refraction	1–42	
+ parallax	8	1–34
true alt. of ⊙'s center.		29– 3–16[15]
		90–
Zenith distance		60–56–44[16]
	° ′ ″	
⊙'s decln at Greenwich	23–25–18	
increase for 78°– 50′– 19″[17]	11	23–25–29
Lat. of Willis's Mountain		37–31–15[18]

Th:J.R's observn of Dec. 18. gives Lat.		37–35–10[19]
19.		37–31–15[20]
		75– 6–25[21]
mean		37–33–12.5[22]
Th:J's observation Nov. 21. gives		37–33– 5[23]
difference		7.5″
Lat. of Monticello	38– 8	
W's Mount[n]	37–33– 5	
difference	34–55 = 40.15 miles	

	° ′	
*	58– 9	by the instrum[t]
–	3–20	error of instrum[t]
	58– 5–40	
÷ 2.	29– 2–50	

†	58–13	by the instrum[t]
–	3–20	error of instrum[t]
	58– 9–40	
÷ 2.	29– 4–50	

MS (Roger W. Barrett, Chicago, 1947); written entirely in TJ's hand on both sides of a single sheet; undated.

On 20 Nov. 1811 TJ was at Mill Brook, the residence of his son-in-law John Wayles Eppes, located in eastern Buckingham County about three miles from Willis's Mountain. He was staying at Poplar Forest on 18 and 19 Dec. 1811 (*MB*, 2:1271, 1272).

TH:J.R.: Thomas Jefferson Randolph. The geographical (GEOGR.) mile is defined as one minute of arc along the equator, or approximately 1,850 meters (*OED*).

[1] Reworked from "32–35–40."
[2] Reworked from "29–2–10."
[3] Reworked from "29–3–10."
[4] TJ here canceled "observn."
[5] Reworked from "35."
[6] Reworked from "45."
[7] Reworked from "32–35–40."
[8] Reworked from "32–34–19."
[9] Reworked from "57–25–41."
[10] Reworked from "78°–34′–20″."
[11] Verso begins with this word.
[12] Reworked from "78°–34′–20″."
[13] Reworked from "37–36–30."
[14] Reworked from "29–3–10."
[15] Reworked from "29–1–36."
[16] Reworked from "60–58–24."
[17] Reworked from "78°–34′–20″."
[18] Reworked from "37–32–55."
[19] Reworked from what appears to be "37–37–13."
[20] Reworked from what appears to be "37–32–15."
[21] Reworked from "75–9–28."
[22] Reworked from "37–34–14."
[23] Reworked from "37–32–[. . .]."

Petition of Albemarle County Residents to Virginia General Assembly

[before 19 Dec. 1811]

To the General Assembly of Virginia the memorial & Petition of the subscribers Inhabitants of the county of Albemarle humbly Represents, That a spirit for the extension & improvement of domestic manufactures exists at present throughout the state of Virginia with an ardor which requires only a slight degree of Legislative[1] encouragement to render it permanent; & place us in some respects independent of Foreign nations. Your Petitioners beg leave to state that, influenced by the spirit above mentioned, much of their attention has of late been devoted to the increase & improvement of their flocks of Sheep; & many of them at great expense & trouble have improved the quality of their wool by the introduction of the best breeds from Spain & other foreign countries.

That nothing is calculated to repress their present ardor in the breeding of sheep, but the ravages they are subject to from Dogs, who in one night may not only devour their property to an immense amount, but may damp & perhaps forever destroy all future enterprise & energy in the same cause. The only remedy for this evil, they concieve is to lessen the number of dogs so that what remain, being better fed, will have no inducement to plunder, & the only way to lessen their number must be by partial Taxation.

Therefore, as well to protect & encourage the raising of Sheep, as to indemnify the ravages committed on them by dogs, your Petitioners pray for the passage of a Law conformable to the following outlines, which they leave to the wisdom of the Legislature to make General or not, but which they pray may become at any rate a law for the county of Albemarle, & such other counties as may petition to the Same effect.—

"Let each Houskeeper in the county keep one dog free of Tax: but for every second dog lay a Tax of fifty cents & for every dog over two, on the same farm lay a Tax of one dollar for each. This tax to be collected in the usual manner but the money to be retained in the hands of the Sherrif to be hereafter appropriated."[2]

"When a person shall sustain a loss among his sheep by dogs, let three freeholders, (in the manner directed for the appraisement of Estrays) asscertain his loss; taking into consideration the quality & breed of the sheep. Their certificate to be filed With the clerk, & the court at the end of each year to appropriate the money arising from the Tax on dogs towards defraying these losses. If the money is sufficient[3] let the losses be defrayed in full, if not let it be in due proportion, & if there is an excess, let it go towards defraying the expenses of the county, as the court shall think proper."

"In Towns, (if the law is made general) let the money go towards paving their streets, or any other way the corporation shall think best."

Your Petitioners indulge The hope that your honorable Body can see no objection[4] to making an Evil thus remedy itself; which besides diminishing the danger to be apprehended from mad Dogs, (a consideration by no means unimportant) and calculating that such a Law would reduce the present number of Dogs one half, upon a fair estimate, in the article of food alone, would produce to the county of Albemarle a clear saving of Ten Thousand Dollars ꝑ annum.

And your Petitioners &C &C—

D. Shiner	Frank Carr	J Rodes
John H. Craven	Martin Dawson	John a Michie
D: Carr	Wm Woods	William Gillaspy
Henry Chiles	Micajah Woods	Ths M Randolph
George Divers	Thos Eston Randolph	John Rothwell
Samuel Carr	David Wood	Rbn Lindsay
P. Minor	Jno Rogers	Eli Alexander
	Z Shackleford	J Bullock

James Scott
Thos Amonett
John Gilmer
John Watson
James McKinney
Immanuel Poor
Charles Yancey
Charles Flanagan
Jonathan Barksdale
Reuben Maury
Th: Jefferson
David J Lewis
Robt C Nicholas
Jno, H, Wood
W Stevens
Wm Dunkum
John Goss
Jo^{s} Mills
John S Abell
James Henderson
Pleasant Dawson
John Nicholas
Geo Gilmer
Christopher Hudson
Lewis Mahanes
Wm Broadhead
Benj Mathews
James Roberts
James Jefferies
A Brodhead

John Gillum
Richd Shackelford
Thos Carter
Robt Gillack
Allen Dawson
Jonathan Browning
John Smith
Phillip Darrell
Harrison Wood
Robt W. Cullock jr
Nelson Barksdale
John Fretwell
John Lewis
C Peyton
James Horsley
Charles Lively
Nowel Kerby
Thos Johnson
Eli Austin
Benajah Gentry
<*Wiley Dickerson*>

[*Signatures on Dupl:*]

John Patterson
Reu. Johnson
W^{m} A, Shelton
Nelson Freeland
Silas H Smith
Thomas Daniel
Tandy Morris
Saml Shelton

Jesse Thomas Ju^{r}
Nathaniel Goolsby
Jno Coles
W. C. Nicholas
Christopher Hudson

MS (Vi: RG 78, Legislative Petitions, Albemarle Co.); in an unknown hand except for seventy-four signatures, one of which is canceled; undated; endorsed: "Petition from Albemarle for preservation of sheep rec^{d} Decr 19th 1811. ref^{d} to

Props[s] (reasonable) reported Bill drawn." Dupl (Vi: RG 78, Legislative Petitions, Albemarle Co.); in a different hand from MS, with thirteen signatures; undated; endorsed: "Petition from Albemarle."

The Virginia House of Delegates received this petition on 19 Dec. 1811 and referred it on 31 Dec. to its Committee of Propositions and Grievances, which reported on 15 Jan. 1812 that it was "reasonable." A bill was accordingly drafted, presented on 23 Jan., and rejected on 7 Feb. 1812. The failed statute had the same provisions and sometimes drew on the language of the recommendations in the petition while leaving blanks for the amounts of the fines and adding language requiring that lists of taxable dogs be kept, authorizing magistrates to order the killing of dogs traveling with slaves or dogs that killed or injured sheep, and fining owners who concealed dogs that had been ordered killed (*JHD*, 1811–12 sess., 42, 53–4, 82, 122; Dft bill in Vi: RG 79, House of Delegates, Rough Bills; in an unidentified hand; endorsed: "A bill to prevent the destruction of Sheep in this commonwealth Presented Jan[y] 23[d] 1812. [Rejected—]").

On 26 Jan. 1814 the Virginia legislature passed a similar law, entitled "An Act to prevent the destruction of Sheep in this Commonwealth," which levied a $1 tax on DOGS above six months of age. All housekeepers could keep one dog tax-free, and persons occupying plantations could have two. Part of the proceeds were to go to "the overseers of the poor, or trustees of charitable institutions." Furthermore, any "magistrate, having sufficient proof that sheep have been killed or worried by any dog or dogs" was "required to order the same to be killed" or face a fine of $2 a day for each such dog. The act applied to many but not all Virginia counties. Ironically, Albemarle and Bedford were among those exempted (*Acts of Assembly*, 1813–14 sess., 55–6).

[1] Word omitted from Dupl.

[2] Omitted closing quotation mark editorially supplied.

[3] MS: "sufficent." Dupl: "sufficient."

[4] Preceding two words omitted from Dupl.

From John W. Campbell

DEAR SIR! Petersburg 20th Dec: 1811

After reviewing the papers contained in the volumes you were pleased to lend me, I have concluded to decline their publication, principally from the reasons suggested in your letter, that they would at this day, be not interesting to the mass of readers.

I return the volumes, with my sincere thanks for the loan of them.

I am

Dear Sir With the highest respect & esteem yr. mo: obdt Ser[t]

JOHN W. CAMPBELL

RC (DLC); endorsed by TJ as received 29 Dec. 1811 and so recorded in SJL.

For the PAPERS authored by TJ and now returned to him, see TJ to Campbell, 1 Oct. 1809, and note. TJ's LETTER of 3 Sept. 1809 warned him that reprinting these writings might not return a profit.

From John W. Campbell

Dear Sir! Petersburg Dec: 20th 1811

I have taken the liberty of enclosing you a proposal for a work which I expect to publish during the next Summer.

I have progressed in this work, as far as the year Seventy Six, but for the period, subsequent to that, I find it extremely difficult to procure materials.

I would be much gratified by your advice as to the best sources of information; [an]d if you have any thing, that would yield [any?] assistance, particularly in the period subsequent to the revolution, you would do me a singular favour by lending it for a few months.

Excuse my freedom, & accept for your health and happiness the best wishes of

Dear Sir Yr mo: obdt Svt John W. Campbell

RC (DLC); damaged at seal; endorsed by TJ as received 5 Jan. 1812 and so recorded in SJL.

The enclosed PROPOSAL, not found, was a prospectus for Campbell's *History of Virginia, from Its Discovery Till the Year 1781: with Biographical Sketches of all the most distinguished characters that occur in the colonial, revolutionary, or subsequent period of our history* (Philadelphia, 1813).

From Pierre Samuel Du Pont de Nemours

Monsieur, 20 Xbre 1811.

J'ai eu l'honneur de vous adresser ces jours derniers une Lettre assez étendue que Mr Barlow veut bien vous envoyer par la Frégate des Etats-Unis La Constitution.

J'apprends aujourd'hui que cette même Frégate portera en Amérique Mr de Correa de Serra, Portugais distingué, l'un des meilleurs Correspondans de notre classe à l'Institut, et qui Serait comme vous également bien placé à la premiere.

quand nous avons eu l'honneur de vous nommer Associé étranger, nous êtions Classe des Sciences morales et politiques. C'était une troisieme espece d'Académie qui valait bien les deux autres, où vous êtiez un membre très éminent, et où Mr de Correa Se serait aussi fort bien trouvé.

L'Histoire nous reste: C'est une très belle attribution. Pour ne la point perdre, nous n'en abusons pas; et même nous en usons gueres. Cependant la Classe S'est une fois Souvenue que cette noble Science était de Son domaine, et elle ne S'y est pas montrée inférieure à ce qu'on devait attendre d'elle.

C'est encore un genre d'étude où Mr de Corréa se ferait remarquer.

S'il n'était pas déja de notre Société philosophique de Philadelphie, je prendrais la liberté de le recommander à elle et à vous comme bien digne d'y entrer.

Mais à ce titre, il vous est déja connu et affilié.

S'il[1] reste aux Etats-Unis, il Sera pour eux une Excellente acquisition.

S'il passe au Bresil, après avoir Sejourné aux Etats-Unis, il y portera l'estime que votre nation et votre liberté inspirent, et le tendre interet que mérite la douceur de votre Gouvernement.

Vous verrez bientôt que c'est un homme qui n'avait pas besoin que je vous le recommandasse[2]

Je crois que c'est moi qui avais besoin qu'il Sût que je vous Suis extrêmement attaché, et que vous m'accordez quelque bienveillance.

Je vous renouvelle l'hommage de mon respect.

DuPont (de Nemours)

EDITORS' TRANSLATION

Sir, 20 December 1811.

I had the honor of sending you a few days ago a rather lengthy letter that Mr. Barlow is going to forward by way of the United States frigate The Constitution.

I found out today that this same frigate will carry to America Mr. Corrêa da Serra, a distinguished citizen of Portugal, one of the best correspondents in our class at the Institut, and a man who, like you, would have been equally well placed in the first class.

When we had the honor to elect you a foreign associate, we were the class of the moral and political sciences. This was a kind of third academy, as good as the other two, of which you were a very eminent member, and into which Mr. Corrêa would also have fit perfectly.

History remains with us, which is a precious responsibility. In order not to lose it, we do not abuse it; indeed, we hardly use it at all. However, the class remembered that this noble science was once within its scope, and it has proved equal to what was expected of it.

This is another field of study in which Mr. Corrêa would have been noticed.

If he were not already a member of our philosophical society in Philadelphia, I would take the liberty of recommending him to you and to the society as a man very worthy of joining it.

But he is already known to and affiliated with you.

If he stays in the United States, he will prove to be an excellent acquisition by your country.

If he goes to Brazil after spending some time in the United States, he will take with him the esteem inspired by your nation and your liberties, and the tender interest merited by the mildness of your government.

You will soon see that he is a man who does not need a recommendation from me

I would want him to know that I am very attached to you, and that you look kindly upon me.

I renew my regards and my respect. DUPONT (DE NEMOURS)

RC (DLC); at head of text: "a Monsieur Jefferson Ancien President des Etats-Unis"; endorsed by TJ as received 31 July 1813 and so recorded in SJL, which adds that it was delivered "by Mr Correa de Serra." Tr (DeGH: H. A. Du Pont Papers, Winterthur Manuscripts); posthumous copy. Translation by Dr. Genevieve Moene.

At this time Du Pont's section of the Institut de France was responsible for ancient literature and HISTOIRE.

[1] Preceding two words replaced in Tr with "Il" ("He").

[2] Tr: "recommande" ("recommend").

From Alexander von Humboldt

MONSIEUR, Paris à l'Observatoire ce 20 Dec. 1811.

J'arrive hier de Vienne où mon frere est Ministre du Roi de Prusse et ou j'ai passé un mois pour voir mes parents. J'ai eté bien heureux de retrouver à mon retour l'interessante lettre que Vous avez daigné m'écrire, Monsieur, et que Vous avez accompagné d'un cadeau auquel je mets le plus grand prix. Les notes sur la Virginie seront placeés dans la bibliotheque que nous avons formé mon frere et moi. c'est un titre de gloire pour moi que d'avoir joui de la bienveillance, j'ose dire de l'amitié d'un homme qui a etonne ce siecle par ses vertus et sa moderation. Craignant que la Fregatte ne parte, comme on me l'a fait craindre je ne puis ajouter que peu de lignes. J'ose Vous offrir la fin de mon Receuil d'Observations astronomiques et la 6me et 7me livraison de l'Essai sur la Nouvelle Espagne avec les Atlas correspondants. J'avois envoyé et fait envoyé par mes libraires les cahiers précédens par differentes voyes: peutetre Vous Sont ils à la fin arrivés; je Vous supplie cependant de m'ecrire avec la plus grande franchise ce qui Vous manque pour être au complet. J'espere que les communications seront plus sures dans la suite J'ai achevé les deux tiers de mes ouvrages, j'exprime en ce moment la partie historique. Mr Arrowsmith à Londres m'a volé ma grande Carte du Mexique: Mr Pike a profité d'une maniere peu genereuse de la communication qui lui a eté faite sans doute à Washington de la copie de ma Carte: d'ailleurs il a estropié tous les noms. Je suis affligé d'avoir a me plaindre d'un citoyen des Etats Unis qui d'ailleurs a deployé un si beau courage. Mon nom ne se trouve pas dans son livre et un leger coup d'oeil sur la Carte de Mr Pike Vous prouve d'où il a puise. Ma fortune a souffert moins par mes voyages que par des évenemens politiques: c'est perdre bien peu que de perdre sa fortune Je trouve des consolations dans le travail dans des souvenirs et dans l'estime des hommes qui reconnoissent la purete de mes intentions. Je suis vivement interessé comme Vous à la grande lutte de l'Amerique espagnole. Il ne faut pas s'etonner que la lutte soit sanglante, lorsqu'on pense que les hommes portent partout l'empreinte de l'imperfection des institutions sociales et que les peuples d'Europe depuis trois siecles ont cherché leurs securité dans le ressentiment mutuel et la haine des Castes. Je ne quitterai l'Europe qu'après avoir achevé mon ouvrage: les journaux me font voyager au Thibet, je balance entre plusieurs projets, mais je desire le plus percer en Asie. Je charge de cette lettre mon ami Monsieur Correa de Serra, membre de la Societé Royale[1] de Londres et Correspondant de l'Institut qui va s'etablir a Philadelphie. C'est un homme d'une ame éleveé, d'un esprit juste et fort et un des plus grands botanistes du siecle, quoique il n'ait que très peu publie. J'ose le recommander à Votre amitié et je Vous supplie de le recommander a Vos amis en Pensylvanie. Agreez, mon digne et respectable ami, l'hommage de mon admiration et de ma reconnoissance.

HUMBOLDT

EDITORS' TRANSLATION

SIR, At the Observatory in Paris, 20 December 1811.

I just came back from visiting my relatives for a month in Vienna, where my brother is a minister of the king of Prussia. On my return I was quite happy to find the very interesting letter that you so kindly wrote me, accompanied by a gift that I prize most highly. The Notes on Virginia will be placed in the library established by my brother and me. I am proud to have enjoyed the kind attention, I dare say the friendship, of a man whose virtues and moderation have amazed his century. I can only add a few lines for fear that the frigate may leave, as I have been told. I make bold to offer you the conclusion of my book of astronomical observations and the sixth and seventh parts of the Essay on New Spain, with corresponding maps and charts. I had sent, and had my publishers send, the preceding portions in various ways. Perhaps they have finally arrived. In any event I pray you to tell me most frankly what you are missing from the complete set. I hope for more reliable means of communication in future. I have finished two thirds of my work and am presently writing the historical section. Mr. Arrowsmith, of London, stole my large map of Mexico. Mr. Pike took advantage in a less than generous way of a copy of my map that someone gave him, most probably in Washington. As a matter of fact, he has mangled all the names. I am grieved to have to complain about a citizen of the United States, especially one who has shown such admirable courage. My name is not to be found in his book, and a glance at Mr. Pike's map shows from where he took it. My fortune has suffered less from my travels than from political events. To lose one's fortune is to lose very little. I find some consolation in my work, in my memories, and in the esteem of people who recognize the purity of my intentions. I am as keenly interested as you are in the great struggle in Spanish America. We should not be surprised that the contest is bloody when we recall that men all over the world bear the imprint of their imperfect social institutions and that for three centuries Europeans have sought safety in the mutual resentment and hatred of one caste for another. I will leave Europe only after I have finished my work. The press has me traveling to Tibet. I am hesitating between several projects, but I most desire to penetrate Asia. I entrust this letter to the care of my friend, Mr. Corrêa da Serra, a member of the Royal Society of London and a correspondent of the Institut, who is moving to Philadelphia. He is a man with a lofty soul and a just mind, one of the greatest botanists of the century, although he has published very little. I venture to recommend him to your friendship and entreat you to commend him to your friends in Pennsylvania. My worthy and respectable friend, please accept the tribute of my admiration and gratitude.

HUMBOLDT

RC (DLC); dateline at foot of text; endorsed by TJ as received 31 July 1813 and so recorded in SJL, which adds that it was delivered "by Mr Correa de Serra." Translation by Dr. Roland H. Simon. Enclosures: (1) conclusion of Humboldt, *Recueil d'observations astronomiques, d'operations trigonométriques et de mesures barométriques faites pendant le cours d'un voyage aux régions équinoxiales du nouveau continent, depuis 1799 jusqu'en 1803*, 3 vols. (Paris, 1808–09). (2) parts 6–7 of Humboldt, *Essai politique sur le royaume de la Nouvelle-Espagne: ouvrage qui presente des recherches sur la geographie du Mexique*, 2 vols. (Paris, 1808–19; Sowerby, no. 4157).

Humboldt apparently deposited the recently received copy of TJ's *Notes on the State of Virginia* in the BIBLIOTHEQUE ("library") of the University of Berlin (now the Humboldt-Universität), an institution that Humboldt and his brother Karl Wilhelm had founded in 1810 (Paul R. Sweet, *Wilhelm von Humboldt: A Biography* [1980], 53–4, 58–9; Hermann Klencke and Gustav Schlesier, *Lives of the Brothers Humboldt, Alexander and William*, trans. Juliette Bauer [1852], 99–100). Aaron ARROWSMITH issued the *New and Elegant General Atlas, comprising all the new Discoveries, to the present Time* (Philadelphia, 1804; Sowerby, no. 3836) that Humboldt regarded as plagiaristic. Zebulon Montgomery PIKE was the author of *An Account of Expeditions to the Sources of the Mississippi, and through the Western Parts of Louisiana . . . And a Tour through the Interior Parts of New Spain* (Philadelphia, 1810; Sowerby, no. 4169; Poor, *Jefferson's Library*, 7 [no. 371]).

On 26 Dec. 1811 Humboldt wrote TJ another letter, not found, but recorded in SJL as received from Paris on 31 July 1813 "by Mr Correa de Serra."

[1] Manuscript: "Royle."

From Micajah Harrison

DEAR SIR State of Kentucky Mount sterling Decr 21st 1811

I trust you will excuse the freedom I have taken in addressing you on a subject, by no means interesting to you, having however full assurance of your obliging disposition, and knowing the deference, deservedly given to your opinion in all cases; I have been encouraged to take the liberty of requesting your opinion on the following subject, upon which there is a difference of opinion between myself and some others in this little Village—"Is the cause of the Vapour & fogs, owing to a thick, Dense & heavy atmosphere or, a thin, light & unelastic atmosphere?"—

Your Condescending to gratify us with your opinion, will be gratefully acknowledged, by myself and a few friends of this place, to whose inspection alone it shall be submitted—

With sentiments of the highest respect & Esteem I am yr: ob^t Servt

MICAJAH HARRISON

RC (MHi); endorsed by TJ as received 5 Jan. 1812 and so recorded in SJL.

Micajah Harrison (1776–1842), a native of Virginia, moved to Kentucky in 1786 and participated eight years later in Gen. Anthony Wayne's campaign against the Indians. He was appointed clerk of the newly formed Montgomery County (with Mount Sterling as the county seat) in December 1796 and served in that capacity for nearly three decades. Harrison also farmed and briefly operated a tavern (*WMQ*, 2d ser., 14 [1934]: 176; *The Biographical Encyclopedia of Kentucky of the Dead and Living Men of the Nineteenth Century* [1878], 140; Carl B. Boyd and Hazel M. Boyd, *A History of Mt. Sterling, Kentucky, 1792–1918* [1984], 5, 19, 213).

From Thomas Sully

SIR Philadelphia Decr 22nd 1811

An association has lately been formed in this City consisting of Artists, & Amateurs, residing in different parts of the Union; Under the Title of Society of Artists of U.S.

I am requested to communicate to you in the name of the Society. That you were unanimously elected an Honorary member at a special meeting held on the 15th inst:

Your love for the Arts & Sciences, and your long & unremitted exertions to promote the Independence & prosperity of our Country are known to all the World—A Society having for its object the cultivation of the fine Arts throughout this extensive, & flourishing

Republic, cannot fail to meet your approbation, and receive your cordial cooperation.

The establishment of Schools in the various branches of the Arts on liberal principles, and periodical Exhibitions of the Works of American Artists, will, it is believed have a tendency to form a correct taste in this Country.—By calling into Action Native genius, many prejudices will be removed with respect to foreign productions: And the application of the fine Arts to useful purposes, is acknowledged by all who are acquainted with the principles, & progress of Civilization, to be of great importance.

The members of this infant Institution are convinced that their success depends much upon their own exertions; at the same time they are aware that the countena[nce] and support of the most distingushed patriotic characters in the Country: will not only powerfully aid them in the Arduo[us] pursuits in which they are engaged but will also have a tend[ency] to unite & give confidence to all who are immediatly interested in the prosperity of the Institution.

I herewith transmit a Copy of the Constitution of the Society.

By order of the Committee of Corresponde[nce]

Thos Sully. Secy

——Committee of Correspondence——

Rembt Peale
Geoge Murray
Benjn Trott.
Robt Mills
Gideon Fairman
Wm Rush
Thos Sully.

RC (MHi); edge trimmed; in an unidentified hand, with signature and committee membership list in Sully's hand; between dateline and salutation: "Thomas Jefferson Esqr"; endorsed by TJ as a letter from Sully received 1 Jan. 1812 and so recorded in SJL. Printed in Richmond *Enquirer*, 25 Feb. 1812. Enclosure: *The Constitution of the Society of Artists of the United States, Established at Philadelphia, May, 1810* (Philadelphia, 1810).

Thomas Sully (1783–1872), painter, was a native of Horncastle, England, who immigrated to America with his parents in 1792. Building on initial training by his friend Charles Fraser, his brother-in-law Jean Belzons, and his brother Lawrence Sully, he took up art as his profession in 1801. A visit to Gilbert Stuart in 1807 and a trip to England, 1809–10, contributed to his further artistic development. After setting up studios in Richmond and New York, late in 1807 Sully relocated permanently to Philadelphia. He became a United States citizen in 1809. Sully gave art lessons, operated a picture gallery, and produced more than twenty-six hundred works during his lengthy career. Among the most famous are a painting of George Washington crossing the Delaware and portraits of TJ (1821), Andrew Jackson, Lafayette,

James Monroe, and Queen Victoria (*ANB*; *DAB*; Edward Biddle and Mantle Fielding, *The Life and Works of Thomas Sully (1783–1872)* [1921]; Bush, *Life Portraits*, 76–9; Sully to TJ, 6 Apr. 1821; TJ to Sully, 17 Apr. 1821; *Philadelphia Inquirer*, 6 Nov. 1872).

Rembrandt Peale (1778–1860), painter, was the third son of Charles Willson Peale. Like his father, he became a well-known and highly regarded portraitist. Peale executed numerous likenesses in Baltimore, Charleston, New York, and Philadelphia before traveling in 1802 to England, where he studied at the Royal Academy and under Benjamin West. He produced many portraits of George Washington, starting with one taken from life in 1795, and his two life portraits of TJ, painted in 1800 and 1805, are among the third president's most recognizable images. Peale was a founder of the Pennsylvania Academy of the Fine Arts in 1805. During two trips to France between 1808 and 1810, he painted many French notables, including Napoleon and Pierre Samuel Du Pont de Nemours. In 1814 Peale moved to Baltimore and there opened a museum and art gallery. Eight years later financial difficulties forced him to sell the museum to his brother Rubens and relocate to New York City, where in 1826 he helped found the National Academy of Design. Peale also exhibited history paintings, served as president of the American Academy of the Fine Arts, 1836–38, and published drawing manuals, travel accounts, and memoirs. He died in Philadelphia (*ANB*; *DAB*; Peale, *Papers*; Bush, *Life Portraits*, 37–41, 54–6; *PTJ*, 33:114, 433–4; Peale to TJ, 13 July 1813, 8 Jan. 1824, 7 Dec. 1825; TJ to Peale, 29 Nov., 16 Dec. 1825; Philadelphia *Daily Evening Bulletin*, 4 Oct. 1860).

George Murray (d. 1822) and Gideon Fairman (1774–1827), were both engravers and inventors. They helped found the banknote engraving firm of Murray, Draper, Fairman & Company in Philadelphia about 1810. Murray was a native of Scotland who moved to Philadelphia about 1800. Fairman was born in Connecticut and moved to Philadelphia from Albany in 1810. He also painted portraits (George C. Groce and David H. Wallace, *The New-York Historical Society's Dictionary of Artists in America 1564–1860* [1957], 219, 462; William Dunlap, *History of the Rise and Progress of the Arts of Design in the United States* [1834; repr. 1969], 2:48–9, 143–4; *List of Patents*, 26, 79, 237; Washington *Daily National Intelligencer*, 9 July 1822; Philadelphia *United States Gazette*, 20 Mar. 1827).

Benjamin Trott (ca. 1770–1843), artist, specialized in miniature portraits. A native of Boston, he was a friend of both Sully and Gilbert Stuart and worked in Philadelphia for extended periods, including 1806–19 (*ANB*; *DAB*; Dunlap, *Arts of Design*, 1:414–7; Washington *Daily National Intelligencer*, 29 Nov. 1843).

William Rush (1756–1833), sculptor, was a lifelong resident of Philadelphia who made his reputation carving figureheads and ornaments for merchant vessels and United States Navy frigates. With the passage of the Embargo Act in 1807, he began creating architectural statues and busts of notables such as his cousin Benjamin Rush, TJ, Lafayette, James Madison, and George Washington. TJ received a plaster cast of Rush's bust of Andrew Jackson as a gift in 1820. In 1794 Rush helped to organize the Columbianum, a short-lived art academy. He carved replicas of mastodon bones to complete skeletons for Charles Willson Peale's museum in 1801, sat on Philadelphia's city council, 1801–26, and was a founder of the Pennsylvania Academy of the Fine Arts in 1805 (*ANB*; *DAB*; Pennsylvania Academy of the Fine Arts, *William Rush, American Sculptor* [1982], esp. 128–9, 152–3, 170–1, 176; James Ronaldson to TJ, 1 Feb. 1820; Philadelphia *United States Gazette*, 19 Jan. 1833).

The Society of Artists of the United States, which was founded in Philadelphia in May 1810, conducted classes and held several annual exhibitions. It was incorporated as the Columbian Society of Artists on 16 Feb. 1813, with TJ's name first on a long list of incorporators (act of incorporation in *Acts of the General Assembly of the Commonwealth of Pennsylvania* [Philadelphia, 1813], 73–6; Tr in Minute Book of Society of Artists of the

United States [MS in PPAFA]). The society was essentially moribund by 1815, and finally dissolved five years later (Edward J. Nygren, "The First Art Schools at the Pennsylvania Academy of the Fine Arts," *PMHB* 95 [1971]: 225–36; Latrobe, *Papers*, 3:65).

According to the Society's minutes, TJ was unanimously elected an honorary member on 11 Dec. 1811 (not THE 15TH INST), George MURRAY having nominated him. On 5 Feb. 1812 Murray successfully moved that the above letter, a second Sully letter of 6 Jan. 1812, and TJ's 8 and 25 Jan. 1812 replies be "recorded in the Books of the Society, and that they also be published in the Newspapers" (Minute Book of Society of Artists of the United States, MS in PPAFA, pp. 46, 52).

To James Leitch

Dec. 24. 11.

6.℔ oznabrigs thread
3.℔ blue & green thread, of the size of oznabrigs thr[d]

TH:J.

RC (ViCMRL, on deposit ViU: TJP); dateline beneath signature; written on a small scrap; at foot of text: "M[r] Leitch." Not recorded in SJL.

From Lafayette

MY DEAR FRIEND La grange december 26[h] 1811

The Arrival of the Constitution frigate Has Blessed me with a very welcome Compensation for your Long Silence—I Have first Enjoy'd the kind Letters directed to me, then took a share in those to mde de tessé and to my friends Humboldt and tracy—they Have Given me So much to think and to Say that I feel the insufficiency of Epistolary Correspondance, and more than Ever the Need of personal Conversation—I ought However first to Apologize for my Having teazed you with Complaints—you will, I Hope, Excuse me in favor of the friendly Sentiment which, on Every opportunity, made disappointment So painful—I Heartily thank you for the particulars You Give me Respecting your Health, your mode of life, and Beg you, my dear Jefferson, to Be very minute in favoring me with all the detaïls that Concern you—our friend mr Barlow will write the Latest politics—He Has Been Remarkably well Received By the Emperor, and all the people about Court—His Representations[1] Have Been attended to with that Regard and welcome which made us Expect Every day the favourable promised Answer—Such was His very pleasant Situation when I Left Him a few days Ago. I Hope He Has By this time Got materials for the Return of the frigate, and Hasten this Letter to improve the Opportunity.

Permit me to introduce to you mr Correa, a portuguese Gentleman, whose Eminent merit, Amiable qualities, and Liberal Sentiments Have Endeared Him to a Great number and the very choice of friends which will Recommend Him to your Good Opinion—I know nothing Can gratify Him So much as to Be presented to you, and I find a particular pleasure in putting under your Care this worthy New inhabitant of the united States.

Whatever Be the motives or Result of the Bloody wars Now Raging in Europe, it is a Happy prospect to See Before us the whole American Continent Advancing to independance and freedom—Such, I trust, must Be the End of the actual movements in the former Spanish Colonies—the shakles of their Several Aristocrasies, the present intrigues of the British Government, the unhappy measures Hitherto adopted Against Neutral trade will no doubt Embarass the Revolution—But while Such a model as the united States Stands Before those new Erected Societies, European institutions Being So Little Attractive, it is to Be Hoped their prejudices and Habits will yeald to Good Sense, and Good Exemple—we did not, you and I, flatter ourselves it Would Come on So Soon, an[d] from this instance we may Conclude that if Liberty too often Meets Rocks and Stoppages, it, at other times, finds its way where it Had Not Been intended.

of My personal Concerns I Have little to Say—my fourteen children and grand children Live with me in these Rural Retirements—I gave you an Account of my Arrangement With Mm Baring parish, and grammont. it Has not Suited mr Ridgeway to do the like—the whole mortgage in which He was for a third part Has Remained unpaid and unliquidated—a Late attempt to find monney in Amsterdam on my Lands Has failed—I am much obliged to the kind interest our friend mr Barlow takes in this affair.

My Son and daughters Beg Leave to Be Respectfully Remembered to you and to mrs Randolph whom I Beg you to present with my Best Respects—you know, my dear Jefferson, How Affectionately I am Your old and Grateful friend LAFAYETTE

RC (DLC); edge trimmed; endorsed by TJ as received 31 July 1813 and so recorded in SJL, which adds that it was delivered "by Mr Correa de Serra."

[1] Manuscript: "Reprentations."

From James Ronaldson

SIR Edin^r^ Decr 26–1811

Fearfull letters from so many different places may impress you with doubts of the character of the writer—I shall even tell you what I been about—The want of Antimony (indespensible in the Letter foundry) induced me to visit France, first to procure an immedeately supply, and in the next place to make arrangements for a regular supply for the future, with this adventure we had reason to be pleased although only partially successfull,[1] for on leaving France, the ship was taken by the English and although released by the Admiral on the Station, my Captain during the time the vessel was in possession of the English privately[2] threw over $8 or $900 worth, which at the time he said he would pay if the ship was released, but since his arrival in the US Denies & refuses payment—our future supply has not always escaped the British Cruisers, a parcle on board the Meteor has been condemned and will be sold some time soon at Portsmouth.—for my present appearance in Scotland I had no motive but after an absence of 17 years to visit my Father & Mother, and see if their Wigwam was prepared for the Decr of life I arr^d^ here ab^t^ last of Novr and propose returning in Feby—

The country, manners of society & &^c^—have in 17 years undergon considerable alteration, And as my mind has not remain'd stationary, but been as respects society traveling on an oposite direction the difference apears more remarkable. Perhaps in no part of the world has practical Agriculture arrived at higher perfection than in the ‡Lothians of Scotland, under the inconveniencies of a short wet summer they contrive to produce good grain and in considerable quantity the operative system is in great perfection, the Plowmen, labourers &^c^ are all expert at their respective branches, but while the land is well plowed judicously crop'd, manuired often, & drained with that kind of stone filled and covered ditches that last 15 to 25 years; it surpriseing[3] the few permanent improvement that have been made, I mean that specis of improvement to be expected from the Landlords Houses, wall fences, Trees, Culvert drains, banking and streighting of Creeks although rents in the past 25 years, have tripled, the Landlords have done little or nothing of this kind.—But this is still less remarkable than to find, a large majority of these gentlemen are in debt; men in possession of estates yealding from 10 to £120000.0.0 Sterg ℔ Ann are borrowing money!! 100 Acres of

‡Counties of East, West & Mid Lothian

middling good land will rent at £3.10 ℔ acre[4]—and requires the tennant to have from 6—to £10 Sterg of stock ℔ acre for it—The tennant retains of the landlords rent 10 ℔Cent this he pays into the tax office with 5 ℔ Cent out of His own pocket so government draw 15 ℔Cent out of all the lands—besides this the tennant pays his window, home, Dog taxes

It does not apear to me that people live easier than they did, nay the contrary, but street begging is not so prevailent, what causes this diminution I can't tell however it does exist and is allways a disgrace to society, nothing can look worse than a poor sailor having lost a leg, Arm or eye sight, obliged[5] to beg for bread, it is surprising the ingratitude of Commercial states to this class of men—There should be an hospital in each of the martime states of the union for the reception of such as receive injuries or are worn out by age in the Marcantile or National service this would insure a set of sailors superior to any in the world, and if the Hospital was connected with a farm many of 'em could do a little towards defraying their expence; and thise hospitals if well conducted would become favourites with Mariners, and returning from foreign countries they would bring with them the seeds and plants of these places by which means the hospital garden, farm,[6] & the whole nation would be enriched, this degression on behalf of a much neglected injudicious managed class, breings forward a train of other reflections that are more interesting to the writer than the affairs of Britains, of course he cannot help giving way to his feelings The mangement of Soldiers as respects dress is certainly very injudicious those here have a sugar loaf conical cap without any brim, and a small projection of leather to preserve the eyes from[7] the sun, this may be very well for reviews and please Miss molly folks, but it is ill calculated for preserving the health and activity of a man obliged to be out at all hours[8] and exposed to every sort of weather. these hats or caps in place of sheltering the neck, leave it exposed and conducts all the water that has fallen on the head down the neck and back, subjecting the poor wearer to agure, billous fiver, flux, &c &c and every soldier should have a couple of good flannel shirts made of smooth wool such as would be agreeable to the Skin—inatention to these things has filled the hospitals with sick British in Portugal, formerly reputed the healthiest country in Europe, and if continued will have equally mortal effects in the US—The condition of those at orleans particularly requires round hats & flannel shirts—The present appearance rather menacing war require attention[9] to be turned that way—War prisoners are not now in the same predicament they were as when sold for slaves killed or eaten, but they are still bad enough, shut up in a narrow space, poorly fed, ill cloathed and idle, nay denyed the previledge of working to improve their condition is too[10] bad; and should be corrected.—In Britain Prisoners of war are denyed all materials that would enable them to make articles that would interfere with her own manufactures—persons have been condemned to imprisonment for furnishing French prisoners of W[ar] with straw! out of which they made Bonnets for sale[11]—Now I propose that the persons authorised to look after the citizens of the US who have the misfortune of being prisoners of war in foreign countries—Should be instructed to provid them with spinning wheels, cards, knitting needles, wool, flax & Cotton, with these simple means the poor fellows could Cloath[12] their bodies & beds. some pasteboard needles & paint would give them the materials for hats;—They should be furnished with flour and make it into bread themselves, and in place of beef the Oxen or sheep should be given them alive; that offal we dispise would be to persons so scantily fed a great comfort it is now lost, and as they performed the bussiness of Bakers & Butchers this saving could be added to their allowance, the sheep and Ox skins would furnish them a humble substitue in mokosens for shoes—It has allways been a parctice with nations ingaged in war to use what power they had to put out of the Battle as many of their enemies as possible, and shurely the most humane is the best—for this reason the US should give to every enemy who came over 100 acres of land without imposing on the comer over, any obligation but his remaining quiet and industrious he should not be required to take up, arms in your caus excpt he chose, nor be permited, to sell his land untill the peaze this regulation is to prevent his going off with your money and again aiding the enemy,[13] Consistancy; There is now confined in London waiting trial a number of Englishmen, who being made prisoners by the French, entered into that service and were taken at Isle of France when that place was captured by the English—Some days ago a party of Dainish Prisoners of war marched through Edin^r^ from a Depot of Prisoners in the interior—to join the British ships of war they are to serve on board; these Daines having entered into the British service.—The marine lights app[ear] better than those of the US The tower erected on the Bell Rock 10 or 12 mi[les] out into the German ocean deserves to rank with the wonders of the age and does honor to every one concerned in its establishment it stands on a small rocky shole that is bare at about half tide, the tide there riseing and falling 20 feet, the reflectors are parabolic concaves of 2 feet over and 11 or 12 inches deep made of Copper covered with a thick plating of silver finely polished and Lighted with a well trimed argand lamp, the price of one of the largest and best reflextors is from 30 to £40 Sterg in the Bell Rock lanthern there is 16—one half of which are covers with a Blue or Red Glass and the frame in which all the 16 stand revolving alterately present a bright & a coloured light—Every effort should be made on the part of the US to cherish the imployment of her Citizens at home and secure a market for her agricultural products beyond the controll of European Nations,—In France you are told America and her Governmt are devoted to England; in Britain nothing is talk'd of when America the subject of conversation, but the US is the devoted sevant of France; and neither of these nation are to be contented but by joing the war on their[14] to which there is very little encourgement—Britain with a great & Successfull fleet France with an equally surprising army, have added nothing to the comfort independence, security, happiness, either of their own people—or others,[15] and those who have embarked with or against them have all been ruined—The Ship this goes by I shall send you a parcle of seeds. the tree seed are of the kinds most esteem'd here and no doubt will thrive in the US. the Greens & turnips should be allowed to Seed—I could wish some of 'em sent to such regions in the US whose winter is rainey not frosty (Kentucky Tenenesse &c)—I have ordered the merchs to procure some of the new grass so much talked of I think called Feron it is a jointed grass thrives in rich moist lands and is said to produce very great crops the seeds will be principally usefull—I wish to send them to George McIntosh of Norfolk and desire him to take half of them, he has some ground and they may by this means be saved to the country—the seeds will be sent to the care of the Collector at Norfolk who will be desired to forward them to you or deliver them to your order—I know in this letter I committed the sin of repetition, but it is chargeable to a conviction of the importance of the subjects aluded to—America has no friends in the Governments of Europe and every thing Should be done to place the US independent of them either during peace or in war, war is their trade and study; to reout and beat them, it will be necessary that the US adopt new principals and no Nation has Such means of atacking the moral qualities of man and it will be found better to operate on their minds than bodies Men here are not well informed about the US no doubt—the government know well supplies of provisions sent to Spain & Portugal but very few of the people do—and 95 ℘Cent of them suppose the country could not support its self independent of Britain for 6 months, that every town on the Coast could be distroyed, not a ship permited to look out of Port—that America has no manufactures, and her circumstances will not permit her to become one these 100 Years—that her statesmen know this well, and that the imports duties will not be advanced least the Members of Congress should lose their popularity and the Government is so weak it could not prevent Smuggling—&c &c

With most ardent wishes for Your health and happiness—and the prosperity of All good governments—I am Respectfully

JAMES RONALDSON

It has been said that the P.R. useth much Brandy—

RC (DLC); dateline added in an unidentified hand prior to mailing; edge torn and mutilated at seal; postscript written perpendicularly along right margin of last page; addressed: "Thomas Jefferson Montecello" and "Capt Rindge Concordia"; franked and postmarked; endorsed by TJ as a letter of 26 Dec. 1812 received 9 Mar. 1812 and so recorded (under correct year of composition) in SJL.

The lighthouse at BELL ROCK, located eleven miles from shore in the Firth of Forth, had been put into operation earlier this year (*Literary Panorama* 11 [1812]: 311–6). FERON: fiorin grass. The COLLECTOR AT NORFOLK was Larkin Smith.

P.R.: "Prince Regent," later George IV of Great Britain.

[1] Manuscript: "successull."
[2] Word interlined.
[3] Reworked from "It surprises me."
[4] Preceding two words interlined.
[5] Manuscript: "obligled."
[6] Manuscript: "fram."
[7] Manuscript: "form."
[8] Ronaldson here canceled "in the day."
[9] Manuscript: "attentiion."
[10] Word interlined.
[11] Preceding two words interlined.
[12] Manuscript: "Coath."
[13] Manuscript: "ememy."
[14] Thus in manuscript.
[15] Manuscript: "gthers."

To William & Samuel Craig

GENTLEMEN Monticello Dec. 27. 11

An absence of 6. weeks occasions this late acknolegement of your favor of Nov. 29. covering a letter from Doctr Stephenson of Belfast. and asking my directions with respect to a small box from him containing 2. plants of a grass which I had asked under the belief it's introduction would be useful to our country. if the box be as small as I expect, so that it might not be an abuse of the mail to send it by that, it will be the quickest & most likely conveyance to ensure success in raising the plant. if too large for the mail, I must pray you to send it by some vessel bound to Richmond addressed to Messrs Gibson & Jefferson of that place who will forward it to me. the propriety of the one or the other conveyance I must request the exercise of your discretion on. Accept my thanks for your attention to this matter & the assurances of my great respect. TH: JEFFERSON

PoC (MHi); at foot of text: "Messrs Wm & Saml Craig"; endorsed by TJ.

To John Low

SIR Monticello Dec. 27. 11.

An absence of 6. weeks from home has occasioned the delay of acknoleging the reciept of your two letters of Nov. 29. & Dec. 15. the former announcing to me the forwarding a set of the Encyclopaedia, published in New York, which, it says, I subscribed for a few years ago. there is certainly some mistake in this matter. possessed as I am of every Encyclopedia which has ever been published in Europe in the English or French languages, and of Dobson's published in America, I long since made it a pointed rule to subscribe for no more Encyclopaedias. to this rule I feel conscious of having strictly adhered, and my memory does not furnish me with the least trace of having broken thro' it in the case of the one you mention. besides this I always noted in a list I kept for that purpose every book for which I subscrib'd. on this there is no note of any such subscription. these several testimonials give me a confidence that I never subscribed for this work. I must therefore request you to examine again your subscription list and see whether my name be really on it, and whether it be in my own handwriting. the latter question is suggested by the fact that in some other cases it has been found that some of the circulators of subscription papers have set my name on their list on the supposition that it might encourage some to subscribe, & with no view of ever calling on me really as a subscriber. so in the present case I suspect error only not fraud. my subscriptions having ever been in my own handwriting, you may perhaps yourself know my signature, many at Washington must know it, & some at New York, particularly mr Remsen of the bank of Manhattan, who was chief clerk to the office while I was Secretary of State, mr Gelston collector of New York & others. if contrary to my belief I have really subscribed, it puts an end to the question, and I take the work and will make your remittance as soon as the fact is ascertained. otherwise I adhere to my rule and will return the 3. vols. I have recieved. but if I have been really a subscriber, let me beseech you not to forward it by mail. this is an abuse of the privilege of franking which I am in duty bound to prevent. the work may be as conveniently forwarded from N. York as from any other place, to Richmond, to the address of Messrs Gibson & Jefferson of that place, by any vessel from N.Y. to Richmond, where I can give orders respecting it. the time of your stay in Washington, mentioned in your letter being elapsed, I address this to N. York. Accept the assurance of my respect.

TH: JEFFERSON

PoC (DLC); at foot of first page: "Mr John Low"; endorsed by TJ.

Thomas DOBSON's *Encyclopædia; or, A Dictionary of Arts, Sciences, and Miscellaneous Literature*, 18 vols. (Philadelphia, 1798; Sowerby, no. 4891) was based on the third edition of the *Encyclopaedia Britannica*.

To William Mann

SIR — Monticello. Dec. 27. 11.

An absence of 6. weeks in a distant county is the cause of this very late acknolegement of your letter of Nov. 11. covering the copy of a spa[1] in Chancery by Gourley against a group of defs among whom I am named, without being able to conjecture the cause of it. you are free to consider the spa as served on me personally. I observe that mr Nicholas is a def. and presume he will not let us suffer before we are apprised of the matters with which we are charged. Accept the assurance of my respects.

TH: JEFFERSON

PoC (MHi); at foot of text: "M[r] William Mann"; endorsed by TJ.

Mann's letter to TJ was dated 12 Nov. 1811, not NOV. 11.

[1] Abbreviation for "subpoena."

From William W. Clayton

28th Dec[r] 1811—

I have been Very unfortunate Coming from Fredericks[bg] on my way near to your Place in Bedford I lost my Horse died on the Road

I was Taken sick and Compelled to stay on The Road untill my money Is nearly Exausted I wish To Get to M[r] Clays near To your Possessions in Bedford a few shillings wou[d] aid me

W, W, CLAYTON

RC (MHi); at foot of text: "Co[l] Th[os] Jefferson"; endorsed by TJ: "Clayton W. W."

William Willis Clayton was a cousin of Editha Landon Davies Clay. She and her husband, Charles Clay, were TJ's near neighbors at Poplar Forest (Mary Denham Ackerly and Lula Eastman Jeter Parker, *"Our Kin": The Genealogies of Some of the Early Families who Made History in the Founding and Development of Bedford County Virginia* [1930], 347–8, 350, 354).

To George Hay

DEAR SIR Monticello Dec. 28. 11.

On my return after an absence of 6. weeks in Bedford I find here your favor of the 5th informing me of the dismission of Livingston's suit. as this has been for want of jurisdiction, without any investigation of the merits of the cause, the public mind will remain unsettled & uninformed as to the justice of the case, and their impression produced by Livingston's squalling as if his throat had been cut, will be uncorrected. I believe therefore it is a duty to myself as well as the public to lay the case before them, altho it is with infinite reluctance that I shall present myself on that arena: and with the more as I have not the courage & really not the time, to reform the Commentaries on the case which I sent you, and to put them into a more popular dress. they were written for those to whom the matters they contain were familiar; to common readers they will appear unnecessarily erudite, and pedantic. but I repeat that I am too tired of the subject to go over it again. so I think I must publish it as it is, and must I suppose send it to N.Y. as I know no press but that which reprints the Edinburgh review which can print correctly any language but English. I must request you therefore to return me the defence I put into your hands as also all the documents & papers that I may return them to their proper deposits. I am under great obligations to my counsel & to yourself particularly for the trouble they have had with this case, and as soon as I get through a mass of letters & other matters of business accumulated during my absence, I shall make them my just acknolegements for their attention to it. Accept the assurances of my great esteem & respect. TH: JEFFERSON

PoC (DLC); at foot of text: "Mr Hay"; endorsed by TJ.

COMMENTARIES: TJ's Statement on the Batture Case, 31 July 1810. The New York publisher who reprinted the EDINBURGH REVIEW was Ezra Sargeant.

To Hugh Nelson

DEAR SIR Monticello Dec. 28. 11.

The suit of Livingston against myself having been dismissed from court for want of jurisdiction, the merits of the case still unexplained to the public, I am apprehensive the impression made by Livingston's squalling may be strengthened by the false inference that I wished to get rid of the case in that way, which is not true. I believe therefore it is due to myself, & still more to the public, to lay the case before them, by publishing the Commentaries on it which I had prepared for the use of my counsel, and which I had inclosed to you for perusal. it will doubtless be satisfactory to our citizens at large to see that no wrong has been done to Livingston, that the ground of his complaint has been merely my maintaining the national right to the beach of the Missisipi adjacent to N. Orleans, and keeping it from such intrusions as might restrain individuals from making lawful uses of it, and preserve the city & country from destruction: and that in doing this I only obeyed the prescriptions of the law both as to matter & manner. it is with infinite reluctance indeed that I think of presenting myself on this arena; yet I believe it a duty, and with that view ask the return of the MS. I put into your hands. Accept the assurance of my friendly esteem & respect. TH: JEFFERSON

PoC (DLC); at foot of text: "the honble Mr Nelson"; endorsed by TJ.

To William Lambert

SIR Monticello Dec. 29. 11.

An absence of 6 weeks has prevented my sooner acknoleging your two favors of Nov. 14. & 22. which I found here on my return, the former with a letter from Bishop Madison. I am very thankful for your calculations on my observations of the late Solar eclipse. I have for some time past been rubbing off the rust of my mathematics contracted during 50. years engrossed by other pursuits, and have found in it a delight and a success beyond my expectations. I observed the eclipse of the sun with a view to calculate my longitude from it, but other occupations had prevented my undertaking it before my journey; and the calculations you have furnished me with shew it would have been more elaborate than I had expected, and that most probably I should have foundered by the way. one thing I do not understand, why you preferred using the external rather than the internal contacts. I presume the Bishop sent you the whole of the observations & the note on them which I shall subjoin to this. you will there percieve I had little confidence in the external contacts, but an entire one in the forming & breaking of the annulus. I have no telescope equal to observing the eclipses of Jupiter's satellites, and as soon as I have fitted up a little box for my instruments, I shall amuse myself with the further ascertainment of my longitude by the lunar observations, which have the advantage of being repeated ad libitum, and of requiring less laborious calculations. Accept the assurances of my esteem & respect TH: JEFFERSON

PoC (DLC); at foot of text: "M[r] William Lambert"; endorsed by TJ; with PoC of Tr of enclosure on verso. Enclosure: extract from TJ to Henry A. S. Dearborn, 15 Nov. 1811.

To Bishop James Madison

DEAR SIR Monticello Dec. 29. 11.

Your favor of Nov. 19. arrived here just as I had set out for Bedford, from whence I returned a few days ago only, & found your letter here. I thank you for mr Lambert's[1] calculation on my observations of the late eclipse of the sun. I have been for some time rubbing up my Mathematics from the rust contracted by 50. years pursuits of a different kind, and thanks to the good foundation laid at College by my old master & friend Small, I am doing it with a delight & success beyond my expectation. I had observed the eclipse of Sep. 17. with a view to calculate from it myself the longitude of Monticello; but other occupations had prevented it before my journey. the elaborate paper of mr Lambert shews me it would have been a more difficult undertaking than I had foreseen, & that probably I should have foundered in it. I have no telescope equal to the observation of the eclipses of Jupiter's satellites. but as soon as I can fit up a box to fix my instruments in, I propose to amuse myself with further essays to fix our longitude by the lunar observations, which have the advantages of multiplied repetitions & less laborious calculations. I have a fine theodolite & Equatorial both by Ramsden, a Hadley's circle of Borda, a fine meridian and horizon as you know. once ascertaining the dip of my horizon I can use the circle, as at sea, without an artificial horizon. do you think of ever giving us a second edition of your map? if you do I may be able to furnish you with some latitudes. I have a pocket sextant of miraculous accuracy, considering it's microscopic graduation with this I have ascertained the lat. of Poplar Forest, (say New London) by multiplied observations, & lately that of Willis's mountains by observations of my own, repeated by my grandson, whom I am carrying on in his different studies. any latitudes within the circuit of these three places I could take for you myself, to which my grandson whose motions will be on a larger scale, would be able to add others. my unremitting occupations while you were engaged in the first publication put it out of my power to furnish you with some local draughts which might have aided you, to wit some very accurate surveys of James river from Cartersville about 10. miles upwards, some of the river in this neighborbood, some county lines, the country between New London & Lynchburg E[t]c. Accept my friendly salutations & assurances of great & continued esteem & respect. TH: JEFFERSON

PoC (DLC); at foot of first page: "Bishop Madison."

The reflecting circle of Jean Charles BORDA was a surveying instrument that French scientists used to measure the length of the meridional arc, the standard on which they based the metric system (*DSB*). TJ, who regarded the instrument as an elaboration of methods developed by John Hadley, obtained one in 1807 from William Jones, of London (Jones to TJ, 17 Oct. 1807 [DLC]; TJ to Robert Patterson, 21 Mar. 1811). A MERIDIAN is an astronomical instrument consisting of a telescope with a large graduated circle that is used to determine a star's ascension and declination. Madison's 1807 MAP of Virginia was posthumously republished with additions and corrections in Richmond in 1818. MY GRANDSON: Thomas Jefferson Randolph.

[1] Manuscript: "Lambard's."

From Nicolas G. Dufief

MONSIEUR, A Philadelphie ce 30 X[bre] 1811

Vous trouverez ci-inclus le premier Supplement au catalogue que j'ai eu l'honneur de vous acheminer aussi-tôt après Sa publication. Je viens de recevoir le calcul intégral & différentiel de La Croix, mais comme vous voulez toutes ses œuvres, je présume que cet ouvrage ne vous conviendra pas.

Je profite de cette occasion pour vous prier d'agréer au renouvellement de l'année mes vœux pour votre santé & votre Prospérité

Votre très-respectueux Serviteur N. G. DUFIEF

EDITORS' TRANSLATION

SIR, Philadelphia 30 December 1811

You will find enclosed the first supplement to the catalogue that I had the honor to forward to you immediately after its publication. I have just received Lacroix's integral and differential calculus, but since you want all of his works, I presume that it will not suit you.

I take advantage of this opportunity on the eve of the New Year to convey my wishes for your health and prosperity

Your very respectful Servant N. G. DUFIEF

RC (DLC); endorsed by TJ as received 5 Jan. 1812 and so recorded in SJL. Translation by Dr. Roland H. Simon. Enclosure not found.

A MANUAL

OF

PARLIAMENTARY PRACTICE:

FOR THE

USE OF THE SENATE

OF THE

UNITED STATES.

BY THOMAS JEFFERSON.

SECOND EDITION.

WITH THE LAST ADDITIONS OF THE AUTHOR.

WASHINGTON:

PUBLISHED BY WILLIAM COOPER; AND BY

JOSEPH MILLIGAN, GEORGETOWN.

1812.

Title Page of Jefferson's Manual of Parliamentary Practice

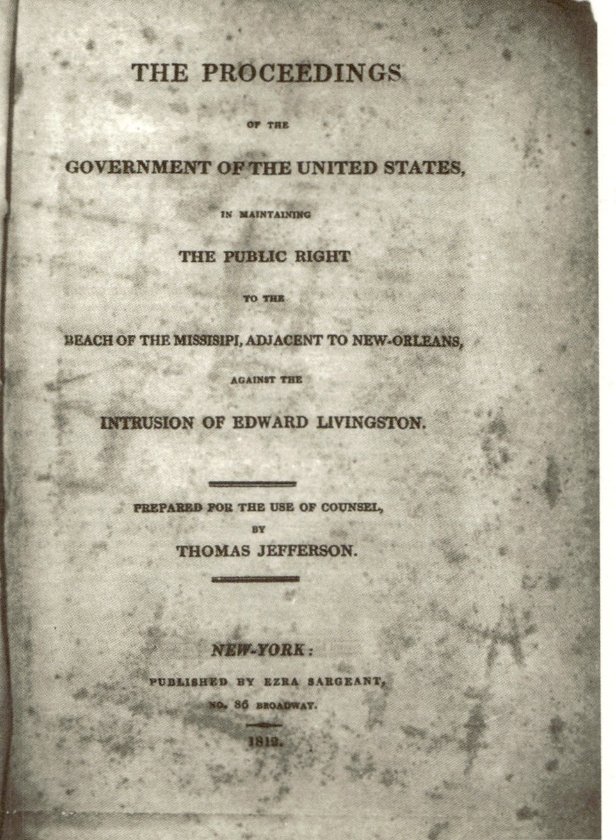

THE PROCEEDINGS

OF THE

GOVERNMENT OF THE UNITED STATES,

IN MAINTAINING

THE PUBLIC RIGHT

TO THE

BEACH OF THE MISSISIPI, ADJACENT TO NEW-ORLEANS,

AGAINST THE

INTRUSION OF EDWARD LIVINGSTON.

PREPARED FOR THE USE OF COUNSEL,

BY

THOMAS JEFFERSON.

NEW-YORK:

PUBLISHED BY EZRA SARGEANT,

NO. 86 BROADWAY.

1812.

Title Page of Jefferson's Pamphlet on the Batture Case

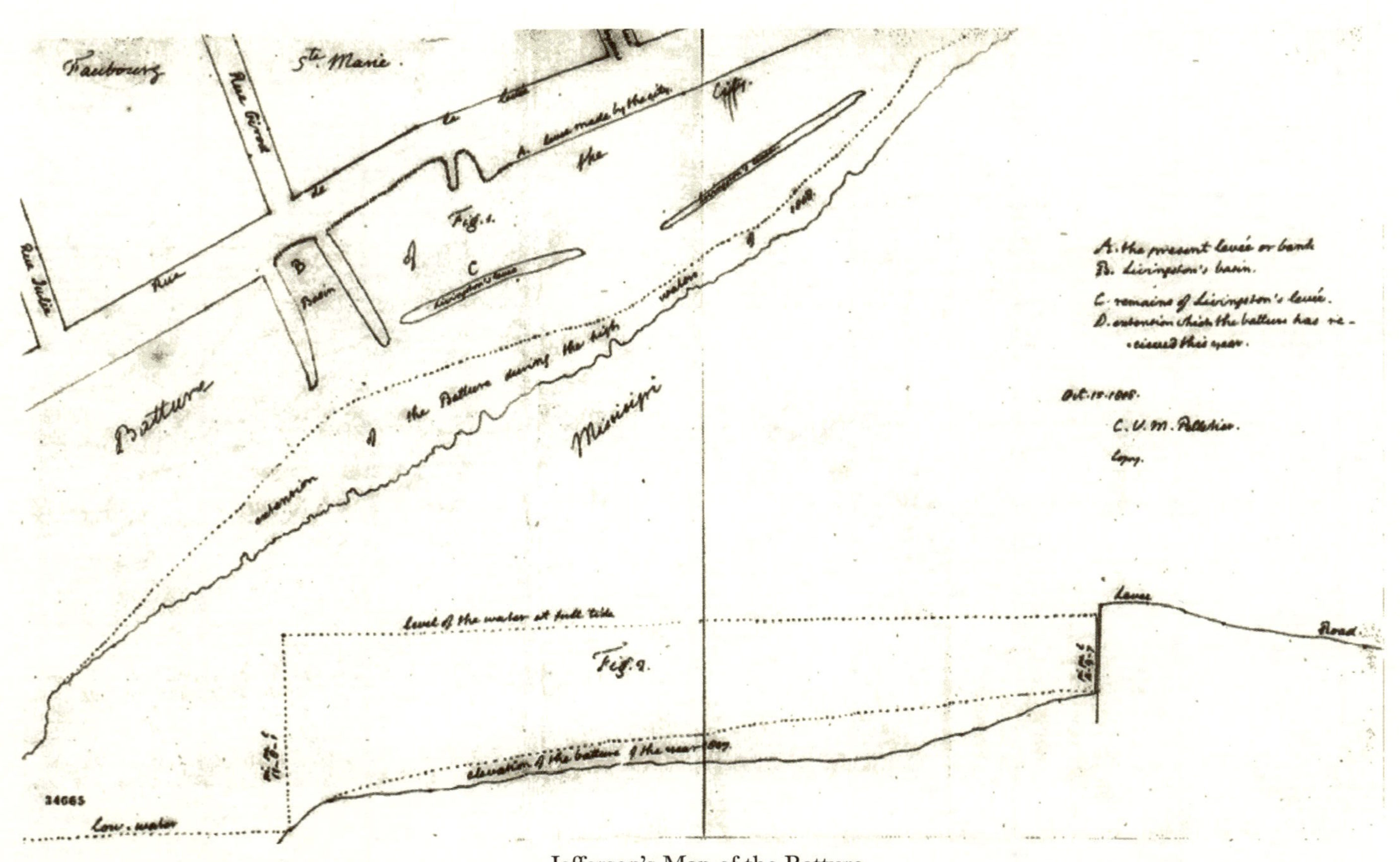

Jefferson's Map of the Batture

Edward Livingston by John Trumbull

a. Land Roll. 1810.

1052¾ Monticello. viz. 1000.a. patented by Peter Jefferson. 1735. July 19.
27½ recd in exchange by Th:Jefferson from Nicholas Lewis } being part of ... acres
25¼ purchased by Th:J. from Richard Overton ... } pat. by Nich. Meriwether
1052¾

574¾ Montalto. viz. 470½ part of 483. purchased by Th:J. from Edwd Carter the remaining 12½ havg been convd to Nich. Lewis in exchange.
40. purchased by Th:J. from Thomas Wells.
61¼ purchased by Th:J. from Benj. Brown &
3. by estimation, being the bed of the public road 30.f wide from Th:J's corner on it to it's crossing of Moore's creek.
} being parts of 9350. acres patented by John Carter Sep. 28. 1730.

150. Tufton ... patented by Peter Jefferson 1755. Sep. 10.
150. Portobello ... patented by Peter Jefferson 1740. Sep. 16.

1162¼ Milton viz. 728¼ patented by
434. patented by Bennett Henderson
1162¼
} purchased by Th:J. from the representatives of Bennet Henderson.

222. on McGehee's road & Henderson's branch patented by Th:Jefferson 1788. Apr. 12.
196. Ingraham's. on the waters of Buck island creek. patented by Th:Jefferson. 1788. Apr. 12.
819½ Lego. purchased by Th:J. from Tho. Garth, being Edwin Hickman's fourth part of 3277. as patented by Smith, Hickman, Graves and Clarke. 1734. May. 25.
485. on the Shadwell mountain, patented by Th:Jefferson. 1789. July 23.
400. Shadwell. purchasd. by Peter Jefferson from Wm Randolph, part of 2400. a. patd. by him 1735. July 1.
5212. in one contiguous body.
400. Pouncey's. patd. by Peter Jefferson, whereof 100.a. having been sold to Wm Speers was repurchased from his son John Speers by Th:Jefferson
4. Limestone quarry. on Plumbtree branch, purchased by Th:J. of Robert Sharpe, being part of 400. acres patented by Crawford.
66⅔ Limestone on the waters of Hardware, an undivided sixth of 400.a. patd by Philip Mayo 1749. Sep. 1.
5682⅔ whereof 3574$\frac{5}{12}$ are in St. Anne's parish
2108¼ are in the parish of Fredericksville.
5682⅔

4164½ acres. Poplar Forest. viz. 2558½ part of 4000.a. patd by William Stith Mar. 5. 1747. and Sep. 10. 1755. [1441½ a. the residue thereof, with 8½ a. adjoining patented by Th:J. Mar. 27. 1797. having been conveyed to T.M. Randolph & Martha ux.]
2558½
800.a. on a branch of Buffalo creek patented by Th:Jefferson May 23. 1797.
183. purchased of John Robertson by John Wayles
380. purchased of the same John Robertson by John Wayles, having been patd by Richd Callaway May 12. 1759
214. purchased of Daniel Robertson by John Wayles by whom they were patented Aug. 1. 1772.
29. recd in exchange from Benj. Johnson for 32. a. of the preceding tract by deed of
4164½

157. natural bridge, in Rockbridge. patented by Th:J. July 5. 1774.
10,004⅙ in the whole

4. lots in Beverley town, Henrico. viz. No. 57. at the foot of the hill, 107. & 108. on the public road, and 151. includes the ferry landing, being the uppermost lot of the town on the river.
a moiety of lot 335. in Richmond, containing 825. square yards purchased by Th:Jefferson of William Byrd. sold to D. Higginbotham

Jefferson's Farm Book

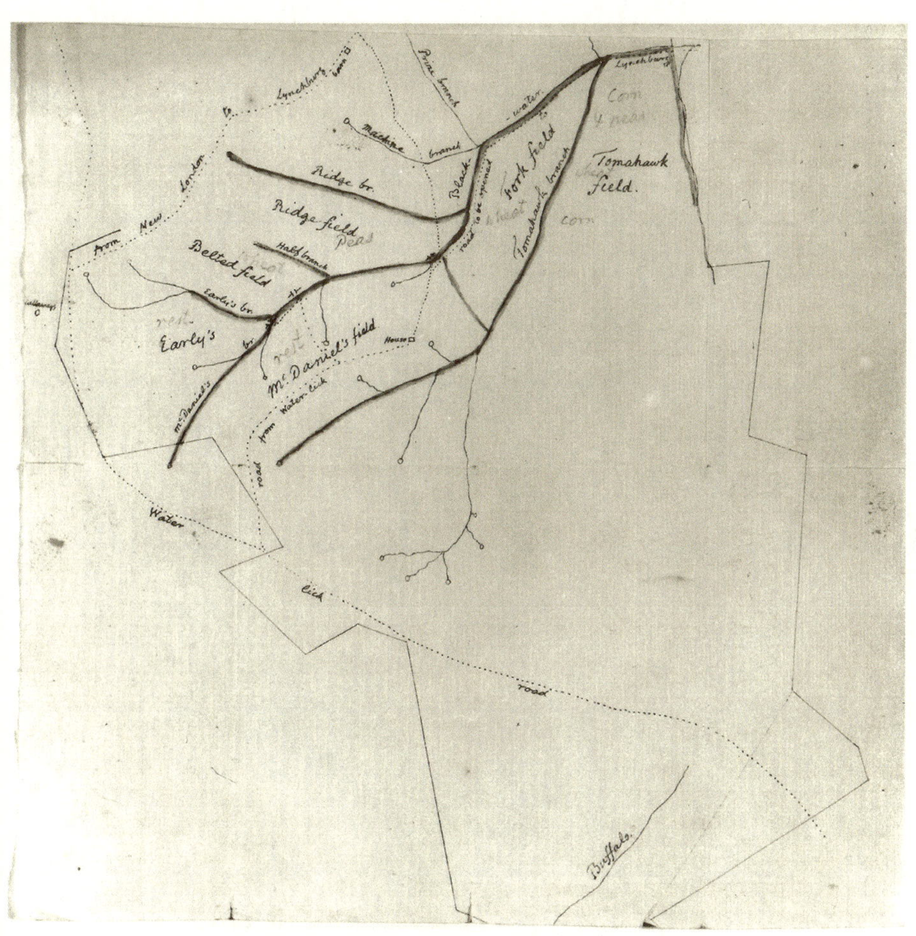

Jefferson's Map of Tomahawk Plantation

Table with a Revolving Top

Astronomical Case Clock

John Adams by Gilbert Stuart

To Gideon Granger

Dear Sir Monticello Dec. 30. 11.

I have often been extremely mortified at the abuse of my right of transmission by mail, committed by booksellers and sometimes by foreigners in sending packages of books, which I have always forbidden when apprised in time. a recent instance is so gross as to require my special mention of it to you. a mr Low of New York, publisher of an Encyclopedia has sent on 3. quarto volumes by mail, which were to be followed by I do not know how many others. I wrote back immediately to him to prevent further transmissions by mail, and I pray if any in the mean time should come to[1] the general post office, that you will be to good as to stop them there & give them house room till other arrangements with mr Low may enable me to say what is to be done them. I have reason to believe they are not put into the mail but at Washington to which place they are otherwise brought. if that be the case perhaps it would be better you should refuse to recieve them, which will most effectually prevent further trouble. excuse my troubling you with this detail from the uneasiness I have often felt before at the indiscretions of others in perverting a privilege indulged to me for very different purposes, & never used by myself as to large packages but where they concerned the government or public. I salute you with constant friendship & esteem Th: Jefferson

P.S. since writing the above another package is recieved which seems to contain 5. or 6. vols I hope Low will have stopped all others.

PoC (DLC); adjacent to signature: "M[r] Granger"; endorsed by TJ.

[1] Preceding two words interlined in place of "pass thro'."

From Andrew Logan

Sir, Lancaster Dec. 30, 1811.

Forgive an intrusive young man for taking the liberty of writing to you on a subject which is of So little importance both to you and to the community generally—that it is possible you may deem it not worth an answer.—In the course of last week I had a political contest with a gentleman in Lancaster; he states to me that you sold to Englishmen all the stock of the U. S. Bank that is possessed by foreigners, and declares you to be the soal cause of the Congress not chartering that bank, and he also stated to me that without the concent of any authority from government you sold these shares of stock which were reserved for the benefit of U.S. Our contention was warm and maintained with equal warmth on both sides. I had some grounds for believing he would have resorted to desperate measures, but as I appeared resolutely determined to meet him in any way I presume he has given his rage to the empty wind, and suffered it to be wafted to distant regions. the disput arose on a bill that was drafted by a committee from the house of representatives of this state for the chartering of said bank.—

It is a surprising circumstance that the Legislature of this state have not got their eyes open with respect to banking.—

Respected and reverenced father . . . . . I am a young man of only a tolerable education recieved in western Pennsylvania in the borough of Cannonsburgh at Jefferson College 15 miles from the residence of my father at the age of 16 I was taken from school where I only had remained for 18 months but had made tolerable progress in the Latin for the time. I was apprenticed to E: Pentland editor of a gazette in the town of Pittsburgh, where I served a regular apprenticeship from thence I went to Phila[d] in the fall of 1809 and in July last visited Baltimore Washington Alexandria Anapolis and Norfolk and have kept a Journal of all my travels thro' those places and in Sept. last came to Lancaster, and have been impressed with the idea of going to sea, as the printing business is become so dull in this and other states that it is almost impossible to make a decent living at it.—I have long thought of making application to the Secretary of the Navy for the office of 2d lieutenant if a war should insue I flatter myself I should not be the last in stepping forward to vindicate the honor of my beloved country. I wait your reply before I decide on what course to pursu for a living I possess some property in the western country, though I and it are all at your disposal command me and I will obey you. I look to you for information, as a father I intreat you to instruct me. I am acquainted with M[r] Boileau and all the officers of state and can procure their recommendations to any officer in the US.

I have the honor to be

Your obedient and very humble servant ANDREW LOGAN

RC (MoSHi: TJC-BC); ellipsis in original; addressed: "Hon. Thos. Jefferson Esqr Montecello Virginia"; franked; postmarked Lancaster, 30 Dec.; endorsed by TJ as received 5 Jan. 1812 and so recorded in SJL.

Andrew Logan (ca. 1791–1870), journalist, reputedly claimed descent from the Mingo chief Logan. He did not enter the United States Navy. Logan published the *Beaver Gazette*, 1813 and 1816–18, and the *Crisis*, 1813–16, in Beaver, Pennsylvania, and he sat on the town council in 1816. He moved to Ohio and edited the *Cleaveland Gazette*, 1818, and the *Cleave-*

land Register, 1818–20, the former being Cleveland's first newspaper. After returning to Beaver, Logan published the *Beaver Republican*, 1826–34, and served as the town's postmaster, 1832–38. He ultimately moved to Davenport, Iowa, where he printed its first newspaper, the *Iowa Sun, and Davenport and Rock Island News*, 1838–42, and then took up farming (Brigham, *American Newspapers*, 2:1445; Gertrude Van Rensselaer Wickham, *The Pioneer Families of Cleveland, 1796–1840* [1914], 1:210–1; Joseph H. Bausman, *History of Beaver County Pennsylvania* [1904], 1:461, 2:662; J. Fraise Richard and Thomas Henry, *History of Beaver County Pennsylvania* [1888], 381; Luther F. Bowers, "The Iowa Sun," State Historical Society of Iowa, *Palimpsest* 19 [1938]: 313, 322; *Davenport Democrat*, 9 July 1870).

After the Bank of the United States lost its bid to have its federal charter renewed early in 1811, its trustees tried to obtain a state charter. A memorial seeking such a charter was presented to the Pennsylvania HOUSE OF REPRESENTATIVES on 13 Dec. 1811 and a bill to this effect had its first reading a week later, but it was defeated on 20 Jan. 1812. Thirteen pro-Bank legislators signed a protest against this decision on 25 Jan. 1812, but neither that nor a last-ditch effort to obtain a charter in New York succeeded in saving the institution (*Journal of the Twenty-Second House of Representatives of the Commonwealth of Pennsylvania* [Lancaster, 1811 (i.e., 1812)], 69, 103, 271, 302–4; Donald R. Adams Jr., *Finance and Enterprise in Early America: A Study of Stephen Girard's Bank, 1812–1831* [1978], 13–5).

Ephraim PENTLAND edited the Pittsburgh *Commonwealth*, 1805–10 (Brigham, *American Newspapers*, 2:964). Nathaniel Britton BOILEAU was secretary of the commonwealth of Pennsylvania, 1808–17 (*Princetonians*, 1784–90, pp. 335–49).

To Jeremiah A. Goodman

SIR Monticello Dec. 31. 11.

The people arrived here on the evening of Saturday the 28th with every thing well except 1. hog tired & killed on the road. the articles for Dick to carry back will be now soon ready to put on board his waggon, but it is now raining, so that it is not likely he will set off today. the inclosed paper will tell you what they are & what is to be done with them. we are in very great want of the pair of oxen from Poplar forest, as only 1. pair of those we have are worth a farthing for work. as soon as you can spare the other pair I must get you to send them here. the day I left Poplar Forest I met many carts with a pr of oxen & a horse carrying a hhd of tob° to Lynchbg and with great ease. it occurred to me that instead of making another waggon as I hinted to you, we had much better adopt this mode of carrying our tob° to market, & wheat also. each plantation might equip 2. such carts, so as with the [wa]ggon they might send 5 hhds of tob° or 160. bushels of wheat a day to market. if you see no difficulty in this you had better engage the wheels, to be made strong as those I saw there, to be ready as soon as may be. every consideration urges the sending all our tob° to Richmond without the loss of a moment which can be avoided. I mentioned to mr Darnell to have the stock taken off of the clover immediately. I shall be glad to recieve by post the list of stock at both places as soon as it is taken. Accept my best wishes

TH: JEFFERSON

RC (ViU: TJP); torn at seal; addressed: "Mr Jeremiah A. Goodman Poplar forest Bedford by Dick." Enclosure not found.

Jeremiah Augustus Goodman (ca. 1780–1857) was hired by TJ as overseer at his Lego plantation on 25 Dec. 1809. Late in 1811 TJ transferred him to Poplar Forest, where he remained until TJ dismissed him at the end of May 1815. After leaving TJ's service Goodman returned to Albemarle County. In 1830 and 1850 he owned seventeen and sixteen slaves, respectively, and his real-estate holdings toward the end of his life were valued at $6,000 (Woods, *Albemarle*, 210; *MB*, esp. 2:1250, 1267, 1317n; Goodman to TJ, 16 June 1815; DNA: RG 29, CS, Albemarle Co., 1830, 1850, 1850 slave schedules; Albemarle Co. Will Book, 9:3–6 [full name in father's will], 24:96–8, 25:330–1).

Goodman's 13 Jan. 1812 reply, not found but recorded in SJL as received from Poplar Forest on 22 Jan. 1812, may have included a discussion of an exchange of one hundred pounds of flour from the Shadwell Mill then under the management of Thomas Mann Randolph and James McKinney (Account with Randolph and McKinney, [10 June 1812]).

To Jean Guillaume Hyde de Neuville

SIR Monticello Dec. 31. 11.

An absence of 6. weeks from home has prevented my earlier acknolegement of your letter of Nov. 22. I am happy to learn from that that Madame[1] d'Houdetot continues in life and health. there was no person in France from whom I recieved more civilities or for whom I entertained higher regard, and it would at all times be pleasing to me to shew my sense of it by services to those for whom she interests herself. your wishes therefore become mine, and I have communicated the case of your friend in a letter to the President. but if you could engage Col^o Williams to recommend, it would be more than equal to all other recommendations. whatever he would desire in such a case would be done by the Secretary at war without further enquiry, and I think he would be readily disposed to comply with your wishes. I shall be happy if any aid I can give on this occasion may be useful to your friend or gratifying to yourself, and pray you to accept the assurance of my great esteem & respect TH: JEFFERSON

PoC (DLC); at foot of text: "M. de Neufville"; endorsed by TJ.

Jean Guillaume Hyde de Neuville (1776–1857), later made a baron, was a French royalist and diplomat. He lived in exile in the United States, 1807–14, but kept informed of European events through his extensive contacts with other Bourbon sympathizers. After returning to France, Hyde de Neuville became a member of the Chamber of Deputies in

1815 and served as ambassador to the United States, 1816–22, and to Portugal, 1823–24. He visited Monticello late in 1818. Hyde de Neuville was again elected to the Chamber of Deputies in 1823. He was named Count of Bemposta in 1824 for his role in stopping a coup d'état in Portugal. Four years later Hyde de Neuville became minister of the French navy, retiring after the fall of the Bourbon monarchy in 1830 (*DBF*; Françoise Watel, *Jean-Guillaume Hyde de Neuville (1776–1857) Conspirateur et Diplomate* [1997]; Hyde de Neuville to TJ, 22 Dec. 1807 [DLC], 3 Dec. 1818; TJ to James Madison, 31 Oct. 1812).

Hyde de Neuville's letter to TJ of NOV. 22, not found, is recorded in SJL as received from New Brunswick on 22 Dec. 1811. TJ enclosed it to James Madison on 31 Dec. 1811. Hyde de Neuville was seeking an appointment to the United States Military Academy at West Point for Charles Despinville, the son of his FRIEND and relation Charles, comte d'Espinville. The younger Despinville became a West Point cadet in July 1813, and he later rose from third to first lieutenant as an artillery officer in the United States Army, serving from 1817 to 1830 (Hyde de Neuville to TJ, 19 Oct. 1812; Heitman, *U.S. Army*, 1:369; *JEP*, 3:103, 105, 108, 4:91 [18, 19 Dec. 1817, 14 Apr. 1830]).

[1] Manuscript: "M."

To Irenée Amelot De Lacroix

SIR Monticello Dec. 31. 11.

A long absence from home has prevented my sooner acknoleging the reciept of your letter of the 10th. I have this day written to the President of the US. on the subject of it. but, Sir, it is important on these occasions to send testimonies of character, which I would advise to obtain from those who not only know you, but are known themselves to the government. these papers come under regular review when the decision is to be made between the candidates. I do not recollect whether you have become formally a citizen, and sincerely wish the same provisions in favor of citizens exclusively which stood in your way in a former law may not find place in those now under consideration. Accept the assurance of my great respect & esteem.

TH: JEFFERSON

PoC (DLC); at foot of text: "M. Amelot de Lacroix"; endorsed by TJ.

Irenée Amelot De Lacroix, Baron de Vanden Boègard (b. ca. 1775) served under Napoleon in Egypt and at the decisive battles of Marengo and Austerlitz. He aided in a spirited defense of the island of Guadeloupe and served as an aide-de-camp to Gen. Jean Victor Moreau. Lacroix ultimately attained the rank of colonel in the French army. He followed his friend Moreau into exile and was in Boston by 1807, where he became a merchant, published several military treatises, and opened a military school. Lacroix subsequently lived in Portsmouth, New Hampshire, and New York City, and he obtained United States citizenship. He failed in repeated petitions to TJ and others for a military appointment. During the War of 1812 Lacroix apparently received government permission to raise a corps of French volunteers in New York City, but the undertaking failed. In the winter of 1813–14 the United States government briefly detained him after he accepted a major general's commission from a group of Mexican revolutionaries, releasing him after he agreed to decline the post (*Portrait of Colonel I. A. De La Croix, Baron de Vanden Boègard: written by his former Secretary, and Afterwards his Adjutant Major*, trans. Maria De Lacroix [Baltimore, 1814]; Lacroix to TJ, 29 Sept. 1807, [ca. 2 Dec. 1807], 12 Mar. 1808, and TJ to Lacroix, 21 Dec. 1807, 3 Feb. 1809 [DLC]; Madison, *Papers, Pres. Ser.*, 5:333–5, 388–9, 469; Sowerby, no. 1163; New York *Columbian*, 6 July, 30 Oct. 1811, 9 Oct. 1812; Alexander J. Dallas to James Monroe, 10 Jan. 1814 [DNA: RG 59, MLR]; Monroe to Dallas, 15 Jan. 1814 [DNA: RG 59, DL]).

SJL records Lacroix's LETTER OF THE 10TH of December, not found, as received from New York on 29 Dec. 1811. TJ enclosed it to James Madison on 31 Dec. 1811. The FORMER LAW of 12 Apr. 1808 stated that newly commissioned army officers had to be citizens of the United States or one of its territories ("An Act to raise for a limited time an additional military force," *U.S. Statutes at Large*, 2:481–3).

To James Madison

DEAR SIR Monticello Dec. 31. 11.

It is long since I have had occasion to address a line to you, and the present is an irksome one. with all the discouragements I can oppose to those who wish to make me the channel of their wishes for office, some will force themselves on me. I inclose you the letters of several merely to be placed on the file of candidates & to stand on their own ground, for I do not know one of them personally. Gerna indeed, the recommender of Arata, I once saw at Paris. he was a bookseller from Dublin, and I got him to send me some books from thence, & that is all I know of him. le Compte despinville I never saw nor heard of before; nor have I ever seen de Neufville his recommender; but he brot me a letter of introduction from the Countess d'Houdeton, an old lady from whom I recieved many civilities & much[1] hospitality while in France. she was the intimate friend of Dr Franklin, and I should feel myself obliged to render any civilities or personal services in my power to one of her recommendation. De la Croix I never saw. but he is a very able military man as far as I can judge from many excellent pamphlets & essays in the newspapers written by him, and Genl Dearborne thought him a valuable man. I write to him & to de Neufville that they must send certificates of character to the Secretary at war, and I pray you to consider me only as the postrider bearing their letters to you.

The prospect of the death of George III. still keeps up a hope of avoiding war. we have had a bad fall for our wheat. I never saw it look worse. we have had but $\frac{3}{4}$ I. of rain in the last 8. weeks. your message had all the qualities it should possess, firm, rational and dignified, and the report of the Commee of foreign relations was excellent. they carry conviction to every mind. heaven help you through all your difficulties. TH: JEFFERSON

RC (DLC: Madison Papers); endorsed by Madison. PoC (DLC); at foot of text: "The President US."; endorsed by TJ. Enclosure: Anthony Gerna to TJ, 10 June 1811, and enclosure. Other enclosures are accounted for at notes to TJ to Jean Guillaume Hyde de Neuville and to Irenée Amelot De Lacroix, both 31 Dec. 1811.

The LETTER OF INTRODUCTION from Elisabeth Françoise Sophie de La Live de Bellgarde, comtesse d'Houdetot, is not recorded in SJL and has not been found. TJ is referring to Madison's annual MESSAGE to Congress of 5 Nov. 1811 (Madison, *Papers, Pres. Ser.*, 4:1–5). The House committee on FOREIGN RELATIONS suggested that Congress complete and perfect the military establishment; raise an additional ten thousand regulars; authorize the president to accept the services of up to fifty thousand volunteers; give him the power to call portions of the militia into federal service as needed; repair all naval vessels not in service; and allow American merchant ships to arm themselves (*Report of the Committee, appointed on so much of the Message of the President of the United States, as relates to our Foreign Relations* [Washington, 1811], 8).

[1] Reworked from "so many civilities & so much."

To Oliver Pollock

SIR Monticello Dec. 31. 11

Your letter of Nov. 19. arrived here probably a day or two after I had set out on a journey from which I have but recently returned. I lose no time in answering it. I really feel every disposition to do you justice by bearing witness to the services you rendered while agent for Virginia at N. Orleans, which my memory could enable me to do with sufficient certainty. but the obliteration from that of matters of detail cannot appear strange after a lapse of more than 30. years, and the unremitting & anxious occupations I was engaged in during the subsequent scenes of the revolutionary war, after them again in Europe, & latterly in our own country: during all of which the current events sufficed to engross my whole attention, while nothing called for a recurrence to the transactions in which you were interested, so as to retrace the impressions in my mind. I remember in general that you were Agent for the state of Virginia at N. Orleans, that you paid large sums for the state to enable Genl Clarke to carry on his expedition, that this was essential to it's success, and that we entertained at that time a lively sense of these services. I think I settled some of your claims myself, while Governor, & certified them to the legislature with a recommendation of your case. so far I remember.

I have read your Memorial to the legislature, & observe in the 2^{d} page a fact stated which I think belongs to my predecessor Govr Henry, & not to myself. you say that 'Govr Jefferson finding it expedient to support the military designs of Genl Clarke authorized him to draw on you, & yourself again to draw on Penette & co. of Bordeaux.'[1] all this relates to Govr Henry. Clarke's military designs were authorised & fully executed in his time. I remember Rocheblave, taken at Kaskaskia was a prisoner in Williamsburg while Govr Henry lived there, and Hamilton, Hay, & a 3^{d} person whose name I forget, taken at Vincennes, after being long on their road, were delivered to me very soon after I entered on office. Penette too of Bordeaux had been employed by Govr Henry, & his misconduct was known too soon after I came in for me to have made much use of him. it is possible however I may have authorised some draughts on him for the subsequent support of Clarke in his acquisitions. I mean by this nothing more than a correction of fact: for of Clarke's expedition I had approved previous to his entering on it. it was an idea of his own, & he came down from his native county to propose to Govr Henry to raise volunteers himself & undertake the reduction of the Illinois posts. Govr Henry approved the design, but considering secrecy as essential to success, could not ask authority from the legislature, but consulted Col^{o} Mason, R. H. Lee, some others, & myself, who not only advised it, but pledged ourselves to Clarke to use our best endeavors in the legislature, if he succeeded, to induce them to remunerate himself & his followers in lands. he was satisfied with this, succeeded & was remunerated. Clarke's authorisation therefore to draw on you, for the support of his military designs, & yours to reimburse yourself by draughts on Penette, must have been derived from Govr Henry. the fact is of little importance, but merely for the sake of correctness. I go into no examination of the particular claim stated in your Memorial. of that I know nothing. but I have such confidence in the justice of our legislature that I am satisfied if the claim be rightful, right will be done. Accept the assurance of my esteem & respect. TH: JEFFERSON

PoC (DLC); at foot of first page: "Oliver Pollock esq."; endorsed by TJ.

Henry HAMILTON, lieutenant governor of Canada and commandant of the British outpost at Detroit, and Major Jehu HAY were among those captured at Vincennes by George Rogers Clark in April 1779 (*PTJ*, 2:256–8, 3:333).

[1] Omitted closing quotation mark editorially supplied.

Instructions for Poplar Forest Management

1811. Dec.

The crop of the Tomahawk plantation for 1812.

Corn, oats & peas. the Shop field, the best parts of it 64. acres
the Eastern parts of McDaniel's field 36. acres
100.

of the above, put about three fourths into corn, of the best parts, the rest in oats & peas.

there will still remain about 16. a^{s} of the Shop field for Burnet.

Wheat & oats. the Ridge field 130. a^{s} Early's 54. Upper Tomahawk 25. in all 209. acres

tobacco. half of the 2. year old ground 15. a^{s} the ground on the road cleared & not tended last year 10. acres about 2. now cut down, & perhaps some parts of the meadow ground. as this is more than can be tended, perhaps the 10. a^{s} on the road, or part of them may go into corn.[1]

In general I would wish 4. a^{s} of meadow ground to be prepared, to be tended one year in tob^{o} and 8. or 10. a^{s} of high ground to be tended 2. years in tob^{o} which will give from 20. to 24. a^{s} of tob^{o} every year. the high land for this year 1812. is to be cleared on the South side of Tomahawk creek, between the upper & lower fields. but as to the Meadow ground, I wish as much as possible to be prepared, of that which is easiest to prepare, & to be tended in tob^{o} pumpkins, peas or whatever will best suit it, & clean it, to be sown in timothy in the Fall. the parts already clean should be sown this spring.

All the ground which is in wheat, or which will be in oats, & turned out to rest, is to be sown in clover in February, and Burnet, if I can get seed, is to be sown in the old South hill side of the Shop field.

An acre of the best ground for hemp, is to be selected, & sown in hemp & to be kept for a permanent hemp patch

The laborers for the Tomahawk plantation are to be the following. Men. Dick, Jesse, Gawen, Phill Hubard, Hercules, Manuel, Evans. Women. Betty, Dinah, Cate's Hanah, Gawen's Sal, Aggy, Lucinda, Dinah's Hanah, Amy, Milly.

Nace, the former headman, and the best we have ever known, is to be entirely kept from labour until he recovers, which will probably be very long. he may do any thing which he can do sitting in a warm room, such as shoemaking and making baskets. he can shell corn in the corn house when it is quite warm, or in his own house at any time.

Will & Hal, when they have no work in the shop, are to get their coal wood, or assist in the crop. they will make up for the loss of Hanah's work, who cooks & washes for me when I am here. the smiths should make the plantation nails of the old bits of iron.

Edy is not named among the field workers, because either she or Aggy, whichever shall be thought most capable, is to be employed in weaving, and will be wanting to clean the house and assist here a part of the day when I am here. until a loom can be got ready both may be in the ground.

Bess makes the butter during the season, to be sent to Monticello in the winter. when not engaged in the dairy, she can spin coarse on the big wheel. Abby has been a good spinner. they may each of them take one[2] of the young spinners, to spin with them in their own house, & under their care. in that way one wheel will serve for two persons. the spinners are to be Maria (Nanny's) Sally (Hanah's) Lucy (Dinah's) and Nisy (Maria's). this last may spin at her grandmother Cate's & under her care; and so may Maria who is her niece, & whose mother will be there. they had better spin on the small wheel.

2. cotton wheels will suffice for Abby & Bess and the 2. girls with them, & a flax wheel apiece for each of the other two girls. hemp should be immediately prepared to set them at work, & a supply be kept up; and as there will be no wool to spare[3] till May, mrs Goodman may employ the wool spinners for herself till then, if she chuses. whatever terms have been settled between mrs Bacon & mrs Randolph, shall be the same with her. (I do not know what they are) and as a compensation for teaching Aggy or Edy to weave, I propose to give her the usual price for all the weaving she may do for me, the first year, considering it as her apprenticeship: and that afterwards she shall have the same proportion of her time as she is to have of the spinners.[4]

Several of the negro women complain that their houses want repair badly. this should be attended to every winter. for the present winter, repair, of preference those of the women who have no husbands to do it for them. the removal of so many negroes from this to the other place will require a good deal of work there to lodge them comfortably. this should be done at once, by the gangs of both places joined.

10. bushels of clover seed to be got early from Cofe, for the 2. plantations. fresh seed.

The ground laid off for my garden is to be inclosed with a picquet fence, 7. feet high, & so close that a hare cannot get into it. it is 80. yards square, & will take, I suppose about 2400. rails 8.f. long, besides the running rails & stakes. the sheep to be folded in it every night.

As soon as a boat load of tob^{o} is ready, it must be sent down to Gibson & Jefferson in Richmond, & an order given the boatmen on them for the price of the carriage. good enquiry should be made before hand for responsible faithful boatmen. mr Griffin knows them well; mr Robinson also will advise.

If a physician should at any time be wanting for the negroes, let our neighbor Dr Steptoe be called in. In pleurisies, or other highly inflammatory fevers, intermitting fevers, dysenteries, & Venereal cases, the doctors can give certain relief; and the sooner called to them the easier & more certain the cure. but in most other cases they oftener do harm than good. a dose of salts as soon as they are taken is salutary in almost all cases, & hurtful in none. I have generally found this, with a lighter diet and kind attention restore them soonest. the lancet should never be used without the advice of a physician, but in sudden accidents. a supply of sugar, molasses and salts should be got from mr Robinson & kept in the house for the sick. there are 2. or 3. cases of ruptures among the children at the two plantations, to which the Doctor should be immediately called, & great attention paid to them, as if not cured now, they will be lost for ever.

The work horses are to be equally divided between the 2. places, and one more apeice to be purchased if good ones can be got on good terms and on credit till the sale of our tob^{o} say April or May. a pair of well broke oxen, not above middle age is to be set apart for Monticello; & the rest equally divided. the cattle, sheep, & hogs to be equally divided as to numbers, ages, sexes E^{t}c but when the cows begin to give milk in the spring of the year, reserving at Bear creek enough for the overseer & negroes, the surplus milch cows must come to Tomahawk for the butter season, to make a supply for Monticello. the carts & tools equally divided.

Of the 28. hogs at Bear creek, the 39 in the pen at Tomahawk & 8. more expected at the same place, in all 75. 30 of the fattest must be sent to Monticello, 2 be given to the 2. hogkeepers Jame Hub^{d} & Hal, 28. be kept for the negroes & harvest, & 15 to furnish the allowance to the 2 overseers, & what remains of the 15 after furnishing them, to be kept for my use while here.

the offal of the 28 hogs for the negroes and of those for myself will serve them, it is expected 6. weeks or 2. months before entering on the distribution of meat to them regularly.

MS (NN: George Arents Tobacco Collection); written entirely in TJ's hand on both sides of a single sheet; partially dated.

TJ probably prepared this memorandum to guide the work of Jeremiah A. Goodman, his new overseer in charge at Poplar Forest.

The SHOP FIELD at Tomahawk Plantation is referred to as the Fork field in the map reproduced elsewhere in this volume and in later documents. A COFE is a hawker or peddler (*OED*). MR ROBINSON: Archibald Robertson. The TWO PLANTATIONS at Poplar Forest were Bear Creek and Tomahawk.

[1] Remainder of text in a different ink.
[2] TJ here canceled "or two."
[3] Reworked from "spin."
[4] Recto ends here.

Burgess Griffin's List of Blankets and Beds Distributed to Poplar Forest Slaves

[ca. 1811–1812]

Blankets given in 1809		in 1810	
At black water		At black water	
Betteys Cate & marey	1	Nase	1
hall	1	Abbey	1
old bettey isl[d][1]	1	Little dick Will's[2]	1
yellow dick. Aggy's[3]	2	will	1
Big hanner Cate's[4]	1	Sukey	1
Sukeys Children	1	Aggay	1
Austern	1	Seasor	1
florow	1	Big lucy (Alb)[5]	1
fanney	1		8
Eday	1		
	11		
At bar creke 1809		At bar creke 1810	
Rachal	1	Going Sal Will's[6]	1
merrear Cate's[7]	1	hubarts Sal	1
Cate hubart	1	Eve Alb[8]	1
	3	purch[d][9] mat Caffs Jim	1
total	14		4
		total	12

Blankets gven in 1811	
At black water	
yellow dick	1
Cate & marey Isl^{d} Betty's[10]	1
old bettey	1
hall	1
Big hannah	1
Austan	1
Bess	1
little Cate[11] Sucky's[12]	1
	8.
At Bar Creeke 1811	
Cate hubert	1
Mareear	1
Rachal	1
Dannel	1
Rubin	1
	5
total	13

Beds given out in 1809	
At black water	
Diner	1
hannah	1
Lucinder	1
olde bettey	1
Eady	1
	5
At bar creeke 1809	
Rachal	1
Cate hubrt	1
	2
	7
At black water in 1810	
Nanney	1
florow	1
lucy	1
	3
At bar creeke 1810	
Eve	1
mureear	1
Goings Sal	1
	3

MS (ViU: TJP-ER); in Griffin's hand, with additions by TJ; undated; written on both sides of a single sheet, with first side consisting of blanket lists for 1809 and 1810; endorsed by TJ: "Pop. Forest. Griffin's list of blankets & beds given 1809. 10. 11."

Griffin probably prepared this list in connection either with handing over his responsibilities as overseer at Poplar Forest to Jeremiah A. Goodman late in 1811 or with the settlement of his accounts with TJ, which he completed on 11 Sept. 1812 (*MB*, 2:1282).

BIG HANNER: Big Hannah. AUSTERN: Augustine. SEASOR: Caesar. FLOROW: Flora. BAR CREKE: Bear Creek. GOING: Gawen. MERREAR: Maria. MAT CAFFS JIM: TJ's slave James (b. 1772), whom he had purchased in 1806, worked at Poplar Forest and was later moved to Lego (*MB*, 2:1194).

[1] Word (abbreviation for "island") added by TJ.

[2] Word added by TJ.

[3] Word added by TJ.

[4] Word added by TJ.

[5] Word (abbreviation for "Albemarle") and parentheses added by TJ.

[6] Word added by TJ.

[7] Word added by TJ.

[8] Word added by TJ.

[9] Word added by TJ.

[10] Preceding two words added by TJ.

[11] Word interlined in place of "dick."

[12] Word added by TJ.

Lists of Slaves at Poplar Forest

[1811–1812]

Bear creek

43. Jame Hubbard
47. Cate
71. Armistead. Hubard's
74. Caesar. Bess's
    Austin
76. Maria. Cate's
78. Nanny.
83. Flora. Will's
88. Cate. Betty's
    Cate. Suck's.
    Fanny. Will's.
    Sally. Cate's.
90. Daniel. Bess's
92. Mary. Betty's.
93. Reuben. Hanah's.
94. Stephen. Suck's.
97. Cate. Rachael's
98. Maria. Nanny's
99. Nisy. Maria's
01. Phil. Nanny's
04. Gawen. Flora's
    Johnny. Maria's
06. Milly. Nanny's
    Davy. Suck's Cate's.
    Aleck. Flora's.
07. Rachael. Fanny's.
08. Billy. Cate's Sally's
    George Dennis. Nanny's
    Billy. Flora's.
09. Isaac. Maria's
10. Anderson. Sally's.
    Anderson. Nanny's
11. John. Suck's Cate's.
    Rhody. Fanny's.
    Boston. Flora's.

Tomahawk.

47. Bess.
49. Betty
53. Will
    Abby.
66. Dinah.
67. Dick.
    Hal.
70. Hanah. Cate's
72. Jesse.
73. Nace. Cate's
77. Sal. Will's
78. Gawen. Betty's.

    Phil Hubard?[1]

89. Aggy. Dinah's.
91. Lucinda. Hanah's.
92. Edy. Will's.
94. Manuel. Will's.
    Evans. Dinah's
    Hercules. Betty's.
96. Hanah. Dinah's
97. Amy. Will's
    Milly. Sal's
98. Sally. Hanah's
99. Ambrose Suck's
    Lucy. Dinah's.
    Billy. Hanah's
01. Betty. Sal's
02. Jamy. Dinah's.
04. Prince. Suck's
    Abby Sal's
05. Jamey Hanah's.
    Briley. Dinah's
06. Joe. Suck's
    Edy. Sal's[2]

08. Phil. Hanah's.
09. Martin. Sal's
Shepherd. Suck's
Melinda. Lucinda's
Edmund. Hanah's
11. Moses. Sal's

35.

40.[3]

Tomahawk

Hall. Bess's. 67. Sep.
Hanah. Cate's. 70. Jan.
Sally. 98.
Billy 99.
Jamy. 05.
Phil. 08.
Edmund. 09.
Lucinda. Hanah's. 91. June
Melinda. 09. Aug. 8.
Nace. Cate's. 73.
Phil Hubard.
Will. ab[t] 53.
Abby. ab[t] 53.
Edy. Will's. 92. Apr.
Manuel. Will's. 94.
Amy. Will's. 97.
Gawen. Betty's. 78. Aug.
Sal. Will's. 77. Nov.
Betty. 01. Jan.
Abby. 04. Nov.
Edy. 06. Aug.
Martin. 09. Jan. 31.
Moses. 11. Apr.
Milly. Sal's. 97. Mar.
Dick. 67.
Dinah. 66.
Aggy. 89.
Evans. 94.
Hanah. 96.
Lucy. 99.
Jamy. 02.
Briley. 05.

Bear creek

Jame Hubbard. ab[t] 43.
Cate. ab[t] 47.
Armistead. Hubard's 71.
Cate. Rachael's 97. Aug.
Maria. Cate's. 76. Oct.
Nisy. 99.
Johnny. 04. Sep.
Isaac. 09. Nov.
Sally. Cate's. 88. Aug.
Billy. 08. Aug.
Anderson. 10. Apr. 14.
Reuben. Hanah's. 93.
Austin. Betty's. 75. Aug.
Flora. Will's. 83.
Gawen. 04. July
Aleck. 06. Sep.
Billy 08. Oct.
Boston. 11. Dec. 1.
Fanny. Will's. 88. Aug.
Rachael. 07. Feb.
Rhody. 11. July.
Caesar. Bess's. 74. Sep.
Cate. Suck's. 88. Mar.
Davy. 06. June
John. 11. June 1.
Daniel. Suck's. 90. Sep.
Stephen. Suck's. 94.
Cate. Betty's. 88. Mar. 8.
Mary. Betty's. 92. Jan.
Nanny. 78. July
Maria. 98. Feb. 24.
Phil. 01. Aug.

Bess. ab[t] 47		Milly. 06. May.
Ambrose. 99.	children of Suck, the daughter of Bess.	George Dennis. 08. May.
Prince. 04. Mar.		Anderson. 10. Aug.
Joe. 06. May		
Shepherd. 09. Apr.		
Betty. ab[t] 49.		
Hercules. Betty's. 94. Nov. 20.		
Jesse. 72. Nov.		
40.		35

MS (PPRF); written entirely in TJ's hand on both sides of a single sheet, creased down the middle; undated.

This document may have been prepared for the use of incoming overseer Jeremiah A. Goodman. It was certainly compiled after the birth of BOSTON on 1 Dec. 1811 and probably before the birth of Edy's daughter Nancy on 15 Feb. 1812 (Betts, *Farm Book*, pt. 1, 131). TJ sorted his Poplar Forest slaves on the basis of their residence at his Bear Creek and Tomahawk plantations and then listed them twice, grouped by age and by family. The number given before or after the name of each slave represents the year in which he or she was born, and the number at the bottom of each column represents the total number of slaves in that column.

[1] TJ canceled "88. Cate. Betty's" on the line above this entry and "Cate. Suck's" on the line below it.

[2] Preceding two words written over "Milly. Nanny's," erased.

[3] One side of sheet ends here.

List of Landholdings and Monticello Slaves

[ca. 1811–1812]

[1000].	a.[s] pat[d] 1735.	1743.	Abram.
27½	purch[d] from N. Lewis	49.	Caesar.
25¼	Overton	53.	John.
470½	part of 483. Carter	55.	Davy.
40.	Wells	56.	Amy.
61¼	Brown	57.	Doll.
3.	bed of road. Brown	58.	Isabel.
150.	Tufton. pat[d] 1755.	59.	Betty Brown.
150.	Portobello pat[d] 1740.	60.	Ned.
[1]927½	the Montic[o] tract		Lewis.
[1]162¼	the Hendersons	61.	Nance.
222.	on Henderson's bra.	64.	Jenny. Ned's
196.	Ingraham's.	68.	Isaac.
[1]580¼	the Milton tract.		Bagwell.

400. a^{s} Shadwell
819$\frac{1}{4}$. Lego.
485. Shadwell mount^{n}
400. Pouncey's
4. Limestone. Sharp's
133$\frac{1}{3}$ d^{o} Hardware
5749$\frac{1}{3}$

Bedford & Campbell
214. Dan. Robinson
2650. part of Pop. For.
[2]864. N. of Tomahawk.
534. part of Pop. For.
380. Callaway's pat.
183. Jno Robinson's
800. Buffalo.
1897. S. of Tomahawk
29. Johnson
[4]790

[85.] [Charles.]
Ben.
John Bedf. Dinah's
Davy Bedf.
86. Bartlet.
Ned.
87. Ursula
Edy.
88. Lewis j^{r}
Mary. Bagw's.
Fanny.
89. Aggy. Charles's
90. Dick. Ned's
Jesse.
Abram j^{r}
91. Nancy. Rach's
Lilly.
92. Gill.

Jenny. Lewis'.
69. Critta.
70. Peter Hemings.
71. Minerva.
72. Jame Bedf^{d}
73. Sally. Hem.
Rachael B. Oct.
75. John Hem.
76. James.[1] Isab's.
Mary. Jerry's.
Rachael. Doll's.
77. Jerry.
79. Cretia.
Moses. Isab's.
Eve.
80. Mary. Moses'.
Joe.
81. Wormly.
Dick. Bedf.
82. Shepherd.
83. Lucy. Phill's.
Barnaby.
Burwell.
84[.] Davy[.] Is[ab's.][2]
1799. Robert.[3]
1800. John. Cretia's.
Nanny. Bagw's.
Isabel. Lew's.
Thrimson.[4] Isab's
Israel. Ned's
Isaiah. Jerry's
01. William. Moses'.
Harriet. Sally's
Mary. Bet's
Lovilo. Isab's.
Joe. Rachael's[5]
02. Jerry. Jerry's
Randal. cretia's.
03. Davy. Moses's.
Moses. Ned's
04. Jupiter. Jerry's.
05. James. Edy's

Sally Lew's
Moses. Bedf. Dinah's.
93. Edwin.
Virginia.
Thenia.
94. Scilla.
Dolly. Doll's
Solomon.
95. Thruston.
James. Lew's
Esther.
96. Philip. Suck's
Nace. Maria's
James. Ned's
Suckey.
97. Sanco. Eve's.
Indridge.
Evelina.
Lazaria.[8]
Bec.
[98.] [Bev]erly.
[Aggy. Ned's.]

Madison. Sally's.
Joe. Ursula's.
Robin. Lucy's.
Henry. Cretia's.
Washington. Mary B's.
Eliza. Rach's
Lania. Bedf. Rachael's[6]
06. Willis. Bagw's
Jossy. Eve's.
Calia. Moses'.
Sucky. Ned's
07. Anne. Ursula's.
Milly. Cretia's
Maria. Edy's
Sandy. Lucy's
Gloster. B. Rachael's[7]
08. Archy. Bagw's.
Eston. Sally's.
Ellen. Rach's.
09. Dolly. Ursula's
Burwell. Eve's.
Stannard. Lilly's.
Lilburn. Cretia's.
Ellen. Fanny's.

MS (ViFreJM); possibly incomplete; written entirely in TJ's hand on both sides of a single sheet; edges frayed, with missing text supplied from Betts, *Farm Book*, pt. 1, 127, 130; undated, but composed after the death in October 1811 of TJ's slave Anderson and after the transfer to Poplar Forest in 1811–12 of Phill Hubbard (Betts, *Farm Book*, pt. 1, 130).

A page from TJ's Farm Book depicting another list of his landholdings is reproduced elsewhere in this volume.

BRA.: branch.

[1] *Farm Book*: "Jamey."

[2] Recto ends here.

[3] In *Farm Book* TJ here canceled "Billy Bedford."

[4] Corrected to "Thrimston" in *Farm Book*.

[5] Entry interlined.

[6] Entry interlined.

[7] Entry interlined.

[8] Corrected to "Maria" in *Farm Book*.

Resumption of Correspondence with John Adams

JOHN ADAMS TO THOMAS JEFFERSON,
1 JAN. 1812

EDITORIAL NOTE

By the latter part of the 1790s Thomas Jefferson and John Adams had become bitter political opponents. The friendship they had forged as congressional and diplomatic colleagues, fellow revolutionaries, and members of George Washington's administration did not survive the strain of Jefferson's victory in the 1800 presidential election. Adams left the nation's capital just before Jefferson's inauguration in March 1801, and with the exception of brief notes they exchanged shortly thereafter, no letters passed between the two men for more than a decade. Jefferson tried to heal the breach after Abigail Adams wrote to console him for the loss of his daughter Maria in 1804, but to no avail. The eventual repair of their damaged relationship is attributable to the efforts of their mutual friend Benjamin Rush.

On 17 Oct. 1809 Rush wrote Adams that he had had a dream in which a "renewal of the friendship & intercourse" between the two ex-presidents took place, a reconciliation prompted, he added, by a short letter from Adams to his former rival. Adams encouragingly replied that he had "no other objection to your Dream, but that it is not History. It may be Prophecy." Early in 1811 Rush advised Jefferson of his ardent wish that "a friendly and epistolary intercourse might be revived" between the two men, expressing his firm belief that "an Advance on your Side will be a Cordial to the heart of Mr. Adams." These initiatives bore no fruit at the time. In the summer of 1811, however, Jefferson's neighbors Edward Coles and John Coles visited Quincy, and Adams there told them that "I always loved Jefferson, and still love him." After these words reached Jefferson, he was moved on 5 Dec. 1811 to write Rush about the continued warmth and depth of his feelings for his old friend. Sensing an opportunity, Rush soon passed the pertinent passages from Jefferson's letter along to Adams. An olive branch having been extended, Rush implored Adams to write to Jefferson and for the two men to "embrace each other! Bedew your letters of reconciliation with tears of affection and joy. Bury in silence all the causes of your separation. Recollect that explanations may be proper between lovers but are never so between divided friends." The letter printed below renewed direct contact between Adams and Jefferson and reestablished one of the most celebrated epistolary conversations in American history, one that continued until the last year of both men's lives (Lyman H. Butterfield, "The Dream of Benjamin Rush: The Reconciliation of John Adams and Thomas Jefferson," *Yale Review* 40 [1950]: 297–319; TJ to Adams, 8 Mar. 1801, and Adams to TJ, 24 Mar. 1801, *PTJ*, 33:213, 426; Rush to Adams, 17 Oct. 1809 and 16 Dec. 1811, Rush, *Letters*, 2:1021–3, 1110–1; Adams to Rush, 25 Oct. 1809 [CtY: Franklin Collection]; Rush to TJ, 2 Jan. 1811; TJ to Rush, 16 Jan. 1811, and note; Adams to TJ, 17 Apr. 1826. Portraits of Adams and Rush are reproduced elsewhere in this volume.

John Adams to Thomas Jefferson

Dear Sir Quincy January 1st 1812.

As you are a Friend to American Manufactures under proper restrictions, especially Manufactures of the domestic kind, I take the Liberty of Sending you by the Post a Packett containing two Pieces of Homespun lately produced in this quarter by One who was honoured in his youth with Some of your Attention and much of your kindness.

All of my Family whom you formerly knew are well. My Daughter Smith is here and has Successfully gone through a perilous and painful Operation, which detains her here this Winter, from her Husband and her Family at Chenango: where one of the most gallant and Skilful Officers of our Revolution is probably destined to Spend the rest of his days, not in the Field of Glory, but in the hard Labours of Husbandry.

I wish you Sir many happy New years and that you may enter the next and many Succeeding years with as animating Prospects for the Public as those at present before us. I am Sir with a long and Sincere Esteem your Friend and

Servant John Adams

RC (DLC); addressed: "Thomas Jefferson Esqr late President of The United States Montecello Virginia"; franked; postmarked Quincy, 6 Jan.; endorsed by TJ as received 14 Jan. 1812 and so recorded in SJL. FC (Lb in MHi: Adams Papers). PoC of Tr (DLC); in TJ's hand; conjoined with PoC of Tr of TJ to Adams, 21 Jan. 1812. Enclosed in TJ to Benjamin Rush, 21 Jan. 1812.

John Adams (1735–1826), president of the United States, 1797–1801, was born in Braintree (now Quincy), Massachusetts, graduated from Harvard College in 1755, and taught school briefly before his admission to the bar in 1758. He married Abigail Smith in 1764. Adams first achieved prominence by drafting resolves and writing a series of newspaper essays opposing the Stamp Act in 1765. Three years later he moved his family to Boston, where he became a representative in the General Court. That body elected Adams to both the First and Second Continental Congresses, where he distinguished himself as an advocate of American nationhood and served with TJ on the committee that prepared the Declaration of Independence. In 1778 he traveled to France to help negotiate a treaty of alliance. Adams returned to Massachusetts the following year and took the lead in writing a constitution for the state before traveling back to France to continue negotiations. After concluding peace with England, he became the first American minister to the Court of Saint James in London. Returning to the United States in 1788, Adams was a vocal supporter of the new federal constitution and served as the first vice president of the United States, 1789–97. He succeeded George Washington as president in the latter year, but his administration was plagued by difficult relations with France and divisive struggles within the Federalist party that contributed to his defeat for reelection by TJ, his vice president (*ANB*; *DAB*; *Sibley's Harvard Graduates*, 13:513–20; Lyman H. Butterfield and others, eds., *Diary and Autobiography of John Adams*, 4 vols. [1961]; Butterfield, Richard Alan Ryerson, C. James Taylor, and others, eds., *Adams Family Correspondence* [1963–]; Robert J. Taylor, Ryerson, C. James Taylor, and others, eds., *Papers of John Adams* [1977–]; David McCullough, *John Adams* [2001]).

The PIECES OF HOMESPUN were John Quincy Adams's *Lectures on Rhetoric and Oratory, Delivered to the Classes of Senior and Junior Sophisters in Harvard University*, 2 vols. (Cambridge, Mass., 1810; Sowerby, no. 4659). Their arrival after Adams's covering letter initially caused TJ to take the playful reference to homespun at face value (TJ to Adams, 21, 23 Jan. 1812). Adams's daughter Abigail Adams SMITH had recently undergone surgery for breast cancer. Her HUSBAND was Revolutionary War veteran William Stephens Smith (*ANB*; McCullough, *John Adams*, 601–2).

From Thomas Erskine Birch

ILLUSTRIOUS & MOST RESPECTABLE SIR. Jan. 1st 1812

Some time in Novr last I transmitted by the mail to your address a copy of the Virginian Orator, in which was inclosed a letter. Separate from the packet there was delivered to the stage-driver, at the same time, a letter to G & R Waite of Baltimore in which was inclosed 3 tickets in the "Susquehanna Canal lottery" all of which had drawn prizes, but by a reference to the post Office register in which they were all to be deposited, it appears that the temptation was too strong for the stage-driver to withstand, for they were never deposited & it appears that neither of them have reached the place of their destination.—The author of the Virginian Orator thought he could not pay a greater tribute of respect to the man who had rendered the unremitted service of 40 years to his country than by teaching the American youth to lisp the fame of the man of Monticello as Pope did the "Man of Ross."

The Ode which is particularly addressed to yourself, and other parts alluding to your administration and retirement, were the only wreath that an obscure friend could offer;

Such as it is—ah might it worthier be,
Its scanty foliage all is due to thee.

From some of your literary friends, I have had the satisfaction to hear, that the parts concerning yourself were more acceptable to them, than all the lapidary adulation of modern epitaphs. And when your body shall be consigned to the tomb I said with Ovid

"Carminibus vives in omne tempus meis."

With sentiments of high regard & all due consideration, the Author takes the liberty of transmitting another copy with this letter, requesting you to accept of this small tribute of respect.

From, illustrious Sir, Y[r] M[o] Ob[t] & very humble Ser[t]

THO[S] E BIRCH
Preceptor of Anchor & Hope
Academy Wythe County V[a]

RC (MHi); dateline at foot of text; addressed: "Tho[s] Jefferson Esq[r] late President of the U.S. Monticello Albemarle V[a]" by "Mail"; franked; postmarked Montgomery Court House, 17 Jan. 1812; endorsed by TJ as received 19 Jan. 1812 and so recorded in SJL. Enclosure: enclosure to Birch to TJ, [Nov. 1811].

G & R WAITE OF BALTIMORE ran a lottery and exchange office (William Fry, *Fry's Baltimore Directory for the Year 1812* [Baltimore, 1812], 79). Alexander POPE eulogized the MAN OF ROSS (John Kyrle, an English landed gentleman) as a benefactor of the poor (*Of the Use of Riches: An Epistle To the Right Honorable Allen Lord Bathurst* [London, 1732; later forming the third of Pope's *Moral Essays*], 16–8). CARMINIBUS VIVES IN OMNE TEMPUS MEIS: "thou shalt live for all time in my song," from Ovid, *Tristia*, 1.6.19 (*Ovid with an English translation: Tristia. Ex Ponte*, trans. Arthur Leslie Wheeler, Loeb Classical Library [1924], 36–7).

From Benjamin Galloway

SIR. City of Washington Jan 1st 1812.

The enclosed poetical production was placed in my hands a few days ago by an English Lady, M[rs] Mary D[e]Butts accompanied with an earnest request that I would cause it to be forwarded to you. The abovementioned Lady is the Wife of Doctor Richard D[e]Butts whose residence is in the State of Maryland immediately opposite the Town of Alexandria. The enclosed Extract is a verbatim et literatim Copy of an original Letter from the Author of the Poem (M[r] Northmore) to M[rs] D[e]Butts. The circumstance alluded to, which will probably prevent M[r] Northmore from ever carrying into effect the design he had once contemplated of visiting the United States, is, that he has lately entered into the Holy Estate of Matrimony with a Miss Welby, the neice of M[rs] Mary D[e]Butts. In conformity to the anxious wish and sollicitation, that a sure conveyance should be afforded of forwarding said work to you, I have delivered it to M[r] Secretary Munroe: who has promised [to] carry M[rs] D[e]Butt's wishes (quo ad hoc) into [e]xecution. The Author is an intimate acquaintance of said Lady; is an independant country Gentleman, of eight thousand pounds per Year; a real Whigg, M[rs] D[e]Butts at the time of placing the Volume in my hands with the accompanying Extract intimated to me, that an acknowledgment by you of the having received said Poem, would be infinitely gratifying to the Author, as well as proof positive, that She had faithfully executed the commission with which her Friend had honoured her.

Wishing you every earthly felicity

I am, Sir, with consideration and respect Yours et cetera

BENJAMIN GALLOWAY

RC (DLC); margin damaged; dateline at foot of text; endorsed by TJ as received 12 Jan. 1812 and so recorded in SJL. Enclosure: Thomas Northmore to Mary DeButts, stating that "I beg your acceptance of my Poem of Washington & will trouble you to send the other Copy to your late upright & enlightend President M[r] Jefferson a man whose name I have introduced with merit & approbation into my work, and whose political Career will I am certain be mentioned by Posterity with applause. It would have been my pride to have seen him & conversed with him, and I once indulged the hope, but now it will probably never be in my power" (Tr in MHi; undated extract; at foot of text: "extract of a Letter from Thomas Northmore Esq[r] N[o] 16 Orchard Street, Portman Square London").

The POETICAL PRODUCTION being transmitted to TJ, Northmore's *Washington, or Liberty Restored: A Poem, in Ten Books* (London, 1809; Sowerby, no. 4303), suggested that in promoting "The cause of freedom, and the cause of man," TJ "shalt be another Washington" (book V, lines 292–5), and alluded in a footnote to "The high respect in which Washington held this enlightened friend of the human race" (2d ed. [Baltimore, 1809], 136).

MARY D[E]BUTTS, born Mary Anne Welby in Lincolnshire, England, married Samuel DeButts in 1785. RICHARD D[E]BUTTS was their first son. The family moved in about 1792 to Prince Georges County, MARYLAND (Fillmore Norfleet, *Saint-Mémin in Virginia: Portraits and Biographies* [1942], 158–9; ViU: DeButts Family Letters). Thomas Northmore's brief marriage to Penelope WELBY actually ended with her death in 1792. He married Emmeline Eden in 1809 (*ODNB*).

From Hugh Nelson

DEAR SIR Washington Jany 1. 1812

Your favour of the 28[h] Ulto was receivd this morning. I must apologise for the liberty of detaining your manuscript so long: but it was done upon the presumption that you wou'd not want it, during its detention; and that if any effort shou'd be made in Congress a recurrence to the manuscript wou'd be of importance to myself, in combating M[r] L—s pretension before the legislature of the Nation. I shall return to Albemarle for a few days, as soon as we dispose of the Bills now before us, for military preparations: This will be effected I think in a very few days. As I do not think it quite wise to trust the Book to the mail: I will venture to detain it until I return. It gives me pleasure to learn that this work will be laid before the public: I must state that I have found some misconceptions relating to this Question, prevailing here: which I am sure, the examination of the question made by yourself, published, wou'd dispel. Mr L— and his friends have been active, I doubt not, in propagating crises and impositions on this Subject. These will be certainly removed by the publication of the Work—

accept my assurance of great respect and friendship

Hugh Nelson

RC (DLC); endorsed by TJ as received 5 Jan. 1812 and so recorded in SJL.

The PRETENSION was Edward Livingston's claim to the batture at New Orleans. On 11 Jan. 1812 President James Madison signed a bill to raise an additional MILITARY force (*U.S. Statutes at Large*, 2:671–4).

To John Crawford

Sir Monticello Jan. 2. 12

Your favor of Dec. 17. has been duly recieved, & with it the pamphlet on the cause, seat, & cure of diseases, for which be pleased to accept my thanks. the commencement: which you propose by the Natural history of the diseases of the human body is a very interesting one, & will certainly be the best foundation for whatever relates to their cure. while Surgery is seated in the temple of the exact sciences, medecine has scarcely entered it's threshold. her theories have passed in such rapid succession as to prove the insufficiency of all, & their fatal errors are recorded in the necrology of man. for some forms of disease well known and well defined, she has found substances which will restore order to the human system; & it is to be hoped that observation & experience will add to their number. but a great mass of diseases remains undistinguished, & unknown, exposed to the random shot of the theory of the day. if on this chaos you can throw such a beam of light as your celebrated brother has done on the sources of animal heat, you will, like him, render great service to mankind.

The fate of England, I think with you, is nearly decided, and the present form of her existence is drawing to a close. the ground, the houses, the men will remain; but in what new form they will revive & stand among nations, is beyond the reach of human foresight. we hope it may be one of which the predatory principle may not be the essential characteristic. if her transformation shall replace her under the laws of moral order, it is for the general interest that she should still be a sensible & independant weight in the scale of nations, & be able to contribute, when a favorable moment presents itself, to reduce under the same order her great rival in flagitiousness. we especially ought to pray that the powers of Europe may be so poised & counter-poised among themselves that their own safety may require the presence of all their force at home, leaving the other quarters of the globe in undisturbed tranquility. when our strength will permit us to give the law of our hemisphere, it should be that the meridian of the mid-Atlantic should be the line of demarcation between war & peace, on this side of which no act of hostility should be committed, and the lion & the lamb lie down in peace together.

I am particularly thankful for the kind expressions of your letter towards myself, and tender you in return my best wishes & the assurances of my great respect & esteem. TH: JEFFERSON

PoC (DLC); at foot of first page: "Doct[r] Crawford."

Crawford's BROTHER Adair Crawford was a physician and chemist in London whose *Experiments and Observations on Animal Heat, and the Inflammation of Combustible Bodies; Being an Attempt to Resolve these Phænomena into a General Law of Nature*, 2d ed. (London, 1788; Sowerby, no. 842) achieved some prominence (*ODNB*). TJ's biblical reference to THE LION & THE LAMB paraphrases Isaiah 11.6: "The wolf also shall dwell with the lamb, and the leopard shall lie down with the kid; and the calf and the young lion and the fatling together; and a little child shall lead them."

To Donald Fraser

Monticello Jan. 2. 12.

Th: Jefferson presents his compliments & thanks to mr Frazer for the copy of the Compendium inclosed to him. for those who read little, abridgments are necessary; & even for those who read most it is convenient to have them at hand to save troublesome research. it will therefore find it's scale of usefulness. he salutes mr Frazer with respect.

PoC (DLC); dateline at foot of text; endorsed by TJ.

To John Pitman

SIR Monticello Jan. 2. 12.

Your favor of Dec. 4. has been duly recieved, & with it your addresses to the Tammany & Philermenian societies. in the former I find all those sentiments of republican patriotism which distinguish every branch of the Tammany societies, and on which depend all the hopes of man of seeing one good government at least exist on the earth. I will add on the subject of the poem that if Homer & Virgil had employed their sublime geniusses in the cultivation of that spirit of peace & philanthropy which has inspired your muse I verily believe there would have been less of war & bloodshed in the world, and Plato would probably not have proposed to exclude Poets from his republic. for these pamphlets as well as for the very obliging expressions of your letter towards myself personally, accept my thanks and the assurances of great respect & esteem.

Th: Jefferson

RC (RPB); at foot of text: "M[r] John Pitman jun[r] Providence." PoC (ViW: TC-JP); endorsed by TJ.

To Thomas Erskine Birch

Sir Monticello Jan. 3. 12.

I duly recieved the favor of your letter wherein mention was made of a volume inclosed in it which had been committed to the press by yourself about the close of my administration, but which did not accompany the letter. whether omitted inadvertently, or more bulky than is admitted into the mail, or separated by the way and still to come on I do not know. whatever it's contents may have been, I should have perused them with all the satisfaction I derive from whatever flows from the pen of pure republican patriotism. that such sentiments must be yours, your course thro' the war is a sufficient pledge. for the song of the poet I have no pretensions of having furnished the brilliant materials. my humble object has been to endeavor honestly to deserve the approbation of my fellow citizens. in this consciousness I tender you thanks for whatever indulgencies you may have expressed towards me, and with these the assurances of my great respect.

Th: Jefferson

PoC (DLC); at foot of text: "M[r] Tho[s] Erskine Birch"; endorsed by TJ.

To Joseph Hunter

Sir Monticello Jan. 3. 12.

I have two clocks out of order, and requiring something to be done to them, probably not much, as they will go for a while when put in motion, but stop again after awhile. presuming that your business leads you sometimes to our court, I should be glad whenever you come if you would call & set these to rights. indeed having 4. or 5. of these in the house we never pass the year without some repairs being necessary, which may furnish further occasion of troubling you hereafter. accept my best wishes. TH: JEFFERSON

PoC (MHi); endorsed by TJ as a letter to "Hunter." Recorded in SJL as a letter to Joseph Hunter, of Warren.

Joseph Hunter was a resident of Warren in Albemarle County who repaired clocks for TJ on three occasions in 1812 and 1813 (*MB*, 2:1278, 1290, 1291; TJ to Hunter, 20 June 1813; Hunter to TJ, 20 June 1813; DNA: RG 29, CS, Albemarle Co., 1810, 1820).

From Joseph Milligan

DEAR SIR Georgetown January 3rd 1812

I hope you will pardon me but as the manuel is out of print and many applications for it I wished to know whether I might have your permission to print a new edition during the present Session of Congress: the booksellers both of Baltimore & Philad have applied to me for it therfore I wished to say to them whether I might Calculate on supplying them from the New edition I proposed with your permission to print it on a fine wove Flax 8vo I wrote you on that Subject on the 2nd December last which perhaps has not reached you, I have spoken with Mr S. H. Smith on the Subject of a new edition last winter at which time I purchased the few remaining Copies of the first Edition as he is out of business he seemed to think it advisable for me to have a new edition printed if I could obtain your permission with best wishes for your health & happiness I am

with high respect & Esteem Your obidient Servant

JOSEPH MILLIGAN

RC (DLC); at foot of text: "Thomas Jefferson Esqr Monticello"; endorsed by TJ as received 5 Jan. 1812 and so recorded in SJL.

Notes on a Conversation with Nathaniel H. Hooe

1812. Jan. 6. memm. mr Hooe offd me Tom for 450. D I offered him that sum paiable at 2. annual instalments, which he declined. I told him that at half cash & half on 12. mo. credit I would give but 400.D.

MS (MHi); entirely in TJ's hand; on address leaf of Hooe to TJ, 10 Sept. 1811.

From James Monroe

DEAR SIR washington Jany 6. 1812

A circumstance has occurr'd with which it may be useful for you to be made acquainted, merely to put you on your guard. you have doubtless seen a letter publish'd in the gazettes, which is imputed to Gen[l] Wilkinson & said to be written from this place in 1803. to Mr Power at N. Orleans, requesting him to use the Gen[l]'s influence with the Sp[h] authority there to prevent the restoration of the Deposit. It is understood that the authenticity[1] of the letter is admitted, & the explanation given of the measure, which I have recently & casually heard, is the circumstance with which I wish you to be acquainted. It is this, that the letter was written with yours & Gen[l] Dearborne's knowledge & approbation, & that a copy of it was at that time deposited in the war office. Knowing of this explanation you will be prepar'd, by reflection, for the answer which ought to be given to any application that may be made to you on the subject. You need not answer this—I write in haste for the mail—very respectfully yr friend

& servant JA[S] MONROE

RC (DLC); endorsed by TJ as received 8 Jan. 1812 and so recorded in SJL.

A number of newspapers had recently quoted from an 1803 letter from Wilkinson to Thomas POWER that the latter presented as evidence when he testified at Wilkinson's court-martial. Headed "*Private and strictly Confidential*," the extract read "Should a change of circumstances which are talked of, but not expected by me, produce a change of policy in the Councils of Spain and the opening of the port be contemplated, I beg you to interest yourself in my name (confidentially) to prevent the measure until I arrive near you. You can speak freely to the Marquis de Cassa Calvo or the Intendant for me. I have strong motives for this request" (Richmond *Enquirer*, 12 Dec. 1811).

[1] Manuscript: "authenticy."

From Thomas Sully

SIR Philadelphia Jan[y] 6th 1812—

In my Letter to you dated the 22[d] of December, I had the honour to communicate in the name of the Society of Artists of the United States, the information that you were elected an honorary member of that body; I have now the pleasure of informing you that at their last annual meeting held on Jan[y] 2[d] for the choice of Officers, you were elected their President for the present year.

You will no doubt Sir perceive that the establishment of a new institution, embracing a wide field, and combining a variety of very important objects, will also be attended with many difficulties; to obviate which, the founders of this infant Society have endeavoured to call to their aid all the talents, and resources within their reach.

The local situation of this country, as well as the form of its gouvernment, renders it necessary that we should establish our Society on principles somewhat different from similar institutions, formed under other circumstances, and existing under different patronage, and various forms of gouvernment. The Artists in this Country can never expect to be supported by individual patronage; It is to the public only that they look for incouragement; and they expect to receive it only in proportion as the application of their labour has a tendency to promote the public good.

In this country there are but few Artists who are eminent in the higher branches of the Arts; and those being scattered over a vast extent of country, it was found impossible to form any thing like a National institution without calling in the aid of amateurs; and the progress already made by this association has sufficiently proved the propriety of such a measure

I have no hesitation candidly to acknowledge that the Society expect to recieve much benefit from your acceptance of the office of President, although at a distance, and your time doubtless employed in important persuits; we nevertheless hope to derive much solid advantage from such communications as your leisure may permit you to make on the subject of the Arts.

The general concerns of the Society (as you will percieve by a copy of the constitution sent) are conducted by four Vice Presidents, and a Secretary, all of whom are artists and are selected from the four principal branches of the arts,—Viz—Architecture, Painting, Sculpture, & Engraving; such an arrangement was considered necessary in order to prevent jealousy among the different professions, and to strengthen in every possible manner the bond of union.

The business of the Society is generally transacted by Committees, and it has hitherto been conducted in such a manner as cannot fail to insure success: and we may venture to hope that our country will soon be independent in works of taste and elegance, as she already is in all the Mechanical and useful arts.

I have the honour to be

With great respect Y^r^ Ob^t^ Ser^t^ THO^S^ SULLY. Sec^y^

By order of the Committee of Correspondence.
Remb[t] Peale.
Benj[n] Trott.
Geo[e] Murray
Rob[t] Mills
Tho[s] Sully—

RC (DLC); between dateline and salutation: "Thomas Jefferson Esq[e]"; endorsed by TJ as a letter from Sully received 22 Jan. 1812 and so recorded in SJL. Printed in Richmond *Enquirer*, 25 Feb. 1812.

To Samuel & James Leitch

MESS[RS] SAM[L] & JAMES LEITCH Monticello Jan. 7. 12.

I intended to have seen you at court yesterday, but having no other call there, I concluded on second thoughts it would be easier to write a letter than ride half a dozen miles and wade in the mud of the court yard. your account should have been paid at some of my earlier epochs of recieving money, had it been sooner communicated to me. it shall be discharged in the course of the winter, after getting my crop to market, partly in money, partly perhaps by some intermediate supplies of nails. Accept the assurance of my esteem & respect

TH: JEFFERSON

PoC (MHi); endorsed by TJ.

A letter of 1 Jan. 1812 from the Leitch partnership, not found, is recorded in SJL as received from Charlottesville on 2 Jan. 1812. On 4 Mar. 1812 TJ paid $100 on his ACCOUNT with the firm (*MB*, 2:1274).

To Joseph Milligan

SIR Monticello Jan. 7. 12.

Your letter of Dec. 2. arrived here during an absence of 6. weeks from home, and on my return I thought to postpone an answer till I could accompany it with a remittance. as this however will require some 2. or 3. weeks yet, & in the mean time your letter of the 3[d] arrives, I now acknolege the reciept of both. I am perfectly willing that you should print another edition of the Parliamentary Manual, indeed I have no right to refuse it, because no copy right was retained, or would have answered any view I had in publishing it. if it can be made to promote order & decorum in debate it will do great good. when I compiled it, I had never yet seen the 4th vol. of Hatsell. a subsequent perusal of that volume enabled me to make some useful additions which I had printed, & now inclose you a copy of them. these should be inserted in the text of the new edition in their proper places. but I wonder you should think of printing them in 8vo. it is essentially a book for the pocket, & which members will carry to their house in their pocket occasionally, & some habitually. for this purpose I found it convenient to trim off all the margin of the former edition & reduce one of them to the size of 5. by 3.I. that of the additions now inclosed[1] which I found much more convenient. should you want any copies for present demand you can have them, I believe, from mr Pritchard bookseller of Richmond, with whom I deposited all my remaining copies for sale. I am glad you propose to reprint the Scientific dialogues. they are so much superior to any book we have on the same subject and scale, that as soon as known, it will take place of all other.   a mr Cabell of this state applied to me to know where he could get a copying press. I told him of the one I had deposited with you for sale. he was on his way to the legislature in Richmond and said he would write for it. I shall as promptly as a country residence permits remit you the amount of your account.

Accept the assurance of my respect   TH: JEFFERSON

RC (NHi: Miscellaneous Jefferson Manuscripts); addressed: "Mr Joseph Milligan Bookseller Georgetown Columb."; franked; postmarked Milton, 9 Jan. 1812. PoC (DLC); endorsed by TJ.

Although TJ's ADDITIONS NOW INCLOSED have not been found, a comparison of the 1801 Samuel H. Smith edition of *A Manual of Parliamentary Practice* with Milligan's 1812 edition found approximately three more pages of text in the latter (*PW*, 33, 349).

[1] Preceding six words interlined.

Decision of Virginia Court of Appeals in *Peyton v. Henderson*

Virginia to wit,

At a Court of Appeals held at the Capitol in Richmond the seventh day of January 1812

Craven Peyton Applt. against John Henderson Appee	}	upon an appeal from a decree pronounced by the Superior Court of Chancery held in Richmond the eighth day of June 1805

This day came the appellant, by his counsel, and the appellee being solemnly called, came not, and the Court having maturely Considered the transcript of the record of the decree aforesaid and the arguments of the appellants counsel, is of opinion that there is no error in the said Decree, therefore It is Decreed and Ordered that the same be affirmed.

Which is Ordered to be certified to the said Superior Court of Chancery.[1]

A Copy,
Teste,
H, DANCE C,C,A

Tr (ViU: TJP, final document [p. 50] in *Peyton v. Henderson* Court Record [1804–12]); in the hand of Harrison Dance, clerk of the Virginia Court of Appeals. 2d Tr (ViU: TJP-LBJM); entirely in George Carr's hand; also certified by William W. Hening. 3d Tr (same, p. 41); entirely in Carr's hand; with subjoined notation that the decree had been certified by Hening on 26 Feb. 1812 as clerk at a session of the Superior Court of Chancery for the Richmond District; on verso of 2d Tr. Enclosed in Dance to TJ, 10 July 1812.

This decision ended legal efforts to overturn John Henderson's asserted right to run a canal through lands at Milton that TJ had purchased from the Henderson heirs through the agency of Craven Peyton (Peyton to TJ, 6 Aug. 1809, and note; Robert F. Haggard, "Thomas Jefferson v. The Heirs of Bennett Henderson, 1795–1818: A Case Study in Caveat Emptor," *MACH* 63 [2005]: 1–29).

[1] Preceding thirteen words omitted in 2d Tr.

From Gideon Granger

DEAR SIR General Post Office January 8. 1812

I have just received yours of the 30th. Ult: and given instructions to the Postmaster of the City if any Such bundles arrive for the future, to detain them and notify me, and you may be assured I shall keep them Carefully as well as apprise you of their being in my possession.

With great esteem and Respect GIDN GRANGER

RC (DLC); in a clerk's hand, signed by Granger; at foot of text: "Thomas Jefferson Esq Monticello Va"; endorsed by TJ as received 12 Jan. 1812 and so recorded in SJL.

From William Lambert

SIR, City of Washington, January 8th 1812.

I have the honor to transmit an abstract of the calculation of the longitude of Monticello west of Greenwich, founded on the apparent times of the internal contacts of Sun and Moon on the 17th of September last, as contained in your letter of the 29th of December; and having ascertained the elements with scrupulous exactness, tested by various rules, the accuracy of the result, according to the data furnished, may be confidently relied on.

	° ′ ″
Lat. of Monticello, by observation 38.° 8.′ 0.″ N. reduced, (320 to 319)	37.57.33.341.
Constant log. to reduce the Moon's equat. hor. parallax, for the lat. and ratio	9.9994827.
	° ′ ″
Obliquity of the Ecliptic, Sept. 17th 1811	23.27.42.690
	h. m. Sec ° ′ ″
Estimated longitude of Monticello, supposed near the truth	5.15.20 = 78.50.0.W.

---

	h. m. S.		° ′ ″ dec.
Annulus formed	1.53. 0.	=	28.15.00.000
Estimated long. from Greenwich	+5.15.20		
Corresponding time at Greenwich	7. 8.20.		☉'s R.A. 174.26.55.519.
Right ascension of the meridian,			♎, 22.41.55.519.
Altitude of the nonagesimal,			46.44. 3.732
Longitude of the nonagesimal,			♎. 2.41.31.560
Moon's true longitude			♍. 24. 2. 7.711
" true distance à nonagesimal, (West)	° ′ ″		8.39.23.849.
" hor. parallax, reduced, (320 to 319)	0.54.5.916		
Sun's hor. parallax,	– 0 .8.700		
hor. parallax ☽ à ☉,			0.53.57.216
☽'s parallax in longitude, (correct)			0. 5.58.862
" apparent distance à nonagesimal,			8.45.22.711
" true latitude, north ascending			0.37.20.676.
" apparent longitude			♍. 23.56. 8.849.
Sun's longitude,			♍. 23.57. 7.341.
diff. of apparent longitude, ☽ west of ☉,			+ 0. 0.58.942
☽'s parallax in latitude (correct)			0.36.58.430
" apparent latitude, north,	′ ″ dec.		0. 0.22.246.
" horizontal Semidiameter	14.45.595	} Semidiam. corrected.	′ ″ 14.52.803
Augmentation,	+ 0.10.185		
Inflexion of light	– 0. 2.977.		
☉'s Semidiameter,	15.57.246.		
Irradiation of light	– 1.623	Semidiam. corrected.	15.55.623
difference of Sun and Moon's Semidiameters, corrected			1. 2.820.

---

	h. m. Sec.		° ′ ″ dec.
Annulus broken,	1.59.25	=	29.51.15.000
Sun's right ascension, (corresponding time at Greenwich)			174.27. 9.923.
Right ascension of the meridian,			♎, 24.18.24.923.
altitude of the nonagesimal,			46. 5.42.940
Longitude of the nonagesimal,			♎, 4.12.14.333.
Moon's true longitude,			♍, 24. 5.17.322.
" true dist. à nonagesimal, (West)	° ′ ″		10. 6.57.011
" hor. parallax, reduced	0.54. 5.942		
Sun's hor. parallax,	– 0. 8.700		
hor. parallax ☽ à ☉,			0.53.57.242

☽'s Parallax in longitude (correct)		0. 0.54.272.
" apparent distance à nonagesimal		10.13.51.283.
" true latitude, north ascending		0.37.38.905
" apparent longitude		♍. 23.58.23.050
Sun's longitude,		♍, 23.57.23.018.
diff. of apparent longitude, ☽ East of ☉,		– 0. 1. 0.032.
☽'s parallax in latitude, (correct)		0.37.24.643.
" apparent latitude (north)	′ ″ dec.	0. 0.14.262.
" horiz. Semidiameter,	14.45.604.	
Augmentation,	+10.028.	Semid. corrected, 0.14.52.655
Inflexion of light,	– 2.977	
Sun's Semidiameter,	15.57.247.	Semid. corrected. 15.55.622.
Irradiation of light	– 1.623	
difference of Sun and Moon's Semidiameters, corrected.		0. 1. 2.967

1st internal contact

	″		
diff: of Semid[s]	62.820		
☽'s apparent lat.	22.246		
Sum,	85.066	log.	1.9297560
diff.	40.574	log.	1.6082478
		2)	3.5380038
			1.7690019.
☽'s apparent lat. co.sine, ar. comp			+0.0000000
diff: of apparent ☉ and ☽, +	″ 58.749		1.7690019.
Parallax in longitude	–5.58.862.		
true diff. of long. ☉ & ☽,	–5. 0.113.		

2d

	″		
diff. of Semid[s]	62.967		
	14.262		
	77.229.	log	1.8877804
	48.705.	log.	1.6875735
		2)	3.5753539
			1.7876769.
			0.0000000
diff. of app. long.			1.7876769.
	′ ″ – 1. 1.330.		
Parallax in long.	– 6.54.272.		
true diff. long.	– 7.55.602.		

The Moon's hourly velocity of the Moon from the Sun, at a middle time between the formation of the annulus and the true conjunction of the Sun and Moon at Monticello, was 27.′ 6.″ 0328; and between the breaking of the annulus and the true conjunction, 27.′ 6.″ 0505. dec.

As 27.′ 6.″ 0328 to one hour, or 60 minutes, so is true diff. of long. ☉ and ☽, 5.′ 0.″ 113. to the interval of apparent time, which subtracted from 11. m. 4. Sec. 443. dec which subtracted from 1. h. 53. m. 0, S. the time of the formation of the annulus, gives 1. h. 41. m. 55. Sec. 557. dec the time of true conjunction of Sun and Moon at Monticello, by the first internal contact.

As 27.′ 6.″ 0505. to one hour, or 60 minutes, so is true difference ☉ and ☽, 7.′ 55.″ 602, to 17. m. 32. Sec. 960, which subtracted from 1. h. 59. m. 25. Sec gives 1. h. 41. m. 52. Sec. 040, dec. the time of true conjunction, by the second internal contact.

	h. m. Sec. dec	
1st	1.41.55.557.	
2	1.41.52.040.	
Mean true conjunction at Mont.	1.41.53.798	
ditto at Greenwich,	6.57.14.915.	° ′ ″ dec.
Longitude in time, West,	5.15.21.117.	= 78.50.16.755.

Another method.

Moon's apparent motion in lat. during the annular appearance, ″ dec 7.984. log + 10 = 10.9022205

″ apparent motion in longitude,	″ dec 118.974	log.	2.0754521.
tangent, angle inclination,	° ′ ″ 3.50.21.108		8.8267684
Moon's apparent motion in longitude		log.	2.0754521.
angle of inclination, ar. co. cosine			+ 0.0009757
Chord of transit,	″ 119.242	log.	2.0764278.

diff. of Semidiameters,	″ 62.820	(t)
&	62.967	(u)
Sum,	125.787.	(v)
diff.	0.147	(w)

As chord of transit,		″ 119.242.	log. co. ar.	7.9235722
To	(v)	125.787.	log	2.0996358
So	(w)	0.147	log	9.1673173
To	(x)	0.155.	log	9.1905253

Chord of transit, –x, = ″ 119.087. half 59.5435 (r)

d° +x, = 119.397. half, 59.6985 (s)

Log. (r)	″ 59.5435	+ 10	11.7748343			
Log. (t)	62.820		1.7980979			
Angle of conjunction	° ′ ″ 18.35.11.714		9.9767364			
″ of inclination,	+3.50.21.108					
Central angle	22.25.32.822.	cosine	9.9658480.	sine.	9.5814791.	
diff. of Semidiameters	″ 62.820	log.	1.7980979.	log.	1.7980979.	
diff. of apparent longitude,	+58.069	log	1.7639459	log.	1.3795770	
					app. lat. ″ 23.965.	

(s)	59.6985	log. + 10	11.7759634
(u)	62.967	log.	1.7991061

angle of conjunction,	° ′ ″ 18.32.20.714.	Cosine	9.9768573		
Angle of inclination	–3.50.21.108				
Central angle,	14.41.59.606	cosine	9.9855469	sine	9.4044164
(u)	62.967	log.	1.7991061	log.	1.7991061
diff. of apparent long.	–60.905.	log.	1.7846530	log.	1.2035225
					″ 15.978. app. latitude.

Parallax in long.	′ ″ dec. –5.58.862	Parallax in long.	′ ″ –6.54.272
diff. of app. long.	+0.58.069	diff: of app. long.	–1. 0.905
true diff. long. ☉ and ☽,	–5. 0.793.	true diff. long. ☉ & ☽,	–7.55.177.

As hourly velocity ☽ à ☉, 27.′ 6.″ 0328 to one hour, or 60 minutes, so is true diff. long. –5.′ 0.″ 793. to 11. m. 5. s. 949, which subtracted from 1. h. 53. m. 0. S. gives 1. h 41. m. 54. Sec. 051. dec. the time of true conjunction of Sun and Moon at Monticello, by the formation of the annulus.

As hourly velocity ☽ à ☉, 27.′ 6.″ 0505. to one hour, or 60 minutes, so is true difference of longitude, –7.′ 55.″ 177, to 17. m. 32. Sec. 021. dec, which subtracted from 1. h. 59. m. 25. S, gives 1. h. 41. m. 52. Sec 979 the time of true conjunction, by breaking of annulus.—

	h. m. Sec. dec.	° ′ ″ dec.
By formation of annulus	1.41.54.051	
" breaking of ditto	1.41.52.979.	
True conjunction ☉ & ☽, at Monticello,	1.41.53.515.	
" at Greenwich,	6.57.14.915	
Longitude in time, West	5.15.21.400 =	78.50.21.000
By first method		78.50.16.755.
Mean result		78.50.18.877.

The above may be considered as an accurate determination of the longitude of Monticello, by the internal contacts, supposing the latitude of the place, the apparent times of formation and breaking of the annulus, and the Sun and Moon's positions in the Nautical almanac, to be correctly given. The last method may be explained by the following figure.—

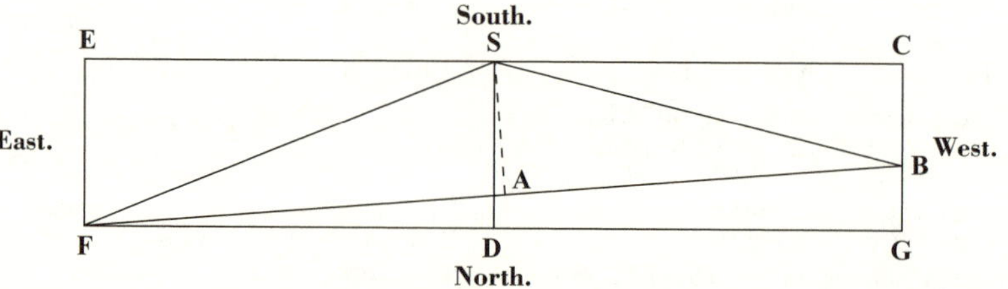

The line **ESC**, = **FDG**, represents a small portion of the ecliptic, passing through the center of the Sun, **S**, equal to the Moon's apparent motion in longitude from the Sun, during the appearance of the annulus.

F, the Moon's center at the formation, **B**, at the breaking of the annulus.

FS, the difference of the Sun and Moon's semidiameters (corrected) at the beginning, **BS**, at the end. **EF**, the Moon's apparent latitude at the beginning, **CB**, at the end of the annular appearance. **SA**, the nearest approach of the centers of ☉ and ☽. **GFB**, the angle of inclination, **FAB**, the chord of transit, or the Moon's motion in the apparent orbit. **ASF**, the angle of conjunction at the beginning, **ABS**, at the end. **FSE**, and **BSC**, the central angles, from which, the difference of apparent longitude of Sun and Moon, **SE**, at the formation, and **SC**, at the breaking of the annulus, may be correctly ascertained, as in the foregoing process.

I am, Sir, with great respect, Your most obedient servant,

William Lambert.

RC (DLC); on two folio sheets; at foot of text: "Thomas Jefferson late President U.S." Enclosed in Lambert to TJ, 9 Jan. 1812.

To Thomas Sully

Sir Monticello Jan. 8. 12.

I have duly recieved your favor of Dec. 22. informing me that the Society of Artists of the US. had made me an honorary member of their society. I am very justly sensible of the honor they have done me, & I pray you to return them my thanks for this mark of their distinction. I fear that I can be but a very useless associate. time, which withers the fancy, as the other faculties of the mind and body, presses on me with a heavy hand, and distance intercepts all personal intercourse. I can offer therefore but my zealous good wishes for the success of the institution, and that, embellishing with taste a country already overflowing with the useful productions, it may be able to give an innocent & pleasing direction to accumulations of wealth, which would otherwise be employed in the nourishment of coarse[1] and vicious habits. with these I tender to the society & to yourself the assurance of my high respect & consideration.

Th: Jefferson

PoC (DLC); at foot of text: "Mr Thomas Sully." Tr (PPAFA: Minute Book of Society of Artists of the United States, p. 83). Printed in Richmond *Enquirer*, 25 Feb. 1812.

[1] Tr: "course."

From William Lambert

Sir, City of Washington, January 9th 1812.

The inclosed abstract of calculation relative to the longitude of Monticello from Greenwich by the apparent times of internal contacts of Sun and Moon on the 17th of September last, will, it is hoped, be accepted by you as an accurate result, admitting the data to be correctly stated. Having in a former communication, given rules for ascertaining the altitude and longitude of the nonagesimal, Moon's parallaxes, &c. I did not suppose it necessary to repeat the operation in this; permit me to request, that you will send a copy of this abstract, if approved, to bishop Madison, at Williamsburg.

You will find that by the internal contacts, Monticello is farther west than the external contacts made it; and you may, if you judge proper, take a mean of the results; but if, as you suggest, there are doubts of the accuracy of the times of the beginning and end of the eclipse, it will be better to depend on the inclosed statement alone, until future observations offer to correct it.

I am, Sir, with sincere and great respect, Your most obedient servant,
WILLIAM LAMBERT.

RC (DLC); addressed: "Thomas Jefferson, late president [of the U. States, and] President [of the American philosophical Society, Monticello, Virginia]" (trimmed, with missing portion conjectured from address of Lambert to TJ, 23 Apr. 1812); endorsed by TJ as received 12 Jan. 1812 and so recorded in SJL. Enclosure: Lambert to TJ, 8 Jan. 1812.

From John Low

DEAR SIR
New york, Jany 9th 1812.

Your favour of the 27th Decr has this day come to hand, acknowledging the receipt of my two former letters from Washington.—I can assure you that you have certainly Subscribed for a Set of the Encyclopædia, and in your own hand writing.—In order to convince of the fact I shall take the liberty of calling upon Mr Remsen, and Mr Gelston, for the purpose of shewing them the Signature, and request of them to mention, in writing, whether, in their opinion, the writing is genuine.—Mr Madison did not recollect his Subscription until I presented his signature, and he no doubt also Saw your Signature, they being near each other.—I am extremely sorry I committed a mistake, by Sending them by mail, but knew of no other way, and was informed by D[r] Mitchell and the Post Master at Washington, that they could be sent on that way according to privilige—I also understand by your letter, that you have only received 3 Vol[s]—the whole set consists of 7 Vol[s] which I made up in two parcels, one of which must be at the post office next your place, I suppose at Milton—The comparison between the Signature on the Subscription and your letter, is a perfect one—The Subscription was obtained by my father, who is since dead, otherwise some circumstances, perhaps, at the time, might be mentioned, which would refresh your memory concerning it.—

I remain yours
Respectfully
J[NO] LOW.

RC (DLC); addressed: "Hon[ble] Tho[s] Jefferson, Montacillo Vir[a] via Milton V[a]"; franked; postmarked New York, 13 Jan.; endorsed by TJ as received 22 Jan. 1812 and so recorded in SJL; with enclosure on verso of address leaf.

ENCLOSURE

Certificate of Henry Remsen and David Gelston

We have seen Mr Jefferson's name to a subscription for publishing a new Encyclopædia or Universal Dictionary of Arts & Sciences by John Low. It is the first on the subscription and we think it genuine. New York January 11th 1812

HENRY REMSEN
DAVID GELSTON

MS (DLC); in Remsen's hand, signed by Remsen and Gelston.

Henry Remsen (ca. 1763–1843), banker and real-estate investor, was a clerk in the United States Office of Foreign Affairs by 1784 and served as chief clerk in the Department of State during the first part of TJ's tenure as secretary of state. He left that post in 1792 to become first teller of the New York branch of the Bank of the United States. Remsen became a cashier at the Manhattan Bank about 1801 and served as its president from 1808 until about 1825. They seldom corresponded after TJ's retirement, but Remsen maintained a friendly relationship with TJ throughout his career (NN: Remsen Papers; *PTJ*, 12:418, 612, 23:425–6; William Duncan, *The New-York Directory, and Register, for the year 1793* [New York, 1793], 125; William Duncan, *The New-York Directory, and Register, for the year 1795* [New York, 1795], 176; *Longworth's New York Directory* [1801], 258; [1825], 355; Waldron Phoenix Belknap Jr., *The De Peyster Genealogy* [1956], 89, 101; New York *American Citizen*, 18 Feb. 1808; Nathan Miller, *The Enterprise of a Free People: Aspects of Economic Development in New York State during the Canal Period, 1792–1838* [1962], 199, 200, 201; New York *Evening Post*, 20 Feb. 1843).

From Robert Patterson

SIR Philadelphia Jan[y] 10th 1812.

I have rec[d] & read your interesting communication of the 10th Nov[r] with great satisfaction, and have laid the same before the Committee appointed on the subject of your former communication; who, I am sure, will give it that consideration which it so highly merits. In the meantime, Sir, you will permit me to make a few observations, which may not, however perfectly agree with the ideas which you have expressed on the subject.

1. I cannot perceive any satisfactory reason for rejecting the cylindrical pendulum, which you formerly recommended as a standard of lineal measure, and giving the preference to a bob-pendulum. In the former, the proportion between the whole length of the cylinder and the virtual length of the pendulum, or distance between the center of suspension & center of oscillation, can be exactly found; and such a description of it can be given in words as will enable an artist to make an accurate imitation—neither of which is the case in the bob-pendulum.

2. It is not necessary that the whole length of the pendulum should be made the unit of measure:—Any given part thereof may, with equal convenience be used for this purpose. And, on many accounts, I cannot help giving the English foot a decided preference, as the unit of long measure in the U. States; and that its parts & multiples should continue the same as they have done time immemorial. Any material change, either in the unit or division of weights or measures, would perhaps be impracticable Even in France, under the strong government of Napoleon, the old weights & measures, I am credibly informed, are still generally in use, except in their public offices.
3. Neither is it at all necessary that the pendulum should be so regulated as to make exactly 86400. oscillations in a mean solar day, in a given latitude, and at a given temperature—a problem which in practice would be very difficult to accomplish—Let a cylindrical pendulum rod of any given metal, (except iron which will be affected by magnetism) of a convenient length, (say about 5 English feet) its diameter being in a given proportion to its length, (say 1 to 120) having its center of suspension (a knife-edge) at a given proportional part of its length, (say $\frac{1}{120}$ part) below the upper extremity, be attached to a good clock in any given latitude (say 40° N. which is not far from the mean latitude of N. America) at any given height above the level of the sea, at any given temperature of the atmosphere;—and by a few repeated experiments, let the number of oscillations in a sidereal day (which on many accounts should be preferred to a solar day) be carefully ascertained. Then on this pendulum-rod let the unit of lineal measure (the English foot) be marked, and its proportion to the whole length of the pendulum-rod exactly ascertained & noted—a problem of easy solution by the aid of a proper instrument. Now from the above and other well-known data, the same unit of measure may be marked on any other cylindrical pendulum, under any other given circumstances: and thus a very accurate & comparable standard of measure is easily obtained, communicable by words to distant nations or future ages.
4. Instead of opening a correspondence on this subject, with the learned societies of other nations or countries, as a preliminary step, would it not be preferrable, after sufficiently maturing the system, to bring it before our own national legislature, and induce them to give it a legal sanction? Our standard of weights and measures being thus fixed, it might be a proper diplomatic business to obtain from all other civilized or commercial nations, an exact comparison between their standards & ours.
5. I am not quite satisfied with respect to the accuracy of deducing the

standards of weight or capacity from that of lineal measure; since any little, unavoidable error in the latter will be greatly increased in the former—I have therefore a scheme, tho not yet sufficiently matured, which was suggested by my son Robert, now in Europe, for a comparable standard of weight, and consequently of capacity, independent of lineal measure—It is a drop of pure water; not thro a hole or aperture, for the size of this (which could not with sufficient accuracy be described in words) would affect the weight of the drop; but from a solid conical point of pure gold of a given angle—And let any given number of these drops, at a given temperature compose the unit of weight (say that number which from a mean of several tryals would exactly weigh an avoirdupoise ounce)[1]—And very happily for this system, no property of a body can be ascertained with so much accuracy as its weight.

The reason why I would prefer the accustomary units, subdivisions & multiples of measure, to any other, however superior in an abstract point of view, is the strong prejudices against any innovation in long established habits & customs. This prejudice would operate powerfully with the legislature itself, in preventing them from enacting a law embracing any material innovations; but still more powerfully with the people at large against complying with such a law.

And after all, Sir, the decimal division of weights and measures, possesses no advantage over the present vulgar division, except that they afford somewhat of a greater facility in arithmetical computations.

I shall, Sir, esteem it a high favour to hear from you again on this Subject—

I have the honour to be, Sir, with the most perfect respect & esteem Your obedient Servant R. PATTERSON

RC (DLC); at foot of text: "Thomas Jefferson Monticello"; endorsed by TJ as received 22 Jan. 1812 and so recorded in SJL.

[1] Omitted closing parenthesis editorially supplied.

From Thomas T. Hewson

SIR, Philad[a] Jan[y] 11th 1812.

The American Philosophical Society lately held its annual meeting for the election of Officers. On this occasion the Society reiterated its expressions of respect for your person, by again unanimously electing you to the Presidential Chair, in the confident expectation, that your patronage and assistance would still be extended to the promotion of useful knowledge, more especially, at this momentous period, when every patriotic citizen is desirous of living at home, and in peace.

The commands of the Society afford me an opportunity of offering the assurances of my personal respect and veneration for your character

Thos T Hewson secretary

RC (DLC); addressed: "Thos Jefferson Monticello. Virginia"; franked; postmarked Philadelphia, 12 Jan.; endorsed by TJ as received 22 Jan. 1812 and so recorded in SJL.

The American Philosophical Society reelected TJ to its PRESIDENTIAL CHAIR at its 3 Jan. 1812 meeting (APS, Minutes [MS in PPAmP]).

To James Monroe

Dear Sir

Monticello Jan. 11. 12.

I thank you for your letter of the 6th. it is a proof of your friendship, and of the sincere interest you take in whatever concerns me. of this I have never had a moment's doubt, and have ever valued it as a precious treasure. the question indeed whether I knew or approved of Genl Wilkinson's endeavors to prevent the restoration of the right of deposit at N. Orleans could never require a second of time to answer. but it requires some time for the mind to recover from the astonishment excited by the boldness of the suggestion. indeed it is with difficulty I can believe he has really made such an appeal; & the rather as the expression in your letter is that you have 'casually heard it,' without stating the degree of reliance which you have in the source of information. I think his understanding is above an expedient so momentary and so finally overwhelming. were Dearborne & myself dead, it might find credit with some. but the world at large, even then, would weigh for themselves the dilemma, whether it was more probable that, in the situation I then was, cloathed with the confidence & power of my country, I should descend to so unmeaning an act of treason, or that he, in the wreck now threatening him, should wildly lay hold of any plank. they would weigh his motives and views against those of Dearborne and myself, the tenor of his life against that of ours, his Spanish mysteries against my open cherishment of the Western interests; and, living as we are, & ready to purge ourselves by any ordeal, they must now weigh, in addition, our testimony against his. all this makes me believe he will never seek this refuge. I have ever & carefully restrained myself from the expression of any opinion respecting Genl Wilkinson, except in the case of Burr's conspiracy, wherein, after he had got over his first agitations, we believed his decision firm, & his conduct zealous for the defeat of the conspiracy, and altho' injudicious, yet meriting, from sound intentions, the support of the nation. as to the rest of his life, I have left it to his friends & his enemies to whom it furnishes matter enough for disputation. I classed myself with neither, and least of all in this time of his distresses, should I be disposed to add to their pressure. I hope therefore he has not been so imprudent as to write our names in the pannel of his witnesses.

Accept the assurance of my constant affections

TH: JEFFERSON

RC (DLC: Monroe Papers); addressed: "James Monroe Secretary of State Washington"; franked; postmarked Milton, 13 Jan. 1812; endorsed by Monroe. PoC (DLC).

From Colin Buckner

DEAR SIR, Lynchburg Jany 12th 1812

Being about to become a member of the family of Mr Christopher Clark, and being a Stranger here, I have thought it a duty I owe to that Gentleman to obtain a letter from an acquaintance who is known to him, you are the only one near this to whom I can apply,—Col° Taylor who gave me a letter to you at the time I received an appointment in the Army, will forward me a letter for Mr. Clark by next Mail and I am anxious to deliver yours at the Same time.—your Compliance will add to the obligations which I am already under to you.—

With Respect & Esteem I am Sir yr. mo. Ob. Servt

COLIN BUCKNER

RC (MHi); endorsed by TJ as received 15 Jan. 1812, but recorded in SJL as received the previous day.

Colin Buckner (ca. 1778–1836) was appointed by TJ a captain in the 5th Infantry Regiment, United States Army, effective 1 July 1808. He served on the Canadian frontier during the War of 1812, rose to major in January 1814, transferred later that year to the 20th Infantry, and was honorably discharged on 15 June 1815. Buckner subsequently settled in Lynchburg, where he served as a director of the local branch of the Farmers' Bank and sat on the committees that prepared to celebrate Lafayette's visit in 1825 and mourn TJ's death the following year. At his own death Buckner's personal estate included more than thirty slaves and was valued in excess of $20,000 (Heitman, *U.S. Army*, 1:259; *JEP*, 2:99, 107, 544, 580 [25 Jan., 2 Feb. 1809, 14 Oct., 7 Nov. 1814]; *Richmond Enquirer*, 10 Jan. 1832; William Asbury Christian, *Lynchburg and Its People* [1900], 81, 85; Lynchburg Will Book, B:210–1, 254–5; *Lynchburg Virginian*, 10 Mar. 1836; gravestone inscription in Lynchburg Presbyterian cemetery).

The earlier introductory letter Buckner mentions from COL° TAYLOR, not found, may have been from John Taylor of Caroline, who held that rank in the militia during the American Revolution. At the time of his 1808 military appointment, Buckner was apparently living near Taylor's residence at Port Royal (Buckner to William H. Cabell, 19 July 1808 [Vi: RG 3, Governor's Office, Letters Received]).

From William P. Newby

SIR, Tufton. January 13th 1812

you found on my return that I had not Stated the number of Hogs kill'd we ware not done killing at the time the return was filed. I now present to you the number with the total wt

No 1. 40 Hogs wt 4.967[1]
No 2. 22 do wt 1.838[2] Small hogs
6.805[3]

WM P. NEWBY

Measure of the barn.
30 feet Long
26 feet, wide
2 feet deep with corn

RC (MoSHi: TJC-BC); addressed: "T. Jefferson Monticello"; endorsed by TJ: "Newby Wm P."; with calculations by TJ adjacent to postscript:
"26
30
780
2
1560 f.
−1/5 312
1248 bush
÷ 5 250. barr. corn
1/2| 125."

William P. Newby (ca. 1789–1857) was a native of Lancaster County who served as overseer at TJ's Tufton farm after the departure of William McGehee in mid-November 1811 and before William Ballard took this position at the beginning of December 1813. Negotiations to return Newby to TJ's employ as an overseer at Poplar Forest in 1815 failed. He settled in Culpeper County and at his death left a personal estate appraised at slightly more than $27,000, including approximately twenty-six slaves (TJ to Thomas Mann Randolph, 26 Aug. 1811; TJ to Newby, 20 Jan., 21 June 1815; Newby to TJ, 22 Apr. 1815; DNA: RG 29, CS, Culpeper Co., 1820, 1850; Culpeper Co. Will Book, T:556–7, U:58–68).

TJ's papers include a brief, undated memorandum by Newby consisting of measurements for a "New corn house 11 feet wide 11 feet 4 In Long 9½ feet deep" (MS in MoSHi: TJC-BC, in Newby's hand and signed by him; written on a scrap from one of TJ's address covers; endorsed by TJ: "Newby Wm P.").

[1] TJ here added a calculation: "128 ℔ averge." The correct figure is 124 pounds.

[2] TJ here added a calculation: "83 ℔ averge."

[3] Below this number TJ added a calculation: "110 ℔ average."

From James Barbour

SIR Richmond Jany 14th–12

The partiality of my Country having bestowed on me, the station of Chief Magistrate of the Commonweal, the wish, nearest my heart, is to conduct myself in such a manner, as to evince, that its confidence has not been, entirely, misplaced. On the one hand, I wish to exercise no power not granted by the constitution; on the other not to abandone one, which may have been conferred by that instrument. Going into the Government with these views I was immediately called on to decide a question of importance, and one, to me, of delicacy likewise, as I am to fix by my determination, my own powers—The question to which I allude is this—The Council being equally divided can I consider myself advised—or in other words have I a right to incline the scale by my own vote. The Constitution being doubtful, much must depend upon the Cotemporaneous exposition. As you went early into the administration and the case must have occurred frequently during your continuance in the Government, I have taken the liberty to request that you will have the goodness to inform me what was the exposition given to the Constitution at that time—I would not have troubled you had not my researches into the Journals of the Council, been ineffectual—I would trouble you still more, by requesting, that you would be kind enough to furnish me with your opinion upon this Subject—If I Should be deemed intrusive you will have none to censure but yourself. The repeated civilities and evidences of regard which you have on all occasions Shewn have prompted me to solicit at your hands this new favor—

I beg you to believe that I entertain for you the highest respect and affection JS: BARBOUR

RC (DLC); endorsed by TJ as received 19 Jan. 1812 and so recorded in SJL.

James Barbour (1775–1842) read law in Richmond and was admitted to the Virginia bar in 1793. He represented his native Orange County in the House of Delegates, 1798–1803, 1804–05, and 1807–12, with service as Speaker, 1809–12. Barbour served three terms as governor of Virginia, 1812–14, sat in the United States Senate, 1815–25, became secretary of war under John Quincy Adams, 1825–28, and was minister plenipotentiary to Great Britain from 1828 until Andrew Jackson recalled him the following year. He began his political career attacking the Alien and Sedition Acts and supporting strict-construction Republicanism, but his experience as a wartime governor altered his outlook, and he came to support protective tariffs, the Second Bank of the United States, internal improvements, and other measures to strengthen domestic manufacturing and commerce. Barbour defended states' rights during the 1819–21 crisis over the admission of Missouri as a slave state but helped to orchestrate a compromise. He chaired national presidential conventions that nominated Henry Clay in 1831 and William Henry Harrison in 1839.

Barbour served as president of the Agricultural Society of Albemarle, 1824–26, and published the results of his experiments in scientific agriculture at Barboursville, his 5,000-acre Orange County estate. He also supported the University of Virginia and other efforts to encourage public education. In 1817 TJ provided Barbour with an architectural design that he used at Barboursville, but their correspondence during TJ's retirement was primarily political (*ANB*; *DAB*; *DVB*; *PTJ*, 31:325–6; Charles D. Lowery, *James Barbour, A Jeffersonian Republican* [1984]; Leonard, *General Assembly*; Rodney H. True, "Minute Book of the Agricultural Society of Albemarle," *Annual Report of the American Historical Association for the Year 1918* [1921], 1:304, 307, 310, 324; Barbour to TJ, 29 Mar. 1817; Washington *Daily National Intelligencer*, 14 Sept. 1842).

Barbour ran for governor in 1811, but the General Assembly reelected George William Smith. After Smith died in the Richmond Theatre fire on 26 Dec. of that year, Barbour was elected to THE STATION OF CHIEF MAGISTRATE on 3 Jan. 1812 (*DVB*; Richmond *Enquirer*, 4 Jan. 1812). The Virginia CONSTITUTION as adopted by the Convention of 1776 called for an eight-member "Privy Council, or Council of State," elected by joint ballot of both houses of the legislature "to assist in the Administration of Government" by advising the governor on his exercise of executive power. Four members were "sufficient to act" (*PTJ*, 1:380–1).

To Randolph Jefferson

DEAR BROTHER Monticello Jan. 14. 12.

When I saw you last I mentioned to you that among a stock of family medecines & conveniences which I laid in by the advice of Dr Wistar when I left Philadelphia[1] he had put up, I thought, some bougies of better form than common. on searching I have found one of them, which I now send you. Doct^r Walker will be the best judge of it's merit. should you have a return of your complaint I hope you will by all means follow his judicious advice of using the lunar caustic, as the only means of giving permanent relief, and of ensuring a continuance of life. in his hands the operation will be safe, & altho' the pain will be great, yet we should make up our minds to the sufferings we are doomed to meet, and meet them with firmness and patience.

On my arrival here I found a letter announcing the death of mr Marks. I sent for our sister as soon as she could leave that neighborhood, & she is now here; but in very low health indeed, & scarcely able to walk about the house.

I had an opportunity yesterday of sending your watch to Richmond. present my respects to my sister

Yours affectionately TH: JEFFERSON

PoC (ViU: TJP-CC); at foot of text: "R. Jefferson"; endorsed by TJ.

The letter ANNOUNCING THE DEATH of TJ's brother-in-law Hastings Marks was probably Lancelot Minor to TJ, 18 Dec. 1811, not found but recorded in SJL as received from Louisa on 22 Dec. 1811. SJL also records TJ's missing letter of 28 Dec. 1811 to his widowed SISTER Anne Scott Marks. On that same day he sent his slave Wormley Hughes to bring her to Monticello, where she resided for the remainder of her life (*MB*, 2:1272).

[1] Preceding four words interlined.

To William Thornton

DEAR DOCTOR Monticello Jan. 14. 12.

We are all busied in the country with our houshold manufactures of clothing. I do not believe one fifth of the coarse clothing has been bought this year from the importers which has been heretofore bought, and the next year nobody counts on wanting a single yard of coarse goods (blankets excepted) & but little will be wanted of goods of midling qualities. for the fine we must depend on the town manufactories. most of us are still however at the old spinning wheel & hand cards. a few neighbors of us are setting up some spinning jennies, next in simplicity to the spinning wheel. but I have seen in the hands of a friend an advertisement of a machine much simpler than the jenny, & which will do about 6. times the work of a spinning wheel. it's price, 15. Dollars shews there cannot be much work about it. this promises to be exactly what we want. but does it answer what is announced of it? this question I have presumed your friendship would induce you to answer for me, to give me your opinion of the machine & some idea of it, that I may know if it is worth the trouble of sending for it. if we could but have as simple a carding machine we should be fixed. why would not 2. circular cards in peritrochio, fixed thus, answer? 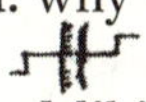 one turned by each hand in the same or opposite directions ad libitum? or plain cards on 2. cylinders, one to be turned by each hand? or 2 cards on plain surfaces, & prone, shoved backwards & forwards as in polishing marble? I copy the advertisement on the other side & tender you the assurances of my continued friendship & respect TH: JEFFERSON

RC (DLC: Thornton Papers); with 1st Tr of enclosure on verso; addressed: "Doctr William Thornton Washington Col." PoC (DLC); with PoC of 1st Tr of enclosure on verso; endorsed by TJ. Enclosure: description of Ebenezer Herrick's machine: "The Domestic Spinner. Ebenezer Herrick of West Stockbridge county of Berkshire, Mass. has lately recieved a patent for an invention greatly improving the art of spinning wool & cotton. the machine is called the Domestic Spinner. it will spin from 6. to 8. threads at a time. the expence of one machine together with the right of using the same, will not exceed 15. Dollars. mr Herrick says any person can spin one run & a half per day on each spindle, with the same labour requisite to spin 2. runs on a common wheel" (1st Tr in DLC: Thornton Papers, in TJ's hand, partially dated, at head of text: "Extract from the Delaware

Watchman. Wilmington Mar. 16.," on verso of RC of covering letter; PoC in DLC, on verso of PoC of covering letter; PoC of 2d Tr in DLC, in TJ's hand, subjoined to PoC of TJ to Ebenezer Herrick, 20 Feb. 1812; 3d Tr in DLC: TJ Papers, ser. 10, in TJ's hand; printed in Wilmington *American Watchman and Delaware Republican*, 16 Mar. 1811, with one minor variation in wording; see also Herrick to TJ, 24 Mar. 1812).

James Hargreaves patented the spinning JENNY in England in 1770 (*OED*). An axis IN PERITROCHIO is another way to describe the mechanical power or elementary machine called the wheel and axle (*OED*).

From John Barnes

MY DEAR SIR, George Town 15th January 1812

I regret exceedingly—at the lapse of time, since I had the pleasure of receiving your last favr dated the 3d July—I have also to regret the want of intelligence—respecting the uncertain fate of the two years Annual Remittance for Paris—viz—Bowie & Kurtz 14h feby 1810. on Baring Brothers & Co London—60 days sight. for £200 sterling—as well Bowie & Kurtz—13th April 1811—on Wm Murdock London at, 60 days sight. also for £200 Sterling—both drawn in my favr and by me endorsed to Messrs Hoffingan & Co Bankers in Paris, for Genl Kosciuskos sole use & Benefit; inquiring of Messrs Bowie & Kurtz: they assure me—neither of these Bills—by their late advices had—been presented—for payment, make me Apprehensive some fatal circumstance has intervened to obstruct the due course of their Negociation—and the more so—as the good Genl was Accustomed—on Receipt—thereof to favr me, with a line of acknowledgm: indeed the delay of the latter Remittance by Messrs Barlow & Warden, may yet be considered in season to be Accounted for—but the former is quite 'unaccountable'[1]—under these uncertainties—it—would not be adviseable to forward his present Annual remittance—untill advices will Warrant its probable safty—Nevertheless it may be proper to receive—his Dividend due 1st Inst at Bank of Pennsa to be ready—should any favable advices—reach you in course of this or insuing month—submitting these several Occurances to your consideration—I am wth great Respect & Esteem—

Dear Sir—Your most Obedt servant— JOHN BARNES—

RC (ViU: TJP-ER); at foot of text: "Ths Jefferson Esqr"; endorsed by TJ as received 22 Jan. 1812 and so recorded in SJL.

TJ's LAST FAVR to Barnes is dated 29 June, not the 3D JULY 1811.

[1] Omitted opening single quotation mark editorially supplied.

From John Dortic

Sir New York January 15th 1812.

Your honour of the 1st october last reached my home during my absence, while travelling through Virginia, where I went as far as Richmond. Probably I Should have proceed farther had I not been called back by unexpected business

I make this apology, Sir, to prove to you that I could not Sooner convey to you my thanks for the kindness of your answer to the inquires I had taken the liberty to trouble you with. My excuse, for thus troubling you, is my knowledge of your regard for the prosperity of your country

Be pleased, Sir, to accept the tribute of my best thanks for your favour which is far beyond what I had a right to expect

My observations in my Journey have convinced me that I had a true idea when I thought that the State of Virginia was one of the best in the union for the cultivation of the vines. Its advantages can not, I believe, be Surpassed by any; every thing is in its favour, Soil, aspect and mildness of the Climate, and I coincide, Sir, with you that the banks of James River Should to have the preference.

The culture of the vines must be considered as one of the most advantageous to this country and, therefore, ought to be encouraged by the Legislatures of the States on which rests the hope of Succeeding.

The quality, at first, is not so much to be looked for as the quantity. Brandy being one of the principal objects the quality will be the next consideration.

In the course of a few years the wine made in this country would give grounds to lay heavier duties, on foreign wines, and when the Vineyards yield a full crop and of a considerable value to the owner, the land tax could be proportioned to the revenue

Tired as I am of the European System of plaguing[1] the honest marchand, as Soon as I get rid of Some difficulties, I am under by the British and French Decrees, I will choose a Spot in Some part of your State for the purpose of making wine by the Shortest and most economical Way, and I hope that my knowledge in that line Will procure me a certainity of being more Successful than any body else

Having desired of my friends in France Some bundles of Fontainebleu Chasselas, Should they come in good Season, I Should be much flattered, Sir, if you give me leave to forward you a part of them. I Shall in that case direct them to Aer McRae Esqr in Richmond late American consul in Paris where I had the favour of being acquainted with him and Whom I have had the pleasure to visit in this city on his arrival from England. I promised him Some of the Said plant.

As Soon as I have a good prospect on the business I wish to have Settled, and perhaps before the Winter be over, I will go again to Virginia to know by myself the State of the Weather and vegetation in the months of march and April the Success depending great deal on that circumstance

I have the honour to be With Respect Sir Your most obedient Servant JOHN DORTIC

RC (DLC); addressed: "Thomas Jefferson Esquire Monticello"; franked; postmarked; endorsed by TJ as received 22 Jan. 1812 and so recorded in SJL.

MARCHAND: merchant; trader. FONTAINEBLEU CHASSELAS is a synonym for Chasselas Doré or Golden Chasselas, an early bearing white grape extensively cultivated in Europe and America at this time (Hatch, *Fruit Trees*, 154).

[1] Manuscript: "plaging."

To John B. Magruder

SIR Monticello Jan. 15. 12

We have had made for you several months ago a parcel of nails, to

wit, 150. ℔	VIII[s]	@1/	£7–10
140.	X[s]	@11½[d]	6–14–2
			14– 4–2

yesterday a person called in your name on the subject of the nails, but he talked of another balance of £29. some shilling which he claimed and seemed very importunate to have something decisive done on it: I told him no such balance existed, that except the article of plank which John Perry had undertaken to replace to you and the balance of £14–4–2 which these nails were to pay, every thing between you & me had been settled and paid; but as he seemed totally uninformed of our accounts, I found it useless to say more than that I would write to you. you know Sir that no article of any account between you & me has ever been disputed except those between 1803. Nov. 14. and 1804. June. 12. a paiment of 146.34 D = £43–18 Dec. 16. 1805. cleared every thing to that date, except the articles abovementioned which you charged at £46–3–9. & I allowed at only £27–8–5 making a difference of £18–16–8.[1] as to this we made a particular arrangement to be fulfilled by John Perry which therefore is unconnected with our subsequent accounts. you had rendered me your subsequent acc[t] from 1805. Aug. 3. to 1807. Sep. 29, which being mislaid you were so kind as to send me another. both of these I have now before me. the debets amount to £43–7–6$\frac{3}{4}$. the first gave me credit for nails to Oct. 1. 1808. £14–1–7$\frac{1}{2}$. the second gave the same credit and added a subsequent one to 1810. Nov. 6. of £15–1–10 making together £29–3–5$\frac{1}{2}$ & leaving a balance in your favor of £14–4–1$\frac{1}{4}$ this you desired to recieve in some spikes, & the rest equally divided between 8^{s} & 10^{s}. not having any spike rods, nor having recieved any since I had the balance made up in 8^{s} & 10^{s} which have been waiting for you ever since. a part of these the young man took away yesterday, & the rest will be delivered when called for. this, you know Sir, is an exact statement of every thing between us, and that the claim of any balance of 29.£ by the young man is totally void of foundation. I shall be very glad to have the rest of the nails taken away & that we should mutually sign a discharge, in order that no puzzle may arise hereafter about matters which you & I know to be settled. I am uninformed whether John Perry has replaced the plank and recieved from you the money I had paid for it; but when I formerly enquired of him he assured me you should have it on demand according to what had been settled between yourselves. Accept the assurance of my respect.

TH: JEFFERSON

PoC (MHi); at foot of first page: "Mr Magruder"; endorsed by TJ.

John Bowie Magruder (d. 1815) lived in Prince Georges County, Maryland, before moving to Virginia by 1792 and purchasing property along the Rivanna River near the boundary between Albemarle and Fluvanna counties. Four years later he began constructing a dam and gristmill, expanding his operation in 1799 to include additional mills, soon known as Union Mills, which adjoined his estate of Cumber, later Union Hall. In 1802–03 Magruder provided TJ with plank wood, probably for mill construction at Shadwell. Their difference of opinion over the cost eventually led TJ to return the wood. TJ later enlisted Magruder's aid to settle a similar disagreement with Isaac Shoemaker. Magruder was also a lay Methodist preacher who officiated at marriages in eastern Albemarle County, 1803–05. In 1812 he joined TJ and others to engage the services of weaver William McClure. At his death Magruder owned land on both sides of the Rivanna River and approximately fifteen slaves (DNA: RG 29, CS, Prince Georges Co., Md., 1790; *Bulletin of the Fluvanna County Historical Society* 10/11 [1970]: 26–8; TJ to Magruder, 26 Mar. 1803, 23 Sept. 1804, 14 Nov. 1805, 24 Sept. 1807 [MHi]; John Vogt and T. William Kethley Jr., *Albemarle County Marriages, 1780–1853* [1991], 1:20, 3:701; Woods, *Albemarle*, 260–1; *MB*; Fluvanna Co. Deed Book, 3:279, 4:39; Fluvanna Co. Will Book, 2:189–92, 204–6).

A letter from TJ to Magruder of 10 June 1811, not found, is recorded in SJL, as is Magruder's missing reply of 19 June 1811 received from Fluvanna on 23 June 1811. For TJ's PARTICULAR ARRANGEMENT, see TJ to John M. Perry, with Notes on Agreement with Perry, 20 Jan. 1810.

[1] Thus in manuscript. The correct figure is £18.15.4.

From Richard Barry

SIR January 16th 1812.

I have wrote you a letter about two weeks before Christmas, not hearing from you since I fear it has not come to your hands yet the contents of it was praying you would be so good as to let me have the ballance of my account Indeed Sir, I would not call on you now but I am building a house and I find it will take all my little earnings to meet the demands of it

I remain with Sincere Wishes for your happines a friend

RICHARD BARRY

RC (MHi); at foot of text: "Thomas Jefferson Esqr"; endorsed by TJ as received 22 Jan. 1812 and so recorded in SJL.

From Samuel J. Harrison

SIR Lynchbg Jany 16. 1812

Mr Griffen tells me that you have directed your Overseer, to Send your present Crop of Tobo to Richmond; which I am Sorry to hear; as I had intended to make you a Liberal offer for it: and as it is not yet too late, I hope you will say by Return of Mr Griffen, what price you will take for it—you Know the prospects are against the Probability of Tobaccoes getting Very high: To that I Dare Say (if you are disposed to Sell here) that we Should not likely disagree: that at any rate I will expect you to propose a price—Should the overseer have Engaged Boats to take it down I will take them off his hand.

I am Sir Yr Mo ob S S J HARRISON

RC (MHi); endorsed by TJ as a letter from "Harrison Saml H." received 22 Jan. 1812 and so recorded in SJL.

The OVERSEER at Poplar Forest was Jeremiah A. Goodman.

From Henry Wheaton

SIR, Providence, R.I. 17. Jan. 1812.

I beg your attention to the enclosed Address, written by a friend, and which as I know you to be sensibly alive to everything which concerns the welfare of science, I flatter myself you will read not without pleasure—as it indicates the growing respectability of the healing art among us.

With my prayers for the continuance of your life and health I remain sincerely with great respect your humble servant, and admirer.

HENRY WHEATON.

RC (DLC); addressed: "The Hon. Thomas Jefferson Monticello" and "Mail"; franked; postmarked Providence, 22 Jan.; endorsed by TJ as received 2 Feb. 1812 and so recorded in SJL. Enclosure not found, assigned Sowerby no. 988 and unidentified there as well.

From John Melish

SIR Newyork 18 Jan^ry 1812

I duly received your esteemed letter of the 10th March; and I now write you with pleasure, from an opinion that the subject is congenial to your present pursuits.—

I have lately returned from a very extended Tour to the Western Country, and now intend to prepare my whole Travels for the Press, as you will see by the enclosed Prospectus, and Plan.—I have commenced procuring Subscribers here with considerable success, and intend soon to visit the Seat of government in prosecution of that object, when I will, perhaps, also go into Virginia. In the meantime it will [be][1] of considerable importance if You will permit me to add your name to the List of Subscribers, for one or more Copies; and it would be esteemed a very particular favour if you would condescend to give me any information regarding the chance of procuring Subscribers in Your State. The design of the work I submit to your judgement without Comment. I intend to have it also published in Britain, provided I can make arrangements to that effect; and my object is to render a service to the Inhabitants of both Countries.—

Being a stranger to you it may be proper to accompany this with proper references.—I am well acquainted with the following Gentlemen, and they can attest the Correctness of my principles & Conduct—I am with much esteem

Sir Your mo: ob. Ser JOHN MELISH

Walt: Morton Esq Secretary Phenix Insurance office New y^k
John Aird Esq Deputy Clerk Supreme Court— Do
Col: Duane Editor of the Aurora Philadelphia
Geo: Mauray Engraver Do

RC (DLC); at head of text: "Thomas Jefferson Esq"; endorsed by TJ as received 2 Feb. 1812 and so recorded in SJL. Enclosures: (1) Melish, *Proposal to Publish by Subscription* his new work entitled *Travels in the United States of America, in the Years 1806 & 1807, and 1809, 1810, & 1811; including an account of passages betwixt America and Britain, and Travels through Various Parts of Britain, Ireland, and Upper Canada*, 2 vols. (Philadelphia, 1812; Sowerby, no. 4034), to be published in octavo for $5 in boards, and to include a full account of his travels and the results of his extensive interviews with local inhabitants, as well as maps, plates, and appendices reviewing the existing geographical and travel literature, summarizing the United States Constitution, and providing statistical information and documents important to an understanding of political economy; noting that during his travels he had observed the impact of "the stoppage of the foreign trade" on the maritime states and come to believe that "*internal manufacture and commerce* would, in all probability, be substituted for *foreign commerce*" in the near future; and observing that as a result the western states were now "a most important field for inquiry," thanks to their fertile soil, moderate climate, natural resources, sparse population, and abundance of cheap land, which made them both a likely source of industrial strength and an expanding market for eastern manufactures (undated broadside in DLC: TJ Papers, 192:34219). (2) Melish, *Outlines of Travels in the United States . . . Plan of the Work*, detailing the subjects to be covered in each of more than one hundred chapters (with chapter 31 of the first volume to describe his visit to TJ at the President's House in Washington, where he got a "Polite reception, and information as to the state of the country, Roads, Bridges, Canals, Manufactures, Health, &c") and in appendices (undated pamphlet in DLC: TJ Papers, 192:34215–8).

[1] Omitted word editorially supplied.

From Ferdinando Fairfax

DEAR SIR, [ca. 20 Jan. 1812]

I comply the more readily with Doctor Thornton's request (that I would express to you my opinion of Barret's machine for Roving and Spinning) from knowing your desire to patronise and promote the Useful Arts, and the readiness with which you communicate information of their improvements. As I know, and have every year occasion to observe, how many <u>un</u>important Patents are obtained, and how many empty pretenders are employ'd in puffing their merits, I am cautious of deciding in favor even of those that I wish to adopt and best understand. Of Barret's machine, which I have seen in operation, I may with propriety say, that it deserves high commendation, for simplicity of combination, ease of movement, and efficiency of its objects; which are the most desirable of all that belong to the art of Spinning—namely, to prepare the roving with great nicety, to spin the threads (of yarn as well as cotton, which few machines can do) of exact size, evenness, and equality of twist (depending on a measured number of revolutions) and to untwist again each of those threads, and draw them as fine by successive operations of the same kind, as may be required. It consists of as few parts, simply combined & easily made and repair'd, as I can conceive possible, to effect those objects; and any ingenious Woman can learn in a day its use: but I would recommend to any gentleman, not having a regular factory, to have it worked pretty much under his own eye, and kept in a locked apartment when not in use; knowing that the fingers of the prying & curious are hardly less injurious to a nice machine, than those of the wilfully mischievous. Indeed the common Spinning-wheel must be kept with care: and how much better will the one in question repay every care!

With very high consideration D[r] Sir,—&c F: FAIRFAX

P.S.

The model of the machine of which you wrote to Doctor T. being in itself imperfect, may give me a less favorable opinion of its merits than it deserves: But being so cheap, it may be worthwhile to procure one for Experiment (ie Hearrick's).

RC (DLC: TJ Papers, 194:34602); undated; on verso of last page of RC of William Thornton to TJ, 20 Jan. 1812; at head of text: "The Hon[ble] Tho[s] Jefferson Esq."; endorsed by TJ as received 26 Jan. 1812 and so recorded (as a letter of 20 Jan. 1812) in SJL.

Ferdinando Fairfax (1769–1820) was born in Fairfax County and soon became a godson of George Washington. As the heir of his uncle George William Fairfax, he inherited large tracts of land in the Northern Neck of Virginia and what is now West Virginia in 1787. He endeavored to expand an iron-ore mining operation into a large foundry, established a ferry service at his property fronting the Shenandoah River, and in 1810 unsuccessfully sought federal office. Fairfax was a proponent of African colonization, a founding trustee of the Charlestown Academy in 1797, and a justice of the peace (*PTJ*, 24:368–9, 28:12–3; Donald Jackson and Dorothy Twohig, eds., *The Diaries of George Washington* [1976–79], 2:154; William D. Theriault, "Shannondale Springs," *West Virginia History Journal* 57 [1998]: 1–3, 21–3; Fairfax, "Plan for liberating the negroes within the united states," *American Museum, or, Universal Magazine* 8 [1790]: 285–7; Fairfax to TJ, 9 Sept. 1804 [DLC], 20 Apr. 1818; Madison, *Papers, Pres. Ser.*, 3:79; Charles Town, Va. (now W.Va.), *Farmers' Repository*, 27 Sept. 1820; Washington *Daily National Intelligencer*, 28 Sept. 1820).

From William Thornton

DEAR SIR City of Washington Jan[y] 20th 1812–

I have this Day had the honor of your Letter of the 14th Inst: enquiring into the goodness of the Domestic Spinner by Ebenezer Hearrick. Having been very much confined by sickness I sent to the office for the Drawing of Hearrick's machine. It may possibly answer, but I think it cannot spin fast the length of the thread every motion being very short. It consists of a Frame, a principal Band wheel, a revolving Cylinder & six spindles, a lathe which holds the Spindles—levers which raise the horizontal Bars—Pulleys or wheels round which pass the Cords fastened to the Levers—Weights and an Arm that carries the threads from the points of the Spindles downwards. I do not perfectly understand its operation & fear its want of efficiency. I think it is a good deal like the spinning Billy. There is a spinning machine in the office invented by m^{r} Oliver Barrett of New York State, which is more like the Spinning Jenny, but which will also rove the wool & spin 12 threads. It may be made for about $25, & does excellent work. I think very highly of the machine & the Inventor told me he would sell the different Counties of Virginia for $500 each. He charges the patent right of each machine $20—so that it would be the cheapest for several Individuals to join, put in $50 each & purchase the County. If a purchase be made I could get a machine executed here very well as a model & it could be sent for by a single Horse Cart, for it is light. Judge Cranch gave $50 for one of 12 Spindles, & is so much pleased with it that he is going to establish a manufactory of Cloths, & to use this machine. It will rove as much in one Day as will keep the Spinner three Days in spinning it; & of any fineness. It is such a machine as will render our merino wool of great value. Its very great simplicity will prevent it from going out of order, & it may be made to spin 20 threads as well as 12.—In New York State it may be made well at the rate of 200 Doll^{s} a Dozen without the Spindles wch cost 25 Cents each; & the rest of the iron work which cost ab^{t} 5 Doll^{s} more, making the whole about 25 Doll^{s} for a 12 Spindled machine: but here, where labour is high a machine would cost between 30 & 40.—Lame or old negroes would spin very well with it. The wool requires carding, but one Carding machine erected at your mills would serve a whole neighbourhood, & I could engage you a Carding machine.—The price I have by enquiry found, for one for the finest as well as coarsest wool is about $400.—If the Gentlemen of your County would incline to buy the patent right, & have a machine made as a Pattern it might afterwards be made very cheap, & as I think Patents will be renewable it will be still cheaper by the renewal.—I think you have sketched a very good Card, but it will require to be further thought of to perfect it.—I have requested my respected Friend m^{r} Fairfax to give you also his opinion. He went to my office, examined both very particularly and will subjoin his Opinion.—

I have applied to the Congress to permit m^{r} Charles Whitlow to cultivate the Ground destined for a Botanical Garden at the junction of the President's Square & Capitol Park So. of the mouth of the Tiber & to occupy it till demanded by Congress, he being obliged to give it up on demand, they paying the valuation of the Improvements

& for the collection of plants.—m[r] Whitlow is the person who has made so many valuable Discoveries in this Country of new Plants, and lately one of immense Importance as a substitute for Flax & Hemp. The Plant I have no doubt will supersede Flax & Hemp compleatly. It grows about 5 or 6 feet high and is perennial. It produces 500 for one, & can therefore be propagated with great rapidity. It produces ab[t] a thousand pounds W[t] of good Flax p[r] Acre. It does not require rotting to be ready for manufacturing, & loses very little in preparing. It may be spun into thread equal to N[o] 44 equal to 10 Doll[s] a lb, and is still very strong. It makes ropes & Cables so much stronger than the best Russia hemp as to decide that a nine Inch Cable would equal a 12 Inch cable of the hemp.—It is sufficiently soft, especially when bleached, to make the finest & strongest paper.—m[r] Whitlow has taken out a Patent for the uses to which he has applied it, and has had a very large Sum offered for it, but he prefers selling it to the different States and values Virginia at 10,000 Doll[s]. I think it is one of the most valuable Discoveries that has been made for a very long time.—m[r] Whitlow has a very valuable Collection of Plants viz 2500 Species ready to bring here from the Botanical Gardens of the Universities of Edinburgh & Cambridge, with a superb Collection of the most valuable Fruit Trees. Currants as large as common Grapes &c &c—

I am dear Sir with the highest respect and consideration yours sincerely &c WILLIAM THORNTON

RC (DLC); at foot of text: "Honorable Thomas Jefferson"; endorsed by TJ as received 26 Jan. 1812 and so recorded in SJL; with RC of Ferdinando Fairfax to TJ, [ca. 20 Jan. 1812], on verso of last page.

In the United States House of Representatives on 20 Jan. 1812, Samuel Latham Mitchill presented a petition from CHARLES WHITLOW requesting "permission to occupy the grounds, in the city of Washington, destined to a Botanic garden, and to be given up on the demand of the Government, he being paid for the improvements, plants, trees, and shrubs, introduced into the same, at their valuation by independent persons." A bill to this effect was introduced in the House on 25 Feb., but the Senate discharged the petition from further consideration on 1 Apr. 1812 (*JHR*, 8:134, 202; *JS*, 5:90). Whitlow received a patent on 11 Jan. 1812 for a "new species of plant applicable to many uses, particularly for the uses of flax and hemp, &c.," a discovery Thornton regarded as being of IMMENSE IMPORTANCE (*List of Patents*, 109).

Charles Whitlow (Whitlaw) was a botanist and inventor who came to America from Great Britain in 1794. By 1809 he was a nurseryman in New York City, selling shrubs and fruit trees imported from London. Whitlow energetically promoted a plant he claimed to have discovered in 1810, which came to be known as *Urtica Whitlowi*. It was later described as *Urtica Canadensis*, and its modern name is probably *Laportea canadensis*. Whitlow followed up his 1812 federal patent by petitioning the New York State Assembly to support his ongoing plant research, which he claimed "promises more advantages to the arts and manufactures than any other discovery of modern years." The state legislature duly incorporated the Urtica Whitlowi Society on 12 Apr. 1813, but skepticism soon emerged regarding his discovery. Critics dismissed it as the common nettle. Nonetheless, two years later Whitlow successfully patented "certain plants of the *genus urtica*" in Great Britain. In 1816–17 he came to the United States on an extensive botanical lecture tour. Whitlow returned to Great Britain, published regularly on agriculture and nutrition, and invented a medicated vapor bath, but he never completely shed his reputation as a charlatan (*New-York Gazette & General Advertiser*, 16 Nov. 1809; Thornton to TJ, 8 May 1812, 19 Feb. 1817; Brattleborough, Vt., *Reporter*, 6 Feb. 1813; *Journal of the Assembly of the State of New-York* [Albany, 1813], 112, 119, 570–1; *Laws of the State of New-York, passed at the Thirty-Sixth Session* [Albany, 1813], 302–4; Whitlow to James Monroe, 23 Dec. 1813 [DNA: RG 59, MLR]; *Transactions of the Society for the Promotion of Useful Arts, in the State of New-York* 3 [1814]: 77, 79–80; *Repertory of Arts, Manufactures, and Agriculture*, 2d ser., 26 [1815]: 127; *Tradesman; or, Commercial Magazine* 5 [1815]: 474–5; Philadelphia *Poulson's American Daily Advertiser*, 2 Dec. 1816; *New-York Columbian*, 30 May 1817; *New-York Spectator*, 12 Sept. 1817; *Transactions of the Literary and Historical Society of Quebec* 3 [1824]: 85; Richard Peters to James Madison, 24 Aug. 1818 [DLC: Madison Papers, Rives Collection]; Francis W. Gilmer to TJ, 15 Sept. 1824; Whitlow, *A Short Review of the Causes and Effects of the Present Distress* [1839], esp. 33).

To John Adams

DEAR SIR Monticello Jan. 21. 1812.

I thank you before hand (for they are not yet arrived) for the specimens of homespun you have been so kind as to forward me by post. I doubt not their excellence, knowing how far you are advanced in these things in your quarter. here we do little in the fine way, but in coarse & midling goods a great deal. every family in the country is a manufactory within itself, and is very generally able to make within itself all the stouter and midling stuffs for it's own cloathing & houshold use. we consider a sheep for every person in the[1] family as sufficient to clothe it, in addition to the cotton, hemp & flax which we raise ourselves. for fine stuff we shall depend on your Northern manufactures. of these, that is to say, of company establishments, we have none.[2] we use little machinery. the Spinning Jenny and loom with the flying shuttle can be managed in a family; but nothing more complicated. the economy and thriftiness resulting from our[3] houshold manufactures are such that they will never again be laid aside; and nothing more salutary for us has ever happened than the British obstructions to our demands for their manufactures. restore free intercourse when they will, their[4] commerce with us will have totally changed it's form, and the articles we shall in future want from them will not exceed their own consumption of our produce.

A letter from you calls up recollections very dear to my mind. it carries me back to the times when, beset with difficulties & dangers, we were fellow laborers in the same cause, struggling for what is most valuable to man, his right of self-government. laboring always at the same oar, with some wave ever ahead threatening to overwhelm us & yet passing harmless under our bark we knew not how, we rode through the storm with heart & hand, and made a happy port. still we did not expect to be without rubs and difficulties; and we have had them. first the detention of the Western posts: then the coalition of Pilnitz, outlawing our commerce with France, & the British enforcement of the outlawry.[5] in your day French depredations: in mine English, & the Berlin and Milan decrees: now the English orders of council, & the piracies they authorise: when these shall be over, it will be the impressment of our seamen, or something else: and so we have gone on, & so we shall go on, puzzled & prospering beyond example in the history of man. and I do believe we shall continue to growl, to multiply & prosper until we exhibit an association, powerful, wise, and happy, beyond what has yet been seen by men. as for France & England, with all their preeminence in science, the one is a den of robbers, & the other of pirates. and if science produces no better fruits than tyranny, murder, rapine, and destitution of national morality, I would rather wish our country to be ignorant, honest & estimable as our neighboring savages are.—but whither is senile garrulity leading me? into politics, of which I have taken final leave. I think little of them, & say[6] less. I have given up newspapers in exchange for Tacitus & Thucydides, for Newton & Euclid; & I find myself much the happier. sometimes indeed I look back to former occurrences, in remembrance of our old friends and fellow laborers, who have fallen before us. of the signers of the Declaration of Independance I see now living not more than half a dozen on your side of the Patomak, and, on this side, myself alone. you & I have been wonderfully spared, and myself with remarkable health, & a considerable activity of body & mind. I am on horseback 3. or 4. hours of every day; visit 3. or 4. times a year a possession I have 90 miles distant, performing the winter journey on horseback. I walk little however; a single mile being too much for me; and I live in the midst of my grandchildren, one of whom has lately promoted me to be a great grandfather. I have heard with pleasure that you also retain good health, and a greater power of exercise in walking than I do. but I would rather have heard this from yourself, & that, writing a letter, like mine, full of egotisms, & of details of your health, your habits, occupations & enjoiments, I should have the pleasure of knowing that, in the race of life, you do not keep, in it's physical decline, the same distance ahead of me which you have done in political honors & atchievements. no circumstances have lessened the interest I feel in these particulars respecting yourself; none have suspended for one moment my sincere esteem for you; and I now salute you with unchanged affections and respect. Th: Jefferson

RC (MHi: Adams Papers); at foot of first page: "John Adams, late Pr. US"; endorsed by Adams as answered 3 Feb. 1812. PoC (DLC). PoC of Tr (DLC: TJ Papers, 194:34560–1); entirely in TJ's hand; subjoined to PoC of Tr of Adams to TJ, 1 Jan. 1812. Enclosed in TJ to Benjamin Rush, 21 Jan. 1812.

For the SPECIMENS OF HOMESPUN, see Adams to TJ, 1 Jan. 1812, and note. The British DETENTION OF THE WESTERN POSTS within American territory after the end of the Revolutionary War was a source of friction until they were relinquished under the Jay Treaty of 1795 (*PTJ*, 7:432, 440, 8:58–9n, 28:399–400). At PILNITZ (Pillnitz) in 1791 the rulers of Austria and Prussia declared their willingness to intervene in French affairs (William Doyle, *The Oxford History of the French Revolution* [1989], 156–7; *PTJ*, 22:161–2, 26:601–3). TJ became a GREAT GRANDFATHER in 1810 when Ann C. Bankhead gave birth to her first child, John Warner Bankhead (Shackelford, *Descendants*, 73, 75).

[1] PoC of Tr: "our."

[2] PoC of Tr: "of these we have none, I mean company establishments."

[3] PoC of Tr: "thriftiness attending our."

[4] PoC of Tr: "she will, her."

[5] Manuscript: "oulawry."

[6] PoC of Tr: "speak."

From Mathew Carey

Sir, Philad[a] January 21. 1812.

Your parliamentary Manual has been for a long time out of print, & in demand. I have written to the publisher, M[r] S. H. Smith, to enquire whether he has any objection to a republication of it. And wish to be informed by you, whether, if he consents to its being reprinted, you have any alterations or improvements to make in it.

I am, sir, very respectfully, Your ob[t] h[ble] serv[t]

Mathew Carey

RC (MHi); at head of text: "Thomas Jefferson, Esq[r]"; endorsed by TJ as received 26 Jan. 1812 and so recorded in SJL.

Mathew Carey (1760–1839), bookseller, publisher, and author, was born in Dublin, Ireland. Apprenticed to a bookseller and newspaper publisher in 1775, during the ensuing decade Carey wrote an anonymous pamphlet denouncing the anti-Catholic legal code; spent a year in Paris, where he worked briefly at Benjamin Franklin's Passy press and met Lafayette; established a nationalist newspaper after his return to Ireland; and was imprisoned for sedition. To avoid a further prosecution for libel, Carey immigrated to Philadelphia in 1784. With financial assistance from Lafayette, Carey published the Philadelphia *Pennsylvania Evening Herald*, 1785–88. His other publishing ventures, which proliferated after he gave up his printshop in 1794, included the *Columbian Magazine*, 1786–87, the *American Museum*, 1787–92, bibles, reprints of English works, and new works by Americans, including Mason Locke Weems's *A History of the Life and Death, Virtues and Exploits, of General George Washington* (1800). Carey also published the second American edition of TJ's *Notes on the State of Virginia* (1794). He broke with the Federalists over Jay's Treaty in 1795, was generally sympathetic to the Republicans thereafter, but sought to promote interparty reconciliation with his 1814 publication, *The Olive Branch: or Faults on Both Sides, Federal and Democratic*. Carey was elected to the American Philosophical Society in 1821. Especially after his retirement in 1822, he wrote extensively in support of protective tariffs and internal improvements. TJ subscribed to the *American Museum* and regularly purchased books from Carey. During TJ's retirement his correspondence with Carey generally concerned itself with book orders, with occasional commentary on their contents (*ANB*; *DAB*; James N. Green, *Mathew Carey: Publisher and Patriot* [1985]; *PTJ*, 17:261–2, 19:606, 25:467; *MB*, esp. 2:811, 1376; Sowerby, esp. nos. 3539, 4903; Poor, *Jefferson's Library*, 4, 7, 11 [nos. 114, 348, 708]; Brigham, *American Newspapers*, 2:923, 930–1, 1388; APS, Minutes, 20 July 1821 [MS in PPAmP]; Washington *Daily National Intelligencer*, 20 Sept. 1839).

To Benjamin Rush

Dear Sir — Monticello. Jan. 21. 12.

As it is thro' your kind interposition that two old friends are brought together, you have a right to know how the first approaches are made. I send you therefore a copy of mr Adams's letter to me & of my answer. to avoid the subject of his family, on which I could say nothing, I have written him a rambling, gossiping epistle which gave openings for the expression of sincere feelings, & may furnish him ground of reciprocation, if he merely waited for the first declaration; for so I would construe the reserve of his letter. in the course of the spring I can have a good occasion of writing to him again, on sending him a law case of Livingston against myself, which having been dismissed out of court, for want of jurisdiction, remains unexplained to the world. this explanation I shall print for my own justification; and a copy may not be unamusing to one who is himself a profound lawyer. ever affectionately yours — Th: Jefferson

RC (DLC); addressed: "Doct[r] Benjamin Rush Philadelphia"; franked; postmarked Milton, 23 Jan. 1812; endorsed by TJ as a letter to Rush that was "returned to me after his death by his family." PoC (DLC). Enclosures: (1) John Adams to TJ, 1 Jan. 1812. (2) TJ to Adams, 21 Jan. 1812.

To James Barbour

DEAR SIR Monticello Jan. 22. 12

Your favor of the 14th has been duly recieved, and I sincerely congratulate you, or rather my country, on the just testimony of confidence which it has lately manifested to you. in your hands I know that it's affairs will be ably & honestly administered.

In answer to your enquiry whether in the early times of our government, where the council was divided, the practice was for the governor to give the deciding vote? I must observe that, correctly speaking, the Governor not being a counsellor, his vote could make no part of an advice of council. that would be to place an advice on their journals which they did not give, & could not give because of their equal division. but he did what was equivalent in effect. while I was in the administration, no doubt was ever suggested that where the council, divided in opinion, could give no advice, the Governor was free and bound to act on his own opinion, and his own responsibility. had this been a change of the practice of my predecessor mr Henry, the first governor, it would have produced some discussion, which it never did. hence I conclude it was the opinion & practice from the first institution of the government. during Arnold's & Cornwallis's invasion, the council dispersed to their several homes, to take care of their families. before their separation, I obtained from them a Capitulary of standing advices for my government in such cases as ordinarily occur: such as the appointment of militia officers, justices, inspectors Etc. on the recommendations of the courts; but in the numerous & extraordinary occurrences of an invasion, which could not be foreseen I had to act on my own judgment, and my own responsibility. the vote of general approbation at the session of the succeeding winter, manifested the opinion of the legislature that my proceedings had been correct. Genl Nelson, my successor, staid mostly, I think, with the army; and I do not believe his council followed the camp; altho' my memory does not enable me to affirm the fact. some petitions against him for impressment of property without authority of law, brought his proceedings before the next legislature. the questions necessarily involved were Whether necessity, without express law could justify the impressment, and, if it could, Whether he could order it without the advice of council. the approbation of the legislature amounted to a decision of both questions. I remember this case the more especially, because I was then a member of the legislature, & was one of those who supported the governor's proceedings; and I think there was no division of the house on the Question. I believe the doubt was first suggested, in Governor Harrison's time, by some member of the council, on an equal division. Harrison, in his dry way, observed that instead of one governor & eight counsellors, there would then be eight governors & one counsellor, and continued, as I understood, the practice of his predecessors. indeed it is difficult to suppose it could be the intention of those who framed the constitution that, when the council should be divided, the government should stand still: and the more difficult as to a constitution formed during a war, & for the purpose of carrying on that war: that so high an officer as their governor, should be created and salaried, merely to act as the clerk and authenticator of the votes of the council. no doubt it was intended that the advice of the council should controul the governor. but the action of the controuling power being withdrawn, his would be left free to proceed on it's own responsibility. where from division, absence, sickness or other obstacle, no advice could be given, they could not mean that their governor, the person of their peculiar choice & confidence, should stand by, an inactive spectator, and let the government tumble to pieces for want of a will to direct it. in Executive cases, where promptitude and decision are all-important, an adherence to the letter of a law against it's probable intentions, (for every law must intend that itself shall be executed) would be fraught with incalculable danger. judges may await further legislative explanations. but a delay of Executive action might produce irretrievable ruin. the state is invaded, militia to be called out, an army marched, arms & provisions to be issued from the public magazines, the legislature to be convened, and the council is divided. can it be believed to have been the intention of the framers of the constitution, that the constitution itself & their constituents with it should be destroyed, for want of a will to direct the resources they had provided for it's preservation? before such possible consequences all verbal scruples must vanish, construction must be made secundum arbitrium boni viri, and the constitution be rendered a practicable thing. that exposition of it must be vicious which would leave the nation, under the most dangerous emergencies, without a directing will. the cautious maxims of the bench, to seek the will of the legislator in his words only, are proper & safest for judicial government. they act ever on an individual case only, the evil of which is partial, & gives time for correction. but an instant of delay in Executive proceedings may be fatal to the whole nation. they must not therefore be laced up in the rules of the judiciary department. they must seek the intention of the legislator in all the circumstances which may indicate it, in the history of the day, in the public discussions, in the general opinion & understanding, in reason, & in practice. the three great departments having distinct functions to perform, must have distinct rules adapted to them. each must act under it's own rules, those of no one having any obligation on either of the others. when the opinion first begun that a governor could not act when his council could not, or would not advise, I am uninformed. probably not till after the war; for had it prevailed then, no militia could have been opposed to Cornwallis, nor necessaries furnished to the opposing army of La Fayette.—these, Sir, are my recollections & thoughts on the subject of your enquiry to which I will only add the assurances of my great esteem & respect. TH: JEFFERSON

RC (NN: Barbour Papers); at foot of first page: "H. E. Governor Barbour"; lacks address cover. RC (DLC: John Tyler Papers); address cover only; addressed: "His Excellency Governor Barbour Richmond"; franked; postmarked Milton, 27 Jan. 1812. PoC (DLC).

Long before ARNOLD'S & CORNWALLIS'S INVASION, on 13 Nov. 1779 the Virginia Council of State approved a CAPITULARY OF STANDING ADVICES authorizing TJ to conduct routine business in its absence. The General Assembly passed a resolution OF GENERAL APPROBATION of his conduct as governor on 12 Dec. 1781 (*PTJ*, 3:183–4, 6:135–7). On 5 Jan. 1782 the legislature indemnified former governor Thomas Nelson for his IMPRESSMENT OF PROPERTY WITHOUT AUTHORITY OF LAW (*JHD*, 1781–82 sess., 74; *Acts of Assembly*, 1781–82 sess., 18). SECUNDUM ARBITRIUM BONI VIRI: "according to the judgment of a good man." Use of this phrase to describe discretion in the exercise of executive power evoked the long-standing legal tension between technical and discretionary administration of justice (Roscoe Pound, "Justice According to Law," *Columbia Law Review* 13 [1913]: 696–713).

From Jean Guillaume Hyde de Neuville

MONSIEUR N/york 22 Janvier 1812

Veuillez agreér mes Sinceres remerciments pour la réponse obligeante que vous avez bien voulu faire à ma lettre, je ne doute point du Succès de ma reclamation puisqu'elle est appuyeé par vous.

Jai lhonneur d'être avec autant de reconnoissance que de respect Monsieur Votre três humble et três obt. Serviteure

G. HYDE NEUVILLE

EDITORS' TRANSLATION

SIR New York 22 January 1812

Please accept my sincere thanks for the obliging answer you kindly gave to my letter. I have no doubt about the success of my claim with your support.

I have the honor to be with as much gratitude as respect

Sir your very humble and very obedient servant G. HYDE NEUVILLE

RC (DLC: TJ Papers, 212:37820, misfiled at 22 Jan. 1818); dateline at foot of text; endorsed by TJ as received 2 Feb. 1812 and so recorded in SJL. Translation by Dr. Roland H. Simon.

To John Adams

DEAR SIR Monticello Jan. 23. 12.

The messenger who carried my letter of yesterday to the Post-office brought me thence, on his return, the two pieces of homespun which had been separated by the way from your letter of Jan. 1. a little more sagacity of conjecture in me, as to their appellation, would have saved you the trouble of reading a long dissertation on the state of real homespun in our quarter. the fact stated however will not be unacceptable to you: and the less when it is considered as a specimen only of the general state of our whole country and of it's advance towards an independance of foreign supplies for the necessary manufactures.

Some extracts from these volumes which I had seen in the public papers had prepared me to recieve them with favorable expectations. these have not been disappointed; for I have already penetrated so far into them as to see that they are a mine of learning & taste, and a proof that the author of the inimitable reviews of Ames & Pickering excels in more than one character of writing. the thanks therefore which I had rendered by anticipation only in my letter, I reiterate in this Postscript on a knolege of their high merit, & avail myself of the occasion it furnishes of repeating the assurances of my sincere friendship & respect. TH: JEFFERSON

RC (MHi: Adams Papers); addressed: "John Adams late Presid[t] of the US. Quincy. Mass."; franked; postmarked Milton, 27 Jan. 1812; endorsed by Adams as answered 10 Feb. 1812. PoC (MHi).

The TWO volumes enclosed in Adams to TJ, 1 Jan. 1812, were forwarded to TJ by Gideon Granger with a brief covering note dated 16 Jan. 1812 from the "Gen[l] post Office": "M[r] T. Munroe Sent me the package which accompanies this, and perceiving it was from M[r] Adams I thout best to forward it without delay" (RC in DLC; endorsed by TJ as received 22 Jan. 1812 and so recorded in SJL). In 1809 John Quincy Adams had published an anonymous series of letters in the *Boston Patriot* criticizing the extreme Federalist views of Fisher AMES. These letters were collected and published as *American Principles: A Review of Works of Fisher Ames* (Boston, 1809). A year earlier the younger Adams had published similarly critical comments on his fellow Massachusetts senator, Timothy PICKERING, as *A Letter to Harrison G. Otis, Esquire; from John Q. Adams, a Senator of the United States, in Reply to Timothy Pickering* (New York, 1808; and other eds).

From Pierre Samuel Du Pont de Nemours

Mon très respectable ami, 25 Janvier 1812.

un livre de la plus haute importance m'a êté prêté par Mr Warden;[1] et je voudrais bien qu'il m'eut êté donné de votre part.

Ce Sont les Commentaires Sur Montesquieu.

Un autre Américain m'a dit qu'on croyait aux Etats-Unis qu'il était d'un de mes enfans et Seulement traduit en anglais par vous.

Plut-à-dieu qu'un de mes Fils eut êté capable de le faire! mais quoique tous deux aient de l'esprit, de la raison, assez d'instruction, beaucoup de morale, ils sont l'un et l'autre trop entraînés par leur travail journalier pour faire un tel Livre.

C'est l'ouvrage d'un grand Homme d'Etat; et c'est vous qui l'avez fait.

Vous y avez mis une petite dédicace comme s'il était offert par un Francais aux Etats-Unis.[2] Vous aurez cru que ce qui paraitrait pendant quelque tems venir d'une autre nation frapperait davantage; et en effet il est rare que les plus éclairés des Hommes Soient dans leur Pays des Prophètes aussi bien écoutés qu'ils méritent de l'être.

mais il n'y a pas en Amérique un Français et il n'y en a pas même en France un Seul, qui eut pu Suivre tant de discussions du premier ordre avec une Si Sévere logique et une Si étonnante profondeur.

Je n'en ai encore bien lu que le premier, le Second, le troisieme, le quatrieme, le cinquieme, le Sixieme, le Septieme,[3] le huitieme et le treizieme chapitre. Je n'ai que parcouru les autres. mais je les lirai et relirai tous plus d'une fois et avec la plus sérieuse attention.

Pardonnez moi d'avoir commencé par ceux qui ont plus de rapport à mon travail habituel[4] et aux matieres que nous avons déja traitées ensemble.

Pardonnez moi, avec encore plus d'indulgence, Si relativement au treizieme Chapitre, qui renferme de Si interessantes considérations sur notre derniere correspondance, je me permets à montrer quelques observations.—Je les Soumets à mon Frere, à mon noble compagnon, à mon Maitre dans ma propre Science.

Vous avez vu avec génie que donner à la République le cinquieme, ou le Sixieme, ou telle autre partie aliquote du Revenu des terres, c'êtait lui donner précisement la même partie aliquote de leur capital. Vous avez le premier dit cette vérité: Elle est à vous dans la Science de l'Economie politique.

mais il n'est pas vrai que cette concession Soit un fardeau pour les Propriétaires des terres. Vous avez très bien reconnu qu'elle n'en est pas un pour leurs Successeurs, qui n'héritent, n'achettent et ne vendent que la portion qui leur appartient dans la terre qu'ils administrent et qu'ils exploitent.

Elle n'en est pas même un pour les premiers Propriétaires qui font cette concession, quand ce Sont réellement eux qui la font, et quand elle ne leur est pas extorquée par une autorité arbitraire qui prend plus que les besoins publics n'exigent pour être raisonnablement et complettement Satisfaits.—Car le besoin public de la Sureté personnelle et de la garantie de toutes les especes de propriétés est Si grand, que même les plus absurdes et les plus oppressives des taxes Sont préferables au pillage réciproque et universel qui aurait lieu Si l'autorité d'un Gouvernement et une[5] force publique ne S'y opposaient pas.

Ainsi les Taxes ne Sont pas toujours un mal, comme le dit par une expression trop forte le Chapitre XIII; Elles n'en Sont un en général que pour la portion qui excède les véritables besoins publics;

et comparativement qu'autant que la forme de leur perception les rend trop couteuses, vexatoires, litigieuses, chargeés de Fraix inutiles,[6] gênant la liberté des personnes, interrompant l'action du travail.

d'où Suit que la concession faite par les propriétaires à l'Etat politique d'une partie quelconque du revenu du territoire, concession qui laisse à toutes les especes de travaux la plus grande liberté dont ils puissent jouir, et la plus vive concurrence qui puisse les animer, qui fait par conséquent cultiver les terres le mieux et au meilleur marché qu'il Soit possible et en rend pour leurs Proprietaires le revenu le plus haut possible, loin de leur faire aucun tort et de leur causer aucun mal, est au contraire pour eux un très grand bien, le plus grand bien qu'ils puissent désirer.

Quelques Personnes ont pensé qu'il vaudrait mieux donner à l'Etat des domaines qu'il ferait cultiver; et l'immunité des Propriétaires du reste du Territoire en paraitrait à la pluspart d'entre eux plus assurée.—C'est ce dont je vous ai parlé au Sujet de la Constitution financière des Egyptiens.

mais comme un Gouvernement, même le plus parfait qu'on pût imaginer, ne Saurait être qu'un très médiocre cultivateur parce que les Soins de l'administration générale et les détails de l'Agriculture sont trop disparates; comme il aurait, pour mettre en valeur tant de terres, besoin de trop d'Agens Sans interêt à la chose et gagnant leurs gages avec le moins de peine qu'ils pourraient, il faudrait lui donner beaucoup plus de terres, ou Selon votre judicieuse observation une bien plus grande part du Capital de la nation pour qu'il en tirât le même revenu. Et il faudrait aussi lui donner un trop grand capital disponible pour mettre, même mal, ces terres en valeur.[7]

Encore les Propriétaires des autres terres auraient toujours à craindre que dans l'urgence des besoins publics et pour Se procurer plus promptement de l'argent, le Gouvernement ne vendit Souvent à vil prix et hors de Saison[8] les productions des terres qu'on lui auraît concédeés, ne fit ainsi tomber la valeur du produit des biens fonds des simples Citoyens, ce qui dérangerait les entreprises et toutes les Spéculations de l'Agriculture et du Commerce.

Il pourrait arriver aussi que le Gouvernement ayant mal cultivé les Terres qu'on lui aurait données ne leur fit pas produire tout le revenu qu'on aurait voulu lui assigner, et que cela ne conduisit à recourir aux Taxes, aux Excises, aux duties, aux diverses manieres de lever de l'argent qui tourmentent les Personnes et gênent ou arrêtent le travail. Cest ce qui est arrivé dans toute l'Europe, où tous les Souverains ont commencé par avoir des domaines, et ont ensuite introduit les impôsitions désordonnées, ruineuses, destructives de la liberté des hommes et des actions.

Qu'il faille aux Gouvernemens une part dans les revenus de leur Nation: c'est ce que l'on ne peut pas contester, puisque l'existence d'un Gouvernement est un des premiers besoins de la Société.

que cette part ne doive pas être arbitraire, qu'elle doive être levée avec la plus grande équité proportionnelle, c'est ce qui n'est pas moins clair, et qui Se trouve effectué lorsque c'est précisement la même partie aliquote de tous les revenus territoriaux, ou comme vous le dites très bien de tous leurs capitaux qui est assignée au maintien de la chose publique.

Et que la levée se fasse au meilleur marche possible quand ce Sont les Propriétaires qui restent chargés de la culture, c'est ce qui résulte de ce qu'ils ont déja le capital nécessaire à l'exploitation,[9] les chevaux, les charrues, les granges, les ouvriers, et qu'il ne leur en coute pas plus en cultivant leur très grande part de la Récolte et du revenu qu'elle produit, de cultiver aussi la petite part de l'Etat, qui reste indivise entre tous les membres de la Société pour leur utilité commune.

Je Suis affligé que dans votre beau et Savant Chapitre Sur les taxes, vous n'ayez pris aucune conclusion. Vous les présentez toutes comme mauvaises presque comme également mauvaises. Cependant il en faut; et ne pas Se déterminer Sur celles qu'il faut, c'est laisser dans la Société une grande Source d'indécision de querelles et d'erreurs.

La multitude de gens qui veulent avoir des fonctions publiques, exercer une autorité, pousse par beaucoup de Sophismes aux impôsitions les plus compliquées, les plus dispendieuses, les plus vexatoires.

Vous êtes, et vous devez vous sentir, digne de fixer l'opinion.

Il me Semble que vous êtiez d'autant plus obligé de vous reconnaitre cette dignité, et d'en faire usage, que, ayant adopté Sur la production des richesses la Théorie de Smith et celle de Mr Say, qui Supposent que le travail et que tout travail est producteur de richesses, on pourrait en induire que vous croyez aussi tout Travail contribuable et impôsable pour les Fraix du Gouvernement que vous avez Si bien nommé national.

Je répugne cependant à me persuader que cette doctrine pour le payement des contributions puisse trouver place dans votre pensée.

Elle rentrerait dans l'inconvénient de l'income Tax d'Angleterre par laquelle Suivant des opinions arbitraires on frappe Sur ce que l'on croit le bénéfice particulier ou les gages de tous les travaux:

ou dans celui des excises et des duties par lesquelles on Se flatte de faire contribuer tout le monde, parce que l'on vexe en effet[10] tout le monde, que l'on interrompt tout le commerce, que l'on taxe, soit toutes les consommations, Soit quelques consommations, et que l'on dénature tous les prix des productions et des marchandises.

Une Taxe arbitraire Sur des gains ou des Salaires Simplement présumés, non prouvés, Serait tout-à-fait opposée à votre délicate et juste Sensation du droit des Hommes à la Liberté individuelle et à l'indépendance du travail qu'ils jugent à propos de faire.

Et vous Savez mieux que personne que rançonner le commerce, intervertir Son ordre naturel, ajouter artificiellement au prix nécessaire des ventes et des achats, (indépendamment des fraix énormes et des vexations inséparables de ce genre de perceptions), ce Serait nuire à la production des richesses dans une proportion bien plus forte que la Somme qu'on léverait ou qu'on Se procurerait[11] par ce moyen. Car on ne peut faire changer le prix de la portion de marchandises qui circule entre les divers degrés de magaziniers, de voituriers, d'Artisans et de Consommateurs, Sans déranger ceux des fraix de culture et des ventes à la premiere main: ce qui condamnerait à la Stérilité toutes les terres médiocres.

Il faut une régle de perception Simple, claire, facile à comprendre, qui laisse à tous les citoyens la faculté de vérifier la recette faite au nom de l'Etat, et de Savoir Si on leur[12] demande ou non plus que n'exige la Loi; au Gouvernement le moyen de S'assurer que Ses préposés n'abusent pas; et à toute la Nation la certitude de ne pas payer en fraix inutiles les verges avec lesquelles on la fouetterait,

Cette connaissance et cette clarté Sont un avantage indubitable de la concession Sociale d'une portion aliquote du Revenu ou du Capital des terres pour les dépenses[13] de la République.

Si l'on veut Savoir à quel point cette concession est d'ailleurs fondée en principe et en raison, il faut examiner plus profondement la nature et les fruits des divers Travaux. Et peut-être votre Génie Si propre à cet examen trouvera-t-il que ni Smith, ni Mr Say, n'ont considéré la chose Sous toutes Ses faces.

Il est certain qu'aucun travail ne peut être prolongé qu'autant que la vente, ou l'utilité de ce qui en résulte paye, au taux fixé par la concurrence, non Seulement le Salaire des Ouvriers qui l'ont exécuté, mais encore l'intérêt, de même au prix courant, du Capital qu'on y a employé.—Et il est également certain que le Salaire est un profit pour les ouvriers, et l'interêt de l'argent ou du Capital avancé, un profit pour le Capitaliste qui l'a fourni.

Mais il ne S'en Suit pas que ce travail, Si utile à ceux dont on y emploie les forces, l'esprit, ou l'argent produise toujours de nouvelles richesses pour la Société, pour l'humanité.

un gain n'est pas une création; un profit n'est pas un produit.

Vous avez très bien montré, dans votre beau Chapitre du Luxe, qu'il y a des Travaux fort avantageux pour ceux qui les font, et plus qu'inutiles, nuisibles en ce qu'ils inspirent des gouts Séducteurs pour des jouissances de pure vanité, qui n'ajoutent ni à la masse des Subsistances, ni à celle du chauffage, ni à celle des logemens ou des vêtemens commodes et comfortables.

Malthus reconnaissant, avec les Economistes français, que la mesure de la Subsistance est celle de la population, parce qu'il est impossible d'employer plus d'Ouvriers qu'on ne peut en nourrir, a trouvé, comme les Economistes aussi, qu'il ne fallait pas confondre et ranger Sur la même ligne[14] tous les travaux utiles; moins encore ceux qui ne[15] Sont qu'agréables.

Il en est parmi[16] les utiles qui méritent[17] le premier rang. Ce Sont ceux qui font naitre l'espece de Richesses nécessaires à la Subsistance des hommes, à l'entretien, Malthus dit à la maintenance du travail. Les Economistes ajoutent que ce Sont ceux dans lesquels les hommes échangent leur travail contre la faculté productrice dont dieu a doué la nature; et peuvent ainsi mettre dans le commerce, procurer à l'espece humaine, des choses qui auparavant n'existaient pas. Ce Sont ceux là qu'ils appellent Producteurs de Richesses; et Sous cet aspect ils embrassent outre les Subsistances, les combustibles, et les matieres premieres des bâtimens, des Vêtemens, des meubles, des outils.

La manipulation de ces Subsistances et l'emploi de ces matieres premieres; occupent une multitude d'hommes. Ceux-ci pour obtenir une part dans les Subsistances et les autres matieres[18] que la terre ne leur avait point donneés, qu'elle avait produites et vendues à la Sueur et aux capitaux des Entreprenneurs de culture, ou d'autres travaux productifs, ceux-ci dis-je emploient en Seconde ligne leur travail Sur ces matieres premieres, construisent les maisons, fabriquent les machines, les ustensiles, les meubles, filent, tissent la laine, le chanvre, le lin, la Soie, en font des étoffes et des vêtemens, travaillent même sur les Subsistances déja produites comme les meuniers, les boulangers et les cuisiniers.

Ils disent aux premiers possesseurs des productions, donnez moi à manger, et en consommant les subsistances qui existaient, que je tiendrai de vous, je ferai pour vous et pour moi même avec les matieres premieres qui existent aussi, une multitude de choses qui vous Seront d'une grande utilité.

d'autres disent tout simplement: donnez-moi à manger, et je vous donnerai du plaisir: ce ne sont pas ceux qui font le moins bien leurs affaires.

Mais, quoique le plaisir Soit le premier ingrédient du bonheur, nous Sommes déja convenus que l'augmentation du plaisir et même du bonheur donnés en échange de richesses à consommer, et qui ont êté consommées, n'est pas une production de Richesse.

Ceux qui nous donnent de même en échange des alimens et des autres récompenses de leur travail le plaisir de jouir des differens objets d'utilité ou de commodité qu'a fabriqué leur industrie—ont-ils par cette fabrication produit des Richesses?

"Oui" répond le vulgaire, "car ces effets mobiliers nés de leur travail, Sont incontestablement des richesses."

Ce Sont des richesses réunies et conservées, répliquerai-je devant le profond penseur Jefferson, non pas produites.

Les Fabricateurs de ces choses Si utiles, quelquefois Si précieuses, ont ajouté à la valeur des matieres Sur lesquelles ils ont travaillé celle de leurs gages; cest à dire de toutes les consommations que la concurrence leur a permis de faire, et de plus l'interêt des capitaux avancés pour leur travail: interêt dont le taux se fixe aussi par la concurrence. Leur Savante industrie en se déployant Sur la matiere premiere, et y incorporant, pour ainsi dire, toutes les consommations qui ont entretenu et Soldé leur travail, en ont fait des Objets de jouissance durable.

Les nations S'enrichissent ainsi; par ce que la sage économie qui a fait employer des consommations nécessaires à Solder un travail utile, vaut mieux que la déperdition de consommations Semblables au payement de jouissances frivoles et dont il ne résulterait qu'un plaisir passager.—L'économie est un moyen de S'enrichir et non pas de produire des richesses.

On fait très bien de Se procurer, par le bon emploi de la récolte qu'a produit l'année immédiatement précedente, des choses d'un long usage, dont la matiere et le prix des façons, provient des récoltes de plusieurs années antérieures.

Mais, encore une fois, additionner n'est pas multiplier: conserver, accumuler, n'est pas produire.

Conserver, additionner, transformer, acquerir des richesses, sont des choses à la portée de l'intelligence et du travail de l'homme.—En produire n'appartient qu'à dieu.—dieu Seul, en organisant la nature, l'a rendue productrice.—Il ne nous a laissé de travaux qu'on puisse appeller producteurs de richesses nouvelles que ceux par lesquels nous appliquons nos efforts notre raison, notre esprit, notre peine, à profiter de cette belle propriété de la nature, à recueillir ce qu'elle nous donne, ou nous vend.

Dans les plus riches ouvrages des Arts, il n'y a rien qui pût contribuer à ce que Malthus appelle la maintenance, ou l'entretien, d'aucun travail, Si les Travaux de la culture et de la pêche, ou dans les déserts de la chasse, êtaient Suspendus ou infructueux.

Tout au contraire, la Surabondance de quelques repas a fourni le premier Capital, au moyen duquel on a eu le loisir, dans l'état le plus Sauvage, d'employer l'intelligence et un travail d'industrie à fabriquer avec une matiere premiere quelques objets de jouissance durable, armes ou instrumens, que leur matiere et la subsistance du Travailleur avaient précedé, qui de ces deux richesses précédentes, jointes l'une à l'autre, ont fait une Seule et même richesse.

Ces armes et ces instrumens ont facilité un nouveau travail, une plus abondante récolte de chasse ou de pêche, qui a pu Salarier un travail plus grand encore.

Dès qu'une récolte quelconque a pu payer plus que Ses fraix, il y a eu un produit net; et ce produit net a formé un capital que Son Possesseur a pu employer, Selon Sa volonté, ou à produire de nouvelles richesses en Subsistances, ou à cumuler des richesses en objets de jouissance durable, ou dépenser et dissiper en Simples jouissances personnelles.

Tant que la culture n'a pas êté établie, on n'a pas eu besoin d'impôt.—Chacun gardait aisément Sa petite propriété mobiliaire avec ses propres forces et Ses propres armes.

Mais quand les récoltes ont couvert les champs, il a fallu une force publique pour les préserver des voleurs et des gaspilleurs du dedans, pour les protéger contre les brigands du dehors.

Or comme on ne peut pas alimenter les hommes dépositaires, directeurs ou agens de la force publique avec des effets mobiliers qui donnent des jouissances durables à ceux qui ont d'ailleurs de quoi vivre, mais ne Sont propres à nourrir personne, il a fallu que ce fussent les récoltes que l'on gardait qui fournîssent la Subsistance aux Administrateurs, à leurs employés, à leurs Soldats, et qui les payassent directement ou indirectement.

Il l'a fallu d'autant plus que l'on ne pouvait pas l'empêcher.

Car aussitôt que la culture a en produit plus de Subsistances que n'en exigeaient les besoins des Cultivateurs, Si leur propriété a été respectée (Sans quoi il n'y aurait plus eu de culture et la Société civilisée n'aurait pu S'établir,) les hommes qui n'avaient point de récoltes ont naturellement du offrir et ont offert leurs Services aux Entreprenneurs de culture, pour en obtenir un partage dans cette Surabondance de récoltes et de Subsistances que les cultivateurs ne pouvaient pas consommer.

Ces offres de Services ont été très Salutaires, en opérant une distribution plus étendue des récoltes, en encourageant la culture par le débit de Ses productions, en faisant naitre de nouveaux liens de bienveillance et de Secours réciproques, en procurant à la Société un grand nombre d'objets de jouissances durables, moins nécessaires que les Subsistances, mais qui adoucissent la vie et ajoutent beaucoup au bonheur.

Cependant comme il S'agissait d'échanger des Services contre la nourriture et la vie, l'agréable et l'utile contre l'indispensable, les offres de Services aussi multipliées que les besoins les plus urgens, ont par la nature de la chose fixé le prix de ces Services offerts aussi bas qu'aient pu l'ordonner et le permettre la concurrence entre les gens qui désirent des alimens d'une part, et celle entre les gens qui de l'autre part trouvent le Service utile ou agréable.

Ce bas prix, ou plus tot ce juste prix des Services, juste puisque c'est la concurrence puisque ce sont des conventions libres qui l'ont fixé, quand il ne va pas[19] jusqu'à la pauvreté, (il en est longtems préservé dans les pays où les gouts ne Sont pas fastueux et où une Sage[20] éducation a répandu de bons principes de morale) ce juste[21] prix des Services est très utile au genre humain; car c'est lui qui permet d'étendre la culture Sur des terres d'une fertilité médiocre, dont les récoltes assurent la Subsistance à une multitude de familles qui ne pourraient pas exister Si les Salaires êtaient plus chers.—ce que nous disons ici du Service des hommes est également applicable à l'interêt des capitaux: c'est un point Sur lequel l'opinion est déja depuis longtems plus éclairée, car il est bien reconnu que le bas prix de l'interêt de l'argent est d'un extrême avantage pour la Société

Mais puisque l'impérieuse concurrence tariffe toujours l'interêt des Capitaux et le salaire des Services aussi bas que l'exige[22] l'ensemble des circonstances Sociales où se trouve la nation, il S'en Suit qu'aucune autre Autorité que celle de la concurrence ne peut restreindre ni le prix des Salaires, ni celui de l'interêt des Capitaux.—Cela n'est pas plus possible que de fixer avec efficacité, par des ordres ou des loix, Soit trop haut, Soit trop bas, le prix des Services, ou des denrées, ou la valeur des monnaies. Il est nécessaire et inévitable que l'on parvienne à échapper en mille[23] manieres à la prétendue fixation quand elle n'est pas juste. Si elle êtait juste, elle Serait inutile, et encore nuisible comme gênante.

Même dans les Pays où il y a des Esclaves, et où tous les droits des hommes Sont violés à leur égard, à ce que l'on imagine dans l'interêt de leurs maitres, il a êté prouvé par Franklin, et avec plus de détail par les Philosophes français, que le travail de l'Esclave, comparé à ce que coutent Son acquisition et sa dépense, à la durée de Sa vie, et à son produit, est moins profitable à son Propriétaire et lui revient plus cher que ne Serait celui de l'homme libre réglé par la concurrence.

Il n'existe donc aucun moyen de faire porter des impôts Sur les travailleurs ou sur le loyer de l'argent, quelle que Soit l'aisance[24] que la concurrence leur laisse. car rien ne peut les empêcher de S'en récompenser, ainsi que des gênes et des vexations, ainsi que de l'interêt des interéts[25] cumulés à chaque cascade que font les excises, ou les duties, ou l'income tax, de S'en récompenser aux dépens de ceux qui directement ou indirectement payent tous les Salaires, et directement ou indirectement louent tous les Capitaux.

or, il n'y a pas d'autres Salarians, d'autres Payeurs définitifs dans la Societe, que ceux qui par l'alliance de leur travail et de leurs[26] Capitaux avec la bonté de Dieu et la fertilité de la nature font naitre des Productions propres à nourrir des Hommes, et comme dit malthus, à maintenir le travail.

Les habitans du monde n'ont pour vivre que la récolte du monde.

C'est en cela que consiste toute la Théorie de l'Impôt. C'est ce qui montre que, dans la pratique, il ne peut y avoir aucune Institution plus propre à donner au travail toute Sa liberté à l'influence des Capitaux toute Son utile énergie, à ne laisser aucune place aux injonctions arbitraires et aux vexations, à maintenir la bonne intelligence des gouvernés avec les gouvernans et la tranquillité publique, à prévenir les dissentions civiles, à établir et à conserver entre toutes les classes de citoyens la bonne foi et une amiable moralité, qu'une raisonnable constitution de finances à partage de revenus, ou comme vous le dites, de Capitaux terriens. Et vous avez montré que ce noble Sacrifice Sera l'exemption d'impôt pour toute la Postérité.[27]

Il y faudra venir quand vos manufactures Seront établies et vos douanes devenues improductives; et je regrette beaucoup que, dans un livre aussi profond que le vôtre et qui aura une Si prodigieuse autorité, vous ayez comme évité de jetter là dessus aucune idée préliminaire.

Je m'explique cette réserve en me rappellant que vous m'avez dit que dans vos Etats du nord-Est, qui Sont les plus riches, les plus réellement puissans, les plus éclairés même sur toute autre matiere, la contribution territoriale est encore odieuse. Je n'en suis que plus affligé pour votre grande et belle République. C'est un reste de préjugés anglais: et je sais que les préjugés ne doivent être attaqués que l'un après l'autre, doivent l'être d'abord par les Simples Philosophes avant que ceux qui Sont en même tems connus pour hommes d'Etat hazardent de se compromettre en les combattant de front.

Je vois avec plaisir que vous avez plus de tems devant vous que je ne l'avais cru, que votre Systême actuel de Finance[28] peut durer encore un certain nombre d'années, que la conquête du Canada pourra le prolonger, et vous laisser le loisir nécessaire pour éclairer l'opinion de vos concitoyens.

J'ai vu par les mémoires de montgomery Pike que vous Serez forcés à cette conquête pour n'être pas cernés par les entreprises, les établissemens et les petits forts de la Compagnie anglaise du Nord-Ouest, et conserver la liberté de vous étendre au moins jusqu'aux Rocky-Hills qui seront la limite naturelle entre les Etats unis et les colonies que l'Angleterre commence au nord de la Californie.—mais tout retardement possible d'hostilités est toujours à désirer. Il faut y regarder beaucoup quand il s'agit de voter la mort d'un Si grand nombre d'hommes innocens, étrangers ou compatriotes. Il faut Si vous le pouvez[29] avoir mis vos ports en bon état de défense.—Fondez, forez, tournez de gros canons de fer très doux[30]—Vous ne manquez ni de métal, ni de charbon de terre ou de bois pour la fonte, ni de chutes d'eau pour mettre en mouvement ces énormes tours. Adoucissez le Fer avec des Fourneaux de réverbere beaucoup plus haut que ceux qu'on a employés jusqu'à ce jour, et qui le tiennent plus longtems en fusion.[31] Notre Société d'encouragement vient d'ôter à nos fers médiocres[32] leur aigreur, et le danger de casser ni à chaud, ni à froid, par cette Seule méthode.

Les projets de Mr de Pusy n'ayant pu encore être exécuté à

New-york, il y faut Suppléer par des Batteries flottantes construites et défendues de maniere qu'on ne puisse les incendier: Sans quoi cette belle ville Serait écrasée par les bombes et le canon.—Je ne connais pas bien vos autres Ports. Mais je Suis trop certain que celui là[33] ne pourrait autrement éviter un extrême péril, ou plustôt sa ruine totale.

que dieu vous bénisse et vous défende! Il a donné à votre nation le courage et un grand Sens, auxquels elle doit ce que vous avez le premier nommé un Gouvernement national; et votre livre est une belle consolidation de ce Gouvernement qui n'existe qu'imparfaitement en Angleterre et dans Sa pureté que chez vous.

Conservez-le et propagez-le. Les livres comme le vôtre, et ils seront toujours très rares, y Servent et y serviront bien plus que les Sénats même, et Surtout que les Armées.

Je vous remercie de me l'avoir fait lire. Je vous remercie du plus profond de mon ame de l'avoir composé.

J'aurai beaucoup de peine à le rendre à Mr Warden. Je ne m'en séparerai que la larme à l'oeil—Je vous prie de permettre qu'avant de me déterminer à ce Sacrifice je prête l'ouvrage à Mr Barlow et au Général La Fayette.

Ménagez votre Santé. Vivez et travaillez au moins vingt ans encore.—Je n'en espere pour moi même que dix: mais par la nature de ma santé et de ma maladie, la fortifiante et animante goutte, j'ai quelque espoir aussi de travailler jusqu'à mon dernier jour.

agréez ma reconnaissance, ma vénération, mon extrème respect.

DuPont (de Nemours)

Résumé Sur la nature des dépenses, des travaux et des Richesses.

Premier Capital en Subsistances.

Travail qui en les consomant recueille ou produit d'autres Subsistances.

Sil n'en recueille ou n'en produit pas plus qu'il n'en a consommé, il y a consommation et production perpétuelle de Subsistances et de richesses Sans aucune augmentation. L'homme vit du produit de Son travail.

Surabondance de Subsistance.—Produit net. Accroissement de capital et de richesses: tant en Subsistance qu'en matieres premieres. commencement de fabrication d'armes et d'outils.

Emploi de l'augmentation du Capital, des Subsistances, des[34] matieres premieres, des armes des outils[35] et du travail, à produire et recueillir d'autres Subsistances et d'autres matieres premieres.

Dépenses et travail qui produisent des richesses.

nouvelle augmentation de Subsistances, de produit net et de population. Fabrication plus animée d'objets de jouissance durable.

augmentation des capitaux, quand ceux qui les emploient ou les prêtent ne dépensent pas tout le fruit de leur usage ou de leur loyer.

dépenses qui distribuent les richesses en Salariant des hommes et du travail.

Emploi des Salariés

1° à produire d'autres richesses, Subsistances ou matieres premieres. Travaux producteurs de richesses.

2° à conserver des richesses en formant avec elles une multitude d'objets de jouissances durables, lesquels en S'accumulant accroissent les capitaux, quoiqu'ils ne Soient pas des productions,[36] mais de Simples additions et conservations de richesses, qui procurent du bonheur à tous les Hommes Sans pouvoir en faire vivre un seul de plus. Travaux à la fois distributeurs et conservateurs ou accumulateurs de richesses[37]

3° à Salarier des Travailleurs qui ne rendent que des Services agréables Sans production, ni conservation de richesses, et tout au contraire en dissipation des capitaux qu'on y emploie et dont les ouvriers ne peuvent économiser que de faibles parcelles. Travaux qui ne sont que distributeurs de richesses

Les Travaux distributeurs de richesses dans lesquels les moins utiles Sont ordinairement ceux qui donnent le plus de profit aux Serviteurs ou salaries qu'ils font participer à la distribution, ne donnent à aucun Salarié que ce qui est payé par un autre homme.

Ils n'operent que des transformations de richesses, quand ils Sont utiles.

Ils ne peuvent augmenter la population.

Les Travailleurs n'y Sont que des gagistes. Ils ne peuvent être imposés véritablement par aucune Autorité; car il leur faut leurs gages, Et Si on les vexe, il leur faut de plus l'indemnité de la vexation.—Franklin dit qu'ils mettent tout cela dans leurs Factures.

Les Travaux producteurs de richesses S'allient avec dieu et la nature, recueillent les Subsistances et les matieres premieres, payent Seuls tous les autres Travaux, peuplent seuls l'univers.

Quand une nation Se livre principalement à des Travaux d'industrie pour l'usage des autres nations, elle peut avoir une prosperité éphemere et même éblouissante. mais Sa population est toujours mêlée et affligée de pauvres, et la subsistance de Ses citoyens est toujours en danger.

Elles peuvent acquerir de grands capitaux Sans que ces capitaux puissent y assurer constamment la maintinance du Travail.—Ces nations ne Sont que comme des villes, auxquelles il[38] faut des campagnes nourricieres; et quand ces campagnes qui les nourrissent[39] Sont dans un autre pays, à moins que la nation manufacturiere[40] ne Soit très petite, qu'elle n'ait par mer les communications les plus faciles, et que la liberté du Commerce ne Soit généralement respectée (ce dont nous Sommes bien[41] loin) Son independance politique, et même Son existence physique n'ont aucune bâse[42] assurée.

d'ailleurs ce n'est pas entendre les principes de la Richesses des nations que de s'arrêter[43] à observer qu'un Peuple particulier peut s'enrichir en se mettant par Son travail d'industrie aux gages des autres Peuples. ce métier Servile et hazardeux ne prouve rien pour la production des Richesses.—Il S'agit de la Terre entiere que la Science de l'Economie politique[44] doit peupler et enrichir, dont elle doit rendre les habitans aussi Solidement, aussi durablement, autant progressivement heureux que leur nature le comporte.[45]

Pardon, Si je me répète. dans ces importantes matieres, on ne peut trop S'efforcer d'être clair et démonstratif.[46]

Jefferson n'est pas fait pour S'arrêter Sur les traces de Smith et de Mr Say au point où ils ont Stationné. Quoique tous deux, et Surtout le premier, Soient des hommes d'un très éminent mérite, il a la tête encore plus profonde et les reins plus forts qu'eux.

EDITORS' TRANSLATION

My very respectable friend, 25 January 1812.

A book of the highest importance has been loaned to me by Mr. Warden, and I very much wish that it had been given to me by you.

It is the commentaries on Montesquieu.

Another American told me that it was believed in the United States to have been written by one of my children and only translated into English by you.

I wish to God that one of my sons were capable of writing it! But, although they are both gifted with wit, reason, enough education, and high ethical standards, they are too occupied with their daily tasks to write such a book.

It is the work of a great statesman, and it is you who wrote it.

You added a little dedication to it as if it were offered by a Frenchman to the United States. You believed that that which appeared, for a time, to come from another nation would make a bigger impression; and indeed, the most enlightened men rarely become prophets in their own country and are seldom listened to as well as they deserve.

But no Frenchman, either in America or France, could have pursued so many first-rate discussions with such rigorous logic and astonishing depth.

Thus far I have only read carefully the first, second, third, fourth, fifth, sixth, seventh, eighth, and thirteenth chapters of this book. I have only skimmed the others. But I will read and re-read them all more than once with the most serious attention.

Forgive me for having begun with those that are closest to my usual research and the topics we have already discussed.

Forgive me, with even more indulgence, if I now take the liberty of making a few observations regarding Chapter Thirteen, which contains so many interesting considerations connected with our most recent correspondence.—I submit them to you, my brother, my noble companion, my master in my own science.

You have the genius to see that to give the republic a fifth, or sixth, or any other portion of landed income is to give it precisely the same percentage of its capital. You were the first one to expound this truth: it belongs to you in the science of political economy.

But it is not true that this concession is a burden on landowners. You state very clearly that it is not a burden on their heirs, who inherit, buy, and sell only the portion they own of the land they manage and develop.

It does not even burden the landowners who first make this concession, if it is not extorted from them by an arbitrary authority that takes more than the public requires to be reasonably and completely satisfied.—The public's need for personal safety and protection of property is so great that even the most absurd and oppressive taxes are preferable to the reciprocal and universal plunder that would take place if the authority of the government and the public sector did not oppose it.

Therefore, taxes are not always a bad thing, as is too strongly stated in Chapter XIII. They are generally bad only when they exceed the true needs of the public;

and comparatively bad only when their form makes them too costly, vexing, litigious, and burdened with useless fees, which causes them to interfere with personal freedom and interrupt one's labor.

It follows from this that the concession by landowners of a part of their landed income to the political state leaves to every type of work the greatest liberty that can be enjoyed and the strongest competition that can animate it. Consequently, land is cultivated in the best and least expensive manner possible, and it provides landowners with the greatest possible income. Far from wronging or harming them in any way, it is, on the contrary, a very good thing for them and the best thing they could desire.

Some thought it would be best to give the state land to cultivate; in this way, those who owned the rest of the country would be guaranteed immunity from taxation.—This is what I mentioned to you regarding the financial constitution of the Egyptians.

But because a government, even the most perfect one that can be imagined, could only be a very mediocre farmer, since the general administration of the state and the details of agriculture are too dissimilar, and because the government would require too many agents, who would have no interest in the matter and would obtain their salaries with as little effort as possible, it would be necessary to give the government much more land, or, as you judiciously observed, a much larger portion of the nation's capital, in order to provide it with the same income. It would also be necessary to hand over to the government an excessive amount of capital to develop these lands, even badly.

Furthermore, the owners of nonpublic lands would still have to fear that the urgency of public finance and the necessity of raising money rapidly would induce the government to sell the produce of the land that had been granted to it at low prices and out of season, which would lower the value of the crops grown by common citizens and upset all the enterprises and speculations of agriculture and commerce.

Having developed the land under its control badly and failed to raise the expected level of income, the government might still resort to taxes, excises, duties, and various other ways of raising money that torment people and impede or stop them from working. This happened all over Europe; monarchs started out owning land, and then they introduced taxes that were disorganized, ruinous, and destructive of all liberty.

Governments indisputably need a portion of their nation's income, since the existence of a government is one of the first needs of society.

It is no less clear that this portion must not be arbitrary, and that it must be raised with the greatest equity. This goal is achieved when the share of landed income, or, as you so rightly say, of capital that is thus allocated is precisely the same as that which is assigned to the maintenance of public affairs.

Because landowners who are responsible for agriculture already have the capital necessary to develop land and maintain horses, ploughs, barns, and workers, and as it does not cost them any more, while cultivating their very large share of the harvest, to farm in addition the small portion belonging to the state (which remains undivided for the use of all), the tax is collected in the best possible way.

I am distressed to see that you came to no conclusions in your beautiful and scholarly chapter on taxes. You present them as all being bad, and almost all of them equally bad. They are necessary, however, and to fail to determine which ones are proper is to leave society in a state of indecision and cause disputes and errors.

The multitude of people who want to hold public office and exercise authority advocate, through the use of a lot of fallacious arguments, the most complicated, costly, and vexatious taxes.

You are, you know, eminent enough to guide public opinion.

I think that you should have acknowledged your status and used it because, regarding the production of wealth, you adopted the theories of Mr. Smith and Mr. Say, which imply that every kind of labor produces wealth. From this one might infer that you believe all labor to be liable for the costs of government, which you so aptly called national.

I am reluctant, however, to believe that you really hold this doctrine regarding the payment of taxes.

It would return us to the inconveniences of the English income tax, which arbitrarily strikes at the personal profits or salaries of labor:

or those of excises and duties which, because they require contributions from everyone, vex everybody, interrupt all commerce, tax either some or all consumer goods, and distort the prices of all products and merchandise.

An arbitrary tax on profits or presumed, but unproven, salaries would be completely opposed to your delicate and just sense of the rights of men, individual liberty, and the freedom to work as people see fit.

And you know better than anyone that to ransom commerce, invert its natural order, artificially inflate the necessary price for buying and selling goods (independent of the enormous cost and annoyances inseparable from this kind of taxation), would harm the production of wealth in a much larger proportion than the amount being raised or procured in this manner. Because one cannot change the price of the portion of merchandise that circulates between various types of shopkeepers, carriers, craftsmen, and consumers without disturbing the cost of agricultural products and their price when first sold, all mediocre lands would be condemned to sterility.

What is necessary is a rule of collection that is simple, clear, and easy to understand, that leaves every citizen with the ability to verify the profits made in the name of the state and to know whether or not they are being asked to give more than is required by law: a rule that enables the government to ensure that its employees are not abusing their powers and that guarantees the nation that it is not paying useless fees for the rods used to beat it.

This knowledge and clarity are doubtless an advantage of the social concession of a portion of landed income or capital to pay the expenses of the republic.

If one wants to know to what extent this concession is actually founded on principle and reason, one must examine in greater depth the nature and fruits of various kinds of labor. And perhaps your genius, which is so suitable to this examination, will discover that neither Mr. Smith nor Mr. Say have considered this question from every angle.

Work cannot go on unless the sale or usefulness that results from it pays for, at a rate set by competition, not only the salaries of workers but also the interest on the capital invested.—It is also certain that a salary is a profit for the workers, and the interest on the money or capital invested is a profit for the capitalist who invested it.

But it does not follow that this labor, so useful to those who invest their strength, mind, or money in it, always produces new wealth for society or humanity.

A gain is not a creation; a profit is not a product.

You have shown very well, in your learned chapter on luxury, that some work that is very advantageous to those who do it is not just useless, but harmful—because it inspires seductive tastes for the enjoyment of pure vanity and adds nothing to the mass of subsistence, the means of heating or housing people, or the provision of practical and comfortable clothing.

Malthus admitted, as do the French *économistes*, that the measure of subsistence is population, because it is impossible to use more workers than can be fed, and he found, as do also the *économistes*, that one must not confound and put all useful labor in the same basket; even less so labor that is merely pleasant.

Some useful kinds of work deserve to be placed in the first rank. They are the ones that give rise to the kind of wealth necessary for the subsistence of men, to their upkeep, Malthus says the maintenance of work. The *économistes* add that these are the kinds of work that men exchange for the productive faculty that God gave to nature, and that can therefore be put into commerce, and procure for mankind things that did not previously exist. This is the labor that they call productive of wealth; and under this heading they include, besides subsistence, fuels and raw materials, buildings, clothes, furniture, and tools.

The manipulation of subsistence and use of raw materials occupy a multitude of men. In order to obtain a portion of the supplies and other materials that the land has not given them, which it had produced and sold through the sweat and capital of agricultural entrepreneurs or through other productive work, these men, I say, utilize raw materials to build houses, make machines, utensils, and furniture, and spin and weave wool, hemp, linen, and silk, with which they make fabrics and clothes. Some even use agricultural products already in existence, as is the case with millers, bakers, and cooks.

They tell the first owners of these products: give me something to eat, and by consuming the subsistence that existed, that I will get from you, I will do for you and for myself, with the raw materials that also exist, a multitude of things that will be very useful to you.

Others simply say: give me something to eat, and I will give you pleasure: these are not the ones who do worst in business.

However, although pleasure is the first ingredient of happiness, we have already agreed that an increase in pleasure and even in happiness given in exchange for goods that will be, or already have been, consumed, does not produce wealth.

Those who, in the same manner, give us the pleasure of enjoying various useful or convenient objects manufactured by their labor in exchange for food or other products, have they produced wealth?

"Yes," answers the ordinary man, "because these objects created by their labor are unquestionably riches."

They are gathered and preserved riches, is my response to the profound thinker Mr. Jefferson, but they have not been produced.

The manufacturers of these very useful, sometimes very precious things, have added to the value of the materials with which they worked that of their salaries, that is to say, the value of all the consumption that competition allowed them to make, and furthermore the interest on the capital advanced for their labor, which is also determined by competition. Their learned industry, by applying itself to raw materials, and by incorporating, in a manner of speaking, all the consumptions that sustained and rewarded their labor, have produced objects that will be enjoyed for a long time.

Nations become rich in this manner; because the wise economy that used necessary consumptions to pay for useful labor is better than one that loses such consumptions through paying for frivolous enjoyments whose pleasures are only fleeting.—Economy is a means to get rich but not to produce riches.

One is wise to obtain, through the good use of the crop produced the preceding year, durable goods, the materials and labor costs of which are provided by crops from several preceding years.

But, again, to add is not to multiply. To conserve and accumulate is not to produce.

To conserve, add, transform, and acquire wealth are things that are within the reach of the intelligence and labor of man.—To produce them belongs only to God.—Only God, by organizing nature, made it productive.—God defined work that is productive of new wealth as that to which we apply our efforts, reason, and mind in order to profit from nature's bounty and collect what it gives or sells us.

Even the richest works of art contain nothing that can contribute to what

Malthus calls the maintenance, or upkeep, of labor, if agriculture, fishing, or hunting were suspended or unfruitful.

On the contrary, the surplus from a few meals provided the first capital, with which mankind was able, even in its most savage state, to use intelligence and labor to manufacture with raw materials some objects of lasting enjoyment, weapons or implements; these workers, by bringing together the two preceding forms of wealth, transformed them into one and the same wealth.

Weapons and implements made labor easier, increased the productivity of hunting and fishing, and allowed the financing of even more work.

As soon as any crop was able to pay more than its cost, a net product resulted, and this net product formed a capital that its owner was able to use as he wished to produce new wealth, to accumulate wealth through objects of lasting enjoyment, or to spend and dissipate in simple personal pleasure.

Until agriculture was established, one did not need taxes.—Each person easily kept his little parcel of land with his own strength and weapons.

But once crops covered the fields, public officials were needed to protect them from thieves and squanderers from within and brigands from without.

Because investors, directors, or public agents cannot be fed by objects that provide lasting enjoyment to those who have another source of livelihood but who do not have the means to feed anybody else, surplus crops had to provide sustenance for administrators, their employees, and soldiers, and to pay them directly or indirectly.

It was all the more necessary in that it could not be prevented.

As soon as agriculture produced more than was needed by the farmers and their property was respected (without which there would have been no more agriculture, and civilized society could not have been established), men who did not have crops had to and did offer their services to agricultural entrepreneurs in order to get a share of the crops and foodstuffs that they could not themselves consume.

These offers of services were very beneficial in that they effected a broader distribution of crops, encouraged agriculture through the sale of its productions, gave rise to new links of kindness and reciprocity, and provided society with many objects of lasting enjoyment, which were less necessary than subsistence, but rendered life sweeter and happier.

However, these services were exchanged for food and life; that which is pleasant and useful was traded for something indispensable; offers of service thus governed by the most urgent needs naturally set their price as low as competition could make or allow it, between, on the one hand, people who desire food, and, on the other, those who find such services useful or pleasant.

The low, or rather fair, price offered for these services—fair because it is controlled by competition and freely made contracts—when it does not lead to poverty (and it does not for a long time in countries where tastes are not luxurious and a wise education has spread good moral principles) is very useful to mankind. This fair price allows agriculture to spread to lands of mediocre fertility, where crops insure the means of subsistence to a multitude of families that could not survive if salaries were higher.—What we are saying here about services, about the labor of men, is equally applicable to the interest on capital: on this point opinion has been enlightened for a long time, because it is well known that a low price, or rate, of interest is very advantageous to society.

But because imperious competition always drives the interest on capital and the salary for services as low as is required by the totality of the social circumstances in which the nation finds itself, it follows that no authority other than competition can restrain the price or rate of salaries, nor the price or rate of interest on capital.—It is equally impossible to fix with efficiency, by orders or laws, either higher or lower, the price of goods and services or the value of money when the proposed fixation is not fair. It will necessarily and inevitably be thwarted in a thousand different ways. If it were fair, it would be useless, and also harmful, because bothersome.

Even in countries with slaves, where the rights of men are violated in what is imagined to be the interest of their masters, Franklin has proven, as the French *philosophes* have in greater detail, that the work done by a slave, compared to the cost of his acquisition and upkeep during his lifetime, is less profitable and eventually costs his owner more than that of a free man, regulated by competition.

No way can therefore be found to tax workers or the rent of money in a free-market economy. Nothing can prevent them from compensating themselves for all such constraints and vexations, as the interest compounds at each succession of excise taxes, duties, or income tax, or from rewarding themselves at the expense of those who directly or indirectly pay all salaries and rent out all capital.

The only employers or ultimate payers in society are those who combine their work and capital with the grace of God and the fertility of nature to create products capable of feeding men and, as Malthus says, of maintaining labor.

The inhabitants of the world can live only on the world's harvest.

This is what the whole theory of taxation means. It shows that, in practice, no institution is more capable of giving labor complete freedom, of granting capital all of its useful energy, of leaving no room for arbitrary injunctions and annoyances, of maintaining a good understanding between the governed and their governors, of preserving public tranquility, of preventing civil disorders, and of establishing and conserving good faith and friendly morality between all classes of citizens than a reasonable structure of finances based on the sharing of revenue, or, as you call it, landed capital. And you have shown that this noble sacrifice will mean tax exemption for all posterity.

You will have to come to it when all your manufactures are established and your customs duties have become unproductive; and I deeply regret that in a book as profound as yours, and which will have such a prodigious authority, you somewhat avoided throwing any kind of preliminary light on this subject.

I understand this reserve when I remember your telling me that in your northeastern states, which are the richest, most powerful, and even most enlightened ones on all other matters, land taxes are still considered odious. I grieve for your great and beautiful republic. This attitude is a remnant of English prejudice: and I know that prejudices must only be attacked one at a time, and, first, by simple philosophers, before men who are also known as statesmen can venture to compromise themselves by tackling them head-on.

I see with pleasure that you have more time at your disposal than I had thought; that your current financial system can last for some years; and that the conquest of Canada will further prolong it and give you the leisure necessary to enlighten the minds of your fellow citizens.

I learned from the memoirs of Montgomery Pike that you will be forced to make this conquest in order to avoid being surrounded by the businesses, establishments, and little forts of the English North West Company and in order to remain free to extend your territories all the way to the Rocky Mountains, which are the natural border between the United States and the colonies that England is establishing in northern California.—But any possible delay to the outbreak of hostilities is always desirable. It is necessary to think twice before causing the death of so many innocent men, whether foreigners or fellow citizens. If you can, you must put your ports in a good state of defense.—Smelt, drill, and finish big cannon from very soft iron.—You lack neither metal, coal, nor charcoal for smelting, nor do you lack waterfalls to drive enormous derricks. Soften the iron with reflector furnaces that are much taller than the ones hitherto in use and that keep the iron molten longer. Our society for encouraging manufactures has just learned how to remove the brittleness from our mediocre iron and, through this method, to keep it from breaking, whether hot or cold.

The plan of Mr. de Pusy has not yet been put into effect in New York, making it necessary to compensate with floating batteries, built and defended in such a manner that they cannot be set on fire. Otherwise, this beautiful city could be destroyed by bombs and cannons.—I do not know your other ports well, but I am quite certain that there is no other defense from this extreme danger or, rather, total ruin.

May God bless and protect you! He gave your nation courage and a great deal of common sense, qualities that allow it to have what you were the first to proclaim: a national government; and your book is a beautiful exposition of a type of government that exists only imperfectly in England and in purity exclusively in your country.

Preserve and propagate it. Books such as yours, and they will always be rare, are of use to it and will serve it much better than senates and considerably better than armies.

I thank you for letting me read it. I thank you from the bottom of my soul for having written it.

I will find it hard to return it to Mr. Warden. I will part with it with tears in my eyes.—I request that before I must make this sacrifice, I may loan the book to Mr. Barlow and General Lafayette.

Take care of your health. Live and work for at least twenty more years.—I expect to live only ten more years myself: but because of the nature of my health and of my sickness, the fortifying and animating gout, I also have some hope of working until the end of my days.

Please accept my gratitude, veneration, and utmost respect.

DuPont (de Nemours)

Summary of the nature of expenses, labor, and wealth.

First capital in subsistence.

Labor that by consuming collects or produces other supplies.

If labor neither collects nor produces more than it has consumed, there is a perpetual consumption and production of subsistence and of wealth without any increase. Man lives off the product of his labor.

Overabundance of subsistence.—Net product. Increase of capital and wealth: in subsistence as well as in raw materials. Beginning of the manufacture of weapons and tools.

Use of the increase of capital, supplies, raw materials, weapons, tools, and labor, in order to produce and collect other supplies and raw materials.

Expenses and labor that produce wealth.

New increases in subsistence, net product, and population. Increase in the manufacture of objects of lasting enjoyment.

Increase of capital, when those who use or loan it do not spend the whole fruit of its use or rent.

Expenses that distribute wealth by paying a salary to men and labor.

Use of wage-earners.

1. to produce other wealth, supplies, or raw materials. Labor productive of wealth.

2. to conserve wealth, by manufacturing a multitude of objects of lasting enjoyment, which, by multiplying, increase capital, even though they are not products, but simple additions to and conservators of wealth, which brings happiness to all men, without allowing even one more man to make a living. Labor: at the same time distributors and conservators, or accumulators of wealth.

3. to pay workers who provide only pleasant services, who do not produce anything, nor conserve wealth, but who, on the contrary, squander the capital used for these services and are only able to save a very small part of this capital. Labor that only distributes wealth.

Labor that distributes wealth, of which the least useful kind is usually that which provides the largest profits to servants or wage-earners included in the distribution, gives wage-earners only what is paid to other men.

They only effect transformations of wealth when they are useful.

They cannot increase population.

Workers are only wage-earners. They cannot really be taxed by any authority, because they need their wages to live. If vexed, they will also require a vexation indemnity.—Franklin says that they put all this in their bill.

Labor producing wealth allies itself with God and nature, collects subsistence and raw materials, pays on its own all other labor, and is the only type that populates the universe.

When a nation engages primarily in industrial production for the benefit of other nations, it can enjoy a short-lived and even dazzling prosperity. However, part of its population is always afflicted with poverty, and the subsistence of its citizenry is always in jeopardy.

These nations can acquire a large amount of capital, but it cannot guarantee the maintenance of work.—They are like cities that need the countryside to feed them; when the countryside that supplies them is located in another country, unless the manufacturing nation is very small, has very easy access to seaborne transportation, and freedom of commerce is generally respected (and we are far from this state of things), its political independence and even physical existence are not at all assured.

In any case, one does not understand the principles of The Wealth of Nations if one focuses on the possibility that a particular nation can become rich by being paid by other nations. Working for other nations is a servile and hazardous occupation that proves nothing with regard to the production of wealth.—The science of economics must populate and enrich the entire globe; it must make the inhabitants of the whole planet as solidly, lastingly, and progressively happy as their nature allows.

Forgive me if I repeat myself. In these important matters, one cannot try too hard to be clear and conclusive.

Jefferson is not one to stop where Mr. Smith and Mr. Say halted. Although both of them, and especially the former, are men of eminent worth, Jefferson has an even more profound mind than they do, and his back is stronger than theirs.

RC (DLC); at head of text: "a Thomas Jefferson ancien Président des Etats-Unis"; endorsed by TJ as received 27 May 1812 and so recorded in SJL. FC (DeGH: Pierre Samuel Du Pont de Nemours Papers, Winterthur Manuscripts); in a clerk's hand, with a few revisions by Du Pont. Translation by Dr. Genevieve Moene. Enclosed in John Graham to TJ, 23 May 1812, or James Madison to TJ, 25 May 1812.

Du Pont mistakenly concluded that TJ was the author of Destutt de Tracy's COMMENTAIRES SUR MONTESQUIEU, anonymously published as *Commentary and Review of Montesquieu's Spirit of Laws*, a translation TJ had helped revise and for which he had written the preface (editorial note to TJ to William Duane, 12 Aug. 1810). Du Pont's letter ruminated further on issues about which he had already written TJ at length (Du Pont to TJ, [ca. 28 July 1810]). The explorer Zebulon MONTGOMERY PIKE published *An Account of Expeditions to the Sources of the Mississippi, and through the Western Parts of Louisiana . . . And a Tour through the Interior Parts of New Spain* (Philadelphia, 1810; Sowerby, no. 4169; Poor, *Jefferson's Library*, 7 [no. 371]). French engineer Jean Xavier Bureaux DE PUSY, whose wife was a stepdaughter of Du Pont, drafted plans for the fortification of the approaches to New York harbor in 1800 during a visit to the United States (*PTJ*, 31:265, 32:56–7, 246–7).

[1] Preceding three words interlined.

[2] Remainder of paragraph reworked from "parce que ce qui paraît venir d'une autre nation frappe davantage, et qu'il est rare que les plus éclairés des Hommes Soient dans leur Pays des Prophètes aussi respectés qu'ils méritent de l'être" ("because that which appears to have come from another nation makes more of an impression, and because in their own countries the most enlightened men are rarely treated with the respect to which they are entitled as prophets").

[3] Preceding eleven words interlined in RC, and preceding ten omitted in FC.

[4] Preceding eight words interlined in place of "Sont plus relatifs à mon propre travail" ("relate more to my own work").

[5] Preceding seven words interlined.

[6] Preceding five words interlined.

[7] Sentence interlined.

[8] Preceding five words interlined in place of "prix" ("price").

[9] Preceding ten words interlined.

[10] Preceding two words interlined.

[11] FC substitutes "proposerait" ("would propose") for this word.

[12] Preceding three words interlined in place of "avec certitude Si on lui" ("with certainty if one to it").

[13] Word interlined in place of "maintiens" ("maintenance").

[14] Remainder of sentence interlined in place of "même entre les travaux utiles" ("even among the useful industries").

[15] Manuscript: "ne ne."

[16] Manuscript: "parmi parmi."

[17] Preceding five words interlined.

[18] Preceding four words interlined.

[19] Sentence to this point interlined in place of "Ce bas prix de services, quand il ne va pas" ("The low price of services, when it does not").

[20] Word interlined in place of "bonne" ("good").

[21] Word interlined in place of "bas" ("low").

[22] Preceding five words interlined.

[23] Preceding thirteen words interlined.

[24] The text from this point through "l'alliance de leur travail" in next paragraph was written on a separate piece of paper and pasted over the text that it replaces.

[25] FC here adds "des capitaux toujours chers et" ("of capital always expensive and").

[26] Du Pont here canceled "propres" ("own").

[27] Sentence interlined.

[28] Preceding two words interlined.

[29] The text from this point through the end of the next paragraph was written on a separate piece of paper and pasted over the text that it replaces.

[30] In FC this sentence continues "et adoucissez le fer dans de très-hauts fourneaux de réverbère" ("and soften the iron in the best reverberating blast furnaces").

[31] Preceding two sentences not in FC.

[32] FC here reads "indigènes" ("indigenous").

[33] In FC remainder of sentence reads "courrait le plus grand danger" ("runs the greatest danger").

[34] Manuscript: "des des."

[35] Preceding four words interlined.

[36] FC substitutes "producteurs" ("producers") for this word.

[37] Sentence interlined.

[38] The text from this point to the end of the document was written on a separate piece of paper and pasted over the text that it replaces.

[39] Preceding three words not in FC.

[40] Preceding two words interlined by Du Pont in FC in place of "nation."

[41] FC substitutes "très" ("very") for this word.

[42] In FC remainder of sentence reads "sur laquelle on puisse compter" ("on which one can count").

[43] FC: "se borner" ("restrain oneself").

[44] FC here adds "peut et doit" ("can and must").

[45] Preceding six words interlined by Du Pont in FC.

[46] Preceding two words not in FC.

To William Eustis

DEAR SIR Monticello Jan. 25. 12.

I reject a multitude of applications for recommendations to office, but now and then a case occurs which cannot be declined. the inclosed letter is from a friend of my youthful days, & one of our most worthy citizens. of the son I know little, but if like his father he should be a good man. the father seems to speak of him with the candor for which he is remarkeable. mr Duval having staid with me one evening has given me an opportunity of observing that he is sensible and gentlemanly. the father speaks of a captaincy. but the son is of a very juvenile appearance & slender form to head a company. however he will present himself & you will judge. accept the assurance of my great esteem & respect

TH: JEFFERSON

PoC (DLC); at foot of text: "The Secretary at War"; endorsed by TJ. Enclosure: William DuVal to TJ, 17 Jan. 1812, recorded in SJL as received from Buckingham on 24 Jan. 1812, but not found.

John Pope DUVAL, of Virginia, was commissioned a first lieutenant in the 20th Infantry Regiment, United States Army, on 9 Apr. 1812, promoted to captain on 31 Jan. 1814, and honorably discharged on 15 June 1815 (Heitman, *U.S. Army*, 1:391; *JEP*, 2:247, 248, 489, 503 [8, 9 Apr. 1812, 17 Feb., 4 Mar. 1814]).

To Benjamin H. Latrobe

DEAR SIR Monticello Jan. 25. 12.

I was on a visit of six weeks to a distant place of mine when the elegant work of mess[rs] Franzoni & Andrei arrived, & an attack of rheumatism subsequent to my return has prevented till now my acknolegements for it, and what acknolegements can I make adequate to it's merit? the one formerly contemplated is unworthy of a thought, and nothing in that line to which my resources are competent, would be it's equivalent. can there be a hope of any occasion ever occurring in which I can be useful to them? and make them thus sensible of the value I set on their exquisite medallion? of my thankfulness for it and my wish for some occasion of rendering them any service in my power? until this occurs I shall consider myself much their debtor: and as what has past on the subject has always been thro' yourself, I must sollicit thro' the same channel a conveyance of these sentiments to them with the assurance of my respect. nor am I at all unmindful how much it is to your good will that I owe this beautiful performance. but the occasions of being thankful to you have been so frequent that an expression of my sense of them can be but a matter of repetition. such as it is however accept it as a cordial offering, & with it the assurance of my great esteem & respect. TH: JEFFERSON

PoC (DLC); at foot of text: "M[r] Latrobe"; endorsed by TJ.

To Thomas Sully

SIR Monticello Jan. 25. 12.

My letter of Jan. 8. conveying my thanks to the Society of Artists of the US. for having thought me worthy of a place among their associates, could scarcely have reached your hands, when I recieved your second favor announcing the further honour of being named their President. the gratification of this mark of their partiality to me would have been high indeed, could it have been mixed with some hope of my being useful to them. it would have lessened the uneasiness of unmerited distinction. no one is more sensible than myself that it is to the lively fancies of it's younger members, to their zeal & energy, and not to the languid imagination & wearied faculties of age, that the Society must owe it's future successes. I can only give them the tribute of my thanks and best wishes, with the assurance of the readiness & pleasure with which I shall avail myself of any occasion which may occur of rendering them service. in communicating these sentiments to the society, I pray you to accept for yourself those of my great consideration & respect. TH: JEFFERSON

PoC (MHi); at foot of text: "Mr Sully." Printed in Richmond *Enquirer*, 25 Feb. 1812.

To Colin Buckner

SIR Monticello Jan. 26. 12.

I recieved your favor of the 12th by our last post and avail myself of it's first return to inclose you the letter desired. if I conjecture rightly the nature of the connection likely to take place between mr Clarke & yourself, I congratulate you on it, having heard very favorable report of the link which will constitute the connection, & knowing the extreme worth of mr Clarke himself. I shall be gratified if I am in any degree instrumental in promoting your happiness, and tender you the assurances of my great esteem & respect

TH: JEFFERSON

PoC (MHi); at foot of text: "Capt Buckner"; endorsed by TJ. Enclosure: TJ to Christopher Clark, 26 Jan. 1812.

To Christopher Clark

DEAR SIR Monticello Jan. 26. 12.

On a suggestion that it may be interesting to Capt Colin Buckner, & perhaps to yourself, I have been requested to make him the subject of a letter to you. my personal acquaintance with him is small. when Congress, towards the latter end of my administration, authorised the raising some new regiments, Capt Buckner was one of the competitors for a command I remember that his recommendations were among the most satisfactory that we recieved as to any character, and that he was one of the first to whom it was decided to give a Captain's commission. Col^o Monroe's recommendation of him from his personal acquaintance was strong & decisive. from that time till I met with him on my late visit to Bedford I had no particular information respecting him. having seen him several times during that visit I was entirely impressed with the belief that he had fully merited the favorable opinion which had led to the commissioning him. I have thought it a duty to bear witness to what I know of him, and shall be gratified if it can be useful to him or to yourself. and avail myself of the occasion to assure you of my great esteem & respect

TH: JEFFERSON

PoC (DLC); at foot of text: "Christopher Clarke esq."; endorsed by TJ. Enclosed in TJ to Colin Buckner, 26 Jan. 1812.

To Samuel J. Harrison

SIR Monticello Jan. 26. 12.

Your favor of the 16th came to me by post, & not by mr Griffin as it would seem to infer. the new method of selling tobacco by the hogshead renders it difficult for me to sell mine in Lynchburg, as it would require a journey & considerable stay in an inclement season: and if to be sent to Richmond the earlier it goes off the better. I therefore left orders to hurry it down. another reason, I acknolege, induced me to make no offer of it at Lynchburg. from the very small competition at that market, the prices there are far below those of Richmond. if I could recieve there the Richmond price with only a fair deduction of expences, I should certainly prefer selling there. on the present occasion, as I had fixed, to messrs Gibson & Jefferson, a minimum price of 8.D. at Richmond, I will offer to you what shall not have been forwarded down the river at the same price, deducting a dollar a hundred for expences, say for 7.D. a hundred paiable in Richmond in 60. days from the delivery of each parcel at the warehouse of Lynchbg. this last article is proposed merely to prevent the delay of the whole sum because the last lingering hogshead or two cannot be got ready but tardily. I should not in fact call for any part until the principal mass should have been delivered. if you think proper to accept this offer, on shewing this letter to mr Goodman at Poplar Forest, he will consider it as an instruction to deliver the tobo at the warehouse to your order. I should expect also that you would be so good as to drop me a line of notification by post. Accept the assurances of my esteem & respect

TH: JEFFERSON

PoC (MHi); at foot of text: "Mr Saml J. Harrison"; endorsed by TJ.

To Thomas T. Hewson

SIR Monticello Jan. 26. 12.

Our last post brought me your favor of the 11th informing me that the American Philosophical society had again done me the honor of electing me to their Presidential chair. I feel continued gratitude for these repeated marks of their good will, & consider them as renewed obligations to devote myself to their service in any way in which they can make me useful. I regret indeed that the occasions are so infrequent. in doing me the favor of conveying to the society a repetition of my thanks, I pray you to accept for yourself the assurances of my great esteem & respect. TH: JEFFERSON

RC (PPAmP: APS Archives); addressed: "Thomas T. Hewson Secretary of the Amer. Philosophical Society Philadelphia"; franked; postmarked Milton, 27 Jan. 1812; endorsed in part: "Elect Prest Read 7 Feby 1812." PoC (DLC); endorsed by TJ.

To John Barnes

DEAR SIR Monticello Jan. 27. 12.

I have just recieved your favor of the 15th and learn with concern that a doubt can exist that our friend Genl Kosciuzko may have failed to recieve his remittance of 1810. for as to that of 1811. mr Barlow's safe arrival ensures it.

of that of 1810. the 1st 2d & 4th of Exchange were sent by different opportunities thro' the department of state, and altho' I trust they have been recieved, yet I return you the 3d which I had not thought it worth while to send to him. perhaps it may not be amiss now to send it with your next remittance. what convinces me however of it's having been recieved is the following paragraph in the General's letter to me of March. 1. 1811. in answer to one of mine explaining to him the liberty I had taken with a part of his funds. he says 'I approve what you have done with my funds. my entire confidence is in you. I only request that the interest be regularly paid, and I wish it were possible to send it through some other channel than England, for thro' that I lose a great deal & I am not rich.' certainly if he had failed to recieve his remittance of the preceding year, he would have mentioned it. we shall have an excellent opportunity of sending the next by mr Morton of Bordeaux who tells me he shall return with the opening of the spring[1] and I hope you may effect it thro some channel other than English. my part of it shall be ready in time, my crop being now beginning to go to market. I inclose you an order for the dividends due at the bank of Pensva the 1st instant.

The kind interest you took in my embarrasments on my leaving Washington induces me to inform you that of the 8000.D. for which I went into the bank of Richmd I paid 2000. the first year, 3000. the last, and with the crop of tobo now on it's way to market shall pay the remaining 3000: which will clear me out of the bank, the interest having been regularly kept down. the next year I hope I may begin on the General's. nor am I unmindful that I still owe a balance to you. but my whole tobacco fund having been pledged to the bank has kept me constantly streightened as to others. the moment these funds are liberated you shall be among the first thought of. It is long since I have written to you. the truth is that the necessary attention to my affairs within doors & without, does not leave as much time for my writing table as suffices for the pile of letters always awaiting and pressing for answers. the concern I feel nevertheless in your health & happiness is ever the same, and be assured if any occasion should arise in which I could serve you, there is no one living on whom you may count with more certainty. your abundance of kindness to me has made impressions which no time will weaken. I salute you with affection & respect. TH: JEFFERSON

PoC (DLC); at foot of first page: "mr Barnes"; endorsed by TJ. Enclosures not found.

TJ translated part of Tadeusz Kosciuszko's letter of MARCH. 1. 1811, which was written in French.

[1] Remainder of sentence interlined.

To Richard Barry

SIR Monticello Jan. 27. 12.

Your former letter arrived while I was on a six weeks visit to Bedford. that of Jan. 16. is just now recieved. I am just now beginning to get my crop to market, and will not fail to send you the balance I owe you out of the earliest sales. I cannot exactly say, but I presume this will be within some 3. or 4. weeks. farmers you know have no banks to go to, and therefore depend on resources which always require some little notice. wishing you always prosperity & health I tender you the assurance of my continued esteem TH: JEFFERSON

PoC (MHi); at foot of text: "Mr Richard Barry"; endorsed by TJ.

To Mathew Carey

SIR Monticello Jan. 27. 12.

The Parliamentary Manual, originally compiled for my own personal use, was printed on the supposition it might be of use to others, and have some tendency to settle the rules of proceeding in Congress, where, in the lower house especially they had got into forms totally unfriendly to a fair extrication of the will of the majority. no right over it was therefore wished to be retained by myself, nor given to others. it's reimpression consequently is open to every one, nor have I any thing to add to it but what is contained in the inclosed paper. when I first printed it, I had never seen Hatsell's 3d volume. a subsequent perusal of that suggested the inclosed amendments which should be incorporated with the text of the original in their proper places. I believe that mr Milligan of Georgetown is now engaged in printing an 8vo edition. I think he has erred in the size of the volume. almost the essence of it's value is in it's being accomodated to pocket use. Accept the assurance of my esteem & respect

TH: JEFFERSON

RC (Christie's, New York, 2004); at foot of text: "Mr Matthew Cary"; endorsed by Carey as received 4 Feb. and answered 14 Feb. 1812. PoC (DLC); endorsed by TJ. Tr (NjVHi); in an unidentified hand, signed by TJ. Enclosure not found.

TJ mistakenly referred to John HATSELL'S 3D VOLUME rather than the fourth (*PW*, 33–4).

From John B. Magruder

DEAR SIR Jan 27h 1812

Your Letter of the 15 Inst is now before [me.][1] I observe its contents and observe that the stattments therein contain'd are perfectly correct so farr as they respect the A/c's and Nails. I am very sorry that the young Man who you saw; should have (through in attention to the situation of the accounts betwen us) made the Errowneous demand which he did; which occation'd you the trouble of writeing to me on the subject. Mr Bacon some Month past inform'd me that the Nails you directd him to have made for me were ready, and as I had been so negligent as to let so long time relaps without sending for them, I thought it probable that they were disposed of (and if they had been as I had so Long neglectd to send for them I should have had no just right to Complain).[2] I therefore direct'd the young Man to call on M[r] Bacon and know if they were on hand and if they were not, at what time they[3] would be ready; that I was in want of them, and would send for them (If the weather would admit) at any time he would appoint. In regard to the Plank, I have been allways ready and disireous to receive it and Return the Money that you paid me for it ever since you informd me that you prefurd setling the A/c in that way to paying me the price I charged for it. I have had conversation with M[r] Perry on the subject of the Plank; but from what has passd betwen us I think I have no right to concider him in any other capacity than your Agent in the Busyness. I shall be very glad to receive the Plank and return the Money at any time you may think proper to have the plank deliv[d]. To the best of my Recollection it was agreed on betwen us, that as the Plank which had been deliver[d] to your order was saw'd both as to Length Bredth thickness and Quality to suit your purpose—That which was to be return'd to me was to be Merchantable. That is to say the Length to be from 18 to 20 feat Long and upwards if conveniant, from 5 to 6 Inches wide and one and Quarter Inch thick the Quality as near the Quality of that deliver'd you as Possable. The Price to be reduced and advance'd[4] in Proportion to its thickness.

I am Dear sir yours with sincere Respect

John B. Magruder

RC (MHi); endorsed by TJ as received 15 Feb. 1812 and so recorded in SJL.

[1] Omitted word editorially supplied.

[2] Manuscript: "Compain." Omitted closing parenthesis editorially supplied.

[3] Manuscript: "the."

[4] Manuscript: "advace'd."

From George Hay

Sir, Richmond. Jan[y] 29. 1812—

I ought to ask your pardon, and I do ask it for having So long delayed to answer your last letter, and to comply with the requisition which that letter contained. You will be disposed to grant it, I am Sure, when I inform you that much of my time has been occupied by business in Court, which pressed most heavily upon me, and much of it devoted to duties arising from the recent calamity which this City has Sustained.

I shall deposit at the Stage office this evening all the books and documents received from you. The list is Subjoined—

I am with great respect Y[r] mo: ob: Se. Geo: Hay.

1. The manuscript defence
2. 4 printed pamphlets tied together marked by you N° 1.
3. 4. d° d° d° d° —unmarked—the first being "addresse au conseil Legislatif &c"[1] by Poydras.
4. a printed pamphlet marked on the title page by myself—A
5. one bound octavo, labelled "Batture 1808"[2]
6. one d° thin quarto d° d° d°
7. Collection of pamphlets printed & written: the first leaf containing an address or direction to "The honl Albert Gallatin &c"[3]
8. a quarto printed pamphlet entitled "Examen de la Sentence &c"
9. d° entitled Memoire a Consulter &c
10. d° entitled—Pieces probantes—

RC (DLC); endorsed by TJ as received 2 Feb. 1812 and so recorded (as a letter of 30 Jan.) in SJL. Enclosure: TJ's Statement on the Batture Case, 31 July 1810. Other enclosures described at enclosure to Robert Smith to TJ, 4 June 1810, note to William C. C. Claiborne to TJ, 11 Aug. 1810, and enclosure to TJ to George Hay and William Wirt, 23 Mar. 1811.

The RECENT CALAMITY was the Richmond Theatre fire of 26 Dec. 1811 (Richmond *Enquirer*, 31 Dec. 1811).

[1] Omitted closing quotation mark editorially supplied.

[2] Omitted closing quotation mark editorially supplied.

[3] Omitted closing quotation mark editorially supplied.

To Jacob Franklin Heston

SIR Monticello Jan. 29. 12.

I recieved from you, not long since, a small volume on Moral & Political truth, for which be pleased to accept my thanks, but especially for the favorable opinions expressed towards myself in the dedication. so far as intentions faithfully directed to the public good may have merited approbation, I feel conscious that I have just claim to it. of all beyond that I have no right to judge. It were much to be wished that the objects of poetry had generally been as praiseworthy as yours. had the Muses, instead of singing battles & bloodshed, & thus nourishing in weak, but ardent minds a thirst for murderous fame, employed their fascinations in the praise of probity, benevolence, moral virtues generally, & the freedom of man, millions of human lives would have been preserved, and an ambition kindled to excell in virtue, as now in arms.

Accept the assurance of my esteem & respect.

TH: JEFFERSON

PoC (MHi); at foot of text: "Mr Jacob Franklin Heston."

From Gibson & Jefferson

Sir Richmond 30th Jany 1812.

Your letter of the 5th Inst relative to your crops of flour and Tobacco, we observe was replied to by Mr Ligon on the 9th: we regret we did not sooner notice the quotations he gave you of the prices of the latter as we do not consider them applicable to such a crop as yours, but merely for small crops or scattering Hhds picked up at the Warehouses, we should have no doubt of obtaining your limits provided the quality has not been overrated, some small select parcels have been sold at $7 which is the highest we have yet heard of, it will be very material to have it down as soon as possible, as every one is anxious to make immediate shipments—You must have misunderstood the information given to you by Mr Jefferson as to the price at which your crop sold last year in this place—it was shipp'd by Mr Rutherfoord and Mr Mutter who bought it of Mr Harrison in a parcel of 200 Hhds at 9$—

We are with respect

Sir Your obt Servts— Gibson & Jefferson

RC (ViU: TJP-ER); in Patrick Gibson's hand; at head of text: "Thomas Jefferson Esqre"; endorsed by TJ as received 2 Feb. 1812 and so recorded in SJL.

SJL records missing letters from TJ to Gibson & Jefferson of 2 Jan. 1812 and of the 5th inst. Letters from the firm to TJ of 2 Jan. 1812 and of the 9th, not found, are both recorded in SJL as received from Richmond on 12 Jan. 1812.

To John W. Campbell

Sir Monticello Jan. 31. 12.

Your favor of Dec. 20. was between two & three weeks on the road. with it I recieved safely the returned volume which you have certainly done wisely not to reprint. I shall gladly become a subscriber for your work; but it is not in my power to furnish any materials. exactly at the date to which your letter states your work to be arrived (1776) I began to be called from home, & was thenceforward sometimes at Philadelphia, at Williamsburg & in foreign countries, & scarcely ever at home. so that even the collection of newspapers which I had continued to 1776. ceased at that period. what materials I had preceding that period, I lent to mr Burke, & have never been able to recover them. as from that period you enter into the revolutionary war, the materials become wider spread. during the years 1779. 80. 81. while

I was governor of Virginia I made it a point in a continued series of letters to Gen[l] Washington & the President of Congress to give them a connected detail of the military proceedings in this state. the copies of my letters in the council office are probably lost: but the originals are among General Washington's papers & in the Secretary of state's office (Col[o] Monroe's) General Stevens of Culpeper who was in command, has probably interesting papers. I recollect no other deposits of any consequence. Accept my best wishes for the success of your work and the assurance of my respect Th: Jefferson

PoC (DLC); at foot of text: "M[r] John W. Campbell"; endorsed by TJ.

John Jay and Samuel Huntington served successively as PRESIDENT OF CONGRESS during TJ's Virginia governorship.

From John Moody

Honorable Sir Richmond January 1812—

I have written on to washington to Obtain a Majors Commision in the Service to Several friends—at this Crisis of publice affairs my pulse Beats high I am willing to offer my[1] Sevices in a Suitable Station and the above would be an Eligeable one, I will take it particularly kind if you will be So Very Oblidgeing as to write a few Lines of Reccomendation in my favour to the proper placee as I have Very few Acquaintance at washington, M[r] J. Monroe I have written to and one or two Others

with the Highest Respect I am your most Ob[t]

John Moody

RC (DLC: TJ Papers, 195:34631); partially dated; endorsed by TJ as received 2 Feb. 1812 and so recorded in SJL.

John Moody (ca. 1747–1826) was a Revolutionary War veteran who settled in Richmond in 1786 and belonged in the 1790s to the Richmond mercantile firm of Moody & Price. In 1798 he was attacked in print for his Republican views. Moody regularly wrote to both TJ and James Madison in search of patronage. By 1806 Moody sold millstones in his own shop in Richmond, and in 1810 he became an agent for the inventor Oliver Evans. As such, he granted licenses for the use of Evans's patented milling machinery (*PTJ*, 29:429n; *MB*, 2:989; Madison, *Papers, Congress. Ser.*, 17:198–9; Madison, *Papers, Sec. of State Ser.*, 2:450; Richmond *Enquirer*, 11 Jan. 1806; Leesburg *Washingtonian*, 2 Oct. 1810; Moody to TJ, 20 Nov. 1821, 20 Sept., 1 Dec. 1824, 31 Jan. 1825; TJ to Moody, 27 Nov. 1821; *Richmond Enquirer*, 3 Oct. 1826).

Moody's letter to James MONROE has not been found. He asked Monroe for patronage on at least two other occasions (Moody to Monroe, [ca. Jan. 1801] [Vi: RG 3, Governor's Office, Letters Received], 4 Oct. 1814 [DNA: RG 59, LAR, 1809–17]).

[1] Manuscript: "my my."

From Tadeusz Kosciuszko

MON CHER ARISTIDE 1 Fevrier. 1812 a Berville

J'ai eu l'honneur et le sensible plaisir de reçevoir vos deux lettres et celle de Mr Barnes avec une lettre d'echange.

En les relisant dans ma solitude (car je suis a la campagne a 16 lieux de Paris près de Fontainebleau) Jai vu que vous avez fait beaucoup pour la suretè de votre Pays et beaucoup pour les connoissances dans tous Les genres nècèssaires. Mais qui me dira positivement que votre Gouvernement Rèpublicain durerat longtems; Si L'èducation de la jeunesse n'est pas établie sur la base fixe des principes Republicains sur La morale et La justice, et Surveillèe par Le Congrès même afin qu'aucun Professeur ne puisse s'en écarter. Vous savez que les enfants sont plus suscèptibles d'une imprèssion solide et durable, que l'âge mure ou l'intèrêt parle avec tant de force qu'aucune autre considèration le plus honorable ne l'emporte pas; C'est dans cet âge tendre que se grave mieux tous Les devoirs de la sociètè et envers sa Patrie, C'est de cette Éducation que vous devez ésperer d'avoir les plus grands défensseurs de votre Pays et les Soutiens du Gouvernement Rèpublicain. Vous ne devez pas attendre autant des Villes maritimes corrompues par le commerce étrangér et par l'opulence, ils seront S'ils ne le sont dèja pour le Gouvernement Monarchique. Vos estimables Quakkers ne feront rien ils sont des hommes Moreaux mais non pas Citoyens. Votre véritable force consiste dans les habitants de l'intèrieur ou il y a des moeurs des vertus sociales susceptibles de grandeur d'Ame et de génerosité si vous renforcez ces qualites par une éducation strictement surveillér alors votre but sera rempli, et vous vèrez sortir de votre Pays autant de Hèros que de la Grece et plus sages que de Rome.

Je vous embrasse tendrement et agreez L'assurance des Sentiments d'Estime, dattachement et de haute Consideration que je vous ai voués pour la vie T: KOSCIUSZKO

Adressez vos Lettres pour moi à Mr Hotinger à Paris

EDITORS' TRANSLATION

MY DEAR ARISTIDES 1 February. 1812 Berville

I have had the honor and distinct pleasure of receiving your two letters and that of Mr. Barnes with a letter of credit.

Rereading them in solitude (for I live in the country sixteen miles from Paris, near Fontainebleau) I saw that you have done much for both the security of your country and the advancement of knowledge in every necessary field. But who can assure me that your republican government will endure for

long, if the education of its young people is not established on the set basis of republican principles, morality, and justice, and watched over by Congress, so that no professor may deviate from them? You know that children are more susceptible to sound and durable impressions than those who have reached their maturity, to whom personal interest speaks with such force that no other more honorable consideration can win them over. The social and patriotic duties are best taught to those of tender age. From this education you must hope to find the best defenders of your country and supporters of your republican form of government. You must not expect as much from maritime cities corrupted by foreign trade and riches; they will favor monarchical government, if they do not already do so. Your esteemed Quakers will do nothing; they are moral men but not citizens. Your true strength lies in the people living inland, where mores and social virtues capable of grandeur of soul and generosity exist. If you reinforce these qualities through a strictly supervised education, then you will reach your goal and see the emergence in your country of heroes as numerous as in Greece and wiser than in Rome.
I embrace you tenderly. Please accept the assurance of the sentiments of esteem, attachment, and high consideration that I have dedicated to you for the rest of my life T: Kosciuszko

Address letters for me to Mr. Hottinguer in Paris

RC (MHi); dateline adjacent to signature; endorsed by TJ as received 16 Apr. 1812 and so recorded in SJL. Translation by Dr. Roland H. Simon.

ARISTIDE (Aristides), known as "the Just," was a fifth-century B.C. Athenian statesman.

To Benjamin Galloway

Sir Monticello Feb. 2. 12.

I duly recieved your favor of the 1st [ult.][1] together with the volume accompanying it, for which I pray you to accept my thanks, and to be so kind as to convey them to mrs Debutts[2] also, to whose obliging care I am indebted for it's transmission. but especially my thanks are due to the Author himself for the honorable mention he has made of me. with the exception of two or three characters of greater eminence in the revolution[3] we[4] formed a group of fellow laborers in the common cause, animated by a common[5] zeal and claiming no distinction of one over another.

The spirit of freedom breathed thro' the whole of mr Northmore's composition is really worthy of the purest times of Greece and Rome. it would have been recieved in England in the days of Hampden & Sidney with more favor than at this time.[6] it marks a high and independant mind in the author, one capable of rising above the partialities of country, to have seen in the adversary cause that of justice and freedom, and to have estimated fairly the motives and actions of those engaged in it's support. I hope & firmly believe that the whole world will, sooner or later, feel benefit from the issue of our assertion of the rights of man. altho' the horrors of the French revolution have damped for a while the ardor of the patriot in every country, yet it is not extinguished; it will never die. the sense of right has been excited in every breast, and the spark will be rekindled by the very oppressions of that[7] detestable tyranny employed to quench it. the errors of the honest patriots of France, & the crimes of her Dantons & Robespierres, will be forgotten in the more encouraging contemplation of our sober example and steady march to our object. hope will strengthen the presumption that what has been done once may be done again. As you have been the channel of my recieving this mark of attention from mr Northmore, I must pray you to be that of conveying to him my thanks, and an assurance of the high sense I have of the merit of his work and of it's tendency to cherish the noblest virtues of the human character.

On the political events of the day I have nothing to[8] communicate. I have retired from them, and given up newspapers for more classical reading. I add therefore only the assurances of my great esteem & respect.

TH: JEFFERSON

PoC (DLC); at foot of first page: "Benjamin Galloway esq." Reprinted (without year) in *Richmond Enquirer*, 18 Sept. 1816, from unidentified issue of the Fredericktown (now Frederick), Md., *Political Examiner*.

[1] PoC: "inst." *Enquirer*: "ult."

[2] *Enquirer*: "Mr De Butts."

[3] Preceding three words interlined.

[4] *Enquirer*: "he."

[5] Preceding five words omitted from *Enquirer*.

[6] Sentence omitted from *Enquirer*.

[7] *Enquirer* here adds: "very."

[8] TJ here canceled "say."

From Joseph Milligan

DEAR SIR Georgetown February 2nd 1812

As you will See by the Enclosed proof of the first 12 pages of the Manual I have had it printed to meet your Idea as to Size and think that it is certainly a great[1] improvement as it may be bound like the Volume of the British spy herwith sent So as to make an elegant pocket Volume I have not yet got the house of representatives to take a Vote on ordering a certain Number for the house but I hope to have it brought before them in a week—I went this day to get Mr Burwell to give me some instructions in what manner to bring it before the house but he had just Set out for Baltimore but I hope he will be back in a few days, I have just been with our mutual friend Mr John

Barnes who is in good health and desires his respects with the best wishes for your health and happiness

I am with respect Your obedient Servant JOSEPH MILLIGAN

RC (DLC); at foot of text: "Thomas Jefferson Esqr Monticello Vi^a"; endorsed by TJ as received 15 Feb. 1812 and so recorded in SJL. Enclosure: proofs, not found, for pp. 1–12 of Milligan's edition of TJ, *A Manual of Parliamentary Practice: for the Use of the Senate of the United States* (Georgetown, 1812).

Milligan enclosed a VOLUME of *The Letters of the British Spy*, an anonymous work by William Wirt that looked at American society through the eyes of a fictional British visitor. Originally printed in the Richmond *Virginia Argus*, Aug.–Sept. 1803, it appeared in several editions beginning later that year.

[1] Manuscript: "grat."

To Charles Pinckney

DEAR SIR Monticello Feb. 2. 12.

Your favor of Dec. 18. is duly recieved and I am happy to learn from it that you are well and still active in the cause of our country. S. Carolina remains firm too to sound principles. of her orthodoxy I shall never doubt. you have the peculiar advantage of gathering all your aristocracy into Charleston, where alone it can be embodied, and where alone it can be felt. we are to have war then? I believe so, and that it is necessary. every hope from time, patience & the love of peace is exhausted, and war or abject submission are the only alternatives left us. I am forced from my hobby, peace until our revenue is liberated. then we could make war without either new taxes or loans, and in peace apply the same resources to internal improvement. but they will not give us time to get into this happy state. they will force us, as they have forced France to become a nation of souldiers, & then the more woe to them. but all this is for future history. mine is drawing to it's close. age begins to press sensibly on me, and I leave politics to those of more vigour of body and mind. I give up newspapers for Horace & Tacitus, and withdraw my mind from contention of every kind, perfectly secure that our rulers & fellow citizens are taking all possible care of us. they will still have many years of aid from you, and that they may be years of health, honor & happiness is my sincere prayer. TH: JEFFERSON

PoC (MHi); at foot of text: "Charles Pinckney esq."; endorsed by TJ.

From John Adams

Dear Sir Quincy February 3. 1812

Sitting at My Fireside, with my Daughter Smith, on the first of February My Servant brought me a Bundle of Letters and Newspapers from the Post office in this Town: one of the first Letters that Struck my Eye, had the Post Mark of Milton 23. Jany 1812. Milton is the next Town to Quincy and the Post office in it is but three Miles from my House. How could the Letter be So long in coming three miles? Reading the Superscription I instantly handed the Letter to Mrs Smith. Is not that Mr Jeffersons hand? Looking attentively at it, She answered it is very like it. How is it possible a Letter from Mr Jefferson, could get into the Milton Post office? Opening the Letter I found it, indeed from Monticello in the hand and with the Signature of Mr Jefferson: but this did not much diminish my Surprize. How is it possible a Letter can come from Mr Jefferson to me in Seven or Eight days? I had no Expectation of an answer, thinking the Distance So great and the Roads So embarrassd under two or three Months.—This History would not be worth recording but for the Discovery it made of a Fact, very pleasing to me, vizt that the Communication between us is much easier, Surer and may be more frequent than I had ever believed or Suspected to be possible.

The Material of the Samples of American Manufacture which I Sent you, was not Wool nor Cotton, nor Silk nor Flax nor Hemp nor Iron nor Wood. They were Spun from the Brain of John Quincy Adams and consist in two Volumes of his Lectures on Rhetorick and oratory, delivered[1] when he was Professor of that Science in our University of Cambridge. A Relation of mine, a first Cousin of my ever honoured, beloved and revered Mother Nicholas Boylston, a rich Merchant of Boston bequeathed by his Will a Donation for establishing a Professorship, and John Quincy Adams having in his Veins So much of the Blood of the Founder, was most earnestly Solicited to become the first Professor. The Volumes I Sent you are the Fruit of his Labour during the Short time he held that office. But it ought to be remembered that he attended his Duty as a Senator of the United States during the Same Period. It is, with Some Anxiety Submitted to your Judgment.

your Account of the flourishing State of Manufactures in Families, in your Part of the Country is highly delightful to me. I wish the Spirit may Spread and prevail through the Union. Within my Memory We were much in the Same Way in New England: but in later Times We have run a gadding abroad too much, to Seek for Eatables, Drinkables and wearables.

your Life and mine for almost half a Century have been nearly all of a Piece, resembling in the whole, mine in The Gulph Stream, chaced by Three British Frigates, in a Hurricane from the North East and a hideous Tempest of Thunder and Lightening, which cracked our Main mast, Struck three and twenty Men, on Deck[2] wounded four and killed one. I do not remember that my Feelings, during those three days were very different from what they have been for fifty years.

What an Exchange have you made? of Newspapers for Newton! Rising from the lower deep of the lowest deep of Dulness and Bathos to the Contemplation of the Heavens and the heavens of Heavens. Oh that I had devoted to Newton and his Fellows, that time which I fear has been wasted on Plato and Aristotle, Bacon (Nat) Acherly, Bolingbroke,[3] De Lolme, Harrington Sidney, Hobbes, Plato Redivivus Marchmont Nedham, with twenty others upon Subjects which Mankind is determined never to Understand, and those who do Understand them are resolved never to practice, or countenance.

your Memoranda of the past, your Sense of the present and Prospect for the Future Seem to be well founded, as far as I See. But the Latter, i.e the Prospect of the Future, will depend on the Union: and how is that Union to be preserved. Concordiâ Res parve crescunt, Discordiâ Maximæ dilabuntur. Our Union is an immense Structure. In Russia I doubt not a Temple or Pallace might be erected of Wood, Brick or Marble, which Should be cemented only with Ice. A Sublime and beautiful Building it might be; Surpassing St. Sophia, St Peters St. Pauls, Notre Dame or St. Genevieve. But the first Week, if not the first day of the Debacle would melt all the Cement, and Tumble The Glass and Marble the Gold and Silver, the Timber and the Iron into one promiscuous chaotic or anarchic heap.

I will not at present point out the precise Years Days and Months when; nor the Names of the Men by whom, this Union has been put in Jeopardy. your Recollection can be at no more loss than mine.

Cobbets, Callenders, Peter Markoes, Burrs and Hamiltons may And have passed away. But Conquerors do not So easily disappear. Battles and Victories are irresistable[4] by human Nature. When a Man is once acknowledged by the People in The Army and the Country to be the Author of a Victory; there is no longer any Question. He is undoubtedly a great and good Man. Had Hamilton, Burr obtained a recent Victury, neither you, nor Jay nor I Should have Stood any

Chance against them or either of them more than a Swallow or a Sparrow.

The Union is Still to me[5] an Object of as much Anxiety as ever Independence was. To this I have Sacrificed my Popularity in New England and yet what Treatment do I Still receive from the Randolphs and Sheffeys of Virginia. By the way are not these Eastern Shore Men? My Senectutal Loquacity has more than retaliated your "Senile Garrulity."

I have read Thucidides and Tacitus, So often, and at Such distant Periods of my Life, that elegant, profound and enchanting as is their Style, I am weary of them. When I read them I Seem to be only reading the History of my own Times and my own Life. I am heartily weary of both; i.e. of recollecting the History of both: for I am not weary of Living. Whatever a peevish Patriarch might Say, I have never yet Seen the day in which I could Say I have had no Pleasure; or that I have had more Pain than Pleasure.

Gerry Paine and J. Adams, R. R. Livingston, B. Rush and George Clymer and yourself are all that I can recollect, of the Subscribers to Independence who remain. Gerry is acting a decided and a Splendid Part. So daring and So hazardous a Part; but at the Same time So able and upright, that I Say "God Save The Governor": and "prosper long our noble Governor."

I walk every fair day. Sometimes 3 or 4 miles. Ride now and then but very rarely more than ten or fifteen Miles. But I have a Complaint that Nothing but the Ground can cure, that is the Palsy; a kind of Paralytic affection of the Nerves, which makes my hands tremble, and renders it difficult to write at all and impossible to write well.

I have the Start of you in Age by at least ten Years: but you are advanced to the Rank of a Great Grandfather before me. Of 13 Grand Children I have two William and John Smith, and three Girls, Caroline Smith Susanna and Abigail Adams, who might have made me Great Grand Children enough. But they are not likely to employ their Talents very Soon. They are all good Boys and Girls however, and are the Solace of my Age. I cordially reciprocate your Professions of Esteem and Respect. JOHN ADAMS

Madam joins and Sends her kind Regards to your Daughter and your Grand Children as well as to yourself.

P.S. I forgot to remark your Preference to Savage over civilized Life. I have Something to Say upon that Subject. If I am in an Error, you can Set me Right, but by all I know of one or the other I would rather be the poorest Man in France or England with Sound health of Body and Mind than the proudest King, Sachem or Warriour of any Tribe of Savages in America.

RC (DLC); endorsed by TJ as received 19 Feb. 1812 and so recorded in SJL. FC (Lb in MHi: Adams Papers).

Adams was recalling a HIDEOUS TEMPEST he experienced during his voyage to France in 1778 (Lyman H. Butterfield and others, eds., *Diary and Autobiography of John Adams* [1961], 2:275–6). British political theorist Henry Neville published PLATO REDIVIVUS in London in 1681. CONCORDIÂ . . . DILABUNTUR: "harmony makes small states great, while discord undermines the mightiest empires" (Sallust, *The War with Jugurtha*, x. 6, trans. John C. Rolfe, Loeb Classical Library [1921; repr. 1995], 148, 149). PETER Markoe was a resident of Philadelphia who wrote plays and political poems and satires (*ANB*). John Randolph of Roanoke and Daniel Sheffey both represented Virginia districts in the United States House of Representatives at this time, but neither hailed from the EASTERN SHORE. Robert R. LIVINGSTON was appointed to the committee that drafted the Declaration of INDEPENDENCE but returned home to New York before the document was signed (*ANB*).

[1] RC: "delived." FC: "delivered."

[2] Preceding two words interlined in RC.

[3] RC and FC: "Bolinbroke."

[4] RC and FC: "irresisable."

[5] Preceding two words interlined in RC.

To Albert Gallatin

DEAR SIR Monticello Feb. 3. 12.

You are to consider me in this letter as a witness & not a sollicitor. it is written at the request of a mr James Dinsmore who lived in my family 10. years as a housejoiner, did all the housejoinery of my house, being one of the ablest of his calling, and one of the best men I have ever known. while I lived in Washington he applied to me for a Surveyor's place for his brother John Dinsmore in the Western country. I recommended him to mr Briggs, who employed him, and I think has since spoken of him to me in very high terms. John's health is now so much declined that he is become unequal to the labor of surveying, & is therefore settled on his farm with his family at Attacapas. the place of reciever of the public monies there[1] is become vacant and he wishes it. I know nothing of him personally, but observing that similar[2] dispositions run much in families, I am disposed from a knolege of his brother, to expect he is a good man also. but mr Briggs can give you his character from his own knolege. if a better man applies, you will of course give it to the better man. if none better, the object of this letter is to draw your attention to him. and, if not on this occasion, you may perhaps on some other, make advantageous use of him.

ever affectionately Yours TH: JEFFERSON

RC (NHi: Gallatin Papers); addressed: "Albert Gallatin Secretary of the Treasury Washington"; franked and postmarked. PoC (DLC); endorsed by TJ.

TJ recommended JOHN DINSMORE to Isaac Briggs after appointing the latter surveyor of United States lands south of Tennessee (TJ to Briggs, 20 Apr. 1803, and Briggs to TJ, 2 May 1803 [DLC]).

[1] Word interlined.
[2] Word interlined.

To James Leitch

Feb. 3. 12.

1. doz. teacups of the pattern laid by
1. doz. saucers to d^{o}
1. doz. coffee cups as near the pattern as you have
1. doz. saucers to d^{o}
the paper laid by

TH:J.

RC (ViCMRL, on deposit ViU: TJP); dateline beneath signature; written on a small scrap; at foot of text: "Mr Leitch." Not recorded in SJL.

To Ezra Sargeant

SIR Monticello Feb. 3. 12.

Observing that you edit the Edinburgh Review, reprinted in N. York, and presuming that your occupations in that line are not confined to that single work, I take the liberty of addressing the present letter to you. if I am mistaken, the obviousness of the inference will be my apology. Mr Edward Livingston brought an action against me for having removed his intrusion on the beach of the river Missisipi opposite N. Orleans. at the request of my counsel I made a statement of the facts of the case and of the law applicable to them, so as to form a full argument of justification. the case has been dismissed from court for want of jurisdiction, and the public remain uninformed whether I had really abused the powers entrusted to me, as he alledged. I wish to convey to them this information by publishing the justification. the questions arising in the case are mostly under the civil law, the laws of Spain and of France, which are of course couched in French in Spanish, in Latin & some in Greek, and the books being in few hands in this country I was obliged to make very long extracts from them. the correctness with which your edition of the Edinburgh Review is printed, and of the passages quoted in those languages induces me to propose to you the publication of the case I speak of. it will fill about 65. or 70. pages of the type & size of paper of the Edinburgh Review. the MS. is in the handwriting of this letter, entirely fair and correct. it will take between 4. & 5. sheets of paper, of 16. pages each. I should want 250. copies struck off for myself, intended principally for the members of Congress, and the printer would be at liberty to print as many more as he pleased for sale, but without any copy right, which I should not propose to have taken out. it is right that I should add that the work is not at all for popular reading. it is merely a law argument, & a very dry one; having been intended merely for the eye of my counsel. it may be in some demand perhaps with lawyers, & persons engaged in the public affairs, but very little beyond that. will you be so good as to inform me if you will undertake to edit this, and what would be the terms on which you can furnish me with the 250. copies. I should want it to be done with as little delay as possible so that Congress might recieve it before they separate, and I should add as a condition that not a copy should be sold until I could recieve my number & have time to lay them on the desks of the members. this would require a month from the time they should leave N. York by the stage. in hopes of an early answer I tender you the assurances of my respect.

Th: Jefferson

PoC (DLC); at foot of first page: "M[r] Ezra Sargeant."

Ezra Sargeant (1775–1812), printer, publisher, bookseller, and merchant, was born in Leicester, Massachusetts, and living in New York City by 1802. TJ subscribed to his reprint edition of the British quarterly periodical, the *Edinburgh Review* (*New York Genealogical and Biographical Record* 45 [1914]: 277; New York *Daily Advertiser*, 29 Apr. 1802, 7 May 1803, 31 May 1805; *Longworth's New York Directory* [1803], 254; Sowerby, no. 4733; New York *Commercial Advertiser*, 24 June 1812; Hudson, N.Y., *Northern Whig*, 29 June 1812).

From Samuel J. Harrison

SIR Lynchbg Feby 5th 1812

I rec[d] your Letter of the 26th ult[o] yesterday, & Accept your proposal of Seven Dollars ℔ 100[t] for your present Crop of tob[o]—Ten H[hds] only, are in: & none Sent to Richmond as you Seem to have expected—I think the price you make me give too high, Either for the Richm[d] market or future prospects: & Shall therefore Submit it to your Discretion, to lower the price of the Stemed—it is allways lower than Leaf—

I Shall be allways ready to make the payments agreeable to your Letters.—

Y[r] M[o] ob sr S J Harrison

RC (MHi); endorsed by TJ as received 10 Feb. 1812 and so recorded in SJL.

From Henry Andrews

Southington Febuary 7th 1813 [1812], (State of Connecticutt)

Sir

Prehaps you will be surpriz[d] and no doubt condem the author of the following lines either as an impudent person or at least conclude him conducted by an overheated immginaton but Sir I beg you to pardon the intrusion and listen a moment to the solicitation of a youth who has through the malice of Enemies together Connected with the frailities of inexperience too much to be regretted by the wise and good enlisted himself under the banners of Poverty—I can affirm solemly that I am concienciously free from any heinous crimes, but my own imprudent Conduct in dissappaton has in a manner withdrawn from me the Confidence and Esteem of those whom I once could respect as friends—

My parents both died when I was quite young & I have at present no Relative living except an uncle—who whould I think[1] restore me to his Confidence provided I could & would by a compleat refformation become worthy of his friendship—

I wish Sir to procure some employment whereby I may become usefull to Society and my Country for at present "hungry ruin has me in the wind"[2]—What little Education I am possess[d] of I have obtain[d] in the mercantile business, however I would willingly except of any employment that my abillities would admit of or even enter into the Service of the United States army after a proper and suitable Education and endeavour to defend the rights and lyberty of my fellow Citizens as I think my age (being 22) (if not my Courage)[3] would recommend—

I consider you Sir as having been the Common father of my Country and therefore offer to trouble you. I should be Happy to have you find some employment for me either with yourself, or friends, but if not agreeable would beg you to pity my situation and favour me with advice & information. I fully see the folly of my past conduct and sincerely pray for assistance from the aiding hand of a friend to snatch me from destruction & despair

I shall remain in this place a sufficient time to recieve a line from you and beg you to Condecend to honour me in that respect

I Subscribe myself—your Humble Serv[t] HENRY ANDREWS

RC (MHi); misdated; between dateline and salutation: "Thomas Jefferson Esq[r]"; endorsed by TJ as a letter of 7 Feb. 1812 received 19 Feb. 1812 and so recorded in SJL.

Thomas Otway used the expression "HUNGRY Ruine had it in the wind" in *The History and Fall of Caius Marius. A Tragedy. As it is Acted at the Duke's Theatre* (London, 1680), 6.

[1] Preceding two words interlined.

[2] Omitted closing quotation mark editorially supplied.

[3] Omitted opening parenthesis editorially supplied.

From James Madison

DEAR SIR Washington Feb[y] 7. 1812

I have rec[d] several letters from you which not requiring special answers, I now beg leave to acknowledge in the lump. I have delayed it in the hope that I might add something on our public affairs not uninteresting. If there be any thing at present of this character it will be found in the inclosed paper from N. York. We have no late[1] official information from Europe; but all that we see from G.B. indicates an adherence to her mad policy towards the U.S. The Newspapers give you a Sufficient insight into the measures of Congress. With a view to enable the Executive to step at once into Canada they have provided after two months delay, for a regular force requiring 12 to raise it, and after 3 months for a volunteer force, on terms not likely to raise it at all for that object. The mixture of good & bad, avowed & disguised motives accounting for these things is curious[2] eno', but not to be explained in the compass of a letter. Among other jobbs on my hands is the case of Wilkinsons. His defence fills 6 or 700 pages of the most collossal paper. The minutes of the Court, oral written & printed testimony, are all in proportion. A month has not yet carried me thro' the whole.

We have had of late a hard winter & much Ice which still lies on the water in view. The re-iterations of Earthquakes continue to be reported from various quarters. They have slightly reached the State of N.Y. and been severely felt W. & S. Westwardly. There was one here this morning at 5 or 6 minutes after 4 OC. It was rather stronger than any preceding one, & lasted several minutes, with sensible tho very slight repetitions throughout the succeeding hour.

Be assured of my best affections JAMES MADISON

RC (DLC: Madison Papers); endorsed by TJ as received 15 Feb. and so recorded (as a letter of 12 Feb.) in SJL. Enclosure not identified.

On 6 Feb. 1812 Madison signed a bill authorizing the president to raise and organize a VOLUNTEER FORCE. A supplement to the bill was approved on 6 July 1812 (*U.S. Statutes at Large*, 2:676–7, 785–6). General James WILKINSON's court-martial proceedings concluded on 25 Dec. 1811. On 14 Feb. 1812 Madison publicly stated that Wilkinson's conduct had been objectionable, but he nonetheless approved the general's acquittal and ordered that his sword be returned to him (*Annals*, 12th Cong., 1st sess., 2125–37; DNA: RG 94 and 153, Records relating to Wilkinson's 1811 and 1815 Courts-Martial).

[1] Word interlined.
[2] Word copied above the line for clarity.

From Randolph Jefferson

DEAR BROTHER.— woodlawn Feby 8: 12

I Received yours of the 6 instant, and am extreemly oblige to you for the things you were so kind as to send me. which came to hand safe, I have not had a tetch of my complaint since I saw you, and have Greatly mended in flesh. I have rode down to snowden on horse back and I found it not disagree a tall with me, tho I rode very slow, and once I went down in the gigg all appeard to a Gree exceedingly well with me so far. as soon as the roads Gits in good order we will come over I expect it will be the last of next month or the first of april, I am very sorry to hear of my sister marks low state of health, but hope she will recover after a little time after the weather Gits a little warmer, if my health should continue to keep as it is I will endeavour to come over next month. if your shepards bitch has any more puppys I must Git the favour of you to save me one dog puppy my wife and family Joins in love and Respect to all of you

I am your most affectionatly.— RH; JEFFERSON

NB if you sent my watch to Fast Bender it is more then probable that she went to the Flames with the rest of the watches in his shops as his shop were burnt about the eighttenth of Jany.

RC (ViU: TJP-CC); endorsed by TJ as received 2 Mar. 1812 and so recorded in SJL.

This letter responds to TJ's letter of 14 Jan. 1812, which Randolph evidently received on THE 6 INSTANT. On 16 Jan. 1812 FLAMES swept through downtown Richmond, destroying several stores, shops, and tenements, including the space occupied by Mr. J. H. Fasbender (Richmond *Enquirer*, 18 Jan. 1812; DNA: RG 29, CS, Henrico Co., 1820).

To William Eustis

Dear Sir Monticello Feb. 9. 12.

I take the liberty of forwarding to you the inclosed letter which proposes to place three young gentlemen on the list of candidates for military appointments in the new army to be raised. of them personally I know nothing. with their family I am well acquainted. it is among the very respectable ones of our state in point of character, standing & property. the writer of the inclosed letter is of my intimate acquaintance, and his personal knowlege of the young men is as satisfactory to me as my own would be. Accept the assurance of my great esteem & respect. Th: Jefferson

PoC (DLC); at foot of text: "The honble The Secretary at War"; endorsed by TJ.

The inclosed letter, not recorded in SJL and not found, was from Philip Turpin (TJ to James Pleasants, 9 Feb. 1812; Pleasants to TJ, 25 Feb. 1812).

To Hugh Nelson

Dear Sir Monticello Feb. 9. 12.

I am sorry to be troublesome to you on the subject of my manuscript; but if I do not get it printed before Congress rises I shall fail in the most material part of my object; and proposing to get this done in New York, the distance of the place of impression will add considerably to the delay. I will therefore pray you to send it by return of post, as no conveyance is, I think, safer than the mail. our neighborhood furnishes nothing new & worthy of communication. war is the common expectation as soon as the militia can enter Canada.

I go so little from home that I am not able to give you any information from Belvoir. accept the assurances of my great esteem & respect.

Th: Jefferson

PoC (MHi); at foot of text: "The honble M[r] Nelson"; endorsed by TJ.

To James Pleasants

Dear Sir Monticello Feb. 9. 12.

The inclosed letter being directed to you in conjunction with mr Randolph & myself, I now forward it. your personal knolege of the young gentlemen will perhaps enable you to serve them, and especially your presence at the seat of appointment. I have no personal acquaintance with them, but have written to the Secretary at War inclosing a letter from D[r] Turpin respecting them.   our neighborhood furnishes little matter of communication, and I go too seldom from home to collect that little. I find my neighbors expect war, approve of it & are willing to meet any taxes except the stamp-tax. I hear some wishing the whiskey tax (which every sober man will favor) could be levied solely on licenses to be issued for selling that liquor. the objection to this tho' weighty, are not as strong as to the domiciliary searches. Accept the assurance of my esteem & respect.

TH: JEFFERSON

PoC (ViW: TC-JP); at foot of text: "The honble James Pleasants"; endorsed by TJ.

The INCLOSED LETTER, not recorded in SJL and not found, was from a Mr. Harrison (Pleasants to TJ, 25 Feb. 1812).

From John Adams

DEAR SIR Quincy Feb. 10 1812

I have received with great pleasure your favour of the 23 of January. I suspected that the Sample was left at the Post Office and that you would Soon have it. I regret the Shabby Condition in which you found it: but it was the only Copy I had, and I thought it Scarcely worth while to wait till I could get a Sett properly bound.

The Dissertation on the State of real homespun was a feast to me, who delight in every Information of that kind. In a moral œconomical and political point of View, it ought to be considered by every American Man Woman and child as a most precious Improvement in the Condition and prosperity of our Country.

Although you and I are weary of Politicks; you may be Surprised to find me making a Transition to Such a Subject as Prophecies. I find that Virginia produces Prophets, as well as the Indiana Territory. There have been lately Sent me, from Richmond two Volumes, one written by Nimrod Hewes and the other by Christopher Macpherson; both, upon Prophecies, and neither, ill written. I Should apprehend that two Such Mulattoes might raise the Devil among the Negroes in that Vicinity: for though they are evidently cracked, they are not much more irrational than D[r] Towers[1] who wrote two ponderous Vollumes, near twenty years ago to prove that The French Revolution was the Commencement of the Millenium, and the decapitation of The King of France but the beginning of a Series, immediately to follow, by which all The Monarchies were to be destroyed and Succeeded by universal Republicanism over all Europe: nor than D[r] Priestly who told me Soberly, cooly and deliberately that though he knew of Nothing in human Nature or in the History of Mankind to justify the opinion, Yet he fully believed upon the Authority of Prophecy, that the French Nation would establish a free Government and[2] that The King of France who had been executed, was the first of the Ten Horns of the great Beast and that all the other Nine Monarks were Soon to fall off after him; nor than The Reverend M[r] Faber who has lately written a very elegant and learned Volume to prove that Napoleon is Antichrist; nor than our worthy Friend M[r] Joseph Wharton of Philadelphia, who in consequence of great Reading and profound Study has long Since Settled his opinion, that the City of London is or is to be the Head Quarters of Antichrist; Nor than the Prophet of The Wabash, of whom I want to know more than I do, because I learn that the Indians the Sons of the Forrest are as Superstitious as any of the great learned Men aforesaid and as firm believers in Witchcraft as all Europe and America were in the Seventeenth Century and as frequently punish Witches by Splitting their Sculls with the Tomahawk, after a Solemn Tryal and Adjudication by the Sachems and Warriours in Council.

The Crusades were commenced by the Prophets and every Age Since, whenever any great Turmoil happens in the World, has produced fresh Prophets. The Continual Refutation of all their Prognostications by Time and Experience has no Effect in extinguishing or damping their Ardor.

I think, these Prophecies are not only unphilosophical and inconsistent with the political Safety of States and Nations; but that the most Sincere and Sober Christians in the World ought upon their own Principles to hold them impious, for nothing is clearer from their Scriptures [than][3] that Their Prophecies were not intended to make Us Prophets.

Pardon this Strange Vagary. I want only to know Something more than I do about the Richmond and Wabash Prophets.

called to Company and to dinner I have only time to repeat the assurances of the Friendship and Respect of JOHN ADAMS

RC (DLC); at foot of text: "M[r] Jefferson"; endorsed by TJ as received 23 Feb. 1812 and so recorded in SJL. FC (Lb in MHi: Adams Papers).

Nimrod Hughes (HEWES) published *A Solemn Warning To All Dwellers Upon the Earth* in Virginia in August 1811. In this pamphlet he described visions foretelling the "destruction of one third of mankind" on 4 June 1812. Hughes was a white Protestant (Susan Juster, *Doomsayers: Anglo-American Prophecy in the Age of Revolution* [2003], 196–

200, 210–12). Christopher McPherson (MACPHERSON), a free mulatto who adhered to Hughes's prophecies, published a memoir about the same time (*A Short History of the Life of Christopher McPherson*, 2d ed. [Lynchburg, 1855]). Joseph Lomas TOWERS was the author of *Illustrations of Prophecy* (London, 1796; repr. Philadelphia, 1808; Sowerby, no. 1548). The first American edition of George Stanley FABER, *A Dissertation on the Prophecies That Have Been Fulfilled, Are Now Fulfilling, Or Will Hereafter Be Fulfilled* was published in Boston in two volumes in 1808. The PROPHET OF THE WABASH was known by his Shawnee name, Tenskwatawa, or simply as "the Prophet." He began having visions in 1805, and along with his older brother Tecumseh, a prominent warrior, he advocated giving up the use of European goods and urged the creation of a pan-Indian political and military alliance. Tenskwatawa's village, Prophetstown, was located in Indiana near the confluence of the Wabash and Tippecanoe rivers (*ANB*).

[1] Preceding two words added by Adams in a blank he left for the purpose.

[2] Preceding ten words written perpendicularly along left margin of first page and keyed to this point in text with a dagger.

[3] Omitted word editorially supplied.

From Ezra Sargeant

SIR, New York Feb[y] 10. 1812

Your favour of the 3rd Inst. has been duly recieved—I will engage to furnish two hundred & fifty copies of the pamphlet mentioned say from 65 to 70 pages of the same type and size of paper of the Edinbergh Review, for one hundred and thirty Dollars. All the care possible shall be taken to have it correct, in fact the proof reading shall go through the same channel as the Reviews. It will require about three weeks to print them, and get them ready for delivery at the stage office here. I will also engage that a copy shall not go out of the office short of the time you mentioned

I am Sir Your Obt. St E: SARGEANT.

RC (MHi); at foot of text: "The Honb[le] Tho[s] Jefferson Monticello"; endorsed by TJ as received 19 Feb. 1812 and so recorded in SJL.

From James Barbour

DEAR SIR Richmond Feb[y] 11th 1812

With sincere thanks, I acknowledge the receipt of your letter in answer to mine—The prompt compliance with my request, coupled with the very satisfactory view you have given me of the subject referred to in my Communication to you, has laid me under fresh obligations; and is an additional evidence of your friendly disposition—Every impression of my mind was perfectly in unison, with the opinions you express. A want of confidence in the correctness of my Judgement, with some precedents to the contrary, produced my embarrassment—The cogent reasons you assign in favor of your opinion has removed my difficulties; and I shall unhesitatingly pursue the course which has for its support such high authority.

I beg you to be assured of my regard and attachment

JS: BARBOUR

RC (DLC); endorsed by TJ as received 16 Feb. 1812 and so recorded in SJL.

From Benjamin Rush

DEAR SIR Philadelphia Feb: 11th 1812

Few[1] of the Acts of my life have given me more pleasure than the one you are pleased to acknowledge in your last letter.

I wish in your reply to Mr Adams's letter you had given him the echo of his Communications to you respecting his daughter Mrs Smith and her husband. The former has been saved from certain death by a painful operation, and the honor & interest of the latter lie near his heart. I wish he could be provided for in the new Army. He possesses with a fine martial Appearance, military talents and knowledge. I well recollect upon his return to America After visiting the Continent of Europe, being much struck with his details of the improvements in the Art of War with which he had taken pains to make himself acquainted during A residence of some weeks at Berlin.

It will give me pleasure to hear of a frequent exchange of letters between you and Mr Adams. I associate the idea of your early friendship for each other, founded upon a Sympathy of just opinions and feelings, with every retrospect I take of the great political[2] moral & intellectual Atchievements of the Congresses of 1775 and 1776.

Health, respect and friendship! from Dear Sir yours truly, and Affectionately

BENJN RUSH

RC (DLC); at foot of text: "Thos Jefferson Esqr"; endorsed by TJ as received 19 Feb. 1812 and so recorded in SJL.

TJ and Adams were both members of the Continental Congress in 1775, and Rush joined them in 1776 (*Biog. Dir. Cong.*).

[1] Rush here canceled "eforts."

[2] Word interlined.

From Gibson & Jefferson

SIR — Richmond 12th Feby 1812—

We have received your note by Mr Johnson there are at present no ploughs to be procured here, Saml[1] Adams is in daily expectation of receiving some of Peacock's—Vail & Rogers likewise expect a supply of the Cary plough—we have been equally unfortunate in our search after Burnet seed, the only chance of obtaining it, is from Mr Graham, who informs us that he does not know until he sees his Overseer whether he will have any to spare—We have sold your 59 barrels flour at $9\frac{3}{4}$\$—

Your obedt Servts — GIBSON & JEFFERSON

RC (MHi); in Patrick Gibson's hand; at head of text: "Thomas Jefferson Esqre"; endorsed by TJ as received 16 Feb. 1812 and so recorded in SJL.

[1] Reworked from "John."

From Charles Simms

SIR — Alexandria Feby 12th 1812

I have at length met with an opportunity of shipping in a vessel from this Port to Richmond a quarter Cask of wine, a bag of almonds, a box of olives and a box of marble, which I received for you from Salem—and which I have consigned to the care of Messrs Gibson and Jefferson of Richmond the charges for duties Freight & drayage on those articles amount to \$$15\frac{93}{100}$, which I have requested them to remit to me

I have the Honour to be very respectfully Sir Yr Obedt Servt

CH. SIMMS

RC (MHi); endorsed by TJ as received 21 Feb. 1812 and so recorded in SJL.

From John Barnes

DEAR SIR, — George Town 13th Feby 1812.

Your much esteemed favr 27th Ulto received the 1st Inst persuade me the sett of ex for 1810. has reached the good Genls Banker. shd any demur in point of paymt in either sett, the Genl no doubt woud've Noticed it. his observations tended only to the loss of ex. in their negociation between Paris & London. If even that were 15 per Cent, still however the Gen[l] should take into the Acco[t] the Rate of ex—, say 10 ℔[Ct] under par at which I purchased them. On the present Occasion I have address[d] a letter to my friend M[r] Geo Taylor Jun[r] Broker in Philad[a] for his advice and Assistance in Regard to Bills of ex— on Paris directing him to Apply to M[r] David Parish, of whom M[r] Coles in 1809. purchased a sett for me, in fav[r] of the Gen[ls] Banker—I expect his Answer daily—

By last nights Mail, I recd from the Cash[r] Bank of Penn[a] the Gen[ls] half years Dividend—due the 1st Ult[o] for $400. is $80 above the Usual divid[d]

It most assuredly Afford me great pleasure in perciving the prosperous situation of your funds—arising from your persevering exertions in Reducing your former accumilated debts—to so pleasing a state of adjustment and withal the future flattering prospect—must surely be a happy consolation—to the feelings of a gratefull mind emerging from such embarrassm[ts] while many Others—under like circumstances,[1] would have suffered themselves to bend beneath a lesser weight of difficulties, without reflecting on the future direfull Consequences.— No Apology is Necessary for your not writing me sooner, your engagem[ts] are so Various; more interesting[2] and pressing—

I cannot sufficiently express my Acknowledgements for the manner, & singular favors I have recd and your still continued Offers of Services,—which bating—only 20 years from 80. I should probably be tempted to solicit—

But as Time! keeps equal pace, with our age—as Usual, my present Hope and wish is—to gather up carefully the Scattered fragments, and retire to the friendly City from whence I came—for believe me, my present situation however Respectable, do not, nor has not, for these 3 yrs passed, Neated me little more—than a dollar ℔ day—not quite—$400—per Annum.

and the Only friend here I wish to serve and to succeed me, is—my respectable Deputy—M[r] William Morton—fully Competent to the Complicated business of the Office—having been Eleven years steadily employed therein—and whose services—are deserving of the Salary I allow him $800. per Ann[m].—Gen[l] Mason, as well the Merch[ts] and others in George Town his fast friends and well wishers— why then! you will Naturally Answer—do you not, address the President on the subject.—I did!—with great diffidence—Attempt it, 12 M[os] since—but as I expected the President, very Candidly & justly Observed—that—in these Cases, he could not, by any means—whatever allow himself to promise any thing of the

Kind. of course, I begged to be understood—not by any means to bias his choice—but only to Observe to him M[r] Mortons qualifications & situation—& withal added, should no Other Candidate interfer with his choice—&[a] . . . It is under these particular circumstances and Views alone,—I Venture to solicit your Benevolent Offer—should a favorable Opportunity be Affording you—in the Course of the insuing summer—either at Orange, or Monticello.

I pray you My Dear Sir—excuse the freedom I have taken in addressing you—on so delicate a[3] subject—but convinced as I am of y[r] friendship towards me, I have Ventured to unbosom myself on this interesting Occasion, in behalf of a Worthy young Man, whom my Anxious wishes are to serve, and in whom, should the Office of Collector be conferred—will I am persuaded, do Honor to the trust reposed in him—

with great Respect, and Esteem—I am Dear Sir—Your mst Obed[t] serv[t]

John Barnes.

PS. this Instant, Mr Taylors Answer recd informs me—there are no Bills on Paris for Sale in Philad[a]—advises me to Apply at Baltimore—which I shall attend to, and advise the result,

JB—

Thursd[y] Even[g] 13 Feb[y] 1812

RC (ViU: TJP-ER); ellipsis in original; postscript on verso of address cover; addressed: "Thomas Jefferson Esquire Monticello—Virginia"; franked; postmarked Georgetown, 15 Feb.; endorsed by TJ as received 19 Feb. 1812 and so recorded in SJL.

THE CASH[R] BANK OF PENN[A] was Jonathan Smith.

[1] Manuscript: "cumstances."
[2] Manuscript: "intereting."
[3] Manuscript: "a a."

From Nathaniel G. Ingraham, Alexander Phoenix, William Nexsen, and John Redfield

Sir — New York Debtors Prison 13 feb[y] 1812

Four of your fellow Citizens overwhelmed by the calamities of the times, with large families totally destitute of the means of Subsistence, are incarcerated by the government of their Country for—debt. Attached to the Republican Administration of that government by every tie which can direct & controul the affections of man, they have thro' a series of misfortunes & sacrifices supported & maintained all the measures of its policy for the last three Years. The same events which have arrested the prosperity of the nation, have deprived us of our liberty & our families of every comfort. We surrendered ourselves under the Insolvent laws of this State. We gave under them to our Creditors, the whole of our property & were legally discharged. We were content to begin the world anew, & labor with our hands for the support of the dear relatives entitled to our protection; (& with every wish to pay, as we could, our debt to the Government; who will also receive the shattered remains of our fortunes from the hands of our Assignees.) When we had stript them & ourselves of every Dollar we were thrown into this Prison to eat the bread of dependance or starve on the scanty allowance of charity—

It is true our debt to the government is large. We owe them one hundred & forty thousand Dollars; but we have heretofore paid into the Treasury upwards of three hundred & sixteen thousand dollars—We have not therefore been idle or unprofitable servants; & had it not been for circumstances which have baffled the wisdom & power of the nation and almost destroyed its resources, we should now have been surrounded by the comforts of wealth & looking forward to a prosperous futurity—

For the last nine months, suits have been going on against us, & none are yet matured into judgments. We have now been seperated from our families nearly four months, during which time we have made every exertion by offering to give confessions of Judgment,—to release all errors,—to sign & seal whatever might be demanded of us, that we might bring our case before the Secretary of the Treasury—we were willing to submit to any exaction, to make any sacrifice of present feeling or future interest to restore to our suffering families the benefit of our industry & care—

But the Judge of this District is sick & gone to Charleston. The District Attorney for the same reason is absent at New Orleans & his Agent here refuses to remove one step from the ordinary track—Driven thus by necessity & almost by despair we have carried before the National Legislature our appeal to the humanity, if not to the justice of our country. The feelings of Husbands & Fathers compel us to seek thro every channel, the means of making that appeal with success. And to whom Sir can the wretched victims of foreign injustice & rapacity, suffering under all the horrors of imprisonment, apply for assistance with greater freedom, than to the Man of the People, to the author of the declaration of American Independance—

We make the application Sir without fear & beseech you to interest yourself in the behalf of your fellow Citizens who, for their misfortunes alone, have been cut off from Society, deprived of the enjoyment of pure air & the use of their own limbs. Suffer us not to be compelled to a life of uselesse inactivity & sloth—a burden to humanity!

To You Sir it must be well known that the Judicial system established within this State, approximates more closely than in any other part of the United States, to that of Great Britain. Indeed in many respects its Legislature have neglected to adopt the amelioration of the antient system, introduced into that Kingdom within the last twenty years, & to which in all probability the American revolution gave birth by the diffusion of political light & knowledge. The State of New York is I believe the only State in the Union which suffers the incarceration of a Citizen, without providing for him the means of subsistence; which leaves him in this situation for years, charged with no crime, at the mercy of private revenge. The Charity of good men is severely taxed to gratify the malice of the bad—In no other state in the Union could the confinement of a Citizen, reduced to utter penury have continued thro five long years for a debt of fifty Dollars! of which there is now in this Prison a living instance!

But Sir we are intruding too long upon your patience—We must be allowed to hope that You will not be an indifferent spectator of oppression upon the liberty of the Citizen, committed even under the imposing form of law. We implore your aid with the Government & your friends in Congress to effect our deliverance from this monument of the Shameful neglect of those rights on which are bottomed all the political institutions of our Country—We only[1] ask for the liberty of relieving society from the burden of supporting us & our families—Accept Sir, the prayers of the unfortunate for your happiness—

NATH^L G. INGRAHAM
A: PHOENIX
W^M NEXSEN J^R
JOHN REDFIELD JUNIOR

RC (MHi); in Phoenix's hand, signed by Ingraham, Phoenix, Nexsen, and Redfield; addressed: "His Excellency Thomas Jefferson Monticello Virginia"; franked; postmarked New York, 15 Feb.; endorsed by TJ as received 23 Feb. 1812 and so recorded in SJL.

The four signatories were all insolvent New York City merchants. Nathaniel G. Ingraham (ca. 1761–1827) moved from Connecticut to New York City by 1795. He went bankrupt in 1801, successfully resumed trade before the troubles described above, and made his last appearance in city directories as an auctioneer in 1827 (DNA: RG 29, CS, Middletown, Conn., 1790; William Duncan, *The New-York Directory, and Register, for the year 1795* [New York, 1795], 109; New York *Daily Advertiser*, 16 Apr. 1801; MiU-C: Phoenix Family Papers; Madison, *Papers, Pres. Ser.*, 3:169–70; *Longworth's New York Directory* [1827], 269; *New-York Evening Post*, 25 Aug. 1827).

Alexander Phoenix (1778–1863), Ingraham's brother-in-law, was a New Jersey native who graduated from Columbia

College in 1795, became an attorney by 1803, and later replaced his brother Sidney Phoenix as a member of Ingraham, Phoenix & Nexsen. After the firm went bankrupt, he became a Congregational minister, moved to Massachusetts, and accepted a call in 1824 from a church in Chicopee. Phoenix moved to New Haven, Connecticut, in 1835, and finally to Harlem, New York, about 1841 (MiU-C: Phoenix Family Papers, including letters written from debtors' prison late in 1811, his 6 Nov. 1811 insolvency certificate from the New York City courts, and the 12 Jan. 1824 offer from a committee of the Church of Christ at Chicopee; Milton Halsey Thomas, *Columbia University Officers and Alumni 1754–1857* [1936], 116; *Longworth's New York Directory* [1803], 236; S. Bourne Jr., *A Sermon occasioned by the death of Rev. Alexander Phoenix* [1864]; New York *Independent*, 3 Sept. 1863).

William Nexsen, one of several contemporary New Yorkers of that name, was active as an auctioneer by 1803 (*Longworth's New York Directory* [1803], 225). John Redfield was a grocer in New York City in 1810 and filed an insolvency petition in the state courts the following year (*Longworth's New York Directory* [1810], 309; Albany *Balance, and State Journal*, 3 Sept. 1811).

The firm of Ingraham, Phoenix & Nexsen, auction and commission merchants and traders, was established in 1803. It declared bankruptcy in 1811 with losses totaling $467,547.61. All three principals were then committed to debtors' prison along with Redfield, who had become liable as surety for the company's customhouse bonds (MiU-C: Phoenix Family Papers, esp. Articles of Agreement establishing Ingraham, Phoenix & Nexsen, 15 Feb. 1803, and Full Account and List of Losses sustained, 11 Oct. 1811; New York *Columbian*, 10 Sept. 1811). They had their case brought BEFORE THE NATIONAL LEGISLATURE in a petition noting that the firm had prospered until the "present unfavorable state of the relations between this country and commercial nations of Europe" had caused them to lose "the whole of their private estates, and become corporately and individually insolvent" (*JS*, 5:57 [14 Feb. 1812]). The matter was referred to Albert Gallatin, whose report stated that the United States was owed $141,000 for "duties on merchandise imported, from the month of May, 1810, to the month of March, 1811"; that the firm had diverted this sum to other creditors; and that its principals along with their surety Redfield had accordingly "been imprisoned for want of bail at the suit of the United States." He concluded that his legal authority as treasury secretary to release prisoners indebted to the United States did not extend to Ingraham, Phoenix, and Nexsen, because they had not yet been formally arrested after the issuance of judgments on their revenue bonds, and that their failure to accord the United States its legal priority as a creditor also acted against them. Redfield not being subject to the latter concern, Gallatin suggested that he was a stronger candidate for legislative relief (*Report of the Secretary of the Treasury, on the Petition of Nathaniel G. Ingraham, and others, of New York. April 9th, 1812* [Washington, 1812]). An act releasing Redfield while reserving all government claims on his property passed on 24 Feb. 1813, and Ingraham, Phoenix, and Nexsen secured their release after a similar bill became law on 3 Mar. 1813 (*U.S. Statutes at Large*, 6:117, 119).

[1] Word interlined.

From Hugh Nelson

DEAR SIR, Washington Feby 13. 1812—

I must beg your pardon for having led you into an Error in my former letter concerning your manuscript. Your letter was recd at the

Capitol, where having no opportunity of examining my Books and papers brot from home, having intended to bring the manuscript with me, it was taken for granted that it was put up and brot here. But on examination it was found that I had left it at home in my desk. I have written on to Robert Smith a young Gentleman who lives with me who is at school, at Mr Maury's,[1] to whom I have also sent the Key of my desk, to get the manuscript from my desk and to deliver it to yourself forthwith—I have been in weekly expectation of finding a few days to run home: but the urging of Important business has prevented me.

With great respect[2] and esteem I remain, Dear sir, yr hbl st

HUGH NELSON

RC (DLC); endorsed by TJ as received 19 Feb. 1812 and so recorded in SJL.

[1] Preceding seven words interlined.
[2] Manuscript: "respct."

From Mathew Carey

SIR, Philada Feb. 14. 1812

I have recd Your favour of the 27th ult. & thank you sincerely for Your polite attention to my request. If Mr Milligan has the Parliamentary Manual in the press, I shall not interfere with him. I am, respectfully,

Your obt hble servt MATHEW CAREY

RC (MHi); at head of text: "Thomas Jefferson, Esqr"; endorsed by TJ as received 19 Feb. 1812 and so recorded in SJL.

To Samuel J. Harrison

SIR Monticello Feb. 14. 12.

Your favor of the 5th has been recieved by which I learn that the sale of my tobacco is closed by your acceptance of the offer in my former letter. with respect to the proposal to reduce the price of the stemmed tobo I do not remember whether that was done in our last year's bargain. if it was, it shall be done in the bargain of this year, my intention having been to sell this year on the same terms as the last, with only the more accomodated change in the dates of paiment. you would of course understand that my offer could extend only to my own part of the tobo not to that of the overseers, which is not quite an eighth, unless they chuse it. for that you must be so good as to enquire from themselves. I inclose you an order for the tob° and tender you the assurances of my respect & esteem

Th: Jefferson

PoC (MHi); at foot of text: "Mr Samuel J. Harrison"; endorsed by TJ. Enclosure not found.

In LAST YEAR'S BARGAIN, TJ sold Harrison his Bedford tobacco for "7.D. per ~~Cwt~~" (*MB*, 2:1263).

To John Melish

Sir Monticello Feb. 14. 12.

Your favor of Jan. 18. came duly to hand. I very willingly become a subscriber to your intended publication, judging from the table of contents, and your familiarity with the subjects treated of, that the work cannot fail to be useful to ourselves by pointing out advantageous pursuits not yet attended to, and to Great Britain by shewing what their ignorance and injustice have lost to them here, and laying open to their wiser successors the interests they yet may cherish by peace & justice, advantageously for both nations.[1] with respect to the probability of your obtaining subscriptions in this state I am less able to inform you than any other person, being chiefly confined at home by the natural effects of age. at Richmond I should expect many might be obtained; so also in the country, but so sparse as to render difficult the collection either of the signatures or the sums.

a good agent in Richmond, with which the whole state communicates, might do a good deal without going from home. with my wishes for your success accept the assurances of my respect.

Th: Jefferson

PoC (DLC); at foot of text: "Mr Mellish"; endorsed by TJ. Extract printed in Richmond *Enquirer*, 3 Apr. 1812, preceded by editor Thomas Ritchie's endorsement of Melish's upcoming publication and announcement that he was acting as Melish's agent in Richmond.

[1] Extract from *Enquirer* ends here.

To Henry Wheaton

Monticello Feb. 14. 1812.

Th: Jefferson presents his compliments to Dr Wheaton and his thanks for the Address he was so kind as to inclose him on the advancement in Medecine. having Little confidence in the theories of that Art, which change in their fashion with the Ladies caps & gowns, he has much in the facts it has established by observation. the experience of Physicians has proved that, in certain forms of disease; certain substances will restore order to the human system; and he doubts not that continued observation will enlarge the catalogue, and give relief to our posterity in cases wherein we are without it. the extirpation of the smallpox by vaccination, is an encouraging proof that the condition of man is susceptible of amelioration altho we are not able to fix it's extent. he salutes Dr Wheaton with esteem & respect.

PoC (DLC); dateline at foot of text.

From John B. Chandler

DEAR SIR Moble 15th Febuary 1812

I Rec^d a Letter from Mr Shoemaker Stating that thay Beeing som miss under Standing in the Settelment of your accounts I Cant Say what entreys mought Be in the Books but I Can Say that in the whole Time I was employd in Mr Shoemakers Business I Kneaver Knew any thing But Carcet[1] Entrey in his Books

I Shold be in in the Spring and If a berth cold be procourd in you mills I Shold be wondres hapey To embrace it as this cuntrey dose not Suit me as To helth

on my Way in I Shold do my Self the Pleasur of Callling on you and Seeing you as I have Som Private comunication to make to you which I have Know doubt will be Satisfacturey To you when you come to heere them.

I am Dear Sir your most obedent & Umble Servent

JN^O B. CHANDLER

RC (MHi); between dateline and salutation: "Thos Jefferson Esqr"; endorsed by TJ as received 25 Mar. 1812 from Mobile and so recorded in SJL.

On 12 Oct. 1807 TJ paid $40 to "Chandler & Shoemaker" for "work on dam" (*MB*, 2:1213).

[1] Chandler may have intended "correct."

To James Leitch

Feb. 15. 12.

Cloaths for the bearer Burwell, such as he shall chuse.

TH:J.

RC (ViCMRL, on deposit ViU: TJP); dateline beneath signature; written on a small scrap; adjacent to signature and dateline: "M[r] Leitch." Not recorded in SJL.

Burwell Colbert (1783–ca. 1862), butler, painter, and glazier, became one of TJ's most trusted slaves. When and how he acquired the surname Colbert, which TJ seems never to have used, is unknown. He was the son of Betty Brown and the grandson of Elizabeth Hemings. Colbert began his working life in the Monticello nailery, where he rose to foreman. He received training as a painter and glazier and thereafter did interior and exterior work at Monticello and Poplar Forest. Beginning during TJ's presidency, he was the head house servant at Monticello, in which capacity he supervised the housemaids, porters, and waiters, acted himself as chief waiter, and kept the keys to the cellar storerooms. During TJ's retirement Colbert was also his personal servant and accompanied TJ on his trips to Poplar Forest. He was one of two slaves to whom TJ began paying an annual $20 gratuity in 1812, and TJ sometimes borrowed money from him. Colbert married his first cousin Critta, the daughter of Nance Hemings and the property of TJ's son-in-law Thomas Mann Randolph. They had eight children before her death in 1819. TJ freed Colbert in the codicil to his will and gave him $300 to help establish him as a painter and glazier. At the sale that dispersed TJ's estate in 1827, Colbert purchased a mule, engravings of TJ and Lafayette, and household wares. He subsequently worked at the University of Virginia and for several of TJ's friends and family members (Stanton, *Free Some Day*, esp. 120–5, 143, 155–9; Betts, *Farm Book*, pt. 1, 30; *MB*, esp. 2:968n, 1277; TJ's List of Gratuity Payments to Burwell, [ca. 14 Apr. 1826]; TJ's will and codicil, 16–17 Mar. 1826; Sarah N. Randolph to Cornelia J. Randolph, 7 Dec. 1865 [NcU: Nicholas P. Trist Papers]).

To Harmer Gilmer

DEAR SIR Monticello Feb. 16. 12.

I have been for some time desirous of getting a few particular plants from mr M[c]Mahon, the gardener, of Philadelphia, which can only be removed at this season, & by the stage, as no other conveyance is quick enough. but without the care & patronage of some passenger they would never get to me. understanding that you will be returning to our neighborhood immediately, & by the stage, I cannot deny myself the appeal to your goodness to recieve them from mr M[c]Mahon & take charge of them in the stage. they are but few, & small, & will be packed in moss in a small close box, so as to give no other trouble but to see them removed with your baggage from stage to stage. as they may add to the charge of your own baggage, the cost shall be reimbursed on your arrival here. if you are so good as to take this charge for me, it would be necessary for you to call on mr M[c]Mahon and inform him of the day of your departure, that he may know when to take the plants out of the ground, as it would increase their risk to take them sooner than necessary. I hope the rarity of such an opportunity will excuse me for imposing this trouble on you. Accept the assurance of my esteem & respect TH: JEFFERSON

PoC (MHi); at foot of text: "M[r] Harmer Gilmer"; endorsed by TJ.

Harmer Gilmer (1787–1812), the son of TJ's friend George Gilmer, of Pen Park in Albemarle County, was a medical student at the University of Pennsylvania (*PTJ*, 12:454; Woods, *Albemarle*, 207; Archibald Alexander, *A Discourse occasioned By the Burning of the Theatre in the City of Richmond, Virginia, on the twenty-sixth of December, 1811* [Philadelphia, 1812], iii; Albemarle Co. Will Book, 5:221–2).

To Bernard McMahon

SIR Monticello Feb. 16. 12.

In your letter of March last, as on various other occasions, you were so kind as to offer to supply my wants in the article of plants, and in my answer of April 8. I mentioned a few articles, as also the mode of conveyance, which could not occur till about this time. an opportunity now presents itself of the most fortunate kind. mr Harmer Gilmer, a student of medecine now in Philadelphia, and my neighbor, will be setting out on his return to us very soon after you recieve this. he will come in the stage and will, I am sure, take charge of any small box you may be so good as to put under his care. I write to him on this subject. never expecting so good an opportunity again, & so seasonable a one, I will still add a little to my former wants so as to put me in possession once for all of every thing to which my views extend, & which I do not now possess.

seeds. Auricula. double Anemone. double Carnation. Mignonette. eggplant. Sea Kale

bulbs. Crown imperial. double Ranunculus.

plants. Hudson & Chili strawberries. fine gooseberries. Cape jasmine.

trees. Cedar of Lebanon. balm of Gilead fir. Cork tree. Spanish Chesnut or Maronnier of y[e] French.

one plant of the Cape jessamine, & one or two of the trees will suffice. the seeds may come in a letter packet by mail; the bulbs, plants & trees (if the latter be chosen small) in a small & light box, packed in moss which mr Gilmer will take charge of: and if you will be so kind as to inform me of the amount in the letter by the mail, it shall be promptly remitted. mr Gilmer will be so near his departure as to require immediate dispatch.

Among other plants I recieved from M. Thouin, was the Brassica sempervirens, or Sprout Kale. one plant only vegetated, the 1st year, but this winter I have 20. or 30. turned out for seed. I consider it among the most valuable garden plants. it stands our winter unprotected, furnishes a vast crop of sprouts from the beginning of December through the whole winter, which are remarkably sweet and delicious. I inclose you a few seeds, a part of what the original plant gave us; the next year I hope to have a plenty. I send it because I do not percieve by your catalogue that you have it. Accept my esteem & respect

TH: JEFFERSON

PoC (DLC); at foot of text: "Mr McMahon"; endorsed by TJ. Dft (DLC: TJ Papers, 192:34238); undated; subjoined to RC of McMahon to TJ, 10 Mar. 1811; consisting of plant and seed list: "dble Anemone. Auricula dble Carnation
dble Ranunculus. Crown Imperial
Mignonette.
sea kale egg plant
Chili Hudson strawberries
Gooseberries
Cape Jasmine
Cork tree. Cedar of Lebanon
Balm of Gilead fir. Spanish chesnut. Maronnier
seeds. dble Anemone
Auricula.
dble Carnation
Mignonette
Sea Kale
egg plant
bulbs. dble Ranunculus
Crown imperial.
plants. Hudson } strawberries
Chili }
gooseberries
Cape Jasmine
Cedar of Lebanon
balm of Gilead fir
Cork tree
Spanish Chesnut. Maronnier."

TJ received seeds of SPROUT KALE from André Thoüin in the spring of 1811 and cultivated the plant on the lower platform of his garden by the following year (Betts, *Garden Book*, 469 and plate 33 opp. p. 474).

To John M. Perry

SIR Monticello Feb. 16. 12.

Mr McGruder has written to me urgently on the subject of the plank due him: I must therefore press you to execute that contract immediately, that I may at length be done with it. he says he is ready to return the money on recieving the plank, and as I presume, on his recieving the stocks from you, as he is to do the sawing himself. be so good as to let me know what I may say to him. Accept my best wishes.

TH: JEFFERSON

PoC (MHi); at foot of text: "Mr John Perry"; endorsed by TJ.

From John Harvie

DEAR SIR February 17th 1812[1] Woodford County Kentucky

The dreadful blow which has thinned my family has occasioned a remissness in my writing to you; but your goodness, I know, will forgive the omission in the cause, which has produced it. Perhaps this letter will not reach you by the time that your claim against me is due. I hope however that a short procrastination of payment will occasion you no sensible inconvenience I have written to Doct. Brockenbrough of Richmond who is my agent in Virginia that I should request you to forward on my note to him for payment. As communications from this country by mail are extremely liable to miscarriage I have thought this the most eligible mode of discharging the debt and I hope that it meets with your concurrence. As you have most probably an agent at Richmond, and at all events almost daily opportunities of communication to that place I inferred that the fixing upon it for the cancellation of your claim would not thwart any of your arrangements Under that impression I now ask the favour of your sending on the note to Doct. Brockenbrough for payment. As soon as that has taken place an answer acknowledgeing its occurrence would be most acceptable to yours most respectfully

JOHN HARVIE

RC (MHi); at foot of text: "Thomas Jefferson Esqr"; mistakenly endorsed by TJ as a letter of 12 Feb. received 9 Mar. 1812 and so recorded in SJL.

The DREADFUL BLOW Harvie sustained was the loss of a brother, a sister, and a niece in the Richmond Theatre fire of 26 Dec. 1811 (Marion Dewoody Pettigrew, *Marks-Barnett Families and Their Kin* [1939], 178, 179; Richmond *Enquirer*, 31 Dec. 1811).

[1] Remainder of dateline beneath signature.

From Thomas W. Maury

DEAR SIR. Albemarle 18th February 1812

Excuse if you please, the liberty I take, in introducing to your acquaintance the Bearer Robert N. Smith, who is the nephew & ward of The Honble Hugh Nelson, and charged by that gentleman with some communication to you

I am very respectfully Sir.

yr mo: obt THOs W. MAURY

RC (MHi); at foot of text: "Thomas Jefferson Esqr Monticello"; endorsed by TJ as received 19 Feb. 1812 and so recorded in SJL.

Thomas Walker Maury (ca. 1780–1842), attorney and educator, was admitted to the bar in 1800. He was appointed a county magistrate in 1816 and represented Albemarle County in two sessions of the Virginia House of Delegates, 1815–17. TJ attended the school of his grandfather, Rev. James Maury, and some of TJ's grandchildren attended the younger Maury's school. He was secretary of the commission that met at Rockfish Gap in 1818 to choose a location for the new University of Virginia. Late in life Maury lost his estate to his creditors (Woods, *Albemarle*, 269, 377, 381; *MACH* 18 [1959/60]: 42; Leonard, *General Assembly*, 281, 285; *MB*, 2:1377, 1379; *Albemarle County Cemeteries*, 3:152; *Richmond Enquirer*, 8 Mar. 1842).

Robert Nelson Smith (1794–1877), a son of Augustine Smith and Alice Grymes Page Smith, was raised by Hugh Nelson in Albemarle County. In 1815 he married Mary Margaret Fry, also of Albemarle, and two years later the couple moved to Kentucky, where Smith headed a school near Louisville. In 1844 he moved to a farm in Lafayette County, Missouri (*Memoir of Col. Joshua Fry, sometime Professor in William and Mary College, Virginia* [1880], 49; *VMHB* 23 [1915]: 89).

SJL records receipt on 6 Aug. 1811 of an undated letter to TJ, not found, from Maury's uncle Benjamin Maury.

From Francis Adrian Van der Kemp

Sir! Olden barneveld (N. york State) Febr. 18. 1812.

I do not search for an apologÿ, in sending you included imperfect Sketch of a work, which I ardently wished, to see executed bÿ a masterlÿ hand If to former favours—which can not be obliterated by me—you would join another by condescending to gratifÿ me with your opinion and Strictures I should feel myself ÿet higher indebted to your Patronage—while—I should consider—to have not Laboured in vain—if one of your[1] literarÿ friends—here or in Europe was induced by you, to undertake and discharge this arduous task.

Manÿ years past you honoured with a flattering approbation—a few loose Philosophical hints—on some points of Nat: Hist—discussed by you and the Count de Bufton—send to you by my frend the Chanc. Livingston. Encouraged by the remarks of my Correspondents—I have retouched these so often—that it is now a work of considerable bulk by what it was then. Did I dare to presume, that I could once more submit it to your judgment, without a too great Sacrifice of your precious time, I would endeavour—to give it a revision in the course of this year—altho by the uncouth garb in which it appears—I have not a distant prospect of publishing.

Permit me to assure you, that I remain with high regard and consideration

Sir! Your most obed: and obliged Servant

Fr. Adr. van der Kemp.

RC (DLC); dateline adjacent to signature; endorsed by TJ as received 1 Mar. 1812 and so recorded in SJL.

Francis Adrian Van der Kemp (1752–1829) was born at Kampen in the Netherlands. He served in the Dutch military, attended the University of Groningen, 1770–73, left the Dutch Reformed church in the latter year, and graduated in 1775 from a Baptist seminary in Amsterdam. Van der Kemp actively supported both the Dutch and American patriot movements. He was imprisoned in 1787 for his antimonarchical activities and immigrated to the United States in May 1788 carrying letters of introduction from TJ. Van der Kemp became a naturalized citizen in 1789. A Federalist, he corresponded regularly with John Adams and DeWitt Clinton. In 1805 Van der Kemp was elected to the American Philosophical Society. He settled at Olden Barneveld (now Barneveld), Oneida County, New York, where he farmed, served as a justice of the peace and master in chancery, and was briefly a federal revenue surveyor. He and TJ exchanged ideas on religion and the writing of history. In 1816 Van der Kemp persuaded TJ to let him publish anonymously in an English Unitarian periodical the latter's "Syllabus," an outline of his understanding of the doctrines of Jesus. Van der Kemp himself published a number of shorter works and translated a large body of early New York Dutch records, the manuscript of which was lost in a fire after his death. His grander designs for publishing expansive historical works did not come to fruition (*ANB*; *DAB*; Harry F. Jackson, *Scholar in the Wilderness: Francis Adrian Van der Kemp* [1963]; Helen Lincklaen Fairchild, *Francis Adrian Van der Kemp, 1752–1829: An Autobiography, Together with Extracts from his Correspondence* [1903]; *PTJ*, 12:632–3, 655, 656, 16:285; APS, Minutes, 18 Jan. 1805 [MS in PPAmP]).

Robert R. Livingston sent Van der Kemp's LOOSE PHILOSOPHICAL HINTS to TJ on 29 Mar. 1801, describing them as an "essay" by a "clergyman of much learning" (*PTJ*, 33:497–8).

[1] Manuscript: "yuer."

ENCLOSURE

Francis Adrian Van der Kemp's Synopsis of a Proposed Book

Contemplated work[1]

"Moral and Physical causes of the Revolutionarÿ Spirit, in the latter part of the 18th centurÿ, with their probable issue on both Continents

Ardua quæ pulcra"

(Rough outlines dotted)[2]

General observations (Preliminarÿ)

Previous Situation[3] of Europe and America 1750

General Sketch of Europe—Since its invasion bÿ the Northern Nations.[4]

Establishment of the Feudal System

Its[5] extent and ramifications—even thro the church-establishments. Its nature Strength,[6] means, advantages, abuses, consequences. Its partial overthrow. Means, communes, corporations.[7] Its consequences in various parts of Europe, mediate, immediate—in England on the Continent.

Henrÿ vii—Ferdinand & Isabella—Louis xii[8] Henrÿ iv.

Sullÿ—Richelieu—Mazarin.

Parliaments—Nat: Assemblys[9]—England—France—Spain
origin—design—power—existence[10]
Coroll:
Humbling of Vassals—increase of the Power of the People—
In the cities—countrÿ.
Resurrection of Letters—Birth of the Spirit of inquirÿ
Its causes—Monasteries—Learned Greeks in Italy—Lorenzo
di Medicis—discoverÿ of the Pandects—effects[11]
consequences—Italy—Germanÿ—France—England.
Lord Bacon—Newton—Leibnitz—Wolff.
Reformation
occasion—means—Success. Its consequences
Italÿ—Germanÿ—France—England.
Discoverÿ of America—Doubling of the cape the good Hope—
circumnavigation of the globe
Colonisation—its nature, in what different from that of the Ancients—
manner—views—consequences
Commerce—Gold—Silver—Banks—Public credit—Bills of exchange
View of Europe under Louis xiv. xv. Cromwell—William iii—Anne
Louvois—Colbert—Walpole—Alberoni.
State of Religion—morals—Sciences.
Papal[12] Power—Since the reformation till the annihilation of the Jesuits
Pope—clergÿ—mendicants—Jesuits
Benedict xiv. Clement xiv—Bourbons—Austria
Bavaria
Protestants—hierarchÿ
continent[13] calvinists—Bern—Geneva—Holland[14] Lutherans[15]
Saxonÿ[16]
England—Episcopacÿ—Puritans—Dissenters Prognostic.
Tolerance Advocates—principles[17]
Morals—Sciences—men of Lettres—Views—efforts—Success
General Observations[18]
Civilians (Publicists)
Grotius—Puffendorf—Burlamaqui—Du Vattel—Bynkershoek
Conring—Heineccius.
Eccles: Law—Erastus—Hobbes—Thomasius—Boehmer[19]
General bent on the continent of Europe, to imitate French fashions, manners, Language, admire their Literature, and adopt their principles.
Spirit of Philosophising and levelling in Europe. Its Spread—its disguises
France—Germanÿ—England.
Libertÿ of the press—Advocates—principles—abuses—means
Particular—Typographÿ
Modern Philosophÿ
Oeconomists. Principles, views, methodical plans, means, Success.
La Riviere—Mirabeau—Vauban—St. Pierre
Ephemerides—Cadastre—Victor Amadeus 1732 Dooms-day Book
Encÿclopedists D'Alembert, Diderot, Helvetius—&c.
views means—open—clandestine, zeal, intrigues—intolerance.
Protectors—Frederic ii—Catherine ii Leopold &c.[20]

Generality of the revolutionarÿ Seeds in both Continents. Proofs
Stupend[21] effects, above human conception, execution, calculation.[22]
Proofs.
Particular consideration of the principal hotbeds—America—France
their proprietÿ[23]
Coroll[24] Proofs of an overruling providence.
Diffusion of incorrect information among the lower classes in the cities—without an adequate counterpoise of an improvement in morals
Prevalence of Political disquisitions and discussions
Studÿ of antiq: first Nation: then Eccles: civil in everÿ countrÿ—followed by that of Nat: Historÿ—Natu: rights of men—origin of Society—Government &c
Montesquieu—Rousseau—Condorcet—Turgot—Mablÿ—Adams.
Knowledge of the English Constitution—Books
Locke—de Lolme—Sidneÿ—Burgh—Price
Commerce
England—Holland—France—North of Europe:
Consequences
Abuse of Power: Exertions to extend it: Continent—England
Loose principles in Religion and morals
Sapping of the throne and church—confounding ranks
ridiculing orders
Proofs—England—continent.
Clubs—(Political)—of the middle and lower classes.
Revolutionarÿ Hotbeds in miniature—[25]
Mercenarÿ writers, anonÿmous Pamphleteers
Diminution of pomp and Splendour of Royalty—replaced by confidence in a numerous Armÿ
Standing armies
Origin—means—final tendencÿ—without, within—
Consequences on the mass of the Nation—Libertÿ—Population—commerce—agriculture—Finances
"Pectore Si fratris gladium"[26]
Diminished influence of the Clergÿ—causes—consequences
Nobility—
Dependance on court favour—by which even the Shadow of an intermediate power between the King and its Subjects was removed.
Increased Luxe and corruption of morals—Proofs
Insolence of the common People
General view of Europe in 1763—England—France—Prussia, Russia &c
Peace between the powers engaged in the 7 years war,[27]
Revolutions
Geneve—
Situation from the middle of the 18th centurÿ—the intentions yet good, the manners[28] visiblÿ declining—Its causes—means.
Factions—France—Aristocratic[29] Swiss cantons—Mediation
Venice—
Since long in a State—approaching dissolution—causes means annihilated without resistance.
Genoa—Tuscanÿ[30] Lucca[31] Lombardÿ Sicilys[32]

Swisserland Dissentions—civil—religious
depopulation—causes—consequences—
French influence—dismembrement Mediatorship[33]
Sweden Dissentions—Vergennes—Revolution—Sudermanland
Expulsion of Gustavus—Bernadotte[34]
Corsica Struggle—conquest.[35]
Poland Dissidents—confederates—mediating Powers—Partition 1772[36]—
Catharine ii Frederic ii Maria Theresia
Revolutionarÿ trial[37]—issue 1793
Progress of the revolutionarÿ Spirit among crowned heads.
Pretext of resusutating the Republics of Greece.
Catherine ii Joseph ii
Russia—Tartars—Prognostic[38]
Revolutionarÿ Spirit in America
First Congress in Albanÿ 1754 a Federal representative[39] Government in Embryo.
causes—pretended—remote—occasional—efficient
origine—progress—views of both parties—Great Brittain
N. America—
France Holland
Situation of France
Louis xvi[40]—Power of the crown—Parliaments—Opposition
Lawÿers (gens de robe) Lettres de cachet—Vergennes
Finances Henrÿ iv Louis xiv. xvi—Sullÿ—Colbert—Neckar
Its causes[41]—means of redress—issue.
Clergÿ—Situation—arch-bishop of[42] Toulouse—Toleration
Edict of 1786.
Nobility—numerous—Duc's D'Epernon—Sullÿ Henrÿ IV
Pedigrees in the Royal Librarÿ 1785—La maison du Roi—
Battles of Lawfeld—Rouceux.
Luxurious indolence
Enormous civil List:[43] Prodigality of the court—Princes
Ministers—cupidity of the Courtiers—influence of women—
Pusillanimity of the best part of the Communalty[44] in the beginning of the contest.
Profligacÿ of morals in the Capital—Populace—Police
Remedies—means—inefficacÿ by their want in energÿ proprietÿ
inadequacÿ
Views of the court and Nation at the origin of the American Contest.[45]
Revolution in Holland—
Situation in 1700–1748—Stadhouderat—William[46] V—Louis of Brunswick Views—Armÿ W. India Regiments[47] Navÿ Amsterdam
Van Berckal 1766–1775. militarÿ Jurisdiction Extent—abolishment.
van der Capellen—Scotch-Brigade
corvees—abolishment—opposition—armed volunteers—clubs organised—illimited convoys—Naval Stores—French[48] intrigues
La Vauguion—Berenger Brittish—Yorke.
Provisional Treaty with N. America. 1782
The Scheldt—Peace bought by moneÿ, adviced—Shared by France.

Factions—animosity—dreams as if France and Great-Brittain courted, disputed her alliance, while the only question was, who Should become their master.

Germanÿ

weakness of its chief—Power of the Members—Imperial capitulations vain formularies. convulsions—Symptoms—dissolution—Confederacÿ of the Rhine.

America. Individuals French, Dutch, German, Poles—

Peace 1783—American Independence—[49] Federal Constitution causes[50]

Troubles in Braband

causes—Suppression of monasteries—Edict of Toleration Joseph ii Clergÿ—van Eupen—van der Noot issue—[51]

General view of Europe[52] in 1783

Progress of the Dutch Revolution—Prussia—England—France—Stadholderian, Aristocratic—Democratic Faction views—means—arms issue 1787. coup de grace 1795 Revolutionarÿ mumerÿ—death mockerÿ—remotion of the carcase—Burÿal 1 apr. 1810—

Java Daendals conquest. 1811[53]

Revolution in France 1787.

Assembly of Notables 1789. church Estates declared Nat: property—States General—Nat: Assemblÿ—Double representation of the Commons—Dissention among the 3 orders—fluctuating policÿ of the court—Rëunion of the 3 orders in one Deliberative Assemblÿ—Exclusion of the 3^d^ order (Tier Etat) from their usual meetings. Nat: Assemblÿ at Tennis-court oath "not to Separate—till a constitution was formed".—issue—

Revolutionarÿ Progress—issue

Guarding—arresting—imprisoning—beheading of the king—familÿ—massacres.[54]

Constitution of 1793—Gobel—Arch-Bishop of Paris abjures the Christian Religion—abolition of the Christian æra

Factions—Feuillans—Mountain—Girondists—Jacobins—

Sanguinarÿ government—Robespierre

victories—views—means

Directorÿ—Consuls—Emperor—conquests—means—end

Interior Situation of the Empire[55]

Fall of the Ecclesiastical[56] Powers and Hierarchÿ

Papal 1798 Roman Republic Pius vii 1802 concordat genius—views—final overthrow

Protestants Holland—abolishing of the Nat: church 1796[57]

England—Hoadleÿ &c[58]

Portugal

Internal Situation[59]—Foreign relations—with Great-Brittain Since the Treatÿ of John Methuen in 1703—with France Since 1793. Treaty of Madrid 1801–1804—Taleyrand's diplomatic engines—1808—Junot's invasion—Flight of the Royal familÿ—Brazils—conquest expulsion of the French—issue

Spain

Bourbon race of Faineants—Situation comparative under Philip ii with that of Philip v Charles IV—internal—external

Griefs—resources—Ferdinand vii Napoleon—Struggle[60]
Revolutionarÿ attempt in Peru—Inca Tupac Amaru—issue
execution 1781—New insurrection 1801 in the plains of Riombamba
South-America (Spanish)
Situation in 1812[61]
Effects and Consequences in Both Hemispheres
Europe—French Empire—Continent—Great-Brittain
America United States—South-America—W. Indies
Asia Indostan
Africa Slave trade—Missionaries—Cape the good Hope—Europ: Settlement[62]
General Observations
Religion—manners—Sciences—commerce—Population
Conclusion. Situation in 181[63]

MS (DLC: TJ Papers, 195:34711–2); written entirely in Van der Kemp's hand on both sides of two folio sheets; undated. Printed anonymously in Cambridge, Mass., *General Repository and Review* 4 [1813]: 390–7; at head of text, with brackets in original: "Sketch of a desired work. [We insert the following at the request of a very respectable correspondent, who says—'If this sketch deserve your approbation, I shall be gratified if you procure it a place, under the article of Intelligence, in the next number of the Repository. I am tired of copying it, and in my opinion it would be a valuable work if well executed.']."

ARDUA QUÆ PULCHRA: "Things that are beautiful are difficult to achieve." PECTORE SI FRATRIS GLADIUM: the full quotation is from Lucan's *Pharsalia* lines 376–8: "Pectore si fratris gladium iuguloque parentis Condere me iubeas plenaeque in viscera partu Coniugis, invita peragam tamen omnia dextra" ("if you bid me bury my sword in my brother's breast or my father's throat or the body of my teeming wife, I will perform it all, even if my hand be reluctant") (Lucan, *The Civil War [Pharsalia]*, trans. J. D. Duff, Loeb Classical Library [1928, repr. 1988], 30, 31).

[1] *General Repository*: "SKETCH OF A DESIRED WORK."

[2] Parenthetical phrase not in *General Repository*.

[3] Reworked from "Station."

[4] *General Repository* here adds "Value and necessity of studying the annals, records, ballads, romanzas, and other writings of the middle age."

[5] *General Repository* here adds "origin."

[6] Manuscript: "Strenght."

[7] Word preceded in *General Repository* by "gilden."

[8] *General Repository*: "Louis XI."

[9] *General Repository* here adds "Cortes."

[10] *General Repository* here adds "fate."

[11] *General Repository* here adds "mediate, immediate."

[12] Word preceded in *General Repository* by "Continent."

[13] Word not in *General Repository*.

[14] *General Repository* here adds "Calvin, Synod of Dort."

[15] *General Repository* here adds "Denmark."

[16] *General Repository* here adds "Brandenburg."

[17] *General Repository* here adds "continent; England; Locke, Noodt, Bayle, Barbeyrac, Goodricke."

[18] *General Repository* here adds "with regard to religion, commerce, learning, politics."

[19] *General Repository* here adds "Vander Marck," followed by a new section on "Diplomatic history. Treaties of Munster, Nymeguen, Ryswick, Utrecht, that of the Pyrenees, Tilsit. Prospect of a general solid treaty; its basis. Mabillon, Montfaucon, Muratin, Leibnitz, Datt, Vertot, Dumont."

[20] *General Repository* here adds "British share in the general corruption; Bolingbroke, Hume, &c."

[21] *General Repository*: "Stupendous."

[22] Preceding two words not in *General Repository*.

[23] Word replaced in *General Repository* by "peculiar influence."

[24] Manuscript: "Corall." *General Repository*: "Corollary."

[25] Preceding four words interlined in manuscript and omitted in *General Repository*.

[26] Preceding four words not in *General Repository*.

[27] *General Repository* here adds "*Revolutionary spirit;* its developements. Man—a rational, social, moral being. Scholium. Corollary. Progress of the human mind. Social compact; its basis, requisites, boundaries; unalienable rights—safety of life, security of property, civil and religious liberty. Theories to obtain and secure these possessions in the highest degree of perfection to all the associated. Means, obstacles. *Contour* of the *Tableau.* Its parts; executive, legislative, judicial; tribunal of correction. Their cement, ornaments, means of preservation; symptoms of disease, danger, remedies, crisis, encouragement, prospect."

[28] *General Repository*: "morals."

[29] Word in front of "France" in *General Repository*.

[30] *General Repository* here adds "Leopold."

[31] *General Repository* here adds "Sardinia."

[32] *General Repository* here adds "St. Marino."

[33] *General Repository* here adds "Denmark; revolution in 1660, Acta Regia, present situation."

[34] *General Repository* here adds "Peace with England. Acknowledgment of Ferdinand VII. of Spain."

[35] *General Repository* here adds "Paoli, Marboeuf."

[36] *General Repository*: "1792."

[37] *General Repository* here adds "Kosciousco."

[38] *General Repository* here adds "Project of an armed neutrality; its conception, birth, and death."

[39] Manuscript: "representativ."

[40] *General Repository*: "Louis XV."

[41] *General Repository* here adds "of their derangement."

[42] *General Repository* here adds "Aix; Autun."

[43] *General Repository* here adds "golden book."

[44] *General Repository*: "commonalty."

[45] Preceding five words replaced in *General Repository* by "beginning of the American revolution."

[46] *General Repository* here adds "IV."

[47] *General Repository* here adds "commerce."

[48] *General Repository* here adds "influence and."

[49] *General Repository* here adds "Washington."

[50] *General Repository* here adds "morbid features, cure, prognostic. Its finances, Hamilton; the United States considered as a naval power, its history, its prospects, as a commarcial [commercial], its regulations; as a continental power, its prospects, interests. Its manufacturing exertions, prospects, obstacles, Robert R. Livingston, Humphreys, Custis. Shoals and beacons. Its literary state, wants, means."

[51] Section on Brabant not in *General Repository*.

[52] *General Repository* here adds "and America."

[53] Preceding four words not in *General Repository*.

[54] *General Repository* here adds "general massacres, Paris, in the country."

[55] *General Repository* here adds "external relations. Sweden, Denmark, Prussia; war in 1812–13."

[56] Word replaced in *General Repository* by "Papal."

[57] *General Repository* here adds "Saxony, toleration, edict."

[58] *General Repository* here adds "dissenters, catholic question" and inserts new section: "*Russia.* Situation, internal, relative, at the peace of Tilsit in 1805, Alexander, peace with England, acknowledgment of Ferdinand VII, war with Napoleon, treaty with Prussia, 1813. *England.* Situation, constitution, house of Stuart, Hanover; power;—priding herself in her strength as long she remains shielded by Providence; war with North

America, its cause, 1812, motives, interests of both nations."

[59] *General Repository* here adds "revolution in 1640."

[60] *General Repository* here adds "Lord Wellington, issue."

[61] Section from "South America (Spanish)" to this point replaced in *General Repository* by "Caraccas, Buenos-Ayres, Carthagena, Mexico; situation in 1813."

[62] Preceding two words not in *General Repository*.

[63] Final digit in year canceled and illegible. *General Repository*: "18**."

To Edward Gantt

DEAR DOCTOR Monticello Feb. 19. 12

Your's of Jan. 21. came by our last post, & I have with pleasure forwarded your application to the President. your letter gave me the first information of your removal to the Westward, and I learned from it with real concern the circumstances which had induced it. on my going to live in Washington, my first enquiries were into the mode of practice of the Physicians there, of whom I should of course find it necessary to employ one sometimes. I did not ask the public opinion, but merely the facts of their practice. the result was an unhesitating preference of yourself, tho' then equally unknown to me personally as the others, and I never found cause to doubt the correctness of my preference. I can add that your leaving that residence afterwards gave me very sincere concern. as you carried with you my high esteem and respect, so my cordial wishes attend you in your new situation, that you may find it as advantageous as your worth and skill have a right to command. Accept my affectionate and respectful salutations. TH: JEFFERSON

PoC (MHi); at foot of text: "Doct^{r} Gantt"; endorsed by TJ.

Edward Gantt (ca. 1741–1837), physician, was born in Prince Georges County, Maryland, and graduated from the College of New Jersey (later Princeton University) in 1762. He studied medicine at the universities of Edinburgh and Leiden, receiving an M.D. from the latter in 1767. In 1790 Gantt owned twenty-three slaves at a plantation in his native county that he inherited from his father in 1785. Later he moved to Georgetown and was attending physician at the President's House from 1801 until about 1806. Gantt worked with TJ to introduce and encourage smallpox vaccination. He spent his last years in Kentucky (*Princetonians, 1748–68*, pp. 377–8; *BDML*, 1:342; Gantt to TJ, 17 Aug. 1801 [DLC]; *MB*, 2:1118–9, 1144; Silvio A. Bedini, *Thomas Jefferson: Statesman of Science* [1990], 311–4).

Gantt's missing letter to TJ of JAN. 21., recorded in SJL as received from Louisville, Kentucky, on 15 Feb. 1812, evidently contained his APPLICATION for a military appointment for his son (TJ to James Madison, 19 Feb. 1812; Madison to TJ, 6 Mar. 1812).

To James Madison

Dear Sir Monticello Feb. 19. 12.

Your's of the 12th has been duly recieved. I have much doubted whether, in case of a war, Congress would find it practicable to do their part of the business. that a body containing 100. lawyers in it, should direct the measures of a war is, I fear, impossible; and that thus that member of our constitution, which is it's bulwark, will prove to be an impracticable one from it's cacoethes loquendi. it may be doubted how far it has the power, but I am sure it has not the resolution, to reduce the right of talking to practicable limits.

I inclose you a letter from Foronda. you may be willing to see what part he takes in the proceedings in Spain. if you have time & inclination to read his folletos, papelles & papelitos, I will send them to you. I have not yet looked into them.

Altho' I reject many applications to communicate petitions for office, yet some lay hold of the heart, or from other circumstances cannot be declined. but in the crowd of military appointments perhaps there may be less objection to communicate them. the inclosed letter from old Doctr Gantt is one of these cases. you knew him personally & his merit; his letter will inform you of his misfortunes and his virtuous anxieties for his family. as I can add nothing to your knolege of his case & the information of the letter, I shall leave his application on those grounds and conclude with the tribute of my constant affection & respect Th: Jefferson

RC (DLC: Madison Papers, Rives Collection); torn at seal, with portions of two words supplied from PoC; at foot of text: "The President of the US." PoC (DLC); endorsed by TJ. Enclosures: (1) Valentín de Foronda to TJ, 30 Nov. 1811. (2) Edward Gantt to TJ, 21 Jan. 1812 (see TJ to Gantt, 19 Feb. 1812, and note).

TJ misrecorded Madison's letter of 7 Feb. 1812 in SJL as one of the 12th. cacoethes loquendi: "passion for speaking." folletos, papelles & papelitos: "pamphlets, papers, and scraps."

To John B. Magruder

Sir Monticello Feb. 19. 12.

I did not recieve your letter of Jan. 27. till the 15th inst. I immediately wrote to mr Perry pressing a performance of his contract without further delay. I inclose you his answer and hope he will do what he therein promises. Accept the assurances of my esteem & respect.

Th: Jefferson

PoC (MHi); at foot of text: "M[r] Magruder"; endorsed by TJ. Enclosure: John M. Perry to TJ, 18 Feb. 1812, not found, but recorded in SJL as received from Albemarle the same day.

A letter of 23 Apr. 1812 from John M. Perry to TJ, not found, is recorded in SJL as received from Charlottesville the same day. For a sense of its possible contents, see TJ's 19 Apr. 1812 notes printed at his 20 Jan. 1810 letter to Perry.

To Lancelot Minor

SIR Monticello Feb. 19. 12.

The letter which you mention to have written about ten days ago has not yet been recieved. that of the 16th by mr Sea came to hand last night. I will first observe in answer to your enquiries, that the personal property of the estate; and especially that which is liable to waste may, & ought to be sold without waiting the probat of the will. this may be done by any agent of the estate, but particularly by one named an executor. M[rs] Marks has been ill of a fever 3. or 4. days, but former conversations with her, with a slight one on the receipt of your letter have put me fully into possession of her opinions & wishes. we both think the whole personal property except the negroes[1] should be sold immediately, either for cash or credit as you think best, the debtors & creditors be called on by advertisement or otherwise to give in their accounts duly proven, and that those whose demands are admitted should be induced if possible to accept assignments of the bonds given for the property sold <u>in full satisfaction</u> of their debts. the object of all this is to close the business, and relieve you from further trouble within as short a time as possible. the tob[o] had certainly better be prized and sent to mr Anderson in Richm[d] for sale as you propose. we think the negroes should remain to take care of things till the sale & then come up here. if you will be so good as to inform me of the day of sale, I will send for them within a day or two after. there will be no impropriety in sending them out of the county before the Probat as they can as well be appraised here as there. I would by all means advise a summons to be served on Cap[t] Paine, witness to the will, and to make this a proper foundation for an attachment, should he not obey the summons, it would be well to tender him the legal allowance for his attendance, which I believe is 53. cents, by the person who serves the summons. he may not perhaps be aware that if the will should fail to be proved and the devisee thereby lose the land or other property, the whole value of them will be recoverable & will be demanded from him. the inhumanity of refusing testimony in the case of the dead, would make it a duty to enforce this. until the will is proved it would be useless for mrs Marks to go to qualify as executrice. she will do it the first court after probat. her qualifying, as it will constitute her a legal defendant to any suit which a claimant might wish to bring, will confirm & assume on herself all our acts done with her approbation and relieve us from being charged as Executors de son tort, as the law would otherwise term us. she is too unwell to be consulted for a list of the kitchen & houshold furniture, but relies that the negroes who were about the house can give full information of it. in answer to a question of mr Sea's as to fowls she says the mr Winston's were desired to take such as they chose, & she gave the rest to the negroes who had had the trouble of raising them. the negro man Aaron being willing to take corn for the clothes due him, you will be so good as to settle with him in that or any other way you please; and in general altho for your satisfaction I have stated our opinions on the subjects before mentioned, yet we wish you not to be restrained by them, but to act in all cases as circumstances shall render best in your judgment, and in all cases I take on myself all responsibilities & especially pecuniary ones for your acts, deeming the trouble you will have, quite a sufficient burthen without adding jeopardies of any sort to them. if you will be so good as to send me either the original deed of Clarke, if recorded, or a copy if not, and a notice where particularly he lives[2] I will prepare a new one & send it to Kentucky to be executed by mrs Clarke for her dower, being the proper method of obtaining her relinquishment. till this is obtained, & till probat of the will it would be unsafe to sell the land, much as we desire it. mrs Marks thinks there are 80. acres of Slaughter's[3] land. the deed will show how much of Clarke's. I shall satisfy mr Sea for the trouble of his journey on delivering him this letter. Accept the assurances of my great esteem & respect. TH: JEFFERSON

RC (NN: Thomas Jefferson Papers); addressed: "Mr Lancelot Minor Louisa by mr Sea"; endorsed by Minor.

Lancelot Minor (1763–1848) was a farmer who lived at Minor's Folly in Louisa County. He frequently served as a trustee, executor, guardian, or agent for his neighbors ("Minor Family," *WMQ*, 1st ser., 9 [1900]: 53; *MB*; Vi: Minor Family Papers; *Richmond Enquirer*, 5 Dec. 1848).

Minor was NAMED AN EXECUTOR of the estate of TJ's brother-in-law Hastings Marks. The will, dated 16 Dec. 1805 and proved 9 Mar. 1812, states that "I Hastings Marks of Louisa County do hereby make and declare this my last will and testament in manner following that is to say first it is my desire that all my just debts should be paid out of my estate, secondly, I give and bequeath all my estate both real and personal that remain after paying my debts as aforesaid to my wife Nancey Marks to her and her heirs forever, lastly I do constitute and appoint my friends, Thomas Jefferson Thomas M Randolph & Lancelot Minor my executors and my wife Nancey Marks my executrix to this my last will and testament" (Louisa Co. Will Book, 5:386–7).

EXECUTORS DE SON TORT: persons

acting as executors of an estate without legal authority (*Black's Law Dictionary*). On this day TJ paid Sea $3 for THE TROUBLE OF HIS JOURNEY (*MB*, 2:1273).

Letters from Minor to TJ of 5, 16, 23 Feb., 6, 8, 15 Mar., and 26 Apr. 1812, not found, are recorded in SJL as received from Louisa County on 20, 18 Feb., 1, 10 Mar. (two letters received that day), 1 Apr., and 4 May 1812, respectively. SJL also records missing letters from TJ to Minor of 8 Jan. and 4 Mar. 1812.

[1] Preceding three words interlined.
[2] Preceding seven words interlined.
[3] Manuscript: "Slaugter's."

To Oliver Barrett

SIR Monticello Feb. 20. 12.

Being desirous of getting a Spinning machine simpler than any of those made on the Arkwright plan, so simple indeed as that we can use and keep it in order in our families in the country where we have nothing but very coarse workmen, I consulted Dr Thornton of the Patent office on the subject. he recommends yours as coming more nearly within my views than any other and carrying about 20. threads[1] which induces me to wish to get one. he says that you furnished one to Judge Cranch of Washington[2] at the price of 50.D. of which 20. goes for the patent right and that the workmanship is about 25. or 30.D. will you be so good as to answer this letter and to inform me if he is correct as to the number of threads & price. if he is I wish you to prepare me one immediately for 20. threads, and on reciept of your letter I will immediately remit you the price to any address you direct in New York, and will expect you to forward the machine well packed to the address of Gibson & Jefferson merchants at Richmond to be forwarded to me. Doct^r^ Thornton further mentioned that you would sell your patent right to a county for 500.D. I imagine you judge of our counties by those of N. York, which are perhaps 5. times as large & populous as ours. we have about 100 counties which may average 5000 souls of white population each. 500.D @ 20.D. a machine, patent price, would suppose 25[3] machines in a county, which are 5. times as many as could be sold at 50.D. each. if the machine answers as well as Dr Thornton says, I think it probable that at 100.D. to a county you would sell twenty county rights where you would one at 500.D. this is mentioned for your consideration, my object being only to get a single one to use in my family Accept the assurance of my respect TH: JEFFERSON

PoC (MHi); at foot of text: "Mr Oliver Barrett. New York"; endorsed by TJ.

Oliver Barrett (ca. 1783–1818) patented his Domestic Roving and Spinning

Machine on 3 Dec. 1811. He sought to profit from the machine by selling exclusive rights within specific territories to designated agents. According to one such agent, the machine processed wool "fine enough for broadcloths, or sufficiently coarse for carpeting and *rose blankets*—and cotton may be spun fine enough for domestic purposes." A child of twelve or fourteen years could be taught its use in two or three days and it was "simple in construction and operations, and not liable to be put out of repair—and may be built with any number of spindles." Barrett also patented a mill for fanning wheat and clover seed in 1808 and a cloth-felting machine in 1812. The patents all placed him at different locations in the state of New York, at Sandy Hill (later Hudson Falls), Schaghticoke in Rensselaer County, and Troy, and at some point he was also postmaster of nearby Mechanicville. Barrett died at Venice, near Sandusky, Ohio (*List of Patents*, 63, 103, 118; Hartford *Connecticut Courant*, 9 June 1812, 4 May 1813; *New-York Columbian*, 9 Sept. 1818).

[1] Preceding five words interlined.
[2] Preceding two words interlined.
[3] Number interlined in place of "a."

To Henry Dearborn

DEAR GENERAL Monticello Feb. 20. 12.

The inclosed letter will explain to you it's object, which I have thought would go safest to Boston first under the friendly protection of your cover, and that you would be so good as to add any thing to the superscription which may be necessary to carry it thro' the post office safely to it's address. this favor I ask of you. I saw with great joy your nomination to the command of the military force of the US. there is no one to whose hands I would rather it should be committed, or with whom it will be more safely or skilfully employed. I sincerely congratulate you on it. at the same time I hope arrangements may be made with the government, confidentially, to secure to you the office you hold or something better on your retiring from your military employ. wishing you every advantage & honour which this appointment can bring, I add the assurances of my constant friendship & respect TH: JEFFERSON

RC (MiD-B); at foot of text: "Gen[l] Dearborne"; endorsed by Dearborn. PoC (DLC); endorsed by TJ. Enclosure: TJ to Ebenezer Herrick, 20 Feb. 1812.

President James Madison's NOMINATION of Dearborn as a major general, United States Army, had recently been confirmed (*JEP*, 2:206, 207 [20, 27 Jan. 1812]).

To Ebenezer Herrick

SIR Monticello Feb. 20. 12.

I subjoin the copy of an advertisement taken from a newspaper, which induces me to write this letter requesting you to forward one of the machines therein described, well packed, to the address of Messrs Gibson and Jefferson merch^ts^ at Richmond for me. they will send it on to me. I inclose you 15. Dollars, the price mentioned in the advertisement, in bills of the bank of Richmond, which the mercantile intercourse between Boston & Richmond will certainly afford opportunities of exchanging.

the same intercourse doubtless furnishes opportunities of sending the machine to Richmond by vessels going constantly from Boston to Richmond for coal, flour, corn E^t^c. be so good as to drop me a line of answer by post, and accept the assurance of my respects

TH: JEFFERSON

PoC (DLC); adjacent to signature: "Mr Ebenezer Herrick West Stockbridge county of Berkshire Mass."; with enclosure subjoined; endorsed by TJ. Enclosure: enclosure to TJ to William Thornton, 14 Jan. 1812. Enclosed in TJ to Henry Dearborn, 20 Feb. 1812.

Ebenezer Herrick was aged between sixty and seventy and living in Hancock, Berkshire County, Massachusetts, at the time of the 1830 census (DNA: RG 29, CS). On 17 Aug. 1810 he received a patent for "The domestic spinner," the invention DESCRIBED in the enclosure, and on 22 Oct. 1813 he received another for his improvements to the stocking loom (*List of Patents*, 85, 129).

From Archibald Robertson

DEAR SIR Lynchburg 20 Feby 1812

The sudden & untimely end of our friend Mr Wm Brown has placed us in rather a disagreeable situation as to money matters—we are therefore under the necessity of making application to those in arrears, Be assured it is with reluctance that we call on you at this time, from what pass'd when I last had the pleasure of seeing you—any aid that you can give us will be thankfully received, & beg you will excuse so unexpected an application—I remain

very respectfully Your mo ob^t^ St A. ROBERTSON

RC (ViU: TJP); endorsed by TJ as received 26 Feb. 1812 and so recorded in SJL.

A letter from Brown & Robertson to TJ of 17 Dec. 1811, not found, is recorded in SJL as received from Lynchburg on 18 Dec. 1811.

To Henry Flood

[SIR?] Monticello Feb. 21. 12.

Your letter of Jan. 29. is just now recieved, having been three weeks on the road. I have this day written by the mail to my overseer at Poplar forest to send off two boys on horseback with bags as soon as he recieves my letter. I shall probably be on myself nearly as soon as he will be sending for the seed, and will leave the price of it with you as I pass. with my thanks for your attention to this matter be pleased to accept the assurance of my esteem & respect

TH: JEFFERSON

PoC (MHi); salutation faint; at foot of text: "Maj[r] Flood"; endorsed by TJ as a letter to Henry Flood.

Henry Flood (ca. 1756–1827) operated a tavern in Buckingham County where TJ often dined or stayed the night when traveling to and from Poplar Forest. Noah Flood also kept a tavern, located about 11½ miles from the former, and which establishment is being referenced is not always clear (*MB*, esp. 2:1161, 1305; Chambers, *Poplar Forest*, 140–1; *Richmond Enquirer*, 24 July 1827).

Flood's letter to TJ of JAN. 29, not found, is recorded in SJL as received from Buckingham on 19 Feb. 1812.

To Jeremiah A. Goodman

SIR Monticello Feb. 21. 12.

I have just recieved a letter from Maj[r] Flood informing me that his neighbor M[r] Duval will spare me from 6. to 8. bushels of Burnet seed. you will therefore be pleased to send off two boys on horseback to bring it. they should take bags which will hold 4. bushels each. the seed is as light as chaff. it is sown half a bushel to the acre. Major Flood's is 34. miles from Poplar Forest on the great main road leading from New London to Richmond.

M[r] Harrison has doubtless informed you that I have sold my tobacco to him, except the overseer's parts, which they will decide on for themselves. I hope the spinning and weaving has got well under way. I am informed from Richmond that there is not a single yard of cotton or oznabrigs to be had there, nor is there another yard ordered or expected. we have no chance therefore of clothing the negroes next winter but with what we shall make ourselves. I shall be with you as soon as the season is so far advanced as to be out of danger of my being taken on the road by snow or cold weather. Accept my best wishes. TH: JEFFERSON

P.S. I pray that not a possible moment may be lost in delivering the tobacco at the Warehouse for mr Harrison, noting the days every hogshead is delivered there, because that fixes the paiments

PoC (MHi); adjacent to signature: "M[r] Jeremiah A. Goodman"; endorsed by TJ.

To William Eustis

[Dea]r Sir Monticello Feb. 23. 12.

The inclosed presents one of those cases which it is not in my power to refuse being the channel of communicating. the writer is the son of a very early and intimate friend & fellow-student, to whom, were he living, I ought to refuse nothing. of the writer personally I never heard any thing, nor ever saw him: but I think he must be personally known to mr Nelson & mr Basset, two of our representatives in Congress. I have moreover written to him to advise his sending on to you certificates of character. should I be the means of adding to your list of candidates one of as much worth as was his father, I shall have the double pleasure of rendering service to a friend & to the public. Accept the assurance of my esteem & respect. Th: Jefferson

PoC (DLC); salutation faint; at foot of text: "The Secretary at War"; endorsed by TJ. Enclosure: Francis Willis to TJ, 6 Feb. 1812, not found, but recorded in SJL as received from "Gloster" on 21 Feb. 1812.

To Francis Willis

Sir Monticello Feb. 23. 12.

Your favor of Feb. 6. came to hand by our last post, and I have this day written to the Secretary at War on the subject of your request. I ought however to observe to you that it will be necessary for you to forward on to the Secretary at War letters or certificates of character from persons to whom you are personally known; and if they are from persons known at Washington, it will be so much the better. I have referred him to mr Nelson and mr Basset of Congress, on the presumption that you are personally known to them. I should further observe that the US. having institutions for the instruction of Midshipmen in the Navy, and Cadets in the Artillery, all their officers for those departments are now taken from those two corps; so that no person who has not been of those corps can have an appointment. it is only in the new regiments that persons can enter without having passed thro' the lower grades. I shall be happy if on this occasion I may have been useful to the son of one who was among my early & most intimate friends, and with every wish for your success I tender you the assurance of my respect. TH: JEFFERSON

PoC (MoSHi: TJC-BC); at foot of text: "Francis Willis esq."; endorsed by TJ.

Francis Willis (b. 1768) was the eldest son of TJ's college friend Francis Willis (1744–91), of White Hall, near Gloucester Court House (Lyon G. Tyler, "The Willis Family," *WMQ*, 1st ser., 6 [1897]: 27–9; *PTJ*, 16:165–6; *MB*, 1:73). He did not receive a military appointment.

For Willis's missing FAVOR OF FEB. 6., see TJ to William Eustis, 23 Feb. 1812.

From Palisot de Beauvois

MONSIEUR, Paris 23 fevrier 1812.

j'ai prie la liberté de m'adresser a vous pour vous prier de me faire obtenir justice dans une demande Légitime et qui avait été rejettée par la Cour de New-Kent dans les réclamatîons de la Succession de mon beau frere. m. P. Piernetz.[1] j'espérais, monsieur, parmi les dépeches arrivées depuis quel ques temps de votre païs trouver une Lettre de vous, j'en suis d'autant plus Surpris que la personne qui avait été chargée de mes Lettres est de retour de son voyage, et m'a assuré que toutes les Lettres, qui lui avaient été confiées, ont èté fidelement remises.

puis-je espérer, Monsieur, que vous voudres bien m'accorder votre protectîon dans une cause aussi juste diriger, M. M. Oster et Pauly et me marquer si je puis esperer que justice me sera rendu.

j'ai L'honneur d'etre avec la plus haute consideratîon Monsieur, Votre très humble et tres obeiss[t] Serviteur

PALISOT DE BEAUVOIS
membre de L'institut
rue de Turenne n° 58.

EDITORS' TRANSLATION

SIR, Paris 23 February 1812.

I have taken the liberty of writing you to request your assistance in making a legitimate claim against the estate of my brother-in-law, Mr. P. Piernet, which was rejected by the court of New Kent County. I was hoping, Sir, that I would find a letter from you among the dispatches that arrived some time ago from your country. I am all the more surprised as the person who had been put in charge of my letters has returned from his trip and assured me that all the letters that had been entrusted to him were faithfully delivered.

May I hope, Sir, that you will be so kind as to grant your protection to so just a cause? Send word to Messieurs Oster and Pauly, and tell me if there is hope that justice will be done.

I have the honor to be, Sir, with the highest consideration,

Your very humble and very obedient servant

PALISOT DE BEAUVOIS
member of the Institut
Rue de Turenne number 58.

RC (DLC); endorsed by TJ as received 27 May 1812 and so recorded in SJL. Translation by Dr. Roland H. Simon. Enclosed in John Graham to TJ, 23 May 1812, or James Madison to TJ, 25 May 1812.

[1] Preceding three words added in margin.

From Charles Yancey

D^R^ SIR. Hopefull Mills 23rd Feby 1812

I sent you word by my son Ralph H Yancey, that I expected to be able to Supply You with Clover Seed; it has eventually turned out, that I cannot: & I have thought it best to Notify You, fearing a Reliance on me Might prevent a Supply from another Quarter. I am Respectfully, with Regard & esteem Your friend, & most Obedient Servant. CHARLES YANCEY

RC (MHi); endorsed by TJ as received 2 Mar. 1812 and so recorded in SJL.

A letter from Yancey of 20 Feb., not found, is recorded in SJL as received 27 Feb. 1812.

From Thomas Erskine Birch

Anchor & Hope Acad.
MOST RESPECTABLE SIR. Wythe 24th Feb. 1812

A few days previous to recieving your letter of the 3d of Ult, I was aware that the Virginian Orator, which I sent, had not been recieved by you, as no register had been entered in any Post Office. Your letter confirmed it, & I found that the book was taken, & the letter that was inclosed in the book sent on, & recd by you: I accordingly sent another book, & letter, but am doubtful whether you have recd either. If you have recd the last letter & the book again miscarried, be so kind as to inform me, & I will send another book by a gentleman who will do himself the honor of putting it into your hands, who will in abou[t] 4 weeks start for Charlottesville

I have the honor to subscribe myself, illustrious Sir, Y[r] mo Ob[t] & Very humble Ser[t] THO[s] E BIRCH

PS.

If you have rec[d] both my lette[rs] & neither of the books, I consider myself in rather an awkward situation, until I am assured th[at] you have rec[d] one. T E B

RC (MHi); dateline between signature and postscript; edge trimmed and torn at seal; endorsed by TJ as received 9 Mar. 1812 and so recorded in SJL.

From James Pleasants

DEAR SIR, Washington, February 25th 1812.

Yours, enclosing m[r] Harrison's letter on the subject of commissions for Doctor James & his brothers was receivd several days since; I immediately waited on the secretary at war & had a conversation with him on the subject, from which I think one of them will receive a commission. There would have been no doubt as to the others, but as the applications from that state were considerably more numerous than the vacancies to be filled, the Secretary seemed to think it would not be proper to appoint two or more in one family, whilst a number must necessarily be rejected; this consideration was strengthened by the circumstance of its being necessary for the benefit of the recruiting service, to distribute the Company officers over the Country as equally as practicable.

The report of the comm[ee] of ways & means, nearly in conformity with the letter from the treasury depertment, will be taken up this day; there will be opposition, produced by local circumstances, to different parts of the proposed taxes; but I think there is no doubt but a considerable majority will be found in favour of additional revenue enough to pay the interest on the necessary loans, in some form or other—I believe war is expected by the best informed men here; the hopes from the prince[1] of Wales becoming unshackled in the exercise of the regal functions being much diminished.

It is proper that I should apologise to you in this place for not answering a letter receivd from you some time since on the subject of making a title to the Beaverdam lands to W Bentley—I communicated the contents of your letter to Bentley soon after it was receivd, but he never did any thing in the business—In the course of that year I was servd with a Sp[a] from the Federal court to answer a Bill filed by the heirs of W[m] Ronald, the object of which was to prohibit me as surviving trustee in that deed from making a deed to Bentley, on the ground of his having purchased the land for the benefit of the heirs of Ronald, and paid for it with their money—I answered the Bill on which I believe no decree has ever yet been made. As soon as any thing is done I will make it known to you, that means may be taken to secure the balance due. With Sentiments of Greatest respect,

I am very sincerely, y[r] ob[t] &c[a] JAMES PLEASANTS JR

RC (MHi); endorsed by TJ as received 1 Mar. 1812 and so recorded in SJL; notation by TJ above dateline: "Bentley William."

DOCTOR JAMES & HIS BROTHERS may have been relatives of Philip Turpin. TJ had forwarded a letter to Secretary of War William Eustis from the elder Turpin in connection with this request for patronage, and on 12 Mar. 1812 Beverly Turpin was appointed a second lieutenant in the light dragoons, United States Army (TJ to Eustis, 9 Feb. 1812; Heitman, *U.S. Army*, 1:976; *JEP*, 2:219 [25 Feb. 1812]). On 17 Feb. 1812 Ezekiel Bacon submitted the REPORT OF THE COMM[EE] OF WAYS & MEANS to the United States House of Representatives. It consisted of a two-year plan for raising revenue through a new government loan as well as additional taxes. On 14 Mar. 1812 President James Madison signed legislation approving the loan, which was to be raised by public subscription and was not to exceed eleven million dollars at six percent annual interest (*Annals*, 12th Cong., 1st sess., 1050–6; *U.S. Statutes at Large*, 2:694–5). On 20 Jan. 1812 TREASURY secretary Albert Gallatin had presented the House with a plan to raise revenue by both direct and indirect taxes (*ASP, Finance*, 2:523–7). TJ wrote to Pleasants about the TITLE TO THE BEAVERDAM LANDS on 26 Jan. 1810. The plaintiffs in *Ronald's Heirs v. Barkley* FILED an amended bill in the United States Circuit Court for the Virginia District on 6 Apr. 1810, and Pleasants ANSWERED on 11 Sept. 1811 (Vi: USCC-RB, 13:608, 609). The complicated case was not decided until 1818 (Marshall, *Papers*, 8:209–16).

[1] Manuscript: "pince."

Preface to Statement on the Batture Case

[*Ed. Note*: Following the dismissal of *Livingston v. Jefferson* by the United States Circuit Court on 4 Dec. 1811, TJ decided to publish his 31 July 1810 Statement on the Batture Case as a public justification of his actions. He did not alter the text substantially, but he added a preface that he dated 25 Feb. 1812 (DLC: TJ Papers, 195:34668) before sending the manuscript the following day to Ezra Sargeant, a printer in New York City. The entire pamphlet, published as *The Proceedings of the Government of the United States, in maintaining the Public Right to the Beach of the Missisipi, Adjacent to New-Orleans, against the Intrusion of Edward Livingston. prepared for the use of counsel, by Thomas Jefferson* (New York, 1812; Sowerby, nos. 3501, 3508; Poor, *Jefferson's Library*, 10 [no. 604]) will appear with commentary on its textual evolution in a forthcoming volume of *The Papers of Thomas Jefferson: Second Series* on the controversy over the Batture Sainte Marie.]

From John Barnes

Dear Sir George Town 26th Febuary 1812.

since the receipt of M[r] Geo Taylors Advises respecting Bills of exchange on Paris, I have made sundry inquiries at Baltimore &[a] but have not obtained any satisfactory Acco[t]—even those few who are disposed to draw—I find ask a high advance say 10 per Cent above par—Under present Circumstance I should presume it adviseable[1] to wait a M[o] or two—in expectation of a more favorable change of Circumstances in the[2] Political as well, the Commercial transaction depending—and sh[d] a favorable Opport[y] present you to inform the good Gen[l] least he might Attribute this delay—to some Neglect—of mine—

most Respectfully

I am Dear Sir your very Obed[t] John Barnes.

RC (ViU: TJP-ER); at foot of text: "Th: Jefferson Esq[r] Monticello"; endorsed by TJ as received 1 Mar. 1812 and so recorded in SJL.

Tadeusz Kosciuszko was the good gen[l].

[1] Manuscript: "adiseable."

[2] Manuscript: "in the in the."

To Ezra Sargeant

Sir, Monticello. Feb. 26. 12.

Your letter of the 10th has been recieved. I must acknolege that the price of the printing is higher than I had expected, being something over half a dollar a piece on so large a purchase as 250. copies of a pamphlet of about 70. pages. however I am ignorant of the expences of printing, and the motives for the publication overlook small considerations. I now therefore forward the MS. for publication on the terms of your letter. on giving it a last revisal, I found that a topographical sketch of the ground in question would be indispensable. I therefore prepared one, of the size of a single 8[vo] page, in the simplest form, and with the least writing possible, so as not to add sensibly to the time or cost of the publication.

When done, I would request you to make up 144. copies into one packet addressed to mr Patrick Magruder Clerk of the House of Representatives at Washington; another of 35. copies addressed to Samuel A. Otis Secretary of the Senate, and a third of 71. copies addressed to myself at this place. this last packet, which will not be larger than a common 8[vo] vol. may be put into the mail. with respect to those for mr Otis & Magruder, I imagine that it will be practicable to find some person going on in the stage from N. York to Washington who will take charge of them as a part of their baggage, and that this may be done with a few days delay only. be so good as to let me know as soon as you can ascertain when the work will be ready for delivery, as also whether any and what additional sum will be required for the map, and I will have the whole sum remitted you immediately by my correspondent in Richmond. Accept the assurance of my respects. TH: JEFFERSON

PoC (MHi); at foot of text: "Mr Ezra Sarjeant"; endorsed by TJ. Enclosure: TJ's Statement on the Batture Case, 31 July 1810, including his 25 Feb. 1812 preface.

TJ's TOPOGRAPHICAL SKETCH has not been found, but a map based on it, labeled "The Fauxbourg St Marie from Lafon's Map and the Beach, or Batture from Pelletier's Survey," appeared as the frontispiece to Jefferson, *Proceedings*.

From Patrick Gibson

SIR Richmond 27th February 1812—

I received your favor of the 24th and shall attend to your instructions relative to your old Albemarle crop, I expected to have given you the requisite information for this mail, but find the hands at Shockoe so much engaged, that it cannot be open'd until the last of the week—fine Tobaccos sell very readily at from 7 to 9$ at this last price m^r Bruce sold his crop; at the same time Tob^o of tolerably good quality can with difficulty be disposed of at 4 & 5$—Our flour market is at this time very dull, several sales have been made at 9⅜$ there is however so little to be expected down the river and our millers have so small a stock on hand, that I think there is a probability of its reviving—

The Wine, Almonds & 2 boxes are received from Alexandria and shall be sent up by Johnson with the molasses & corks, and likewise ten bushels burnet seed the 10^lbs of bar tin was sent by m^r Johnson the 12th Ins^t, Adam's ploughs have arrived but he has received none smaller than N° 4 (the smallest size is N° 1) be pleased to inform me whether the N° 4 will answer—The nail rod &c has not yet arrived I cannot account for the delay as the bill of Loading is dated the 19th Decem^r—You will receive inclosed 100$ in ten dollar notes.—

Accept my sincere thanks for your kind expressions of sympathy and condolance, altho' vain and ineffectual in restoring me to happiness, they are yet received with the deepest sensibility, and impart no small degree of alleviation in this severest of trials.—I pray you Sir freely to command my services, whenever they can be useful to you—I am with great respect & esteem—

Your Ob^t Servt PATRICK GIBSON

RC (ViU: TJP-ER); endorsed by TJ as received 1 Mar. 1812 from "Gibson & Jefferson" and so recorded in SJL.

Patrick Gibson (ca. 1775–1827), merchant, emigrated by 1797 from England to Richmond. There he took TJ's cousin George Jefferson into his firm, which later became the partnership of Gibson & Jefferson. In 1811 Gibson was appointed a director of the Bank of Virginia. TJ employed his firm to handle his Richmond commissions from 1797 until 1820. After George Jefferson's death in July 1812, Gibson became one of TJ's most prolific correspondents (George Jefferson to TJ, 8 Mar. 1811; Fillmore Norfleet, *Saint-Mémin in Virginia: Portraits and Biographies* [1942], 107, 165–6; *MB*, esp. 2:975–6; Vi: Gibson Family Papers; *Richmond Enquirer*, 20 Dec. 1827).

TJ's FAVOR OF THE 24TH, not found, is recorded in SJL as a letter to "Gibson & Jefferson." TJ had evidently expressed SYMPATHY AND CONDOLANCE to Gibson for the death of his wife, Elizabeth Sanderson Gibson, in the Richmond Theatre fire of 26 Dec. 1811 (Baltimore *Weekly Register*, 11 Jan. 1812).

From Bernard McMahon

DEAR SIR. Philadelphia Feby 28th 1812

I duly received your kind letter of the 16th ins^t and am much obliged to you for the Brassica sempervirens.

This morning I done myself the pleasure of sending you by Mr Gilmer a box containing the following articles.

2 Roots Amaryllis Belladonna
6 Pots of Auriculas, different kinds.
1 d^o of a beautiful Polyanthus
32 Roots best Tulips of Various kind
32 d^o Best double Hyacinths assorted.
40 plants of the Hudson Strawberry, the best kind we have here I have none nor have I seen any in America of the large Chili strawberry—
4 roots Lilium superbum. L.
4 small plants Gooseberries, large red fruit & the best I have ever seen.
Some roots Amaryllis Atamasco L.

The labels are laid in with the above and the numbers attached to the following.

N° 1 Ribes odoratissemum (mihi). this is one of Capt Lewis's, and an important shrub, the fruit very large, of a dark purple colour, the flowers yellow, showey & extremely fragrant.

Nº 2 Symphoricarpos leucocarpa (mihi) This is a beautiful shrub brought by C. Lewis from the River Columbia, the flower is small[1] but neat, the berries hang in large clusters are of a snow white colour and continue[2] on the shrubs, retaining their beauty, all the winter; especially if kept in a Green House. The shrub is perfectly hardy; I have given it the trivial english name of Snowberry-bush.

Nº 3 The Yellow Currant of the river Jefferson; this is specifically different from the other, but I have not yet given it a specific[3] botanical name.

Nº 4 Cape of Good hope Grape Vine, according to Mr Peter Legaux, who says he received it originally from thence. This I am confident, from several years observation, is the variety of grape most to be depended on for giving wine to the United States, but particularly to be cultivated for that purpose in the middle and eastern states.

Nº 5 An improved variety of the Cape grape, somewhat earlier and better for the table, and equally good for making wine.

I am verry sorry that I cannot at present supply all your wants, but shall as soon as in my power; and that the opportunity which now offers does[4] not admit of a conveyance for many articles which I wish to send you. I hope you will do me the favor of informing me whenever you hear of a favorable opportunity, for conveying them[5] Excuse the confused manner in which I write, as there are several people in my store asking me questions every moment.

I would thank you to informe me whether you take the Glocester Nut to be a distinct species, as announced by Michx f. (Juglans laciniosa) or whether, if only a variety, it is nearer allied to the Juglans tomentosa Michx or to the J. squamosa Michx fi. the J. alba of his father.

I send you a few seeds by this mail, and shall send some more in a few days.

I am Sir,

With gratitude, esteem & respect Your sincere wellwisher,

BERND McMAHON

P.S. you will please to excuse me for not making any charge for the few articles sent; such I could not think of.

RC (DLC); endorsed by TJ as received 4 Mar. 1812, but recorded in SJL as received a day later.

TJ planted the sweet-scented currant (RIBES *odoratissimum*) (with MIHI meaning "mine," presumably for names assigned by McMahon himself); the common snowberry (SYMPHORICARPOS *albus*); and YELLOW CURRANT (*Ribes aureum*) on 12 Mar. 1812 (Betts, *Garden Book*, 474–5). TJ received the Alexander (cape or CAPE OF GOOD HOPE) grape from Pierre LEGAUX and planted it on 11 May 1802 (Betts, *Garden Book*, 277 and plate 17 opp. p. 226). François André Michaux (MICH^{x}, with F and FI probably meaning "fils" or "son") and his FATHER, André Michaux, cataloged native American trees and the numerous members of the *Juglandaceae* (hickory and walnut) family (*Hortus Third*, 226, 613).

1 Manuscript: "smll."

2 Word interlined in place of "hang."

3 Manuscript: "specfic."

4 Word interlined in place of "will."

5 Word interlined in place of "several other articles which I wish to send you."

To John B. Magruder

SIR Monticello Feb. 28. 12.

I have just been informed that you have red clover seed for sale. if you will be so good as to inform me if it be so, and the price, if the latter suits, I will take 10. bushels.—mr Randolph also wants, but I do not know how much. if on learning the price I conclude to take, I will send for the seed tomorrow or Monday, and at the same time will send you an order on Gibson and Jefferson of Richmond for the amount. accept the assurance of my respect TH: JEFFERSON

PoC (MHi); at foot of text: "Mr John B. Magruder"; endorsed by TJ as a letter of 28 Mar. 1812. Recorded in SJL at 28 Feb. 1812.

From P. T. Jones (for John B. Magruder)

DEAR SIR Union mills Feby 28th 1812

Your letter has Just come to hand contents particularly attended to We have no clover Seed to dispose of at present—Mr Magruder is gone to Richmond and intends to get some for Some of his acquaintances but I suppose[1] not so much as will supply your dem^{d} The probability is, that if he should get, the price will be high

yrs Respectfully P. T. JONES

RC (MHi); addressed: "Mr Thomas Jefferson Albemarle Monticello"; endorsed by TJ (with brackets in original) as a letter from "[Jones for] Magruder John B." received 28 Feb. 1812 and recorded in SJL as a letter received from Magruder that day.

1 Preceding two words added in margin.

To Patrick Gibson

Dear Sir Monticello Mar. 1. 12.

I recieved yesterday your favor of Feb. 27. and one hundred Dollars inclosed in it. it was only one of the smallest size of Peacock's ploughs which I wished to recieve: consequently his N° 4. would not answer my purpose.

I have usually got my stock of red clover seed from the other side of the Blue ridge, but am quite disappointed there this year; and am therefore obliged to apply for it at your market where I am told there is plenty but high in price as is general this year. I must pray you to procure & send me in tight barrels ten bushels, as it is an article of such necessity as to render the price but a secondary consideration. if Johnson's boat should be at Richmond, or mr Randolph's I would have it sent by them; but if not there, then by the very first boat coming to Milton, as the season for sowing is now passing. Johnson was guilty of a gross breach of promise in not taking down a load of flour for me as expected when I wrote my last letter to you. he has promised to do it in the course of this week. Accept the assurance of my esteem & respect Th: Jefferson

PoC (MHi); at foot of text: "M[r] Gibson"; endorsed by TJ as a letter to Gibson & Jefferson and so recorded in SJL.

To Jeremiah A. Goodman

Sir Monticello Mar. 1.

Our distress on the article of hauling obliges me to send for the yoke of steers which were to come from Poplar Forest. you know our situation and will I hope send us a pair which will do solid service. of those which mr Griffin sent while you were here, we have never been able to make any thing. I have given Moses leave to stay a day with his friends. I suppose he can bring on the back of his steers as much corn as will bring them here, on your furnishing him a bag. I wrote to you on the 21st of February by post; but as I know that letters linger long on the road sometimes, I will repeat here one article of my letter which was pressing. Maj[r] Flood has informed me that mr Duval, his neighbor, can furnish me with 6. or 8. bushels of Burnet seed. two boys on horseback should therefore be sent off immediately with bags which will hold 4. bushels each. the seed is as light as chaff. it is sown half a bushel to the acre. Major Flood's is 34. miles from Poplar Forest on the great main road leading from New London to Richmond.

I inclose some lettuce seed, and shall be glad if you will sow about 8. or 10. feet of one of the beds behind the stable, and do the same on the 1st day of every month till the fall. Accept my best wishes

TH: JEFFERSON

RC (PWacD: Sol Feinstone Collection, on deposit PPAmP); partially dated; addressed: "Mr Jeremiah A. Goodman at Poplar Forest near New London by Moses." PoC (MHi); endorsed by TJ as a letter of "Mar. 1. 12." and so recorded in SJL.

MOSES, one of TJ's slaves, was born in Bedford County in 1792. He was moved to TJ's Lego farm in Albemarle County about 1811. Thomas Jefferson Randolph leased him from TJ in 1817 and purchased him from TJ's estate ten years later (*MB*, 2:1246; undated invoice from 1827 estate sale, Jefferson-Kirk Manuscripts, on deposit ViU:TJP).

Goodman's response of 5 Mar. 1812, not found, is recorded in SJL as received from Poplar Forest on 9 Mar. 1812.

From Joseph Hunter

SIR Warren March 1st 1812

I received a letter from you some time ago thro the hands of Col Nicholas requesting me to call and repaire your clocks which letter I should have answered last court but haveing no business there I had no recollection of the day until the Citizens ware gon. I have now to informe you that my situation is such that I cannot attend as I would wish to the calls of my Pattrons, but if it will not be too late for you I will indevour to call on you at April court at which time if it is not in my power to do so you shall be informed of it by Youres respectfully

JOSEPH HUNTER

RC (MHi); endorsed by TJ as received 2 Mar. 1812 and so recorded in SJL.

From Joseph Léonard Poirey

[*Ed. Note*: On 1 Mar. 1812 Joseph Léonard Poirey addressed TJ a letter from Rue Mézieres number 4, Paris (RC in DLC, endorsed by TJ as received 27 May 1812 and so recorded in SJL, enclosed in John Graham to TJ, 23 May 1812, or James Madison to TJ, 25 May 1812; Dupl in DLC, dated Paris, 1 Mar. 1813, endorsed by TJ as received 18 Aug. 1813 and so recorded in SJL) that was nearly identical to one he had sent on 6 Dec. 1803 (DLC). In these letters he sought TJ's assistance in obtaining financial compensation for his services during the American Revolution.]

Poirey served as Lafayette's military secretary during the American Revolution. He participated in battles at Petersburg, Jamestown, and Yorktown. Poirey then returned with Lafayette to France, where he served as captain secretary general in the French National Guard and later as secretary general of the Paris troops. In 1790 the United States Senate confirmed President George Washington's nomination of Poirey to the brevet rank of captain, and the following year he was admitted into the Society of the Cincinnati. His requests for compensation were finally honored via federal statute in 1819 (*PTJ*, 12:529; Washington, *Papers, Pres. Ser.*, 4:571–2; Linda Grant De Pauw and others, eds., *Documentary History of the First Federal Congress* [1972–], 2:71; Ludovic Guy Marie du Bessey de Contenson, *La Societe des Cincinnati De France et La Guerre D'Amerique 1778–1783* [1934], 245; TJ to Poirey, 8 Mar. 1819).

To Archibald Robertson

SIR Monticello Mar. 1. 12.

Yours of Feb. 21. has been duly recieved. I think in conversation with you at Lynchburg, I stated to you that on winding up my affairs at Washington I was obliged to apply to the bank of Richmond for a large sum, for which I pledged to my endorser my Bedford crops of tobacco, and that with what they had yielded the two preceding years, the crop now at market would clear me of the bank. that for the present year therefore I could only furnish you about 600.D. from another fund, by an order on mr Harrison of Lynchburg paiable the 1st day of April for lands he bought of me. the sale I have made of my crop of tobacco, exactly ensures my discharge of my bank debt, so that after this year my Bedford resources will be liberated, and will enable me to do justice to others, for which my anxiety is as great as it can be. intending to be at Poplar Forest before this order is payable, I had put off sending it to you. I now inclose it however, lest I should be delayed, with an assurance that after the present year I shall not permit this debt to linger.

Accept the assurance of my esteem & respect

TH: JEFFERSON

PoC (ViU: TJP); at foot of text: "Mr Robertson"; endorsed by TJ as a letter to "Robertson, Brown &," and so recorded in SJL. Enclosure not found.

From Isaac A. Coles

DEAR SIR, Washington Mar: 2d 1812.

I received a few days ago by the Constitution from my old friend Mr Walsh of Cette, the enclosed letter, from which you will percieve that the old Gentleman has declined sending the wine you wrote for, until our commerce shall be placed on a footing of more security—through Mr Morton however it may be obtained at any time; and I know that it will give him pleasure to execute any commission with which you may honor him—

I called on the Collector at Alexandria to [e]nquire after your wine from Baker, & was told that it had been sent round to Richmond to the Care of Messrs Gibson & Jefferson about ten days before—It has no doubt arrived before this, & in all probability you will get accounts of it before the receipt of this letter.

The military nominations for Virginia have not yet been sent to the Senate—I send you below a list of the persons who have been recommended by the delegation—The proposition to lay a tax on Salt was on friday rejected by the House; but it is said that the vote will be reconsidered to day, and that it will now pass by a respectable Majority—I am Dr Sir with sincere and respectful attachment

truly yrs I. A. Coles

Thos Parker
Hugh Mercer } colonels

James Baytop
James Preston } [Lieutenant] Colos

I. A. Coles.
Geo: Humphries
Thos Smith
Woodford } Majors.

RC (DLC); mutilated at seal; postscript written perpendicularly in left margin; at foot of text: "Thos Jefferson esqr"; endorsed by TJ as received 5 Mar. 1812 and so recorded in SJL.

On 2 Mar. 1812 the United States House of Representatives reversed its 28 Feb. negative of a resolution calling for a TAX ON SALT of domestic manufacture and recommended a duty of ten cents per bushel (*JHR*, 8:211, 215; *Annals*, 12th Cong., 1st sess., 1113–4).

ENCLOSURE

Peter Walsh to Isaac A. Coles

Dear sir Cêtte 1 December 1811

I have only received within these few days your favour of the 4th april which I believe came by the Frigate Constitution which arrived in October at cherbourg with Mr Barlow and Mr Warden. It is not possible for me to send the Wine which you, Mr Jefferson and Mr Cabell have ordered of me till a change of measures towards our Vessels are adopted by the English, who at present take all those that fall in their way with French Goods on board. My Friend at Bordeaux, in answer to the application I made him for room for said Wines on board of Some one of the Vessels at that Place, has written me that none of their Captains can be prevailed upon to take any Goods on Freight, and that the most of them are returning in Ballast.—

It grieves me to be thus deprived of the means of Complying with yours and the Gentlemen above mentiond's Commands, but you may depend on it's being done as soon as there may be Safety therein and on my endeavours to give you satisfaction in the quality, wishing much for occasions to shew the Esteem and regard with which I am

Your Friend & hble St PETER WALSH

have the goodness to inform Mr Jefferson and Mr Cabell of what precedes

RC (DLC); addressed: "I. A. Coles Esquire Enniscorthy near Charlottes Ville Virginia"; notation by TJ on address leaf: "alba flora."

Walsh had written to William Lee, the American commercial agent at BORDEAUX (Walsh to TJ, 10 Oct. 1811).

From Gibson & Jefferson

SIR Richmond 2nd March 1812

we send you by mr. Johnson a Hhd of molasses—10 Bus Burnett Seed the quarter Cask wine & 2 Boxes rec^d from Alexandria—a Bag of Corks & 12^lb of almonds to serve untill we can [send][1] the bag (which was rec^d from Alexandria[2]) which was by mistake put into a waggon with some other things & Sent to Lunenburg—

respectfully GIBSON & JEFFERSON
℔ JAMES LIGON

RC (ViU: TJP-ER); in Ligon's hand; addressed: "Thomas Jefferson Esqr Monticello" by "mr Johnson"; endorsed by TJ as a letter from Gibson & Jefferson received 8 Mar. 1812, but recorded in SJL as received from the firm two days earlier.

[1] Omitted word editorially supplied.
[2] Manuscript: "Alexandia."

From John Low

DEAR SIR, New York. March 2^d 1812.—

Sometime ago I rec^d yours of the 27th Decr last, informing me of your not recollecting of subscribing to the Encyclopædia I sent on, and requesting me to shew your signature to some persons who might be acquainted with it—About the middle of January I answered yours, and waited upon Mr Remsen & Mr Gelston of this city and who examined the signature and said it was genuine, and procured their signatures in my letter to that effect.—Fearful, however, my letter had not come to hand I take the liberty of troubling you with this, in order to ascertain whether it has or not, so that, if not, I may send on another certificate of those Gentlemen.—Be pleased to let me know as soon as convenient, and oblige

Yours with respect,

RC (DLC); at foot of text: "Tho[s] Jefferson Esq[r]"; endorsed by TJ as a letter from "Low John" received 12 Mar. 1812 and so recorded in SJL.

From Charles Willson Peale

Dear Sir Farm Persevere March 2[d] 1812

In a former letter I stated to you my folly in attempting to eradicate weeds from my farm by cuting them down with a briar-hook, by which exertion I had almost lamed my right arm—by using it only in light work the effects at last are almost whooly removed, and I have learned that the best mode to free land from weeds, is to plow late in the fall and early in the spring; to manure and sow plenty of good seeds to take place of weeds. Plowing deep I think is also important. Potatoes which we planted on long straw did not produce so well as those with stable manure, they were however of a better flavor—the season proved too dry for that mode. I have also learned that a small farm well worked and well manured, will produce as much profit, as one much larger, tended as is too commonly done, slovenly. I do not expect to get more than one field in good order yearly. By a good rotation of Crops to prepare them for fine grass, then having a stock of Cattle to procure manure. I shall give this spring 5 bushels of plaster to the acre on one field, on others $2\frac{1}{2}$ where I intend to plow in the clover instead of mowing it a second time.

Although I find pleasure on a farm, yet the interests of the Museum are not neglected, as my Son Rubens is well informed in many essential parts of Natural history, and he is also industrous.

I send you an Essay to promote domestic happiness. The circumstance that led me to write on that subject, was meeting at a friends house with a young man intoxicated, who was indeavoring to make apologies for his conduct, he was sensible of his error and almost frantic with grief on his situation; he wished to communicate to his friend that he was not happy at home. a few years back he had failed in the merchantile line, he possesses an amiable heart and abilities of a superior grade—I was acquainted with his parents before the revolution war, and I wished to serve the family—and having heard that his wife and some of his relations treated him harshly, determined[1] me to give them some advice, I left him with his friend, and went immediately to his house, his wife was not at home—being obliged to return to the farm, I thought to write them a letter; entering on the subject I found it must necessarly be a lengthy one, and beleiving such advice as I wished to communicate would also be useful to other families, determined me to print it, The subject is important, and many good precepts are found in divers[2] authors diffused with other matters. It has been my wish to do as much good as I possibly could in a short Essay, should I be so fortunate as to make some converts from bad habits, I may make some additions which are omited in order to save[3] expence in printing of this essay.

I have my doubts about engrafting the peach on plumb Stocks—I find that the worm also feeds on the Plumb, perhaps nearly as much as on the Peach tree. It appears to me that in this instance as in some others, your nature menders only mar the opperations of nature. Trees of this intended improvement perhaps do not give so good fruit, or thrive much longer.

The worms that used to destroy the Elm in the state-house yard are now nearly passed away, very little damage was done by them last summer—I have seen the same progress with some other Insects which have destroyed vines. we hear very little about the hessian-fly of late. Can you find no inducement to visit Philad[a]? It would give me a great deal of pleasure to see you at the Museum, your Garden must be a Museum to you.

accept my best wishes for your health, and believe me with much esteem y[rs] C W Peale

RC (DLC: TJ Papers, 195:34715–6); damaged at seal, with missing text supplied from PoC; addressed: "Thomas Jefferson Esq[r] Monticlla Virginia"; endorsed by TJ as received 6 Apr. 1813 and so recorded in SJL. PoC (PPAmP: Peale Letterbook). Enclosure: Peale, *An Essay to promote Domestic Happiness* (Philadelphia, 1812; repr. in Peale, *Papers*, 3:127–47).

In his endorsement TJ interlined "13" above the year in "Mar. 2. 1812.," because he received the letter so late that he wrongly suspected that it was misdated.

[1] Manuscript: "determed."
[2] Word interlined in place of "different."
[3] Peale here canceled: "some of the."

From John Brockenbrough

Sir, Richmond Mar: 3. 1812

By a letter just received from my friend Mr. John Harvie I am informed that he is indebted to you $— and I avail myself of the first mail to request you to direct the manner in which you wish the debt to be discharged. I will either pay the money to your order, or, if you prefer it, transmit it in Bank-notes by mail—

I am, very respectfully, Sir, Yo. mo: ob[t]

John Brockenbrough

RC (DLC); at foot of text: "Ths. Jefferson Esq"; endorsed by TJ and recorded in SJL as a letter from John "Brackenridge" received 9 Mar. 1812, with both later corrected to read "Brockenbrough."

John Brockenbrough (1773–1852) served as the first cashier of Richmond's Bank of Virginia, 1804–12, and as president, 1812–43. Born into a prominent Essex County family, he received a medical degree from the University of Edinburgh in 1795. Two years later he married Gabriella Harvie Randolph, the widow of Thomas Mann Randolph (1741–93). Through this marriage Brockenbrough became the stepfather of Thomas Mann Randolph (1792–1848), the half brother of TJ's son-in-law of the same name. Brockenbrough soon abandoned medicine to manage his wife's properties and pursue other business interests that came to include ironworks in Richmond and the Warm Springs in Bath County. He sat on a state committee to study domestic manufactures in 1808, corresponded with and admired John Randolph of Roanoke, and was active in the Richmond Junto, a loosely organized group of prominent city Republicans. As president of the Bank of Virginia, Brockenbrough helped secure funding for Central College in 1818, and he served as a manager of a failed effort to salvage TJ's finances by means of a lottery in 1826 (*DVB*; *PTJ*, 30:437–8; Brockenbrough to Joseph C. Cabell, 31 Jan. 1818 [ViU: TJP]; Brockenbrough to TJ, 1 Mar. 1826; Richmond *Daily Dispatch*, 8 July 1852).

From Benjamin Rush

Dear Sir Philadelphia Feb[y] [Mar.] 3rd 1812.

In a letter which I received a few days ago from M[r] Adams, he informs with[1] a kind of exultation, that After a correspondence of five or six & thirty years had been interrupted by various Causes, it had been renewed, and that four letters had passed between you & him. In speaking of your letters he says "they are written with all the elegance, purity and Sweetness of Style of his youth and middle age, and with (what I envy more)—a firmness of finger, and Steadiness of chirography, that to me, are lost for ever."—

It will give me pleasure as long as I live to reflect, that I have been in any degree instrumental in effecting this reunion of two Souls destined to be dear to each Other, and animated with the same dispositions to serve their country (tho' in different ways) at the expense of innumerable Sacrifices of domestic ease, personal interest, and private friendships.—Posterity will do you both justice for this Act. If M[r] Adams's letters to you are written in the same elevated and nervous Style, both as to matter and language that his letters are, which he now and then addresses to me, I am sure you will be delighted with his correspondence. Some of his thoughts electrify me. I view him as a mountain with its head clear and reflecting the beams of the sun, while all below it is frost and Snow.—

Health, respect & friendship! from Dr Sir yours truly & Affectionately BENJN RUSH

RC (DLC: TJ Papers, 195:34638); misdated; endorsed by TJ as a letter of 3 Mar. (misdated Feb.) 1812 received 11 Mar. 1812 and so recorded in SJL.

John Adams showed his EXULTATION in a letter that fancifully hailed Rush as "Dreamer," "Mediator," and "Conjurer," and went on to report that, as a result of the "Sorceries and Necromances" employed by Rush, "a Correspondence of thirty five or thirty Six years Standing interrupted by various Causes for Some time, has been renewed in 1812 and no less than four Letters have already passed between the Parties; Those from Jefferson written with all the Ellegance, purity and Sweetness, I would rather Say Mellifluity or Mellifluidity [*preceding seven words interlined*] of his youth and middle age: and what I envy Still more with a firmness of Finger and a Steadiness of Chirography, that to me is lost, forever." In a postscript on the coining of new words, Adams also remarked that "I approve Jeffersons Word 'Belittle['] and hope it will be incorporated into our American Dictionaries" (Adams to Rush, Quincy, 10 Feb. 1812 [RC courtesy of Hans Peter Kraus, New York City, 1966, at foot of text: "Dr Rush"; FC in Lb in MHi: Adams Papers]).

1 Manuscript: "with with."

From Larkin Smith

DEAR SIR Norfolk 3d March 1812

A small package of Garden seed was this day delivered to me, with your address; by a very safe conveyance to Richmond I have committed it to the care of Mr James Barbour, with a request that he would transmit it to you without loss of time, as the season for sowing the seed has commenced.

Permit me to avail myself of this occurrence to express to you my unabated devotion, and high respect for your great public services, and private worth; and to offer[1] at all times any services that it may be in my power to render to you in this place.

I have the honor to be Dear Sir with great Esteem & respect Your Obt Servant LARKIN SMITH

RC (MoSHi: TJC-BC); at foot of text: "Thomas Jefferson Esqr Monticello"; endorsed by TJ as received 21 Mar. 1812 and so recorded in SJL.

1 Smith here canceled "every."

From George McIntosh

Honoured sir Norfolk March 4th 1812

Mr James Ronaldson of Philadelphia being at this time in Scotland, has addressed to me, by the Ship Concordia from Leith, twelve Goose berry bushes—Six of which he requests me to forward to you, or to dispose of according to your orders—which on hearing from you, will give me great pleasure in performing—I am proud Sir, in being reconed amongst the list of your admirers and wishing you every enjoyment, and tranquility, in your retirement, will be the continued prayer of

Hon^d sir

your Sincere, $obed^t$ Humb Servant George McIntosh

RC (MHi); at head of text: "Thomas Jefferson esq^r"; endorsed by TJ as received 15 Mar. 1812.

George McIntosh (1768–1863), a native of Scotland, was a dry-goods and hardware merchant and landowner in Norfolk. In 1860 his estate had an estimated value of $600,000 (George McIntosh family Bible [1979 typescript in Vi: Miscellaneous Bible Records Collection]; *Simmons's Norfolk Directory* [Norfolk, 1801], 22; Thomas C. Parramore, Peter C. Stewart, and Tommy L. Bogger, *Norfolk: The First Four Centuries* [1994], 120–1, 129–30, 452–3n; Norfolk *Commercial Register*, 5 Nov. 1802; *The Norfolk Directory* [Norfolk, 1806], 23; Norfolk *American Beacon and Commercial Diary*, 26 Sept. 1817; *Richmond Enquirer*, 10 Apr. 1832, 29 Sept. 1835; DNA: RG 29, CS, Norfolk, 1850, 1860; Samuel S. Cobbs, "Burials in Cedar Grove and Elmwood Cemeteries Norfolk, Virginia" [1993 typescript at ViN], 3:14).

From John Bradbury

Sir New York 5 March 1812

The term of my mission to Louisiana having expired I arrived here a fortnight ago from St Louis in the hope of receiving my Family in the ensuing Spring: I am here informed that the Government of the United States have it in contemplation to establish a Botanic Garden at the City of Washington and that no appointment is as yet made of a Person to Superintend it.

If this information is correct I would willingly offer myself to those in whom the power of making the appointment is Vested, but suppose I am totally unknown to them; If Sir you deem me qualified to fill the Station you will render me greatly your Debtor by making this my wish known to those who have authority in this business—

I shall only add on this Subject that my extensive acquaintance amongst the Naturalists in Great Britain together with what plants I have acquired in Louisiana would enable me to assist the establishment considerably

I ascended the Missouri last Summer to a little above the Mandan Nation; and found the Soil and aspect of the country changed after passing the River Platte and consequently abounding in natural productions almost wholly different from those to the eastward of that River. The Plants which I there collected and which do not appear to be discribed in the last Edition of the Systema Naturæ exceed 100 Species Some of which are beautiful. In Zoology I think I shall add two Species of Crotalus a Talpa a Sciurus, and an animal with cheek Pouches as Mus Bursorius of Linnæus, but differing from that animal Specifically yet agreeing in Generic character and both so mu[ch] disagreeing with the Genus Mus that I am of opinion they must constitute a new Genus betwixt Mus & Arctomys

I have an ardent wish to ascend the Arkansas & Red Rivers confident that their Borders would afford a Rich harvest. If I can obtain the Situation mentioned above perhaps an opportunity may be afforded me whether or not there is any probability that I may I beg Sir you will have the goodness to cause me to be informed by Letter to the Post office Newark State of New Jersey

I am Sir Your most obliged Servant JOHN BRADBURY

RC (DLC); edge torn; endorsed by TJ as received 11 Mar. 1812 and so recorded in SJL.

John Bradbury (1768–1823), naturalist, was born in Stalybridge, England. From an early age he studied natural history and botany, and he was elected to the Linnean Society of London. Bradbury came to America to explore Kentucky and the Louisiana Territory in search of plants and seeds for the Liverpool Botanic Garden. In August 1809 he visited Monticello, and he later traveled west with members of John Jacob Astor's fur-trading company. Delayed in part by the War of 1812, Bradbury did not return to England until 1816. There he was dismayed to discover that Frederick Pursh had already published descriptions of plants that Bradbury had discovered, using specimens he had shipped to Liverpool. In 1817 Bradbury published an account of his travels. He returned to the United States shortly thereafter, spent some time in Saint Louis, and settled in Kentucky (Charles Boewe, "John Bradbury [1768–1823], Kentucky's Forgotten Naturalist," *Filson Club Historical Quarterly* 74 [2000]: 221–49; Rodney H. True, "A Sketch of the Life of John Bradbury, Including his Unpublished Correspondence with Thomas Jefferson," APS, *Proceedings* 68 [1929]: 133–50; William Roscoe to TJ, 25 Apr. 1809; TJ to Meriwether Lewis, 16 Aug. 1809; H. W. Rickett, "John Bradbury's Explorations in Missouri Territory," APS, *Proceedings* 94 [1950]: 59–89; James P. Ronda, *Astoria & Empire* [1990]; Bradbury, *Travels in the Interior of America, in the Years 1809, 1810, and 1811; including a Description of Upper Louisiana, together with the States of Ohio, Kentucky, Indiana, and Tennessee, with the Illinois and Western Territories, and containing Remarks and Observations useful to Persons Emigrating to Those Countries* [Liverpool, 1817]; TJ to William H. Crawford, 29 Feb. 1816).

From Joseph St. Leger d'Happart

Sir! march 5th 1812, near Green'sburgh, westm[d] County

In Jan[y] 1809. I attended an Indian of the Tawa-nation, left very ill, in Somerset. on their return from the Seat of Gov[nt] & way home, him & friends, call'd at my home, & their interpreter (m[r] armstrong) ask'd me, whether I had made out my bill & on my telling him, I had Sent it on, he replied, you had authoris'd him, to discharge it but as I had forward it, it undoubtedly would be paid. Since that Sir! however, my bill ($189.69.) has been Several times inclos'd, detain'd in the war office & return'd, without any acceptance. The first time, not knowing the custom of the country, I had address'd it to m[r] Gallatin, who direct'd me, to the Secret[y] at war, m[r] Dearborn, but at that period, m[r] Eustis, preceded him & told maj: Craig, Pittsburgh, "its first bearer," it would be honor'd, provided I Should annex to it, a certificat from the justice of the peace, Somerset, attesting I was the physician; which I did, besides the Signature of the prothonotary or recorder & a few lines from a gentleman of the profession: Still, I am So far depriv'd of that Sum, the last answer of m[r] Eustis, being, there was no funds. How then to proceed? I do not know, but as the Sum would, at this present time, be exceedingly usefull, I beg leave to inclose the whole transaction to you Sir! (in the last form, I drew & got it return again, with the Same former answer, "There was no funds.") and in hope, as you had desired m[r] armstrong, to Settle it,[1] you will do me the favor, to enable my receiving its amount.—As in these back-woods, we always are in want of our pecuniary faculties, if you Should be So kind, as to render me that Service, it Surely would be gratefully acknowledg'd, as your former civilities, at francis's-hotel, Philadelphia, 1800. remain engrav'd in my mind. I have the honor to be,—Sir! your's most respectfully

S[T] Leger d'Happart

FC (PPiU: d'Happart Papers); entirely in d'Happart's hand; at head of text: "Thomas Jefferson, esq[re]"; dateline beneath signature, with "Copy" adjacent to it. Recorded in SJL as received 1 Apr. 1812. Enclosure not found. Enclosed in TJ to James Madison, 17 Apr. 1812.

Joseph St. Leger d'Happart spent eighteen months in a French prison before immigrating to the United States, arriving in Boston early in 1796. He became a clerk and in 1797 obtained United States citizenship, but he soon quarreled with his employers. The British seized a ship owned by d'Happart in 1805. Two years later he was confined to debtors' prison in Philadelphia. D'Happart won his release in 1808 and lived thereafter in southwestern Pennsylvania (PPiU: d'Happart Papers; *Appeal of J. L. D'Happart to the Public, in consequence of his business with Messrs. William, James & Nathaniel Fellows Cunningham, Boston*

[Boston, 1797]; *New-York Commercial Advertiser*, 10 Oct. 1805; d'Happart to TJ, 11 June 1808 [DLC], 20 June 1812).

D'Happart used the verso of the FC of this letter for his retained copy of a letter to William Findley, written from Greensburg, Pennsylvania, 22 May 1812, enclosing TJ to d'Happart, 17 Apr. 1812, asking Findley to call on President James Madison and "collect the amount of my claim, which is $189.69," and specifying that the payment should be forwarded "in a check on Pittsburgh-Bank or in any other manner you may consider perfectly safe" (FC in PPiU: d'Happart Papers; entirely in d'Happart's hand; at foot of text: "To the Honorable Wm Findley, Member of Congress City of Washington"; endorsed by d'Happart).

TAWA-NATION: the Ottawa nation. In March 1809 William Eustis succeeded rather than PRECEDED Henry Dearborn as secretary of war.

[1] Preceding two words interlined in place of "Sollicit."

From José Corrêa da Serra

SIR Washington city 6 March. 1812

When i Left Europe two months ago, several of your correspondents and friends in that part of the world favoured me with Letters of recommendation to you, knowing how ardently i wished the honour of your acquaintance. Mr Thouin gave me also his Last publication on grafting, that i might present to you on his part. Not having the advantage of finding you in this place as i was Led to believe in Europe, and being obliged to go as soon as possible to Philadelphia where i intend to reside, i send you Mr Thouin's book, that you may not be deprived of the pleasure of reading it, and keep the Letters with me, which i shall have the honour of presenting to you in the course of this summer when i intend to undertake the pilgrimage of Monticello. The present Letter and Mr Thouin's book i leave here at the care of Mr Gallatin. I am most devoutedly

Sir Your most obedient h^e serv^t

JOSEPH CORRÊA DE SERRA

RC (DLC); endorsed by TJ as received 18 Mar. 1812 and so recorded in SJL. Enclosure: enclosure to André Thoüin to TJ, 7 Dec. 1811. Enclosed in Albert Gallatin to TJ, 10 Mar. 1812.

José Corrêa da Serra (1751–1823), botanist and diplomat, was born in Portugal and educated in Italy, where he was ordained in the Catholic priesthood. In 1779 he was a founder and first secretary of the Royal Academy of Sciences of Lisbon, in which capacity he edited the first three volumes of a pioneering collection of early Portuguese documents, *Collecçaõ de Livros Ineditos de Historia Portugueza, dos Reinados de D. Joaõ I., D. Duarte, D. Affonso V., e D. Joaõ II* (Lisbon, 1790–93). Corrêa da Serra became a fellow of the Royal Society of London and the Linnean Society of London. Anticipating persecution for his liberal political views, he fled his native land in 1795. He lived in London until 1801 and then in Paris before relocating to the United States in 1812. Corrêa da Serra was elected to membership in the American Philosophical Society even before his arrival, settled in Philadelphia, and was welcomed by a scientific and political community that valued his broad interests and insatiable intellectual curiosity. He befriended TJ and visited Monticello regularly during his extensive travels, and he was made an honorary member of the Agricultural Society of Albemarle. From 1816–20 Corrêa da Serra resided in Washington as Portugal's minister plenipotentiary to the United States. He eventually grew disenchanted with American politics and values. In 1820 he returned to Europe, expecting to proceed to Brazil as a councillor of state to the Portuguese monarch there, but he ultimately settled in Lisbon in 1821 after the royal court returned to that city (João Romano Torres, ed., *Portugal–Dicionário Histórico, Corográfico, Heráldico, Biográfico, Bibliográfico, Numismático e Artístico* [1904–15], 6:837–8; Michael Teague, *Abade José Correia da Serra: Documentos do seu Arquivo [1751–1795], Catálogo do Espólio* [1997], esp. 34; Richard Beale Davis, *The Abbé Corrêa in America, 1812–1820: The Contributions of the Diplomat and Natural Philosopher to the Foundations of Our National Life* [1955; repr. 1993]; Léon Bourdon, *José Corrêa da Serra: Ambassadeur du Royaume-Uni de Portugal et Brésil à Washington 1816–1820* [1975]; Ana Simões, Maria Paula Diogo, and Ana Carneiro, *Cidadão do Mundo: Uma Biografia Científica do Abade Correia da Serra* [2006]; APS, Minutes, 17 Jan. 1812 [MS in PPAmP]).

When Corrêa da Serra first visited TJ in July 1813, he presented him LETTERS OF RECOMMENDATION from André Thoüin, Pierre Samuel Du Pont de Nemours, and Alexander von Humboldt, respectively dated 7, 20, and 20 Dec. 1811.

From James Madison

DEAR SIR Washington Mar. 6. 1812.

I return the letter from Foronda inclosed in yours of the 19th Feby. I find I shall not be able to read his lucubrations[1] in print. The letter[2] from Dr Guantt is in the hands of the Secry of war, and will not be unheeded; but the course the nominations have taken makes it doubtful whether the wishes in behalf of his Son, can be fulfilled.

You will see that Congs or rather the H. of Rs have got down the dose of taxes. It is the strongest proof they could give that they do not mean to flinch from the contest to which the mad conduct of G.B. drives them. Her perseverence in this seems to be sufficiently attested by the language of Ld Liverpool & Mr Perceval, in their parliamentary comments on the Regent's message. The information from F. is pretty justly described in the paragraph inserted in the natl Intelliger after the arrival of the Constitution. The prints herewith inclosed are forwarded to you at the request of Thoms Gimbrede (of N. York) the author.

[Be assured of my great & affectionate esteem

JAMES MADISON]

RC (DLC: Madison Papers); closing and signature clipped, but replaced in pencil in an unidentified hand; at foot of text: "Mr Jefferson"; endorsed by TJ as received 9 Mar. 1812 and so recorded in SJL. Enclosure: Valentín de Foronda to TJ, 30 Nov. 1811. Other enclosure printed below.

Madison had forwarded a letter from Edward Gantt (GUANTT) (described at TJ to Gantt, 19 Feb. 1812) to William Eustis, the SECRY OF WAR. On 4 Mar. 1812 the United States House of Representatives approved resolutions supporting additional TAXES in the event of war (*Annals*, 12th Cong., 1st sess., 1147–56). On 7 Mar. 1812 the Washington *National Intelligencer* began publishing extracts from the PARLIAMENTARY COMMENTS that followed a speech by the British prince regent, the future George IV. Dispatches from France that arrived with the United States frigate CONSTITUTION on 22 Feb. 1812 included news that Napoleon had received American envoy Joel Barlow favorably (*National Intelligencer*, 25 Feb. 1812).

[1] Manuscript: "lucrubations."

[2] Reworked from "Your letter of subsequent date."

ENCLOSURE

Thomas Gimbrede's Engraving of the First Four American Presidents

[30 Jan. 1812]

Engraving (ViCMRL).

On 3 Mar. 1812 Gimbrede sent copies of this engraving to James Madison from New York, stating that he "conceived that a print representing the four Presidents; would be very desirable and pleasing to the dispassionate and true Americans" and asking that Madison "forward two of them to the honourable Thos Jeffersson—ex-president of the United States" (RC in DLC: Madison Papers; printed in Madison, *Papers, Pres. Ser.*, 4:225).

From James Madison

DEAR SIR [9 Mar. 1812]

As the Intelligencer will not publish the Message & documents just laid before Cong^s^ for the present Mail, I send you a copy of the former. It is justified by the Documents, among which are the original credential & instructions[1] from the Govr of Canada, and an original dispatch from the Earl of Liverpool to him approving the conduct of the Secret Agent. This discovery, or rather formal proof of the Co-operation between the Eastern Junto, & the B. Cabinet will, it is to be hoped, not only prevent future evils from that source, but extract good out of the past.

RC (DLC: Madison Papers, Rives Collection); signature and dateline clipped; at foot of text: "Mr Jefferson"; endorsed by TJ as a letter of 9 Mar. 1812 received 11 Mar. 1812 and so recorded in SJL. Enclosure: Madison to United States Congress, 9 Mar. 1812, transmitting documents showing that, during a period when the United States was observing peaceful neutrality toward Great Britain and the British minister was making amicable professions during negotiations here, that nation had employed a secret agent at Boston to foment disaffection and resistance to the law and prepare the way for a British invasion to destroy the Union and bring New England into a political connection with Britain; and concluding that in addition to its effect on the public councils, this discovery should render the Union even dearer to its citizens (Tr in same, in the hand of Edward Coles; printed in Madison, *Papers, Pres. Ser.*, 4:235–6, and other texts described there).

The DOCUMENTS that accompanied Madison's message, published in the Washington *National Intelligencer* on 10 Mar. 1812 and reprinted as a *Message from the President of the United States, transmitting Copies of Certain Documents obtained from a Secret Agent of the British Government, employed in Fomenting Disaffection to the Constituted Authorities, and In Bringing About Resistance to the Laws; and eventually, in Concert with a British Force, to Destroy the Union of the United States* (Washington, 1812), and again in *ASP*, *Foreign Relations*, 3:545–54, dated from 1809–12 and purported to show that John Henry, a former officer in the United States Army, had received INSTRUCTIONS FROM THE GOV^R^ OF CANADA, Sir James Craig, and approval from Robert Jenkinson, the EARL OF LIVERPOOL, for a SECRET mission to ascertain whether some northeastern states might secede from the Union in the event of an Anglo-American war. Madison and Secretary of State James Monroe negotiated the purchase of the pertinent papers from Henry for $50,000 and passage to France on an American warship (Samuel Eliot Morison, "The Henry-Crillon Affair of 1812," *Proceedings of the Massachusetts Historical Society* 69 [1947/50]: 207–31; Madison, *Papers, Pres. Ser.*, 4:117n).

[1] Manuscript: "intructions."

From James Monroe

Dear Sir washington march 9. 1812

The President will communicate to day to the Congress, the discovery which has been lately made to the government, of an attempt of the British gov^{t}, thro' the gov^{r} gen^{l} of Canada [or at least by him, with the subsequent approbation of that gov^{t}] to promote division & disunion, in the year 1809., the period of difficulty under the embargo, by means of a secret mission to Boston, the object of which was to intrigue with the disaffected. The agent a captain John Henry formerly an officer of the U States, of the Corps of Artilery, appointed in 1798. & having served till 1802. has made the discovery himself, & deliverd up all the original documents. He had been promised reward & honor for his service in that affair; & been disappointed, and revenge for the injury, is among the strong motives, to the measure on his part. The compromitment of the British gov^{t} is complete to the extent stated; and the compromitment of some leaders of the federal party, by designation & strong circumstances, tho' without naming them, equally clear. He insisted that the people with whom he communicated had not broken their faith with him, as the British gov^{t} had, & that therefore, he could not give them up. The documents carry with them the complete evidence of authenticity. It is not probable that they will be contested. many will shrink, from the tendency they will have, with those acquainted with the events of that period, in the Eastern states, to draw attention to them. I will send you a copy of the documents as soon as they are published, which will be forthwith.

The intimation which I gave you, of the vindication said to have been set up by gen^{l} Wilkinson of himself against a certain charge, was taken from a member of Congress, who had rec^{d} it, from D^{r} [Kent?], a particular friend of the general. As it was not relied on in the trial, it is probable that it was merely the suggestion of a friend, who hasarded it, to meet a document which was making an unfavorable impression against him. I hope that you continue to enjoy good health. It would give me great pleasure to be able to make a visit to my farm for a few days & to have an opportunity of seeing you & other friends.

I am dear Sir with great respect & esteem sincerely your friend

Jas Monroe

RC (DLC); first set of brackets in original; one word illegible; endorsed by TJ as received 12 Mar. 1812 and so recorded in SJL.

From William Watson

D^R SIR March 9th 1812

Mr Bacon was Stating to me last Cort that it was Contrary to your orders for Joseph to plate aney more trees without your orders, he Requested me when ever I sent to send a not with the trees and send them to you or him self and they sold be done, when ever I wanted them, and that he wold take my plating by the year, and take it out in my shop, I am very glad the arangment is maid in this way

Mr Lilley & M^r freeman had previously told me tha Joseph had liberty to plate some trees in his own time this was the reson I got hm to plat for me I am your obt servant

W^M WATSON

NB I shold be glad to hav som done by wednesday next

RC (MHi); dateline beneath signature; endorsed by TJ as received 9 Mar. 1812 and so recorded in SJL.

William Watson (d. 1853) was a saddler and harness maker in Albemarle County. He owned property in Charlottesville and was the county jailer, 1811–28 and 1832–41 (Woods, *Albemarle*, 338–9, 380; Mary Rawlings, ed., *Early Charlottesville: Recollections of James Alexander 1828–1874* [1942], 8; *MB*; Albemarle Co. Will Book, 22:193–4, 271–3).

From Charles Christian

RESPECTED SIR, Police office, New York 10th March 1812

I beg leave to offer the enclosed for your patronage. Nothing is left after discharging the demands on Mr Cheetham's estate for his children. your name Sir woud be a host and a passport to the benevolence of the Republicans of this City, It would prevent the Sins of the father being visited on the children, for however, unfortunately, a concurrence of circumstances, and strong passions, impelled Mr Cheetham as a Public writer into error, he was in heart a Republican and an admirer of your virtues.

All whom I have yet solicited have contributed, and it has but this moment occurred to me that I ought in the first instance to have submitted the subscription to you. Were you yet at the head of the Government, I Should not have obtruded this request, and were you Sir, not Mr Jefferson I should not have ventured it at all.

However, Sir, you may be pleased to view this request, made in behalf of five orphans, I beg the favor of a return of the enclosed.

With the highest respect and veneration, I have the honor, Sir, to remain your Obed[t] and very humble Servant

CHARLES CHRISTIAN

RC (MHi); dateline beneath signature; at head of text: "Thomas Jefferson Esq[r]"; endorsed by TJ as received 18 Mar. 1812 and so recorded in SJL. Enclosure not found.

Charles Christian (d. 1829), cabinetmaker and auctioneer, emigrated by 1798 from Great Britain to New York City, where he served intermittently as a police justice and justice of the peace from approximately 1810 until about 1821. He rose in the state militia from lieutenant in 1803 to brigadier general in 1820 (*Longworth's New York Directory* [1798]; [1829], 143; Kenneth Scott, *Early New York Naturalizations: Abstracts of naturalization records from federal, state, and local courts, 1792–1840* [1981], 19; New York *Morning Chronicle*, 6 Apr. 1803; New York *Commercial Advertiser*, 3 Mar. 1810; New York *Columbian*, 13 Jan. 1813; New York *Statesman*, 17 June 1813; *New-York Evening Post*, 2 May 1821, 13 Aug. 1829; Hugh Hastings and Henry Harmon Noble, eds., *Military Minutes of the Council of Appointment of the State of New York, 1783–1821* [1901–02], esp. 1:666, 3:2203).

James CHEETHAM, a prominent New York City newspaper editor, died in 1810, followed a year later by his wife, Rachel Cheetham. He had strongly supported TJ's election to the presidency but eventually joined DeWitt Clinton in opposing the national administration (*DAB*; New York *American Citizen*, 20 Sept. 1810; Albany *Balance, & State Journal*, 1 Jan. 1811; *New-York Weekly Museum*, 5 Oct. 1811; Madison, *Papers, Pres. Ser.*, 3:375).

From Henry Dearborn

DEAR SIR Washington March 10th 1812

My Son has enclosed to me your letter of the 20th ult[o] and informs me that he had sent your letter to the man it was intended for, and requested him to send the machine to his care at Boston and he, my Son, would ship it to Richmond.—be pleased Sir to accept my most sincere thanks for your friendly & flattering observations in relation to my appointment in the Army, I shall accept the appointment from a sence of duty, but with a strong conviction of the weight of responsibility that attaches to the proposed command. I am neither so vain as to think my self as well qualified as I ought to be, or so ambitious as to covit, at this time of life, a place that requires superior tallents, with all the ardour and vigour of youth. I concider my appointment as confined to one department only, and not as a Commander in Chief, otherwise I should not have consented to accept it.—The communications made yesterday by the President to Congress has produced such an explosion as must have a very strong effect on our political parties, and as the facts are fully established beyond all possible doubt, I think it must in a great measure break down our Northern[1] Junto, the names are from tenderness or policy, kept back, as you will receive the perticuliers in the paperes I will not trouble you with them.—The Clinton party are hostile & active, no means are, or will be, omitted for rendering the measures of the President unpopular, or his reelection doubtfull, but with the exception of two or three in Virginia and a very few others in other States, New-York will stand alone, unles they receive the aid of the Tories.—altho I retain some faint hope of avoiding war on honorable termes, the grounds for such hopes are diminishing from day to day. our preperations are slow, but the course is so strongly mark'd out as to leave no chance for retreating, we shall commence the war clumsily, but shall do better & better every year.—

please to accept Sir my most sincere wishes for a long continuence of your life & happiness. H. Dearborn

RC (DLC); between dateline and salutation: "Mr Jefferson"; endorsed by TJ as received 18 Mar. 1812 and so recorded in SJL.

Dearborn's son, Henry A. S. Dearborn, forwarded TJ to Ebenezer Herrick, 20 Feb. 1812, to its addressee.

[1] Manuscript: "Nothern."

From Donald Fraser

Sir— [ca. 10 Mar. 1812]

As the tender Ivy, when boreas blows, naturally, entwines the Sturdy Oak for Support, So, poor literary wights, like my self, must, occasionally, look up to their Superiors in Station & influence.

Having, in the course of last year, lost by Robbery & mis-placed confidence, in depraved men, most of the fruits of many year's arduous industry, both in School & at the desk—I am now, at Sixty years of age reduced to penury!—I have now, two works ready for the Press, by which I might clear a few hundred dollars; But, am utterly unable to purchase the necessary paper.

I must, therefore relinquish these works, or dispose of them for a triffle to some avaricious Book-seller.

I am, at present, very desirous to obtain the office of an Inspector of the customs here, which neats 730$ pr annum.

When, my relation, the Hon. Alexander McRae, passed through this place, a few months Since, on His return from France;

I informed him of the disasters which I had met with, & my intention of applying for a birth in the custom-house; likewise, that I could obtain recommendations from DeWitt Clinton & Some other respectable characters in the Republican ranks—Mr McRae, observed "that he understood that M[r] Clinton & David Gelston, the Collector were not upon the most friendly terms; that I had better apply to the late President of the United States, or Some highly influential character that he had no doubt of my obtaining my object—He further added, that if I did not obtain a recommendation from Such a quarter that he would write to his intimate friend The Secretary of State, to write a few lines to David Gelston,[1] to request of him, as a personal favour, to confer the office on[2] me.

The affability & Benevolence of Your character, induces me to hope, that you will pardon, the Seeming impertinences of, the freedom of the following request;—Namely, that you would have the goodness, to favour me with a few lines to David Gelston Esq[r] as your name, as it ought, will have great weight with the Collector: M[r] Clinton, Gen[l] Morton, R. Riker Esq[r] & Sulvanus Miller Esq[r] are Gent, [of][3] good Standing here.—

Should you think proper to aid a poor, & almost broken-hearted old man; may that Almighty Being, who delights in benevolent actions, reward you, not only temporally here, but, eternally hereafter.

Is, the hearty wish, of one, who has th[e] honor to be, venerable Sir, your obedient & humble Servant. D FRASER

P.S. I taught a School in Fluvanna county virginia, when Your Self was Governor of that State—as the enclosed Certificate will evince—George Thompson, and, if my memory Serves me some of the other Subscribers were members of the Legislature

I have through life, been honest and industrious, imprudent & unfortunate!

RC (DLC: TJ Papers, 195:34726–6a); undated; torn at seal; addressed: "Hon. Tho[s] Jefferson Late President of the United States Monticello"; franked; postmarked New York, 10 Mar.; endorsed by TJ as received from New York on 18 Mar. 1812 and so recorded in SJL. Enclosure not found.

NEATS: to make a net gain (*OED*). On 2 May 1812 Fraser asked SECRETARY OF STATE James Monroe to recommend him to David Gelston (DNA: RG 59, LAR, 1809–17). GEORGE THOMPSON represented Fluvanna County in the Virginia House of Delegates, 1779–82, 1785–88, and 1790–91 (Leonard, *General Assembly*).

[1] Manuscript: "Gelson."
[2] Manuscript: "one."
[3] Omitted word editorially supplied.

From Albert Gallatin

DEAR SIR Washington 10th March 1812

Mr Correa, an interesting and learned Portuguese, who has lately arrived in the Constitution & is recommended to us by Barlow, Humboldt &a, has requested me to transmit to you the enclosed letter and work. He intends to pay you his respects in person this summer.

You have seen from your retreat that our hopes and endeavours to preserve peace during the present European contest have at last been frustrated. I am satisfied that domestic faction has prevented that happy result. But I hope nevertheless that our internal enemies, and the ambitious intriguers who still attempt to disunite, will ultimately be equally disappointed. I rely with great confidence on the good sense of the mass of the people to support their own Government in an unavoidable war, and to check the disordinate ambition of individuals. The discoveries made by Henry will have a salutary effect in annihilating the spirit of the Essex junto, and even on the new focus of opposition at Albany. Pennsylvania never was more firm or united. The South & the West cannot be shaken. With respect to the War, it is my wish and it will be my endeavour so far as I may have any agency, that the evils inseparable from it, should, as far as practicable, be limited to its duration; and that, at its end, the United States may be burthened with the smallest possible quantity of debt, perpetual taxation, military establishments and other corrupting or anti Republican[1] habits or institutions.

Accept the assurances of my sincere and unalterable attachment & respect.

Your obedt Servt ALBERT GALLATIN

RC (DLC); dateline adjacent to signature; at foot of text: "Mr Jefferson"; endorsed by TJ as received 18 Mar. 1812 and so recorded in SJL. Tr (NHi: Gallatin Papers). Enclosure: José Corrêa da Serra to TJ, 6 Mar. 1812, and enclosure.

[1] Reworked from "antient Republican."

From Patrick Gibson

SIR Richmond 11th March 1812

Having at length succeeded in getting your Tobacco reviewed I shall now give you my opinion of it corroborated by the judgement of some of my friends who are more in the habit of purchasing and shipping—

N°s 2593 & 2032	bright-col^{r} good order & well flav^{d} worth about		$6\frac{1}{2}\$$
" 2031	dark " mix'd & tolerably well flav^{d}	"	4 "
" 2033	" " " ragged tho' "	"	3 "
" 2030	" " " and sour	"	2 "
" 2029	" " " with mould		$1\frac{1}{2}$"
" 2034	stemmd very mean dirty & bad flav^{r}		1 "

these are the prices which I think might be expected for such Tobacco, if a purchaser could be met with, which I suppose might be found amongst our manufacturers the first two are the only Hhd^{s} worth shipping I shall however wait your instructions respecting them—The ten bushels Cloverseed order'd in yours of the 1st were sent on the 6th by C: Peyton's Billy to the care of Mr Higginbotham—

The Nail rod & bar iron has at last arrived and shall be sent up by Johnson

Flour has become very dull, a sale could not now be made at more than 9$ cash this fall is in consequence of an impression that an embargo may shortly be expected; and the accounts received this morning from Washington, respecting the conspiracy has tended to increace that apprehension I am with great respect

Your ob^{t} Servt PATRICK GIBSON

RC (ViU: TJP-ER); at foot of text: "Thomas Jefferson Esqre"; endorsed by TJ as a letter from Gibson & Jefferson received 15 Mar. 1812.

SJL records missing letters from David HIGGINBOTHAM of 14 Feb., received from Milton on 15 Feb. 1812, and of 7 Mar., received from Milton presumably on that date but listed as received 6 Mar. 1812.

To Matthew Wills

SIR Monticello Mar. 11. 12.

Understanding from mr Randolph & others that you are disposed to undertake to carry flour from the Shadwell mills to Richmond at half a dollar a barrel, I send the bearer with this letter to inform you that I have at those mills about 234. barrels of flour, 120. of which are now ready, about 60. will be ready by the return of the boats from the 1st trip, and the residue not till after the 20th of April. I shall have also 4. or 5. hhds of tob^{o} to be got ready as fast as the weather permits. you shall have the carriage of all this if you can take off the first 120 barrels immediately, or, if your boats are absent, then on their first return home, and the rest as it will be ready. I shall further have annually about 5. or 600. barrels to carry down which, if I find punctuality I shall be willing to send by your boats. while carrying the present parcel I have no doubt you will readily get other loading from Milton if you chuse to undertake it. be pleased to write me by the bearer whether I may rely on you & on what day your boats will be here. Accept my respects TH: JEFFERSON

PoC (MHi); at foot of text: "Cap[t] Matthew Wells"; endorsed by TJ.

Matthew Wills was a son of Elias Wills, a prominent Fluvanna County landowner (Minnie Lee McGehee and Ellen Miyagawa, "The Story of Wilmington," *Bulletin of the Fluvanna County Historical Society* 50 [1990]: 52, 54; Fluvanna Co. Deed Book, 4:539; Richmond *Enquirer*, 27 June 1807; DNA: RG 29, CS, Fluvanna Co., 1810, 1820).

From Samuel J. Harrison

SIR Lynchbg Mar 13. 1812

your Dft in favor of Brown & C[o] pay[e] the 1st of next Month for $600. has appeard & wishing it Should be Honor'd have accepted it, & Shall pay it at maturity.

If you have intended this Dft as a part of the last payment for the Land, (which from its having been made payable at the Same time it would Seem that you have) I here inform you that I do not expect to make that payment untill the Title Shall be fully clear'd—Scott having Sued both you & me for a Valuable part of the Tract.

Now however frivolous this Suit may be thought to be; yet I ought not, nor Can I believe that you wish me to be Involved in any Trouble about it; which would Evidently you Know be the Case, in the Event of your Death, before the Suit Shall be Decided.

I am Sorry that Scott is So Troublesome, and hope you will not think hard of me for withholding the £400. untill I Shall have Received an undoubted Title to the Land; for I asure you it would be but little Consequence to me, did I not believe that Justice to myself & Family Required that I Should do So.

I here Enclose you the Bond for the last Payment, which has been allways Ready for you had M[r] Griffin applied as you directed him.[1]

The $600. will of course be deducted out of the Tob[o]—

Y[r] M[o] ob S[t] S J HARRISON

RC (ViU: TJP); endorsed by TJ as received 1 Apr. 1812 and so recorded in SJL. Tr (ViU: TJP); entirely in TJ's hand; at head of text: "letter from mr Sam[l] J. Harrison to Th: Jefferson." Enclosure not found.

On 29 Feb. 1812 TJ drew an order on Harrison for $600 in favor of Archibald Robertson, partner of the late William BROWN, to be credited to his "store acct." (*MB*, 2:1273; TJ to Robertson, 1 Mar. 1812).

[1] Paragraph omitted in Tr.

From John Jacob Astor

Sir, New York, 14 March 1812.

I am induced to take the liberty of addressing you, from a belief that it will afford you some satisfaction to be informed of the progress which has been made in carrying on a trade with the Indians, which at it's commencement was favoured with your approbation.

Since I had the pleasure of speaking to you first at Washington concerning it, my constant study has been to attain the object; and for this purpose I sent a ship in November 1809 to Columbia River, the captain of which had several times been there, and enjoyed both the esteem and confidence of the Indians. He took with him a cargo for trade, while in the mean time he was to prepare the Indians for a friendly reception to some white men who would come to stay with them. From thence he was to proceed to the Russian settlement, with a proposition to the Governor for the purpose of friendly intercourse and mutual benefit in trade.

In June 1810 I sent a party of men, say about seventy in number, to ascend the Missouri, with a view to make Columbia River and meet the people who had gone by water, as well as to ascertain the points at which it might be most proper to establish posts for trade, &c.

In September 1810 I sent a second ship to Columbia River, with sixty men and all the means which were thought necessary to establish a post at or near the mouth of that river.

In October 1811 I sent a third ship with above sixty men and all necessaries, to fix a post and to remain at or near Columbia River, and to cooperate with those who had gone before.

The first ship made her port, and from thence made a visit to Count Barranoff, Governor of the Russian settlements in North West America. My propositions met with attention, and I have received from him a letter approving of my plan; but for a final arrangement he referred to the Government and the Russian American Fur Company at St Petersburg. The ship made a voyage to Canton, sold her furs, and returned to Columbia River to meet the one which sailed in 1810, and to concert with her. I hope to hear from them in about three months.

The last account which I had of the party which ascended the Missouri was by letter of 17 July last, about 180 miles below the Mandan[1] Village, where they left the Missouri, and took the Big River in a southern course, this being recommended as nearer and easier to the south branch of Columbia River than the route taken by

Mr Lewis: they were well provided, and had procured near a hundred horses to transport their baggage.—The accounts as to ultimate success were fair and encouraging, and they had no doubt of meeting their friends who went by sea; which I think they must have done in October last.

In June 1809, when Mr Daschkoff was sent to this country, he was charged by his Government to remonstrate to ours against a trade carried on by citizens of the United States to the North West Coast, supplying the Indians with arms & ammunition, which not only afforded the means of killing one another with greater facility, but also endangered their own settlements.—As the Government could not well prevent this, I proposed a plan to Mr Daschkoff which it was thought would meet the end required, namely, an agreement between the American Fur Company of this country and the American Fur Company of Russia, that the former should supply the latter with all articles which they needed from this country and from Europe, (thus becoming their carriers &c) and to have an establishment at or near Columbia; but not to trade with natives near the Russian settlements, and by no means to supply them with arms or ammunition. On the other hand the latter not to deal with any transient traders or ships, nor with the natives at or near Columbia River. This plan was submitted to the Governor of the Russian settlements on the North West Course, who approved of it.

When Count Pahlen came to this country, he also was charged by his government to speak to our government on this Subject.[2] I communicated the plan to him, who was so much pleased with it that he transmitted it to his Court. I sent a gentleman for this purpose to St Petersburg, who presented it to Count Romanskoff, who also is much pleased with it, but there exists some difficulty as to a condition which I had proposed, namely, that the Russian Government should allow the American Fur Company to carry their articles of fur from this country to Russia free of duty, or subject to a moderate duty only (at present they are prohibited). The Government seems well enough disposed to grant this, but it appears there was an engagement entered into between them and the Fur Company at the time of its formation, prohibiting the entry of furs except by the Russian Fur Company, who had not yet felt inclined to consent to the admission. There was however still some hope: to all the other propositions they were ready to agree. Should this plan succeed, I think we shall do very well as far as respects that part of our business.

With respect to our Trade on the frontier and in the Interior, I have not been so fortunate: on the contrary great and insurmountable difficulties are thrown in our way by the present restrictions on our commerce.

After negociating with the Michilimackinac Company for nearly three years to purchase them out, and not succeeding, I had determined to risk an opposition; and accordingly in October 1810 I ordered a quantity of goods from England for this trade, and made engagements with several Indian traders and others, to carry on the business. The people of Canada being informed of this, & knowing that an opposition would be very injurious, and at the same time seeing that I was determined to push one, they proposed to sell to the American Fur Company the property and establishments they had in the Indian country within the territory and boundaries of the United States, together with that at St Joseph's, on condition that we should not for five years trade beyond those boundaries or in British dominions in opposition to them; and that for five years the trade within those limits should be carried on upon joint account. This agreement was completed, and by it the American Fur Company became possessed of the property before mentioned: but as the assortment of goods on hand at St Joseph's, Michilimackinac and other places, was very incomplete for outfits in the interior, it became necessary to obtain a further supply, and we were in hopes that by some change in our political situation we might be enabled to bring in our goods which we had ordered from England, and which had been Transported to St Joseph's (for in consequence of the President's proclamation they had been shipped, though before the 2 Feby 1811, to Canada instead of New York.) But very unfortunately for us our expectations have not been realised. On application to the President in August last we were informed that Congress had left no power with the Executive to grant permission. The consequence has been, that the Indians have been very badly and not half supplied; and though in the mean while we have been under the necessity of retaining in pay the people we had engaged, as well as of keeping up all our establishments at the usual expense, yet we have been unable to carry our business to more than a fourth of it's usual extent.

This dead expense is a serious loss to us, beside the interest on a stock on hand, chief part of which is unsaleable from want of other articles; while on the other hand the useful & saleable commodities lie locked up at Montreal and St Joseph's. If we had only a part of them in the Indian country or at Michilimakinac, we could make out to keep the Indians[3] contented, and keep the trade together in our own hands. But unless this is the case, we shall be under the necessity of selling our property to great sacrifice (as the articles are not saleable except for the Indian trade) either to the British agents for the Indian department of that Government, or to the Canada traders: thus totally relinquishing the trade to them.—

I have been thinking to apply to Congress for relief, at least to get permission to transport our property from the island of St Joseph to the Indian country within the territory or boundary of the United States.

Whether such application would be likely to meet with success, or whether in the present state of things it would be proper to make it, I have not been able to determine. I am so much embarrassed I know not what to do. It is probable that unless our Government do something by which the Indians may get their usual supplies (and which are not now to be had in the United States) there will be great uneasiness on their part, if not actual hostility: for they will become desperate by those privations: under which indeed they cannot exist.—

Perhaps, Sir, you will condescend to give some advice to me how to proceed. The Government, say the President and heads of Executive Departments, are well informed of the situation of the American Fur Company, as no step of importance has been taken without their previous approbation: they know of my plan with the Russians, as well as of my arrangements in the Interior.

The party which ascended the Missouri is under the direction of a very respectable gentleman from Trenton, New Jersey, by the name of Hunt.

The North West Company of Canada having received information of our intention to establish a post at Columbia, sent a party of forty men in 1810 from Lake Superior, with intent to be before us; but they were prevented by Indians in the Rocky Mountains from proceeding further, and were obliged to return. Another party has been sent in 1811 from the same place and for the same object, consisting of sixty men. We shall know next summer how far they have succeeded; at all events I think we must be ahead of them.

By what I can learn there is a great deal of fur on the west side of the mountains, and a considerable business is to be done on the coast with the Russians.

I am with Great Respect Sir your very Humble Servt,

JOHN JACOB ASTOR

N.B. I will thank you To consider that part of my Comunication which relates to the contemplated[4] arrangement with the Russians as Privet

RC (DLC); in a clerk's hand, with closing, signature, and postscript by Astor; above postscript in Astor's hand: "Thomas Jefferson Esqr"; endorsed by TJ as received 25 Mar. 1812 and so recorded in SJL.

John Jacob Astor (1763–1848), merchant, was born in Germany, moved to London in 1779, and settled in New York City in 1784. There he began his career importing musical instruments but quickly moved into the fur trade. By 1787 Astor had begun making trips to Montreal, where he established a warehouse and entered into agreements with local traders. He soon became a leading trader in the Montreal and London markets, and late in the 1790s he began trading directly with China. A millionaire by 1807, Astor sought assistance from local and federal officials, including DeWitt Clinton and Albert Gallatin, in establishing an American fur-trading company that would bypass Canadian traders. His efforts to set up fur-trading outlets on the West Coast failed, and following the War of 1812 Astor concentrated on the Great Lakes region. After a brief involvement in the administration of the Second Bank of the United States, in 1819 he entrusted the management of his American Fur Company to partners and moved to Europe. When he returned to the United States in 1834, Astor sold his fur-trading company and devoted himself to his extensive real-estate holdings in New York City, where he opened the Astor House hotel in 1836 (*ANB*; *DAB*; James P. Ronda, *Astoria & Empire* [1990]).

The meeting between TJ and Astor AT WASHINGTON probably occurred in July 1808 (Astor to TJ, 27 Feb. 1808, TJ to Astor, 13 Apr. 1808, and TJ to Meriwether Lewis, 17 July 1808 [DLC]; Daniel D. Tompkins to TJ, 9 May 1808 [MHi]). In NOVEMBER 1809 Astor sent out the ship *Enterprize*, under Captain John Ebbets. Wilson Price Hunt commanded the land expedition he sent in JUNE 1810. The ship dispatched to the Columbia River in SEPTEMBER 1810 was the *Tonquin*, and the THIRD SHIP, sent in October 1811, was the *Beaver*. Aleksandr A. Baranov wrote Astor tentatively APPROVING OF MY PLAN on 8 Aug. 1810. The GENTLEMAN Astor sent to Saint Petersburg to present his plan to COUNT ROMANSKOFF (Nicolas de Romanzoff) was his son-in-law Adrian Benjamin Bentzon (Bashkina, *United States and Russia*, esp. 687–9, 728–32, 797–9, 820; Ronda, *Astoria & Empire*, 72, 78, 101, 211). The PRESIDENT'S PROCLAMATION of 2 Nov. 1810 reimposed restrictions on American trade with Great Britain and moved Astor to have his trade goods shipped from Europe to CANADA INSTEAD OF NEW YORK. A subsequent United States statute of 2 Mar. 1811 exempted American-owned ships and goods that departed from British ports prior to 2 Feb. 1811 (Madison, *Papers, Pres. Ser.*, 2:612–3; *U.S. Statutes at Large*, 2:651–2).

[1] Manuscript: "Mandam."
[2] Preceding three words interlined.
[3] Astor here canceled "contained."
[4] Manuscript: "contenplated."

To John Barnes

DEAR SIR Monticello Mar. 15. 12

Having several small sums to pay in George town, in order to spare Messrs Gibson & Jefferson the embarrasment of making so many fractional remittances, I have taken the liberty of desiring them to include the whole in a round sum of 200.D. and inclose it to you, presuming on your usual goodness that you will make the distribution for me, to wit

to Henry Foxall	55.46½
Richard Barry	70.52
Joseph Millegan	65.12½
R. C. Weightman, exact sum unknown, but it is under	8.89
	200.

as you will recieve this in a few days, I shall write to the several persons to call on you. Accept the assurance of my constant and affectionate regard TH: JEFFERSON

PoC (DLC); at foot of text: "M[r] J. Barnes"; endorsed by TJ.

To John Brockenbrough

SIR Monticello Mar. 15. 12.

I recieved duly your favor of the 3[d] and about the same time one from mr Harvie of the same purport with your's respecting his bond for 176.90 D now due. I now inclose you the bond, the amount of which, if paid to mess[rs] Gibson & Jefferson of Richmond, will be the same as if paid to myself, and will give you the least trouble.

I cannot pass over this occasion of writing to you, without expressing my acknolegements to the bank over which you preside, for their great indulgence to me. the sum of 8000.D. necessary for me on calling in my accounts on my departure from Washington, they were so kind as to accomodate me with. the crop of my tobacco made in Bedford the last year, and actually sold, enables me as soon as it's amount is due to pay the remaining 3000.D. on my existing note. I have thus been enabled to discharge without distress or disadvantage an amount of debts which I could not have raised on a sudden without painful sacrifices of feeling & of fortune, and for this I am indebted to them, and I assure you of my due sensibility for this great service rendered me. permit me to add the tender to yourself of my great esteem & respect TH: JEFFERSON

PoC (DLC); at foot of text: "D[r] Brockenbrough"; endorsed by TJ. Enclosure not found.

The $176.90 NOW DUE was part of Harvie's payment to TJ for the Southwest Mountain tract (*MB*, 2:1274; Agreement with John Harvie, 17 Feb. 1810).

Account with Mary Daingerfield and Nathaniel H. Hooe

[before 15 Mar. 1812]

1809

Dr Mr Thos Jefferson in Accpt with Mrs Mary Daingerfield & Nathl H. Hooe

January 1st			Reced from the Bank of		
To hire of 7			Fredericksburg Octob^{r} 1st 1810	$250	
men & a woman	$508	00	Interest on same for 9 months	11	25
	536	87	February 10th 1811 Reced from		
Balance &			the bank of Fredericks burg	250	
Interest due	28	87	Interest on the same for		
			13 month^{s} & 10 days	16	66
			balance of hire for 1809	8	
			Interest[1] on same for 2 years		96
January 1st 1810				$536	87
To hire of Tom &					
Edmund	$131	00			
	137	70			
Balance due	6	70	November 10th 1811		
			then Reced of the Bank of		
			Fredericksburg	131	
January[2] 1st 1811			Interest on same for 10^{m} &		
To hire of Tom	$74	00	ten days	6	70
Am^{t} agree on by us				$137	70
for Gaol[3] Fees	20				
EE[4]	$129	57			

MS (MHi); in Hooe's hand; undated; notation by Hooe on verso: "Mr Thos Jefferson With Nathl H. Hooe"; endorsed by TJ: "Hooe Nathan^{l} acc^{t} 129.57."

TJ used this account to calculate that a payment of $131.50 to Hooe would cover his obligations "in full to Jan. 1. 12.," including interest to the end of March 1812, and he accordingly arranged for such a payment to be made (*MB*, 2:1274; TJ to Patrick Gibson and to Hooe, both 15 Mar. 1812).

[1] Manuscript: "Interes."
[2] Manuscript: "Jannuary."
[3] Manuscript: "Goal."
[4] Abbreviation for "errors excepted."

To Patrick Gibson

DEAR SIR Monticello Mar. 15 12.

I safely recieved the clover seed by mr Peyton's boat Johnson again disappointed me in taking down 36. barrels of my flour, instead of the full load of both his boats. I shall no longer trust to him alone therefore, but on the return of the Milton boats (all of which went down at the same time) shall employ others to take down the whole. in truth I begin to be uneasy lest the market should fail, and wish you to sell as fast as you recieve it, so as to secure the price going. Dr Brockenbrough will pay you on my account for John Harvie on demand 176.90 D

I have drawn on you this day in favor of D. Higginbotham for 82. D 15 c and having some debts in other states which ought now to be paid, I must pray you to make remittances for me as follows.

to John Low, bookseller of New York	75
to John Barnes of George town	200.
to the bank of Fredericksbg for Nathaniel H. Hooe of K. George	131.50
	406.50

I accordingly write to these persons that they will recieve from you shortly these sums respectively. Accept the assurance of my great esteem & respect. TH: JEFFERSON

P.S. I have re-opened my letter to acknolege the rect of yours of the 11th since writing the above. I wish you to sell the whole of the tobo mentioned in it, for the best price you can get, be that what it may: and also to sell my flour as you recieve it for the price prevailing, which may be on a credit of 30. or 60. days, if it will make sensible difference in the price.—mr McIntosh of Norfolk will forward to you by the stage a small package of plants sent me from Scotland. I will pray you to pay the postage, & forward them along to Milton by the stage, as the season for planting them is fast passing by.

PoC (DLC); adjacent to signature: "Mr Gibson"; endorsement by TJ partially cut off. Recorded in SJL as a letter to Gibson & Jefferson.

SJL records a missing letter of 15 Mar. 1812 to David HIGGINBOTHAM. It probably contained TJ's instructions that a total of $82.15 be paid as follows: $30.82 for "acceptance for James Salmons [i.e., Sammons]. ante Oct. 7."; $13.33 for "a cow bot. by E. Bacon"; $13 for "a cow bot. of Turner by E. Bacon"; and $25 for "my assumpsit for J. Salmons to Turner Oct. 7." (*MB*, 2:1275). Fleming Turner described the latter two transactions in his own records, listing an account with TJ consisting of a September 1811 debt of $25 "To James Salmonds order on you paye 1st March 1812" and another of $13 described as "your bond paye 1st March

1812 above left in hands David Higginbotham for collection," balanced by $38 to TJ's credit in March 1812 "By my dft on David Higginbotham in favour of Murphy Brown & C° and at My Cr. with them in a/c" (ViU: Fleming Turner Account Book [1806–23], 25–6).

To Nathaniel H. Hooe

DEAR SIR Monticello Mar. 15. 12.

I thought, when you were here, I should certainly have got my crop of flour[1] to Richmond in the course of that month. I have not however got one third of it down even yet. but I avail myself of it's first proceeds to desire Messrs Gibson & Jefferson to remit to the bank of Fredericksburg for your order 131. D 50 c including interest to the last of this month. this remittance you may accordingly expect within a few days.

I have written to Boston for the Spinning machine of which you gave me a note, and to New York for one under a much higher character, carrying 20. spindles, roving for itself, and costing but 25.D. in addition to the patent price which is 20.D. more. Accept the assurance of my esteem & respect. TH: JEFFERSON

PoC (MHi); at foot of text: "Nathl H. Hooe esq."; endorsed by TJ.

No correspondence between TJ and Hooe regarding a SPINNING MACHINE has been found.

[1] Manuscript: "flower."

To John Low

SIR Monticello Mar. 15. 12.

Your letter of Mar. 2. is just now recieved; the former one, after long lingering on the road, had been also recieved, and had compleatly removed all doubts as to my subscription. I presume it had taken place probably 9. or 10. years ago, before the multitude of those applications had obliged me to keep an account of them. the lapse of time and other occupations had compleatly erased it from my memory. expecting soon to have another remittance to make to New York I had delayed yours, with a view to include both in one draught: but now desire my correspondents in Richmond, Messrs Gibson & Jefferson to remit you, without further delay seventy five dollars, which you will accordingly recieve from them in the course of not many days after your reciept of this. regretting the trouble & delay which the default of my memory has occasioned you, I pray you to accept the assurance of my respects. TH: JEFFERSON

PoC (DLC); at foot of text: "Mr John Low"; endorsed by TJ.

To George McIntosh

SIR Monticello Mar. 15. 12.

I am this moment favored with your's of the 4th inst. informing me you had recieved some plants for me from mr Ronaldson. I had before recieved a letter from him notifying me that he had forwarded them. I will ask the favor of you to commit them to the Richmond stage addressed to messrs Gibson & Jefferson of Richmond who will pay the portage & forward them to me. they will come much safer if you can get some passenger to take them under his patronage by the way. I presume they are properly packed; if not, a light box, and wet moss inveloping them, would be the best mode of preserving them, the expence of which will in like manner be reimbursed by messrs Gibson & Jefferson. Accept my thanks for your attention to this object, and still more especially for the kind expressions of your letter towards myself. it is very soothing to me to learn that my ministry in the public affairs has been satisfactory to my fellow citizens. I tender you in return the assurance of my thankfulness & respect. TH: JEFFERSON

PoC (MHi); at foot of text: "Mr McIntosh"; endorsed by TJ.

From James Barbour

DR SIR Richmond March 16th 1812

The accompanying collection of garden Seeds was forwarded to me by Colo Larkin Smith of Norfolk. He suggested to me the necessity of sending them as Soon as possible as the time for Sowing them had, probably, arrived. Supposing the Stage both the safest and most expeditious conveyance I avail myself of that opportunity. I hope you will receive them in the time.

I tender you my best respects, JS: BARBOUR

N B. Just as I had finished this note a waggon from Milton passed and I have confided the Seeds to him—R. Johnston.

JB

RC (MHi); endorsed by TJ as received 21 Mar. 1812 and so recorded in SJL.

To Henry Foxall

Dear Sir Monticello Mar. 16. 12.

The stove arrived safely; I have set it up and find it to answer perfectly. the room is very small where it is placed, and is fully warmed by it in a few minutes. a room of larger size would require the stove to be larger. I certainly like it better than any stove I have ever seen, & not doubting that when it becomes known it will be in great demand, I expect you will find it worth while to make one or two sizes above this. I have a large dome-room of 24.f. diam. which needs a stove, but a large one. I have not yet learned how to prevent it's smoaking in the first moments of lighting the fire. I have desired Mess[rs] Gibson & Jefferson of Richmond to remit a sum of money to mr Barnes for the paiment of this and two or three other debts there & I have desired mr Barnes to pay you out of it 55.46½ D the amount of the bill sent me. Accept the assurance of my great esteem & respect

Th: Jefferson

PoC (MHi); at foot of text: "M[r] Henry Foxall"; endorsed by TJ.

To Joseph Milligan

Sir Monticello Mar. 16. 12

I duly recieved your favor of Feb. 2. with a specimen of the size & type you proposed for the Manual, and think you have done prudently in accomodating it to the pocket rather than the shelf of a library. I have desired my correspondents, Mess[rs] Gibson & Jefferson of Richmond, to remit for me to mr Barnes a sum of money, out of which I have requested mr Barnes to pay you sixty five Dollars 12½ Cents the amount of your account. it will be some few days after your reciept of this before the remittance will get to his hands. should you reprint the Scientific dialogues I shall be glad of a copy. this would be better in 8[vo] to stand along side of other books on the same subject which are mostly in 8[vo]. Accept the assurances of my esteem & respect

Th: Jefferson

PoC (DLC); at foot of text: "M[r] Joseph Milligan"; endorsed by TJ.

Milligan announced the publication of his edition of TJ's *A Manual of Parliamentary Practice: for the Use of the Senate of the United States* (Philadelphia, 1812) later this month (Washington *National Intelligencer*, 24 Mar. 1812). An image of the title page is reproduced elsewhere in this volume.

To Roger C. Weightman

Sir Monticello Mar. 16. 12

You were so kind, some time ago, as to send me a copy of Scott's works (a miniature edition) which came safely to hand. the price was not mentioned, but I have desired mr Barnes to pay it out of a sum which will be remitted him on my account within a few days after your reciept of this. Accept the assurance of my respect

Th: Jefferson

PoC (MoSHi: TJC-BC); date enhanced by TJ; at foot of text: "Mr Weightman"; endorsed by TJ as a letter of 15 Mar. 1812, but recorded under 16 Mar. 1812 in SJL.

To George Divers

Dear Sir Monticello Mar. 18. 12.

I promised to stock you with the Alpine Strawberry as soon as my beds would permit. I now send you a basket of plants & can spare you 10. baskets more if you desire it. their value, you know, is the giving strawberries 8. months in the year. but they require a large piece of ground and therefore I am moving them into the truck patch, as I cannot afford them room enough in the garden. I have recieved from McMahon some plants of the true Hudson strawberry. the last rains have brought them forward & ensured their living. I have been 20. years trying unsuccesfully to get them here. the next year I shall be able to stock you. I have recieved also from McMahon 4. plants of his wonderful gooseberry.[1] I measured the fruit of them 3.I. round. by the next year I hope they will afford you cuttings. about 20. plants of the Sprout kale have given us sprouts from the 1st of December. their second growth now furnishes us a dish nearly every day, & they will enable me this year to stock my neighbors with the seed. we have now got the famous Irish grass, Fiorin, ensured and growing. they make hay from it in Dec. Jan. Feb. I recieved the plants from Ireland about a month ago.[2] I am now engaged in planting a collection of pears. I know you have several kinds of very fine. if your Nursery can spare 2. of each kind I will thank you for them: if not, then some cuttings for engrafting, tying up each kind separately. Affectionately Yours

Th: Jefferson

PoC (MHi); at foot of text: "Mr Divers"; endorsed by TJ.

[1] Reworked from "strawberry."

[2] Sentence interlined.

From George Divers

D[R] SIR Farmington 18th Mar: 1812

I receiv'd the alpine[1] strawberry plants sent by your Servant, for which accept my thanks. I send you seven pear scions.[2] they are small being ingrafted the last spring. two of them is a very good forward pear. the other five are of the best kinds that I have, would have sent you some slips, but I shall engraft Some for myself and shall think of you when I set about it,

The Irish grass you speak of must be a great acquisition, I shall be thankful for a little of the seed of the sprout kale and a few cuttings of the large gooseberry when they can be spar'd, with sincere respect

I am Your friend GEO: DIVERS

RC (MHi); addressed: "Thomas Jefferson esq Monticello"; endorsed by TJ as received 18 Mar. 1812 and so recorded in SJL.

[1] Manuscript: "aspine."
[2] Manuscript: "cions."

From William D. Meriwether

DEAR SIR March 19th 1812

I send by your boy two bushels of malt but it is not sufficiently dried for grinding, and should youe want any more will with pleasure furnish youe with[1] it, barly to sowe if youe are not already supplied

I am much obliged to you for your books on brewing, in hopes that I may profit by them, and will return them as soon as the Season for brewing is over; and remain

Yours Respectfuly W D. MERIWETHER

RC (MHi); dateline beneath signature; addressed: "Thomas Jefferson Esqr Monticello"; endorsed by TJ as received 19 Mar. 1812 and so recorded in SJL.

[1] Manuscript: "wit."

To Thomas Erskine Birch

SIR Monticello Mar. 21. 12.

Your favor of 24th Feb. was recieved a few days ago. soon after the date of mine to you of Jan. 3. your's of the 1st of that month came to hand, as also the volume forwarded with it: for which be pleased to accept the renewal of my thanks, and the confirmation of the favorable expectations I had formed of it's contents.

Every appearance warrants the expectation that the scenes in which you bore a part in the revolutionary war are to be shortly renewed, but under circumstances much more favorable to us. the Actors on the former occasion will from their years be entitled to be spectators only on this. the appropriate function of age on such an occasion is to address it's prayers to heaven that it's favors to both parties may be proportioned to the justice of their respective causes. more I am sure we need not desire. Accept the assurances of my esteem & respect. TH: JEFFERSON

PoC (DLC); at foot of text: "M[r] Tho[s] Erskine Birch"; endorsed by TJ.

To John Bradbury

SIR Monticello Mar. 21. 12

I duly recieved your letter of the 5th inst. and congratulate you on your safe return from your long peregrination. I hope it will not be long before we shall have the benefit of the information it has furnished you.

With respect to the establishment of a Botanical garden at Washington by the General government, be assured it is an idea without the least foundation. no doubt it is desired by every friend of science; and it may be expected by such of them as have not sufficiently contemplated either the powers or the present circumstances of the government. there have been repeatedly applications by individuals, & one of them lately, for the use of some of the public grounds at Washington for the establishment of such a garden, and if the suspicion that it would be converted into a mere kitchen-garden for the supply of the town-market can be removed, it is in the power of the President, and would probably be within his disposition so to dispose of it. but I do not believe the government will or can do more. the setting you right in this fact being the best service I can render you in the case, I do it as a duty & add with pleasure the assurance of my esteem & respect. TH: JEFFERSON

PoC (DLC); at foot of text: "M[r] John Bradbury"; endorsed by TJ.

Early in TJ's retirement William Thornton lamented that nothing had been done to establish a BOTANICAL GARDEN AT WASHINGTON. More recently Charles Whitlow had sought congressional permission to use SOME OF THE PUBLIC GROUNDS for that purpose. Neither he nor Bradbury succeeded (Thornton to TJ, 30 Aug. 1809; *JHR*, 8:134 [20 Jan. 1812]).

To Charles Christian

SIR Monticello Mar. 21. 12

I have duly recieved your favor of the 10th inst. proposing to me to join in a contribution for the support of the family of the late mr Cheetham of New York. private charities, as well as contributions to public purposes in proportion to every one's circumstances, are certainly among the duties we owe to society, & I have never felt a wish to withdraw from my portion of them. the general relation in which I, some time since, stood to the citizens of all our states, drew on me such multitudes of these applications as exceeded all resource. nor have they much abated since my retirement to the limited duties of a private citizen, & the more limited resources of a private fortune. they have obliged me to lay down as a law of conduct for myself, to restrain my contributions for public institutions to the circle of my own state, & for private charities to that which is under my own observation. and these calls I find more than sufficient for every thing I can spare. nor was there any thing in the case of the late mr Cheetham, which could claim with me to be taken out of a general rule. on these considerations I must decline the contribution you propose, not doubting that the efforts of the family itself, aided by those who stand in the relation to them of neighbors and friends, in so great a mart for industry as they are placed in, will save them from all danger of want or suffering. with this apology for returning the paper sent me, unsubscribed, be pleased to accept the tender of my respect

TH: JEFFERSON

PoC (DLC); at foot of text: "Mr Charles Christian." Enclosure not found.

To Donald Fraser

SIR Monticello Mar. 21. 12.

I have duly recieved your letter & now return you the papers it inclosed. I would very willingly serve you in solliciting the office you desire in New York had I a right to take that liberty with any one there. as it is, the only service I can render you is in counselling you as to the most hopeful course of application. it is exactly one of those suggested by yourself. the influence of the Secretary of state, if you can engage it thro' any of your friends, is certainly the most likely to be of avail to you. I have some expectations of seeing him here soon, and will not fail to do you justice in presenting the subject to him. Accept my best wishes for your success & happiness.

TH: JEFFERSON

PoC (DLC); at foot of text: "M[r] Donald Frazer"; endorsed by TJ. Enclosure not found.

From Ezra Sargeant

SIR New York 21 March 1812

Your Excellency will receive by this days mail Seventy one copies of "Proceedings &c" put up in 3 parcels and directed to you at Monticello.

Those directed to be put up for P. Magruder Esq and M[r] Otis I expect to forward agreable to your excellency's direction on tuesday next; a Gentleman of my acquaintance purposing going to the Southwar[d] on that day. Should I however be dissappointed of that opportunity your excellency may rely on my embracing the first chance afterwards.—

With the highest respect I remain Sir Your Excellency's Most ob[t] Humb[l] Serv[t]

E. SARGEANT
p. W. B. GILLEY

RC (MHi); edge trimmed; in Gilley's hand; between dateline and salutation: "Thomas Jefferson Esq[r]"; endorsed by TJ as a letter from Sargeant received 25 Mar. 1812 and so recorded in SJL.

William B. Gilley (ca. 1785–1830) operated a bookstore and publishing house on Broadway in New York City from about 1814 until his death (*Longworth's New York Directory* [1814], 106; [1830], 284; *Catalogue of recent publications for sale by William B. Gilley* [New York, 1819]; *New-York Evening Post*, 25 Nov. 1830).

Sargeant's firm sent SEVENTY ONE COPIES of Jefferson, *Proceedings*, to Monticello separately by post. The title page to this pamphlet is reproduced elsewhere in this volume.

To James Barbour

DEAR SIR Monticello Mar. 22. 12.

Your favor of the 16th was safely delivered last night by the waggoner, together with the packet of seeds you were so kind as to recieve and forward. I pray you to accept my thanks for this friendly care. my friends & correspondents Gibson & Jefferson, would have saved you the trouble of seeking a conveyance for the packet, & would do it on any future similar[1] occasion, if simply sent to them; & would pay all charges. I mention this in the event of your being embarrassed again with such an address. the packet arrived in good time, exactly in the season for planting.

I fear the station you have accepted, altho' almost a sinecure in peace, will be found a laborious and disquieting one in the trials of war now coming upon us. but it is happy for us that the event finds at the helm of our state one who will not sleep at his post. I think you should begin at once to clear the ship for action, & especially to see if sound in all her parts and make provision accordingly. God send you & us a safe deliverance. TH: JEFFERSON

PoC (DLC); at foot of text: "H. Excellency Governor Barbour"; endorsed by TJ.

[1] Word interlined.

From Hugh Nelson

DEAR SIR March 22[d] 1812.

An application is now pending before Congress on behalf of the officers and soldeirs, of the late Virginia line on state establishment, to secure to them the Lands which Virginia had engaged to give them; and for which in many instances Land Warrants were issued, but which have never been satisfied. In the cession which Virginia made to the United States, of her lands lying on the North-West of the Ohio River, a reservation was made, in behalf of the[1] officers and soldeirs of the Virginia Line on continental establishment, of lands lying between the Scioto and little Miami Rivers, sufficient to satisfy their claims. But in this compact of cession, the officers[2] and soldeirs of the state line on state establishment were omitted. It appears however by a transcript from the proceeding of the Legislature of Virg[a] that in the propositions first made on her part to the old Congress; the officers[3] and soldeirs on the state establishment were included, as well as the officers and soldeirs of the state on Continental Establishment. This record is before me, and contains the demand for the state Troops, as well as for the Continental Troops. It was referred to a committee of which M[r] Madison was the member on the part of Virginia. The proposition embracing the claim of the Troops for their bounties in Lands, was denominated the fifth in the series. And the committee of Congress in reporting on the proposals, resolve that this 5th proposition is reasonable: but on reciting this proposition which they do in their report, they have omitted to mention the Troops on that establishment. This omission pervades all the subsequent proceedings: and in the deed of cession made on the part of Virginia, and executed by her Delegates in Congress, of whom I find yourself was one, this class of claimants is totally omitted. In examining the Journals of the old Congress, I find that when any proposition made by Virginia was excepted to by the Committee; that their objections are reported to Congress and acted upon. But it no where appears from the Journals, that this claim is objected to: whence we infer that it was an omission arising from inadvertancy which crept in very early in ye transaction; and was never afterwards rectified. The original resolutions of the Virginia Legislature are dated of the 2d January 1781. I presume they were submitted to Congress very shortly after. I find by recurring to the Journals of the Old Congress, that they were frequently under consideration. The deed of cession was executed on the first day of March 1784, signed by Thomas Jefferson, Samuel Hardy, Arthur Lee and James Monroe.

Altho' you were not a member of the old Congress at the time that this negociation between Virginia and the United States first commenced; I have no doubt that a subject of this Importance attracted your attention, and that you can probably give more information on it, than can be derived from any other source. I have conversed very freely with Mr Madison, but he is so entirely occupeid with his official duties; that it wou'd be almost unkind to attempt to recall him to the Scenes of the old congress: and he had no immediate and particular recollection on this subject.

If it shou'd be in your power to throw any light upon this subject, so as to shew that this omission of the officers[4] and soldeirs of the state Line, arose from accident, or was the result of premeditation and design; it wou'd be greatly serviceable to a class of our meritorious Citizens, who, I am well asured, have experienced in all Instances, your freindship and protection—Excuse me, my dear Sir, for this Liberty. Convinced that our feelings on this subject are in perfect Unison, I venture to impose this Task upon one whose whole life has been devoted to the service of his Country; and whose noblest Gratification has arisen from advancing the good of his fellow Citizens.

I hope ere this, your manuscript which you were so kind as to lend me, has been safely returned. Letters from home inform me that it was carreid to Monticello, on the day after my directions to that effect were receivd.

You see by the public Prints that Congress have acted in consonance with the wishes of the President, in making every exertion to place the Country in a manly attitude to assert its rights. Troops are to be raised; The munitions of War to be provided; and money to meet all these demands is to be suppleid. Yet we are told that the nation will not beleive that Congress are serious and in earnest in making these preparations. That they will not make war eventually. And that all this is Gasconade. That war and The Taxes will produce a revolution in the public sentiment. I consider these as the idle suggestions of those who labour constantly to bring the republican party into contempt; and not the serious sentiments of the firm and steady friends of the administration. If you have leisure to communicate your reflections and information on these Topics I shou'd be highly gratifeid by them.

The infernal machinations of the British Gov^t for many years past, to sow discord and disunion amongst us, and to dismember the Union, is now completely developed in the disclosures made to our Government by Mr Henry. This will be accompanied by one of the printed documents containing the whole of these disclosures.

Dispaches were recd on Friday afternoon by the Eng. Minister. On Saturday he had an interview with Colo. Monroe—We have no certain information of its object. It is rumored that he is instructed to demand the meaning of our military preparations.

With sentiments of profound Respect I remain y^r hble s^t

Hugh Nelson

Can you give us any information about Lewis and Clarkes Journal, when we may expect its publication—many Enquireis are made about it, and I am requested to ask if you can afford any intelligence.

RC (MHi); endorsed by TJ as received from Washington on 25 Mar. 1812 and so recorded in SJL. Enclosure described in note to James Madison to TJ, [9 Mar. 1812].

The phrase "and upon their own State Establishment" was inadvertently omitted in the official copy of the 2 Jan. 1781 RESOLUTIONS OF THE VIRGINIA LEGISLATURE transmitted to the Continental Congress fifteen days later by TJ as governor. The error was repeated in subsequent laws relating to Virginia's formal CESSION to the nation of the Northwest Territory in the spring of 1784 (*PTJ*, 4:386–91, 6:573–4, 579, 580n). On 2 Apr. 1812 Nelson submitted a report to the United States House of Representatives relative to the claims of Virginia veterans which stated that, although his committee could not determine whether the omission of troops on the Virginia state establishment was "casual and inadvertent, or premeditated and intentional," it recommended that provisions be made to satisfy the bounties as they had originally been promised by the Virginia legislature (*ASP*, *Public Lands*, 2:374–5). Congress did not settle the matter until 30 May 1830, when President Andrew Jackson signed an act that set aside up to 310,000 acres of public land for "the relief of certain officers and soldiers of the Virginia line and navy, and of the continental army, during the revolutionary war" (*U.S. Statutes at Large*, 4:422–4).

[1] Manuscript: "of the of the."
[2] Manuscript: "offcers."
[3] Manuscript: "offcers."
[4] Manuscript: "offcers."

To Larkin Smith

DEAR SIR Monticello Mar. 22. 12.

Your letter of the 3d inst. with the packet of seeds you were so kind as to forward, came safely to hand yesterday evening, and of course in good time for being committed to the earth. accept my thanks for this kind attention. and indeed I am afraid it may not be the last, as my foreign correspondents are much in the habit of directing packages for me to the Collector of the port to which the vessel is bound. duties, or any other expences which may have occurred, or may occur on such occasions, will always be immediately remitted by messrs Gibson & Jefferson, my established correspondents at Richmond, on notice of them; who will also recieve such packages, pay charges & forward them to me. I mention this to lessen the inconveniences to which your friendship might expose you on any future similar occasion.

In the multitude of characters with which the course of my life has necessarily brought me into correspondence, I look back with great satisfaction on those whose probity & pure patriotism have marked them as moving above the croud of their fellow travellers; as pursuing, thro' the turmoils of our transient scenes that honorable and virtuous course which gives inward happiness thro' life, confidence in death, and a sweet remembrance after. I can say with truth & sincerity that in this roll of estimable worthies, your name has stood eminent in my view, and has ever nourished sincere wishes for your health & prosperity. with the assurance of which be pleased to accept those of my most friendly esteem & respect

TH: JEFFERSON

PoC (MoSHi: TJC-BC); at foot of text: "Col° Larkin Smith"; endorsed by TJ.

To Francis Adrian Van der Kemp

SIR Monticello Mar. 22. 12.

I am indebted to you for the communication of the Prospectus of a work embracing the history of civilised man, political & moral, from the great change produced in his condition by the extension of the feudal system over Europe thro' all the successive effects of the revival of letters, the invention of printing, that of the compass, the enlargement of science, & the revolutionary spirit, religious & civil, generated by that. it presents a vast Anatomy of fact and reflection, which if duly filled up would offer to the human mind a wonderful mass for contemplation. your letter does not ascertain whether the work is already executed, or only meditated: but it excites a great desire to see it compleated, and a confidence that the author of the Analysis is best able to develope the profound views, there only sketched. it would be a library in itself, and, to our country, particularly desirable and valuable, if executed in the genuine republican principles of our constitution. the only orthodox object of the institution of government is to secure the greatest degree of happiness possible to the general mass of those associated under it. the events which this work proposes to embrace will establish the fact that unless that mass retains a sufficient controul over those entrusted with the powers of their government, these will be perverted to their own oppression, and to the perpetuation of wealth & power in the individuals, & their families, selected for the trust. whether our constitution has hit on the exact degree of controul necessary, is yet under experiment; and it is a most encouraging reflection that, distance & other difficulties securing us, against the brigand governments of Europe, in the safe enjoiment of our farms and firesides, the experiment stands a better chance of being satisfactorily made here than on any occasion yet presented by history. to promote therefore unanimity and perseverance in this great enterprise, to disdain despair, encourage trial, & nourish hope are the worthiest objects of every political & philanthropic work: and that this would be the necessary result of that which you have delineated, the facts it will review, and the just reflections arising out of them will sufficiently ensure. I hope therefore that it is not in petto merely, but already compleated; and that my fellow citizens, warned in it of the rocks and shoals on which other political associations have been wrecked, will be able to direct theirs with a better knolege of the dangers in it's way.

The enlargement of your observations on the subjects of natural history, alluded to in your letter, cannot fail to add to our lights respecting them, & will therefore ever be a welcome present to every friend of science. Accept, I pray you the assurance of my great esteem and respect. TH: JEFFERSON

RC (PHi); addressed: "M[r] Fr. Adr. Van der Kemp at Oldenbarneveld State of New York"; franked; postmarked Milton, 25 Mar. 1812; notation by Van der Kemp on address cover: "Progress de L'Esprit humain" ("Progress of the human spirit"). PoC (DLC).

From Samuel Lukens

RESPECTED FRIEND Montgomery Cty. M.D. 3[d] mo: 23[d] 1812

I stand security to a Man in my Neighbourhood for the sum of $600 which Isaac Shoemaker obtained from him some years ago, I have been urging him to pay the money for some years past, and he has promised so often, and failed, that I no longer have any confidence in him.—I now have to request the favour of being informed, thro' thee, whether Isaac is in thy neighbourhood, or, in Charlottesville, Any information thou canst give respecting him, (or if he is in thy vicinity) the visible property he has about him will greatly oblige thy real friend SAM[L] LUKENS

P.S. My not knowing the name of another individual in thy neighbourhood must apologize for the liberty I have taken.—Please direct to Brookville M.D.

RC (MHi); endorsed by TJ as received 1 Apr. 1812 and so recorded in SJL.

From Ebenezer Herrick

SIR West Stockbridge March 24th 1812

yours of Feb[y] 20th has Just come to hand containing two bills of the amount of 15. Dollars with a request that I would send you one of my machines Also a Copy of an Advertisement taken from a News paper which is not Just as I have published but Sir the plan of the machine is such as to admit of any number of spindles that will best accommodate for familys use the best Recommendation I think will be to say it has done—a young woman my Neighbour has spun last season, over 1000 Runs of good woolen yarn at the rate of from 6 to 9 Runs per day she observes that she can now spin 10. runs per day on the same machine—as to [...] person spining at that rate without some [acqua]intance with it can not be expected as practice is the only way to be expert at any business—as to spining Cotton we have had but small opportunity to ascertain the value of it for that purpose as great numbers of Cotton Factories are in this vicinity—we find it will spin Cotton of a coarse Quality[1] best however—It is great repute here—as to the method of Conveyance by Vessels from Boston to Richmond. I think will be some trouble as I live 150. miles from Boston and but about 25. miles from Hudson—a machine might be sent to New York at any time—I shall delay sending it on until I hear from you again, will then convey it as you may direct please to write me as soon as possible & accept the assurance of my Respect

Ebenezer Herrick

RC (DLC); torn at seal; at foot of text: "Thomas Jefferson Esqr"; endorsed by TJ as received 8 Apr. 1812 and so recorded in SJL.

The COPY OF AN ADVERTISEMENT that TJ sent Herrick (see note to TJ to William Thornton, 14 Jan. 1812) was substantially the same as the version Herrick placed in a Massachusetts newspaper, but omitted a testimonial by Arthur Scholfield that the Domestic Spinner would "answer a very good purpose for private families" and Herrick's description of the machine as "about six feet long, two and an half feet wide, and two feet and an half high." Herrick also stated that one person using his invention could spin "at least one run a day, with the same labor required to spin two runs on a common wheel" (*Pittsfield Sun*, 9 Mar. 1811).

[1] Word interlined in place of "kind."

From Elizabeth Trist

My Dear Sir Birdwood March 24th 1812

The only hope I have of your remembrance of me, is that you are not apt, to forget those whom you have once honor'd with the Appellation of friend, under that impression I can not deny my self the pleasure of once more addressing a few lines to you, not to trouble you with unavailing regrets for the misfortunes and sorrows of those whoese welfare my heart takes the deepest interest in, but to assure you that neither time or situation can ever erase from my recollection the sense I have of your goodness and the happiness I have enjoy'd in your society nor can I ever be indifferent to what concerns your happiness or welfare, and offer my congratulations on the termination of your law suit which tho it has cost you trouble and expence has increased the respect and veneration of your Countrymen

I feel sorry for poor Livingstone tho an imprudent man and I fear not as correct in principle as he ought to be but there are so many amiable traits in his character, that it induces one to varnish over the defects, the recent proof I have had of his kindness and goodness of heart in offering through the medium of his wife to take my Grand sons and to make arangements for their establishment in College I can never forget altho very happy that their Mother did not acceed to the proposal and approve of her detirmination to keep them with her unless she can pay for their Education her self altho, it may be a heart rending circumstance to be denied the means of doing what will be perhaps of importance to their respectability and welfare but I console my self with the hope that they may be honest industrious Men and that the difficulties they may have to struggle with, will eventually be for their advantage it is on their accounts I feel the depression of poverty, for my self I have no apprehensions except that of living too long and becoming burthensome to my friends in the midst of my troubles I have found comfort, and am perfectly content with my situation every thing is in the roughest state immaginable but harmony and contentment with good health the first blessing that Heaven can bestow and we enjoy them untincture[d] with ambition, or mortification of being slighted because fortune has frownd upon us, few things cou'd induce me to mix with the multitude again never from choice If I was worth a Million of Dollars

I hope you have finnish'd all your business on the River and that the mill goes on prosperously since you have got rid of those vagrants I heard with great concern that you had had an attack of the Rhumatism tho it was what I expected from your exposing your self so much on the canal when once that is fixd in your system I shall have no cause to envy your agility the maladies of age are numerous those who escape with a moderate portion of them has reason to be thankful, and so highly favord as you have been, has made you careless of the blessing, I wish you to live long and to have no infirmities that will lessen the pleasure of existance, I want to hear what effect these convulsions of the earth have had upon Monticello whether the shock was severe we felt no more than a little tremour when our nearest Neighbours that were settled on more elevated spots were thrown into the greatest consternati[on] from the dread of their dwellings being destroy'd the account we had of an erruption in Bunkum County N Carolina has been contradicted, but if Mr Peirces information may be credited I can not contemplate any thing more horrid than the situation of those people who were exposed to its violence he seems to think the Mississippi has been form'd by [earthgars?][1] but that may not be exactly his Ideas for the paper was so muteilated that contain'd his narrative that I cou'd not make out one half of it but the same Idea enterd my mind when I enterd that River in 84, I have received letters as late as the 16th Jany from Baton Rouge and 29th

from Orleans neither take any notice of the earthquake which induces me to believe that the shock has not been very severe at either of those places, certain it is that many awful and melancholy events have taken place in the course of a few months, May God preserve you many years to your family and friends is the prayer of your ever grateful E TRIST

RC (MHi); edge trimmed; endorsed by TJ as received 5 Apr. 1812 and so recorded in SJL.

Elizabeth Trist's GRAND SONS were Nicholas Philip Trist and Hore Browse Trist, whose MOTHER was Mary Brown Trist Jones. The VAGRANTS who had managed TJ's mill at Shadwell were members of the Shoemaker family.

[1] Word illegible. Trist may have intended "earth jars," as in "jarrings of the earth."

To James Madison

DEAR SIR Monticello Mar. 26. 12

Your favor of the 6th was duly recieved. the double treachery of Henry will do lasting good both here & in England. it prostrates the party here, and will prove to the people of England, beyond the power of palliation by the ministry, that the war is caused by the wrongs of their own nation. The case of the Batture not having been explained by a trial at bar as had been expected, I have thought it necessary to do it by publishing what I had prepared for the use of my counsel. this has been done at New York, and the printer informs me by a letter of the 21st that he had forwarded by mail some copies to myself, and would send by the stage, under the care of a passenger those I had ordered for the members of both houses. but those sent to me are not yet arrived. from this parcel I shall send some to yourself and the members of the Cabinet, which I have thought it necessary to mention by anticipation, that you may understand how it happens, if it does happen, that others get copies before yourself.—every body in this quarter expects the declaration of war as soon as the season will permit the entrance of militia into Canada, & altho' peace may be their personal interest and wish, they would, I think, disapprove of it's longer continuance under the wrongs inflicted and unredressed by England. God bless you and send you a prosperous course through your difficulties.

TH: JEFFERSON

P.S. I had reason to expect that M. De-tutt Tracy, had, by the last vessel from France sent me some works of his thro' mr Warden, and he thro' yourself.

RC (DLC: Madison Papers). PoC (DLC); at foot of text: "The President of the US."; endorsed by TJ.

The PRINTER was Ezra Sargeant.

To Patrick Magruder and Samuel A. Otis

SIR, Monticello Mar. 26. 12.

The proceedings of the Executive of the US. in the case of the Batture of New Orleans, which have been the subject of complaint on the part of Edward Livingston, not having been explained through the medium of a judiciary trial as was expected,[1] I have thought it due to the nation at large, to the National legislature, and to the Executive to make that explanation public through the ordinary channel of the press. and I have therefore taken the liberty of desiring mr Sargeant of New York, the printer, to send under cover to yourself 144.[2] copies, of which I will ask the favor of you to lay one copy on the desk of each member of the House[3] of Representatives for their acceptance. I salute you with assurances of esteem & respect.

TH: JEFFERSON

PoC (DLC); letter to Magruder, with TJ's emendations to show what went to Otis; at foot of text: "Mr Patrick Magruder Clerk of the H. of R of the US" and (added separately) "Mr Samuel A. Otis Secretary of the Senate"; endorsed by TJ as a letter to Otis and Magruder, but recorded in SJL only as a letter to Otis.

Samuel Allyne Otis (1740–1814), secretary of the United States Senate, 1789–1814, was born in Barnstable, Massachusetts, and graduated from Harvard College in 1759. He read law briefly but established himself as a merchant in Boston by 1762. During the American Revolution, Otis acted as a clothier and deputy quartermaster general for the Continental army. He was a member of the Massachusetts House of Representatives in 1776 and again from 1781–87, including service as Speaker, and he represented the state in the Confederation Congress, 1787–88. Under the new constitution Otis became the first secretary of the United States Senate and, despite his Federalist sympathies, he held the post until his death (*Sibley's Harvard Graduates*, 14:471–80; John J. Waters Jr., *The Otis Family in Provincial and Revolutionary Massachusetts* [1968; repr. 1975]; *PTJ*, 23:114–5; Washington *Daily National Intelligencer*, 23 Apr. 1814).

[1] Preceding three words interlined.

[2] Above this number TJ interlined "35."

[3] Above this word TJ interlined "Senate."

From John Barnes

Dear Sir, George Town 27th March, 1812.

Your favor of the 15h Inst inclosing sundry Accots for payment—as well, Messr Gibson and Jeffersons Order, on Bank of Columbia for $200—recd 23d have been Applied[1]—as follows viz—

To J Milligan for	$65.12½
R. Weightman	6.25.
J Barry	70.50.
	paid 141.87½
Mr Foxall promised to send me ℔ Clerk, his Acct (not yet recd)[2]	55.46½
	would be 197.34.
Mr Barry presented to me, Minute of his former a/c stated by yourself wherein you Credited for a diamond which he has promised to explain to you & I requested him (when so done)[3] to call on me; for payment—	8.80.
	$206.14. whole Amt
deducting Messr G & Js order	200.
will be placed to yr debit wth me—	$6.14. if correct.

no present hopes of succeeding in the purchase of a sett of exchange—on France.—

cannot you induce Mr Warden or some other friend—to procure for me a sett—to the Value of $1000 or 1100—which I shd be inabled to pay for, on accot of the good General! referring you to my late letters of the 13th and 16th Ulto—

I am Dear Sir—most Respectfully—

Your very Obedt servant John Barnes.

RC (ViU: TJP-ER); at foot of text: "Thomas Jefferson Esqr Monticello"; endorsed by TJ as received 8 Apr. 1812 and so recorded in SJL.

Richard barry received $70.52, not $70.50 (TJ to Barnes, 15 Mar. 1812; Barry to TJ, 27 Mar. 1812). Barnes's letter of the 16th ulto was actually dated 26 Feb. 1812.

[1] Manuscript: "Applid."

[2] Omitted closing parenthesis editorially supplied.

[3] Omitted closing parenthesis editorially supplied.

From Richard Barry

SIR Washington March 27th 1812

I received your letter of March the 16th in which there appears to be an Omission of the price of a Diamond purchased for you which cost eight Dollars and eighty cents—which appears by the inclosed settlement I send you I recd from Mr Barnes 70.$\frac{52}{100}$ Dollrs

Sir

There is estimates to be received the 6th of April by Mr Granger for finishing the Hotel I intend giving in one I thank you Sir for a few lines to accompany it, Mentioning your Knowlege of Me I would not trouble Sir but Mr Granger has no personal Knowlege of Me—wishing to hear from you I remain with good wishes for your Happiness RICHARD BARRY

RC (MHi); at foot of text: "Thomas Jefferson Esqr"; endorsed by TJ as received 1 Apr. 1812 and so recorded in SJL. Enclosure not found.

SJL records TJ's missing letter to Barry of MARCH THE 16TH. The federal government had purchased Blodget's HOTEL to house the patent and post offices. A statute passed on 7 Mar. 1812 authorized the postmaster general, Gideon GRANGER, to supervise the necessary renovations (Latrobe, *Papers*, 3:272–3, 274n; *U.S. Statutes at Large*, 2:691–2).

From Charles Christian

SIR, Police office, New York 28th March 1812

Influenced by a desire to ameliorate the condition of five orphan children (the family of the deceased Mr Cheetham) whose transition from affluence to want has been sudden and calamitous, I took the liberty to address you, under date of the 10th Inst, in their behalf. I now beg leave to solicit a return of the subscription[1] paper as the wants of those children have become so urgent as to require an immediate application and circulation of that paper.

I have the honor Sir to remain most respectfully Your obedient and very humble servant. CHARLES CHRISTIAN

RC (MHi); dateline beneath signature; at head of text: "The Hon Thomas Jefferson"; endorsed by TJ as received 1 Apr. 1812 and so recorded in SJL.

[1] Manuscript: "subsciption."

From Samuel A. Otis

SIR Washing. 28th March 1812

I had the honor of yours 26th March, and whenever the documents come to hand I will distribute them as requested, and give you notice. I have no doubt they will be interesting. In reply to my frequent enquiries I hear that you continue in the enjoyment of health, that choicest gift of Heaven. May it accompany you thro' a tranquil old age!

Amongst the various publications by order from our presses, should there be anything that might amuse you, on notice, I will forward it with pleasure.

I have the honor to be

With respect & esteem Your most humble Sert SAM A OTIS

RC (DLC); at foot of text: "Mr Jefferson"; endorsed by TJ as received 1 Apr. 1812 and so recorded in SJL.

From Oliver Pollock

SIR, City Washington 28th March, 1812.

I had the Honor of receiving your letter of Dec. 31st in due Course, for which, as well as in the sentiments, and good wishes therein expressed, I beg you to accept my acknowledgments.

Altho' you were put to some trouble to retrace the events of such antiquity in order to answer my letter as correctly as you could—Yet with all that trouble it seems that you have been mistaken in a very important fact, which, I have reason to believe operated in a considerable degree against me.

The period to which I allude is the authority given to Genl Clarke to draw bills on me, and the authority for me to draw on Penete & Co, your words are as follow. "Clarkes authorization therefore to draw on you, and yours to reimburse yourself by Drafts on Penette & Co must have been derived from Governor Henry. The fact is of little importance, but merely for the sake of correctness."

In regard to your mistake in this, you will be satisfied when you are reminded, that the orders were given by the Council of Virginia, as per letter dated "Virginia Board of Trade. Nov. 6. 1779."[1] You then presided as Chief Magistrate, and of course the letter of authorization must have been signed by yourself, and not by Mr Henry.

Unfortunately the leaves of the letter Book containing this period of time have been cut out, so that there is no proof to be obtained further than what the date affords.

You will perceive by the public prints, that altho' I did not succeed in obtaining my Just claim; yet the Legislature have thought proper to allow me something—and as the want of precision in this matter, certainly operated on the minds of some persons, it is very likely that it was the real cause of my failure.

I am advised by my friends, Justified by truth, and urged by my wants to repeat my application at the next Session—all that I ask is to be enabled, to appear, not only free from doubt, but with Honor before the Legislature—and from the pains already taken, I cannot doubt that you will with promptitude, and pleasure do what is right: That the Justice of the Legislature may be extended to a public Servant, whose pride was once[2] flattered with many public testimonials of patriotic service, and who now asks only a pecuniary reparation for losses which led to ruin, and all countless and incalculable consequences thereof, and who indeed, asks it, not less because it is Justly due, but because it is now all important to the comforts and wants of an aged and zealous public Servant.

With the assurances of my high respect, and acknowledgments for your former polite attention,

I have the Honor to be, Sir, Your Most Ob[t] Serv[t]

OL[R] POLLOCK

P.S. Please, Sir, direct to me here where I now reside

RC (DLC); in a clerk's hand, with signature and postscript by Pollock; addressed by clerk: "Hon[e] Thomas Jefferson Monticello V[a]"; franked; postmarked; endorsed by TJ as received 1 Apr. 1812 and so recorded in SJL.

[1] Omitted closing quotation mark editorially supplied.

[2] Manuscript: "one."

To Oliver Barrett

SIR Monticello Mar. 29. 12.

On the 20th of Feb. I wrote to you requesting you to forward for me to Mess[rs] Gibson & Jefferson of Richmond one of your Spinning machines carrying not more than 20. threads, but fewer if that number increased sensibly it's complicatedness,[1] and assuring you that on knowing from you the price it should be immediately remitted to N.

York to any address you would indicate. this will be by mess[rs] Gibson & Jefferson beforementioned. in consequence of this letter I suspended an order I had given for a machine of a different kind in another quarter. not having heard from you, and apprehending my letter may have miscarried, I repeat the essential parts of it here, and renew my request that you will forward one with as little delay as possible, and in the mean time that you will let me know whether & when I may count on your forwarding one; as the order for the other one of a different kind remains suspended, and the year is advancing during which our winter cloathing should be going on. Accept the assurance of my respect. TH: JEFFERSON

PoC (MHi); adjacent to signature: "M[r] Oliver Barrett"; endorsed by TJ; notation by TJ at foot of text: "inclosed under cover to Gen[l] Bailey." Enclosed in TJ to Theodorus Bailey, 29 Mar. 1812, not found and not recorded in SJL, but acknowledged in Bailey to TJ, 7 Apr. 1812.

[1] Manuscript: "complicateness."

To Patrick Gibson

DEAR SIR Monticello Mar. 29. 12.

The season of paying my debts now coming upon me I requested you in my letter of the 15th to make some remittances for me, to which I am now to add one of 200.D. to Benjamin Jones of Philadelphia, ironmonger, and another of one hundred and thirty Dollars to Ezra Sarjeant of New York printer. I do this on the presumption of the sales of my flour, as it gets down, putting you in funds for me. there are still 150. barrels to go down of which Johnson was taking 40 on board yesterday evening. when he returns he will take another load of it and 5. hhds of tob[o]

I write by this post to mr Jones & mr Sarjeant to inform them that they may expect their remittances from you within a few days after they shall recieve my letters. Accept the assurance of my great esteem & respect. TH: JEFFERSON

PoC (ViU: TJP); at foot of text: "M[r] Gibson"; endorsed by TJ as a letter to Gibson & Jefferson and so recorded in SJL.

To Ezra Sargeant

Sir Monticello Mar. 29. 12

Your letter of the 21st came to hand on the 25th but the 71. copies mentioned as forwarded by the same mail did not come with it, nor by a mail since arrived. I presume they are suffering some temporary delay at some post office and that I shall soon recieve them. in the mean time I hope you have forwarded those for mr Otis & mr Magruder to Washington by the stage under the care of some passenger, this being the only conveyance that combines speed with safety. I have, by the mail of this day, desired messrs Gibson and Jefferson, my correspondents at Richmond, to remit to you one hundred and thirty Dollars, which you may expect to recieve as soon as they can procure a draught or bank-bills negociable at New York. Accept the assurance of my respect Th: Jefferson

PoC (MHi); at foot of text: "Mr Ezra Sarjeant"; endorsed by TJ.

To John Benson

Sir Monticello. Apr. 2. 12

The indiscretion of individuals in sending me packages of books & pamphlets by the mail, which ought not to be burthened with them, and which yet I cannot controul because not made known to me beforehand, has made it necessary for me to request of mr Granger to turn over such packages always to the Fredericksburg stage. the only difficulty in that case is the paiment of the portage from Washington to Fredsbg where the concern changes. for this purpose I ask the aid of your kindness so far as to forward on the packages to Milton with instructions to the Driver to deliver them there to mr Higginbotham mercht of that place, and to recieve from him the whole portage from Washington[1] to Fredsbg as well as that from Fredsbg to Milton. I make this request on the presumption that you have the contract of the mail from Washington to Fredsbg as formerly; if not I must vary my request to that of making this arrangement for me with the contractor whoever he may be. I salute you with esteem & respect.

Th: Jefferson

PoC (DLC); at foot of text: "Mr Benson"; mistakenly endorsed by TJ as a letter to Egbert Benson and so recorded in SJL.

Benson's reply of 8 Apr. 1812, not found, is recorded as received from Fredericksburg on 10 Apr. in SJL, which correctly attributes it to John Benson. SJL also records missing letters from TJ to David HIGGINBOTHAM of 7 Apr. 1812 and Higginbotham's response of 9 Apr. 1812, received from Milton the following day.

[1] Word reworked from "Ale."

To Gideon Granger

DEAR SIR Mont° Apr. 2. 12.

I rec[d] yesterday yours of Mar. 28. and I thank you for the information respecting the packages. they contain pamphlets stating the conduct of the Executive in the case of the Batture which I have had printed at my own expence for the information of Congress and the officers of the government. I directed the printer to send by the stage 144. copies to mr Magruder for the Representatives, and 35. to mr Otis for the Senate. he was also to send me 71.[1] to be distributed to officers of the government E[t]c. he informed me he had sent me the last in <u>three</u> packages. I state this because you say there are five packages, and it is possible he may have sent the two for Congress with the three for me. those intended for me whether 3. or 5. I will ask the favor of you to have delivered to the Fredericksbg stage, and in such cases generally to do the same without troubling yourself to write a letter which is an addition to the labour of your office which ought not to be given. I write to mr Benson by this post to make an arrangement for paying the transportation of such packages always at that place. there was formerly a difficulty at Alexandria, by a change there in the concern of the stages. I hope that has been removed since the change of the road from the ferry to the bridge. I am sorry to be so troublesome to you, but I will endeavor to make these incidents as little so as I can. I salute you affectionately. TH: JEFFERSON

RC (DLC: Granger Papers); at foot of text: "Gideon Granger esq." PoC (DLC); endorsed by TJ.

Granger's brief note of MAR. 28. from Washington informed TJ that he had "five large packages addressed to you and Sent to me according to your request" (RC in DLC; endorsed by TJ as received 1 Apr. 1812 and so recorded in SJL). The PRINTER was Ezra Sargeant.

[1] Reworked from "75."

To Samuel J. Harrison

SIR Monticello Apr. 2. 12.

Your letter of Mar. 12. was not recieved till yesterday. it has given me the deepest concern. engagements to make paiments founded solely on your bond, which I deemed as good as a bank note, are now immediately falling due, and I have no resource, on so short warning, but that, to cover me from the mortification, and the consequences of failure. I cannot yet but persuade myself that, on reconsidering this case, you will percieve that the grounds you alledge for witholding paiment are such as neither law nor equity will warrant; that it is impossible it can be just or lawful for you to hold both the land and the price, and that, sensible of this, you will yet comply with your engagement, and relieve me from the distresses, into which the failure will throw me. that Scott may have brought a suit against you and myself is possible, altho' I doubt it, because it has been long said, & yet no process has ever been served on me. however it would be quite in the character of the man, so well known to you, and which no one to whom it is known would consider as justifying the least presumption of right. it is not every frivolous pretension of claim from a third person which authorises the purchaser of property to refuse paiment. it must be a plausible, and even a probable claim. were it otherwise, what a door would be open to breach of engagements, as there cannot exist a title against which unfounded claims may not be set up. and is it possible to urge a more frivolous one than that of a subsequent, against a prior grant? and in a case too where two juries, an ordinary one of 12. men, and a grand inquest of 24. had found it so groundless that they would not even retire for consultation.[1] Again, whatever his pretensions were, you knew them, you were present at the inquests, heard them explained and exposed, witnessed the abandonment of them by Scott's counsel, and their undertaking that I should have no more trouble from them, on my agreeing not to institute any prosecution against Scott. so palpable was all this, that after the verdict of the jury, you accepted the deed, and the possession, made paiment on the ground, of the first £400. and after a year's further consideration, made a second similar paiment. had then mr Scott's pretensions been much more plausible your knolege of them at the time, your conclusion of the bargain with your eyes open, your recieving the title & possession with a full view of them, were a bar to your refusing full execution of the contract on your part. your entering into it with a complete knolege of all these circumstances amounted to a covenant to execute it without regard to them, and to rely, for ultimate security, on my general warranty against all persons whatever. that covenant of warranty still exists, and a consciousness of my own circumstances persuades me that a Chancellor could not be made to believe that if you should pay me the remaining £400. I should not be able to repay it on any eviction of the title. and yet this is the only ground on which he would interpose a suspension. these positions will, I am persuaded, be confirmed to you by any lawyer, of science in his profession, whom you may consult. I hope therefore that, on a review of all these circumstances, you will feel the justice of going through with your contract, and of considering mine to warrant your title a sufficient security, as you considered it at the time of accepting the deed; and the rather as I put you into possession of title papers which prove it all but impossible that any other person can have a title paramount to mine. however, if you really apprehend that, even in the case of my death, my property would not be good for such a sum as £400. I am ready to remove that fear. name the portion of my lands at the Poplar Forest which you shall deem a sufficient security, and name your own trustees, and I will convey it to them with a power to sell it the moment a decision shall be given in favor of Scott's title. or, if you prefer personal security, I will give you as good as the state can furnish. if you think neither of these propositions would sufficiently secure you, then let us put the case at once into it's legal course and settle it without delay. that is to say, let a writ be issued on the bond in my name, apply yourself to the Chancellor with a bill of injunction, which I will answer on the spot, and if the Chancellor gives an injunction, I, of course acquiesce. all this can be done in the course of one fortnight. some one of these three propositions will I trust be acceded to by you. I shall be at the Poplar Forest within about a fortnight from this date, within which time a just revision of the subject will I hope have corrected your first views of it, and dispose you, by doing me justice, to enable me to fulfil my engagements to others, and relieve me from the distressing situation in which a continuance of the refusal will place me. accept the assurance of my esteem & respect. TH: JEFFERSON

PoC (ViU: TJP); at foot of first page: "Mr Saml J. Harrison"; endorsed by TJ. FC (ViU: TJP); entirely in TJ's hand.

Harrison's LETTER OF MAR. 12. was actually dated a day later. TJ conveyed TITLE & POSSESSION of the Ivy Creek lands a year previously (Conveyance of Ivy Creek Lands to Samuel J. Harrison, 9 Feb. 1811).

[1] FC contains the following "Note" at foot of page in TJ's hand, keyed to this point in text with a dagger: "Scott had gone into the middle of a tract of mine of 474. acres, patented many years before,

had surveyed & got a patent for 50. acres, had cleared a field & was preparing it for tob^{o}. I took out a writ of forcible entry; a jury of 12. freeholders met on the land & did not hesitate a moment in giving an unanimous verdict. he traversed it; whereon a grand inquest of 24. freeholders were assembled on the ground the next day, who gave the same verdict without retiring. the sheriff delivered possession to me & I in the same instant to mr Harrison, delivered him the deed, & he made the 1st paiment. it is this claim to 50. a^{s} which is made the ground of stopping the last paiment for 474. acres."

To Hugh Nelson

Dear Sir Monticello Apr. 2. 12.

Your letter of Mar. 22. has been duly recieved. by this time a printed copy of my MS. respecting the Batture has I hope been laid on your desk, by which you will percieve that the MS. itself has been recieved long enough to have been sent to N. York, printed, and returned to Washington.

On the subject of the omission of the officers of the Virginia state line in the provisions & reservations of the cession to Congress my memory enables me to say nothing more than that it was not through inattention as I believe, but the result of compromise. but of this the President, who was in Congress when the arrangement was settled, can give the best account. I had nothing to do but to execute a deed according to that arrangement made previous to my being a member. Col^{o} Monroe being a member with me, is more likely to remember what passed at that time. but the best resource for explanation of every thing we did is in our weekly correspondence with the Governor of Virginia which I suppose is still among the Executive records. we made it a point to write a letter to him every week, either jointly, or individually by turns.

You request me to state the public sentiment of our part of the country as to war & the taxes. you know I do not go out much. my own house & our court yard are the only places where I see my fellow citizens. as far as I can judge in this limited sphere, I think all regret that there is cause for war, but all consider it as now necessary, and would I think disapprove of a much longer delay of the Declaration of it. as to the taxes, they expect to meet them, would be unwilling to have them postponed; and are only dissatisfied with some of the subjects of taxation: that is to say the stamp tax & excise. to the former I have not seen a man who is not totally irreconcilable. if the latter could be collected from those who buy to sell again, so as to prevent domiciliary visits by the officers I think it would be acceptable & I am sure a wholesome tax. I am persuaded the Secretary of the Treasury is mistaken in supposing so immense a deduction from the duties on imports. we shall make little less to sell than we do now, for no one will let his lands be idle; and consequently we shall export not much less; and expect returns. some part will be taken on the export & some on the import. but taking into account the advance of prices, that revenue will not fall so far short as he thinks; and I have no doubt might be counted on to make good the entire suppression of the stamp tax. yet, altho' a very disgusting pill, I think there can be no question the people will swallow it, if their representatives determine on it. I get these sentiments mostly from those who are more in the habit of intercourse with the people than I am myself. Accept the assurance of my great esteem & respect TH: JEFFERSON

PoC (DLC); at foot of first page: "honble mr Nelson."

From James Madison

DEAR SIR Washington April 3. 1812

I have rec[d] your favor of the 26th and have made to the members of the Cabinet the communication you suggest with respect to your printed memoir on the Batture. I learn from the Department of State that some books were rec[d] for you, and duly forwarded. What they were was not ascertained or remembered. If they do not on their arrival correspond with your expectation, let me know, & further enquiry will be made. Mean time there is in my possession, a very large packet, addressed to you, which is probably a Continuation of Humbolts draughts, or other Maps. It was accompanied by no letter to me, and being unfit for the mail, waits for the patronage of some trusty traveller, bound in the Stage towards Monticello. A late arrival from G.B. brings dates subsequent to the maturity of the Prince Regent's Authority. It appears that Percival, &c. are to retain their places, and that they prefer war with us, to a repeal of their orders in Council. We have nothing left therefore, but to make ready for it. As a step to it an embargo for 60 days was recommended to Cong[s] on wednesday and agreed to in the H. of Reps. by about 70 to 40. The Bill was before the Senate yesterday, who adjourned about 4 or 5 OClock without a decision. Whether this result was produced by the rule which arms a single member with a veto ag[st] a decision in one day on a bill, or foretells a rejection of the Bill I have not yet heard. The temper of that body is known to be equivocal. Such a measure, even for a limited and short time, is always liable to adverse as well as favorable considerations; and its operation at this moment, will add fuel to party discontent, and interested clamor. But it is a rational & provident measure, and will be relished by a greater portion,[1] of the Nation, than an omission of it. If it could have been taken sooner and for a period of 3 or 4 months, it might have enlisted an alarm of the B. Cabinet, for their Peninsular System, on the side of Concessions to us; and w^d^ have shaken[2] their obstinacy, if to be shaken at all; the successes on that Theatre, being evidently their hold on the P. Reg^t^ and the hold of both on the vanity & prejudices of the nation. Whether if adopted for 60 days, it may beget apprehensions of a protraction, & thence lead to admissible[3] overtures, before the sword is stained[4] with blood, can not be foreknown with certainty. Such an effect is not to be counted upon. You will observe, that Liverpool was Sec^y^ for the Foreign Dep^t^ ad interim, & that Castlereah is the definitive successor of Wellesley. The resignation of this last, who has rec^d^ no other app^t^ is a little mysterious. There is some reason for believing that he is at variance with Perceval; or that he distrusts the stability of the existing Cabinet, and courts an alliance with the Grenville party, as likely to overset it. If none of that party desert their colours, the calculation can not be a very bad one; especially in case of war with the U.S: in addition to the distress of Br trade & manufactures, and the inflammation in Ireland; to say nothing of possible reverses in Spain & Portugal, which alone would[5] cut up the Percival ascendancy by the roots. From France we hear nothing. The delay of the Hornet is inexplicable, but on the reproachful supposition, that the F. Gov^t^ is waiting for the final turn of things at London, before it takes its course, which justice alone ought to prescribe, towards us. If this be found to be its game, it will impair the value of concessions if made, and give to a refusal of them, consequences it may little dream of.

Be assured of my constant and sincerest attachment

James Madison

I understand the Embargo will pass the Senate to day; and possibly with an extension of the period to 75. or 90 days

RC (DLC: Madison Papers); at foot of text: "Mr Jefferson"; endorsed by TJ as received 8 Apr. 1812 and so recorded in SJL.

On 2 Apr. 1812 the Washington *National Intelligencer* reported receipt of "English papers down to the latter end of February" that announced the end of restrictions on the PRINCE REGENT'S AUTHORITY as well as the composition of the ministry. The EMBARGO FOR 60 DAYS won approval in the United States House of Representatives on 3 Apr. 1812, with the Senate voting the same day to increase its duration to 90 DAYS. Madison signed the final version containing the longer embargo on 4 Apr. 1812 (*Annals*, 12th Cong., 1st sess., 1587–98; *JS*, 5:94, 95 [3, 4 Apr. 1812]; *U.S. Statutes at Large*, 2:700–1).

[1] Word interlined in place of what appears to be "partition."

[2] Word interlined in place of what appears to be "deserted."

[3] Word interlined.

[4] Word interlined in place of "implant."

[5] Reworked from "will." Madison here canceled "withdraw the."

From Samuel A. Otis

SIR Washington April 3d 1812

Agreeably to your request I have this day received & distributed the proceeding on the intrusion of Edward Lewingston &c and have the honor to be

With high respect Your most humble Sert SAM A OTIS

RC (DLC); at foot of text: "Thomas Jefferson Esqr"; endorsed by TJ as received 8 Apr. 1812 and so recorded in SJL.

EDWARD LEWINGSTON: Edward Livingston.

From Theodorus Bailey

DEAR SIR, Post-Office, New York April 7th 12.

By the mail of this morning I had the honor of receiving your note under date of the 29. of March, covering a letter addressed to a Mr Oliver Barrett, inventor of a spinning machine: when your former letter for the same person came to this office, one of my clerks observed, that he had lately distributed a letter addressed to Mr Barrett at Schaghticoke in the County of Rensselaer in this State:—the same direction was consequently given to yours—To attain greater certainty however, as to the particular residence of Mr Barrett, I this day made inquiry at the principal manufactories in this City: but could gain no inteligence other than a belief that the above was the place of his residence. Presuming I should best fulfil your expectations, by covering your letter to Mr Munson Smith, Post Master at Schaghticoke, I accordingly did so; accompanied with a request to him to cause it to be delivered as soon as convenient—and if Mr Barrett could not be found, to return both your letters to me, with such information with regard to Mr Barrett's present residence, as he might be able to give me. the result of my inquiry when received, will be communicated without delay.

With the highest respect & consideration I am most sincerely, your Obedient Serv[t] THEODORUS BAILEY.

RC (MHi); endorsed by TJ as received 16 Apr. 1812 and so recorded in SJL.

TJ's note to Bailey OF THE 29. OF MARCH is accounted for at his letter of that date to OLIVER BARRETT.

To Theodorus Bailey and David Gelston

DEAR SIR Monticello Apr. 9. 12.

I have written to a mr Ebenezer Herrick of West Stockbridge Mass. for a Spinning machine of his invention which he writes me he can more handily send to N. York than to any other port. I have taken the liberty to say to him that if he will commit it to you, you will be so kind as to have it embarked on board some vessel bound to Richmond. should any expence attend this, messieurs Gibson and Jefferson of Richmond, who will recieve the machine will pay it to the Captain.

I had also written to a mr Oliver Barrett of your state for a spinning machine of a different invention by himself. but he, I expect, has some correspondent of his own at N. York who will see to the shipping it. I avail myself always with pleasure of every occasion of assuring you of my continued esteem & respect. TH: JEFFERSON

RC (Mrs. F. deLancy Robinson, Greenport, N.Y., 1947); addressed: "David Gelston esquire New York"; franked; endorsed by Gelston. PoC (MHi); at foot of text: "Gen[l] Bailey"; endorsed by TJ as a letter to Bailey, even though this text is the PoC of the Gelston RC. Recorded in SJL only as a letter to Bailey.

To John Barnes

DEAR SIR Monticello Apr 9. 12

Your favor of Mar. 27. did not get to hand till yesterday. I avail myself of the return of the same post to write the inclosed letter to mr Morton an american merchant established at Bordeaux and who has been very succesful & become very wealthy. he is known to me personally, is a very good man, and at present in this country but about to return shortly to France. he is an intimate acquaintance of mr Isaac Coles who can give you a more particular account of him. I am in hopes he may furnish you not only the present but future means of making your remittances. after reading my letter, to him, be so good as to stick a wafer in it, & put it into the post office.

Mr Barry is right as to the diamond furnished me. I recollect placing it to his credit on the paper left in his hands, but I forgot to note it on the one I retained, & so it escaped me in settling the amount of my balance due him. I am sorry I did so, and made my remittance too small to cover it. it was by no means my intention to have added to your trouble any advance on that account.

I was sorry to learn by your letter of Feb. 13. that your present office yields you so little nett profit. I had hoped it would have afforded you a comfortable income, but the embarrasments thrown on our commerce by the tyrants of Europe baffle all expectation. should you conclude decisively to return to Philadelphia, be so good as to let me know it in advance as much as you can, as it would fix me as to the correspondence I have been seeking there. I salute you with affection & respect. TH: JEFFERSON

PoC (DLC); at foot of text: "Mr John Barnes"; endorsed by TJ. Enclosure: TJ to John A. Morton, 9 Apr. 1812.

From John B. Chandler

DEAR SIR Pinckniy Ville 9the Apl. 1812

I Wrote to you from Moble that I Wold be with you by the Last of this Month but I wold not be abel to be of as Soon as I Supposed but am Now on my way and wold be in albermarl as Soon as I Can perform the Jurney at Least I will be in the State befor my Business Sets in a New and wold be hopey If thay Cold be a berth Procourd in your mills as that be a Cuntrey that I much admire and Wold drauther be ther then aney whear Else

I wrote you that I had funds which I wold be hopey to have the mills or a part which I am in funds Serfishant

and that business I Wold profuir to aney other

I am Dear Sir Your most obedent JNO B. CHANDLER

RC (MHi); at foot of text: "Thos Jefferson Esqr Virginia"; endorsed by TJ as received 3 June 1812 from Pinckneyville and so recorded in SJL.

To Ebenezer Herrick

SIR Monticello Apr. 9. 12.

I received last night only your favor of Mar. 24. altho we generally get our letters from N. York in 6. days. I shall certainly recieve your machine from that port more readily than from Boston. I had named the latter place, because being the seat of government of your state, I had presumed your communications with it more direct. if to the address of Mess[rs] Gibson and Jefferson at Richmond as before desired, you will add that of mr Gelston the Collector at N. York and you send it to him, he will forward it to Richmond. I will thank you to do it speedily as the commencement of my spinning establishment awaits that alone. I presume you have printed directions for the use of it, which will be the more necessary with those who are entirely uninformed of it's principle. a line of information, by post viâ N. York informing me of your having dispatched it will reach me in a week. if you have a careful correspondent of your own at N. York, it might be in his power to dispatch the machine quicker than the multiplicity of mr Gelston's business might permit him to do. Accept the assurance of my respects. TH: JEFFERSON

PoC (DLC); at foot of text: "M[r] Ebenezer Herrick West Stockbridge. Berkshire, Mass."; endorsed by TJ.

To John A. Morton

SIR Monticello Apr. 9. 12.

My friend Gen[l] Kosciuzko, now established at Paris, or rather at or near Fontainebleau, depends for his subsistence chiefly on the produce of stock which he has in our funds and banks. we have occasion to remit him, about this season annually, somewhere about 1000.D. the superintendence of this he left with me, and I have committed to mr John Barnes of George town the immediate care of recieving and remitting to him this income. but we often find it extremely difficult to do this in good bills and without loss, and especially since the channel of England is closed to those operations. at this time no means offer themselves to us: but I have flattered myself that you perhaps could advise us or perhaps yourself furnish us the means. indeed, if your commerce should occasion you to need money here in exchange for money in France perhaps the mutual convenience of yourself & the General might be found in making the remittance annually through the channel of your house. will you do me the favor to answer me especially as to the means of a present remittance, or to inform mr Barnes directly on the subject.

Mr Walsh writes that after trying to send me some wine thro the canal of Languedoc to be shipped from Bordeaux he has not been able to do it. I am in hopes on your return you will be able to assist him in this.

Accept the assurance of my great esteem & respect.

TH: JEFFERSON

PoC (MoSHi: TJC-BC); at foot of text: "Mr Morton"; endorsed by TJ. Enclosed in TJ to John Barnes, 9 Apr. 1812.

John Archer Morton (b. 1772), merchant, was a native of Prince Edward County who traded in Bordeaux and applied unsuccessfully to both TJ and James Madison for the consular post there (*WMQ*, 2d ser., 11 [1931]: 216; *VMHB* 17 [1909]: 314; Mary Lee Mann, *A Yankee Jeffersonian: Selections from the Diary and Letters of William Lee of Massachusetts Written from 1796 to 1840* [1958], 106, 137; Madison, *Papers, Sec. of State Ser.*, 7:152, 234–5; Morton to James Monroe, 14 Apr. 1812 [DNA: RG 59, LAR, 1809–17]).

From Oliver Barrett

SIR — Troy April 10th 1812

With Due reverence I hasten to answer your inquireys, the machine I believe is such as you Wish to Obtain, for when properly made is not likely to Git out of repair without very bad management my price for a machine of 12 Spindles is $50, and $2, for every additional Spindle, Dr Thornton was correct as to the patent fee, which is the Same for a machine of 12 Spindles that it is for 20[1] or 30, as it Gives the purchaseer a Right to build as Large as he thinks propper the Machine I sold to Judge Cranch carries but 12 Spindles, Doct^r Thornton is the Agent for the State of Virginia and has the exclusive Right to make & Sell to any person in the State or to sell the Right to any County in S^d State the method which I have adopted to assertain the Real Value of Co, is this according to the No of inhabitance my rule is three cents on the Population, of Which I shall inform[2] Doct^r Thornton. if the Doctor Wishes I will furnish you With a Machine as soon as I Git orders to that effect if on enquirey of the Doct^r you Wish to write to me again on this subject Pleas to Direct your Letters to me at Troy County Rensselaer N York

Recieve Sir the Sinsere thanks of a friend for the frindly remarks Given to me in your Letter of the 20 Feb^y

OLIVER BARRETT JR

RC (MHi); at foot of text: "Thomas Jefferson"; endorsed by TJ as received 22 Apr. 1812 and so recorded in SJL.

[1] Reworked from "10."
[2] Manuscript: "inforn."

From Gibson & Jefferson

SIR [before 12 Apr. 1812]

We did not write to you by last mail, in consequence of our not having been able to get a purchaser for your Tobacco We have since then disposed of it viz the four worst Hhd^{s} to O Philpotts on 60 ^{d}/. at 2$ and the two best to J: G: Gamble at 6½$, as we could not obtain what we consider'd the value of the remaining Hhd N^{o} 2031, we have requested M^{r} G, who is purchasing for M^{r} Leiper to send it on to him and to request him to allow what he considers its value—we have also sold 58 bls S fine & 1 fine flour at 8 & 8½$—the two last loads of 80 bls: being all low qualities are still on hand,—We have made the several remittances mention'd in your letters of the 15th & 29th—With great respect we are

Your ob^{t} Serv^{ts} GIBSON & JEFFERSON

We had nearly omitted to mention a sale of 34 bls: cross mid^{gs} and 3 straight at 7 & 6$ to M^{r} W: Hancock on 60 ^{d}/s—In great haste

RC (ViU: TJP-ER); in Patrick Gibson's hand; undated; at head of text: "Thomas Jefferson Esqre"; endorsed by TJ as received 13 Apr. 1812, but recorded in SJL as received a day later.

TJ evidently replied to this letter on 12 Apr. 1812, which suggests that his conflicting dates of receipt in endorsement and SJL are both erroneous.

To Patrick Gibson

DEAR SIR Monticello Apr. 12. 12.

Your favor by the last post is recieved. I am sorry a load of my flour has turned out so badly. the mill will have to make it up in good flour in addition to 100. barrels I am still to recieve from it and forward. It is unlucky that the embargo catches me with so much unsold. I expect however that as soon as the merchants have had time to fix on a channel of vent, it will rise again. the clause in the capitulation of Amelia island, for keeping that open[1] as a free port, will offer one resource, and I do not know that the govmt proposes any thing more from the embargo than to keep our ships & seamen out of harms way. the vent of our produce even to our enemies must be desirable; and would be sound policy during actual war. I have sent off 5. hhds of tob° which I will pray you to sell as soon as you can, at least as soon as the embargo panic is over, for what it will fetch. I foresee no chance for an advance of price in that article. I expect you have recieved a sum of 176.90 D from Dr Brockenbrough for me. I shall draw on you to-day in favor of mr Hay, mr Wirt, & mr Tazewell 100.D. each, and I must pray you to send me by the return of post 200.D.[2] in bills of 5. 10. 20.D Accept the assurance of my great esteem & respect TH: JEFFERSON

PoC (DLC); at foot of text: "Mr Gibson"; endorsed by TJ as a letter to Gibson & Jefferson and so recorded in SJL.

Spanish officials at AMELIA ISLAND in East Florida signed articles of capitulation to an American-backed revolutionary force on 18 Mar. 1812. A clause in the agreement stipulated that the ports of East Florida would remain open until 1 May 1813 (Madison, *Papers, Pres. Ser.*, 4:291–6, 326–9).

[1] Word interlined.

[2] Remainder of sentence interlined.

To George Hay

DEAR SIR Monticello Apr. 12. 12.

Livingston's suit having gone off on the plea to the jurisdiction, it's foundation remains of course unexplained to the public. I therefore concluded to make it public thro' the ordinary channel of the press. an earlier expectation of the pamphlets and the desire to send you one induced me, from post to post, to delay acknoleging the reciept of your letter informing me of the dismission, and the more essential acknolegements for your kind aid in this unpleasant[1] affair. considering the infinite trouble which the question of right to the batture, & the immense volume of evidence to be taken at New Orleans would have given to my counsel and myself, I am well satisfied to be relieved from it, altho' I had a strong desire that the public should have been satisfied by a trial on the merits, and the abler discussion of them by my counsel. had the question of right come on, I have no doubt that either the state or the city of Orleans would have considered it as their own cause, & have taken the burthen on themselves. it was in this view I considered your friendly declaration that you would accept no compensation from myself. but the plea on which it was dismissed was entirely uninteresting to the Orleanese, made it merely a private question, and compensation as justly due from myself as in any other private suit of mine. I hope therefore you will do me the favor of accepting the inclosed remuneration, with my grateful thanks for the great & particular attention you paid to this suit, and an assurance that I am deeply impressed with my obligations to you.

I recieved safely the volumes of printed pamphlets but there was a quire of Manuscript documents, which I had stitched together for safe preservation, and which are chiefly originals from the office of the department of state. these I should be glad to recieve as I am bound to return them to the department.

I was served in November last with a subpoena from the court of Chancery at the suit of the executors of mrs Randolph (the mother of mr E.R.) in which mr Norborne Nicholas & perhaps a dozen more with myself, were named defendants. what is it's object I cannot devise, and why I am involved in it.

it is extremely disquieting to me to be thus harrassed with vexatious lawsuits by people who have no claim on earth on me in cases where I have been merely acting for others. will you do me the favor to direct the clerk of the court to send me a copy of the bill, that I may answer it, if necessary. if I am to enter the lists as a substantive defendant, I shall ask the favor of your attention to it. Accept the assurance of my great esteem and respect Th: Jefferson

P.S. Altho' the pamphlets have been some weeks in Fredsbg and expected by every stage, I am still disappointed in recieving them. I detain my letter therefore no longer, but will inclose one separately on it's arrival

PoC (DLC); at foot of first page: "M[r] Hay"; endorsed by TJ.

The inclosed remuneration, not found, was an order on Gibson & Jefferson for $100 (*MB*, 2:1276; TJ to Patrick Gibson, 12 Apr. 1812). E.R.: Edmund Randolph.

[1] Word interlined in place of "troublesome."

Recollections of Patrick Henry

I. THOMAS JEFFERSON TO WILLIAM WIRT, 12 APR. 1812

II. THOMAS JEFFERSON'S NOTES ON PATRICK HENRY, [BEFORE 12 APR. 1812]

EDITORIAL NOTE

In the summer of 1805 William Wirt asked Jefferson to supply him with information for a prospective work on the famed Virginia revolutionary Patrick Henry. In his reply Jefferson agreed to help but warned that his evaluation of his onetime friend and later political adversary would bear a "mixed aspect." Although he regarded Henry as "the best humored man in society I almost ever knew, and the greatest orator that ever lived . . . he was avaritious & rotten hearted. his two great passions were the love of money & of fame: but when these came into competition the former predominated." Having received nothing from Jefferson in the interim, Wirt renewed his request on 18 Jan. 1810. On 12 Apr. 1812 Jefferson finally provided Wirt with his impressions of Henry's personality and career in the second document printed below, which he said that he had composed "a year or two" earlier. Their collaboration did not end here, however. In the summers of 1814 and 1815 Wirt asked Jefferson to clarify various points in his memorandum and furnish additional material. The ex-president crafted lengthy and detailed responses. Wirt's biography ultimately drew on and in places quoted from Jefferson's reminiscences. Wirt sent him portions of the completed manuscript for comment in August 1816, whereupon Jefferson castigated Henry further but admitted that he could "scarcely find anything needing revisal" in Wirt's work. Two months later he found "nothing in it which could be retrenched but to disadvantage." The principal criticism he expressed to Wirt was that he had "practised rigorously the precept of 'de mortuis nil nisi bonum'" [speaking no ill of the dead], which Jefferson saw as "perhaps the distinction between panegyric and history." He was less positive to others in his assessment of Wirt's *Sketches of the Life and Character of Patrick Henry* (Philadelphia, 1817; Poor, *Jefferson's Library*, 4 [no. 131]). In 1824, when the statesman Daniel Webster and Professor George Ticknor of Harvard University visited Jefferson at Monticello, he described the biography as "a poor book written in bad taste . . . [that] gives so imperfect an idea of Patrick Henry, that it seems intended to show off the writer more than the subject of the work" (Wirt to TJ, 23 July 1805 [ViU: TJP], 18 Jan. 1810, 27 July 1814, 21 July 1815, 24 Aug. 1816; TJ to Wirt, 4 Aug. 1805 [ViU: TJP], 14 Aug. 1814, 5 Aug. 1815, 4 Sept., 12 Nov. 1816, 5 Jan. 1818; Daniel Webster's Account of a Visit to Monticello, Dec. 1824).

I. Thomas Jefferson to William Wirt

DEAR SIR Monticello Apr. 12. 12.

Mr Livingston's[1] suit having gone off on the plea to the jurisdiction, it's foundation remains of course unexplained to the public. I have therefore concluded to make it public[2] thro' the ordinary channel of the press. an earlier expectation of the pamphlets and the desire to send you one has delayed, from post to post, my sooner acknoleging your kind aid in this case, and praying your acceptance of the remuneration I now inclose, for the trouble I gave you in reading so much stuff on the subject, and your exertions in the defence. The debt of gratitude however is of a different nature, & is sincerely felt. considering the infinite trouble which the question of right to the Batture, & the immense volume of evidence to be taken at New

Orleans would have given to my counsel and myself, I am well satisfied to be relieved from it, altho' I had had a strong desire that the public should have been satisfied by a trial on the merits, & the abler discussion of them by my counsel.

A love of peace and tranquility, strengthened by age and a lassitude of business, renders it extremely disquieting to me to be harrassed by vexatious lawsuits by persons who have no earthly claim on me, in cases where I have been merely acting for others. in Nov. last I was served with a subpoena in chancery at the suit of the executors of mrs Randolph (mother of mr E.R.) in which mr Norborne Nicholas, & perhaps a dozen others, are also named defendants. the object of this I cannot devine. I never had any matter of business with mrs Randolph,[3] nor ever saw a farthing of hers. I once indeed transacted a single affair of hers, gratis, as a friend, at her earnest sollicitation, to relieve her from pressing distress, and under a regular power of attorney. how this can have subjected me to pass the remainder of my life in a court of Chancery, is as incomprehensible, as it is discouraging to the indulgence of our feelings in the services asked from us by our friends. I have taken measures to get a copy of the bill; and if a substantive defence is required from me, I shall ask the favor of your attention to it, as I have done in the same case of mr Hay.

The inclosed paper written for you a year or two ago, has laid by me with a view still to add something to it. but on reflection, I send it as it is. the additional matter contemplated, respected mr Henry's[4] ravenous avarice, the only passion paramount to his love of popularity. the facts I have heard on that subject are not within my own knolege, & ought not to be hazarded but on better testimony than I possess: and if they are true, you have been in a much better situation than I was to have information of them. I salute you with great & affectionate esteem and respect. TH: JEFFERSON

P.S. Altho the pamphlets have been some weeks at Fredsbg and expected by every stage, I am still disappointed in recieving them. I detain my letter therefore no longer, but will inclose one on it's arrival.

PoC (DLC); at foot of first page: "Mr Wirt"; endorsed by TJ. Tr (MdHi: Wirt Papers). Enclosure: Document II below.

The enclosed REMUNERATION, not found, was an order on Gibson & Jefferson for $100 (*MB*, 2:1276; TJ to Patrick Gibson, 12 Apr. 1812). The SINGLE AFFAIR TJ recalled that involved him in Ariana Randolph's finances was probably his role as a trustee for the payment of her annuity by her son Edmund Randolph, the first attorney general in George Washington's cabinet and TJ's successor as secretary of state. This annuity was one of the debts for which the younger Randolph mortgaged his estate in 1800 (William Mann to TJ, 12 Nov.

1811, and note). Some years earlier, however, on 29 May 1792 Edmund Randolph informed TJ that "an embarrassment in one of my father's pecuniary affairs" necessitated $700. TJ then agreed to endorse a note in this amount to enable his colleague to aid his mother, noting on that date that he had done so "merely as his security that he might receive the money on it from the bank" (*PTJ*, 23:614; *MB*, 2:870).

[1] Tr: "M^r^ L's."
[2] Preceding eight words omitted in Tr.
[3] Tr: "Mr Randolph."
[4] Tr: "M^r^ H's."

II. Thomas Jefferson's Notes on Patrick Henry

[before 12 Apr. 1812]

My acquaintance with mr Henry commenced in the winter of 1759–60. on my way to the college I passed the Christmas holidays at Col^o^ Dandridge's in Hanover, to whom mr Henry was a near neighbor. during the festivity of the season I met him in society every day, and we became well acquainted, altho' I was much his junior, being then in my 17th year, & he a married man. the spring following he came to Williamsburg to obtain a license as a lawyer, and he called on me at College. he told me he had been reading law only 6. weeks. two of the examiners however, Peyton & John Randolph, men of great facility of temper, signed his licence with as much reluctance as their dispositions would permit them to shew. mr Wythe absolutely refused. Rob. C. Nicholas refused also at first, but, on repeated importunities & promises of future reading, he signed. these facts I had afterwards from the gentlemen themselves, the two Randolphs acknoleging he was very ignorant of law, but that they percieved him to be a young man of genius & did not doubt he would soon qualify himself.

He was, some time after, elected a representative of the county of Hanover, & brought himself into public notice on the following occasion which I think took place in 1762. or a year sooner or later. the gentlemen of this country had at that time become deeply involved in that state of indebtment which has since ended in so general a crush of their fortunes. Robinson, the Speaker, was also Treasurer, an officer always chosen by the assembly. he was an excellent man, liberal, friendly, & rich. he had been drawn in to lend, on his own account, great sums of money to persons of this description, & especially those who were of the assembly. he used freely for this purpose the public money, confiding, for it's replacement, in his own means, & the securities he had taken on those loans. about this time however he became sensible that his deficit to the public was become so enormous as that a discovery must soon take place, for as yet the public had no suspicion of it. he devised therefore, with his friends in the assembly, a plan for a public loan office to a certain amount, from which monies might be lent on public account, and on good landed security, to individuals. this was accordingly brought forward in the House of Burgesses, and had it succeeded, the debts due to Robinson on these loans would have been transferred to the public, & his deficit thus compleatly covered. this state of things however was not yet known: but mr Henry attacked the scheme, on other general grounds, in that style of bold, grand & overwhelming eloquence, for which he became so justly celebrated afterwards. he carried with him all the members of the upper counties, & left a minority composed merely of the aristocracy of the country. from this time his popularity swelled apace; & Robinson dying about 4. years after, his deficit was brought to light, & discovered the true object of the proposition.

The next great occasion on which he signalised himself was that which may be considered as the dawn of the revolution, in March 1764.[1] the British parliament had passed resolutions preparatory to the levying a revenue on the Colonies by a Stamp tax. the Virginia assembly, at their next session, prepared & sent to England very elaborate representations addressed in separate forms to the King, Lords, & Commons, against the right to impose such taxes. the famous Stamp act was however passed in Jan. 1765. and in the session of the Virginia assembly of May following, mr Henry introduced the celebrated resolutions of that date. these were drawn by George Johnston, a lawyer of the Northern neck, a very able, logical & correct Speaker. mr Henry moved, & Johnston seconded these resolutions successively. they were opposed by Randolph, Bland, Pendleton, Nicholas, Wythe & all the old members whose influence in the house had, till then, been unbroken. they did it, not from any question of our rights, but on the ground that the same sentiments had been, at their preceding session, expressed in a more conciliatory form, to which the answers were not yet recieved. but torrents of sublime eloquence from mr Henry, backed by the solid reasoning of Johnston, prevailed. the last however, & strongest resolution was carried but by a single vote. the debate on it was most bloody. I was then but a student,[2] & was listening at the door of the lobby (for as yet there was no gallery) when Peyton Randolph, after the vote, came out of the house, and said, as he entered the lobby, 'by god, I would have given 500. guineas[3] for a single vote.' for as this would have divided the house, the vote of Robinson, the Speaker, would have rejected the resolution. mr Henry left town that evening, & the next morning before the meeting of the House, I saw Peter Randolph, then of the Council, but who had formerly been clerk to the house, for an hour or two at the Clerk's table, searching the old journals for a precedent of a resolution of the house, erased, while he was clerk, from the journals, by a subsequent order of the house. whether he found it, or not, I do not remember; but, when the house met, a motion was made & carried to erase that resolution: and,[4] there being at that day but one printer, & he entirely under the controul of the Governor, I do not know that this resolution ever appeared in print. I write this from memory: but the impression made on me, at the time, was such as to fix the facts indelibly in my mind.

I came into the legislature as a Burgess for the county of Albemarle in the winter of 1768.9. on the accession of Ld Botetourt to the government, and about 9 years after mr Henry had entered on the stage of public life. the exact conformity of our political opinions strengthened our friendship; and indeed the old leaders of the house being substantially firm, we had not after this any differences of opinion in the H. of Burgesses, on matters of principle; tho' sometimes on matters of form. we were dissolved by Ld Botetourt at our first session, but all were re-elected. there being no divisions among us, occasions became very rare for any display of mr Henry's eloquence. in ordinary business he was a very inefficient member. he could not draw a bill on the most simple subject which would bear legal criticism, or even the ordinary criticism which looks to correctness of stile & idea: for indeed there was no accuracy of idea in his head. his imagination was copious, poetical, sublime; but vague also. he said the strongest things in the finest language, but without logic, without arrangement, desultorily. this appeared eminently & in a mortifying degree in the first session of the first Congress,[5] which met in Sep. 1774. mr Henry & Richard Henry Lee took at once the lead in that assembly, &, by the high style of their eloquence, were, in the first days of the session, looked up to as primi inter pares. a Petition to the king, an Address to the people of Great Britain and a Memorial to the people of British America were agreed to be drawn. Lee, Henry & others were appointed for the first, Lee, Livingston & Jay for the two last. the splendor of their debut occasioned mr Henry to be designated by his committee to draw the petition to the king, with which they were charged; and mr Lee was charged with the Address to the people of England. the last was first reported. on reading it, every countenance fell, & a dead silence ensued for many minutes. at length it was laid on the table for perusal & consideration till the next day, when first one member & then another arose, & paying some faint compliments to the composition, observed that there were still certain considerations, not expressed in it, which should properly find a place in it. at length mr Livingston (the Governor of New Jersey) a member of the Committee rose & observed that a friend of his had been sketching what he had thought might be proper for such an address, from which he thought some paragraphs might be advantageously introduced into the draught proposed; & he read an Address which mr Jay had prepared de bene esse as it were. there was but one sentiment of admiration. the Address was recommitted for amendment, and mr Jay's draught reported & adopted with scarce an alteration. these facts were stated to me by mr Pendleton & Col[o] Harrison of our own delegation, except that Col[o] Harrison ascribed the draught to Gov[r] Livingston, & were afterwards confirmed to me by Gov[r] Livingston, and I will presently mention an anecdote confirmative of them from mr Jay & R. H. Lee themselves.

M[r] Henry's draught of a petition to the king was equally unsuccesful, & was recommitted for amendment. mr John Dickinson was added to the committee, & a new draught prepared by him was passed.

The occasion of my learning from mr Jay that he was the author of the Address to the people of Great Britain requires explanation by a statement of some preceding circumstances. the 2[d] session of the 1st Congress met on their own adjournment in May 1775. Peyton Randolph was their President. in the mean time L[d] North's conciliatory propositions came over, to be laid by the Governors before their legislatures. L[d] Dunmore accordingly called that of Virginia to meet in June. this obliged Peyton Randolph, as Speaker, to return. our other old members being at Congress, he pressed me to draw the answer to L[d] North's propositions. I accordingly did so, & it passed with a little softening of some expressions for which the times were not yet ripe, & wire-drawing & weakening some others to satisfy individuals. I had been appointed to go on to Congress in place of Peyton Randolph, & proceeded immediately, charged with presenting this answer to Congress. as it was the first which had been given, and the tone of it was strong, the members were pleased with it, hoping it would have a good effect on the answers of the other states. a Committee which had been appointed to prepare a Declaration to be published by Gen[l] Washington on his arrival at the army, having reported one, it was recommitted, & Dickinson & myself added to the Committee. on the adjournment of the house, happening to go out with Gov[r] Livingston, one of the Committee, I expressed to him my hope he would draw the Declaration. he modestly excused himself, & expressed his wish that I would do it. but urging him with considerable importunity, he at length said 'you & I, sir, are but new acquaintances; what can have excited so earnest a desire on your part that I should be the draughtsman? why, Sir, said I, I have been informed you drew the Address to the people of Great Britain; I think it the first composition in the English language, & therefore am anxious this declaration should be prepared by the same pen. he replied that I might have been misinformed on that subject.' a few days after, being in conversation with R. H. Lee in Congress hall, a little before the meeting of the house, mr Jay observing us, came up, & taking R. H. Lee by a button of the coat, said to him pretty sternly, 'I understand, Sir, that you informed this gentleman that the Address to the people of Great Britain, presented to the Committee by me, was drawn by Governor Livingston.' the fact was that the Commee having consisted of only Lee, Livingston who was father in law of Jay, & Jay himself, & Lee's draught having been rejected & Jay's approved so unequivocally, his suspicions naturally fell on Lee, as author of the report; & the rather as they had daily much sparring in Congress, Lee being firm in the revolutionary measures, & Jay hanging heavily on their rear. I immediately stopped mr Jay, & assured him that tho' I had indeed been so informed, it was not by mr Lee, whom I had never heard utter a word on the subject.

I found mr Henry to be a silent, & almost unmedling member in Congress. on the original opening of that body, while general grievances were the topic, he was in his element, & captivated all with his bold & splendid eloquence. but as soon as they came to specific matters, to sober reasoning & solid argumentation, he had the good sense to percieve that his declamation, however excellent in it's proper place, had no weight at all in such an assembly as that, of coolheaded, reflecting, judicious men. he ceased therefore in a great measure to take any part in the business. he seemed indeed very tired of the place, & wonderfully relieved when, by appointment of the Virginia[6] Convention to be Colonel of their 1st regiment, he was permitted to leave Congress about the last of July.

How he acquitted himself in his military command will be better known from others. he was relieved from this position again by being appointed Governor, on the first organisation of the government. After my service as his successor in the same office, my appointment to Congress in 1783. mission to Europe in 84. & appointment in the new government in 89.[7] kept us so far apart that I had no farther personal knolege of him.

Mr Henry began his career with very little property. he acted, as I have understood, as barkeeper in the tavern at Hanover C.H. for some time. he married very young; settled, I believe, at a place[8] called the Roundabout in Louisa, got credit for some little store of merchandize, but very soon failed. from this he turned his views to the law, for the acquisition or practice of which however he was too lazy. whenever the courts were closed for the winter season, he would make up a party of poor hunters of his neighborhood, would go off with them to the piney woods of Fluvanna, & pass weeks in hunting deer, of which he was passionately fond, sleeping under a tent, before a fire, wearing the same shirt the whole time, & covering all the dirt of his dress with a hunting shirt. he never undertook to draw pleadings, if he could avoid it, or to manage that part of a cause, & very unwillingly engaged but as an assistant, to speak in the cause; and the fee was an indispensable preliminary, observing to the applicant that he kept no accounts, never putting pen to paper, which was true. his powers over a jury were so irresistible, that he recieved great fees for his services, & had the reputation of being insatiable in money. after about 10. years practice in the County courts, he came to the General court, where however, being totally unqualified for any thing but mere jury causes, he devoted himself to these, & chiefly to the criminal business. from these poor devils it was always understood that he squeezed exorbitant fees of 50. 100. & 200.£. from this source he made his great profits, and they were said to be great. his other business, exclusive of the criminal, would never, I am sure, pay the expences of his attendance at the court. he now purchased from mr Lomax the valuable estate on the waters of Smith's river, to which he afterwards removed. the purchase was on long credit, & finally paid in depreciated paper, not worth oak leaves. about the close of the war he engaged in the Yazoo speculation, & bought up a great deal of depreciated paper at 2/ & 2/6 in the pound to pay for it. at the close of the war, many of us wished to re-open all accounts which had been paid in depreciated money; & have them settled by the scale of depreciation. but on this he frowned most indignantly; &, knowing the general indisposition of the legislature, it was considered hopeless to attempt it with such an opponent at their head as Henry.[9] I believe he never distinguished himself so much as on the similar question of British debts, in the case of Jones & Walker. he had exerted a degree of industry in that case totally foreign to his character, & not only seemed, but had made himself really learned on the subject. another of the great occasions on which he exhibited examples of eloquence, such as probably had never been exceeded, was on the question of adopting the new constitution in 1788. to this he was most violently opposed, as is well known; &, after it's adoption, he continued hostile to it, expressing, more than any other man in the US. his thorough contempt & hatred of Gen[l] Washington. from being the most violent of all anti-federalists however, he was brought over to the new constitution by his Yazoo speculation before mentioned. the Georgia legislature having declared that transaction fraudulent & void, the depreciated paper which he had bought up to pay for the Yazoo purchase was likely to remain on his hands worth nothing. but Hamilton's funding system came most opportunely to his relief, & suddenly raised his paper from 2/6 to 27/6 the pound. Hamilton became now his idol, and abandoning the republican advocates of the constitution, the federal government, on federal principles, became his political creed. Gen[l] Washington flattered him by an appointment to a mission to Spain, which however he declined; and by proposing to him the office of Secretary of state, on the most earnest sollicitation of Gen[l] Henry Lee, who pledged himself that Henry should not accept it. for Gen[l] Washington knew that he was entirely unqualified for it; & moreover that his self-esteem had never suffered him to act as second to any man on earth. I had this fact from information; but that of the mission to Spain is of my own knolege; because, after my retiring from the office of Secretary of State, Gen[l] Washington passed the papers to mr Henry through my hands. mr Henry's apostacy, sunk him to nothing, in the estimation of his country. he lost at once all that influence which federalism had hoped, by cajoling him, to transfer with him to itself, and a man who, through a long & active life, had been the idol of his country, beyond any one that ever lived, descended to the grave with less than it's indifference, and verified the saying of the philosopher, that no man must be called happy till he is dead.

MS (ViU: TJP); entirely in TJ's hand; undated. Enclosed in Document I above. Extracts printed in William Wirt, *Sketches of the Life and Character of Patrick Henry* (Philadelphia, 1817; Poor, *Jefferson's Library*, 4 [no. 131]), 60–1.

Patrick Henry (1736–99), statesman and orator, was born in Hanover County. He received a modest education in a local school and from his college-educated father. After failing in efforts to establish himself as a merchant and farmer, Henry taught himself law, gained admission to the bar in 1760, and began a flourishing practice that won him local prominence culminating in an acclaimed victory in the Parsons' Cause litigation late in 1763. From 1765 to 1776 he successively represented Louisa and Hanover counties in the House of Burgesses. There he quickly emerged as a leader of the opposition to the Stamp Act. Henry represented Virginia in the First and Second Continental congresses in 1774 and 1775 and was an important figure in the first three and in the fifth (and final) Virginia revolutionary conventions of 1775–76, supporting the last convention's call for independence from Great Britain and its adoption of Virginia's first constitution and Declaration of Rights. He served briefly as a colonel in overall command of the Virginia militia in 1775, but resigned his commission early the following year. Henry was the commonwealth's first governor, 1776–79, and served again from 1784–86. He declined appointment to the 1787 Federal Convention in Philadelphia and led opposition to the new United States Constitution at the Virginia ratification convention of 1788. Henry represented Prince Edward County in the House of Delegates, 1788–90. After refusing several federal appointments, in 1799 he won a final election as a delegate from Charlotte County to the state legislature, but died before it convened (*ANB*; *DAB*; William Wirt Henry, *Patrick Henry, Life, Correspondence, and Speeches*, 3 vols. [1891]; Robert Douthat Meade, *Patrick Henry*, 2 vols. [1957–69]; Richard R. Beeman, *Patrick Henry: A Biography* [1974]; Leonard, *General Assembly*).

PRIMI INTER PARES: "first among equals." DE BENE ESSE: "in anticipation of a future need" (*Black's Law Dictionary*). President George Washington PASSED THE PAPERS offering to appoint Henry envoy to Spain through TJ's hands indirectly, via a 28 Aug. 1794 letter from Secretary of State Edmund Randolph to TJ (*PTJ*, 28:118–9). As recounted by Herodotus, the PHILOSOPHER Solon advised King Croesus that NO MAN MUST BE CALLED HAPPY TILL HE IS DEAD (Herodotus, *Herodotus*, trans. Alfred D. Godley, Loeb Classical Library [1920; repr. 1990], 39).

[1] Manuscript: "1774."

[2] Wirt quoted from "mr Henry moved" to this point in his *Sketches of the Life and Character of Patrick Henry*, 60–1.

[3] In recounting this anecdote in his letter to Wirt of 14 Aug. 1814, TJ gives the amount as "100. Guineas." Wirt used the higher figure in *Sketches*, 61.

[4] Remainder of paragraph quoted in Wirt, *Sketches*, 61.

[5] Preceding six words reworked from "the first Congress."

[6] TJ here canceled "assembly."

[7] Number interlined in place of "93."

[8] Manuscript: "placed."

[9] Manuscript: "Heny."

To Littleton W. Tazewell

DEAR SIR Monticello. Apr. 12. 12.

Mr Livingston's suit having gone off on the plea to the jurisdiction, it's foundation remains of course unexplained to the public. I therefore concluded to make it public thro' the ordinary channel of the press. an earlier expectation of recieving the pamphlets, & the desire of sending you one, has delayed, from post to post, my sooner acknoleging the reciept of your letter informing me of the dismission, and the more essential acknolegement of your valuable aid in it, and praying your acceptance of the remuneration I now inclose. I have learnt from all quarters that your argument was among the ablest ever delivered before that court. considering the infinite trouble which the question of right to the Batture, & the immense volume of evidence to be taken in New Orleans, would have given to my counsel and myself, I am well satisfied to be relieved from it, altho' I had had a strong desire that the public should have been satisfied by a trial on the merits, & the abler discussion of them by my counsel.

I have been so long withdrawn from a familiarity with matters of this kind, that I do not know whether what I propose is agreeable to the scale of remuneration for law services now accustomary. if it be not, I pray you to impute it to it's real cause, ignorance of the present usage, & to be so candid as to drop me a line, and I will make it whatever you would consider as satisfactory. the debt of gratitude is of a different character, and is deeply felt. with the expression of my sense of this be pleased to accept the assurances of my great esteem & respect.

TH: JEFFERSON

P.S. altho' the pamphlets have been some weeks at Fredericksbg and expected by every stage, I am still disappointed in recieving them. I detain my letter therefore no longer, but will inclose one separately on it's arrival.

RC (NjMoHP: Lloyd W. Smith Collection); with postscript added separately to RC and PoC, perpendicularly in left margin; addressed: "Littleton W. Tazewell esq. Norfolk"; franked; postmarked Milton, 12 Apr. 1812; endorsed by Tazewell. PoC (DLC); endorsed by TJ.

The enclosed REMUNERATION was an order on Gibson & Jefferson, not found, for $100 (*MB*, 2:1276, TJ to Patrick Gibson, 12 Apr. 1812).

From Anonymous ("Goodwill")

SIR, District of Columbia, April 13. 1812

You will not doubt the sincerity of the writer when he assures you, that he has been upon his knees before God, during a large part of the night, beseeching the Almighty Soverign to have mercy upon our nation & save our devoted land from the horrors of war, with which we are threatned.

If God saved Nineveh when it was threatened, we know not but we may be saved by looking up to his throne of grace.

As we are assured, that all, who call upon the name of the Lord shall be saved, therefore, if we should not be instrumental in turning away the wrath of God from our land, yet by praying in sincerity we may save our own souls from death & hide a multitude[1] of sins. O Sir, "prepare to meet thy God in peace." Farewell.

RC (DLC); between dateline and salutation: "To the Honorable Thos. Jefferson Esq."; endorsed by TJ as an anonymous letter "against war" received 17 Apr. 1812 and so recorded in SJL.

The unidentified author of this letter also wrote TJ as "Goodwill" on 20 June 1809, "A Friend to the Christian Religion" on 28 Apr. 1811, and anonymously on 1 June and 24 Aug. 1812.

GOD SAVED NINEVEH in the Bible, Jonah 3.10: "And God saw their works, that they turned from their evil way; and God repented of the evil, that he had said that he would do unto them; and he did it not." PREPARE TO MEET THY GOD IN PEACE elaborates on the Bible, Amos 4.12.

[1] Manuscript: "multitue."

From Randolph Jefferson

DEAR BROTHER april 13: 1812

I have bin informd by mr R: patteson who has Just got up from Richmond a day or two past that my watch is safe and in the possession of mr Fass Bender will you be so Good as to send down for her by some person who will be going down shortly that can be depended on to bring her up safe as I expect we shall be over early in may which time the roads will be in Good order to travil and as soon as they are I shall set of over I have one request to ask of you and that is if your bitch has any more puppys by her at this time I would thank you to save me a dog if you have not ingaged them to any other person since you went from heare I have recoverd my health in a great measure to what I was but at times feel the simtoms but after a day or two it leavs me I have not put a drop of any kind of sperits in my mouth since I saw you neither have I seen Docter Walker since I received your letter my wife Joins me in love and Respect to you and family I am Dear brother your

most affectionatily— RH: JEFFERSON

RC (ViU: TJP-CC); dateline beneath signature; addressed: "mr: Thomas: Jefferson monticello politeness mr R: Bell"; endorsed by TJ as received 25 Apr. 1812 and so recorded in SJL.

From Pierre Samuel Du Pont de Nemours

MON RESPECTABLE AMI, Paris 14 avril 1812.

Je continue avec délices la lecture de votre admirable Ouvrage; et j'y ai trouvé dans le livre onzieme la raison qui vous a empêché d'exprimer au treizieme une conclusion.

L'Impôt territorial, ou pour mieux parler, la Constitution domaniale à partage de Revenus, étant, comme vous me l'avez marqué il y a quelque tems, repoussée par l'opinion de vos Etats du Nord, qui cependant sur tous les autres points d'une Saine économie politique

Sont les plus éclairés, vous avez du avoir égard à cette ignorance qu'ils partagent avec presque toutes les Nations.

Vous avez voulu attendre qu'ils fussent devenus capables de comprendre les vérités arithmetiques et morales qui conduiraient à bannir des Finances tout arbitraire, et à garantir pour jamais les Personnes et le travail de toute gêne et de toute contribution.—Votre traduction du mot de Solon: "I have given them the best Laws they Would[1] (et non pas could) receive" est le mot de cette énigme, et du très petit nombre d'autres qui ne sont pas dans votre esprit supérieur; mais dont il a pu être bon encore que, dans votre Pays, vous enveloppassiez vos pensées

Il est une autre vérité très importante que, même en Europe, nous aurions beaucoup de peine à persuader aux Amis de la Liberté générale et des bonnes Loix: c'est que l'on ne peut rien faire de plus avantageux aux dernieres Classes du Peuple, encore priveés de toute Propriéte fonciere, que de leur assurer l'entier et libre usage de leur tems, de leurs forces, de leurs talens, de leurs petits Capitau[x] et de les exempter en conséquence de toute Assemblée politique, de tout exercice militaire, de toute contribution.—Ils voudront longtems prendre part à l'Exercice de la Souveraineté. Leurs Travaux en seront rencheris pour les autres Citoyens, et moins profitables pour eux-mêmes. Les lumieres en seront plus reculées, parceque, tant qu'on les admettra dans les Assembleés électorales, les Préjugés populaires influeront sur les Loix, et donneront au Gouvernement une teinte de cette démocrati[e] pure que vous avez reconnu n'être que l'ébauche d'une Societé civilisée, et ne pouvoi[r], ni ne devoir subsister chez une Nation qu'une profonde étude des droits, des devoirs, et de l'interêt commun aura élevée au plus haut degré de la Science sociale.

Ce qu'il faut partout, et ce à quoi votre Livre contribuera fortement, est d'établir dans toutes les opinions, de rendre egalement manifeste aux derniers comme aux premiers Citoyens, ce que les Gouvernemens doivent pouvoir, et ce qu'ils ne doivent pas pouvoir.

Il faut que les Gouvernans puissent dire: mon Autorité va jusques là. Et que chaque Individu de la Nation gouvernée puisse repondre: Oui; et jusques là elle sera fidèlement respectée; mais Là elle S'arrête; et l'on ne peut tenter de la pousser plus loin Sans prévarication.

Si ce degré de lumiere était général, il deviendrait presque indifferent quelles que fussent les Constitutions;[2] et lorsque les Républiques Se rétabliront, ou plustôt commenceront à s'établir en Europe, elles pourraient ne pas insulter les Rois, et les laisser concourir avec elles à qui gouvernerait le mieux. La concurrence dans l'Art des Gouvernemens aura aussi son utilité: quoique de n'avoir dans les Magistrats revêtus du Pouvoir exécutif et prenant quelque part au Législatif, ni minorité, ni vieillesse, ni faiblesse, ni folie, ni défaut d'instruction, ni Cour dispendieuse, ni vénalité pour les Emplois, Soit une réunion de bien grands avantages.

Votre page 130 m'a fait à ce sujet un plaisir très[3] vif. La sagesse américaine y est reunie à la gayté française, comme dans les livres de Franklin.

Je vous demande avec instance de m'envoyer un autre Exemplaire. J'ai une extrême repugnance à rendre celui que je lis au bon Mr Warden, et cependant je sens qu'il serait parfaitement injuste que je le gardasse.—Si je pouvais l'avoir assez longtems entre les mains, je le traduirais avec tout le Soin possible, Sans aucun espoir de le faire imprimer en Français, à moins que ce ne fût pour votre Louisiane et votre Canada: mais afin que ma Langue ne soit pas privée dun tel ouvrage, ou qu'il ne soit pas traduit tout de travers par quelqu'un qui n'entendrait point ce dont il s'agit, ou par un de ces pauvres Ecrivains qui travaillent pour les Libraires.

Continuez d'éclairer votre Patrie et le monde, de m'aimer, et d'agréer mon très respectueux attachement

DuPont (de Nemours)

P.S. J'ai dit que le, ou les Magistrats revêtus du Pouvoir exécutif devaient prendre quelque part au Pouvoir législatif, et il me semble que ce n'est pas votre opinion.

Voici le motif qui me fait croire qu'ils doivent avoir un droit au moins suspensif, que je regarde moins comme un droit que comme un devoir rigoureux.

Il est défendu par la nature, par la raison, par la justice, de coopérer à l'exécution d'un ordre inique, ou qui nous parait tel.—J'en conclus que tout Pouvoir exécutif a droit de remontrance, et par conséquent de suspension pour cette remontrance, à ce qui lui parait de la part du Pouvoir Législatif une iniquité ou une folie. Et que si le Pouvoir législatif persiste, l'Exécutif n'a pas le droit de l'opposer plus longtems que ne l'exige une discussion raisonnable; mais bien le devoir d'offrir et de donner sa demission.

Pendant la discussion l'opinion[4] publique s'éclaire, et la raison finit par Triompher.

EDITORS' TRANSLATION

My respectable Friend, Paris 14 April 1812.

I continue reading your admirable work with great delight, and I found in book eleven the reason that kept you from expressing a conclusion in book thirteen.

Since the land tax or, to put it better, the territorial constitution for the apportionment of revenues is, as you advised me some time ago, rejected by your northern states, who are the most enlightened on all other points of political economy, you have had to take into account an ignorance that they share with almost all nations.

You wanted to wait until they became capable of understanding the moral and mathematical truths that would lead them to banish all arbitrariness from taxation and forever protect individuals and labor from contributions and constraint.—Your translation of Solon's saying as "I have given them the best Laws they would receive" (not could) is the key to this paradox and to a few others that are not part of your own superior way of thinking, though they are so common in your country that it is best that you conceal your thoughts from them

The friends of freedom and good laws, even in Europe, would not easily be persuaded of another very important truth. It is that nothing more advantageous could be done for the lower classes, still deprived as they are of any property, than to ensure them the full and free use of their time, energy, talents, and meager capital, by exempting them from sitting in political assemblies, serving in the military, or paying taxes.—They will, for a long time, wish to take part in the exercise of sovereignty. In so doing, their work will become more expensive to other citizens and less profitable to themselves. Enlightened thinking will be set back, in that as long as they are admitted into electoral assemblies, class bias will influence the laws and give the government the coloring of a pure democracy, which you have recognized as being only a rough draft of a civilized society and which cannot and must not endure in a nation that has elevated itself to the highest level of social science through a profound study of rights, duties, and the common interest.

Your book will strongly contribute to answering an urgent need for clarifying and impressing upon the minds of all citizens regardless of class what governments must, and must not, be allowed to do.

Those who govern must be able to say: my authority goes this far. And each individual in the nation must be able to answer: Yes; and that far it will be respected; but there it stops; and anyone who attempts to push it farther is corrupt.

If this degree of understanding were widely shared, what kind of constitution people lived under would become almost irrelevant. When republics will be reestablished, or rather when they will begin to be founded in Europe, instead of feeling insulted by them kings might feel challenged to see who could govern best. Competition in the art of governance will also prove useful: although it will be so only where magistrates vested with executive power and taking some part in the legislative power include no youths, no aged persons, no weakness, no madness, no ignorance, no extravagant court, no venality, in sum, many great advantages.

Your page 130 on that subject gave me great pleasure. It blends American wisdom with French good humor, as in Franklin's books.

You must send me another copy. I hate to think of having to return the one I am reading to our good Mr. Warden, but I feel nevertheless that it would be unfair to retain it.—If I could keep it long enough, I would translate it with all possible care, without any hope of having it published in French, unless for Louisiana and Canada. My purpose would be giving my native tongue such a work and preventing it from being badly translated by someone who does not understand what it is about or by one of those wretched scribblers who work for booksellers.

Please continue to enlighten your country and the world, to show your affection for me, and to receive the expression of my very respectful attachment DUPONT (DE NEMOURS)

P.S. I said that magistrates vested with executive power should have some share in the legislative power, and you do not seem to be of that opinion.

Here is why I believe that they must have at least a suspensive veto, which I see less as a right than as an imperative duty.

Nature, reason, and justice forbid cooperation in the execution of an iniquitous order or one that seems to be.—The executive power therefore has the right of remonstrance, and thus of suspending any act of the legislative power that seems nefarious or foolish. If the legislative power persists, the executive has no right to oppose it longer than is needed for a reasonable discussion, but after that it has a duty to offer and tender its resignation.

During the discussion, public opinion will make itself known, and reason will prevail in the end.

RC (DLC); edge chipped; at head of text: "A Thomas Jefferson"; endorsed by TJ as received 27 May 1812 and so recorded in SJL. Tr (DeGH: H. A. Du Pont Papers, Winterthur Manuscripts); posthumous copy. Translation by Dr. Roland H. Simon. Enclosed in John Graham to TJ, 23 May 1812, or James Madison to TJ, 25 May 1812.

The title of the LIVRE ONZIEME of Destutt de Tracy's *Commentary and Review of Montesquieu's Spirit of Laws* is "Of the laws which establish public liberty, in relation to the constitution," and that of the TREIZIEME is "Of the relation which taxes, and the amount of the public revenue, have to public liberty." Destutt de Tracy quoted the ancient lawmaker SOLON on p. 99 as a part of his commentary on the eleventh book. Solon had reportedly stated that he had given the Athenians, not the best laws, but "The best they would receive" (*Plutarch's Lives with an English Translation*, trans. Bernadotte Perrin, Loeb Classical Library [1914–26], 1:443). On PAGE 130 Destutt de Tracy reflected on the "effects of hereditary monarchy."

[1] Manuscript: "Vould."

[2] Tr: "Contributions."

[3] Word interlined in place of "bon" ("good").

[4] Manuscript: "l'opimion."

From "U.M."

SIR Philad[a] 14th April 1812

Your administration was conspicuous for preserving the blessings of peace to your Country—It now appears that we are on the eve of a war with England—If France and Denmark were not equally hostile to our Flag and trade, perhaps the evils of a war ought to be hazarded with Great Britain, if she were the only power that has injured and insulted us—It is now reduced to a certainty that the Prince Regent will not modify the orders in Council, unless France should really repeal her Decrees—That she has not repealed them, is evident from her capturing and burning our vessels to and from Lisbon & England and also in the Baltic—It is now extremely difficult to effect insurance at any premium on American vessels bound to St. Petersburgh; as the French and Danes capture very generally—For such a trade as we now carry on to the Continent, is it worth our while to plunge into a war, that, while it continues will stop all our trade to every part of the world, and when the subjects of the United States have at least 50 or 60 millions of dollars in England and her colonies? The great mass of the People are opposed to war, unless it can be entered on with more flattering prospects—

We now have an Embargo for 90 days, this will, of course, prevent the merchants from sending out any more property and Policy calls for our getting home as much as we can and in the best manner. Our Country is destitute of many articles which our own manufactories call for and without which they cannot be carried on—Such as fine wire for wool cards, tin &c—When our merchants get their property home, they can subscribe to the Loans—The Government during the Embargo can collect a small army and perhaps sometime hence we may be treated better by France—our trade there now is ruinous—the enormously high duties and the expenses, absorb all on some articles—If the Election in Massachusetts prove Federal, it will plainly show that they do not wish war and unless the people are in favour of it, the Government ought not to press it—If we cannot enlist an army for our defence, it will not do to depend entirely on the Militia—Let Congress adjouern and leave a power with the President to continue the Embargo or not as the state of affairs may demand at the expiration of the 90 days—I am an American and I hope free from all bias—If your sentiments coincide with mine I pray you to advise with the President—he will place the greatest confidence in your Judgment—

Respectfully Your friend of Philad[a] U M—

RC (DLC); addressed: "Thomas Jefferson Esq[re] Monticello Virginia ℘ Mail 15th April"; franked; postmarked; endorsed by TJ as a letter "against war" from "Anon. (signed U.M.)" and (probably incorrectly) as received 17 Apr. 1812, and so recorded in SJL.

United States relations with DENMARK had been strained due to confiscations in the BALTIC of American ships suspected of using neutrality as a cloak protecting British goods from seizure (*ASP, Foreign Relations*, 3:328–47; *JEP*, 5:68 [4 Mar. 1812]; Washington *National Intelligencer*, 14 May 1812). On 9 Apr. 1812 United States representative William W. Bibb, a Republican from Georgia, unsuccessfully moved that CONGRESS adjourn briefly so that members could prepare their constituents for the declaration of war that was likely to follow AT THE EXPIRATION OF THE 90 DAYS of embargo (*National Intelligencer*, 11 Apr. 1812; *Annals*, 12th Cong., 1st sess., 219, 1352–3).

From Francis Adrian Van der Kemp

SIR!   Oldenbarneveld 14 Apr. 1812.

I Should be at loss for an apologÿ in writing you again, had not the polite manner—in which you was pleased to bestow on me a new favour required mine Sincere thanks for this condescension. I feel proud—I was highly gratified with this distinction—more So—as it enabled me—by your delicate hint of a radical defect to fill up the gap in this Sketch. It might have been, that in its developing the idea had occurred, as it now was[1] Struck that it did escape mÿ attention in ebauching it. If you deem the Sketch worthÿ preserving—be pleased then to fill it up. Between the <u>General view of Europe in 1763</u> and the following great link <u>Revolutions</u> I Should wish to have inserted—

<u>Revolutiarÿ Spirit</u>—its developement

<u>Man</u>—a rational—Sociable—moral Being.

<u>Scholium</u>—<u>corollarium</u>[2]

<u>Social compact</u>—its <u>basis</u>—its <u>requisites</u>—its <u>boundaries</u>—unalienable rights—Safety of life—Security of property civil and Religious Liberty.

<u>Theories</u>—to obtain—to Secure these possessions—in the highest degree of perfection to all the associated—<u>means</u>—<u>obstacles</u>—<u>remedies</u>[3]

<u>Contour</u> of the Tableau—its <u>parts</u>: <u>Executive</u>—<u>Legislative</u> <u>judicial</u> their <u>cement</u>—<u>ornaments</u>—<u>means of preservation</u> <u>Symptoms of desease</u>—<u>dangers</u>—<u>remedies</u>—<u>Tribunal</u> of <u>correction</u>[4] <u>encouragement</u>[5]—<u>Prospect</u>—

It is only a contemplation—as—if I am not mistaken—I insinuated—I have not a Shadow of hope to accomplish it—mÿ advanced age—mÿ Situation and deep retirement in the western woods would prevent it—and even could I Surmount all these potent obstacles, then yet, I Should not be vain enough to presume—that I could finish it in Such a manner, that a fastidious public would not nauseate at its uncouthlÿ dress—the utmost I have aspired at—after amusing myself a while—is that thro mÿ friendlÿ correspondents a more aspiring genius might undertake the task and create a masterly Statue with a vivifying[6] Scissel from this rude blok—it would be Some flattering praise—when bÿ connoisseurs it was declared marble.

In the general creed, as you delineate it—of goverment's object—I doubt not or we are in unison—it maÿ be, that we varied—in its extension to particular tenets—and then yet—by agreing in what we accorded and with accurate definitions about which we differed—with a liberal dozis of mutual forbearance and concessions—the disparity remaining might appear So insignificant—as not to be worth contention—and it is mÿ Sincere belief could these data be made palatable to Philosophers and Divines—nine tenths of the dissentions among them would evaporate in Smoak: but I do not Soon yet expect a millennium.

I finished Some time ago a historico-Political work—which—I flattered might be of use to my countrÿ—a Sketch of the Achaic Republick—but this dream of enchantment is dispelled. Its intrinsic merit, how partial Self love, and too indulgent friends may be, can not overbalance its incorrect language.—

My friend R. Livingston writes me about the contemplated work—"that it might be best, So to divide the work, as that each part Should make a Separate whole, So that, if anÿ thing Should interrupt the progress of the work what is finished maÿ not be thrown awaÿ, but carrÿ its own interest with it."[7] But the Same objection would remain in regard to its finishing, and I believe not that I Should possess courage enough—to do a thing by halves—to undertake what I could not execute.

I Send last year to Dr. Mease at Philadelphia—at his request for Publication a Dissertation on the use of copper bÿ the Ancients—which—mÿ friend Luzac Should have embellished—had not his fatal death bereft me of his aid. If Dr Mease is discouraged with correcting—of which I Shall not be Surprised—without finding fault with him, I Shall be So free to take hold of an opportunity—if it occurs—to Submit it to your criticisms

If mÿ days are prolonged—having just now finished Literarÿ Sketches on Servetus and Calvin—I hope next[8] winter, to laÿ the last hand at mÿ various essays on Nat. Historÿ. These, if I may Succeed So far, I Should ardently wish, and ask you, to grant me the favour, to Submitt these to your inspection, and request your criticisms upon them. There are manÿ problematical topics—and Some—perhaps hazarded—Speculations—but the chief point is—that I have dared to differ from men as Jefferson and Bufton—and, althow their publication does not yet appear highly presumtif—without—a friend—who would charge himself with the correction—or more favorable circumstances, which might enable me to paÿ a corrector—upon which condition the publication has been offered to me, to acquiesce in this without having first exposed them to your view might appear at least an indelicate return towards a man—by whom I was obliged—before I was one of this So Supereminently Blessed nation.

You certainlÿ are acquainted with Dr Tenney's observation in regard to Some of the So Styled primarÿ colours—This Seems to me a hint which might be pursued bÿ Successful experiments—and perhaps not three onlÿ—but all Seven might, bÿ an ejectment, be driven from their ground: whÿ Should colours more[9] exist in reality in a pencil of Sunraÿs—than in other bodies? The chief difficulty is to divïde the light making—from the heat making raÿs—and this is perhaps not insurmountable. would Such a trial not be a worthÿ amusement for Mount-icello's Philosopher?

Pardon me—if I actuallÿ have abused your indulgence—I promise, to use hence forward more discretion. Permit me to assure that I remain with considerations of the highest regard

Sir! your most obed. & obliged S[t] FR ADR VAN DER KEMP

RC (DLC); dateline at foot of text; endorsed by TJ as received 29 Apr. 1812 and so recorded in SJL.

EBAUCHING: a form of ébauche, meaning an outline drawing or first attempt (*OED*). The additions from REVOLUTIARŸ SPIRIT through PROSPECT to the book synopsis that Van der Kemp enclosed in his 18 Feb. 1812 letter to TJ were included in the version he published in the Cambridge, Mass., *General Repository and Review* 4 [1813]: 393. SCISSEL: metal clippings from coining or other mechanical operations (*OED*); Van der Kemp probably meant "chisel." Samuel TENNEY'S OBSERVATION in his 1791 paper, "Observations on Prismatick Colours" (*Memoirs of the American Academy of Arts and Sciences*, vol. 2, pt. 1 [1793]: 37–9), postulated the existence of four PRIMARŸ COLOURS.

[1] Manuscript: "wa."

[2] *General Repository* here adds "Progress of the human mind."

[3] Word omitted from *General Repository*.

[4] In *General Repository*, preceding three words follow "judicial" above.

[5] Manuscript: "encouragenent."

[6] Manuscript: "vifying."

[7] Omitted closing quotation mark editorially supplied.

[8] Word interlined in place of "this."

[9] Manuscript: "mor."

From William Wirt

DEAR SIR Richmond. April 15. 1812.

I have your favor by the last mail, covering an hundred dollars (a draft on Gibson & Jefferson) as a fee in the suit of Livingston against you. This is much more than an equivalent for any trouble I have had in the case. In truth, I have had no trouble in it. The investigation has been to me both a pleasure and instruction, and in itself, a compleat remuneration. From you I should never have wished a fee in this case. I did not consider it as your case any more than mine or that of any other citizen whom you represented at the time. Even now I am dubious of the propriety of accepting this fee, and it is only the conviction that these costs will not be left by the government to rest on you, that prevents me from returning the draft.

I am glad that your exposition of the Batture question is to be given to the public. It is by far the best piece of grecian architecture that I have ever seen, either from ancient or modern times. I did not think it possible that such a subject could be so deeply and at the same time so airily treated—because I never before had seen such an union of lightness and solidity, of beauty and power, in any investigation. But, for the purposes which are yours in the publication, justice to yourself, to the public and to the rights of New Orleans, the step is certainly proper in a high degree, and must extinguish forever the hopes of Mr Livingston from that sordid and nefarious speculation. I thank you sincerely for the promissed copy of the pamphlet.

I suspect you are mistaken as to the object of the Suit against you by the executors of Mrs Randolph. Since I rec^d^ your letter last night I have not had it in my power to examin[e] the Bill against you, if one be filed, for the court of the Circuit for this county is sitting and I have been closely engaged all day.—But I am concerned for one def^t^ in a suit originally brought by that lady and now depending in the name of her executors, on the ground of a written agreement in the nature of a marriage contract, between her intended husband and her father Mr Jennings, to which agreement I think Mr Wayles was a surety for John Randolph.[1] I write hastily, from memory and am by no means sure of the accuracy of my memory.[2] The suit to which I allude is in the federal court. Ed. Randolph is the main def^t^ & those immediately connected with him have been regarded as sustaining the whole responsibility. This is so much conjecture that I shall say no more about[3] it. I need not add that you can never be drawn into question in any court in which I practise, without every defence which I can render.

For the other subject of your letter I am most thankful;—it is an evidence of your indulgent attention to my requests, which I shall never forget. I despair of the subject. It has been continually sinking under me. The truth perhaps cannot be prudently published by me during my life. I propose at present to prepare it and leave the manuscript with my family. I still think it an useful subject. and one which may be advantageously wrought not only into lessons on eloquence, but on the superiority of solid and practical parts over the transient and gaudy shew of occasion. I wish only it had been convenient to you to enable me to illustrate and adorn my scheme by a short portrait of M^r^ H's[4] most prominent competitors. I have given you too much trouble tho' already to seek you to give you[5] more.—I need only add the prayer which is on my heart that Heaven may crown your future life with that perfect peace to which, if man ever was, you are so justly entitled.

W[M] WIRT

RC (DLC); edge trimmed; endorsed by TJ as received 19 Apr. 1812 and so recorded in SJL. Tr (MdHi: Wirt Papers).

[1] Manuscript: "Randolp."

[2] Manuscript: "memoy."

[3] Manuscript: "abut."

[4] Tr: "M[r] Henry's."

[5] Thus in manuscript. Tr: "to seek to give you."

From William Bentley

SIR, Salem April 16. 1812. Mass.

I have taken the liberty at his request, to introduce M[r] Obadiah Rich, who is travelling in the Southern States. His ardent desire to see the man, in his own country, whom all Europe honours, & all our wise citizens admire, has obliged me to honour myself in writing to M[r] Jefferson.

M[r] Rich has discovered great affection for Natural History, His virtue is pure, & his manners amiable. He is enriched by his travels, & by his uncommon attainments. As one of the most worthy of our New England men, I leave him with the man I delight to honour.

Permit me, with unrivalled esteem of your public & private character, to subscribe myself, Your devoted Servant,

WILLIAM BENTLEY.

RC (DLC); at foot of text: "Thomas Jefferson, Late President of the US. A."; endorsed by TJ as received 19 July 1815 and so recorded in SJL. Enclosed in Obadiah Rich to TJ, 15 July 1815.

William Bentley (1759–1819), Congregational clergyman, was born in Boston, graduated from Harvard College in 1777, served briefly as a schoolmaster, and returned to his alma mater as a tutor in Latin and Greek in 1780. Ordained in 1783, he remained in the same Salem parish for the rest of his life. Bentley was highly skilled in languages, contributed many news digests and commentaries to the *Salem Gazette* beginning in 1794, and kept a voluminous personal diary from 1784 until his death. A Jeffersonian Republican and a liberal Unitarian, Bentley was also an active Freemason and a member of the American Philosophical Society. He bequeathed his library, one of the largest private American collections of his day, to Allegheny College in Meadville, Pennsylvania (*ANB*; *DAB*; *The Diary of William Bentley, D.D. Pastor of the East Church Salem, Massachusetts*, 4 vols. [1905–14]; Bentley to TJ, 17 June 1802 [DLC]; APS, Minutes, 8 Jan. 1811 [MS in PPAmP]; *Salem Gazette*, 4 Jan. 1820).

From Gibson & Jefferson

SIR Richmond 16th April 1812

We received this morning your favor of the 12th Inst and as you direct send inclosed $200 in small notes as ℔ Statement at foot, your drafts in favor of Hay, Wirt & Tazewell shall be duly paid; we have received and passed to your credit $176.90—But little is yet doing in flour and we have hitherto deem'd it adviseable not to offer any for sale; as we have no doubt so soon as the present panic is over, that prices will be better—

With great respect we are Your obt Servts

GIBSON & JEFFERSON

5.	of	20	$100	
8	"	10.	80	
4	"	5	20	$200

RC (ViU: TJP-ER); in Patrick Gibson's hand; at head of text: "Thomas Jefferson Esqre"; endorsed by TJ as received 19 Apr. 1812 and so recorded in SJL.

From James Hamilton

SIR North Carolina Granville Couy Williamsbo 16th April 1812

Mr Robert Hamilton of Petersburg wrote you Some time ago, requesting the favour of you to notify the Subscribers to an obligation given Mr MClure now of your neighbourhood, that the same has been assigned to me, and that the conditions on the part of Mr McLure have been complied with—He has not received an answer from you

As there are several debts which I have assumed to pay for Mr McLure out of the money ariseing from this obligation—and the several persons to whom they are due appear to be very urgent in their applications, You would infinitely oblige me if you would give the necessary notification So that the money may be lodged in the Bank as soon as possible

I am truly sorry to occasion you so much trouble in this business, but I have no other means by which I could give the notice necessary—and in your letter to Mr Macon you were good enough to say that you would take this trouble upon Yourself

The papers have been returned to me & the difficulty I shall find in obtaining the money from the Bank will ever be considerable. having very little intercourse with Richmond—I Will therefore thank you to direct that the money may be lodged in the Bank of Richmond (or rather that of Petersburg if equaly convinient) subject to my order accompanying, the paper subscribed as I shall have to send by a person immediately from this neighbourhood to have the business negotiated

I shall wait for a letter from you, for information when the money is deposited as aforesaid—with respect

I am Sir Your Obed[t] Serv[t] JA[S] HAMILTON

RC (DLC); endorsed by TJ as received 3 May 1812. Enclosure not found.

James Hamilton (d. ca. 1836), merchant, emigrated from Scotland with several of his siblings about 1807 and established himself on an estate called Nine Oaks near Williamsboro, Granville County (later Vance County), North Carolina. In 1812 he formed a business partnership with four of his brothers. Hamilton evidently moved by 1820 to New York City and there continued business under his own name (Patrick Hamilton Baskervill, *The Hamiltons of Burnside, North Carolina, and their Ancestors and Descendants* [1916], 80, 85–7, 133–7; *Longworth's New York Directory* [1820], 214; [1830], 304).

TJ had not received a letter from ROBERT HAMILTON OF PETERSBURG (see TJ to James Hamilton, 4 May 1812).

To Samuel Lukens

SIR Monticello Apr. 16. 12.

The information which you ask respecting Isaac Shoemaker not being acquired by my own knolege, but from the general reports and belief of the neighborhood, I should be altogether unwilling to communicate, but in confidence that you will use it for your own purpose only and not either to his or my prejudice or trouble. when he and his father delivered up my mills about June last, it was understood that he extorted from his father between 4. and 500.D. the greater part of which was a debt from a mr Estis, a tavernkeeper of Charlottesville. he took up his abode with mr Estis—where he has probably lived on that fund. he has lately gone to Staunton, where he has taken and now keeps the principal tavern of that place, on joint account as is said of Estis and himself. it is not believed here that this can be of any continuance. yet the possession of such a house and concern, gives a temporary credit. Accept my best wishes TH: JEFFERSON

PoC (MHi); at foot of text: "M[r] Samuel Lukens"; endorsed by TJ.

Charlottesville tavern keeper Triplett T. Estes (ESTIS) served as jailer of Albemarle County, 1806–10, and as a captain in the militia. He eventually became insolvent (Woods, *Albemarle*, 96–7, 380).

To Reuben Perry

SIR Monticello April. 16. 12.

Having recieved information in March that Jame Hubbard had been living in Lexington upwards of a twelvemonth, I engaged a man (Isham Chisolm) to go after him. he got there five days after Hubbard had run off from there, having committed a theft. he returned of course without him. I engaged him to start a second time, offering a premium of 25.D. in addition to yours, besides his expences. he got upon his tract, & pursued him into Pendleton county, where he took him and brought him here in irons. I had him severely flogged in the presence of his old companions, and committed to jail where he now awaits your arrival. the course he has been in, and all circumstances convince me he will never again serve any man as a slave. the moment he is out of jail and his irons off he will be off himself. it will therefore unquestionably be best for you to sell him. I have paid for his recovery 70.D. all I ask for it is that he may be sent out of the state. Chisolm expects the 50.D. from you. he says he will buy him, if you will take a reasonable price and oblige himself to sell him out of the state. I suppose he would agree to clear you of the purchase and the premium. perhaps you had better go halves with him. I was just setting out to Bedford, but shall now wait till I see or hear from you: provided that be by Saturday sennight the 25th. on that day I must start for Poplar forest where I shall be glad to see you, if you do not come here, and to settle what shall be done. in the mean time I will ascertain what Chisolm will agree to. Accept my best wishes

TH: JEFFERSON

PoC (ViW: TC-JP); at foot of text: "Mr Reuben Perry"; endorsed by TJ.

TJ had sold his runaway slave James HUBBARD to Perry early the previous year (Conveyance of James Hubbard to Reuben Perry, Feb. 1811). TRACT: the course or track traversed by a person or animal (*OED*).

From Hugh White

SIR, Charlottesville 16 April 1812

If this late production of a Neighbour, as a variorum should afford a few moments entertainment. It would rejoice the author

HUGH WHITE

RC (TU). Recorded in SJL as received 17 Apr. 1812. Enclosure not found.

Hugh White (d. 1827) was a Scottish Presbyterian minister who was ordained a Swedenborgian clergyman in 1812. He owned land in both Charlottesville and Milton (Carl Theophilus Odhner, *Annals of The New Church, with a chronological account of the life of Emanuel Swedenborg* [1904], 1:213, 229; Woods, *Albemarle*, 178; Albemarle Co. Will Book, 9:15–6).

On 18 July 1812 White sent what was presumably the same VARIORUM to President James Madison, whose brother he claimed to have tutored in 1775. White described the work to Madison as "a few of his meditations & mental discussions on subjects which in a greater or less extent have occupied the rational faculties of the human race since the origin of the world" (Madison, *Papers, Pres. Ser.*, 5:46–7).

To John Barnes

DEAR SIR Monticello Apr. 17. 12.

I have this moment recieved a letter from Gen[l] Kosciuszko dated Feb. 1. in which he acknoleges the reciept of two letters from me, one from you and a bill of exchange. knowing it would give you pleasure to be ascertained of this, and supposing the General, who is not a man of business, may not have written to you, I drop a line for him. always affectionately yours TH: JEFFERSON

PoC (DLC); at foot of text: "Mr J. Barnes"; endorsed by TJ.

To José Corrêa da Serra

SIR Monticello Apr. 17. 12.

Your favor of Mar. 6. was duly recieved, & with it the pamphlet of M. Thouïn on the subject of engrafting, for which be pleased to accept my thanks. should your curiosity lead you to visit this part of the US. as your letter gives me reason to hope, I shall be very happy to recieve you at Monticello, to express to you in person my great respect, and to recieve from yourself directly the letters of my friends beyond the water introducing me to the pleasure of your acquaintance. to my much valued friend M. Thouïn especially I am indebted for frequent attentions, and particularly in the transmission of foreign seeds, which I place always in the hands of the best gardeners of the US. with a view of having them indigenated here, and of thus fulfilling his benevolent intentions of disseminating what is useful. should you be in correspondence with him, you would do me a great favor in giving a place in your first letter to the assurances of my affectionate remembrance of him. for yourself be pleased to accept the assurance of my high respect and consideration. TH: JEFFERSON

PoC (DLC); at foot of text: "M. Correa de Serra"; endorsed by TJ.

To Joseph St. Leger d'Happart

SIR Monticello Apr. 17. 12.

Your letter of Mar. 5. is but lately recieved. I have inclosed it to the President of the US. which is the only good office I can render you in the case. there must have been some mistake in supposing the not paying your claim was for want of money in the treasury. there has never been a moment when the treasury was without an abundance of money, and I know that at the date of your claim there were several millions in it. Accept my best wishes. TH: JEFFERSON

RC (PPiU: d'Happart Papers); addressed: "Doct^r St Leger de Happart Greensburg Pensylva"; franked; postmarked Milton, 22 Apr. 1812; endorsed by d'Happart as "Receiv'd May 22. Answ'd/ not to be repleid/." PoC (DLC); endorsed by TJ.

D'Happart used the verso of the RC of this letter for his retained copy of a letter to William Findley, written from St. Leger's Retreat, near Greensburg, 20 June 1812, thanking him for assisting in his effort to settle his claim with the government and noting that he had "at last receiv'd" his payment (FC in PPiU: d'Happart Papers; entirely in d'Happart's hand; at head of text: "To the honorable William Findley Member of Congress City of Washington").

To James Madison

DEAR SIR Monticello Apr. 17. 12.

The inclosed papers will explain themselves. their coming to me is the only thing not sufficiently explained.

Your favor of the 3^d came duly to hand. altho' something of the kind had been apprehended, the embargo found the farmers and planters only[1] getting their produce to market and selling as fast as they could get it there. I think it caught them in this part of the state with one third of their flour or wheat, and $\frac{3}{4}$ of their tob^o undisposed of. if we may suppose the rest of the middle country in the same situation, and that the upper & lower country may be judged by that as a mean, these will perhaps be the proportions of produce remaining in the hands of the producers. supposing the objects of the government were merely to keep our vessels and men out of harm's way, and that there is no idea that the want of our flour will starve great Britain, the sale of the remaining produce will be rather desirable, and what would be desired even in war, and even to our enemies. for I am favorable to the opinion which has been urged by others, sometimes acted on, and now partly so by France and great Britain, that commerce under certain restrictions and licences may be indulged between enemies, mutually advantageous to the individuals, and not to their injury as belligerents. the capitulation of Amelia island, if confirmed, might favor this object, and at any rate get off our produce now on hand. I think a people would go thro' a war with much less impatience if they could dispose of their produce, and that unless a vent can be provided for them, they will soon become querulous & clamor for peace. they appear at present to recieve the embargo with perfect acquiescence and without a murmur, seeing the necessity of taking care of our vessels and seamen. yet they would be glad to dispose of their produce in any way not endangering them, as by letting it go from a neutral place in British vessels. in this way we lose the carriage only; but better that than both carriage and cargo. the rising of the price of flour, since the first panic is past away, indicates some prospect in the merchants of disposing of it.—our wheat had greatly suffered by the winter but is as remarkably recovered by the favorable weather of the spring. ever affectionately yours

TH: JEFFERSON

RC (DLC: Madison Papers, Rives Collection); at foot of first page: "The President of the US." PoC (DLC). Enclosure: Joseph St. Leger d'Happart to TJ, 5 Mar. 1812.

[1] Word interlined.

From John S. Stake

HON' SIR New york April 17th[1] 1812

By the advice of many of my Republican friends, I have taken the liberty of addressing you. I am the eldest Son of the late Captain John Stake an old Revolutionary officer, of Well known merrit during our Revolutionary struggles for Liberty and Independance through a seven year's ardurous and Calamitous War: other heroes and other patriots press'd forward in the Same Career of Virrtue and Immortality they where his partners in danger his Companions in glory—

I am now desirous to obtain a Commission in the army and display that valor Which once led our Warriors to defy the thunder of the British Cannon and gloriously triumph in effecting Redress of our injured Country—

Your[2] name as it Justly ought Would have great weight with Both the President and Secretary at War, Will you have the goodness to Write one[3] or either of them a few lines in my Behalf

With Respect I am your[4] Humble st JOHN S STAKE

RC (DLC); endorsed by TJ as received 29 Apr. 1812 and so recorded in SJL.

John S. Stake (b. 1785), a native of New York City, was appointed a second lieutenant in the 13th Infantry Regiment, United States Army, on 1 May 1812. He resigned on 20 Nov. of that year. New York City directories list Stake as a grocer before and after his military service (*New York Genealogical and Biographical Record* 30 [1899]: 165; *Elliot & Crissy's New-York Directory, for 1811* [New York, 1811], 388; Heitman, *U.S. Army*, 1:914; *JEP*, 2:261; *The Citizens Directory and Strangers Guide Through the City of New York* [New York, 1814], 381). His father, an officer in the Continental army and a member of the Society of the Cincinnati, died in 1798 (DNA: RG 15, RWP; *Greenleaf's New York Journal, & Patriotic Register*, 28 Mar. 1798).

[1] Manuscript: "th 17."
[2] Manuscript: "You."
[3] Manuscript: "on."
[4] Manuscript: "you."

Non-Congressional Distribution List for Batture Pamphlet

[19 Apr.–23 June 1812]

The Proceedings of the Govmt on the Intrusion of E. Livingston. sent to the following persons.

Apr. 19. George Hay
William Wirt[1]
Littleton W. Tazewell
Governor Barbour
Judge Tyler
John Wickham
Edm[d] Randolph
Norborne Nicholas
Thomas Ritchie
the President
Secretary of state
of the Treasury
of War
of the Navy
the Atty General.
Postmaster Gen[l]
Caesar A. Rodney.

20. Rob. Smith.
W[m] Duane
Gen[l] Dearborne
John Adams
John Langdon
Rob. R. Livingston.
D[r] Rush.
Judge Tucker
Gov[r] Gerry
Gov[r] Tomkins
Gen[l] Armstrong
Judge Duvall.
Gov[r] Claiborne
James Mather
Moreau de Lislet
Thiery
Derbigny
Bolling Robinson
Benjamin Morgan
D[r] Samuel Brown

21. Joseph Cabell
Judge Cabell
Judge Stuart
Judge Johnston
Judge Homes
J. F. Mercer
J. T. Mason
Gov[r] Homes
Howard
Harrison
John Brown. K[y]
Apr. 23. A. J. Dallas.
Levi Lincoln
Charles Pinckney
D[r] Walter Jones
W[m] Rives
J. W. Eppes
25. James Maury
May. 10. Mrs Trist.
Charles Clay
21. Wilson C. Nicholas
June 6. Ingersol Charles J.
10. Jackson Gen[l] John G.
23. Taylor J.

Th: J. Randolph.
T M Randolph
C. L. Bankhead
Peter Carr
Dabney Carr
Sam[l] Carr.

MS (DLC: TJ Papers, 197:35049); entirely in TJ's hand; partially dated; written in two columns on one side of a single sheet, with second column beginning with entries for 23 Apr. 1812.

In addition to the individuals on this list, TJ arranged for the distribution of Jefferson, *Proceedings*, to every member of the United States Congress (TJ to Patrick Magruder and Samuel A. Otis, 26 Mar. 1812; Otis to TJ, 3 Apr. 1812).

BOLLING ROBINSON: Thomas Bolling Robertson.

[1] Surname reworked from "Wickham."

To Oliver Pollock

SIR Monticello Apr. 19. 12

Your letter of Mar. 28. has been recieved. the supposition hazarded in mine of Dec. 31.[1] that your authority to draw on Penet was probably from Governor Henry, was an inference only from the well recollected facts that Penet was appointed and sent to Europe by Governor Henry, and that soon after I succeeded him I learnt facts which left me without confidence in Penet. I therefore observed still in the same letter that 'it is possible however I may have authorised some draughts on him for the subsequent support of Clarke in his acquisitions.' I do not see, how a fact so cautiously surmised could 'have operated in a considerable degree against you' with our legislature as you express yourself to have believed. if the letter, dated, and consequently drawn for my signature 'at the board of trade' was of Nov. 6. 1779. as you state, the establishment of that fact establishes that it must have been signed by me, because I was in office at that time and proves what I could not recollect but stated to be possible that 'I might have authorised some draughts on Penet for the subsequent support of Clarke's acquisitions.' being without any certain recollection of the fact, I can still only leave it, if it be of any consequence, to be settled by other evidence, my want of recollection being no evidence against it. permit me to repeat the assurances of my esteem and respect.

TH: JEFFERSON

PoC (DLC); at foot of text: "Oliver Pollock esq."; endorsed by TJ.

[1] TJ here canceled: "was not stated."

To John Adams

DEAR SIR

Monticello Apr. 20. 12.

I have it now in my power to send you a piece of homespun in return for that I recieved from you. not of the fine texture, or delicate character of yours, or, to drop our metaphor, not filled as that was with that display of imagination which constitutes excellence in Belles lettres, but a mere sober, dry and formal piece of Logic. ornari res ipsa negat. yet you may have enough left of your old taste for law reading to cast an eye over some of the questions it discusses. at any rate accept it as the offering of esteem and friendship.

You wish to know something of the Richmond & Wabash prophets. of Nimrod Hewes I never before heard. Christopher Macpherson I have known for 20. years. he is a man of color, brought up as a bookkeeper by a merchant, his master, & afterwards enfranchised. he had understanding enough to post up his ledger from his journal, but not enough to bear up against Hypochondriac affections and the gloomy forebodings they inspire. he became crazy, foggy, his head always in the clouds, and rhapsodising what neither himself nor any one else could understand. I think he told me he had visited you personally while you were in the administration, and wrote you letters, which you have probably forgotten in the mass of the correspondencies of that crazy class, of whose complaints, and terrors, and mysticisms, the several presidents have been the regular depositories. Macpherson was too honest to be molested by any body,

& too inoffensive to be a subject for the Mad-house; altho', I believe, we are told in the old Book that 'every man that is mad, & maketh himself a prophet, thou shouldest put him in prison & in the stocks.'

The Wabash prophet is a very different character, more rogue than fool, if to be a rogue is not the greatest of all follies. he arose to notice while I was in the administration, and became of course a proper subject of enquiry for me. the enquiry was made with diligence. his declared object was the reformation of his red brethren, and their return to their pristine manner of living. he pretended to be in constant communication with the great spirit, that he was instructed by him to make known to the Indians that they were created by him distinct from the Whites, of different natures, for different purposes, & placed under different circumstances, adapted to their natures & destinies: that they must return from all the ways of the Whites to the habits and opinions of their forefathers. they must not eat the flesh of hogs, of bullocks, of sheep E^{t}c. the deer & buffalo having been created for their food; they must not make bread of wheat, but of Indian corn. they must not wear linen nor woollen, but dress like their fathers in the skins and furs of wild animals. they must not drink ardent spirits; and I do not remember whether he extended his inhibitions to the gun and gunpowder, in favor of the bow and arrow. I concluded from all this that he was a visionary, inveloped in the clouds of their antiquities, and vainly endeavoring to lead back his brethren to the fancied beatitudes of their golden age. I thought there was little danger of his making many proselytes from the habits and comforts they had learned from the Whites to the hardships and privations of savagism, and no great harm if he[1] did. we let him go on therefore unmolested. but his followers increased till the English thought him worth corruption, and found him corruptible. I suppose his views were then changed; but his proceedings in consequence of them were after I left the administration, and are therefore unknown to me; nor have I ever been informed what were the particular acts on his part which produced an actual commencement of hostilities on ours. I have no doubt however that his subsequent proceedings are but a chapter apart, like that of Henry & Ld Liverpool, in the Book of the Kings of England. Of this mission of Henry your son had got wind, in the time of the embargo, & communicated it to me. but he had learned nothing of the particular agent, altho', of his workings, the information he had obtained appears now to have been correct. he stated a particular which Henry has not distinctly brought forward, which was that the Eastern states were not to be required to make a formal act of separation from the Union, and to take a part in the war against it; a measure deemed much too strong for their people: but to declare themselves in a state of neutrality, in consideration of which they were to have peace and free commerce, the lure most likely to ensure popular acquiescence. having no indications of Henry as the intermediate in this negociation of the Essex junto, suspicions fell on Pickering and his nephew Williams in London. if he was wronged in this, the ground of the suspicion is to be found in his known practices & avowed opinions, as of that of his accomplices in the sameness of sentiment and of language with Henry, and subsequently by the fluttering of the wounded pidgeons.

This letter, with what it encloses, has given you enough I presume, of law and the prophets. I will only add to it therefore the homage of my respects to mrs Adams, and to yourself the assurances of affectionate esteem and respect. TH: JEFFERSON

RC (MHi: Adams Papers); endorsed by Adams as answered 3 May. PoC (DLC); at foot of first page: "John Adams." Enclosure: Jefferson, *Proceedings*. Enclosed in TJ to Benjamin Rush, 20 Apr. 1812.

ORNARI RES IPSA NEGAT: "my theme of itself precludes adornment" (Marcus Manilius, *Astronomica,* 3.39 [*Manilius Astronomica with an English Translation*, trans. George P. Goold, Loeb Classical Library (1977), 166–7]). EVERY MAN THAT IS MAD . . . IN THE STOCKS is a quotation from the Bible, Jeremiah 29.26. David Ross was the MERCHANT who owned and later freed Christopher McPherson (Edmund Berkeley Jr., "Prophet Without Honor: Christopher McPherson, Free Person of Color," *VMHB* 77 [1969]: 180–90). Tenskwatawa was the WABASH PROPHET. John Quincy Adams had COMMUNICATED with TJ regarding rumored New England separatist plots during a visit to the President's House on 15 Mar. 1808 (Adams Diary in MHi: Adams Papers; entry printed in Charles Francis Adams, ed., *Memoirs of John Quincy Adams* [1874–77], 1:521). In July 1809 Timothy Pickering publicly denied allegations that he and his NEPHEW Samuel Williams, a merchant in London and former United States consul there, had conspired to obtain British aid for a potential New England secession from the Union (Baltimore *North American and Mercantile Daily Advertiser*, 3 Aug. 1809).

[1] Reworked from "they."

To John Ashlin

SIR Monticello Apr. 20. 12.

I have just made me a fishpond and am desirous to get some carp fish to stock it. we used formerly when hauling the seyne for shad, to catch some carp also, and I presume therefore that some few are now caught at your place. I send the bearer therefore with a boat, with directions to stay a few days, and procure for me all the carp which shall be caught while he is there. I shall be obliged to you if you can aid him in getting them at as reasonable a price as you can. I presume they will not be higher than what is paid for shad, as they are by no means as good a fish. if through your interest he can be admitted to join in hauling the seyne & come in for a share of shad so as to bring us some, I will thank you, as well as for any other aid you may give him towards his[1] object. Accept my best wishes

TH: JEFFERSON

PoC (MHi); at foot of text: "Mr Ashlin"; endorsed by TJ.

John Ashlin (1762–1823), a resident of Fluvanna County, established a series of mills on the Rivanna River by 1810. He left an estate that included thirteen slaves, a manufacturing mill, a gristmill, a sawmill, a storehouse, and shops (Robert Quarles to TJ, 24 Sept. 1809; TJ to William D. Meriwether, 27 Dec. 1809; McGehee and Trout, *Jefferson's River*, 21, 81–2; Fluvanna Co. Will Book, 2:409–10, 3:16–8, 42–6, 154–6, 202–4; *Richmond Enquirer*, 18 Feb. 1823; Ellen Miyagawa, ed., *Family Cemeteries in Fluvanna County, Virginia* [1996], 4).

On this day TJ gave the BEARER, his slave James, $5 to procure carp (*MB*, 2:1276).

[1] Word interlined in place of "your."

From John Barnes

DEAR SIR, George Town. 20th April 1812.

since I had the pleasure of receiving your favr of the 9th covering one addressed to Mr John A Morton—in Care of Mr Williams—Baltimore which, I forwarded per same mail—

I am most agreably favd with a Letter from the good Genl Koscusko—dated Paris—1st Feby—Acknowledging recpt of Bill of ex for £200 sterling dated 15th April 1811. viz—"I send you great many thanks for it, and I beg you would be so good to send me Regularly—as you do now"—

Under this empression I shd—(I think.) not hesitate—in case of receiving any conditional offer (attended with risque—or empediment to your Acceptance from Mr M—) to purchase good Bill of ex on London—as heretofore—

at all events—to be in readiness to close with either—soon, as it best suits with your conveniency to remit your Annual Interest.—

the very Uncertain time of my closing Affairs here in Case I sh[d] eventually return to Philadelphia is so precarious & difficult to determine that it is impossible for me at this present time to say when—or how—the times are such—we cannot make any Reasonable Calculations—what course to persue—and whether—or Not; I had better, bear the ills—of adverse Fortune! than Risque—to encounter still greater Evils—is, the doubtfull Question.— if the latter—you most assuredly would be promptly informed—and your every command as promptly Obeyed—even While in this uncertain state—permit me again, to assure you, there is scarse an Article of family use you may Require but what I could purchase here (save some few particular[1] ones—) on equal terms—considering freight & risque &[ca]—the many New and elegant Stores on both sides Bridge Street filled with every discription of foreign and Domistic Merchandize wholesale & retail—little short of the greater importing Sea ports—whose abundance—do not proceed—from mere purchases—as heretofore—but as agents on very extensive Consignments, from the great importing merch[ts] at Boston N York Philad & Baltimore &[a] for sale on Commiss[n]—That the retailers who formerly were supplied from those Cities—now purchase—on the Spot—
their groceries from the New range of well built stores along the wharfs—The vast quantities of merchandize—both wet & dry surpasses almost belief—as well in washington—but so it is—that I am fully persuaded I could—with my Usual Attention supply you, or y[r] friends[2]—wants—both Wet and dry—as from Philad[a] (save some few particular Articles—and even those I could procure—and have them sent from thence to Richmond, without your being troubled to write for them—direct—)[3] I have not had to write to Philad[a] for a single Article since[4] you left this—except for Bottled porter—

submitting these Observations—to your better consideration—

I am Dear Sir most Respectfully Yr very Obed[t] serv[t]

JOHN BARNES

P.S. should our Public troubles—increase from bad, to worse, I shall abide where I am—and exert my best endeavours to Merit the Approbation of my friends who may be pleased to fav[r] me—with their Commands—

RC (ViU: TJP-ER); beneath signature: "Th: Jefferson Esq[r] Monticello"; postscript on verso of last page; endorsed by TJ as received 29 Apr. 1812 and so recorded in SJL.

Benjamin and George WILLIAMS were John A. Morton's BALTIMORE agents while he was in France.

[1] Manuscript: "partiular."
[2] Preceding four words interlined.
[3] Omitted closing parenthesis editorially supplied.
[4] Manuscript: "sincee."

To William C. C. Claiborne

DEAR SIR Monticello Apr. 20. 12.

You will probably some time ago have seen in the newspapers that the suit of Edward Livingston against me for maintaining the public possession of the Batture of New Orleans has been dismissed by the District court of the US. at Richmond for want of jurisdiction. my wish was that it should have been tried on it's merits, that the public might have seen thro' that medium that the transaction complained of was one of duty as well as of right. but the court, as I presume thought it wrong to give their time to the discussion of a title to lands not within their jurisdiction. to supply therefore the information which cannot now be passed through that channel, I have published the state of the case as prepared for the use of my counsel, and which I communicated to you when I had the pleasure of recieving you here. had the trial proceeded the questions would have been more ably developed by them. indeed the Jurists of Orleans had left little to be added; and on the whole I trust there will be but one opinion on the case. I inclose a copy of my view of it for yourself, and two others which I pray you to present to the Speakers of the two branches of your legislature, in their private, and not in their official capacities, the subject not being before their houses. it is offered merely as an evidence of my sincere zeal for whatever concerns that interesting country. Accept for yourself the assurance of my great esteem and respect.

TH: JEFFERSON

PoC (DLC); at foot of text: "Gov[r] Claiborne"; endorsed by TJ. Enclosure: three copies of Jefferson, *Proceedings*.

To Derbigny

Monticello. Apr. 20. 12

Th: Jefferson presents his compliments to M. Derbigny and asks his acceptance of the inclosed pamphlet on the subject of the Batture of N. Orleans. this homage is justly due to the first champion who stepped forth in defence of the public rights in that interesting subject, & arrested with so strong a hand the bold usurpations aimed at them. if in rescuing them, as a public functionary, or vindicating them as a private citizen, he has seconded the efforts of M. Derbigny, he owes him acknolegements for having led and pointed the way. he salutes him with great esteem & respect.

PoC (DLC); dateline at foot of text; endorsed by TJ. Enclosure: Jefferson, *Proceedings*. Enclosed in Elbridge Gerry to TJ, 1 May 1812.

Pierre (Peter) Augustin Bourguignon Derbigny (1769–1829), attorney and public official, was born to a noble family in Laon, France, and successively fled the French and Haitian revolutions, arriving in Pittsburgh about 1792. He subsequently lived in Illinois and Missouri before settling in New Orleans in 1797. Derbigny served as official interpreter for the Spanish and American governments. Before statehood he was clerk of the court of common pleas and secretary of the territorial legislative council. Derbigny served in the lower house of the first state legislature, sat on the Louisiana Supreme Court, 1813–20, was secretary of the state, 1820–27, and served as governor from 1828 until his death after a carriage accident. He authored works supporting the retention of existing Spanish and French laws in the territory and state and collaborated with Edward Livingston and Louis Moreau Lislet on the *Civil Code of the State of Louisiana* (New Orleans, 1825). Derbigny was also a key supporter of the public's claim to the Batture Sainte Marie, writing three pamphlets on the subject (*ANB*; *DAB*; Glenn R. Conrad, ed., *Dictionary of Louisiana Biography* [1988], 1:238–40; Michel d'Herbigny, *Pierre Bourguignon-d'Herbigny (1769–1829) Governor of Louisiana and his Descendants in U.S.A.* [1979]; Sowerby, nos. 3475, 3492, 3495; *Terr. Papers*, 9:12–3, 376, 524, 657–8, 1014–6; Derbigny to TJ, 7 Feb. 1805 [DLC]; *New-Orleans Argus*, 8 Oct. 1829; Washington *Daily National Intelligencer*, 31 Oct. 1829).

To William Duane

Sir Monticello Apr. 20. 12.

I inclose you a pamphlet on a subject which has, I believe been little understood. I had expected that it's explanation would have gone to the public thro' the medium of a trial at bar: but, failing in that, I have thought it a duty to give it through the ordinary medium of the press. I wish it could have appeared in a form less erudite. but the character of the question, and of those for whose use I wrote it decided that of the work. had it gone on to trial, my Counsel would have clothed it in a more popular dress.

We are then, it seems, to have no intermission of wrongs from England but at the point of the bayonet. we have done our duty in exhausting all the peaceable means of obtaining justice, and must now leave the issue to the arbitration of force. I have no fear of the award, and believe that this second weaning from British principles, British attachments, British manners & manufactures, will be salutary, & will form an epoch of a spirit of nationalism and of consequent prosperity, which could never have resulted from a continued subordination to the interests & influence of England

I had asked the favor of you in a former letter to let me know what I was in your debt. I am sensible how much the Editors of papers suffer from the irregularities of their subscribers. with myself these would certainly not take place were there a reciever at hand, or even within the state. but the difficulty of making small and fractional remittances to distant states, and the want of a general medium transmissible in a letter, and current in all the states, is a great obstacle, and much greatest with the inhabitants of the country. it has occasioned my discontinuing every paper out of my own state, except yours & the National Intelligencer. having occasion to make a larger remittance to mr Benjamin Jones, an iron-dealer of Philadelphia, I have included with it a sufficient surplus to enable him to pay my arrearages with you, and have desired him to do it; renewing at the same time my request to yourself to inform him of the amount. Accept assurances of continued esteem & respect.

TH: JEFFERSON

PoC (DLC); at foot of first page: "Col° Duane"; endorsed by TJ. Enclosure: Jefferson, *Proceedings*.

To Patrick Gibson

DEAR SIR Monticello Apr. 20. 12.

Your favor of the 16th is safely recieved with the 200. Dollars it inclosed. with respect to my flour on hand it is proper I should adapt my former minimum of 8.D. to the times. I leave the price therefore to yourself entirely, with the observation that it is better to lose a little by selling for less than may perhaps become the market price, than to lose the whole by holding off too long. especially as it is an article which will not keep. if 7.D. can be got I should think it well sold, and you will be the best judge when it will be safest to take even less. Accept the assurances of my esteem and respect

TH: JEFFERSON

PoC (ViU: TJP); at foot of text: "Mr Gibson"; endorsed by TJ as a letter to Gibson & Jefferson and so recorded in SJL.

To Benjamin Jones

Sir Monticello Apr. 20. 12

In my letter of Mar. 29. I informed you I had directed a remittance of Ð:200. out of the surplus of which I should request you to make a paiment for me. this is to Col° Duane for some books, and arrearages of his newspapers. how far back the last go, I do not know: the last paiment to him I find was July 31. 1807. his country paper @ 5.D. a year is the one I take. I have had some books of him also. if you will be so kind as to have the amount of his account asked for, and pay it, I will thank you. I think it will be within the limits of the surplus, unless there be something which I have forgotten; but even if it should be over the surplus be so good as to pay it, and I will have it instantly refunded, on your information.

I tender you the assurances of my esteem & respect.

Th: Jefferson

PoC (MHi); at foot of text: "Mr Benjamin Jones"; endorsed by TJ.

Benjamin Jones (ca. 1767–1849), Philadelphia ironmonger and investor in ironworks and real estate, entered with TJ's nailrod supplier Joseph Roberts into the partnership of Roberts & Jones in 1800. Roberts died late in 1802 and shortly thereafter Jones formed the partnership of Jones & Howell. TJ purchased bar iron and lead from Jones's firm until at least 1815 (*MB*, 2:964n, 1216, 1219, 1310; *Philadelphia Gazette & Universal Daily Advertiser*, 14 Jan. 1800; Cornelius William Stafford, *The Philadelphia Directory for 1800* [Philadelphia, 1800], 104; TJ to Jones, 6 Dec. 1802 [MHi] and 6 June 1815; *Philadelphia Gazette & Daily Advertiser*, 14 Dec. 1802; James Robinson, *The Philadelphia Directory City and County Register for 1803* [Philadelphia, 1803], 134; TJ to Jones & Howell, 10 Aug. 1809; John A. Paxton, *Philadelphia Directory and Register 1813* [Philadelphia, 1813]; will and biographical information in PHi: Jones and Taylor Family Papers; Philadelphia *North American and United States Gazette*, 16 May 1849).

SJL records TJ's letter of mar. 29. as well as letters from Jones to TJ of 21 and 27 Apr., received from Philadelphia on 29 Apr. and 1 May 1812, none of which has been found. On july 31. 1807 TJ arranged for payment of $64.37\frac{1}{2}$ to "Weightman & Duane" (*MB*, 2:1208).

From William Lambert

Sir, City of Washington, April 20th 1812.

By a letter from Mr John Garnett, Editor of the American impression of the Nautical Almanac, at N. Brunswick, in New-Jersey, it is stated, that an error has been discovered (probably at Greenwich) in M. de la Place's computations relating to the true form of the Earth, which being corrected, the ratio of 320 to 319, of the equatorial diameter to the polar axis of the Earth, seems now to be agreed upon as more correct than any of the others formerly used in Astronomical calculations. As this ratio may be considered as a standard, the latitude of any place, north or south, from 0.° to 90°, may be reduced by this Easy process.—

To the constant logarithm 9.9972814, add the log. tangent of the latitude of the place, the sum, (rejecting radius) will be the latitude reduced, according to the above ratio.

But to reduce the Moon's equatorial horizontal parallax, I have found it convenient in practice, to form a table of fixed logarithms to every degree of latitude from 0.° to 90°, which has been constructed on the following principles—

Let the log. of 320, be called (**A**), and the log. of 319, (**B**.) then
A – **B**, = **C**. log. **C**, + log. cotangent lat. place, by observation, –
radius, = log. tangent arch **D**. –
Log. cosine lat. place, by observation, + ar. comp.
log. sine arch **D**, = constant log. for lat: and ratio.

To the constant log. for the lat. add the log. sine of the Moon's equatorial horizontal parallax, the sum, (rejecting radius) will be the log. sine of the Moon's equatorial horizontal parallax, reduced.

As the Moon's equat. hor. parallax never amounts to 1.° 2′—the common log. in seconds and decimal parts, may be substituted for the log. sine; the former is, however, more correct.

Table of logarithms for reducing the Moon's equatorial horizontal parallax, to every degree of latitude from 0.° to 90°, admitting the ratio of the equatorial diameter to the polar axis of the Earth to be as 320 to 319.

Lat. °	Logarithms.	Lat. °	Logarithms	Lat. °	Logarithms.	°	
0	10.0000000.	20	9.9998414.	41	9.9994160	62	9.9989411.
1	9.9999996	21	9.9998259	42	9.9993924.	63	9.9989216.
2	9.9999983.	22	9.9998098	43	9.9993688	64	9.9989026
3	9.9999963.	23	9.9997931.	44	9.9993452	65	9.9988842
4	9.9999934.	24	9.9997757.	45	9.9993215	66	9.9988663.
5	9.9999896	25	9.9997578	46	9.9992977.	67	9.9988489.
6	9.9999851.	26	9.9997394.	47	9.9992740	68	9.9988321.
7	9.9999798	27	9.9997205	48	9.9992503.	69	9.9988159.
8	9.9999737.	28	9.9997011.	49	9.9992267.	70	9.9988003.
9	9.9999668	29	9.9996812	50	9.9992033	71	9.9987853.

10	9.9999591.	30	9.9996609.	51	9.9991800	72	9.9987709.
11	9.9999507.	31	9.9996402.	52	9.9991569	73	9.9987572
12	9.9999414.	32	9.9996191.	53	9.9991340.	74	9.9987442.
13	9.9999314.	33	9.9995977.	54	9.9991113.	75	9.9987320.
14	9.9999207.	34	9.9995759	55	9.9990889.	76	9.9987205
15	9.9999092	35	9.9995538	56	9.9990667.	77	9.9987097.
16	9.9998970.	36	9.9995314.	57	9.9990448	78	9.9986997
17	9.9998841.	37	9.9995087.	58	9.9990233	79	9.9986904.
18	9.9998705	38	9.9994858	59	9.9990021.	80	9.9986819.
19	9.9998563.	39	9.9994627.	60	9.9989813.	81	9.9986742
		40	9.9994394.	61	9.9989610.	82	9.9986673.
						83	9.9986611.
						84	9.9986557.
						85	9.9986511.
						86	9.9986473.
						87	9.9986444.
						88	9.9986423.
						89	9.9986411.
						90	9.9986407.

This table will be found to give the Moon's horizontal parallax, reduced, for any latitude, with greater accuracy, than any, perhaps, heretofore constructed. The application is easy; and for any intermediate minutes and seconds, take the proportional part of the difference from the preceding logarithm, which, in all cases, will be sufficiently exact.

Examples.

Required the log: for lat. 38.° 53.′ 0″—
The log. for 38.° is 9.9994858, and for 39°, 9.9994627, the difference is 231; the prop. part for 53′, is 204,—which subtracted from 9.9994858, gives 9.9994654, a constant log. for lat. 38.° 53.′—
Required the log. for the lat. of Greenwich,
51.° 28.′ 40.″
The log. for 51°, is 9.9991800, and for 52°, 9.9991569, the difference is 231, and the prop. part for 28.′ 40″, is 110, which subtracted from 9.9991800, gives 9.9991690, the constant log. for the lat. of Greenwich.

I am, Sir, with due respect, Your most obed[t] servant,

William Lambert.

RC (PPAmP: APS Archives, Manuscript Communications); written on one sheet folded to form four pages, with text on first three pages and address on the fourth; first three columns of table of logarithms on p. 2 and fourth column on p. 3, with remainder of text adjacent to it; at head of p. 3: "Table Continued"; addressed: "Thomas Jefferson, late president of the U. States, and president of the American Philosop[l] Society, Monticello, Virginia"; franked; postmarked Washington City, 24 Apr.; endorsed by TJ as received 29 Apr. 1812 and so recorded in SJL; endorsed at APS: "Lambert W[m] on an error in the Nautical Almanac read June 19. 1812." Enclosed in TJ to Robert Patterson, 29 May 1812.

Having received Lambert's ASTRONOMICAL CALCULATIONS above and his letter of 23 Apr. 1812 "from the president of the Society," on 19 June 1812 the American Philosophical Society referred them to a committee consisting of "M[r] Patterson Garnet, Allison," which did not return a report (APS, Minutes [MS in PPAmP]; John Vaughan, Report to APS on Papers to be Published, 6 Nov. 1812 [PPAmP: APS Archives]).

To Robert R. Livingston

DEAR SIR Monticello Apr. 20. 12.

I have not hesitated to send you one of the inclosed because I know that your mind will view in it nothing but the abstract question of right; and in the opinion of my fellow citizens on that question it will be my duty to acquiesce. I owe it to you also in return for your excellent book on the subject of sheep, now becoming daily more and more interesting to us. I am embarked a little in that business myself, having made a small beginning in the Merino race, from a ram and three ewes. my principal flock is of the Tunisian breed. the wool of these suits best our common manufactures, which are altogether houshold, there being scarcely a family in the country which does not clothe itself, as far as coarse woollens, or those of midling quality are required. so also as to hemp, flax, and cotton, the last of which has been always manufactured with us extensively, and in considerable perfection. so that were we to have tomorrow with Great Britain peace instead of war I am satisfied we shall no more take from her, in these lines, the worth of a shilling where we have taken that of a pound. the great desideratum with us is the invention of simpler machines; even the Spinning Jenny being too much for our country workmen. I have heard of one by an Oliver Barrett of your state, which the price would indicate to be simple; & another still more so by Herrick of Massachusetts, and I have sent for both. but it is on the puffs of the newspapers which merit as little credit in this as in their other branches of lying. yet I have thought it a duty to my neighbors to take on myself the risk of disappointment. if the machines answer, a service will be rendered them; if they do not I only lose a few dollars. being a farmer myself, I write to you as a farmer, leaving politics to those who are not worn down by them. I reduce myself to the reading 3. or 4. newspapers a week only, and shall soon I believe give up them also. I mark with a white bean the days on which I hear from my old friends, and shall always be happy to learn from yourself particularly that you enjoy health and quiet, with all the comforts which can chear the evening of our days. Accept the assurance of constant and sincere esteem and respect. TH: JEFFERSON

P.S. I ought not to omit informing a brother agriculturalist that I have the Irish fiorin grass growing, from roots recieved from Ireland this spring. I recieved some seed also which is sowed, but not yet up.

RC (NHi: Livingston Collection); postscript added separately to RC and PoC; addressed: (by TJ) "Robert R. Livingston esq." and (by an unidentified hand) "Clermont State of New York"; franked; postmarked Milton, 22 Apr., and New York, 27 Apr.; endorsed by Livingston as "private." PoC (MHi); endorsed by TJ. Enclosure: Jefferson, *Proceedings*.

Robert R. Livingston (1746–1813), statesman, diplomat, and agriculturist, was born in New York City and graduated from King's College (now Columbia University) in 1765. He was admitted to the New York bar in 1770, served as recorder of New York City from 1773 until his revolutionary sympathies led to his removal in 1775, and represented New York in the Continental Congress, 1775–76, 1779–81, and 1784–85. Livingston served with TJ on the committee charged with drafting the Declaration of Independence but left for New York before the document was completed. He played a key role in drafting New York's 1777 constitution and served as the state's first chancellor, 1777–1801, in which capacity he administered the presidential oath to George Washington in 1789. As Congress's first secretary of foreign affairs, 1781–83, Livingston directed the efforts of the American commissioners who negotiated the 1783 Treaty of Paris. In 1788 he made important contributions to New York's ratification of the new federal constitution. Livingston refused TJ's offer of the post of secretary of the navy in 1801 but accepted nomination the same year as minister plenipotentiary to France, serving until 1804 and successfully negotiating the Louisiana Purchase. His lifelong interest in experimental agriculture and mechanical inventions included service as the first president of New York's Society for the Promotion of Agriculture, Arts and Manufactures, 1791–1813, and first president of the American Academy of Fine Arts (later part of the National Academy of Design), 1801–02. Livingston was elected to the American Philosophical Society in 1801. He did pioneering work on merino sheep husbandry and the use of gypsum as fertilizer and, in partnership with Robert Fulton, established a controversial steamboat monopoly on the Hudson and Mississippi rivers. Throughout TJ's presidency the two leaders corresponded frequently on subjects ranging from politics to experimental science (*ANB*; *DAB*; George Dangerfield, *Chancellor Robert R. Livingston of New York, 1746–1813* [1960]; *PTJ*, 6:202, 22:467, 30:653–7, 31:56–7; APS, Minutes, 16 Jan. 1801 [MS in PPAmP]; Washington *Daily National Intelligencer*, 9 Mar. 1813).

TJ began raising sheep of the TUNISIAN BREED, also known as barbary or broadtails, about 1806 (Lucia Stanton, *Sheep for the President* [2000], 3; Thornton to TJ, 30 Aug. 1809).

To James Mather

SIR Monticello Apr. 20. 12.

The suit which mr Edward Livingston had brought against me for maintaining the public right to the Batture of N. Orleans, has been dismissed by the District court of the US. in this state for want of jurisdiction. this was not what I would have wished: but rather that the question of right should have been discussed before the public, from which a compleat justification of it must have resulted. as it is, I have thought myself bound to publish that justification: and as it may add something to the elucidation of a right so interesting to the city of N. Orleans, with which it was my desire, and fully my purpose to have made common cause, could the court have taken cognisance of it, I take the liberty of inclosing you a copy. I am bound further to make here my grateful acknolegements to you for the kind and valuable aid you have been so good as to afford me by forwarding to me the documents necessary for this elucidation. I have great confidence that the several investigations of this case have now placed the right so fully before Congress as to remove all danger of their yielding it: and certainly no other authority is competent to do it, even if they are, which I own I think is more than questionable. Accept the assurances of my great respect and esteem. TH: JEFFERSON

PoC (MoSHi: TJC-BC); at foot of text: "James Mather esquire"; endorsed by TJ. Enclosure: Jefferson, *Proceedings*.

To Louis Moreau Lislet

Monticello. Apr. 20. 12.

Th: Jefferson presents his compliments to M. Moreau de Lislet, and asks his acceptance of the inclosed pamphlet, on the subject of the Batture of N. Orleans. he has taken the liberty of differing from him on a single point; but conscious of the strength of M. Moreau in that field, and of his own weakness he has done it with just respect and diffidence: and deeply indebted for his able information on other questions of the controversy, he has with pleasure expressed his great acknolegements for it. he salutes him with high respect & consideration.

PoC (MHi); dateline at foot of text; endorsed by TJ. Enclosure: Jefferson, *Proceedings*.

Louis Moreau Lislet (1767–1832), attorney and judge, was born in Cap Français on Saint Domingue and educated in law and languages in France. He settled in Orleans Territory about the time of the Louisiana Purchase. In 1805 Moreau Lislet was among the counsel who won a judicial decision continuing the use of Roman civil law in Louisiana. He argued frequently before the highest territorial and state courts and opposed Edward Livingston in the case of the Batture Sainte Marie. Moreau Lislet published an *Explication des Lois Criminelles du Territoire d'Orleans* (New Orleans, 1806; Sowerby, no. 2177), collaborated with James Brown on a *Digeste des lois civiles maintenant en vigueur dans le Territoire d'Orleans* (New Orleans, 1808), joined Henry Carleton in selecting and translating *The Laws of Las Siete Partidas which are still in Force in the State of Louisiana*, 2 vols. (New Orleans, 1820; repr. 1978; Poor, *Jefferson's Library*, 10 [no. 603]) and, with Derbigny and Livingston, prepared the *Civil Code of the State of Louisiana* (New Orleans, 1825). Moreau Lislet served as judge for the parish of New Orleans for a number of years, declined an 1808 appointment to the territorial superior court due to its meager salary, and in 1817 served briefly as state attorney general before resigning to become a state senator (*DAB*; Glenn R. Conrad, ed., *Dictionary of Louisiana Biography* [1988], 1:579–80; *Terr. Papers*, 9:603, 749, 785, 835, 984, 1014; *JEP*, 2:69, 78 [19 Feb., 14 Mar. 1808]; New Orleans *Courier*, 13 Dec. 1832).

For the SINGLE POINT on which TJ differed from Moreau Lislet, see note to Caesar A. Rodney to TJ, 18 Oct. 1810.

To Benjamin Morgan

SIR — Monticello Apr. 20. 12.

Altho' I do not believe that you trouble yourself with law-questions, even those of your own vicinity, yet I send you the inclosed as a testimony of my respect for you.

M[r] Craven Peyton, claimant of the effects of John Peyton now in the hands of mr Duncan, despairing of getting the money out of mr Duncan's hands voluntarily, has desired me to urge recourse to the coercions of the law. indeed mr Duncan's refusing to pay it over till an impossible condition is performed does amount to an unconditional refusal. Lieut[t] Peyton being held under superior orders, cannot be forced to N. Orleans by mr Craven Peyton nor even by any authority of the courts. the laws of no country can require, from those who claim their justice, impossible conditions. after such a lapse of time, and no claim of a creditor brought forward, and nobody knowing, or having reason to suppose that there exists a creditor, for mr Duncan to claim to hold the money until proof produced that there is no creditor, is to claim to hold it till proof of a negative, which is impossible. surely then the laws of Orleans must have provided the means of forcing the money out of the hands of mr Duncan in such a case, and of restoring it to the representatives of the deceased. mr Craven Peyton's suspicions therefore of the unfaithful designs of mr Duncan are not entirely unplausible: and if you think it advisable, I would propose to you to turn the case over to the law. it would at least have the good effect of relieving you from the trouble of it. in that case mr Bolling Robinson whose diligence is known to us, and practises the law as we understand, will recieve the papers from you and take the measures necessary to give a safe issue to the suit to be instituted. if any previous formality is necessary on the part of mr Peyton, he will be ready to do whatever he is advised. I write to mr Robinson to recieve the papers, and to bring suit, if you think mr Duncan will not otherwise part with the money.

I have so often apologised to you for the trouble given you with this business, that a further expression of regret would only be a repetition. I will therefore only add assurances of my thankfulness and of my great esteem and respect. TH: JEFFERSON

PoC (MHi); at foot of first page: "Benjamin Morgan esq"; endorsed by TJ. Enclosure: Jefferson, *Proceedings*.

LIEUT[T] PEYTON: Robert Peyton. BOLLING ROBINSON: Thomas Bolling Robertson.

A letter from Craven Peyton to TJ of 11 Mar. 1812, not found, is recorded in SJL as received from Monteagle the next day.

To Thomas B. Robertson

DEAR SIR Monticello. Apr. 20. 12.

I think I stated to you, while here, the case of mr Craven Peyton, my neighbor, whose brother, John Peyton, had died in your territory, leaving personal property there. another brother Lieut[t] Peyton, took out administration, put the business into the hands of mr Duncan a lawyer, who became his security for the administration, recieved the proceeds of the effects of the deceased and refuses to pay them over to his representatives. at the request of mr Craven Peyton I had asked the favor of mr Benjamin Morgan to recieve and remit the money, at a time when no suspicions existed but that mr Duncan would readily pay them over to those for whom he had recieved them: and I had forwarded to mr Morgan the papers necessary to justify him in doing this. mr Craven Peyton, supposing that he now sees in the conduct of mr Duncan proofs of his intention to keep the money himself, has desired me to procure a suit to be instituted against him, having himself no acquaintance in N.O. I have thought it safer to leave it to the judgment of mr Morgan to decide whether this would be most advisable, and I have requested him, if such be his opinion, to deliver the papers to you for the purpose of coercing a restitution of the money. I have done this on the recollection of your information, while here, that you meant, on your return, to commence the practice of the law. should the laws of Orleans, in the cases of Non-residents, require security for the costs, if you will be so good as to be the security I will be answerable for mr Peyton's indemnifying you. you will of course take your reward out of[1] the proceeds of the suit, the balance of which mr Morgan informed me he could remit thro' his partner at Philadelphia. Having found it expedient to publish the state of the case of the Batture which I shewed you here, I inclose you a copy with assurances of my great esteem & respect

TH: JEFFERSON

PoC (MHi); at foot of text: "Mr Bolling Robinson"; endorsed by TJ. Enclosure: Jefferson, *Proceedings*.

[1] Preceding three words recopied above the line by TJ to correct a malfunction in the polygraph.

To Benjamin Rush

DEAR SIR Monticello Apr. 20. 12.

I do not know if you may have noticed in the Newspapers of a year or two ago that Edward Livingston had brought a suit against me for a transaction of the Executive while I was in the administration. the dismission of it has been the occasion of publishing the inclosed pamphlet, which is sent to you, not to be read, for there is nothing enticing for you[1] in it, but as a tribute of respect & friendship. you have moreover a son whose familiarity with the subject may render a glance of it amusing to him.

The sending a copy of this to mr Adams, as well as the answering some enquiries of his last letter, furnishes occasion for my writing to him a third time. as you have taken a pleasure in watering the tree of conciliation which your friendship for us both planted, I inclose to you my letter to him unsealed for perusal, that you may see how we come on. when read, be pleased to stick a wafer in it and recommit it to the post office. I salute you with constant attachment and respect.

TH: JEFFERSON

PoC (DLC); at foot of text: "Dr Rush"; endorsed by TJ. Enclosures: (1) Jefferson, *Proceedings*. (2) TJ to John Adams, 20 Apr. 1812.

Rush did indeed share TJ's pamphlet on the batture controversy with his SON. Richard Rush soon thanked his father, noting that TJ's essay "discovers wonderful research in him as a mere lawyer and is, unquestionably, as I think, a correct argument. There is more temper in it than is compatible with true dignity, and, unavoidably however, too much minuteness for style. I will acknowledge the receipt of it to him. among other peculiarities of orthography he spells knowledge—knolege" (Richard Rush to Benjamin Rush, 16 May 1812 [PPL: Benjamin Rush Papers, on deposit PHi]).

[1] Preceding two words interlined.

To Jean Baptiste Simon Thierry

Monticello. Apr. 20. 12.

Th: Jefferson presents his compliments to M. Thiery and asks his acceptance of the inclosed pamphlet on the subject of the Batture of N. Orleans. tho' he has ventured to differ from him on a single question, he was too much indebted for his able information on other points of the controversy, not to have made his acknolegements of the aid he derived from it with justice and pleasure. he prays him to accept the assurance of his great respect.

PoC (MHi); dateline at foot of text; endorsed by TJ. Enclosure: Jefferson, *Proceedings*.

Jean Baptiste Simon Thierry (d. 1815) was a native of France who settled about 1804 in Orleans Territory. In 1808 he became the editor of the New Orleans *Louisiana Courier*, which was the official newspaper of the territorial government. Later he served as the Louisiana state printer. Thierry had a gift for polemic and authored both pamphlets and newspaper editorials promoting his outspoken defense of the public right to the Batture Sainte Marie (George Dargo, *Jefferson's Louisiana: Politics and the Clash of Legal Traditions* [1975]; Brigham, *American Newspapers*, 1:185; Claiborne, *Letter Books*, 4:311–2, 359, 371, 5:13–4; Orleans Parish Probate Court Will Book, 2:202).

TJ differed from Thierry on a SINGLE QUESTION regarding the right of alluvion. Thierry asserted in his *Examen des Droits des Etats-Unis et des pretensions de Mr. Edouard Livingston sur la Batture en Face du Faubourg Ste. Marie* (New Orleans, 1808; Sowerby, no. 3477; English translation, Sowerby, no. 3478), 28–9, that despite French royal ordinances, the ancestors of Jean Gravier could claim the right of alluvion under the coutumes de Paris (customs of Paris), which were based in Roman law, and also under Spanish law. TJ noted that the counsel supporting Edward Livingston's claim to the batture had found the French law silent on this point, and he added that the rights in question had been vested in the public "before the Spanish government took place, and could not be anulled by a subsequent law. These gratuitous admissions therefore of M. Thierry, not at all necessary to his argument, and therefore probably not well considered, and in opposition to the opinions and demonstrations of an able brother counsellor, must be disavowed, and the authority of the Ordinance of 1693 insisted on with undiminished confidence. Mr. Thierry himself will perhaps the more readily abandon them, when he sees with what avidity his eagle-eyed adversary has pounced upon them in a letter to some member of the government, in which he considers them as giving up all ground of opposition to his claims" (Jefferson, *Proceedings*, 32–3; the "brother counsellor" was Derbigny).

From John Glass

SIR, New Jersey, Newark 21st April 1812.

Being conscious of the arduous task, which I have undertaken and perhaps the daring presumption to address such an illustrious character, without any previous Knowledge; (only by your writings) I feel myself, as it were constrained to desist from my undertaking; but being emboldened in the anticipation of success, I feel gratified in the consideration that the person to whom this is addressed, has ever encouraged the promotion of literature and the sciences in this our beloved country. But a few minutes have elapsed, since I perused two letters written[1] in answer to those written by Mr Sully, Secry of the society of Artists in the united states at Philadelphia. Those letters reanimated my hopes of success; the sentiments therein contained, breathe the pure air of the love, for the promotion of literature; they also contain the unextinguished zeal of a person, who for the term of eight years, was most popular in America, and in whom the friends of our country reposed the greatest confidence and who previous to the chief magistracy of the United States, had held some of the most important offices in America—with these considerations, and others too numerous here to mention, I am actuated to forward this; although in point of comparison you are exalted and I, as it were abased. I feel a great incumbrance on my mind, in disclosing my views; fearing, lest perhaps, I may be disappointed in my expectations and be plunged into oblivion, and, now honored Sir, I pray you not discard this—my most sedulous attention, has ever been to obtain an education and I trust through the medium of your patronage, I may receive one. For three years past, I have been at Jewelling business; but I have always aspired for something more exalted; not to say, I am too proud a member of the mechanical community; but that I have ever felt concerned about my future usefullness to my country, and as I fear the business, to which I am at present, paying some attention, will be in the course of a few years, of but trivial consequence, and being confident that a good education will always be of greatest imaginable consequence, I feel still more desirious of obtaining one. Dear Sir, I am almost assured of Success in petitioning. Though I feel dubious at times; still I am persuaded to make a bold request. I trust, I am confident in believing, that your desire has ever been to encourage youth in obtaining literature, and perhaps some youth, for the education of whom, you may [be][2] pleased to devote a part of your earthly treasure; may hereafter become conspicuous ornaments of the patronage and generosity of Thomas Jefferson

Esquire. Sir, may I not flatter myself, with the hope of being one of those youth? Ah! could I indulge the thought in reality, I should be elated; but time will determine. This, I trust you will peruse with mature deliberation; it is Dr Sir, to request your patronage and influence for an education which I have long wished for. perhaps in the extensive circle of your acquaintance, there may be men, who would readily assist in the education of a youth, inspired with the love of liberty, who is determined to accelerate and improve every opportunity which may contribute to his advantage It is probable had my father lived, I should not have troubled you, on this most important subject. It pleased the ruler of events, to call him hence when I was quite young; he left a widow and five children to mourn his loss, and of seven children, I was the only Son. God be praised, my mother and sisters have never wanted the neccessaries of life. During the Spring and fall of 1811, I was deprived by death, of my eldest Sisters; the hopes of an afflicted mother and the joy of a brother and two Sisters. I was not at home when they died; but separated by a space of 1000 miles, they have gone tis true, but to a more substantial habitation—My fathers name was John Glass, was born in 1767, and departed this life in the 38th year of his age—I have given you a concise description of our family—There is possibly a considerable portion of my fathers estate, which will consequently, be possessed by my Sisters and myself, I will sacrifice my portion thereof in assisting to receive an education—and now, Dr Sir, possibly you wou[ld] wish to Know my character and abilities—it is a presumptuous undertaking to recommend one's own abilities; therefore let this suffice, untill another communication—as to my character, should I have the exalted honor of receiving an answer to this; I will forward certificates from persons with whom, I have resided for three years past, and whose veracity is unimpeached.—or, should you wish to have a personal conference with me, which I should be very happy of;[3] I would hasten to your residence, if my pecuniary means were adequate, as they are not, I must resort to your generosity—be assured, this is not a fictitious tale; but exactly the reverse. Condescend Dr Sir, to peruse this with mature deliberation, and should you not deem me worthy your encouragement, I pray you, do not expose my name to a frowning world, I am Sir, with the greatest respect yours &^c &^c

John Glass

RC (MHi); mutilated at seal; addressed: "Thomas Jefferson Esqr Monticello—Mail"; endorsed by TJ as received 29 Apr. 1812 and so recorded in SJL.

John Glass (1794–1878), editor, attorney, and insurance broker, was born in Savannah, Georgia. He began work as an apprentice to a jeweler in New Jersey.

During the War of 1812 Glass enlisted in a New York regiment and later transferred to a unit in Georgia, where he completed his service and was honorably discharged in 1815. He had read extensively as an apprentice, and after the war ended he secured employment with a Savannah newspaper and eventually became its editor. Glass later studied law, was admitted to the bar, and practiced until 1830 in Spartanburg, South Carolina. He then relocated to Columbia, where he successively ran a school, served as a banker and broker for an insurance company until its failure, worked as a railroad bookkeeper, and operated a small farm (Brent Howard Holcomb, *Record of Deaths in Columbia South Carolina and elsewhere as recorded by John Glass 1859–1877* [1986], unpaginated introduction by Henry Griffin Fulmer; ScU: Glass Family Papers; Columbia *Southern Christian Advocate*, 5 Oct. 1878).

TJ's LETTERS of 8 and 25 Jan. 1812 to Thomas SULLY had appeared in a number of newspapers before Glass wrote this letter.

[1] Manuscript: "lettas wrtten."

[2] Omitted word editorially supplied.

[3] Glass here canceled "by noticing me."

From George Hay

SIR, Richmond April 21. 1812

Your letter of the 12th inst., was received too late, to be answered by the last mail.—The draft, which it covered, on Messrs Gibson and Jefferson, is returned, cancelled—You will recollect, that the tender of my Services, in Livingstons Suit, was accompanied by an express declaration, that I would receive no compensation from you. This declaration was not made, under the idea, which you have been So good as to Suggest. I meant, neither more nor less than this, that, let the course of the business be what it might, my Services, Such as they were, Should Cost you nothing. I cannot now recede.

I shall be much concerned, if it Should turn out, after farther inquiry and Search, to be the fact, that any part of the documents in your late Suit, have been lost. All that I received, I kept together with great care. With equal care, after the termination of the Suit, I prepared them, for their passage by the mail, and Sent them to the P. office. I certainly have not, now, a Single book, pamphlet, or manuscript belonging to the Cause.

I shall accept your pamphlet on the Subject of the batture, with great pleasure. I hope that Some person will attempt to answer it.

In searching in the Court of chancery for the Suit mentioned in your letter, I found two others, and learnt that the Suit brought by the executor of Mrs A. Randolph is depending in the fœderal Court. I will give you a Short Sketch of these three Suits.

The first is an old Suit, in which there was a decree many years ago, and which is now brought up and opened by a bill of review. It was originally brought by the distributees of the late Col: P. Randolph, against the executors, of whom Mr Wayles was one. The account was Settled, and a final decree entered. This decree established the right of Col. A. Cary, also an executor, to a credit for Several Sums, which the Estate has Since been obliged to pay. The object of the bill of review is to Set aside these Credits. Mr Wayles's representatives do not appear to have any interest in this Suit, & I should not have mentioned it, had I not Seen that an attachment has been awarded against you, which will probably be Served—

The Second Suit is brought, against yourself, and Samuel J. Harrison, for about 50 acres of land, for which, the bill charges, you contrived to get a patent, tho the Complainant had made a prior entry, and altho this fact was known to you. In this case a new Spa[1] is awarded. of this Suit I suppose that you never heard before. The Complainant is one Samuel Scott.—

The third Suit was the subject of your inquiry. Its object is to recover the arrears of an annuity, due to the late Mrs A. Randolph. For the payment of these arrears, Edm: Randolph had executed a deed, perhaps two deeds of trust, in which, inter alios, he mentioned you as a trustee. I suspect that he did this without consulting you. Your name therefore is inserted in the process pro forma only, and So Says Mr Wickham counsel for Gourlay the Executor.—You will of course give yourself no farther Concern about this Suit—

I am, with great respect, Yr mo: ob: Se. GEO: HAY

RC (DLC); endorsed by TJ as received 25 Apr. 1812 and so recorded in SJL.

[1] Abbreviation for "Subpoena."

To James Leitch

Apr. 21.[1] 12

a box of wafers, the largest sized box

TH:J.

RC (ViCMRL, on deposit ViU: TJP); dateline beneath signature; written on a small scrap; at foot of text: "Mr Leitch." Not recorded in SJL.

[1] Number interlined in place of "23."

From John Dawson

DEAR SIR Washington April 22d 1812

Louisiana having become a sister-state I take the liberty of inclosing to you a copy of her constitution, and at the same time, stating to you, with candour, my future plans, and counting, with confidence on your friendly offices, to which I feel that I have a just claim.

You are pretty well acquainted with the history of my political life, which while it has secur'd the approbation of my fellow citizens has provd ruinous to my private fortunes—particularly so was my trip to Europe.

I was regularly educated at Cambridge where I recievd a diploma and all the honours which that University coud bestow—I read law three years diligently and practisd it with success untill calld by my country to the high offices which I have held—I retain some knowledge of the Latin language and have a tolerable acquaintance with the French—under these circumstances it seems to me that I could discharge, with propriety the duties of one of the judges of Louisiana mentiond in the Constitution; and I am persuaded that a letter from you addressd to Governour Claiborne, Mr Poydras, or any other person woud be of great advantage—

Shoud you think proper to write such you will be pleasd to inclose them to me at this place.

With the sincerest regard Your friend and fellow citizen

J DAWSON

RC (DLC); endorsed by TJ as received 29 Apr. 1812 and so recorded in SJL. Enclosure: *Constitution or Form of Government of the State of Louisiana* (New Orleans, 1812).

John Dawson (ca. 1762–1814), attorney and public official, was a native of Caroline County who began his studies at the College of William and Mary and graduated from Harvard University in 1782. His stepfather, Joseph Jones, was the uncle and guardian of James Monroe, and Dawson was a friend and political associate of Monroe and James Madison. He represented Spotsylvania County in the Virginia House of Delegates, 1786–89, opposed the new federal constitution at the state ratification convention in 1788, represented Virginia in the last months of the dormant Confederation Congress, 1788–89, and sat on the Virginia Council of State, 1789–97. In 1789 Dawson was called to the bar in Fredericksburg. He was elected as a Republican to the United States House of Representatives in Madison's former district in 1797 and served until his death. Dawson was unsuccessful in his ongoing quest for a position in the federal government and for a judicial appointment in the new state of Louisiana (*ANB*; *DAB*; Leonard, *General Assembly*; *PTJ*, 16:182, 597, 33:253, 401, 504; Madison, *Papers*, esp. *Congress. Ser.*, 13:262–3, and *Pres. Ser.*, 2:71–2; Claiborne, *Letter Books*, 5:400, 6:156–8, 212–3; Dawson files in DNA: RG 59, LAR, 1801–09 and 1809–17; TJ to William C. C. Claiborne, 2 May 1812; Washington *Daily National Intelligencer*, 2 Apr. 1814).

Dawson traveled TO EUROPE in 1801 to

present the amended commerical Convention of 1800 to the French government for ratification. On his return to the United States in January 1802, the constitutionality of his retention of his congresssional seat while employed by the government in another capacity came into question. Dawson also experienced difficulties recovering the expenses he incurred during this mission (Madison, *Papers, Sec. of State Ser.*, 1:33, 2:352n, 410, 411n, 3:91–2). Article 4, sections 3–4 of the new Louisiana constitution (pp. 17–8) called for three to five JUDGES of the supreme court and an unspecified number of lower-court magistrates.

From Lafayette

MY DEAR FRIEND Paris 22^d^ April 1812

I find the dispatches By the Hornet are Just Going and altho' I mean to write more fully By the Return of the wasp I Hastily Seize the Opportunity to let you know that my family and myself, mde de tessé, who Has Been ill, mr de tessé, m. de mun and m^r^ de tracy[1] are now all well—your Correspondance with washington will inform you of the European news.—Great Continental preparations are moving on and Seem to threaten Russia—our friend mr Barlow Has not Been able to Send a Result of His Negociation for which He keeps the wasp and is promised He will not waït Long—we Hear a British messenger is Gone to America—may He Announce Better dispositions than are Expressed By the ministers of the Regent! no Body More fervently than me wishes the U.S. may Avoid a war.

I Have Been very much Gratified with your Approbation of my Arrangement with Mm Baring and parish. m^r^ du plantier's Letters and other informations Being well weighed it Has Appeared to us Here that it was impossible to make a Sale or loan in America which Has Been Confirmed By m^r^ madison's opinion—the price to Be got in Small portions, upon long Credits, and with Every difficulty of distance and disadvantage of change Seemed to Be from ten to twelve dollars, as opportunities did offer. I Have Been Several years making in Europe fruitless attempts, which the Appearances of a war Had lately Been thought to Reduce to impossibility—your last favor made me think you Believed[2] I was in time to Reap the advantages of delay By a Sale at pointe Coupee.

under those Circumstances, and the pressure of my affairs, the Ruinous Encrease of interest upon interest making it Necessary, Even in probity, to attend to a liberation, I was advised by mr Barlow and other American friends not to miss the opportunity of two English purchasers of my Lands. they Agreed, Considering their loss on the Exchange, to pay twelve dollars, Sixty francs in paris—See, my dear Jefferson, what immense inexpressible obligation I Have to that unexpected American Grant—But the Approbation of the whole world for the use I make of it would Not avail me untill I know I am approved By the friend to whom principaly I owe the provident delivery. Let me add that if my Situation did permit me to Have a plantation at[3] pointe Coupee mr Baring would Readily Restore me to the possession and Even the choice of one or two of His patents.

I Have not yet Received the patent and plan of the precious tract Near the City which Has Ever Been By you Considered as the most important part of the munificent Gift. adieu, my dear Excellent friend I am most affectionately

Yours LAFAYETTE

RC (DLC); endorsed by TJ as received 27 May 1812 and so recorded in SJL. Enclosed in John Graham to TJ, 23 May 1812, or James Madison to TJ, 25 May 1812.

Joel BARLOW advised President James Madison on 22 Apr. 1812 of the sale of Lafayette's lands and of Barlow's detention of the USS *Hornet* in hope of reporting the completion of negotiations in Paris. Unable to secure a treaty by that date, Barlow released the *Hornet* and detained the USS *Wasp* for the same purpose. Madison gave his OPINION on the land negotiations in a 15 July 1811 letter to Lafayette (Madison, *Papers, Pres. Ser.*, 3:380–1, 4:337–9).

[1] Preceding four words interlined.
[2] Word interlined in place of "thought."
[3] Reworked from "Near."

To James P. Cocke

DEAR SIR Monticello Apr. 23. 12

I have just finished a fish pond and wish to get some of the Roanoke chub to stock it. I am told you now possess the pond that was your relation & neighbor mr Cocke's. could you spare me a few to begin with? if you can, I will send tomorrow a light cart with a cask for water, so that the cart may start the next morning and keep the fish out as short a time as possible. I propose so short a term, because I presume you have the means of commanding the fish at any time, and I am to set out for Bedford on Monday or Tuesday. Accept the assurance of my great esteem and respect.

TH: JEFFERSON

PoC (DLC); at foot of text: "James Cocke esq."; endorsed by TJ.

James Powell Cocke (1748–1829) grew up at Malvern Hills, his family home in Henrico County, which he inherited from his father. Cocke sold the property shortly after the American Revolution, and by 1791 he had moved to Springhill in Augusta County. Two years later he purchased land in Albemarle County near the Hardware River and there constructed a house and a gristmill. TJ is said to have planned Cocke's residence, Edgemont, basing it on a design by Andrea Palladio (James P. C. Southall, "Malvern Hills, Henrico County, and Edgemont, Albemarle County," *VMHB* 43 [1935]: 74–91; Lay, *Architecture*; *MB*, esp. 1:276–7; TJ to Cocke, 10 Sept. 1806 [MHi]; Albemarle Co. Will Book, 9:355–6).

ROANOKE CHUB is a regional name for a fish of the genus *Micropterus*, commonly known as Black Bass. TJ was most likely referring to Smallmouth Bass (*Micropterus dolomieu*) (James A. Henshall, *Book of the Black Bass* [1900], 142).

From James P. Cocke

DEAR SIR ap[l] 23[d] 1812

I am sorry to observe that the geting supply of fish is most uncertain, not having made arrang[t] to command them. yet If you will send at the risque be assured I will do my indeavour to procure them. I shall shortly set about some method in order to have them at command & would think the fall would be more proper to remoove them as they are now spawning & much more certain to get them with much esteem am D[r] Sir

y[r] Ob[t] Ser[t] J P COCKE

RC (DLC); at foot of text: "Tho[s] Jefferson Esq[r]"; endorsed by TJ as received 23 Apr. 1812 and so recorded in SJL.

From William Lambert

SIR, City of Washington, april 23[d] 1812.

I transmit to the American philosophical Society, an abstract of such calculations as I have hitherto made to determine the longitude of the Capitol in this city from Greenwich observatory, in England. The variation in the results will be found, on examination, to arise more from probable errors in the data, or in the lunar tables from which the positions in the Nautical Almanac have been computed, than from any mistake in the process or principles of calculation.

The first result is founded on an occultation of a Tauri, (Aldebaran) by the Moon, observed by M[r] Andrew Ellicott, on the 21st of January, 1793; the apparent times of contacts, and the latitude of the place of observation, as extracted from the fourth volume of transactions of the American philosophical society, and furnished by their Secretary, are as follow:—

		h. m. Sec	
January 21st 1793.	Immersion,	at 7.55.49½.	P.M.
	Emersion,	at 9.25.21½	

Latitude of the place, 38°.52′.40″. North.
Estimated longitude, (assumed for the computation, 5. h. 7. m. 35.8 Sec. = 76°.53′.57″.

The British impression of the Nautical Almanac, gives the following calculated times at Greenwich—

	h. m			′	
January 21st 1793	14.32½ Im:	of a ♉, ∗,	12½	N: of ☽'s center.
	14.57½ Em:		14–	

The Moon's positions at noon and midnight, by the meridian of Greenwich, are taken from the Nautical Almanac, and set down, with their successive differences, as follow:—

1793		° ′ ″	° ′ ″	′ ″	″	″
January 20th	Midn:	53.46.59. **A**				
			+ 6.12.35. a1.			
21st	Noon,	59.59.34. **B.**		– 3.14. a2.		
			+ 6. 9.21. b1.		+ 24. a3.	
"	Midn.	66. 8.55. **C.**		– 2.50. b2.		0. a4.
			+ 6. 6.31. c1.		+ 24. b3	
22.	Noon,	72.15.26. **D.**		– 2.26 c2.		
			+ 6. 4. 5 d1.			
"	Midn:	78.19.31. **E.**				

Moon's Latitude (South.)

1793.		° ′ ″	′ ″	′ ″	′ ″	″
January 20th	Midn.	4.46. 3. **A**				
			+ 10.56. a1.			
21.	Noon,	4.56.59. **B.**		– 3.31. a2		
			+ 7.25. b1.		– 0.2 a3	
"	Midn:	5. 4.24. **C.**		– 3.33. b2.		+5. a4.
			+ 3.52. c1.		+ 0.3. b3	
22.	Noon,	5. 8.16. **D.**		– 3.30. c2		
			+ 0.22. d1.			
"	Midn.	5. 8.38. **E.**				

Supposing the positions in longitude and latitude stated in the Nautical Almanac, to be strictly correct, and admitting the ratio of the equatorial diameter to the polar axis of the Earth, to be as 320 to 319, the Star's longitude and latitude, and the true conjunction of the Moon and Star at Greenwich, have been found by calculation, of which the following is an abstract—

For Greenwich.

By the immersion.—

	° ′ ″ dec.
Latitude by observation,	51.28.40.000.N.
" reduced, (320 to 319.)	51.18.10.469.
Obliquity of the Ecliptic, January 21st 1793	23.27.48.324.
Constant log. to reduce the Moon's equat. hor. par: for lat. and ratio	9.9991690.

	° ′ ″ dec.
apparent time of immersion, (Naut. Alm.) 14. h. 32½ m. =	218. 7.30.000.
Sun's right ascension,	304.56.14.484.
Right ascension of the meridian from beginning of ♈,	163. 3.44.484.
ditto, from beginning of ♑, (West)	106.56.15.516.
Altitude of the nonagesimal,	49.57.12.984.
Longitude of the nonagesimal from beg: of ♈,	141.22.37.928.
Moon's <u>true</u> longitude, by the tables,	67.26.46.197.
" <u>true</u> distance from the nonagesimal (West)	73.55.51.731.
" <u>true</u> latitude, (South)	5. 5.30.891.
" equatorial horizontal parallax,	0.55. 6.035
" horizontal parallax, reduced, (320 to 319)	0.54.59.715
" parallax in longitude,	0.40.45.036.
" apparent dist: from nonag: (West)	74.36.36.767.
" parallax in latitude	0.36.20.466
" apparent latitude, (South)	5.41.51.357.
" augmented Semidiameter, arising from app^t alt.	0.15. 3.634.

<u>By the Emersion.</u>

	° ′ ″ dec.
apparent time of emersion, (Naut. Alm.) 14. h. 57½ m. =	224.22.30.000
Sun's right ascension,	304.57.20.165.
Right ascension of the meridian, from beg: of ♈,	169.19.50.165.
ditto, from the beginning of ♑. (west)	100.40. 9.835.
Altitude of the nonagesimal,	47.56.42.656.
Longitude of the nonagesimal from beginning of ♈,	145.50.20.270.
Moon's <u>true</u> longitude,	67.39.31.255
" <u>true</u> distance from the nonag: (West)	78.10.49.015
" <u>true</u> latitude, (South)	5. 5.40.946.
" Equatorial horizontal parallax,	0.55. 5.549.
" horizontal parallax, reduced, (320 to 319)	0.54.59.230.
" parallax in longitude,	0.40.12.942.
" apparent dist: from the nonag. (west)	78.51. 1.957.
" parallax in latitude	0.37.27.504.
" apparent latitude, South,	5.43. 8.450.
" augmented Semid^r arising from app^t alt:	0.15. 2.126.

The difference of apparent longitude and latitude of the Moon and Aldebaran, may be found accurately by the following method, using an assumed latitude of the Star, near the truth.—

		° ′ ″
Moon's apparent lat. at imm: South		5.41.51.357
diff: of lat. ☽ and ∗, (Naut. Alm.)		– 12.30 —
		5.29.21.357
	° ′ ″	
Moon' apparent lat. at emersion,	5.43.8.450.	
diff: of lat. ☽ and ∗, (Naut. Alm)	– 14.0 —	
		5.29. 8.450.
Mean, assumed latitude of the Star,		5.29.14.903.

	° ′ ″
Moon's apparent longitude at emers:	66.59.18.313.
ditto, at imm:	66.46. 1.161.
" motion in apparent longitude	13.17.152.

Moon's motion in apparent long:	797.152 ″	log.	2.9015412. ·
Star's assumed lat. 5.° 29.′ 14.″ 903		cosine	9.9980051.
Moon's motion in apparent long. reduced to same parallel to ecliptic as ∗,	″ dec. 793.499.		2.8995463.

Moon's motion in app^t lat. during transit, 77.″ 093.	log.	1.8870149.
" motion in app: long. reduced, 793.″ 499.	ar. comp. log.	7.1004537.
Angle of inclination, 5.° 32.′ 47.″ 116.	tang.	8.9874686.
Moon's motion in apparent long. reduced 793.″ 499.	dec log.	2.8995463.
Angle of inclination, 5.° 32.′ 47.″ 116. dec	ar. comp: cosine	0.0020380.
chord of transit, 797.″ 231.	log.	2.9015843

Messrs Ferrer and Garnett, in their calculation of the longitude of Kinderhook, in the state of New York, from the solar eclipse of June 16th 1806, found the inflexion of the Moon's light to be –2.″ 977; that quantity will be applied in this case.—

	″	″	″
Moon's augmented Sem^r at imm:	903.634	– 2.977, =	900.657
d° d° at emer:	902.126.	– 2.977. =	899.149.
Sum of the Moon's Semidiameters, corrected			1799.806.

	″		
chord of transit,	797.231	ar. comp. log.	7.0984157.
Sum of Semid^{rs}, corrected,	1799.806	log.	3.2552256.
diff: of Semidiameters,	1.508	log.	0.1784013.
	(x) 3.404	log.	0.5320426.

	″	″
chord of transit,	797.231. ± (x)	800.635. (a)
		793.827. (b)

(a) = 800.635. ″ dec		log. ″	2.9034346.
☽'s cor. sem^{r} at imm. 900.657. × 2 = 1801.314 ″		ar. com. log.	6.7444106.
angle of conjunc^{n}	63.36.37.388. ° ′ ″	cosine	9.6478452
angle of inclinat:	–5.32.47.116.		
Central angle	58. 3.50.272.	at the immersion.	

(b) = 793.827 ″		log.	2.8997258.
☽'s corr: sem^{r} at emers. × 2 = 1798.298. ″		ar. co. log.	6.7451384.
angle of conjunction,	63.48.16.892. ° ′ ″	cos:	9.6448642.
angle of inclination,	+5.32.47.116.		
Central angle	69.21. 4.008.	at the emersion.	

Star's assumed lat: 5.° 29.′ 14.″ 903. ar. co. cosine,	0.0019949.		
☽'s corrected Sem^{r} at immersion, 900.″ 657. log.	2.9545595.	log.	2.9545595.
Central angle at ditto 58.° 3.′ 50.″ 272. cos.	9.7234329.	Sine	9.9287231.
diff: of app: longitude, 7.′ 58.″ 614. = 478.″ 614. log.	2.6799873.	log.	2.8832826.
			} 764.″ 333. dec =12.′ 44.″ 333. diff. of apparent lat.

Star's assumed lat 5.° 29.′ 14.″ 903 ar. co. cosine,	0.0019949.		
☽'s corrected Sem^{r} at emersion, 899.″ 149 log.	2.9538316	log.	2.9538316.
Central angle, at ditto 69.° 21.′ 4.″ 008. cosine	9.5473318.	Sine	9.9711640
diff: of app. long. 5.′ 18.″ 536 = 318.″ 536. log.	2.5031583.	log.	2.9249956.
			} 841.″ 387. = 14.′ 1.″ 387. diff. of apparent lat.

		° ′ ″
Moon's apparent latitude, at immersion, (South)		5.41.51.357.
diff: of apparent lat. found above		– 12.44.333.
Star's lat. by computation from imm. (South)	° ′ ″	5.29. 7.024
Moon's apparent lat. at emersion,	5.43.8.450.	
diff: of apparent lat. as above,	– 14.1.387	
		5.29.7.063.
Mean result Star's lat. (South) by comput:		5.29.7.043.

	′ ″ dec.
Moon's parallax in longitude, at the immersion	– 40.45.036
diff: of apparent longitude ☽ and ∗,	+ 7.58.614.
true difference of longitude ☽ and ∗,	– 32.46.422.
Moon's true longitude, immersion at Green^{wch}	67.26.46.197.
Star's longitude, found by the immersion,	66.53.59.775.
parallax in longitude at the emersion,	– 40.12.942.
diff: of apparent long. ☽ and ∗,	– 5.18.536.
true diff: of longitude ☽ and ∗,	– 45.31.478.
Moon's true longitude at emersion,	67.39.31.255.
Star's longitude, found by the emersion,	66.53.59.777.
″ d^{o} by the immersion,	66.53.59.775.
Mean result Long. of the ∗, by comp^{n} Supposing the ☽'s positions to be correct. }	66.53.59.776.

The difference of apparent longitude of ☽ and ∗, may also be obtained by the following process—

Moon's corrected Semid[r] at imm: in seconds, &c.		″ 900.657	
diff: of apparent lat. ☽ and ∗,		764.333.	
	sum,	1664.990.	log. 3.2214116.
	diff.	136.324.	log. 2.1345723.
			2)5.3559839
			2.6779919.
Star's lat. 5.° 29.′ 7.″ 043. dec. ar. comp. cosine			0.0019933.
diff: of apparent longitude, 7.′ 58.″ 614 = 478.″ 614 =			2.6799852

Moon's corrected Semid[r] at emersion,		″ 899.149	
diff: of apparent lat.		841.387.	
	Sum,	1740.536.	log. 3.2406830.
	diff.	57.762.	log. 1.7616422
			2)5.0023252
			2.5011626.
Star's lat. 5.° 29.′ 7.″ 043. ar. co. cosine,			0.0019933.
diff: of apparent long.	5.′ 18.″ 534. = 318.″ 534.		log. 2.5031559

The true conjunction of Moon and Star at Greenwich happened when the Moon had the same longitude as the Star, which, by accurate calculation, is found to have been at 13. h. 28. m. 16. Sec. 358. dec.

For the place of observation at Washington.

Latitude, by M[r] Ellicott,	° ′ ″ 38.52.40.000 N.
reduced, (320 to 319)	38.42. 9.512.
Const. log. to reduce ☽'s equat. hor. par. for lat: & ratio,	9.9994655
Estimated long. from Greenwich, 5. h. 7. m. 35.8 Sec. =	° ′ ″ 76.53.57. West.

apparent time of immersion, 7. h. 55. m. 49½ Sec =	° ′ ″ 118.57.22.500.
Sun's right ascension corresp[g] time at Green[wch]	304.52.20.420
Right ascension of merid[n] from beg. of ♈,	63.49.42.920.
ditto, from beginning of ♑ (East)	153.49.42.920.
Altitude of the nonagesimal,	72.51.36.375.
Longitude of the nonagesimal, from beg. of ♈,	68.53.15.150.

	° ′ ″
☽'s true longitude, (Naut. Alm:)	66.41.18.569.
" true distance from the nonagesimal, (West)	2.11.56.581.
" true latitude, (south)	5. 4.52.981.
" equat. horizontal parallax,	0.55. 7.767.
" horizontal parallax, reduced	0.55. 3.699.
" parallax in longitude,	0. 2. 3.507.
" apparent distance from the nonag: (west)	2.14. 0.088.
" parallax in latitude,	0.21. 7.919.
" apparent latitude, (South)	5.26. 0.900.
" augmented Semid[r] arising from apparent alt	0.15.15.190.

	° ′ ″ dec.
apparent time of emersion, 9. h. 25. m. 21½ Sec. =	141.20.22.500
Sun's right ascension corresp[g] time at Green[wch]	304.56.15.680.
Right ascension of the meridian from ♈,	86.16.38.180.
ditto from beg. of ♑, (East)	176.16.38.180.
Altitude of the nonagesimal	74.43.18.614.
Longitude of the nonagesimal from ♈,	86.59.20.658
Moon's true longitude, (Naut. Alm.)	67.27. 0.123.
" true distance from the nonag. (West)	19.32.20.535.
" true latitude, (South)	5. 5.31.078.
" Equat. horizontal parallax	0.55. 6.024.
" horizontal parallax, reduced,	0.55. 1.957
" parallax in longitude,	0.18. 5.329.
" apparent distance from the nonag.	19.50.25.864.
" parallax in latitude.	0.19. 9.004.
" apparent latitude (South)	5.24.40.082
" augmented Semid[r] arising from app[t] alt.	0.15.14.021.
Star's latitude, by computation, (south)	5.29. 7.043
Moon's apparent lat. at immersion,	5.26. 0.900.
diff: of apparent lat. ∗ south of ☽'s center,	– 3. 6.143.
Star's latitude (South)	5.29. 7.043.
Moon's apparent lat. at emersion,	5.24.40.082.
diff: of apparent lat. ∗ South of ☽'s center,	– 4.26.961.

For the difference of apparent long. of ☽ and ∗.

Moon's augmented Sem^{r} at imm:	915.190″ – 2.977″ = 912.213″.	
ditto at emers:	914.021 – 2.977. = 911.044.	
Moon's corrected Sem^{r} at immers^{n}	912.213″	
diff: of apparent lat. d°	186.143.	
	1098.356	3.0407431.
	726.070	2.8609785.
		2)5.9017216
		2.9508608.
Star's lat. 5.° 29.′ 7.″ 043	ar. comp. cos.	0.0019933.
diff: of app: long.	+ 14.′ 57.″ 127 = 897.″ 127	2.9528541.

Moon's augmented Sem^{r} at emers:	911.044″	
diff: of apparent lat. at d°	266.961	
sum,	1178.005. log.	3.0711471.
diff.	644.083. log.	2.8089418
		2)5.8800889
		2.9400444
Star's lat. 5.° 29.′ 7.″ 043	ar. comp. cos.	0.0019933.
diff. of app. long.	–14.′ 35.″ 060 = 875.″ 060 dec.	2.9420377.

difference of apparent longitude at imm.	+ 14.′57.″127.
parallax in longitude,	– 2. 3.507.
true difference longitude at the immers^{n}	+ 12.53.620.
difference of apparent long. at emersion,	– 14.35.060.
parallax in longitude,	– 18. 5.329.
true diff. of longitude, at emersion,	– 32.40.389.

The Moon's hourly velocity in longitude, at a middle time between the immersion and estimated time of true conj^{n} at Washington, was 30.′ 37.″ 842, and between the true conjunction and emersion, 30.′ 36.″ 981

---

as hourly velocity, = 30.′ 37.″ 842, to one hour or 60 min: so is true difference of longitude, 12.′ 53.″ 620, to the interval of time, = 25. m. 15.382 Sec, which added to 7. h. 55. m. 49. Sec. 500. dec gives 8. h 21. m. 4. Sec. 882 dec, the time of true conjunction at Washington, found by the immersion.

As hourly velocity, = 30.′ 36.″ 981 dec, to one hour, or 60. min So is true difference of longitude, 32.′ 40.″ 389, to the interval of time, = 1. h. 4. m. 1. Sec. 847 dec, which subtracted from 9. h. 25. m. 21½. Sec gives 8. h. 21. m. 19. Sec 653, the time of true conjunction at Washington found by the emersion.

	h. m. Sec. dec
By the immersion,	8.21. 4.882.
" the emersion,	8.21.19.653.
Mean result true conjunction at Wash[n]	8.21.12.267.
ditto at Greenwich,	13.28.16.358.
Longitude in time	5. 7. 4.091.
	° ′ ″
equal to	76.46. 0.136.

On the foregoing principles, an occultation of n Pleiadum, (Alcyone) by the Moon, on the 20th of October, 1804, has been computed, the apparent times, reduced to the Capitol, are as follow:—

		h. m. Sec.dec	
October 20th 1804	Immersion at	9.22.28.33	P.M.
	Emersion, at	10.17.22.72.	

The British impression of the Nautical Almanac, gives the following calculated times at Greenwich:—

	h. m			
October 20th 1804,	16. 8½. Imm.	of n Pleiad: +	1.⅖ N.	of ☽'s center
	17.15¼. Em:		1⅕ S.	

		h. m. Sec. dec
True conjunction at Greenwich	at	15.50.28.105.
D° at Washington,		10.43. 0.066.
Longitude in time, West,		5. 7.28.039.
		° ′ ″
	equal to	76.52. 0.585.

Annular eclipse of the Sun, observed at a place N. 71.° W. one mile, $\frac{3}{8}$, American measure, from the Capitol, on the 17th September, 1811; the apparent times, as follow:—

	h. m. Sec	
Beginning of the eclipse, at	0.22. 9.	P.M.
Annulus formed at	2. 2. 6	
d° broken, at	2. 6.53	
End of the eclipse at	3.36.53.	

		h. m. Sec. dec
True Conjunction at Greenwich		6.57.14.915.
At Washington,		
By first external contact		1.49.20.078.
" Second ditto		1.48.32.111.
" first internal contact,		1.48.42.823
" Second d°		1.48.28.692.
Results 1st		5. 7.54.837.
2		5. 8.42.804.
3		5. 8.32.092.
4		5. 8.46.223.
Mean Long. of the place of observn		5. 8.28.989
	equal to	77. 7.14.835.
diff: of longitude to the Capitol,		− 1.26.978.
By Solar Eclipse, September, 17th 1811		77. 5.47.857.
" occultation of n Pleiad: Oct: 20. 1804		76.52. 0.585.
" occultation of a Tauri, Jany 21. 1793.		76.46. 0.136.
Longitude of the Capitol W. of Greenwch		76.54.36.193.

This is supposed to be a near approximation to the truth; the errors in the lunar tables being much diminished in their effect, by several observations made at considerable intervals of time.

I am, Sir, with great respect, Your most obedt servant.

William Lambert.

RC (PPAmP: APS Archives, Manuscript Communications); on five folio sheets; addressed: "Thomas Jefferson late president of the U. States, and president of the American philosophical Society, Monticello, Virginia"; franked; postmarked Washington, 24 Apr.; endorsed by TJ as received 29 Apr. 1812 and so recorded in SJL; endorsed at APS: "on the Longitude of Washington read 19th June 1812." Enclosed in TJ to Robert Patterson, 29 May 1812.

For the action taken by the AMERICAN PHILOSOPHICAL SOCIETY, see note to Lambert to TJ, 20 Apr. 1812.

From J. H. Smith

Jefferson County Kentucky[1] April 23d 1812

VENERABLE SAGE AND FATHER OF YOUR COUNTRY.

A conative of the Old Dom[ain?][2] begs leave to address you, and solicit your advice on the following subject.

It appears that a Mr Neef, now resident in the vicinity of Philadelphia of the U.S., as an instructor of youth, has published a system of education, which being radically different from any thing literary that has heretofore been offered to the public, and being in a great measure unintelligible to the Subscriber and his whole circle of acquaintances, and presuming that an object of its declared importance, can not have escaped, Sir, your particular notice and Scrutiny, especially, as said Mr Neef, has been or at least seems to have been known as the above stated character,[3] to the inhabitants of the Union, and particularly the Literate, for the space of ten years or upwards: the subscriber, therfore, in behalf of himself, and at the request of a number of his friends, depending on your clemency for librety so to do, has adopted this mode of soliciting your opinion on this Subject. Your compliance, Sir, with this wish, will add greatly to the Satisfaction of him who has long had the honor of being your devoted friend & humble Servant. Give me leave, Sir, to conclude by praying that, during the balance of your days (which may God happily prolong) you may enjoy the felicities of the earth in as super eminent a degree, as your verious & innumerable Services have been honorable to your self, and superlatively useful to your country and mankind.

J. H. SMITH

RC (MHi); one word illegible; adjacent to signature: "Thomas Jefferson Eesqr"; endorsed by TJ as received 22 May 1812 and so recorded in SJL.

[1] Remainder of dateline beneath signature.

[2] Probably an abbreviation or slip of the pen for "Dominion."

[3] Word interlined, with insertion mark mistakenly placed after comma.

From James Walker

DEAR SIR 23d apl 1812.

The last time that you and myself had any conversatio[n] together with regard to the erection of your saw mill your wish then was that I should commence on the first of april this present month. I have 12 months ago undertaken a large mill to build for Wm Moon

&. calculated on carrying on yours &. Mr. Moons work this summer at the same time. I have[1] engaged a young Man who served an apprenticeship to me for the present year who is a good workman but whose[2] health is such that I fear he will [be][3] of no service to me. I will be with you in a few days &. will either do your work or have it well done by another workman whom I now have in view but have not fully determined with him.—

I am your H. servant: &C. JAS WALKER.

RC (DLC); edge trimmed; dateline adjacent to signature; addressed: "Thomas Jefferson Esqr albemarle"; endorsed by TJ as received 23 Apr. 1812 and so recorded in SJL.

[1] Reworked from "had."
[2] Manuscript: "wose."
[3] Omitted word editorially supplied.

From John Williams

SIR 235 Pearl Street New York April 23rd 1812

A few days since a small package of Coffee, directed to you, came into my hands; the package has been lying in this City for more than a twelvemonth—but from whence it came I am unable to ascertain—I shall be happy to follow any instructions you may give respecting it & am

With great respect
Your obt, humble Servant JOHN WILLIAMS

RC (MoSHi: TJC-BC); dateline at foot of text; at head of text: "Thomas Jefferson Esqr"; endorsed by TJ as received 29 Apr. 1812 and so recorded in SJL.

The mercantile firm of E. Williams operated at 235 Pearl Street for roughly a decade beginning about 1811 (*Longworth's New York Directory* [1811], 325; [1821], 471).

To James P. Cocke

DEAR SIR Monticello Apr. 24. 12.

I am so anxious to save a year, by taking advantage of the present spawning season, not yet over, that I send the bearer to take the chance of your being able by some means to catch some chubs and the rather as his time is not very valuable: insomuch that if a detention of 2. or 3. days could secure my object, I should think it more than an equivalent for his time. I suppose that if taken with a hook & line and the hook carefully withdrawn from the mouth, it would not hurt them, especially if the beard of the hook were filed off. I have therefore furnished the bearer with a line and hooks of different sizes, and altho' he knows nothing about angling, yet with a little of your kind direction he would immediately understand it, and may employ himself in catching them, until you think he has a sufficiency. I am sorry to give you so much trouble, and must rest for the apology on your friendship. Accept the assurance of my great esteem and respect.

TH: JEFFERSON

PoC (DLC); at foot of text: "M[r] Cocke"; endorsed by TJ.

From Joseph Delaplaine

SIR, [ca. 24 Apr. 1812]

I will take it as a particular favour if you will give me your name to the Emporium of Arts & Sciences. The value of the subscription is nothing, it is the honor of having your name I am anxious for.

With much respect your obed. serv[t] JOSEPH DELAPLAINE

RC (DLC: TJ Papers, 191:33940); undated; subjoined to enclosure; addressed: "Honorable Thomas Jefferson Monticello Virginia"; postmarked Philadelphia, 24 Apr.; endorsed by TJ as received from Philadelphia on 29 Apr. 1812 and so recorded in SJL. Enclosure: Delaplaine's call for subscriptions as publisher of the *Emporium of Arts & Sciences*, Philadelphia, undated, indicating that, while this will be the only such work in this country, similar magazines are numerous in Europe and "prove to the artist, manufacturer, and philosopher a constant source of advantage"; pledging that its "elegance of printing, engraving, and paper" will merit American patronage; setting the cost at $7 a year payable semiannually; and announcing that subscriptions are being taken by him and by Edward Parker at 178 Market Street (broadside in DLC; with covering letter subjoined).

The *Emporium of Arts & Sciences* (Poor, *Jefferson's Library*, 14 [no. 920]) was published in Philadelphia from May 1812 until October 1814 and edited first by John Redman Coxe and then by Thomas Cooper. With this letter Delaplaine also enclosed a subscription list, not found, that was probably headed by Coxe's publication prospectus for the *Emporium*, Philadelphia, 1 Apr. 1812. The prospectus, which also appeared in the Philadelphia *Poulson's American Daily Advertiser*, 20 Apr. 1812, stated that the *Emporium* would print practical scientific essays from European authors and American essays "of real merit"; promised to publish on topics ranging from chemistry, mineralogy, and natural philosophy to the arts and agriculture; contended that knowledge amassed by "our transatlantic rivals" could help Americans alter their country's destiny; and explained that the publication would contain eighty pages per issue, with the first number to appear in May 1812. TJ signed the subscription list and returned it to Delaplaine on 30 Apr., and on 15 May 1812 the publisher sent it to President James Madison, who paid for a year's subscription but declined to add his name to the list (Madison, *Papers, Pres. Ser.*, 4:385).

From James Madison

Dear Sir Washington Ap[l] 24. 1812

I have just rec[d] your favor of the 17th. The same mail brings me the "Proceedings of the Gov[t] of the U.S. relative to the Batture" for which you will accept my thanks.

I had not supposed that so great a proportion of produce, particularly of Wheat & flour, was still in the hands of the farmers. In Penn[a] it was known to be the case. In N.Y. almost the whole of the last crop, is in the Country, tho' chiefly in the hands of the merchants & millers. The measure of the Embargo was made a difficult one, both as to its duration &[1] its date, by the conflict of opinions here, and of local interests elsewhere; and to these causes are to be added, that invariable opposition,[2] open with some, & covert with others, which have perplexed & impeded the whole course of our public measures. You will have noticed that the Embargo as recommended to Cong[s] was limited to 60[3] days. Its extension to 90, proceeded from the united votes of those who wished to make it a negociating instead of a war measure, of those who wished to put off the day of war as long as possible, if ultimately to be met, & of those whose mercantile[4] constituents had ships abroad, which would be favored in their chance of getting safely home. Some also who wished & hoped to anticipate the expiration of the terms, calculated on the ostensible postponement of the war question, as a ruse ag[st] the Enemy. At present great differences of opinion exist, as to the time & form of entering into hostilities; whether at a very early or later day, or not before the end of the 90 days, and whether, by a general declaration, or by a commencement with letters of M.[5] & Reprisal. The question is also to be brought forward for an adjournment for 15 or 18 days. Whatever may be the decision on all these points, it can scarcely be doubted that patience in the holders of wheat & flour at least, will secure them good prices; Such is the scarcity all over Europe, and the dependance of the W. Indies on our supplies. M[r] Maury writes me, on the 21st of March that flour had suddenly risen to 16$\frac{1}{2}$ dollars, and a further rise looked for. And it is foreseen, that in a State of war the Spanish & Portuguese flags & papers, real or counterfiet, will afford a neutral cover, to our produce as far as wanted in ports in the favor of G.B. Licences therefore on our part will not be necessary; which tho' in some respects mitigating the evils of war, are so pregnant with abuses of the worst sort, as to be liable in others to strong objections. As managed by the Belligerents of Europe they are sources of the most iniquitous & detestable practices.

The Hornet still loiters. A letter from Barlow to Granger, fills us with serious apprehensions, that he is burning his fingers, with matters which will work great embarrassment & mischief here; and which his instructions could not have suggested. In E. Florida, Mathews has been playing a tragi-comedy, in the face of common sense, as well as of his instructions. His extravagances place us in the most distressing dilemma.

Always & affe^y Yrs JAMES MADISON

RC (DLC: Madison Papers); at foot of text: "Mr Jefferson"; endorsed by TJ as received 29 Apr. 1812 and so recorded in SJL.

Madison's letter from James MAURY was actually dated Liverpool, 20 Mar. 1812 (Madison, *Papers, Pres. Ser.*, 4:256–7). On 14 Apr. 1812 the New York *Commercial Advertiser* reported that, although the USS HORNET had not yet arrived, a letter from Joel Barlow to Gideon Granger advised of "a probability, though not a certainty, of *two* treaties being concluded, between him and the French government, in a few days:—one a treaty of commerce—another a treaty of cession and limits, which will give us a territory from Amelia-Island to the mouth of the Columbia river on the Pacific ocean. His letter was dated the 12th of February; and afterwards a Postscript, dated the 3d March, stating, that the Hornet will be detained a few days, to carry out the treaty. The letters to the government, from Mr. Barlow, are dated the 4th of March. Nothing was then concluded." On 23 Apr. 1812 Secretary of State James Monroe sent Barlow new instructions detailing numerous objections to a commercial treaty with France (DNA: RG 59, DI). Madison concluded that in attacking Amelia Island, George MATHEWS had exceeded his INSTRUCTIONS relating to the possible transfer of East Florida from Spanish to American control, and the president soon disavowed Mathews's actions as United States agent (Madison, *Papers, Pres. Ser.*, 3:122–4, 4:291–6).

[1] Manuscript: "& &."

[2] Madison here canceled: "to every measure."

[3] Number repeated above the line for clarity.

[4] Word interlined.

[5] Abbreviation for "Marque."

From John A. Morton

SIR Baltimore 24th April 1812

The letter which you did me the favour to address me on the 9th Inst. was received by my friends here during my absence on a Journey to the Eastward;—& owing to the irregularity of my movements, did not reach me until my return to this city. No opportunity having occurred for France, I hope this delay in my answer, may not have been productive of any inconvenience or disappointment. I will most willingly afford you every aid in my power, in making your contemplated remittance to General Kosciuzko, but the moment is not favourable to the accomplishment of your views. Bills on France are Scarce & extremely dear, & I believe could not be procured at less than 21$\frac{1}{2}$ Cents to the franc. This disadvantageous exchange would bear hardly on the small income of the General, & be productive of a loss, which it might be an object with him to avoid. It would be gratifying to me to be instrumental in serving the General, & with that view, I offer to furnish M[r] Barnes a bill for the amount you wish remitted, at 20. Cents to the Franc, instead of the Current price of 21½ Cents. This, I presume, will be a more economical method of putting the funds in question, in the possession of General Kosciuzko, than you can adopt through any other channel. As it would be agreable to me to oblige both the General & yourself, I will, with pleasure, make any arrangement you may deem best, for supplying him annually with the produce of his Stock, either by drawing for it from France, or ordering it remitted by my agents in this place. I will not undertake this as a commercial transaction, but to give the General a proof that I feel the interest in his welfare, which he has a right to expect from every American. No expence or charge will ever be made by me or my house, & all we wish is, not to incur absolute loss by the exchange.

Being solicitous to rejoin my family, I shall avail myself of the earliest Safe conveyance for France. On my arrival in Bordeaux, I will endeavour to furnish M[r] Walsh the Means of conveying to you, the wines you directed him to Ship for your account. If my services can, at any time, be useful to you in France, I beg you to command them without reserve. It would afford me much pleasure, to have Opportunities of giving you proofs of the high respect & Sincere esteem, with which I am, most truly,

Your Obed[t] & devoted servant JOHN A MORTON
care of Benj. & Geo. Williams
Baltimore

Permit me, Sir, to offer through you, my respectful Compliments to M[rs] Randolph

RC (MoSHi: TJC-BC); addressed: "Thomas Jefferson Esq[r] Monticello Virginia"; franked and postmarked; endorsed by TJ as received 29 Apr. 1812 and so recorded in SJL.

To William Thornton

DEAR SIR Monticello Apr. 24. 12.

On the reciept of your letter of Jan. 26. recommending Barrett's Spinning machine, I wrote to him for one; but not knowing his particular address, my letter was long getting to him; so that within this day or two only, instead of a machine I have recieved only a letter from him. in this he informs me you have the exclusive right to make and sell them to our state; and adds that if you wish it he will furnish me with a machine of 12. spindles (the size suiting me best) as soon as he gets your orders to that effect. I had before ordered a spinning Jenny, but on the reciept of your letter countermanded it: in consequence my establishment remains suspended until I can get Barrett's machine, and in the mean time[1] a man and his wife whom I hired to conduct it, and who have themselves been brought up to the business, as well as my other subordinate hands are idle. I am very anxious therefore to recieve a machine as early as possible. if you have one ready made, and which you can recommend as well made, you will relieve me much by having it well packed and sent to Messrs Gibson & Jefferson, my correspondents at Richmond, who will forward it to me. if you cannot speedily furnish one, will you be so good as to order one from Oliver Barrett himself. he knows how to forward it. in either case, as soon as it is ready & notified to me I will forward the whole or the divided price to yourself or mr Barrett as you shall direct me. can you do me the favor of informing me immediately[2] when & from whom I may expect one?

Your description of the plant, a substitute for hemp & flax, for the exclusive use of which mr Whitlow has a patent, has thrown all the boys of our neighborhood into great alarm, lest they should not be allowed hereafter to make their trap strings of what they call Indian hemp, which, boys have been in the practice from time immemorial, of applying to their purposes; of this I can give testimony for near 70. years back when I was a boy myself. one of them, in the name of his companions brought me his trap string, to be lodged in the patent office as a caveat against mr Whitlow's claim, if this be the plant he claims. I send a piece only of the string, supposing it sufficient. it is made of the Apocynum Cannabinum of Clayton & Linnaeus.

On the subject of the price of a patent right for a county for mr Barrett's machine, I think he mistakes his interest greatly in asking so much. at 500.D. he will never sell two county rights in this state; whereas at 100.D. he would probably sell from 50 to 100. if the machine be found in practice to answer well. Accept the assurance of my great esteem & respect TH: JEFFERSON

RC (DLC: Thornton Papers); addressed: "Doctor William Thornton Washington Columb."; franked; postmarked Milton, 30 Apr. 1812. PoC (DLC); endorsed by TJ.

Thornton's letter of JAN. 26. was actually dated 20 Jan. 1812. TJ had hired William McClure and HIS WIFE to manage his spinning operations at Monticello (TJ to McClure, 10 Sept. 1811).

APOCYNUM CANNABINUM: Indian hemp (Edmond Charles Genet, "On the economical utility of the Apocinum Cannabinum, or Indian Hemp, and the Asclepias, or Milkweed, natives of the State of New-York," *Transactions of the Society for the Promotion of Useful Arts, in the State of New-York* 3 [1814]: 152–4).

[1] Preceding four words interlined.
[2] TJ here canceled "what."

From Matthew Wills

DR SIR Fluvanna April 24th 1812

Mr Ashlin handed me your letter of the 20th instant wherein you expressed[1] a desire to get Some live Carp and I having the Seine that is halled at Mr Ashlins & Capt Holman on the other Side have endeavoured to procur all the Carps for you that were Caught which were but few Six or eight but not any of them lived but a few hour if you Can advise any way that they Can be Carried a live you Shall have at any time what may be Caught in my Sine & Capt Holmans gratis Mr Ashlin Capt Holman & myself have Sent you by the bearer James Six Shads a piece if you will please accept of them and he has bought twenty at 1/6 each the price Current on the fishing Shore

I am Sir with Sentiments[2] of high esteem Yours

MATTHEW WILLS

RC (MoSHi: TJC-BC); endorsed by TJ as received 26 Apr. 1812, but recorded in SJL as received the previous day.

[1] Manuscript: "expessd."
[2] Manuscript: "Sentimenst."

To John Graham

Monticello Apr. 25. 12.

Th: Jefferson asks the favor of mr Graham to give to the inclosed the safest passage which shall occur, and if possible, through a public vessel, & under cover to our Chargé at London, while we still have one there. the letter is to an old classmate (mr Maury) and ought not to go through an English post office if it can be avoided, being entirely confidential. he salutes mr Graham with esteem & respect, & great thankfulness for his permission to use his kind attentions in the foreign correspondence of TH:J.

PoC (DLC); dateline at foot of text; endorsed by TJ. Enclosure: TJ to James Maury, 25 Apr. 1812.

The CHARGÉ AT LONDON was Jonathan Russell.

To James Maury

My Dear and antient friend
and classmate Monticello Apr. 25. 12.

Often has my heart smote me for delaying acknolegements to you, recieving, as I do, such frequent proofs of your kind recollection in the transmission of papers to me. but instead of acting on the good old maxim of not putting off to tomorrow what we can do to-day, we are too apt to reverse it, & not to do to-day what we can put off to-morrow. but this duty can be no longer put off. to-day we are at peace; tomorrow war. the curtain of separation is drawing between us, and probably will not be withdrawn till one, if not both of us, will be at rest with our fathers. let me now then, while I may, renew to you the declarations of my warm attachment, which in no period of life has ever been weakened, and seems to become stronger as the remaining objects of our youthful affections are fewer. our two countries are to be at war, but not you & I. and why should our two countries be at war, when by peace we can be so much more useful to one another. surely the world will acquit our government of having sought it. never before has there been an instance of a nation's bearing so much as we have borne. two items alone in our catalogue of wrongs will for ever acquit us of being the aggressors; the impressment of our seamen, and the excluding us from the ocean. the first foundations of the social compact would be broken up were we definitively to refuse to it's members the protection of their persons and property, while in their lawful pursuits. I think the war will not be short, because the object of England, long obvious, is to claim the Ocean as her domain, and to exact transit duties from every vessel traversing it. this is the sum of her orders of council, which were only a step in this bold experiment, never meant to be retracted if it could be permanently maintained. and this object must continue her in war with all the world. to this I see no termination, until her exaggerated efforts, so much beyond her natural strength and resources, shall have exhausted her to bankruptcy. the approach of this crisis, is, I think, visible, in the departure of her precious metals, and depreciation of her paper medium. we, who have gone through that operation, know it's symptoms, it's course, and consequences. in England they will be more serious than elsewhere, because half the wealth of her people is now in that medium, the private revenue of her money holders, or rather of her paper-holders, being, I believe, greater than that of her landholders. such a proportion of property, imaginary and baseless as it is, cannot be reduced to vapour but with great explosion. she will rise out of it's ruins however, because her lands, her houses, her arts will remain, and the greater part of her men. and these will give her again that place among nations which is proportioned to her natural means, and which we all wish her to hold. we believe that the just standing of all nations is the health and security of all. we consider the overwhelming power of England on the ocean, and of France on the land, as destructive of the prosperity and happiness of the world, and wish both to be reduced only to the necessity of observing moral duties. we believe no more in Bonaparte's fighting merely for the liberty of the seas, than in Great Britain's fighting for the liberties of mankind. the object of both is the same, to draw to themselves the power, the wealth and the resources of other nations. we resist the enterprises of England first, because they first come vitally home to us. and our feelings repel the logic of bearing the lash of George III. for fear of that of Bonaparte at some future day.[1] when the wrongs of France shall reach us with equal effect, we shall resist them also. but one at a time is enough: and having offered a choice to the champions, England first takes up the gauntlet. the English newspapers suppose me the personal enemy of their nation. I am not so. I am an enemy to it's injuries, as I am to those of France. if I could permit myself to have national partialities, and if the conduct of England would have permitted them to be directed towards her, they would have been so. I thought that in the administration of mr Addington I discovered some dispositions towards justice, and even friendship and respect for us, and began to pave the way for cherishing these dispositions and improving them into ties of mutual good will. but we had then a federal minister there, whose dispositions to believe himself, and to inspire others with a belief, in our sincerity, his subsequent conduct has brought into doubt: and poor Merry, the English minister here, had learnt nothing of diplomacy, but it's suspicions, without head enough to distinguish when they were misplaced. mr Addington and mr Fox passed away too soon to avail the two countries of their dispositions. had I been personally hostile to England, and biassed in favor of either the character or views of her great Antagonist, the affair of the Chesapeak put war into my hand. I had only to open it, and let havoc loose. but if ever I was gratified with the possession of power, and of the confidence of those who had entrusted me with it, it was on that occasion when I was enabled to use both for the prevention of war, towards which the torrent of passion here was directed almost irresistably, and when not another person in the United States, less supported by authority and favor, could have resisted it. and now that a definitive adherence to her impressments and orders of council, render war no longer avoidable, my earnest prayer is that our government may enter into no compact of common cause with the other belligerent, but keep us free to make a separate peace, whenever England will separately give us peace, & future security. but L[d] Liverpool is our witness that this can never be but by her removal from our neighborhood.—I have thus, for a moment, taken a range into the field of politics to possess you with the view we take of things here. but in the scenes which are to ensue, I am to be but a spectator. I have withdrawn myself from all political intermedlings, to indulge the evening of my life with what have been the passions of every portion of it, books, science, my farms, my family and friends. to these every hour of the day is now devoted. I retain a good activity of mind, not quite as much of body, but uninterrupted health. still the hand of age is upon me. all my old friends are nearly gone. of those in my neighborhood mr Divers, & mr Lindsay alone remain. if you could make it a partie quarrée, it would be a comfort indeed. we would beguile our lingering hours with talking over our youthful exploits, our hunts on Peter's mountain, with a long train of etcetera in addition, and feel, by recollection at least, a momentary flash of youth. reviewing the course of a long & sufficiently succesful life, I find in no portion of it, happier moments than those were. I think the old hulk in which you are, is near her wreck, and that, like a prudent rat, you should escape in time. however here, there, and every where, in peace or in war, you will have my sincere affections, & prayers for your life, health and happiness.

TH: JEFFERSON

P.S. I send you a copy of a Memoir of my own on a particular transaction, which I do not offer for your reading, because I do not suppose you trouble yourself with legal or local questions, but for your acceptance as a token of respect from me.

RC (Jonathan Kasso, Melville, N.Y., 2002); faint punctuation supplied from PoC; at foot of first page: "James Maury esquire." PoC (DLC). Enclosure: Jefferson, *Proceedings*. Enclosed in TJ to John Graham, 25 Apr. 1812.

Rufus King was the FEDERAL MINISTER who represented the United States at the British court during most of Henry Addington's 1801–04 term as prime minister (*ANB*). PARTIE QUARRÉE: "foursome."

[1] Sentence interlined.

To John Rodman

Monticello Apr. 25. 12.

Th: Jefferson presents his compliments to mr Rodman and his thanks for the translation of Montgalliard's work which he has been so kind as to send him. it certainly presents some new and true views of the situation of England. it is a subject of deep regret to see a great nation reduced from an unexampled height of prosperity to an abyss of ruin by the long continued rule of a single chief. all we ought to wish as to both belligerent parties is to see them forced to disgorge what their ravenous appetites have taken from others, and reduced to the necessity of observing moral duties in future. if we read with regret what concerns England, the fulsome adulation of the Author towards his own chief excites nausea and disgust at the state of degradation to which the mind of man is reduced by subjection to the inordinate power of another. he salutes mr Rodman with great respect.

PoC (DLC); dateline at foot of text; endorsed by TJ.

John Rodman (1775–1847) was a merchant in New York City by 1801. He spent three years in France before returning to New York City by 1812 to practice law. Rodman served as a major of artillery during the war of 1812 and in 1814 published a translation of the commercial code of France. He was appointed the state's district attorney for the city and county of New York in 1815 and served until 1817, when he resigned and spent another year in France. In 1821 James Monroe appointed Rodman customs collector for the port of Saint Augustine, Florida, and he held this position until 1842. In Florida, Rodman continued to practice law and also served as an alderman for Saint Augustine and a prosecuting attorney for Saint Johns County. He died in New Jersey (Charles Henry Jones, *Genealogy of the Rodman Family* [1886] 34, 53–5; *Longworth's New York Directory* [1801], 264; New York *Public Advertiser*, 26 Sept. 1812; Rodman, *The Commercial Code of France, with the Motives, or Discourses of the Counsellors of State* [New York, 1814]; Rodman to Monroe, 1 Oct. 1814 [DNA: RG 59, LAR, 1809–17]; *Albany Gazette*, 3 Apr. 1815; Rodman to Monroe, 27 Feb., 8 Mar. 1821 [DNA: RG 59, LAR, 1817–25]; *JEP*, 6:57 [28 Apr. 1842]; *Terr. Papers*, esp. 22:17, 50–2, 357–8, 360; New York *Evening Post*, 17 Feb. 1847).

TJ had received *Situation of England, in 1811* (New York, 1812), a TRANSLATION "from the French, by a Citizen of the United States" of Jean Gabriel Maurice Roques, comte de Montgaillard, *Situation de l'Angleterre en 1811* (Paris, 1811). The New York edition was printed by C. S. Van Winkle and copyrighted in that city by John Finch. It contained a preface by the anonymous translator dated New York, 10 Mar. 1812. SJL records no letter from Rodman to TJ, and the way he sent him this book has not been ascertained. Montgaillard's OWN CHIEF was Napoleon.

To Hugh White

Monticello Apr. 25. 12.

Th: Jefferson presents his compliments to the rev^{d} mr White, and his thanks for the pamphlet he has been so kind as to send him. the questions this presents are certainly difficult, and mr White has done what alone can be done, he has presented ingenious views of them. Th:J. has long ago abandoned them as insoluble by understandings limited as ours are, and believes it to be the case wherein, as some one has said before him, ignorance is the softest pillow on which we can lay our heads. he salutes mr White with esteem & respect.

PoC (MoSHi: TJC-BC); dateline at foot of text; endorsed by TJ.

From Theodorus Bailey

DEAR SIR, New york 26. April 12.

I do myself the honor to transmit to you under cover, a letter from the Post-Master at Scaghticoke, in answer to one I addressed to him on the subject of your letters to Mr Oliver Barrett; by which you will know that your letters have been delivered to Mr Barrett.

With the highest consideration and regard

I am Dear sir, most truly yours, THEODORUS BAILEY.

RC (MHi); endorsed by TJ as received 1 May 1812 and so recorded in SJL. Enclosure: Munson Smith to Bailey, Schaghticoke, 21 Apr. 1812, stating that "Yours of 7th April Ins^{t} came to hand with one inclosed for Mr Oliver Barrett which letter I have delivered to him—the former Letter of which you mention as being from Mr Jefferson was receivd in due time & Delivered to Mr Barrett he Says, he has written an answer" (RC in MHi; addressed: "Hon^{e} Theodorus Bailey Esqr P Master N. York"; franked; postmarked Schaghticoke, 21 Apr.).

From Benjamin Rush

DEAR SIR Philadelphia April 26th 1812

Your favor of the 20th instant came safe to hand, but not accompanied with the pamphflet you have mentioned in it. I have read your letter to Mr Adams with pleasure, & shall put it into the post office tomorrow agreeably to your Wishes.—

The daughters of the late Wm Lyman & his only son arrived in this city a few Weeks ago from London. Two of them are now members of my family. The Eldest of them—a most accomplished woman in point of mind is now at Washington, Where she has probably communicated some Anecdotes to Mr Monroe relative to the noted Mr Henry (whom she knew in London) that may serve to extend the Views of the Executive of the mischief intended by him.

I have often heard of the great respect of your daughter Mrs Randolph for Religion. I beg you will present her with the excellent little work which accompanies this letter in defence of the Object of her faith and Affections. It will be invaluable in the hands of her Children. Health, respect & friendship! from

Dear Sir yours very Affectionately BENJ^N^ RUSH

PS: I am now preparing for the press the result of the reading,[1] experience, and reflections of fifty years upon all the forms of madness, and upon all[2] the Other diseases of the mind

RC (MHi); endorsed by TJ as received 1 May 1812 and so recorded in SJL.

William LYMAN was United States consul at London from 1804 until his death on 22 Sept. 1811. His ONLY SON was his namesake William Lyman, and the ELDEST of his five daughters was Jerushia Lyman (*JEP*, 1:476, 477 [11, 12 Dec. 1804]; *Cooperstown Federalist*, 23 Nov. 1811; Lyman's will, 17 Sept. 1811, proved in London, 12 Oct. 1811, Philadelphia Will Book, 3:417–21). Rush enclosed Beilby Porteus, *A Summary of the Principal Evidences for the Truth and Divine Origin of the Christian Revelation* (London, 1800, and later eds.; see Rush to TJ, 15 Mar. 1813). Rush was PREPARING his *Medical Inquiries and Observations, upon the Diseases of the Mind* (Philadelphia, 1812).

[1] Word interlined.

[2] Reworked from "fifty years upon madness, and all."

To William Short

DEAR SIR Monticello Apr. 26. 12.

Your favor of the 19th was recieved yesterday. those of Feb. 20. & Mar. 5. had come to hand before, and were still in my Carton of 'letters to be answered.' the only circumstance in those which pressed for an answer had escaped my memory, until your last reminded me of it, that is to say, the visit proposed by General Moreau. and first I must set to rights the idea that a visit while at Washington would have occasioned embarrasment. not the least. I had considered the incident as a possible one and had made up my mind on it. I should have recieved him with open arms, and should have frankly, stated to Turreau the reason and right of my so doing. I considered the general's not visiting us at Washington as an evidence of his discretion, which could not be taken amiss, because of it's friendly motive: but he would have been cordially recieved; and I wish him to understand this as having been my purpose. with respect to the visit here, I can say with sincerity that I should recieve the General with the greatest pleasure, and a due sensibility of the honor done me.[1] the high estimation in which I hold his character and particularly it's combination of integrity with talents, would ensure this. but my respect for him would shrink from a compliment which was to cost him the labour of such a journey. were indeed the visit to Monticello merely an episode to one to the caves, or Natural bridge, or a promenade of curiosity thro' this part of the country, it's gratification would be pure and unalloyed. lest my silence should be considered by him, as it has been by yourself, as a proof that I was indifferent at least to his visit, I must repose myself on your friendship so far as to give him a true view of my impressions on the subject, and such too as may leave him at perfect liberty to consult his own convenience as well as wishes. should he propose to come, my visits to Bedford 3. or 4. times a year, on each of which I am absent a month, would render some previous idea of the time of his coming necessary to me, to prevent mutual disappointment. the periods of those visits to Bedford being unfixed and immaterial admit his taking his own time. the delays of the post between this and that place are such that[2] no letters arriving during my absence are forwarded thither.

To proceed to the other parts of your letters. the house of Gibson & Jefferson continuing as before, mr Gibson will do for you whatever mr Jefferson has heretofore done. he is a most excellent man, and worthy of any confidence you may have occasion to repose in him.—Threshly's offer of 7.D. to you for your land, and his making the offer to you instead of me, shews he expected to take you by surprise. he is a native Virginian, in commerce, and having asked & recieved previous information from me that the price was 12.D.[3] he came to see the land. he was several days at Monticello.[4] I referred him to the tenants to shew him the land. he happened to apply to Gamble who shewed it to him most unfaithfully. still I do believe he would then have given 10.D. but I thought it worth more, and offered no abatement. after I recieved your desire to let it go at 10.D. I gave him notice of it (he lives at Portroyal) and instead of answering my notice, he has hoped to get it still lower from yourself. I have no fear of getting the 10.D. when the incumbrance of the tenants shall be removed.—the law from which you apprehended danger, respects only lands which the owners have failed to enter on the Commissioners books, to avoid paying taxes your accounts will shew you that the taxes of yours have been regularly paid, and of course that they are on the Commissioners books. the letter from Mad[e] de Tessé with the

Memoires of the Margrave came to hand only the last week. some of my correspondents, booksellers particularly, had so indiscreetly used my privilege of franking, by sending by mail packets more proper for a waggon (one of N. York for instance, sent me 7. 4to vols by mail) that I was obliged to desire the P.M.G[1] to stop all packages larger than an 8vo vol. and commit them to the stage. in this way they experience considerable delays, which has been the case with Me de Tesse's package. the Memoires have run the gauntlet[5] of my whole family, and I shall shortly take them up myself, after which I will forward them to you, a volume at a time.—from the Abbé Rochon I never recieved either letter or book. indeed having never been able to hear of him, tho' I have often enquired, I had concluded he was no longer inter vivos. whatever he has written, whether on coins or any thing else, must be sensible. I found him a very sound-headed man. but the MS. volume you speak of must be beyond the limits prescribed for the mail, and the stage would be too unsafe to be trusted with it unless under the care of a passenger. I shall read with pleasure his Memoire sur la chrystal de Roche, if you can hazard it by mail. I presume it is a prosecution of the effects of the two distinct refrangibilities of the Iceland chrystal, of which he had made two telescopes before I left France, which gave you the distance of any object whose diameter was known, or the diameter if the distance was known.—I set out for Bedford within 3. or 4. days to be absent a month. Accept the assurance of my constant and affectionate esteem.

TH: JEFFERSON

RC (ViW: TJP); at foot of first page: "Mr Short"; endorsed by Short as received 5 May 1812. PoC (DLC).

Short's FAVOR OF THE 19TH of April and THOSE OF FEB. 20 & MAR. 5., none of which has been found, are recorded in SJL as received from New York on 25 Apr., 26 Feb., and 11 Mar. 1812, respectively. They are all listed in Short's epistolary record for 1812 (DLC: Short Papers, 34:6345, with a brief notation that the 5 Mar. letter dealt with "Threshley's [Robert B. Sthreshly's] offer"). Here and with a variant spelling in his 8 Mar. 1811 letter to Short, TJ's apparent use of the word CARTON in the sense of a container made of light cardboard seems to be the earliest recorded in English (*OED*). TJ subsequently received Alexis Marie ROCHON, *Mémoire sur le micromètre de cristal de Roche: pour la mesure des distances et des grandeurs* (Paris, 1807), *Voyages aux Indes Orientales et en Afrique, pour l'Observation des Longitudes en Mer* (Paris, 1807; Sowerby, no. 3805), and at least one other publication as gifts from the author (Rochon to TJ, 7 Aug. 1812; TJ to John Barraud, 25 Dec. 1812; TJ to Robert Patterson, 27 Dec. 1812).

[1] Word interlined.
[2] TJ here canceled "all."
[3] Reworked from "10."
[4] Manuscript: "Monticllo."
[5] Manuscript: "guantlet."

To Matthew Wills

SIR Monticello Apr. 26. 12.

I return you many thanks for the fish you have been so kind as to send me, and still more for your aid in procuring the carp, and you will further oblige me by presenting my thanks to Cap[t] Holman & mr Ashlin. I have found too late, on enquiry, that the cask sent was an old and foul one, and I have no doubt that must have been the cause of the death of the fish. the carp, altho' it cannot live the shortest time out of the water, yet is understood to bear transportation in water the best of any fish whatever. the obtaining breeders for my pond being too interesting to be abandoned, I have had a proper smack made, such as is regularly used for transporting fish, to be towed after the boat, and have dispatched the bearer with it without delay, as the season is passing away. I have therefore again to sollicit your patronage, as well as Captain Holman's in obtaining a supply of carp. I think a dozen would be enough, and would therefore wish him to come away as soon as he can get that number. your favor herein will add my further thanks to the assurance of my esteem & respect.

TH: JEFFERSON

PoC (MoSHi: TJC-BC); at foot of text: "Cap[t] Matthew Wills"; endorsed by TJ.

From Samuel J. Harrison

SIR Lynchbg April 27–1812

your Letter of the 2 Ins[t] was rec[d] in due course, & this answer defered So as to meet you at poplar Forest. your Reasoning has produced no change in my opinion, as to your Right to call for the last payment of the Land—nor can I forbeare Remarking that your Letter Seems not to have been written in that Temper of which you are so charracteristick. I assir'd you that Scott had Sued both you & myself for a part of the Land, which I think aught to have left no Doubt upon your mind of the fact, although the Spa.[1] might not have been Executed upon you. Scott Setts forth in his Bill that his, is the oldest Entry (Say april 1789) and therefore is Intitled to the Land, notwithstanding yours is the oldest patent: that he was Confin'd to his Bed when you ousted him, or you would not have got possession &c &c.

Scotts Claim[2] may be, & probably is unfounded; But having as great Dislike to Law Suits & trouble, as yourself, when Instructing Cap martin to make the Sale, I wished the Title cleared before making the last payment. Your ability to pay, you must be Satisfied, I never for a moment Doubted, but in the Event of your Death before the Termination of the Suit, I should of Course be put to great Trouble. I think Strange of your Suggestion that my withholding this payment can't be justified by Law Nor Equity; when the universal Custom is against you; & courts of Chancery allways grant Relief; and notwithstanding payment is freequeently demanded in Such Cases, yet I had not expected it from you. your proposals as to Security are Equally good—But I can't believe that the Chancellor would Pretend to Decide in the Summary way you have Suggested—as he would thereby, be prejudging Scott, who is before him on the Same Subject; and Certainly aught to be first heard. I certainly Should have felt justified in withholding the 2nd payment, had the Suit been brought before it was made, as the Land Claim'd by Scott is worth more than the money in my hands Besides the injury it would do the Balance of the Tract.

But as I have only withheld this payment to Save me from Trouble & expence, and you have Voluntarily propos'd to put me on Such grounds as to Save me therefrom, in the Event of Scotts prevailing—I here propose that you Shall place in the hands of Trustees, Such part of the Forest Tract, as Shall be Sufficient to make me whole, with Instruction that they promise to Sell the Same for Ready money, for my benefit, So Soon as they Shall be notified, of a Desicion in Scotts favor. It will be proper Still to guard against the Trouble of Valuing the Land, & the Damage, the Balance of the Tract would Sustain by Loping it off—that you Insert in the Trust Deed, Such Specific Sum as it would be right to pay me: which we no Doubt Can agree on—This being done I will Draw upon Richmond for the amount of My Bond forthwith.

I am Sir Respectfully Yr m° ob. S J HARRISON

RC (ViU: TJP); between dateline and salutation: "Ths Jefferson Esquire"; endorsed by TJ as received 12 May 1812 and so recorded in SJL.

1 Abbreviation for "Subpoena."

2 Manuscript: "Clam."

To George Hay

DEAR SIR Monticello Apr. 27. 12.

Yours of the 21st is recieved. I am very sensible of the kindness of the motives on which you decline accepting compensation for the trouble you incurred in defending me at the suit of Livingston. yet the obligations I am under to you would not be lessened by that acceptance. your profession is as laborious as it is honorable, the eminence you have justly attained creates augmentation of expence, and no maxim is more solid than that labour is worthy of it's remuneration. the public rights not having been[1] brought into question on the decision, neither the general government, nor that of Orleans became interested in it. I cannot therefore but intreat your making use of the order which mr Gibson will pay on demand. the zeal and attention you bestowed on the case will leave me still for ever indebted to you.

In the case of the Distributees of P. Randolph v. his exrs mr Wayles's accounts have been settled, and if A. Cary's are not, one exr is not answerable for another. I am almost certain no process has been served on me on the bill of Review. I do not know then how comes an attachment to be the 1st process.

In Ariana Randolph's case, mr Wayles was no security nor any ways concerned, nor am I a trustee, for I could not be made one without my consent, which was never given. I hope therefore both parties will agree to withdraw my name from the suit.

Scott's suit being totally unfounded, will be settled by my answer, when opportunity for that is given me. this is the first knolege I have of being a party to it. I shall set out for Bedford within 3. or 4. days and be absent as many weeks. I shall there see Saml J. Harrison, the other def. and learn what he has done or proposes.

I am sorry to be troublesome to you on the subject of the MS. documents in Livingston's case, all the printed ones being returned to me. the inclosed paper will inform you more particularly what they were, and the ground on which I stand respecting them at the Secretary of State's office. it will probably bring them to your recollection. they were all stitched together in a volume of some mass. perhaps you have delivered them to mr Wirt or mr Tazewell. they can only be mislaid, the volume being too bulky to be lost.

Accept the assurance of my great esteem & respect.

TH: JEFFERSON

PoC (DLC); at foot of first page: "Mr Hay"; endorsed by TJ. Enclosure: List of Batture-Related State Department Documents, enclosed in TJ to Robert Smith, 20 Mar. 1811.

[1] TJ here canceled "justly."

Samuel Scott's Bill of Complaint in *Scott v. Jefferson and Harrison*

[before 27 Apr. 1812]

To the honble Creed Taylor, judge of the Superior court of Chancery for the Richmond district. Humbly complaining sheweth unto your honor your orator Samuel Scott

That on the 15th day of April in the year 1789 he entered with the Surveyor of Campbell county, by virtue of a land office treasury warrant N° 20278. assigned to him by Edmund Tait, for 50. a^{s} of vacant land lying in the county of Campbell, which entry is in the words and figures following. 'April 15. 1789. Samuel Scott, by virtue of a verbal assignment of Edmund Tait for 50. a^{s} part of the aforesaid warrant N° 20278. enters for the vacant land adjoining his own, Wilkenson's, and Timberlake's lines at Trent's road.' 'also all the vacant land between Wayles's 99. acres Christopher Anthony's and Wilkenson's in virtue of the same 50. a^{s}.' copies of which entries subscribed by Wm P. Martin the present surveyor for Campbell county are hereunto annexed and prayed to be taken as a part of this bill. your orator avers that from the time of making the aforesaid entries he was always ready to have surveyed the same, and in fact frequently sollicited the surveyor to appoint a time for so doing, which however the sd Surveyor from time to time neglected, telling your Orator that as he resided in the county of Campbell he would appoint some time convenient to himself, of which your orator should have timely notice, but your orator in fact avers that no notice was ever given him to survey. in this situation the entry remained until the 26th day of April 1803. when your orator being anxious to compleat his title to the sd land, applied to the Surveyor to survey the entry, and on examination it was found that the warrant under which the entry had been made, under which warrant many other entries & surveys had been made, some previous to and others subsequent to the entry of your orator had been returned to the land office; your orator therefore recieved from the Register an exchange warrant for the 50. a^{s} which remained of the original warrant for your orator's entry aforesaid, & under this exchange warrant he made another entry, on the same land on the 26th day of April 1803 and surveyed the same on the 26th day of December 1803 and obtained a patent from the Governor bearing date 15. Octob. 1804 which is hereunto annexed and prayed to be taken as a part of this bill. by virtue of which patent your orator was seised and possessed of the sd land, & proceeded to clear & prepare the same for cultivation. That Thomas Jefferson, herein after called a defendant, by some means, unknown to your orator, obtained a patent for the same land bearing date the day of under which patent the said defendant set up a claim to the land, & actually[1] sued out on the day of a writ of forcible entry & detainer against your orator, and at a time when he was confined to his bed by extreme indisposition & unable to attend to his business, the jury actually dispossessed him, & delivered possession thereof to the sd Jefferson, who shortly thereafter sold the same to Samuel J. Harrison, whom your orator charges to have had full notice of his claim, & whom he prays to make a defendant to this bill. how or by what means the sd Jefferson obtained a patent for the aforesd land, your Orator is utterly unable to conjecture, as no entry for the same is to be found either on the Surveyor's books, or the clerk's office of the county, and your orator verily believes that there never was an entry, neither in the name of the sd Jefferson, nor in the name of any person under whom he claims, for the land or any part thereof, nor was there in point of fact any actual[2] survey: yet so it is, may it please your honor that the said Jefferson with others combining & confederating, hath by some means, and, as your orator expressly charges, not by the regular steps pointed out by law, obtained a patent for the sd land, which patent being of an older date than that of your orator hath preference to his in law, & your orator is wholly remediless concerning the premisses except in this worshipful court of chancery where he is advised matters of this sort are properly cognisable. Your orator humbly concieves that his title to the land in question is founded on the entry made on the 15th April 1789. because that entry was made under a warrant regularly obtained for that purpose, & as no notice was ever given him by the surveyor to survey the same, as by law, & under the custom of the country he ought to have done, he humbly concieves that he hath not lost the benefit of the entry, that the second entry was made under the same warrant, or on an exchange warrant which issued on the same, your orator humbly concieves therefore that his title ought to relate back, & bear inception from the date of the first entry. it is true that your orator's patent issued upon the last survey, & hath reference only to the date of that survey, yet as your orator hath done no act which can amount to an abandonment of his first entry, he trusts that his patent in equity will bear relation to the date of that entry. your orator hath been at much pains to ascertain the steps taken by mr Jefferson in obtaining his patent to the aforesd land without success; that the only entry to be found on the surveyor's books in relation to vacant lands now in the possession of mr Jefferson is one in the words & figures following, to wit, 'March 20. 1770. John Wayles esq. all the vacant lands adjoining to his Poplar forest tract, in one or more surveys' which entry doth not appear to have been made by virtue of any warrant, & is moreover as your orator is advised in terms so vague & general as to be void in law. but what is conclusive as to the present question is that the land now in dispute doth not nor ever did adjoin the Poplar forest tract, in any part of it, but on the contrary lies at the distance of many miles from it. your orator hath been informed that mr Jefferson's patent issued upon a survey purported to have been made by Richard Smith Surveyor of Campbell county. your orator verily believes that there never was a Surveyor for the county of Campbell of that name. he knows of a certainty that since his residence in the county which is about 28. years, there hath been no surveyor of the name of Smith. your orator hath some reason to believe that the defendant's title is derived from Richard Stith, late surveyor of Campbell county, to whom as your orator hath been informed, John Wayles esq. under whom mr Jefferson claims paid a trifling consideration for a pretended entry and survey. your orator hath diligently searched the surveyor's office and the clerk's office & can find no entry except his own herein before referred to; & your orator is firmly persuaded that there never was an actual survey made by mr Jefferson or the person under whom he claims. if therefore the sd Richard Stith, who was the same surveyor with whom your orator made his entry did afterwards enter for the same land, & sell the entry or pretended survey to mr Wayles or mr Jefferson, your orator humbly concieves that the same, so far as concerns the sd Stith, was a fraud upon him, & that a title founded upon the fraudulent conduct of the surveyor ought not in equity to prevail against the title of your orator. In tender consideration whereof, & to the end that your orator may recieve that justice to which he humbly concieves himself entitled, he prays that Thomas Jefferson & Samuel J. Harrison may be made defendants to this bill: that they true & perfect answer make to all the matters and things herein set forth: that the first named def. be required to set forth the several steps taken by himself, or those under whom he claims in obtaining title to the land aforesd; that he say whether he claims under John Wayles esq. & if he does that he set[3] forth the steps taken by the sd Wayles in relation to the sd land, particularly that he be required to produce an authenticated copy of the entry, & the warrant or a copy of the warrant under which the entry was made: that he say whether he doth not believe that mr Wayles purchased the entry of Richard Stith the Surveyor of Campbell, & if he did, at what time & what was the consideration paid? if he claims the sd land by virtue of an entry & survey made in his own name let him say at what time, and with what surveyor the sd entry was made? and that he produce a copy of the entry together with the warrant or a copy thereof under which the same was made: and that the last named def. say whether he had notice of your orator's claim before he purchased the land, or if not before the purchase, at least before paiment was made? and that your honor will be pleased to decree that the said Thomas Jefferson & Samuel J. Harrison may execute to your orator proper conveyance for the said land, deliver the same into his possession and account to him for the rents & profits, and that your honor will grant to him such other relief as according equity & good conscience may seem meet E[t]c and will ever pray E[t]c

Tr (ViU: TJP); entirely in TJ's hand; undated, but seen by Samuel J. Harrison before he wrote TJ on 27 Apr. 1812; endorsed by TJ: "Scott v. Jefferson & Harrison } Bill in Canc. Copy." Enclosure: Land Grant to Samuel Scott, Richmond, 15 Oct. 1804, signed by Governor John Page, by virtue of exchanged treasury warrant no. 1415, issued 23 Apr. 1803 to Scott as assignee of Edmund Tate, and based on a 26 Dec. 1803 survey describing the land as containing 54¾ acres in Campbell County on the south branch of Ivy Creek and "bounded as followeth, to wit: Beginning at pointers, corner to Wilkerson and Johnson (now Couch) thence north forty degrees East one hundred and forty four poles along said Couches line to a hickory his corner, East eighty four poles to a white oak corner to Tiltis, north sixty two degrees east sixty two poles to a white oak corner to Tiltis and Samuel Scott, South thirty eight degrees west thirty poles, south seventy degrees West One hundred and eighty four poles to a hickory corner to said Scott and thence South Seventy six Degrees east fifty eight poles to the beginning, with its appurtenances" (Tr in Vi: RG 4, Virginia Land Office Grant Book, 52:316–7). Enclosed in TJ to George Hay, 13 July 1812.

Samuel Scott (1754–1822), a native of Caroline County, rose to the rank of major in the milita during the Revolutionary War and afterward moved to Campbell County. There he purchased land and by 1790 built a house he called Locust Thicket. Scott developed a reputation both for industriousness and intemperance. He bought land in Bedford County and property in Lynchburg, including a tavern, store, smokehouse, and lumber warehouse. He served as a justice of the peace, and about 1812 he was appointed sheriff of Campbell County, but he delegated these duties. In April 1810 Scott suffered a stroke, after which his family assumed direction of his plantation and business affairs. At the time of his death he owned twenty-nine slaves, but he had already conveyed most of his land to his two sons (National Society of the Daughters of the American Revolution, *DAR Patriot Index* [2003], 3:2382; Chambers, *Poplar Forest*, 61–2; Samuel McGregor Scott file, ViLJML: Family File 3796; S. Allen Chambers Jr., *Lynchburg: An Architectural History* [1981], 16–8; Campbell Co. Will Book, 4:421–5, 5:193–5; *Patrick P. Burton et al. v. Beverly R. Scott and Samuel M. Scott* [1823] court record [Campbell Co. Common Law Order Book, 3:532–85, 4:1–76, typescript in ViLJML: Family File 2437]; Scott's gravestone inscription, Locust Thicket, Lynchburg).

LAND OFFICE TREASURY WARRANT N° 20278, dated 3 Nov. 1783, in part authorized a survey of fifty-four acres of land in Bedford County for Jesse Tate. A survey was accordingly made on 10 Mar. 1798, and on 3 Mar. 1801 Governor James Monroe issued a grant to Tate for this land (Vi: RG 4, Virginia Land Office: Registry of Treasury Warrants; same, Grant Book, 47:469).

[1] TJ here canceled "succeeded."
[2] Manuscript: "actually."
[3] Manuscript: "that the set."

From James P. Cocke

DEAR SIR, Ap[l] 29th 1812

I am conserned that every effort to procure fish for you have been inaffecttual, two has been caught but so managed that they are dead, so soon as I can command them I will advise you & then will endevour to mannage the thing better in the mean time am

D[r] S[r] y[r] friend & Hbl[e] ser[t] J P COCKE

RC (DLC); at foot of text: "Tho[s] Jefferson Es[r]"; endorsed by TJ as received 29 Apr. 1812 and so recorded in SJL.

To John Barnes

DEAR SIR Monticello Apr. 30. 12.

Your favor of the 20th came to hand last night only, and the same post brought me an answer from mr Morton which I inclose for your perusal & consideration, with a request to return it to me. mr Morton is a native of this state, not personally known to me till lately, but long ago much recommended to me by many here; but most particularly by mr Coles, who was much with him in Bordeaux, where his mercantile house is established, and mr Coles assures me it is one of the most solid & succesful there. I take him to be a liberal honorable man, and that he will serve the General with zeal on the principles stated in his letter. I have supposed it would be happy for the General to have so convenient an intermediate between you & himself, because if the chances of war should occasion your remittances to miscarry, Morton will still furnish his necessities with regularity, and take the delay on himself. indeed I presume that money paid by you to his correspondent here (in Baltimore) will be taken by him as a remittance, so as to save you the risque & anxiety of finding bills of exchange, and such as are good. I suggest these things for your consideration, and leave the business of remittance to your own decision altogether. I think bills on London are dangerous and nearly impracticable in France. I believe the negociation of them there is punished with imprisonm[t] if not with death. my money for the General has been ready in the hands of Gibson & Jefferson for 2. or 3. months waiting only your call. I now write to them to remit you immediately 410.D. of which 360. is the General's part, and the remaining 50.D. are for mr E. I. Dupont of Wilmington, to whom I presumed the remittance would be much easier from Geo. town than from Richmond which has little connection with Wilmington. I therefore ask the favor of you to make him the remittance.

I am really glad to find it rather more probable that you should stay at Washington than go to Philadelphia. besides that your office brings you something, and would bring you more if you did not give more to your assistant than the business might be well done for, I think it will be improved whether we have war or peace. your expectation[1] to furnish my necessaries as cheaply as from Philadelphia, is worthy of consideration, and the more because of the superior safety of that channel in the event of war. I shall have time to think of it, as I have not yet got my affairs into a proper train for it.

Accept the assurance of my affectionate esteem & respect

TH: JEFFERSON

PoC (DLC); at foot of first page: "Mr Barnes"; endorsed by TJ. Enclosure: John A. Morton to TJ, 24 Apr. 1812.

TJ's letter to Gibson & Jefferson of 30 Apr. 1812 requesting that the firm remit payment to Barnes for GENERAL Tadeusz Kosciuszko and Eleuthère I. du Pont de Nemours, not found, is recorded in SJL and the substance given in *MB*, 2:1276.

[1] Word interlined in place of "offer."

To Joseph Delaplaine

SIR Monticello Apr. 30. 12.

I send you my subscription, and shall recieve your Emporium with pleasure, and with still greater if the price can be paid to any one in this state. the difficulty of remitting to a distance small & fractional sums has induced me to withdraw from newspapers and other things published out of the state. a regular knolege of the advance of the arts and sciences in Europe which D[r] Coxe is so well qualified to furnish, will certainly be a very acceptable treat to every lover of science. Accept my best wishes for it's success TH: JEFFERSON

PoC (DLC); at foot of text: "M. Delaplaine"; endorsed by TJ.

The enclosed SUBSCRIPTION list is discussed in note to Delaplaine to TJ, [ca. 24 Apr. 1812].

To Eleuthère I. du Pont de Nemours

Dear Sir Monticello Apr. 30. 12.

After having expected for some time that you would be so kind as to inform me of the amount of the keg of powder you sent me, that I might remit it to you, I wrote to you on the 4th of Nov. last, requesting that favor, & that you would add to it the amount of a similar envoy of powder to be forwarded to me, that both parcels might be paid for in one remittance. I had not then learnt the unfortunate accident of the explosion which probably prevented my recieving the second supply. having occasion to make a remittance to mr Barnes of Geo. town, I have included in it 50.D. which I have requested him to forward to you on account of the supply before recieved, and of the second now asked of 25.℔ of powder, of which ½ doz.℔ to be in cannisters for shooting, the rest for blowing rock, a great deal of which work I am to commence immediately, & will therefore ask you to send it without delay to Messrs Gibson & Jefferson of Richmond.

I shall shear this year, 3. fleeces only of imported Merinos, their wool of 1st quality, and about 15. of half blood. I have understood you are concerned in a manufactory of cloth, and will recieve one's wool, have it spun, wove & dyed for an equivalent in the wool. I should be very glad to get mine into so good hands. will you be so kind as to inform me more particularly on this subject. Accept the assurance of my great esteem & respect Th: Jefferson

RC (DeGH: Belin, Du Pont, and Copeland Family Papers); addressed: "E. I. Dupont esquire Eleutherian Mills near Wilmington Delaware"; franked; postmarked Milton, 7 May 1812; endorsed by du Pont. PoC (MHi); endorsed by TJ.

On 19 Oct. 1811 the pounding mill at du Pont's gunpowder factory was damaged by an explosion triggered when someone "introduced into one of the mortars an iron ball" two inches in diameter. A $1,500 reward was offered for information leading to the identification of the culprit (New York *Mercantile Advertiser*, 25 Oct. 1811; John Beverley Riggs, *A Guide to the Manuscripts in the Eleutherian Mills Historical Library* [1970], unpaginated chronology).

To James Leitch

Monticello. Apr. 30. 12.

Th: Jefferson understanding that mr Leitch has olive oil, will be glad of a bottle of it. being to set out on a journey within 2. or 3. days he asks the favor of him to change the inclosed bill. the more of it he can spare in silver, the more convenient it will be for the road.

RC (digital image on eBay website, 11 Apr. 2006, lot posted by Gallery of History, Las Vegas); dateline at foot of text; addressed: "Mr Leitch." Not recorded in SJL.

To John Williams

SIR

Monticello Apr. 30. 12.

If I have had any advice as to the small package of Coffee you mention, it has been so long ago that I cannot recollect it, nor now turn to the paper. I rather suspect it to be a parcel of some particular place or quality sent as a curiosity, perhaps from the new cultivators of that article on Florida point, with some of whom I have had communications on that culture. if you will do me the favor to forward it by water to Richmond, to mess^{rs} Gibson & Jefferson my correspondents there, they will reimburse any expences incurred on it, & will forward it to me. Accept my thanks for your attention and trouble and the assurance of my respect.

TH: JEFFERSON

RC (DLC: Kislak Collection); at foot of text: "Mr John Williams." PoC (MoSHi: TJC-BC); endorsed by TJ.

Appendix

Supplemental List of Documents Not Found

JEFFERSON'S epistolary record and other sources describe a number of documents for which no text is known to survive. The Editors generally account for such material at documents that mention them or at other relevant places. Exceptions are accounted for below.

From John Stewart, "the pedestrian," undated. Recorded in SJL as received 25 Aug. 1811.

From Jonathan Robinson, 6 Feb. 1812. Recorded in SJL as received from Washington on 23 Feb. 1812.

From William Johnson, 24 Feb. 1812. Recorded in SJL as received 28 Feb. 1812.

From Charles Bizet, 5 Mar. 1812. Recorded in SJL as received from Montpellier on 6 Mar. 1812.

From Robert Bell, 16 Mar. 1812. Recorded in SJL as received from Charlottesville on 16 Mar. 1812.

INDEX

INDEX

INDEX

THE PAPERS OF THOMAS JEFFERSON are composed in Monticello, a font based on the "Pica No. 1" created in the early 1800s by Binny & Ronaldson, the first successful typefounding company in America. The face is considered historically appropriate for The Papers of Thomas Jefferson because it was used extensively in American printing during the last quarter-century of Jefferson's life, and because Jefferson himself expressed cordial approval of Binny & Ronaldson types. It was revived and rechristened Monticello in the late 1940s by the Mergenthaler Linotype Company, under the direction of C. H. Griffith and in close consultation with P. J. Conkwright, specifically for the publication of the Jefferson Papers. The font suffered some losses in its first translation to digital format in the 1980s to accommodate computerized typesetting. Matthew Carter's reinterpretation in 2002 restores the spirit and style of Binny & Ronaldson's original design of two centuries earlier.

✧